In Wolf's Clothing
Book Two

JUST SO'S YA' KNOW...

THE *"IN WOLF'S CLOTHING"* trilogy of books is a collection of 60 short stories, ranging in length from 6 to 42 pages each, covering a 21-month span of time through 1977 and 1978, when I was 20 and 21 years old, and trying to become (and rise through the ranks of a career as) a Combat Controller, the Air Force's version of a Navy SEAL. These stories were written and collected over the course of a quarter century, created piecemeal, out of sequence, as the inspiration struck, and as the dictates of free time, personal motivation, and available resources allowed.

I was probably five years into the process before I even noticed the growing size of the collection, and ten years in before I started lining them up in chronological order and filling in the gaps between them to assemble an actual narrative flow. And by then, it was obvious that it was just too much to stuff into a single printed volume. So, after much consideration, I opted to split up the overall anthology into three lesser anthologies covering the three distinct evolutionary periods of that experience.

As such...

* * *

BOOK ONE, subtitled "A Road Full of Forks," covers the first seven months of my military career, and follows my transitions from civilian to military life, from indecisive adolescent to curiously driven young adult, and from scrawny acne-riddled '98-pound weakling' to the physical equivalent of 'Tarzan.'

It describes, over the course of 18 short stories, my passage through Basic Training, then Air Force Air Traffic Control School (and the parallel track of my struggles through Combat Control's entry level training), and finally on through the Army's Jump School at Fort Benning, Georgia.

* * *

BOOK TWO, subtitled "The Wannabe" (which you hold in your hands now), covers the most densely packed period of this series -- just the four months between October of '77 and February of '78 -- and the most 'transitional' period, in terms of all the new and varied and exotic aspects of the job that I was exposed to so quickly. It was my introduction to everything.

It describes, over the course of 24 short stories, my first days on an actual Combat Control Team, then the eight intense weeks of Combat Control School (when I got to do a little of everything they did), followed by the trials and tribulations of a winter Survival School, and even POW School... which in turn planted the first seeds of disillusionment that ultimately led to the end.

* * *

AND BOOK THREE, subtitled "The Pretender," covers all the rest... the remaining 10 months of 1978, described over 18 short stories, and comprised of my last two schools (Water Survival, and the Altitude Chamber), the four months I spent getting an actual air traffic control certification in an actual air traffic control tower, plus all the exercises and operations (and the accident) that ultimately compelled me to try to get out of Combat Control, as well as the devious method I had to use to get out, when all the rules said I couldn't.

* * *

IT WAS AN AMAZING, incredibly transformational, adventurous, and broadly experiential period of my life -- not to mention completely out of character for me, over my head and out of my league -- and requiring the maximum drive and effort of which I was capable just to keep up with these incredible people. And hopefully, each of these 60 little snippets from that extraordinary timeline will be able to convey to you what they meant to me.

Steve Stipp
October, 2017

IN WOLF'S CLOTHING
BOOK 2 - THE WANNABE

IN WOLF'S CLOTHING
BOOK 2 - THE WANNABE

STEVE STIPP

In Wolf's Clothing
Book 2 - The Wannabe - From newbie to neophyte to rookie warrior
So accomplished, he could hardly stand it

Copyright ©2019 by Steve Stipp
All rights reserved.

Published by Rebel Press
Austin, TX
www.RebelPress.com

No part of this publication may be reproduced, stored in a retrieval system, or transmitted in any form or by any means—electronic, mechanical, photocopy, recording, or any other—without the prior permission of the author.

ISBN: 978-1-64339-986-7

Printed in the United States of America

CONTENTS

Prologue 1
Author's Note 35

PART 1: The McChord Combat Control Team 51
Story XIX: *Home, Home Of The Strange* 53
Story XX: *The Naming Of The Spew* 75
Story XXI: *Newbie Zero-One* 97

PART 2: Combat Control School (CCS) 135
Story XXII: *The Gates Of Hell* 137
Story XXIII: *Barely Hanging On* 161
Story XXIV: *The Nitty Gritty* 189
Story XXV: *Over The Hump* 227
Story XXVI: *Into The Field* 247
Story XXVII: *A Survivor Of The Day* 273
Story XXVIII: *Sour Notes* 295
Story XXIX: *Night Moves* 317
Story XXX: *Turning Point* 341
Story XXXI: *Redemption* 363
Story XXXII: *Culminations* 381

PART 3: Back With The McChord CC Team 407
Story XXXIII: *Peaks And Valleys* 409
Story XXXIV: *The Longest Night... Ever* 445
Story XXXV: *And Life Goes On* 495

PART 4: Basic Survival School 515
Story XXXVI: *Welcome To Survival School* 517
Story XXXVII: *Survival School: In The Raw* 539
Story XXXVIII: *Down From The Mountains* 563

PART 5: POW School 587
Story XXXIX: *Prisoner Of War* 589
Story XL: *Torture Avoidance* 609
Story XLI: *Concentration Camp* 651
Story XLII: *Insurrection* 689

Epilogue 709

IN WOLF'S CLOTHING
BOOK 2 - THE WANNABE

*From newbie to neophyte to rookie warrior
So accomplished, he could hardly stand it*

My new team. Combat Control School.
Survival School and POW School.

*"Smart like horse.
Hung like Einstein."*

- My favorite bumper sticker

BOOK TWO

PROLOGUE

1
SURPRISE

December, 1977
Combat Control School (CCS)
In the field, outside Little Rock Air Force Base, Arkansas

I STUMBLE BACK INTO our campsite, numbed as much from boredom as from the wet chill of mid-December in the Ozarks. The ten surviving members of my class have just spent the last two stultifying hours huddled around a field-portable TACAN—that's a TACtical Air Navigation beacon—learning how to tote, assemble and operate the huge goddamned monstrosity under a day-long freezing drizzle.

As for me, I think the only thing I've gotten out of the whole miserable exercise is about an hour-and-a-half of a standing nap. I'm so friggin' exhausted and beaten down, I almost forgot to follow the rest of my classmates back to our camp once the TACAN thing finally ended.

Truth is, the only thing that's gotten me through this day at all is the fact that it's the eighth day out of the final ten that we have to spend in the field before graduation. And even that is something I couldn't possibly care less about anymore. My feet are wet and frozen into muddy popsicles. My camouflaged fatigues are crusted and torn and damp—both sets—which makes changing my sodden clothes a completely useless gesture. I'm hungry, sore, cold, wet and dead tired, and I've only taken a shit twice in the eight days we've been out here. All I want to do right now is get off my feet and slip off into blessed oblivion, mentally reciting the last of my desperate mantras: "*In three days this will all be a memory. In three days this will all be a memory.*

In just three more stinkin' days…"

But it is not to be.

As I shuffle up to the coal mud of our late great fire, Sergeant Hemingway, arguably the crustiest veteran of our instructor cadre, marches into our circle of tents behind me. His weapons and web gear, canteens and ammo pouches clank and clatter proudly, muffled only slightly by a few strategic strips of duct tape layered between them. His cammies still have their *starched creases*, for cryin' out loud. Mine don't look that good when I first pick them up at the dry cleaners.

Now, I'm about as low on the student food chain as you can get, and I am grateful for that anonymity at times like these. Apparently, one of our poor abused student NCOs is about to get him a Grand Atomic Wedgy for some trivial oversight. One of us lower ranking slobs probably has his socks on inside-out or something like that. And as usual, it will be a public spectacle. I don't have the energy to pay it any attention though, and I begin the slow, groaning, creaking descent to my sitting spot on the log beside the charcoal sludge that was once our campfire.

But Sgt. Hemingway grabs my elbow just as I'm reaching the half-stooped phase of my hunker, hoists me back upright, and announces, loudly enough for anyone within gunshot range to hear, "Airman Stipp! Your frag! The truck leaves in twenty minutes! Better hustle!"

He stuffs a piece of paper into my hand—my 'Fragmentary Order' or 'frag'—claps me hard on the back (everybody in gunshot range probably heard that too), and marches off into the mists again.

Wha? Is this some kind of a joke? Did he not notice the one little measly stripe on my uniform, as opposed to the three or four stripes on all the sergeants' sleeves?

Do I really even look *like a leader of men?*

In the center of a slowly contracting circle of fellow students then, I stare dumbfounded at the dirty wad of Xerox paper in my hand. My frag. *Mine!* These are mission orders, the kind that high commanders hand to lower commanders, but *commanders all!* This is a clinical summary of a tactical situation that must be resolved immediately by a team of 'elite specialists'—the ten students of my class, apparently—led by… who? *Me?*

They're giving *me* the frag?

I look around as if they just dropped a dead rat into my palm.

What am I supposed to do with this? A lowly airman. The lowliest airman in the group, in fact. Yet still they've decided to hand this, the final and most difficult frag of the entire course, to me. *To me?!*

What about Sgt. Haley? Or any *of the other sergeants for that matter! I'm not even an NCO!! And if it just has to be me, why'd you wait until JUST NOW to give it to me?!!!*

"Well, what's it say?"

It's Greg Dorn, my best bud from the McChord Team, trying to goose me out of my stupor. My brain stumbles back on track, my throat swallows dry, and I read from the paper.

"Uhhh... '*Southeast Command advises; Green Beret team egressing from hostile territory with multiple prisoners and wounded. Will require mass evac at earliest possible time. Insert one ten-man CCT* ('Combat Control Team'— that's us) *to DZ Delta* (Drop Zone D) *(see map insert 1), ingress overland five kilometers to RP Echo* (that's 'Rendezvous' or 'Rally' Point E) *(see map insert 2), and make contact with friendlies. Establish a secure perimeter, and set up a 2,500 foot LZ* (that's a Landing Zone, or 'runway') *with full lighting and VHF comm for night recovery ops. CCT will direct and protect the C-130 extraction aircraft through landing, loading and departure, then police up the area and egress on foot. Action to commence immediately*'."

I look up, my mouth hanging open. Most of the class—the other lowly airmen at least—are watching me, waiting for words to issue forth. The four student NCOs, on the other hand—Sergeants Haley, Matheson, Donado and Corbin—just scowl at me, as if this was some kind of scheme of mine to steal their moment of glory. I am fully prepared to hand it over to any one of them though, while I go trotting off into the woods to take my third crap of the week, which has suddenly become an urgent priority for me again. But that too, apparently, will not happen.

"Okay then," says Greg, trying once more to jump-start my brain, "Tell us what to do."

Oh yeh... like I *know.*

Still... gawbless his enthusiastic little heart.

My mind whirls into action—in much the same way a helicopter might spin up to speed, if none of its moving parts were actually bolted together— and I start fumbling through impromptu assignments. Fortunately, a couple of my fellow 'Little Fish' are right beside me the whole way, offering suggestions.

"You'll need two pricks," says Goebler (slang for 'PRC-77's... heavy backpack radios), "One primary, one back-up."

"Uh, yeh," I reply.

"I'll take one," says Torrero, volunteering from the back of the circle.

"Okay," I answer, really taking the bull by the horns now.

I half-heartedly get everyone moving, rummaging through their individual gear for their standard combat loads, while I formulate a rough outline of a plan. Greg says he'll pack my stuff up for me, since I'm going to be real busy. Then he disappears with the rest, leaving me standing by the dead campfire, scribbling notes on the back of the frag.

* * *

WITH FIVE MINUTES LEFT to go, and the big deuce-and-a-half truck idling noisily nearby, I finally complete my computations. Several of the guys have already tossed their gear onto the canvas-shelled bed of the truck, and are now hopping and stomping and chuffing great skirls of steam into the chilly air in front of me. I notice none of the NCOs are among them, although one of them is already sitting in the back of the truck looking annoyed.

Now, referring to my notes, I send my peers running to gather up the mission-specific stuff.

I've calculated exactly how many lights we'll need to outline a 2,500 foot long runway, and figured out how many each man will have to carry in his rucksack to get them all to the LZ without breaking anybody's back. I know how many red and green lens covers we'll need to mark the approach and departure ends of the runway. We'll need extra batteries for the PRCs, and some fundamental weather gear for the air traffic control parts of the operation... defused Claymores, trip flares, and extra ammo for the perimeter defense part.

As I call out each item (over the impatient protestations of the instructors waiting by the truck), someone darts out of the crowd and rounds it up. Until at long last, everything on my list has been called and loaded.

And twenty-two minutes after receiving the frag, all ten of us, along with a small mountain of equipment, are huddled under the tarp canopy of the truck, and the tailgate is being slammed shut.

The truck jerks into gear with a whistling diesel sound, and we pull out through the bushes onto the nearby dirt road.

* * *

IT'S A FORTY-FIVE MINUTE drive from our field encampment back to the airfield at Little Rock Air Force Base, forty-five minutes that I spend trying to finalize my calculations while we barrel down the road, rifling a fifty-mile-an-hour wind chill through the group. I am shivering violently, and my penchant for motion sickness is making it tough to look at my list for more than a few seconds at a time while the truck is rolling.

I finally give it up, still about half an hour out from the base, and concentrate instead on fending off the razor-edged cut of the wind. And that's when it really hits me.

I mean, I'd understood it before, but now it's really starting to sink in.

I, Airman Steve Stipp, the lowliest of the low in this hardcore cutthroat class of ate-up warrior wannabes, have just been given a frag. *The* frag. The *last* frag of the entire course. And they've given me only *twenty minutes* to prepare for it, not counting these forty-five nearly useless minutes of hurtling through the snow-dappled Ozark foothills on the way to the base. And that's just plain unfair!

Granted, this frag and its accompanying night jump did not sneak up on us. We knew it was coming, and we knew it was coming tonight. We also knew it was going to be the biggest baddest frag of the course. But we never suspected it would be slapped into the hands of anyone of lesser stature than an experienced and worldly sergeant. And it sure as hell never crossed my mind that it might be handed off to *me*, of all people. One of the few advantages of being the resident cannon fodder in a group like this is that you never have to worry about this level of crap. It's all above your pay grade.

So much for that tonight.

In a fit of creative spite, apparently, the instructors have decided that this last one should go to the dweeb at the *bottom* of the totem pole instead.

C'est moi!

The weather's been bad all day, so probably no jump will happen tonight anyway. And higher winds are expected with the fall of darkness. That should clear out the fog and the overcast, but will probably cancel the parachute portion of the exercise precisely because of the higher wind velocity. So, as long as the jump itself isn't going to happen, wouldn't it be fun to watch the class goober flounder and drown as the anvils are tossed in on him? And why stop with a mere LZ establishment? Let's make it a *night drop! In surly weather! On short notice! Incredibly* short notice... twenty *minutes* instead of the usual twenty-four *hours* that all the other 'frag leaders' got before me. And then let's throw in a *five kilometer covert overland march* to get from the DZ to the LZ!

Just for the hell of it! Let's really bury this dork!

And that's exactly what they've done... stood me at the bottom of the silo, and dumped in the fertilizer. Apparently they're planning on filling it all the way up to the top, too.

* * *

THE GRAY SUNSET DIMS to darkness as we lumber through the base and onto the flightline.

Our classrooms and parachute rigging tables are in a hangar right off the main aircraft parking apron. Everyone is frozen and stiff as the tailgate bangs open and we clamber down onto the pavement. I 'order' a chain of students to pass the gear from the truck to the warmth of the hangar, and the unloading passes quickly.

Inside, the instructors graciously allow us ten minutes to thaw out and take a leak, to fill our canteens and batten down our equipment. I spend this time furiously scribbling more notes, and allocating gear and tasks to each individual man, including myself. Greg nobly volunteers to prep my parachute for me. And that's just as well. Since I'm the one who originally packed it—seven weeks ago, in the parachute packing phase of the class— I'm probably going to die tonight anyway.

When at last the lead instructor bellows for silence and calls me up to the blackboard to give my briefing, I'm still scribbling as I walk up the aisle. But I've got a rough battle plan assembled in my head. And by the time I reach the podium, I'm as ready as I'll ever be.

Again I recap the mission, state our objectives, draw a little map on the board (one of the few things I'm actually good at), and point out our landmarks.

At 2130 (that's 9:30pm, for the unenlightened), *our C-130 drop ship will put us out over this DZ* (the big open field within sight of our camp). *Once on the ground, we will form up and head out, southbound, through these dense woods, for about five klicks* (kilometers), *until we reach this little dirt road here. If our night nav* (navigation) *is on-target, we should hit the road right about here, where it runs straight as an arrow for a little over a mile. We just need 2,500 feet of that straightaway for our LZ.*

Here the team will split and spread out, forming a rough defensive perimeter around our runway-to-be, five men to a side. Each man will have X-amount of Elco lights (the portable gumdrop-shaped runway lights) *that he'll be responsible for placing at the appropriate interval down the length of the runway before assuming his defensive station. The lights will remain off until radio contact has been established with the inbound aircraft, at which time, in sequence* (so as not to completely abandon all of our defensive positions at the same time), *each man will return to activate his assigned lights.*

I address each man on the team individually, one by one, by name, telling him specifically what he'll be carrying, what he'll need to do with it once he gets there, and where his defensive station will be. I lay out our order of march, assigning a point man, a rear guard, two flankers, a second radio man, a compass man, and a pacer (the guy who counts our steps, and keeps track of the distance we've travelled on foot).

It takes just under fifteen minutes to deliver my little oratory. But when it's done, I'm actually feeling pretty damned good about it. It's a viable plan—downright *brilliant*, in fact, considering the absurd time constraints on my preparations—and everyone seems to have absorbed it well, if not a little grimly. Even the instructors have nothing to add except, "All right, ladies. Let's mount up."

I let out a shaky sigh of relief, and head back to my seat. Greg claps me on my shoulder, and hands me my readied parachute. *Good old Greg.*

For most of another fifteen minutes then, the room fills with all the snapping, clicking, bonking, shuffling, stomping sounds of a military machine assembling itself, as the gear is disseminated per my instructions, and each man packs it up and dons his individual 'battle armor.' And when I'm done, I'm one heavy little bastard myself.

In addition to the fifty pounds of my parachute, harness, and reserve, I've got all my web gear hanging from its own belt and harness, including a red-lensed flashlight, a K-Bar combat knife, two pouches (or 180 rounds) of .22 blank ammunition (three banana clips of thirty rounds each to a pouch), a compass and med kit, plus a canteen that I don't notice (until too late) is empty. In addition, almost thirty pounds of runway lights and their batteries, plus lens covers and flares fill my rucksack to bursting.

My GAU-5 (rhymes with "*cow drive*") assault rifle is slung over one shoulder, barrel down, flash suppressor pointed at my foot and tied to my rigging with what amounts to a thin shoestring. And because I'm going to be the glorious 'leader' of this ship of fools, I also get to carry one of the two PRC-77s, which will ride on my back like a car battery once I'm on the ground. *Oy!* And don't forget the layers of cold weather jackets and thermies, plus my field cap, jump helmet, and goggles. I've also painted my face to look like a freshly tossed salad.

If nothing else, I certainly *look* the part of a real Action Jackson field commander.

I'm dazed and frazzled and nervous, but I've got a tenuous feeling that I might have actually pulled this one off, despite all their efforts to overwhelm me, and ignoring the fact that nothing has actually happened yet.

And when, at last, we troop out the doors through a sharp and stiffening wind—under abruptly clear skies, studded with stars and fast-moving cotton puffs torn from the previous overcast—I'm marching, with no small amount of pride, at the head of this column of noble lunatics.

My noble lunatics, at least for the next couple of hours.

It's the only good moment of the day for me. And the last one of the night, as it turns out.

Unbeknownst to me, one great fistful of Cosmic Shit is, at this very moment, hitting one huge Karmic Fan somewhere. And guess who's standing downrange, innocently looking the wrong direction.

2
ACTION JACKSON

AS I TROMP UP the C-130's ramp, that all-too-familiar stench of JP-4 jet fuel wafts out of the windowless cargo hold, and reminds me to take some Dramamine before the flight. This is when I discover that my lone canteen is empty. I'd been too busy back in the hangar to fill it up. So I toss the vile things down my throat now, dry, bitter, and sticking to the back of my tongue.

Only the beginning, my friend. Only the beginning.

One by one, the flight crew cranks over each of the ship's four propellers, and soon the open cargo bay is reverberating with their heavy turbine-powered roar.

Escorted by one of the instructors, I make the rounds of 'my men'—most of whom are still glowering impatiently at me—checking their straps and connections. I feel ridiculous.

At last, I am back at my end of the troop seat, and belted in. We start to taxi, the ramp whines closed, the lights switch to red, and I close my eyes (yet another defense mechanism to fend off the inevitable motion sickness). We trundle and bump over the uneven concrete for several minutes, then rock to a stop. The engines are run up through their final checks, and after another unexplained pause, we taxi into position on the runway.

For some reason though, we sit there for an inordinately long time. But I don't care. My eyes are closed, my earplugs are in, and I'm breathing deep and slow...

Until two of our instructors burst into the compartment, screaming for everyone to get up and out. *Now!*

What? Get out? You mean "out of the way?" "Out of the aircraft?" Which? What? Why?

Did we take off already? No, I think I would have noticed that.

But we *are* abandoning ship apparently, right here and right now. *So quit asking stupid questions, and MOVE!*

I don't feel quite as bad about my own stupidity when I see nearly every other man on the plane bouncing up and down in their seats for the next several seconds. Because we've all managed to release at least one wrong buckle in our haste to unbelt and evacuate. We're *covered* in buckles, after all, so everyone's getting repeatedly yanked back down into their seats as they pop connectors, only to discover that it's not their seatbelt clasps that they've released.

After several embarrassing failed attempts to stand up though, I finally release myself, snatch up my rucksack from the center pile, and join the queue for the exit door.

But there are no inflatable slides on a C-130. No ladders or rolling stairs either. Just a five-and-a-half-foot drop to the concrete, wearing over a hundred pounds of gear, in the dark, and on legs (and arches) stiff from the cold. I crunch to the ground next to the guy who jumped in front of me, and we both limp off the runway into the grass. Fire trucks are already wailing their way out to us.

What the hell?

They sit us in the grass with our backs against our chutes and rucks, and we watch as the little Keystone Kop parody plays itself out in front of us. It lasts for more than half an hour before they finally declare the aircraft safe enough to be towed back to the parking apron.

A blue 'bread van' pulls up and takes the flight crew back to the ramp to crank up another C-130. We, on the other hand, are left to chill even further in the tall wet grass.

A tug drags the first plane away—smoke in the cockpit, they finally tell us—the fire trucks pack up and leave, and we are left alone under the stars.

The wind is brisk and uneven, almost hesitant, but still full of frigid bluster. And the grass is wet. It's now after 10:00pm, but no other aircraft are due in or out, so they leave us right where we are to await our new aircraft.

Eventually, a new C-130 thrums and drones over to us, stopping once again in take-off position on the runway... right where we left off with the last one. I stagger to my feet, and join the others in their slow shuffle over to the lowered cargo ramp and the pool of red light spilling from the interior. I don't even pretend to be interested in my team's snaps and buckles this time, and plop down immediately into my own rearmost seat.

At something like a quarter-till-eleven then, we finally lumber into the sky and turn toward our drop zone.

It should be a ridiculously short flight. After all, it only took forty-five minutes to *drive* it on dirt roads and in a loaded deuce-and-a-half. But the repercussions from that cosmic collision of feces and fan have only just begun to reveal themselves.

* * *

AS PREDICTED BY OUR resident pessimists back at the camp, the wind has stiffened yet again, ricocheting through the mountains and chopping up the skies into turbulent pockets of twenty- and thirty-mile-an-hour gusts. The legal 'wind speed limit' for jumping with the standard round parachutes that we're wearing is thirteen miles an hour. And these winds are *way* over that. But the instructors are yet hopeful, and decide to keep circling until some magical lull presents itself.

Our tactical static-line jump altitude tonight is only fifteen-hundred feet—barely above the darkened mountaintops, and plowing right through the worsening turbulence—so the ride has now not only lengthened, but it has noticeably roughened as well. And there's only so much my closed eyes and a pair of dry Dramamine can handle.

As time stretches out then, and the ten-minute flight slowly elongates to twenty, then thirty, then forty minutes, matter finally triumphs over mind, and my scrumptious lunch (I'd missed dinner in my scramble to set up this glorious mission) decides to return for an encore.

I am prepared for this at least. And after about ten more minutes of my usual futile attempts at resistance—which really only drag out the misery while things rise to their inevitable conclusion anyway—I toss my cookies into the requisite bag and lean back, sweaty and pasty-faced, but at last relieved of that burden. We are required to carry our barf out the door with us though, so I spend a moment securing my little treasure so that it can be easily reached at jump time.

Fifteen minutes later, we're still battering our way through the invisible moguls with no end in sight, and I'm begging the loadmaster for another bag. Having witnessed my previous performance (and I tend to be a rather loud and demonstrative upchucker, I must admit), he is able to locate several more, and gives them all to me.

I use one almost immediately. A little liquid, but mostly just dry heaves. The effort leaves me weak, dizzy, and thirsty though, and all I can think about is how much I'd really like the instructors to just *give up on this one! Let's just turn around and land! Either that or shoot me!*

Give me some live ammo, and I'll do it myself!

But no. If they put this mission off until tomorrow night, I'll have too much time to perfect my dazzling marching orders, and what kind of fun would that be?

* * *

TWENTY MORE WRETCHED MINUTES jostle by then, as this blind, stinking, droning machine blunders through the bumpy skies. And I am audibly moaning now. Though the inner vibration of a gentle moan is usually fairly therapeutic in the quelling of an upset stomach, tonight it's doing absolutely nothing. My guts probably can't even detect the moaning under the assault of this aircraft's relentless grumbling, growling, and hammering through the mountains' lumpy air. But the fact is, I just don't care anymore. I am miserable with a capital *F*, and I can't believe my gut is boiling yet again, preparing for yet another reprise of its trademark Technicolor Yawn®.

This time it's all dry heaves and fluttering abdominal muscles. I twitch and convulse for another couple of minutes, and finally collapse with my empty barf bag in hand. I am utterly drained, sweating like a triathlete, and tumbling at the nexus of a world that is now spinning wildly around me.

I want to weep, but I haven't got the energy. Or the fluids.

So naturally, this is when one of the more malicious of our instructor cadre marches into the middle of the bouncing cargo bay and, holding up three fingers on one hand and a closed fist on the other (to illustrate what '13' *looks* like), announces that the winds are now at precisely "*Thirteen knots!*"

His sinister grin belies the rather amazing coincidence that the winds should just happen to be at exactly the maximum allowable jump velocity...

because of course, *they aren't*. They haven't lessened a single knot. We're still slamming through the same twenty-mile-an-hour buffets we have been for the last hour and a half. Our instructors have simply tired of the circling, not to mention the re-runs of me blowing phantom chunks into this same empty bag, and have opted to just get this over with.

"*Hook! Up!*" he yells.

I swoon to my feet, somehow fumble my leaden rucksack onto its hooks under my reserve chute, tighten my helmet strap, snap my static line onto the anchor cable overhead, collect up my barf bags, and lurch my way down the bucking floor to the side jump door. Sgt. Rabin, the lead instructor on this frag, hauls the door open as I approach, unleashing a raw shaft of hurricane-force winds into the compartment, and thrusts his head out into the thundering slipstream. Hands clutching both sides of the combing, he scans the pitch black universe outside.

I watch him as if in a trance. The freezing torrent of air seems to have placated my stomach somewhat, but the dizziness is slow to subside.

Sgt. Rabin waves me over to the door beside him.

Since I'm the designated 'dashing leader' of this motley crew, this is the part where he shows me how to sight and time the exact moment of exit for the whole team. The standard technique is for me, as the 'Head Honcho,' to wait for just the right instant, then signal my men to "*Go! Go! Go!*". I'll stand on the opposite side of the doorway—right where Sgt. Rabin is now, in the core of the wind tunnel—and usher each man out, following the last man out into the void myself.

Such was our teaching.

Still bleary-eyed and dopey though, I wobble into place next to Sgt. Rabin, and follow his finger out into the darkness. He's shouting something about lights, but I lose most of it in the maelstrom. I can see what he's pointing at though—a broad rectangle of four red lights, sliding through the solid black nothingness out there—the four corners of our drop zone, marked out by the other instructors on the ground. It's interesting to watch, but right now I'm just fixated on the revivifying effect of that screaming Arctic slipstream tearing past me from the doorway. It's slowly clearing my head, and scouring away the deep nausea.

I do notice, however, that the drift of those four points is not bringing them any closer. Rather, they seem to be floating *past* us, like cars on the opposite side of a freeway divider.

I'm puzzling this over in my swooning brain, when Sgt. Rabin smacks my shoulder and shouts, "*Go!*" By this he means, "*Get your men going.*" In my swirling delirium, however, I take it quite literally. And in a mindless lunge, I hurl myself straight out the door into the freezing ether.

I am now, officially, a complete fucking idiot.

What the hell did I just do?

Rather than being the *last* man out the door, I am the first.

For three seconds, I tumble alone through the hard, slick, icy air. Then I am hoisted upward, abruptly but smoothly, by the risers above my shoulders and the straps between my legs (never underestimate the importance of proper testicular placement prior to a jump). The savage roar of the wind is snuffed, replaced by the *snap, pop,* and *ruffle* of an unfurling parachute booming open overhead. And just like that, I am instantly cured of all maladies and imbalances.

Jumping out of an airplane will do that for you, I've discovered.

I am suddenly invigorated! Breathlessly alive, clear-headed... *and most of a damned MILE away from the four red lights to my left! A mile!*

Okay; maybe a kilometer.

I'm barely a thousand feet up in the air now, sinking at twenty-two vertical feet per second, under a chute that will contribute only *ten* miles an hour of forward speed over the ground. And I'm over the frappin' Ozark Mountains and forests (*okay, maybe the Ouachitas*) at nearly midnight, at least a *kilometer* from the damned DZ!

I am dead! And the rest of 'my men' are probably all crowded around the jump door right now, laughing and pointing, drinking champagne, and watching my lonely unbelievably stupid parachute recede into the abyss all by itself.

Well, the least I can do (and by that I mean *the most*) is turn myself toward the distant drop zone, and try to get as close as I can before plowing into some invisible cliff face in the darkness.

I line myself up with the little red lights—which seem to be winking on and off now, as if something were passing in front of them—then turn my attention to my pack release (the so-called 'Red Apple'). I find it, and give it a vigorous heave upward. It releases, and my seventy-five pound rucksack falls away, jerking to a stop at the end of its twenty-foot tether.

I am looking straight down, watching it bounce and swing in the inky blackness below, when something huge *whooshes* by my feet going the other way... *fast!* I twist around in my harness to see what it was. And in the feeble starlight, I barely make out the soft tree-studded swayback of a ridgeline, backing away and rising steadily above and behind me. I have just swooped over the top of a ridge separating our drop zone from the next valley over!

Holy crap! They put me out over the wrong valley!

Couldn't that pilot see how far away those DZ lights were when he hit the "Go!" button? Jesus! I am really screwed!

Then it dawns on me. The speed with which the ridgeline shot past me has given it away.

They put me out "over there" because the winds are still howling at over *twenty F-ing miles an hour! That's why!* They put me out way upwind to allow the winds to carry me back to where I was supposed to be. That ridgeline flashed by me even faster though, because my chute's built-in ten miles an hour of forward speed was being *added* to the wind's twenty- to twenty-*five* mile an hour velocity!

I have to slow the fudge down—like *right now*—before I slam into the ground at over *thirty* horizontal miles an hour!

Quickly, I haul down on my right toggle-line, and the parachute responds with a languid turn to the right. And once the red lights are at my back, I let go of the line.

I'm traveling *backwards* now. The wind is still shoving me toward the DZ at at least twenty miles an hour, but my chute is now countering it with its own *ten* miles an hour. Which means I'm still going to hit the invisible ground at more than ten horizontal miles an hour, while dropping at twenty-two *vertical* feet per second, except that now *I'm going backwards as well!*

Oh, this is going to leave a mark.

But I've done all that I can do, and I look back down between my frozen feet in one last desperate bid to forewarn myself of the impending impact. It's just darkness down there, though. I can barely make out my boots, and with a little imagination, I think I can see my rucksack, swinging like a pendulum, twenty feet further below.

Suddenly I hear a muffled crunch, and my attention is transfixed by my rucksack, which is now bouncing '*away*' from me—trailing '*behind*' me—pulling its line taut in the process.

It has found the ground first! *Of course! I should have...*

WHAM!

My heels hit the ground, and an instant later, my ass and head (apparently interchangeable on this night) smash into it in turn.

With a bone-jarring crash and a bounce, I smack down in the field like a great big camouflaged sack of loose change. I hit and roll onto my side, most of the air bashed from my lungs. Ahead of me, I can see my chute, still fully and firmly inflated, dragging me towards the dark trees. My heavy rucksack is acting like an anchor though, furrowing its way along behind me, and slowing me down. And as I drag along between them, my stunned senses return enough for me to fumble for the riser-release buckles at each of my shoulders. They're always such sticky sons of bitches though, especially when there's any tension on them... like right now.

But tonight the one on the left lets go right away.

My chute goes limp and flutters to the ground.

So do I.

* * *

"**OH... GOD... DAMN,**" I gasp.

I don't tarry long, though. One thing that's been hammered into us since the start of this school is to *Never Be The Last*. There are a hundred push-ups waiting for the last man to the rally point. For the last man to do *anything*, really. And even though I suspect I may be the *only* person from that C-130 that is not still on board it right now, well... a hundred push-ups is a hundred push-ups.

I struggle to my feet, assessing my every ache and pain as I start to disconnect things.

First, my parachute. I withdraw the folded B-4 bag I'd stowed among my crotch straps, and drop it on the ground. I unhook my rucksack tether, and toss the rope into the bag. Then, swooping one arm under the chute's risers, I march toward the deflated canopy, alternating the swoops until the length of suspension lines and silken folds are daisy-chained around my arms from pits to wrists.

I'm only halfway through the process though, when I hear a curious sound wafting against the current of the wind. Sort of a snapping fluttering sound, followed by a discreet "*Oh shit!*" and that flaccid bag-o-meat *ka-flump!* that goes along with a body slamming to Earth. A stream of *ows!* and *shits!* and other gut-punched four-letter utterances accompany a bumping-scuffing-scraping sound, all of which implies the arrival—comparable to mine—of another gallant sky-trooper. Or maybe just his carcass.

At least it looks like I didn't leap alone.

I hurry my post-jump ministrations, dumping my gathered chute into the B-4 bag, breaking the shoestring moorings of my GAU-5, and setting it aside. Then I shuck my harness and helmet, and zip them up with the rest of the parachute paraphernalia in the bag. Only my reserve chute—a tight little 'loaf' of green bundled material about the size of an over-stuffed shoebox—remains outside the bag. I take it now, and hook its two clips onto the handles of the loaded B-4 bag, just as I was taught.

Thump! Crunch! "Aw Christ!" *Scuffle, drag, bump!* "Son-of-a...!"

Ah, another valiant ally has alighted deftly onto the darkened field.

I shrug my way, painfully, into my bloated rucksack, slap my field cap onto my head, chamber a round, and sling the GAU. Then I heave the stuffed B-4 bag over my head, letting it drop onto my shoulders with the connected reserve chute pulled down under my chin—like the arms of a wounded soldier draped over my back—and I begin the long tromp over to the instructor's Jeep, where it's idling at the rally point.

"Oh shit! Oh shit! Oh...!" *Kaflump! Bump-da-bump!*

"Ouch! Mother f...!" *Draaaag!*

Just six more heroes to go.

I accelerate to a jouncing, jangling, flopping trot.

Don't wanna' do no push-ups. Not tonight.

Everything hurts enough as it is.

* * *

THE CONTINUING ARRIVALS FADE in volume as I near the cluster of vehicles where they sit, purring steam into the frosty breeze: a Jeep (for the instructors), a deuce-and-a-half (to carry off our bagged parachutes), and the obligatory 'Meat Wagon' or 'Field Ambulance' (in case of injuries).

It's the rules.

Whump! "Ah fuck!" Somewhere behind me.

Swish! Crunch! Ba-wump! "Ah-gahd! Shit! Son of a bitch!"

Oh yes, the professionals are on the job tonight.

I jog right up to the deuce—to the lilting dulcet tones of a far off voice repeating the word "*Fuck!*," over and over and over again, only slightly muted by distance and the deep grass—and I heft my B-4 bag up onto the truck's bed. And suddenly the remaining weapons and bullets and canteens and coats and radios and rucksacks still hanging on my body don't seem so heavy anymore.

Just to impress any observers with my 'mission focus' then, I immediately drop to one knee, shed the ruck, unlatch its top flap, exposing the damned PRC, and start to set it up.

A faint "*Mother pus-bucket!*" barely rises above the engine noises, along with another "*Shit!*" or two coming from somewhere off across the field. And I can't help but smile... at least a little bit.

Yes, indeedy. The gang's all here!

The radio powers up, and once its little foot-long antenna has been attached, I find our mission freq and do a signal check, knowing that no one's going to answer it. Then, demonstrably satisfied with the state of my communications gear, I hook the handset onto a D-ring on my web gear, package everything up, and pitch it all back onto my aching shoulders again.

As I do, a thin and lonely shout filters in from the outfield.

"Medic! Medic!"

Damn.

And things were going so well.

Cigarette embers arc out of the Meat Wagon's windows as they drop the thing into gear and trundle off into the darkness. Its headlights come on a moment later.

In the meantime, a couple more of 'my guys' jog into the rally point, heave their own bags onto the deuce, and plod over to me, trying gamely to stifle their puffing and panting in front of the lone instructor, Sgt. Myers. Nobody says a thing about my premature ejection from the aircraft.

"Son of a bitch," a less-than-reverent shadow gasps, "There's no way that wind was only thirteen knots up there."

"Thirteen?" Sgt. Myers chuckles from behind the wheel of the Jeep, "Try *twenty*-three, maybe twenty-*five* knots when you went out that door. What the hell's wrong with you dumbasses?"

We all stare at him, slapped speechless, while the steam chugs from our mouths.

Like it was our *idea or something!*

Clearly he's kidding, in a cruel kind of way, but I know he's seriously testing Little Rocky's self-restraint. That's "Rocky"—McChord's own Ricky Spradlin—our class's designated Feisty Runt. Barely over five feet tall, wired and wiry, fun but fearless, but predictably volatile as well. It figures he's one of the first to the rally point. But right now he's glaring at the instructor as if debating between decapitation, castration, or just a good old country ass-whoopin'. But either way—trained, experienced, or not—I'd be hard-put to give the instructor even odds against a wound-up and wailin' Little Rocky.

Another heavily burdened figure lumbers out of the darkness and collapses against the truck's tailgate. It's Percy Hackett, my designated 'pacer' for tonight, and the class's official bitcher.

"Jesus... H... Christ," he wheezes, "That about t'killed me."

"Almost," someone behind me sighs, evidently disappointed.

In the distance, twin spears of red light flare to life and begin to spin.

The meat wagon's emergency lights.

Uh-oh.

Sgt. Myers fumbles with the Jeep's radio for a moment, then mumbles something into the mike that's buried deep in the meat of his huge fist.

"What's up?" Hackett sniffs.

Silence for a moment, while the radio squawks and crackles behind us. Then Rocky speaks up for the rest of us.

"What? You think we know something you don't?"

"Looks like Torrero broke his leg," Sgt. Myers grouses disgustedly, tossing the radio mike onto the floorboard.

Then, turning to face me, he adds, "Better figure out what he's carrying, and how you're going to divvy it up among the rest of you."

His compassion is just breathtaking.

I don't have to say the word "*shit*." Hackett does it for me. Then he slaps the side of his GAU-5 in frustration... and fires a pretend-round into the dirt. *BANG!*

It's a blank—all blast, no bullet, no real-world damage done—but it's still a startling flash of light and a jarring slap to the ears. Everybody jumps, even Sgt. Myers sitting in the Jeep.

"*What the...! Aaaawww!*"

Hackett knows what's coming next.

"Well now, *that* was just fucking brilliant!" Sgt. Myers barks, now standing. "You know the drill, airman! *Drop!*"

"But... I..."

"*Drop!* And give me four-hundred!"

"Four-hundred?!!"

"You heard me! You're number eight. Now drop!"

"Shit."

"And count it off *loud!*"

Hackett snatches the errant weapon off his shoulder, and, thinking better of it only at the last second, refrains from spiking it into the ground, choosing instead to prop it delicately against one of the deuce's tires.

"For some reason, I just don't think that safety's on, airman."

Hackett stops, halfway to the ground, and swivels to snap the rifle's safety on. You can hear his teeth grinding from clear over here. Then he's on his hands and toes, pumping and counting.

"One. Two. Three. Four. Five..."

Four-hundred push-ups. Jesus!

But everybody knows the CCS 'Prime Directive': "*There's no excuse for a weapon going off among your own. It's unprofessional, downright amateurish, in fact. But worse, it's loud! Bad guys can hear it, good guys can get shot. So you will never EVER allow it to happen. Period.*"

The first man to cap one off like that had owed fifty push-ups. But each subsequent bonehead thereafter had to add fifty more to that of the one before (on the presumption that the only thing stupider than a moron squeezing off a round in the middle of his own team is *another* moron doing the same thing after he just saw somebody else doing a million push-ups for it). Hackett is the eighth bonehead in as many days to do it, so...

Four-hundred it is.

I was the *second* bonehead of the class, back on the afternoon of the second day in the field. And looking back on it now, it's a trade-off I'm only too happy to have made—the humiliation of being one of the first to screw up, in lieu of being one of the *last*, and having to do push-ups for the rest of my military career. It is an effective deterrent, however. No one's done it twice.

Then, from out of the midnight gloom comes an impossible silhouette: what appears to be an eight-foot-high mountain of luggage *with legs*, swaying up to the deuce and crumpling onto its bed. It turns out to be good old Greg Dorn, staggering under the burden of his own load *plus* a second B-4 bag bloated with Torrero's discarded jump gear. Greg's breathing hard, but still radiating enough calmness, charisma, and bottled energy to carry it all right back out there again if he was so ordered.

"... Twenty-nine. Thirty. Thirty-one. Thirty-two...," says Hackett.

Greg doesn't even look down as he steps toward me around Hackett's pumping form. He straightens his field cap—*God forbid he should appear at all 'mussed' after the diversions of the last two hours*—and drops his gloved hands to his hips.

"Torrero landed right after me. Landed with the wind. Almost overshot the whole DZ in the dark. Almost went into the damned *trees*. Hit hard and headfirst. I could hear the bone snap from clear over where I was standing. I think it was the... the 'lower leg bone,' whatever it's called..."

"The tibia," says Sgt. Myers.

"Or the fibula," adds Goebler, "There's actually *two* bones in the... lower... um... leg area..."

"Whatever," says Greg, waving off any further interruptions, "They're going to have to evac him to Little Rock General."

"Shit," we all reply in unison.

"... Forty. Forty-one. Forty-two..." says Hackett.

Great. I haven't even started the night overland portion of the frag, and I'm already down to eighty percent of my original force. One guy's getting a bumpy ride off the DZ with his leg in a splint—and as luck would have it, he's the guy that volunteered to carry the other damned prick—and another's just begun an hour's worth of push-ups. The mission clock's about to start ticking as soon as the last ambulatory member of the team reaches the RP and finishes his hundred push-ups for being last. I'm freezing, and hopping back and forth on club feet. It's after midnight in the shivering depths of an Arkansas December, *and I can no longer remember why the fuck I'm here. Damn it!* Right now, at this very moment in time, I've got friends—going to college down in Gainesville, Florida—who are probably getting laid even as we speak. Well, truth be told, knowing them, they're probably playing *Dungeons & Dragons* or something equally geekish. But that's not the point.

The point is that they and the entire rest of the carefree world, for that matter, are comfortable right now, one way or another, whether zoned out in front of their TVs, rolling dice, or making the bedsprings squeak. *Whatever!* Even as we wage our miserable little pretend-war out here on this wind-whipped field, debating alternatives to my brilliant mission plan, and ignoring Hackett's push-ups as they slow and quiet behind us.

He's barely finished his first fifty.

Fuck me. I can just go to hell.

Two more human pack mules stagger out of the darkness, shrug their bags onto the truck, chuckle at Hackett's fading exertions, and approach our huddle with Torrero's rucksack carried between them. And the divvying up begins. His lights and lens covers, the anemometer, and of course, that goddamned prick. As if everyone's loads were not already absurdly heavy enough.

Hackett is on his hands and knees, cursing and gasping furiously—he hasn't quite reached eighty yet, and this is already his third pause—when the last two guys finally barrel out of the shadows, feet thundering, gear flopping and clattering on their backs, racing each other to avoid the ignominy of being the dreaded Last Guy. Sgt. Myers decides that they're both a couple of losers, and now we have *three* exhausted people counting off push-ups together.

Even as they're pumping though, Myers turns and announces to the rest of us that the mission clock has just been started. We now have just two hours to be completely set up and lit up on our anonymous little stretch of dirt backroad, which is still *five klicks away!* Just a tick over three miles.

I sigh, and call for everyone to saddle up and get moving. We've got several minutes of marching just to get to the edge of the DZ where I'd designated our overland to begin. Our two last-place pusher-uppers can catch up to us before we reach the trees, but Hackett is just going to have to be a write-off. At the rate he's going, he won't reach four-hundred before Christmas, and we just can't spare the time. I doubt if that's strictly 'legal'—it's certainly not *realistic*, and most likely not the solution that the instructors were looking for from me—but I don't take the time to think it through.

And off we go… without them… sort of.

Everybody hesitates for a moment or two, no doubt as uncertain as I am about whether we even *can* leave without the others. But when Sgt. Myers offers nothing to disabuse us of the notion, we all shrug and turn southeast, jostling into line of march order as we go, and head for the distant trees.

This is probably a mistake, but then… well… so was giving command of this frag to *me*.

Rocky, my point man, takes the cue, and immediately starts trotting toward the DZ's far corner. The rest of us are hard-pressed to even keep him in sight, as it's always been throughout the entire course whenever Li'l Rocky's had the lead. Behind us, the two Last Guys finish their respective fifty push-ups each (apparently Sgt. Myers softened, and allowed them to split the penalty between them), and they scramble back into their gear to follow us.

Hackett, on the other hand, is a limp rag, paused yet again and gasping, his own count stalled at just over a hundred. Taking all things into account though, Sgt. Myers opts to waive the rest of Hackett's calisthenic debt as well, and releases him to join us.

Hmm. Maybe I just did Hackett a favor by abandoning him.

I bet I'll be finding out right quick just how grateful he truly is for my little 'gift.'

And so begins the overland odyssey.

3
MAX TACTICAL

THE LAST TWO ARRIVALS catch up to us before we've even moved fifty yards. Hackett comes wheezing up to our little parade just before we reach the tree line, and slumps into the number four slot right behind me, puffing, panting, and cussing up a storm.

I don't know what he's getting all huffy about, though. I just got him out of something like three-hundred push-ups by walking off without him like I did. But do you think he appreciates it? *Nooo.*

In a hushed tone, I interrupt his fuming to remind him that (a) this is supposed to be a covert move, so *keep it down*—the instructors are still with us—and (b) here's the edge of the DZ, so start your pace count now. It's the latter point that refocuses his seething energy moreso than the former, and the profanity recedes into the darkness along with the rest of us.

We seem, then, for the moment at least, to finally be on-track. Everybody together—well, all but the one guy who's bouncing over dirt roads in an ambulance as we speak, anyway—everything in its place, and still on-schedule.

Nothing to do now but cover the distance stealthily, and call it a night.

Sometimes I can just be so naïve.

For starters, I now see that I have 'over-tacticalized' the move.

What can I say? This is the first tactical overnight land march we've done since the course began. I have no precedent to follow. Considering the distance to be covered and the time constraints under which we're covering it, it's overkill to keep nine heavily burdened men in a tree-to-tree half-crouch the whole way. Probably not accomplishing much with those two flankers that I've got paralleling us either, about ten yards out on either side of the column. Just begging to lose them somewhere along the line. But right now, with three instructors strolling among us in the pitch black of the forest, and so little time with which to get where we have to go, I can't think of a good 'tactical' way to undo what's been overdone. So we forge ahead as is.

Then Hackett starts bitching again.

Despite the silence that we're all striving so hard for here, not to mention the omnipresence of our accompanying instructors, he's just at the end of his tether. And I can't fault him for that. He's so pissed off, so exhausted, and now so utterly beside himself with the frustration of not being able to keep up a current pace count with all the stopping and starting, ducking and darting, circumnavigating low hills and clambering over invisible fallen logs (not to mention being left behind to finish his push-ups—and that might not have been the *best* way I could've handled that, now that I think about it), he just can't help himself.

I get it. I really do. That doesn't mean that I have to keep putting up with it, though. I'm feeling battered enough myself—so sore, cold, shaky-kneed weak, and deeply bone-tired—that I'm no longer willing to let that kind of unprofessional shittiness, belligerence, and (truth be told) *insubordination* go unchecked. Like it or not, like *me* or not, I am in fact the *leader* of this team and this mission. And after another couple of sharp whispers at him to keep it down, I finally rap the side of my weapon twice—the signal to drop and freeze—and I scamper back beside him.

One of the instructors ambles up next to us in the darkness like a curious cow.

"*What's the count up to now?*" I whisper through my heavy breathing.

"*I don't know,*" he fusses, "*Something like nineteen-fifty.*"

Good. Nineteen-hundred-and-fifty paces. At roughly eleven paces per every ten meters—my own personal measured standard, which is no doubt based on a longer stride than Hackett's—that's roughly a mile. One-point-six klicks out of five. That's good enough for me.

"Fine. You're fired."

"What?!"

"You're fired," I hiss, "*I'll take the pace count from here. You go relieve Donado at rear guard.*"

"What the hell do you think you're...?!"

"Shut up! I'm sick of your bitching. Go to the rear, now!"

Then, without waiting for his next response, I stand up, rap my weapon again, and signal a forward march.

Much better. He ought to really be singing my praises now.

Nobody else says a word; they just tippy-toe past him in the dark. Even Hackett's receding outrage is subdued. I've never done anything like that before in my life, and I'm too mentally and spiritually obliterated to take any pride or relief from it right now. But the rigors of the evening do finally feel a little less trying without the incessant sparks flying off the man behind me.

* * *

THE MARCH ITSELF DOESN'T get even a little bit easier.

We cross several dirt roads along the way. And in each case, Rocky brings us to a stop, and silently signals me with the nature of the problem. I invariably signal him to do a quick 'reconnoiter,' then make the crossing once he's sure it's clear. We all know there's not going to be anybody out on these roads at two in the morning, but you never know what the instructors might pull. Who knows… maybe I'm *not* being 'too tactical' about all this.

Then one by one—with each of us acting 'terribly intent' about not being observed—we dart after him, across the road and into the farside scrub. It takes several minutes to get everybody across this way, and that's annoying for everybody, including me. But I'm not willing to drop our guard now, just because we're all dead exhausted and fed up with this nightmare deployment. After all, the instructors are with us for a reason. If they weren't, we could all just be crashing through the woods, flashlights waving all over the place, shouting dirty jokes at each other, and it wouldn't make any difference as long as we made the LZ in good time. So there's a legitimate purpose to all this hyper-stealthy play-acting.

A couple of small clearings break up the march as well, but we can't just blithely stroll across such open areas just because it'd be easier. People get killed when they make themselves an easy target. So we have to *circle* each clearing, just inside the trees, and that delays things even more.

Fortunately, I'm pretty good at estimating distances, even when they're not line-of-sight. I'm also pretty adept at picking out notable landmarks on the far sides of each clearing from which to resume our straight march, and this precludes me having to 'estimate' when we've circled far enough. And as a final bonus, I'm the only one in the group (that I know of) who seems to understand 'celestial navigation' on night maneuvers, which means I don't have to keep my eyes on my damned compass all the damned time. I can just refer to whatever stars I can see through the trees. It's not true 'navigation' or even 'triangulation'—just a basic familiarity with the constellations and most of the major stars—but it's enough to keep me homing in on the same star each time I look up. And that's enough... or at least it has been so far.

The result of all this is a strong inner confidence that, despite the detours and diversions, we are still on-track and accurately on-pace. I have a very clear picture in my head of the map from which this mission was derived, and I'm certain that I could pinpoint our exact location on it at any time.

Crossing the open strip beneath a promenade of high-tension power lines confirms all this for me. We're a little later getting to it than I'd hoped, but I know right where we are, and it seems there's finally a light at the end of the proverbial tunnel.

* * *

ON THE PRO SIDE of the ledger, my navigational certainty pays off when we finally break out of the woods at the beginning (or the end) of the straightaway portion of our target road... our LZ.

Zoo-hah! Score one for the Steve-meister.

On the *con* side, however, thanks to all my hyper-consciousness on 'max tactical' movement, it has taken us *an hour-and-fifty minutes* just to get here! And the instructors had only given us *two hours* in which to finish the entire mission. Time to scramble.

I call the team into a huddle, set up a quick, close, temporary perimeter, and have the guy who's now carrying Torrero's anemometer take a fast wind reading. While he's doing that, I have Greg Dorn shoot a quick compass bearing down the edge of the road. And when both of them give me their findings, the numbers vary by only ten or fifteen degrees. *Good*. The road is running northeast-to-southwest, with us hunkered down at its northeast end. And the wind is slicing through us from behind, running almost straight down the road itself. So the decision is easy.

"*Okay, this is the departure end of the runway,*" I whisper, "*We'll deploy in reverse order from this point, heading that way.*"

Everyone's heads turn together to look down the length of the road. And that's kinda' cute.

I refer to the pencil markings on my map, barely visible in the scarlet wash of my red-lensed flashlight. And based on my pre-planned runway placement—which is founded on the positions of the tallest trees relative to the aircraft's supposed approach and departure routes—I determine that our *approach* end lights will wind up right about where our fictional 'Green Beret team' is alleged to be waiting.

"*The command post will be down there at the approach end, on this side,*" I continue. "*Corbin, since you've got Torrero's prick now, you switch with Haley and drop your lights here, on the far side of the road. Right over there. Haley, you just drop yours further down, in this area. Just follow the obvious sequence.*"

Haley grunts disgustedly. As the senior-most of the four remaining NCOs, I'm sure it galls him to have to take my orders at all (not to mention the offense of being so casually addressed as "Haley," rather than "*Sergeant* Haley," especially by a low-life like me). Right now though, I just don't give the intercourse of a flying rodent.

"*I'll call 'lights-on' on team channel five as soon as the aircraft calls ten minutes out, okay? Any questions?*"

Nothing but sulking and heavy breathing.

"*Okay then. Let's go.*"

With the instructors moseying casually right down the middle of the road then, we head out. Half the team scampers across to the other side of the road, while my half parallels it on the near side. Every hundred feet or so, two of them—one from each side—appear at the road's opposing shoulders, drop their Elco lights in place, then duck back into the shadows. And after so many lights, with their individual supplies depleted, those two drop out of the moving pack altogether and wait in the weeds, watching over their lights.

It takes almost fifteen painstaking minutes to work our way all the way down to the opposite end of the LZ this way. But when we finally get there, it's just my McChord teammate Sgt. Sal Donado, the instructor duo of Sergeants Myers and Stillman, and me. The rest have all peeled off along the way. I hustle to set up my radio and establish a defensible position, while Sal drops a perpendicular line of three lights stepping away from each side of the runway, and caps them all with green 'approach end' lens covers.

Sgt. Myers, clearly as eager as the rest of us to call it a friggin' night already, walks up to me and immediately starts talking like an inbound pilot calling on my radio.

"Padlock Control, this is Coil Zero-One on point-seven. Radio check, over."

I feel pretty danged stupid talking into my dead handset and pretending like it's not my instructor I'm addressing, but I do it anyway.

"Coil Zero-One, this is Padlock Control. You're loud and clear. Go ahead."

"Padlock," Sgt. Myers answers, "We've been holding out here about fifteen minutes now. What's your status, over?"

This is bullshit, of course. If an aircraft had actually arrived in our vicinity before we were fully set up, its pilot wouldn't have waited until now to contact us. This is just a jab at me personally, pointing out the fact that I've already blown the deadline by five minutes. And right now, that just pisses me off. I act as though he'd never said anything about it at all.

"Coil Zero-One, LZ and assets are in place. Runway zero-five in use. Wind zero-six-zero at one-five, gusting to two-zero. Altimeter unknown. Ready for lights-on at your call."

"Roger that, Padlock. We're three minutes out, on wide-downwind to runway zero-five right now. Lights on, please."

Sgt. Myers is definitely ready to get this night over with. And I am only too happy to oblige. I quickly rechannelize to team channel five, and make one short whispered transmission.

"*Lights on. Lights on.*"

Then Sal and I both hustle over to our own Elcos, and one by one, start snapping them on. At the far distant end of the runway—almost half a mile away from us—where Sgt. Corbin has heard me on the other (Torrero's) PRC, lights begin to wink on at the same time. And shortly thereafter, one by one, then by twos and threes, the lights in between start to fill in.

I'm too preoccupied at first to notice it, but by the time Sal and I are hunkered down around our radio again, our weapons aimed outward as if we're actually thinking about 'defending our position,' it becomes apparent that something's gone wrong. All the runway lights—with the exception of the lines of green *approach* lights Sal and I just set out, plus a single dim red light at the *departure* end—are *white*. Uncapped. There should be two strands of red roll-out lights arrayed similar to our green ones, running perpendicular away from either side of the runway's far end.

But there's not. The *lights* are all there. But with that one dull red exception, they're all white. Sgt. Myers has noticed it too. *Shit.*

Where are the rest of the colored lights?

I call Corbin on the prick, and he says he'll go check.

More time passes. In fact, *six more minutes* transpire, running us further and further past the deadline. But no one can find the missing red lenses… until someone goes and looks at that one red-capped light on the far left. And there they find all six of the red lenses, stacked atop that one light.

This explains why the light had appeared so dim—it was barely eking its way through six layers of red filters—but that doesn't explain how anyone could have *not noticed* an eight-inch-tall stack of lenses towering above a single light. *Dammit!*

Everybody's pissed. The instructors are downright abusive. But the lenses finally get distributed, and our runway is officially declared operative… *two hours and eleven minutes* after the clock started.

* * *

WE HAVE FAILED.

I have failed. And my failure has cost everybody.

Now I'm depressed.

Gawd! It was so close! I almost did it! But…

On top of everything else, now I'm feeling like whale shit too. No longer just cold, aching, dog-tired and overwhelmed by the sudden leap in my responsibilities, I am now mortified and weighed down by guilt as well. Because bottom line, *I have dropped the ball*. For everybody. Which means that we've all failed, and will have to do the whole damned thing all over again tomorrow night.

Shuffling around like zombies, we gather up our scattered equipment and haul it all back to the deuce-and-a-half that has magically appeared in the middle of our runway. Everything is dumped aboard, including all eight of my stooped and growling classmates, and I find my own seat among them, silent and alone in the gloomy crowd.

We are trucked back to our dark campsite somewhere around two or three o'clock in the frigid blustery morning, and retreat to our individual tents.

I don't even undress. I just claw my way into my sleeping bag, coats, gloves and boots still soaked and frozen to me, and collapse into the death sleep of the emotionally riven.

Gah! So... friggin'... close!

And to think of all that it took—all the physical exertion over the last seven weeks, all the mental stress, the perseverance, the pain, the fierce (and uncharacteristic) focus, the relentless pace, the endless *time*—so *much* pushing and driving and never giving up, so much *effort...* all so that I could be *here*, right now, 'enjoying the fruits of my (*unbelievably intense*) labors.'

What! The HELL! Was I thinking?!

Yeh. I was *made* for this kind of work.

BOOK TWO

AUTHOR'S NOTE
A Little Background In The Foreground

1
CATCHING UP TO THE PRESENT

IN AUGUST OF 1976, fourteen months before the point where this book (the second in the trilogy) begins, I was a nineteen-year-old college dropout. I had no goals in mind, no defined aspirations, nothing pulling me in any fruitful direction. Plus, I was still living with my parents in their home in Miami, Florida. And in the midst of all this stalled and listless indecision, a day came when a random tick of a synapse changed everything, and I allowed myself, as I so often did, to be *talked into* something. Something *big* this time.

And in this case, it was *joining the United States Air Force*.

This is not to say that I was coerced, nor that I'd consented against my will. I'd been contemplating a fantasy life as a "jet fighter pilot" for several years. You should've seen me playing those dogfighting games at the arcade. I was damn near invincible! But, regardless of how insipid and childish and uninformed my visions of aviation grandeur might have been, '*I was serious*' (at least in my own head). And I was 'preparing' for it. I'd even been in the ROTC program at the University of Miami... for the whole semester-and-a-half that I was enrolled there.

But by the end of that bicentennial summer, I'd been pretty much disabused of any such notion by a couple of fairly profound realizations: (1) I was extremely motion sensitive (a family trait, from my father's side...

thanks Dad!), and thereby prone to air sickness, and (2) I was no longer in school. After that aforementioned semester-and-a-half of hating every second of college, I'd quit it. And even I, at my most delusional, understood that a degree was a fundamental prerequisite to becoming an officer, and that being an officer was a prerequisite to becoming a pilot in the Air Force. So I'd pretty much written the whole thing off.

Until, on a spur-of-the-moment whim, as I was driving my '70 Ford Maverick past a strip mall that listed an Air Force Recruiter on its sign, I suddenly lunged into the parking lot, and pulled up at the recruiter's door… just to ask him one last question that had *only that moment* occurred to me. Specifically, was there any other way, outside of the conventional track, to become a pilot in the Air Force? Perhaps some 'back door' route that involved a congressman's endorsement, or maybe some specialized hand-to-eye coordination test, or a medical assessment of my spatial awareness, or even something as simple as acquiring a *private* pilot's license *first* before joining the military… anything other than maintaining a C+ average in pursuit of an Underwater Basket-Weaving degree at some backwater college somewhere.

The recruiter thought that was pretty funny.

"No," he confirmed. In order to be a pilot, you had to be an officer. And in order to be an officer, you had to first possess a diploma from *some* institution of higher learning. Period. No roundabout under-the-radar parallel tracks or tangents. No secret winks or handshakes or recommendations from figures of authority. Just 'get that pigskin, then come talk to us.'

And that pretty much ended my military flying dreams for good, right then and there… which was just fine with me. It was what I'd expected, and it only made my lackadaisical rudderlessness easier to accept.

Back to having no idea what to do with myself, a state to which I was already becoming fairly accustomed.

I was rising to head out the door then, when the recruiter slapped a long piece of paper, slathered top to bottom in small print, on his desktop, and said, "But why don't you see what kind of jobs you *would* be qualified for? Come on. Just for curiosity's sake. It'll take you two minutes."

Now I was wishing I'd never acted on that stupid impulse, that I'd just kept right on driving past that stupid strip mall, and let that one stupid little question just die a stupid mystery. But…

Being the unassertive tower of unmotivated jello that I was, I just couldn't think of a polite (or believably fictitious) way to squirm out of it. *Heaven forefend that I should just say "No thanks," and leave*. And I sat back down to read through the list.

Over 200 different *enlisted* jobs, 99.5% of which were entirely unappealing. But since he was waiting, and staring into my face while I read, I finally pointed to the lone exception and said, "*That* might be interesting."

He spun the paper around and read it out loud. "Air Traffic Control. Oo, good one! A *tough* one! Want to see if you'd qualify?"

"Well, ahhh... no," I said. "I... I've got this... this *thing* I've got to..."

"Come on! What could it hurt? Go take a written test. It's free! You pick the date, and they'll provide the boxed lunch. No strings attached, no signature required on *nuttin'*. Just for curiosity's sake. Just to see how you stack up."

Well, he apparently recognized an easily cornered weenie when he saw one, because, just to get that visit over with, I knuckled under and agreed to take the damned test. Once I got out his door though, I figured there was nothing to stop me from just forgetting all about that date. And even if I did go through with it, there was nothing that said I had to act on it. Right?

So *why the hell not?*

* * *

TWO WEEKS LATER, DESPITE all my mental assertions to the contrary, my curiosity did get the better of me, and I wound up slogging through that four-hour knowledge and skills test anyway. I even enjoyed the ham-and-cheese sandwich that came with the boxed lunch. Then, without waiting for the results, I headed out the very next day on a two-week road trip that I'd been talking about with my best friend Eldon. One last 'fling' up the east coast—maybe all the way up to Montreal, Canada, where they were hosting the Olympics that summer—a simple, unplanned, but *grand* adventure for a couple of late-teens looking to put some miles on their virgin driver's licenses, and to obliterate what little money they'd managed to save at their first jobs (along with maxing out his mom's credit card).

Even then, we both knew that Life was about to take over and grind all our little slacker dreams to dust under the boot heel of Reality. So it was pretty much now or never.

And I forgot all about that damned test... until the day we sputtered and wheezed back into my parents' driveway two weeks later, and shut down that nasty cat-piss-smellin', bulldozer-soundin', ass-killin' nightmare of a Maverick for the last time (we'd spilled some lemon tea in the car that smelled like cat piss, we'd blown an exhaust gasket—in *Canada!*—that made it blat like a Harley, and its rock hard bench seats had been murder on our tailbones).

Finally... home!.. after fourteen hellish days on the road.

By then, at the depths of my exhaustion, disgust, and self-loathing, I was ready to do something, *anything* to put my loser-life back on track again. And that's when that test came back to mind.

You know, they should have the results back by now!

The very next day, I returned to that recruiter's office, and sure enough, the results were back! And my overall score was high enough that I'd qualified for *all but two* of those two-hundred jobs (the exceptions being vehicle maintenance and accounting—no surprises there). So if I wanted it, I could sign up *that day* and be a full-time practicing air traffic controller by that same time next year! Maybe not quite the same as being a pilot, *but I'd get to tell pilots where to go!* And at the end of my four-year tour, I'd have a whole career—high-paying and prestigious—waiting for me with the FAA!

Sold!

Suddenly, my life had a direction! And what a cool feeling *that* was!

What a *new* feeling that was.

* * *

ACCORDING TO THE TIMETABLE that the Air Force presented me, I'd be officially sworn in on September 20th, 1976... to their *Delayed Enlistment Program*. Still a civilian for five-and-a-half more months. I'd even still be living at home—still an unemployed college drop-out if that's all I wanted to do with my time—but at least with a military 'start date' now secured for March 2nd, 1977. And if I graduated from Basic Training on schedule, my slot at Air Traffic Control School in early *May* of '77 was assured as well!

Imagine that! Now I was excited.

Of course, it's easy to be excited when your new radical life-altering shift in destiny is still half a year away, far off in the future. Even by late-September, once I'd been sworn in on Delayed Enlistment, my prospects were still just as thrilling. The same with the passage of New Years Day and the steadily accelerating approach of March. All exhilarating.

But by *February* of 1977, I was scared to freakin' *death!*

My theoretical enlistment and departure for Basic Training was rapidly closing on me, and was suddenly no longer quite so 'theoretical' at all. It was real, it was huge, and it was lumbering over the horizon and bearing down on me like an avalanche. Or a tsunami.

Intellectually, I was still excited by it. It would give my life some direction, I'd get to play with airplanes *for a living*, and at the end of my four-year tour, I'd have a career waiting for me on the outside as a *civilian* air traffic controller with the FAA. I'd be set for life, and I'd be the official badass-of-the-block with my friends.

Emotionally, however, I was *terrified*, trying to hide from the tsunami, clinging desperately to the old and familiar, and denying the increasingly obvious and overwhelming approach of the inevitable.

On March 2nd, 1977 then, the theories, the wishful thinking, the denial and the anticipation all vanished, swept up by the inexorable passage of time, *and* the tsunami... *and* my mother's '76 AMC Pacer, for that matter, which delivered me to Miami's Military Induction Center, and left me there alone.

I was definitely in the Air Force now... right where Book One of this trilogy began.

2

WHAT YOU MIGHT REMEMBER FROM BOOK ONE

BY MID-APRIL OF 1977, I was a graduate of Air Force Basic Training. I was exultant in my achievements, and finally comfortable in my new uniform and my new adult skin. From there I was shipped off to Keesler Air Force Base in Biloxi, Mississippi, there to begin Air Traffic Control School at the beginning of May. And I was preparing myself to settle in to my new and hopefully lifelong career, when I once again *allowed myself to be talked into something* even bigger… a heretofore unknown 'alternative career option' called *Combat Control*.

It was a 'spin-off' of air traffic control, a crazy, extremely physical, often *dangerous* deviation from my original plan. But once they had me hooked, I could no longer just walk away from it.

It was the Air Force's very own 'special operations' (or "spec ops") outfit, its version of the Navy's inimitable SEALs, or the Marines' Force Recon, or the Army's Green Berets. And though it flew in the face of everything I'd ever envisioned for myself, and demanded more than anything else I'd ever attempted *in my LIFE*, I still found myself drawn in by all the 'fun' and 'cool' stuff that the recruiter's slide presentation had focused on.

Yeh, that was me at that one particular moment of my existence: stupid, naive, and raw, but *adventurous!*

But mostly stupid.

I'd never heard of Combat Control before. It certainly wasn't *me*, and such an uncharacteristic detour was something I never would have seriously considered in any of the months leading up to my induction into the Air Force. But at that juncture in my life—that wild, tentatively reckless, and strangely invigorating crossroads between the safety and security of adolescence, and the slightly out-of-control freedom of my brand new adulthood—the exotica of jumping out of airplanes, rappelling down cliff faces, skiing glaciers, blowing up bridges, and controlling aircraft into airstrips *that I had built for them myself* just held too great of an allure for me to resist.

So, for all the wrong reasons, I began "Pre-Phase I Combat Control Training" in conjunction with the classes that were beginning at Air Traffic Control School. And it just flat beat the 98-pound weakling right out of me.

* * *

FIVE MONTHS LATER, in September of 1977, I graduated from ATC School *and* completed the Pre-Phase I Combat Control program at the same time. I was feeling like a king, I was built like friggin' Tarzan, and I couldn't help but feel that all the most *fun* stuff was now waiting for me just around the next bend.

From there though, it was straight off to the Army's Jump School at Fort Benning, Georgia... where everything in my new world abruptly turned serious. And suddenly I knew—even then, in all my clueless naïveté—that I had just stuck my head so far into this secret realm that it had *sucked me all the way in*, and from this point on, it was going to be all I could do just to hang on for dear life.

Suddenly I was in *way over my head*.

No longer a mere dalliance and a romp through a landscape of physical extremes—with my involvement in the business being no deeper than my initial curiosity—Jump School suddenly introduced not only physical demands far in excess of any prior experience of mine, but actual *life endangering* activities as well.

Like being hoisted to the *top* of, and dropped to the ground *from* the school's infamous 250-foot towers, not to mention, of course, jumping out of real by-God flying aerospace vehicles, by day and by night. It was enough to give one pause... and maybe even a little diarrhea.

But in the end, by the time I'd graduated from Jump School in early *October* of 1977—which is where the *first* book in this series ended, and where *this* one begins—I was more certain than ever that I had, in fact, chosen the right career field. Because, as extreme as it might have been, the fact was that I not only enjoyed jumping immensely, but I was in the best shape of my life. And if regular old air traffic control was going to make me the 'badass-of-the-block' with my friends back home in Miami, imagine what *this* would make me!

So, as I left Ft. Benning with my freshly minted jump wings gleaming on my chest, I was proud of my accomplishments and energized by my prospects, tempered, unfortunately, by the revelation that my permanent assignment was going to be to McChord Air Force Base (AFB), just south of Seattle, Washington.

That part of the deal I was dreading.

Out of all the scores of Air Force bases around the country, only *seven* even had Combat Control Teams attached to them. And from those seven, I'd only been allowed to choose *three* for my permanent base of assignment. Each of the seven had something about them that sucked though, so *none* of them fully appealed to me. But after much gnashing of teeth and rending of garments, I'd narrowed the grim selections down to...

... Pope AFB, outside Fayetteville, North Carolina (I didn't like being right across the highway from the Army's Fort Bragg, home of the renowned 82nd Airborne and the Army's fearful HALO School, but at least its regular Combat Control Team was one of the closest to my family in Miami)... then Charleston AFB in *South* Carolina (which, while even closer to Miami than Pope AFB, was also the home of the Air Force's Combat Control SCUBA School, which admittedly terrified me worse than *all* their other schools)... and finally, *in last place*, and included solely because I *had* to pick a third (and because this one harbored no other peripheral schools, and was at least situated in a beautiful part of the country) was McChord AFB... just about as far from Miami as it was possible to get, and still be in the continental United States... which seriously depressed me.

Naturally then, the Air Force, in all its infinite wisdom, gave me McChord.

My last choice.

3
THE GUY LEFT BEHIND AT THE END OF BOOK ONE

BUT THE FACT THAT I was so far over my head with all this Spec Ops stuff really didn't bother me at all, simply because *it never occurred to me at the time,* and I wouldn't have really cared if someone had pointed it out. The thrill of my personal evolution over the previous seven months—from surviving the culture shock of Basic Training, to 'mastering' the critical complexities of Air Traffic Control School, including the physical pummeling and stretching and steeling of my body under the Pre-Phase I Combat Control regimen there, and finally my 'conquest' of the rigors and dangers of the Army's Jump School, all so radically outside the scope and scale of my previous life as a civilian—all had led me to believe that I could adapt to *anything,* and *excel* at *everything* if I just put my mind to it. And while that may have even been somewhat true, the fact was that I still wasn't taking the real-world *mission* of Combat Control seriously. I was just in it for the glamour and the coolness and yes, even the occasional *fun.* That was all. And the life experiences that Combat Control was now promising were just too exhilarating for me to let pass by.

So even my uncertainties and *fears* were just being viewed as part of the thrill ride, something I could push my way through and be glad I did afterward... because I was an idiot... or at least an appallingly naive wannabe. And I just didn't have a clue about what I'd gotten myself into.

At the time, the only thing I knew for sure was that I *didn't* want to move to McChord AFB. It was a hundred-million miles from home, it was cold in the winter and rainy the rest of the year. And that's all I could think about as I took off out of Atlanta, fresh out of Jump School, and flew non-stop across the country to lovely socked-in Seattle...

... right where the first story of this book begins.

4
ONE LAST LITTLE POST-SCRIPT

OH, AND ONE MORE thing that I think it's important to note here…

The Combat Controllers of today bear little resemblance to the operators' of *my* day. From everything that I've seen and read, their training is significantly longer and far more grueling now, their standards for admission and retention notably more critical and unforgiving, with physical and psychological demands that are simply relentless. Their capabilities are far more vast, their equipment is the stuff of *science fiction*, and their historical accomplishments have since become the stuff of *legend*.

Not so much in the late 1970s, when I dipped *my* toe in the waters.

According to Wikipedia, my era is described as the 'Post-Vietnam Cold War Period.' The mission of the Combat Control Teams had expanded only slightly since the early *ad hoc* days of the Air Force's inception, when it tore itself loose of the Army, and dragged its 'Pathfinders' along with it, despite the territorial resistance and infighting that nearly doomed it from the start. But overall, its 'prime directive' was still the same… to 'insert' into 'denied areas' by whatever means necessary (by land, sea, or air), and set up advance communications and control assets for the direction and protection of the major forces to follow.

And that's it.

Since 'spec ops' forces *never* stop training, a fully qualified Combat Controller would eventually find himself getting into more 'exotic' spin-offs of the job that weren't directly related to his primary mission (like sniper training, patrol and ambush techniques, hostage rescuing [and taking], and stuff like that), but the meat-and-potatoes of the job were still all about air traffic control in the field, and directing drops. That was in *my* day, anyway.

Nowadays, modern Combat Controllers are almost interchangeable with Navy SEALS and Marine Force Recon troops. They do it all. Nowadays, motivation and dedication are almost more important than their nearly impossible physical demands. And nowadays, the technology and inter-connectivity challenges have created a learning curve far too steep for *my* humble brain to process. But back in *my* time, that wasn't the case.

In other words, mine was a far simpler era with a far less convoluted mission, and physical standards that were actually achievable by mere mortals.

I wouldn't have lasted a *month* in today's CCT environment, and in all honesty, even in my ardent youth, I doubt I ever would have tried.

To me, the Combat Controllers of today are *gods*, superhumans with impossible demands on their impossible array of skills, on their bodies, on their resilience, on their brotherhood, and on their willingness to stand between me and all the evil out there. And so I want it understood that what *I* did in my brief time dabbling among them cannot compare, on *any level*, to what *they* do today on a daily basis. In these regards, they are better than me by every measure.

So what's my (final) point here? It is this…

My story, here among these cathartic pages, is not about heroism or courage. It's not about history-making adventures, nor desperate survival situations, nor deep soul-shattering tales of life-and-death mortal combat. It's not any of the things that a typical military memoir would be about.

Then again, they're not usually very funny either.

No, this is just about my personal experiences swimming in waters that were deeper and darker than I could have ever imagined at the moment I first chose to jump in. It's about the exotica, the complexity, and the life-broadening realms and activities of America's elite warriors, as *experienced* by a blindly naive, unscarred, teetotaling mama's boy, and then later *retold* by a professional-grade smart-ass decades after the fact.

Yeh. Nobody's taking themselves too seriously around here.

So hopefully you'll enjoy it more for the *ride* than the *destination*. These were (often breathtaking) experiences that are just fun to relive, fun to describe, and still astonishing to think that I ever had anything to do with them.

Man, I hope you enjoy this.

BOOK TWO
THE WANNABE

PART 1

The McChord Combat Control Team
McChord Air Force Base, Tacoma, Washington
October, 1977

STORY XIX

HOME, HOME OF THE STRANGE

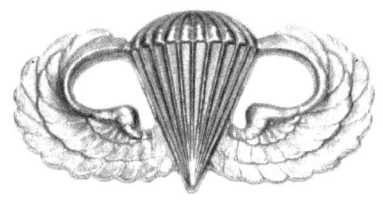

1
FRESH OFF THE PUNKIN TRUCK

October, 1977
McChord AFB, Tacoma, Washington

AH, SEATTLE. LOVELY SEATTLE.

A solid plain of fuzzy white mold beneath our wings.

I can't help it. That's just what it looks like to me: a total horizon-to-horizon undercast deck with a single snow-capped volcano sticking up through it. That's my introduction to the 'beautiful' Pacific Northwest. If the pilot hadn't just announced that we were starting our final approach into SeaTac (the Seattle-Tacoma) Airport, I would never have suspected that we were anywhere near civilization at all.

Dammit!

The deep disappointment from having been assigned a base this far from my home in Miami once again resurfaces. And another glance out the window at the rising undercast just curdles it into something even more slimy and bitter.

I don't want to be here!

But the plane sinks into the cold white soup anyway. And as we continue to descend, the murk outside just gets grayer and grayer and grayer until it blanks out the world altogether.

We break out the bottom barely a thousand or two feet above a dreary wet cityscape, a dismal contrast to the sparkling sunny-blue autumnal ether we'd left above the clouds. I'm sitting in a window seat on the right side of the aircraft, and beyond my wingtip, the lush rolling terrain seems to be drawn up into the overcast like a fistful of sodden quilting being pulled up through the clouds by a giant.

It's a closed environment out there, a bowl of lumpy green curds with a gray lid on it.

Shit.

* * *

OUR LANDING IS UNEVENTFUL, our taxi-in bumpy and boring, then we're at the jetway.

I stand, stooped, under the overhead bins, waiting for the gridlocked center aisle to move, and I attempt to straighten up my rumpled uniform. I'm wearing my casual blues again; short-sleeved sky-blue shirt opened at the neck with a white T-shirt peeking out from behind its unbuttoned collar. Dark blue trousers, my piss-cutter hat tucked up under my belt like a hand towel, and my brand new chrome parachutist badge twinkling silver above my left breast pocket. Which means I'm *looking* better than I *feel* right now.

I can't help it. I'm just dreading everything about this assignment.

There's a guy wearing cammies (camouflaged fatigues) standing in the gate area when I emerge into the concourse. He's tall and rangy—a little dorky-looking, truth be told—with an unruly 'mushroom cap' of curly hair tangled atop his head like a bird's nest. He's also chewing gum and slapping a dark blue beret against his thigh as he tracks the passing ladies.

I approach him, snapping him out of his reverie, and we exchange a manly handshake. Then he reads my name tag out loud.

"You must be Airman Stipp," he says, "I'm Darryl Murton, but everybody just calls me 'Skeeter'." He doesn't say why. "I've got a truck outside to take you to the base, as soon as we get your bags."

"Nice to meet you," I reply, "And all I've got is a duffel."

"Well alright then. Let's head this way, and get you to baggage claim." And he turns to follow the crowd up the narrow concourse—all but his head, that is, which swivels hard left to follow the sashay of a tightly jeaned feminine derriere going the other way.

Subtle, Skeeter is not.

2

JUST A PHASE I'M GOING THROUGH

THE SCENERY IS PRETTY as we barrel south down I-5 into Tacoma. Lush, green, and rolling over the hilly terrain. But the dreary weather saddens it, washing it out like the pale sepia tones of an old photograph. Rain patters the windshield, and every car on either side of us hisses past, either drifting back or charging ahead of us, dulled by its accumulated road film. I keep my eyes out the windows, nodding and issuing "*Uh-huhs*" at all the appropriate junctures in Skeeter's ceaseless blathering, but otherwise leaving my attention fixed on the alien tableau outside.

Skeeter, it seems, is the Team's equivalent of 'Radar' on "*M.A.S.H.*". Fully Phase III qualified and accomplished in almost all aspects of the job, he has nevertheless found himself settled into a more clerical role of late. In other words, his ability to type and keep an organized file cabinet has subtly evolved into a full-time occupation for him, capable of getting him out of any undesirable deployments, exercises, schools, and apparently, judging by his duties of the moment, out of the office as well.

Well, all power to him. Hopefully my own abilities along those lines will lead to a similar evolution down the line.

The verdant roadsides south of Seattle unravel into the flatter, more industrial mosaics of Tacoma—with its belching smokestacks, rundown warehouses, freight yards and dirty looking port (Skeeter warns me about the impending odor, referring to it as the "Tacoma Aroma")—and I finally look away from the passing landscape to interrupt his monologue with a question.

"Yeh, about that Phase III thing… what exactly does that mean? What about Phases I and II, for that matter? Nobody's ever really explained any of that to me yet."

Skeeter seems *thrilled* to have someone actually *asking* him something for once.

"Well," as he explains it—with both hands cavorting through the air as he speaks, making only intermittent contact with the steering wheel, just enough to keep us between the lines of the hurtling interstate—"Phase I CCT," as it was called back at Keesler, wasn't actually Phase I at all. It was more like a "*pre*-Phase I." All prep, no perks.

This much I already knew. I wasn't technically Phase I until I pinned my jump wings on just three days ago back at Fort Benning, Georgia. So, for all the work it took for me to get this far, all that being 'Phase I' really means is that I am now jump qualified, and legal to jump with my team… which is a minimum prerequisite for starting any other training with them. And all it entitles me to is the wearing of an additional set of jump wings on my 'field cap,' plus an extra fifty-five dollars a month in Jump Pay. That's all.

"What's a 'field cap'?" I ask, homing right in on the important stuff. "You mean my *fatigue* cap?"

"No. A field cap is different. It looks kinda' like a green Civil War cap, only smaller. Flat on top, tiny little brim. The Marines wore 'em a lot in Vietnam. You'll get a couple issued to you once you get to the Team. Anyway…"

To become Phase II apparently, you have to complete Combat Control School—CCS—an eight-week ball-buster of a course (two weeks longer than Basic Training) down at Little Rock Air Force Base in Arkansas. And that's where you earn your pretty blue beret.

Typically, however, you have to have been with your team for at least six months or so before they'll even consider sending you to CCS: time to gather a little experience, a little gear, some acceptance from your team, as well as a little clarity as to whether or not this is really the career for you. But once you've reached that point, with your team's concurrence and endorsement of course, then it's off to CCS with you.

And that's when the game really begins.

Presuming that you graduate from that—and a third to a half of all candidates do not—then you're officially Phase II: essentially a trained apprentice-level badass, having been exposed to everything, but mastered nothing, designated as such by the wearing of your brand new beret... but with those same old Army jump wings still affixed.

That's right; *jump wings only*. Not the prized Combat Control 'flash,' the official insignia of the journeyman Phase *III* Combat Controller. No, that comes after something like another *year* back with your team, attending other specialized schools, participating in ever more complex exercises, and racking up time and experience in all aspects of the job, all of which will ultimately have to be checked off for proficiency by a certifying member of your team. And then, and *only* then, once every checkbox on every page of your training records has been signed off, will you be awarded your flash—your parachute-and-lightning-bolt signet, to be proudly displayed on the facing of your beret.

That's apparently what every yeoman Combat Controller, as a minimum, aspires to be... "*Phase III and meant to be, U.S. Air Force CCT.*" Or some such happy Bolshoi.

Phases IV and V get into more supervisory and command levels of proficiency, typically reserved for longer-term and higher-ranking operators, so I don't need to put much thought to those for quite a while yet. If ever.

Hmmm. Interesting.

So, six months or so before they get around to sending me off to CCS, ay? And up to a year after *that* before I will have exhibited sufficient expertise and perseverance for them to brevet me with a CCT flash on my beret, hmm? A total of eighteen months or so... give or take.

Wasn't that about the length of time for which Sgt. Beaudry—my pre-Phase I recruiter and instructor—"suggested" I tough it out? "*Give it about eighteen months or so, then see how you like it.*" Wasn't that what he said?

What a coincidence.

In other words, see it through CCS and a half dozen or so other exotic schools—see it through to a beret anointed with a flash, basically—through all the steps leading up to Phase III ('journeyman') status. See it through to at least that far, then see if you still want out.

So that's what he was saying, the sly old dog.
Hmmm. Okay.
Yeh, I think I'm up for that.

3
SORRY. WRONG ADDRESS.

AS THE MAIN GATE of McChord Air Force Base rolls into view at the bottom of its dip in the road, Skeeter starts wrestling with his pockets. From his right thigh pocket he produces a ratty wallet, from which he then extracts his military ID card. Got to have that to get past the gate guard, of course.

I take the hint, and pry my own wallet out from under my ass.

As I'm doing so, Skeeter reaches into his *left* thigh pocket, and pulls out his beret as well.

What's he need that for? Are we supposed to wear a hat whenever we enter this base?

He slows the truck—just enough to give himself the time needed to don his beret and crank his window down—then we're coasting up to the guard shack, holding up our IDs for the guard's perusal, and exchanging curt pleasantries. And that's when I notice it.

When the SP—the 'Security Police' airman—sticks his head into the window to look at my ID, for a moment the beret on *his* head hovers right next to the one on Skeeter's. And for the very first time, I notice that they are *identical*. Not just vaguely comparable, not just both generally blue-ish, but *twins*. Those two berets are *exactly* the same—dark royal blue.

Only the flashes are different.

Now how the hell did I manage to miss that similarity until only just now? I mean, I saw lots of SPs at Lackland. Of course, that was during Basic Training. I'd never heard of Combat Controllers at the time, and there wouldn't have been any on that base anyway. And my last posting? That was Jump School, on an *Army* installation—Fort Benning—on which there were no Air Force SPs (obviously), and I was the only 'Combat Controller' around. But at Keesler AFB? Air Traffic Control School? There were SPs *and* there was Sergeant Beaudry… although I guess I never saw him wearing any form of headgear. He was always either in work-out togs, or sitting indoors behind his desk. Still… the point is, I never made the connection.

Skeeter doffs his beret as soon as we pull away.

"Does McChord have a 'hat rule' or something?," I ask with an awkward chuckle.

"Nah," he says as he squirrels away his wallet. "I just like to make sure the fuckin' SPs get a *good look* at what a beret looks like on *someone who fuckin' EARNED IT!*"

He's shouting at his mirror by the time he's done.

He looks over at me, and smiles at the big fat question mark on my face.

"Did you know that in all the Air Force, there are only two, *two* job specialties that call for the wearing of a beret as part of the uniform? And you just saw both of them back there. Combat Controllers have had 'em since 1953 after the Air Force first became an independent branch of the services."

Yeh, Sgt. Beaudry had told us that Combat Controllers used to be called "Pathfinders" back when the "Air Corps" had been part of the Army.

"And the goddamned SPs just got 'em about five years ago," he continues, "as part of some stupid-assed, in-house, *esprit de corps*, morale-building circle jerk."

He sighs and grinds his teeth.

"But let's just ignore for now how the SPs are a bunch of goddamned morons, the low-scorers and the wash-outs from all the *other* career fields."—(*seems unlikely, but that's what he says*)—"Let's ignore for now that at *no point* in either their job or their training do they require or ever do anything to actually *earn* a beret. But on top of all that, with an entire rainbow of colors to choose from, especially for a purely ceremonial piece of headgear, as it is in their case—I mean, it's not like they're going to be wearing them in combat or anything..." (*of course, neither would* we)—"It could be *white* for all the difference it makes to them. And with only *one color* out of the *entire spectrum* already taken—*by us*—the fuckers had to go an choose the *exact same color as ours!*"

You know, I'm starting to get the impression that this just might be a bit of a sore subject for old Sgt. Murton here.

"Now no one can tell us apart!" He thumps the steering wheel with both hands. "People see me walking around with *five years* of the most difficult schools in the fuckin' Air Force behind me—with all the jumping and demolitions and special weapons and all the fuckin' survival schools under my belt—and to them, for all they can tell, I'm just another wash-out from the Motor Pool who settled for being an SP instead of working in the chow hall or the damned gym, handing out basketballs!"

Skeeter's eyes dart back to his mirror where the SP is already long gone, out of sight.

"*Fuckers!*"

"And I gather that no one in a position of authority has suggested another color for them?" I ask carefully.

"Oh sure!" he shouts right back. "We've raised a helluva' shit storm! But there's nothing they can do about it now, they say. There are a lot more SPs out there than there are Combat Controllers, and it would cost too damned much money to replace all *their* shit with something different. So if *anybody's* shit is going to be replaced, it's going to be *ours!*"

"Wait. They steal *our beret*, and now they want *us* to change?"

"Damned right! How's that for a kick in the balls?"

"Any idea what the new color's going to be?"

"Nah. No decision yet. But at least it won't be green, black or burgundy. Those are already taken by the Army's Green Berets, their Rangers, and their general Airborne."

Yeh. We wouldn't wanna' take somebody else's color. What kind of low-life bastards would do something like that?

And to think I used to like the SPs.

* * *

THE RANTING FIZZLES OUT as we cruise into the heart of the base. And actually, McChord does appear to be a lovely installation.

I say "*appears to be*" because, for all its beautiful trees, grass, and general foliage—for all its manicured soccer fields, baseball diamonds, and golf courses—it's still muted by this iron gray overcast and the continuous drizzle that's staining everything dark.

Skeeter loops us past a massive brick edifice that he calls "The Castle." It houses our squadron's headquarters, our First Sergeant's and Commander's offices, one of the base's two main chow halls (I'm sorry: 'dining facilities'), and the billets for our 'bachelor airmen' (like me). Then he does a quick drive-by of the Airman's Club, the Base Theater, the Library, the bank and the BX (that's the "Base Exchange," the Air Force's 'department store'), before rolling down a long straight road flanked by some other squadron's barracks on the left side, and five colossal hangars on the right.

Abeam the second hangar, he turns onto a dirt access road that cuts across the grassy infield, and we charge into the hangar's crowded parking lot just ahead of our own wake of flying gravel.

I get a quick peek at the flight line as I step out into the drizzle—all C-130s, it looks like from here, rows and rows of them, parked wingtip-to-wingtip—then I follow Skeeter around to the building's 'front door' on the street side of the structure.

The hangar is depressing enough from the *out*side—five or six stories of featureless and windowless aluminum siding painted a moldering rain-streaked beige—but *in*side it's even worse.

Its vast internal 'cubic acreage' is no longer used to service aircraft, but instead houses several different 'shops,' each one of which has claimed its own little pigeonhole around the outer walls. On first glance, I spot a radio maintenance niche, an electronics storage cage, a row of pre-fab offices with stairs leading up to a collection of desks and cubicles on its *roof*, and a pair of long parachute rigging tables, all looking temporary—or at least improvised—at best. It reminds me of the forts I used to build in our backyard as a kid, cobbled together from scavenged leftovers and discarded lumber.

Great, I've come full circle... to this.

Skeeter threads his way through the rigging tables, bound for the office door at the base of the stairs. It has a photographic enlargement of a CCT flash on it, mounted on cardboard and nailed above a formica nameplate on which "**CPT. J. FORTH**" is etched in white. I'm just spitballing here, but my guess is that my new Team Commander is some guy named Captain Forth, and this is his office, and this is who Skeeter is taking me to meet first.

But that's just a hunch.

Before we reach his little nook though, another cubbyhole's door bangs open at the rear of the space, and out march three of my new fellow teammates in a whirlwind of profanity, boisterous laughter, and big movements. Worn and washed-out cammies, spit-polished jump boots, and a confident glint in their eyes that says they've seen and done it all before, and *what the fuck is it to you!*

Yep, that's what I want to look like some day.

The largest one, a massive Mexican-bandito-lookin' dude—built like a bank vault with stripes, and tanned almost copper—snatches a rolled-up beret from his thigh pocket and wrenches it onto his head in one fluid motion, his eyes locked on me the whole time.

"Whatcha' got there, Skeeter-Peter?," he booms, no doubt impressed as hell by both the dinky little gnat wings on my sleeves and the obviously brand spankin' shiny new jump wings on my chest. "Another sky warrior for the Team?"

'Skeeter-Peter', huh? So that's where 'Skeeter' comes from.

One of his buddies erupts in a single mighty "*Har!*," and stops to appraise me himself. Skeeter flushes (in more ways than one, probably), chuckles self-consciously, and assumes an introductory stance between us.

"Gentlemen, this here is Airman Steve Stipp, fresh off the punkin truck and signing in with us today. Airman Stipp, this here is Sgt. Manny Santos,"—*indicating the towering Mexican bandito whose beret looks tiny now, more like a yarmulke, on that massive blimp-sized head of his*—"Sgt. Joe Montreaux over there... we just call him 'Monty'"—*the shortest of the trio (about my height), square-jawed, gray-eyed, bow-legged, and still smiling after his mono-syllabic outburst of laughter from a moment before*—"and Sgt. Cole

Mabry"—*a tall, somber drink of water who looks like he might have fixed farm machinery his entire life.*

He also looks like he already doesn't like me.

Manny and Joe shake my hand enthusiastically, welcoming me (in a vaguely unsettling way), all the while enlightening me as to Skeeter's general uselessness, unreliability, and homosexual proclivities. Skeeter chuckles again, strangely self-conscious now around these senior sergeants.

Sgt. Mabry, on the other hand—"Cole"—remains dour and distant, calmly donning his own beret on the far side of the rigging table, out of reach.

He and I exchange only a nod.

Manny looks puzzled, though. "Stipp. Stipp," he says, rolling my name around in his mouth for a moment, as if it might taste familiar or something. "Airman Stipp." Then his brow abruptly lifts, and he turns to Skeeter. "Oh, is this the guy?"

"The guy?"

"Yeh, you know. The... the Pope guy. The guy you were talking about this morning?"

The "Pope Guy?" What's he talking about?

I turn to face Skeeter myself. He somehow manages to look even more uneasy, cornered maybe. After a couple of seconds of looking back and forth between Santos and me though, an exaggerated expression of dawning realization suddenly hits him.

"Oh, the *Pope* guy! Yeh, I know what you mean now. Yeh... this is him." And he swings his hand out, as if to say, "*Tah-dah!.*"

"The 'Pope Guy'?" I finally ask out loud.

"Yeh," says Manny with an oblivious chortle, "When we got your notice that you'd be arriving today, we had no idea who you were. We had no orders for you, and we weren't expecting anyone new. So old Skeeter here had to do a little tap dancin', checked a few things out, and it turns out that you were supposed to go to *Pope* Air Force Base! Not here! Ain't that some shit?"

"Pope?" I mutter hopefully. "I'm supposed to be at *Pope?*"

Pope AFB? Fayetteville, North Carolina? The southeast? My first choice? The Air Force didn't screw me after all! It just screwed UP!

"Yeh, somebody in Personnel fucked up and gave you the wrong orders. Sent you here instead of there, ya' lucky bastard."—*huh?*—"Nobody wants

'No-Hope Pope."—*yeh, I do!*—"Man, you skated out of that one by the skin of your dick!"—*aw, see, now there's an image I didn't need in my head right now!*—"Skeeter, you better hurry up and get this man in-processed before they figure out what they did!"

Santos laughs and pounds me on the shoulder.

"Welcome aboard, ya' lucky shit!"

Yeh, but... but...

And the three crusty amigos march out the door and into the drizzle. Skeeter's discomfiture magically vanishes at the same time, and he turns to resume his slalom through the tables and desks to the commander's office.

"He's right," he says, "We need to get you signed in right quick here."

He knocks on the door of Captain Forth's office.

"Look," I stammer, "I don't... I don't want to cause any problems here. I mean, if Pope's where I'm supposed to be, then..."

"Come!" shouts the voice behind the door.

"Don't worry about it," says Skeeter with a wink, "We'll take care of you." Then he swings the door open, and leads me inside.

"But..." *You're missing the point!*, my mind screams. *I* want *to be at Pope! I* don't *want to be here!*

"Cap'n Forth," Skeeter announces, "This is Airman Steve Stipp, signing in today, fresh out of Jump School."

The captain, who looks barely twenty himself, and uncomfortable in his shiny silver bars, rises from his squeaky second-hand chair, and steps around his crappy little hand-me-down desk to shake my hand.

"Welcome to the McChord Combat Control Team, Airman Stipp. I think you're going to like it here."

Skeeter is all smiles.

I return a mincing smile of my own, and accept the proffered hand.

"Thank-you, sir,"—*(*sigh*)*—"Glad to be here."

4

A ROOM WITH A VIEW

THEY'VE ROOMED ME WITH Airman Randy Pogue, another relative newbie on the McChord Team (about six months worldlier than me), whom I take to right away... mostly because he's not here right now. He's actually off at Combat Control School as we speak, way down in Little Rock, Arkansas—McChord's one and only candidate on this class cycle—trying to prove himself worthy of his very own blue beret.

Good luck, Randy! You can tell me all about it when you get back.

Our room is ridiculously huge, probably more than five-hundred perfectly square feet, with a towering ceiling and an enormous white-paned window that overlooks the central flagpole and the triangular-shaped 'square' across the street. It's on the second floor of 'The Castle,' just as Skeeter had said it would be. And all things considered, it ain't bad a'tall.

Everything's big about this place. The corridor outside is broad, carpeted, and brightly lit. The communal 'Day Room'—with its big TV, a couple of ill-stocked vending machines, a card table, and a two-shelf 'library' of severely used paperbacks—is more like a small theater. A nearly *empty* one, what with barely half a dozen cheap vinyl chairs and a single vinyl-padded couch scattered across the floor space. Still homey enough though for the ranks of the financially destitute. Like me.

There's a large communal laundry room with two washers and two dryers—all clearly ancient (probably coal-burning, from the looks of them) and thoroughly abused—an even larger communal bathroom (*not* a 'latrine,' they tell me), and a huge but beautifully accoutered chow hall at the far far end of the extensive hallway system, in a wing of the immense building that's clear over on the other side of the central courtyard. But it's all clean, tidy, and bright. And while perhaps a little austere, sterile, even institutional, it's still friendlier than I'd anticipated on the long flight up here. Not too far off from what you'd expect of a building dubbed 'The Castle' either.

And I am told that the next floor up—the third floor—is the *women's* floor! *Hoo-HOO! How handy!*

Our room has been artfully divided up by Airman Pogue, who used the big wooden lockers, dressers, desks, and beds to reconfigure the clear space between them all into a semi-S-shaped path that leads from doorway to window sill. And he has apparently claimed as his own the furniture nearest the door.

Perfect!
That means I get the window!

* * *

MOUNT RAINIER IS A fourteen-thousand foot snow-capped volcano about forty-five crow-flying miles due east of McChord. It's a great beast of a landmark that just friggin' *owns* the eastern fourth of the horizon. I mean, when it's actually visible—as in, "on one of those rare occasions when the drizzle and low ceilings have actually receded far enough that you can *see* as far as the horizon"—it is a broad, massive, *spectacular* presence. And because it's due east, the sun rises each morning from behind it.

And so it is this morning—Day Three with my new Team.

Following a truly delectable ham-cheese-and-mushroom omelet up in The Castle chow hall, I have donned my brand spankin' cracklin' new camouflaged fatigues, and headed off down the little hill behind the building.

I'm on foot, bound for the team's hangar, about a mile away around the west end of the sprawling flight line. And no sooner do I step out into the crisp mid-October breeze than I realize that I can see long morning shadows on the ground!

Which means *the sun is out! Hah-hah!*

And when I turn to the east, there, like a great monumental cathedral, piled high with snowy buttresses and backlit by God's own Holy Light, is Mount Rainier, still dark with morning shadow on this western facing, crowned by the sun itself and limned with its golden light like a vast halo. The first vestige of the sun I've seen since I got here.

I don't want to walk any further. I don't want to destroy this moment. If I move, the buildings and hangars will be drawn inexorably into the foreground, and there goes this absolutely breathtaking view.

I tell ya', it's almost enough to make you think you're in the right place after all.

Almost.

* * *

TODAY IS APPARENTLY A 'busy work' kind of day. A time-killer. No exercises or deployments or jumps scheduled for today. So Sgt. Santos (that big Mexican-bandito-lookin' dude), and Sgt. Sherrod (a placid, sleepy-eyed 'older' gentleman that everybody calls "Smoke," perhaps because of his ghostlike abilities in the field, or maybe just because of the ever-present pipe that's seldom very far from his face) have improvised a 'class' on the set-up and uses of a 20-man "GP" (or "General Purpose") tent.

Regardless of its make-work nature though, this little hands-on session at least brings most of the team together for the first time since I got here last Monday. And I'm glad to see that they're nothing like the rowdy breed of hard-drinking, wild-carousing, brawling, battling, womanizing, fire-eaters that I'd expected to find in a job like this.

Actually, yes they are. But it turns out that they've got a civilized side as well (or at least a convincingly mature *face* that they can put on whenever the situation warrants), which might just be enough for my naive near-virgin ass to fit in.

For a moment then, when the deuce-and-a-half truck first pulls up on the wet grass and the group converges on it to unload the tent components, I get about a minute-and-a-half to look over the entire team—well, the dozen or so that are out here for this 'class', anyway—as they gather in a loose clot around the tailgate. And I can see now what Skeeter was referring to when he spoke about the different Phase levels and how they're delineated by all the varied hats, badges and flashes.

By far, the vast majority—nine out of the twelve—are capped with blue berets. So apparently, most of the team is at least Phase II, if not Phase *III* certified. *Good to know.*

I see Daryl Murton—"Skeeter"—the guy who picked me up at the airport and helped me get my feet under me once I'd hit the ground. And of course, there's big old Manny Santos—"Wetback," as I heard one of the senior members call him once, though no one else has ever dared call him anything other than Manny in my presence—and his two 'old-head' buddies, scoop-jawed Joe "Monty" Montreaux, and stoic Cole Mabry, the head of the Radio Maintenance side of the operation. I even spot Captain Forth in attendance.

Over there is that old Tech Sergeant—the oldest guy on the team, actually, and its unofficial Supply Sergeant—named Miles Campbell, who took me through his nearly empty equipment storage lockers the other day, and managed to rustle up what few team-specific items I now have in my possession. In other words, he got me my two sets of cammies, my web belt and canteens, my compass, my K-Bar combat knife, and the dapper little 'field cap', with jump wings affixed, that I'm wearing right now. And that's about it. He's promised me a closetful of job-related shit over the next two to four weeks, as the Air Force gets around to replenishing his depleted stock, but until then, those meager pickings will just have to do.

There's the aforementioned Sgt. Sherrod—"Smoke"—doing just what his nickname implies as he supervises the raising of the tent's two endposts with the long ridge beam connecting them. He's a soft-spoken Hardy Kruger type that everyone on the team seems to like and respect, in a fatherly sort of way. And Connor Duncan—who I've heard called both "Dink" and "Ozzy" (or "Aussie," I suppose)—a dumpy, overweight (as in 'beer-gutted') but fun-loving Australian ex-pat, who still managed to out-run me on my first five-mile run with the team yesterday.

There's also a *Chief* Master Sergeant to whom I was introduced this morning, who has since left to attend to other duties while we fiddle with this stupid tent. Skeeter had referred to him as "*the* Chief Roswell," as if anyone who's militarily aware *at all* would know the name, and merely uttering it would spark a gasp of awe from me.

It didn't, though. I've never heard of him. But he apparently *is* quite famous among military circles. He not only holds something like the third or fourth highest *freefall altitude* record in history, but he was also one of the live "test dummies" on the new zero-zero ejection seat trials. He actually rode one of those rocket-propelled seats out of a stationary cockpit simulator *sitting on the ground*... zero altitude, zero airspeed.

Wow! Ballsy!

He's a dignified silver-haired eight-striper now, less than a year from retirement, and the NCOIC ("Non-Commissioned Officer In Charge") for the McChord Combat Control Team. Quite a badge of honor being associated with him, apparently.

Again, good to know.

At the other end of the food chain though, easily identifiable by their distinctly *non*-beret-like field caps, are the young'uns—three of them—mere Phase I rookies like myself, except that each of them has been with the team for at least four months or more now, and are all slated for the next CCS class that'll be cranking up in two or three weeks down in Little Rock. Once they leave for school, I'll be the only Phase I fledgling left on the team.

Of the three, the one I've taken to the quickest is Airman Greg Dorn, partly because of the fact that his room is right across the Castle's hallway from mine, but mostly because of the easy confidence and competence that he exudes just standing there. He looks and acts like he could fix your car just as easily as he could grill you a perfect steak or pull your ass out of a burning building, all without breaking a sweat or expecting any thanks. The guy's, what... nineteen years old and single? And he's already like the Perfect Dad.

Then there's Sgt. Sal Donado, the oldest of the trio. He's a tough, accomplished, New York City Puerto Rican with over six years as a *regular* air traffic controller already under his belt. A late convert, but new to the teams, and thereby a rookie.

And finally, little Ricky Spradlin—"Rocky," I've heard him called—the shortest and feistiest of them all. Barely five feet and a couple inches tall and bleached blond, with large black-irised eyes, and sporting a chipped front tooth that leaves a distractingly angular gap in his mischievous smile,

Rocky has already achieved 'minor legend' status as a result of a recent altercation outside a bar, in which he reportedly had to *jump up* to knock out a giant redneck who stood almost three feet taller than him.

Or so the story goes, anyway.

And in between them all—wearing his brand new unsullied virgin of a beret, with naught but his basic Army jump wings affixed—is the team's one and only Phase *II* member and its official token lunatic, Airman Teddy Heywood.

This guy is Greg Dorn's polar opposite; loud, tactless, insensitive, and hell-bent on nailing down a reputation—hell, make that a *legend*—for outrageousness. Stupid *childish* outrageousness, to be sure, but outrageousness nonetheless.

Take the other day, for instance.

I couldn't believe it when I stepped up into the open cubicle bay atop Cpt. Forth's office just in time to see Teddy whip out his *schlong* and drop it on the desk next to Sgt. Santos, who was trying to concentrate on some paperwork at the time. Without missing a beat though, Santos's fist lashed out and hammered down on the spot where the errant member had landed, only to come up empty. Teddy was already dancing off across the room, cackling loudly and cheering himself on. The boy's a maniac and doesn't want anyone to doubt it for a second. And apparently he's only gotten worse since he graduated from CCS about a month-and-a-half ago.

All these characters are scattered around this teetering half-completed GP tent now, shouting out unhelpful advice to each other, playing grab-ass, and ignoring the light windblown rain that just started up, soaking the grass and chilling the back of my neck. This eclectic dozen, plus two other guys who'll get back Friday from some week-long deployment out to the eastern deserts of Washington state, plus one 'old head' they call "BB" who's currently gone on leave, plus Captain Forth's second-in-command—another captain named Mears, fresh out of CCS himself, and currently off attending some other school—plus Randy Pogue (my roommate-in-absentia, and soon to be the team's newest Phase II guy), and something like four or five other guys not presently in attendance with us here.

And now me.

We 'twenty-plus' make up the entire McChord Combat Control *Team*.

We! Meaning 'these guys *and me.*' *And me!*

I still can't believe I can say that now.

STORY XX

THE NAMING OF THE SPEW

1
FIRST IMPRESSIONS

October, 1977
Moses Lake, Washington

AN HOUR INTO THE flight, and I'm still doing okay. Stomach still upright and content.

I've had to work at it, but so far my efforts have paid off.

I slept away the first half hour or so, starting the minute the plane first powered up out of its parking space back at McChord. Not really 'sleeping,' of course, so much as just keeping my eyes clamped shut, and my thoughts focused on anything that didn't jostle the floor, rumble or roar, or reek of JP-4.

In other words, on anything and anywhere but here.

It got to the point though, where I just couldn't keep myself pinned to the nylon troop seat anymore. My slumped posture had the frame digging into my back, and my ass was killing me.

Plus, since this is my first jump with my new team, my introduction to the Big Leagues, I felt I really ought to at least *pretend* to be up to it.

The rest of the guys had been strolling around the huge empty cargo bay, some shouting to each other—the only kind of 'conversation' possible in the droning hollow bowels of a C-130 in flight—some fiddling with their grease paint, their weapons, or their boot laces, and some actually *eating*. And since first impressions apply even here—perhaps *especially* here—I felt I needed to make some sort of sociable gesture before they opened the jump door over eastern Washington and threw us all out into the wind.

So I got up.

Well, despite my new 'buddies' assertions to the contrary (they'd all insisted that repeated exposure to the unnatural motion of flight would eventually toughen up my sensitive tummy), a wave of nausea promptly ensued. Sort of a personal tradition, I guess. And I chose to combat it with a brisk (but 'leisurely') saunter over to one of the only *three* windows in the entire cargo hold: the tiny round porthole in the left-rear jump door.

It's there that I found an outside horizon to becalm my troubled inner ear. It's there that I found some socially justifiable solitude. And it's there that I've remained ever since, staring down through the thick scratched glass at the passing landscape below.

Great start there, bucko! First jump with your new team, and you're all by yourself back here with your face immersed in this little shaft of light, looking like a prisoner staring out through the bars.

Whatever. It's either that, or the team gets to wear some 'used food' on their boots.

I decide that this 'lone wolf' image is probably just fine among the likes of these guys anyway. *Lone wolf, cowering chihuahua, whatever.*

For now though, the cork is still in the bottle, and that's the immediate priority for me.

* * *

BELOW US, THE SNOW-CAPPED mountains have already sloped away to forest-draped flatlands, scrolling past in slow motion (a C-130 is not a fast aircraft). Now the tight green nap of the trees is thinning out down there, looking more like a lush carpet that's been peeled away in strips, exposing more and more gold and brown as we continue east.

If I angle my view a little more forward, into the direction of flight, I can just make out a dark thread approaching from up ahead. The Columbia River Gorge, if I recall from the map, a deep moat that couldn't quite hold back the westward sprawl of the desert... *in the heart of which* lies the hardscrabble little town of Moses Lake... *beside which* is our vast DZ.

What... fifteen, maybe twenty minutes away?

"*Okay, ladies!*," Santos shouts over hands clapping loudly enough to be heard over everyone's earplugs, "*We're fifteen minutes out! Let's chute up!*"

Well, I guess that answers that question then, doesn't it?

This is different from the way we did things at Jump School. There we did all our 'chuting up' *on the ground*, in that rotting old 'harness shed.' Here we climbed aboard with our chutes just slung over one shoulder, then tossed them under our seats and took off in the unencumbered comfort of our regular old cammies, expecting to don our gear only once the jump was impending. Seemed like a good idea at the time, too.

Now I discover the one minor flaw in that plan. It requires that here and now, in flight, I have to wrangle the parachute on, turning my attention in close, my eyes on my rigging and my connections, my head (and my easily disoriented inner ear) tilted down. Like working on a puzzle in the back seat of a moving car. And that's never been a good combination for me.

Now, as I cross the pitching deck back over to my seat—as I bend over to pull my parachute out from underneath it, and spend a few moments spreading open its straps and harnesses and clips and buckles—as I shrug it onto my shoulders, and stoop to pull its crotch straps up between my legs, and I tug and tighten and shift and adjust everything into snug alignment across my body, I discover just how much of a 'tide' my previous suppressive efforts had been holding back. For, with my eyes no longer closed, or at least watching a horizon that bobs in harmony with the motions my inner ear's detected, all the clashing signals that herald a violent internal eruption have begun to wail.

Sweat suddenly breaks out all over, and my skin goes clammy. The nexus of the spinning gyros in my head shifts dizzyingly forward (and my head *and* stomach both hate 'dizziness'… it's one of the few things on which they can both agree), seeming to take up residence in the crowded quarters behind the bridge of my nose. And with it comes that strange sickly 'odor' that no one but the afflicted can smell. My stomach feels like it's rising, *physically*, floating to the top of my chest cavity as if *on top* of my diaphragm, which in turn triggers the body's natural reflex to breathe deeply and swallow hard.

And I know, from far too frequent personal experience, that an inexorable countdown has just begun. *Dad-gummit!*

This was not the first impression I'd wanted to make with these guys.

But maybe there's still hope—the jump itself! That might just fix it!

I remember, from Fort Benning, the abrupt curative effect that leaping from that doorway had had on my boiling gut then. And I know also how long I am capable of delaying the inevitable, if I can just be still and stay focused enough... if I can hum or moan quietly (the vibrations of which can usually help settle things down a bit), if I can breathe so deeply and steadily that I half-paralyze myself with the numbing effects of hyperventilation. If I can do all that, then I can hold on until they open that door. And if I can get that far, then I can make it to the green light. And if I can just last until *then*, I can get outside, and from there the cleansing tempest should do the rest, blasting the queasiness right out of me... if I can just sit back down, close my eyes again, breathe desperately deep, and just...

"*How you doin' there, Mr. Stipp?!!*"

I look up from my moment of standing-poise (hoping that I wasn't visibly swooning as they'd approached), and find myself facing Sergeants Santos and Campbell, the two Old Heads of the on-board crew today. Santos is smirking—his default facial expression, I've learned—but Campbell is staring concernedly at my face, no doubt gauging the portents being intimated by the pasty white sheen of my skin and the dew of sweat on my upper lip. *Not much point in trying to evade the issue now, I guess.*

I draw a cleansing chestful of air, pat my stomach tentatively, and roll my eyes. Then I lean forward and shout, "*I've been better!*"

Santos leans in himself, and yells into my left earplug, "*Don't puke on the plane, man! They hate it when you do that! They'll land the plane right there in the middle of the desert just to make you clean it up!*"

I'm sure it's intended to lighten the mood, but all it does is elicit a mental picture that only loosens my cork further.

While Santos runs his big meaty hands over my rigging for a last-second safety check (one of his duties as the *jumpmaster du jour*), I turn to Miles and ask, at the minimum necessary volume, if he knows where I might acquire a barf bag.

"*Check with the loadmaster!*" is all he shouts.

So I do.

The C-130's loadmaster—a surly five-striper named Borzinski, with hair scalped down to, well... his *scalp*, and a face chiseled from stern granite—although obviously familiar and friendly with the *regulars* of this team, clearly has no warm spot in his heart for weak-glotted rookies who are threatening to defile his aircraft.

He sniffs, checks a couple of the usual places, then turns back to me empty-handed and disgusted. With *me*, apparently.

Holding his headset in place with one hand, and pushing its mike away from his lips with the other, he shouts, "*I can't find any around here! You're just gonna' have to tough it out, I guess!*"

He starts to reposition his microphone, then stops himself. Swinging it back out of the way again, he adds, "*Ten more minutes! Just hold it for ten more minutes!*"

Sure! No problem! Like I've got a say in the matter.

Then from the end of the troop seat next to me, I hear, "*Ruh-roh!*"

I look left to see Teddy Heywood sitting there, wide smiling mouth chewing on the last bite of a Snickers bar, palms rubbing together in leisurely circles, rolling its wrapper into a ball.

Teddy friggin' Heywood.

Great. Now the court jester's in on it.

* * *

EVEN TAKING INTO ACCOUNT all the blazing testosterone in this group, all the strapping good looks (except for tired old Miles Campbell, of course), all the dash and derring-do (*whatever the hell 'derring-do' is*), and despite all the brazen bravado and shameless machismo practically squirting from the pores of each and every one of these guys, the one out of all of them who made the most profound first impression on *me* on my first day with the team was none other than Teddy friggin' Heywood.

For starters, he *looks* like an impossible freakish cross between Arnold Schwarzenegger and John Denver… Arnold's broad-shouldered muscle-bound body (although not quite so veined and over-inflated), with John's wide toothy grin, mop-top blond hair, even his little round rimless glasses. The two don't go together, *I know*, but then neither does Teddy Heywood, with any*body* or any*thing*.

Then there's the 'philosophy' he evidently lives by, a credo that says that *everything* is funny. *Everything*. And the more shocking, painful, or embarrassing it is to someone else, the funnier it is.

He can be astonishingly insensitive that way, and even infuriating at times. But he apparently always gets away with it. Because, as imposing as he might be physically, and as immature as he might be socially, he still manages to come off as some kind of goofy, harmless puppy that just hasn't quite grown into its big old floppy ears and feet yet. On a 'human' level, I'd put him in the same category as an anatomically over-developed surfer dude: carefree but irresponsible, smart but uninterested in his own intellect, an easy-going but natural 'bronze god' who just presumes that chicks fall at *everyone's* feet.

And it's a good thing, I guess, that he comes off as so amiable and harmless, because this would definitely be the wrong crowd with whom to strike up a sour working relationship. I mean, Teddy's barely above 'rookie status' himself, maybe a few months more than me on this team, but that's all. He might wear a beret these days, but it's still his Army-issued jump wings on its front facing, not a CCT flash.

Yep. You'd better possess some kind of impish charm to get away with that for very long. But somehow, Teddy does.

And that's who's looking up at me now with that patented ear-to-ear shit-eatin' chocolate-spackled grin on his face.

Shit.

* * *

LIKE EVERYONE ELSE, TEDDY has to shout to be heard over the din.

"*You're lookin' a might queasy there, Air-Man Steve! How 'bout a sandwich?!*"

He holds up the drooping remains of a half-eaten baloney-and-cheese, and the oily smell of luncheon meat and mayonnaise boils right up my nose. I try not to recoil too visibly, but deep inside, under all the layers of clothing and tightly cinched harness straps, my stomach is having a private little conniption.

Thanks, Teddy. Thanks a lot.

I swallow deeply, and turn back to the loadmaster. He begrudgingly pulls one headphone cup away from his ear, and I lean in close enough to tickle his lobe with my nose hair.

"*We may wanna' see if we can't rustle up some kind of bag pretty quickly here, Sergeant! 'Cause I don't think I'm gonna' last* two *more minutes, much less ten!*"

There. I said it. Some cookies are about to be tossed on your airplane, Sarge, and I'm the guy who's going to be doing the tossing. So whaddaya' think about them apples, *Mr. Borzinski?*

I try to make eye contact with him, but he's staring hard at the floor and clenching his jaw muscles. He definitely doesn't like having to deal with this, not one little bit. What he doesn't seem to realize though, is that like it or not, deal with it or not, this truly is non-negotiable. And it's fast becoming irreversible.

"*Seriously!,*" I continue, since he hasn't moved yet… hasn't even recovered his ear. "*Is there anything you can think of that we can use?! It doesn't have to be an official labeled 'Barf Bag'! It just has to be watertight! Anything at all! I'll take it!*"

He sighs and casts an angry one-eyed glare at me. Then he straightens up and screams, "*I'll see if I can't find something!*"

Then he stalks away, dragging the endless headphone cord that keeps him in contact with the cockpit.

Teddy finds this delightful. No one else is laughing, but Teddy's centerstage nature has ensured that everyone else is at least *aware* of current events at the front of the plane, and is paying attention as well.

Great.

I sway over to the front passenger door, right behind the cockpit stairs, and peer out through its tiny porthole. One last-ditch effort to hold the tides at bay. But the situation is way past being salvageable by a simple recalibration of my scrambled gyros. My head is warm and sloshing, my skin is pasty and damp, and I can feel the internal emergency valves springing open, one after another in a retreating sequence, starting right behind my quivering diaphragm and working their way up.

'Ruh-roh,' indeed.

I stagger back to my place on the troop seat, one hand's fingertips dragging across the back of the cockpit bulkhead just to keep me upright. I drop into the nylon webbing and lean my head back, eyes closed, breathing ferociously and swallowing constantly. It doesn't fix anything, but it holds things up for an extra minute or two.

Where the hell's that damned loadmaster?!!

* * *

WE CONTINUE TO GROWL through the skies, glacial minutes grinding past. With every exhalation, my churning gut seems to bloat and press a little harder against that 'cork.' And with every shaky *in*halation—and usually an accompanying swallow—I barely manage to tamp that cork back down again.

One step forward, and one step back.

It's a desperate stalemate, but one that could be ended *right now* if somebody would just *find me a goddamned barf bag!*

Finally, despite all the clamoring internal alarms and warning bells telling me not to move a muscle, including my eyelids, I open my eyes again anyway, hoping vainly to find the loadmaster approaching with my salvation in hand. However, not only is he *not*, but I can see that he's back in his original position, leaning against the wall, gabbing away with his good ol' CCT buddy Smoke. And there is nothing even remotely 'bag-like' in his hand.

Son of a bitch!

But at least Teddy Heywood is having a good time.

Sitting directly across from me on the opposite bench, plumped up and kicked back under all his jump gear, his arms draped over his reserve chute like a fat man after a truly grand feast, he's all grinning teeth and eager eyes. Just watching me and waiting for the show. Probably reveling in the waxy sheen on the New Guy's face, and taking mental notes for the many retellings of this story that will doubtless follow.

Unfortunately, just as all my inner signals had warned, this time spent studying my surroundings has accomplished something else... it has tripped the final release valve and triggered the launch sequence. The cork has finally popped, and breakfast is now on its way back up for an encore. It has begun.

Now.

Oh shit.

I sit bolt upright, gasping and swallowing hard and searching for anything—*anything*—that will keep my stomach's contents from decorating this airplane.

T-minus ten seconds and counting! Nine... eight...!

Nothing. I see not a bag, not a bucket, not a box. Not even an unclaimed helmet. I am about to engrave my legacy in the unit's archives... *with vomit.*

... seven... six... five...

I whirl to the left, and sitting next to me is good old Miles Campbell.

"*You okay?!,*" he shouts.

Evidently, judging by his expression, the blood must be visibly draining from my face like the mercury in a thermometer.

"I need a bag, Miles! Right now!"
... four... three...
"Are you... ?!"
... two... one...
Two things happen simultaneously.

First, Sgt. Miles Campbell—exhibiting remarkable speed and alacrity for a man his age (especially one wearing over fifty pounds of parachutes)—leaps from his seat beside me and lunges for the forward bulkhead where a large keg-shaped juice cooler is strapped to the wall, sitting atop a mysterious bed of plastic, one end of which is taped to the wall itself.

And secondly...

... ZERO!...

... ready or not, my countdown ends, and I am forced to let fly an epic chunder of the extreme projectile type, aimed straight across the floor towards Teddy Heywood (purely coincidence, I can assure you—no chance of actually reaching him—*hey, I'm good, but not* that *good*)—just as Miles wheels back around toward me brandishing a huge clear plastic garbage bag (so *that's* what that bed of plastic was under the juice keg) that he apparently just ripped off the wall, tape and all.

He thrusts it at my face, holding it wide open like an airport windsock. And *damn* if he doesn't catch my soured and soaring breakfast right there in *mid-flight!* Open bag swooping toward *me*, flying puke arcing towards *it*.

A hell of an open field snag!

I snatch the bag from him to complete my upheaval on my own, thank-you very much. But the initial saving capture is all his.

Kudos on the ralph-catching there, Miles! Not a drop on the floor! A dazzling save!

In fact, it's modern art!

Did I mention that this is a large *clear* plastic bag?

A ragged stream of pink and tan and orange liquid, hurled with the pressure of a fire hose, splatters across the inside of this *clear plastic bag* like a splash of dirty watercolor paint and egg yolks. And from there—and through each of my many subsequent retches—it slides down the sides, thin and stringy, and pools around the discarded lunch boxes and candy wrappers at the bottom. It is apparently a very gruesome image indeed.

Thank God I *don't have to look at it.* But everybody else does. And the dominos quickly begin to fall from there.

First, and most rewardingly, is Teddy Heywood. His reaction to my billowing 'abstract art' is an abrupt and satisfyingly panicked little 'hiccup'—a wet one that he cannot stop in time—which blurps up an ugly brackish solution like espresso and peanuts (*revenge of the Snickers bar!*) all over his hands as he's raising them to cover his mouth.

This in turn trips a chain reaction among the other guys further down Teddy's bench, the first of whom is quick enough to snatch an empty lunch box out from under his seat, and upchucks into that, another having his own barf bag ready at hand (*the bastard*). I think another guy, down at the *end* of the bench, also gets caught up in the tumbling dominos, but I'm too busy watching Teddy to be sure... because the chain reaction has now rebounded back *to him*.

Already trying to fend off the initial 'urge to purge' just from watching *my* chumming of the trash bag, not to mention that surprising little 'wet burp' of his own, the sight of *three other guys* all harking up their boxed lunches finally overwhelms Teddy's previously untested reserves, and just like that, "*Up from below comes a bubblin' crude.*"

"*Hurl, that is! Gag-reFlexus gold! Vom-I-T!*"

And it's a gully-washer too.

With a loud and helpless gurgle, Teddy is thrown forward in his seat, folding at the gut—although only as far as the reserve chute lying on his belly will allow—and cuts loose a forceful and quite chunky brown geyser of bile that splashes across the floor like the swill of a kicked-over spittoon. The loadmaster roars with disgust, and turns away, unable to watch. So does everyone else, including our Team Commander Captain Forth, who claps his hand to his mouth and staggers aft to the tiny wall-mounted piss bucket bolted to a metal rib just behind the jump door.

Dang. I wish I'd *thought of that. Or the damned loadmaster.*

And I find myself in a most unusual position; sitting on my bench, holding a huge *clear plastic* bag of my own barf in both shaking hands, elbows braced on knees, taking my first steadying breaths after a minute or so of strident heaving, and looking around at a planeload of virtually *disabled* spec ops troops, every one of whom has become 'incapacitated' to some degree or another by first *my*, and then *Teddy's* respective Technicolor Yawns®.

I mean, *at this moment*, now that I've finally stopped yarking myself, there are *five*—count 'em, *five!*—big macho stormtroopers actively bringing their lunches back up, one of whom—good old happy-go-lucky Teddy Heywood—is bucking and thrashing so violently, he looks like he's fighting his way through a *grand mal* seizure, his intermittent bursts of liquefied food mixed with the strange grunts and howls of a wounded animal.

Jesus!

The rest of the team, along with the loadmaster (and now *me*), are busily engaged in averting our eyes, a couple of the guys leaning against the walls with their eyes *closed*, desperately fending off their own encroaching disasters.

Look at me now, Ma! Looky what I did!

* * *

I FEEL BAD ABOUT all this... well *mostly*. So now that my own gut has calmed, I feel compelled to 'assist' in any way I can. And since Teddy is clearly the most adversely affected, it's to him that I first offer my well-used barf bag. It's pretty much a lost cause, of course, since he's already coated the front of his uniform and his reserve chute in watery brown offal, as well as turning the deck between us into a reeking marshland. But *hey, it's the thought that counts, right?*

So I wobble upright and take a step toward him (stopping well short of "Heywood Swamp"), and hold out my bag.

It takes a moment or two before he catches his breath enough to even open his wet and swollen eyes. But the instant he does, he catches sight of me, swaying in the middle of the deck, offering him this four-foot-long puke-streaked bag, and he's off to the races all over again.

"*Ah GAHD!*," he squeaks out, his face turning a bright baboon's-ass red, just before his convulsing gut throws him forward once more, and he picks up right where he left off.

Man, I don't know whether to revel in the poetic justice of it all—the *Instant Karma*—or slit my wrists out of guilt.

I look around the compartment again, and find that everyone (but Teddy) has already resolved their issues, either through downright *heroic* self-control, or by simply getting their 'downloads' out of the way quickly. In fact, big old badass Sgt. Santos is looking right at me with a sinister wall-to-wall smirk torquing his face. I do believe he might have actually *enjoyed* this little opus of mine! Or maybe it's just the humbling of Teddy Heywood that's made his day. Either way, there's a complete lack of sympathy in that twisted grin of his as he straightens up, cups his hands around his mouth, and shouts, "*Five minutes, ladies! Let's get hooked up!*"

So we're still going to do this, then?

Oh, yes! Of course we are.

You don't stop the war for a case of the sniffles, and you don't stop *training* for war over a little bit of untimely purging… even if it is a *mass* purging.

Now normally, I'd be required to carry my spoilage out the door with me. But then normally, the vessel containing my collected inner churnings would not be a four-foot-long mini-parachute in its own right. So I'm not certain the rule applies in this case.

I catch Sgt. Campbell on his way to the portside anchor cable, his static-line clip in hand. And I hold up my lovely prize, accompanied by a shrug of my shoulders and a gesture toward the door that Santos is ripping open even as we 'speak.'

Miles grimaces at the sight of the bag, and shakes his head, "*No.*"

Good. I won't need to carry it out the door with me when I jump.

I cast a wary glance toward the loadmaster, which Miles follows with his eyes. Then he leans in close to the side of my helmet, and yells.

"*Fuck him!*"

I can see that Sgt. Campbell and I are going to get along just fine.

So I roll up my enchantingly transparent bag-o-drippings into a small clay-colored bundle, and wave it over my head to catch the loadmaster's attention. Then, once he's looking my way—and glaring at me with enough heat to spontaneously ignite my underwear from twenty feet away—I make a big showy gesture of tucking my little treasure away among the cross-straps of the nylon webbing at the back of the troop seats.

This is no act of defiance. It's just an attempt to ensure that it can't be blown around the compartment by the winds now storming in through the open door. I'm not leaving it on his plane *just* to piss him off… I'm leaving it because it's just not safe to jump with it.

That's my story, and I'm sticking to it.

Then I join the rest of the team, clipping myself to the anchor cable overhead, and queuing up for the impending jump… with everyone *but Teddy*, that is.

Because Teddy, apparently, can no longer even *stand*.

When I see Smoke pulling Captain Forth aside, shouting into his ear and pointing toward the front of the compartment, I turn to find Teddy Heywood still there, draped over the troop seats like a big bag of wet yard waste that's torn open and spilled half of its contents across the floor. His face is drained of color and shining with a fine glaze of sweat, his crusted lips hanging open and heaving for breath. And with that splash pattern of dark bile fanned across the front of his cammies, heaped atop his reserve chute, and splattered across the floor at his feet, he looks like someone who just got knocked out cold by a well-thrown puke balloon. Though I can't be sure from this far away, it also looks like he's moaning... *loudly.*

Jesus. Just looking at him is enough to make me queasy all over again.

Smoke and the captain walk back to him, lean as close as their noses and gullets will allow (as well as their spit-polished boots), and 'consult' with him for a moment. But with the singular exception of his left arm, which waves them away weakly, he does not move. He is apparently spent, wiped out. Bowled over and plowed under. Decimated by his own fullglottal inversion. But most importantly to his military superiors, he has now been rendered 'combat ineffective,' incapacitated, and unable to follow through with his mission.

In other words, Teddy Heywood is now, by definition, an official 'casualty.' From *vomiting.* From watching *me* vomit, for shit's sake, a prospect which, just a few minutes ago, he'd been downright eager to provoke.

Oh well. Be careful what you wish for, I guess.

I still feel like warmed-over feces myself. I'm sure everyone on this aircraft is reeling from *some* degree of 'BGS' ('Boiling Gut Syndrome'), thanks to my little matinee performance on this, my very first jump with my new team. *Well done, Steve!*

But, wretched spinning disorientation or not, I'm still capable of standing, hooking up, and falling out the friggin' door, misery be damned. We *all* are. Everyone but Teddy, anyway.

Teddy's complete obliteration here is an embarrassment, not only for himself, but for the team as a whole, which must hereafter board any future McChord aircraft with this brand of weakness stamped on its forehead. If Teddy would just drag his ass up off that bench, we could hook him up and *push* him out, and let gravity and the cleansing wind storm do the rest. But for all intents and purposes, he has been gutted and filleted and will not be moved.

"*One minute, gentlemen!,*" shouts Sgt. Santos from the doorway.

Smoke and the captain rise from their futile ministrations, exchange a resigned look with the loadmaster, then head back to the queue. They take their places, clip themselves to the anchor cable, and leave Teddy right where he's sprawled, alone and lifeless, and now at the mercy of one very angry loadmaster (who, as far as I'm concerned, deserves it almost as much as Teddy does). So...

Wow. Two birds with one disgusting stone.
It almost makes it all worthwhile... almost.

* * *

THE LIGHT SWITCHES TO green. And just in time, too. That uncorked caldron at the bottom of my esophagus has had way too much time to boil up another batch of evil. I'm going to need that wallop of fresh air to flash-cleanse my curdling innards again. And the sooner the better.

Our 'stick' charges the door chute-to-chute, each man's reserve pressing against the main of the man in front of him, their boots clomping in harmony, a coordinated shuffling centipede desperately seeking clean air. And I'm right there, eighth in line, in step and driving the queue forward, right along with everyone else.

I'm almost bringing up the rear, with only Smoke Sherrod and another rookie like myself, Greg Dorn, chasing me towards the light. I lead them straight to the door, fling my static line aft, and throw myself out into space—hot, golden, trackless, desert space, bowled and rolling around me as I plummet.

Above and behind me, the dark stinking stovepipe of the C-130 zips out of the picture as if on a bungee cord, swept out of my universe in one swift roaring stroke, taking my nausea and *some* of my humiliation with it.

Whump! My parachute booms open, and abruptly, predictably, and thankfully, all is still and silent once more, including my tender stomach.

Aaaahhh. That's more like it.

The rest of my descent is smooth and revivifying... in a completely mortified kind of way. The 'DZ' at Moses Lake is, well, about the size of the desert itself, which is most of the eastern half of Washington state beyond the Columbia River. It would take a conscious effort to actually miss it. So I quit thinking about it, and instead just settle in to follow the procession of green silk mushrooms in front of me to the ground.

There's a large orange "***T***" down there staked to the desert floor, vinyl panels laid out by Skeeter and Monty, our two teammates who drove that camouflaged pick-up truck and that battered looking Jeep all the way out here into the middle of nowhere. It helps the jumpers pick out not only the center of the DZ, but it also ensures that it's the *correct* DZ as well. That's more important when there are multiple DZs in the area, or in a combat environment when the bad guys might be watching and listening to your communications. But for us here today, it's just for practice.

The jump is short, but not *so* short that I don't have way too much time to contemplate just how badly my first deployment with my new team has gone. I mean, *Jeezy Pete!*, I just triggered a chain-reaction barf-a-thon up there. I grossed out and embarrassed a lot of guys who'd probably never thrown up on a plane before in their friggin' lives. I ruined the jump, the exercise, the *day*, and I probably compromised the team's reputation with the airlift wing that has to fly us everywhere we go as well. Because once that pissed-off loadmaster gets back to the squadron's Ops Shack at McChord, the word will be out among the aircrews about the team's 'chunder-fest' aboard his airplane. And there goes our standing with the Wing. And all because of my quaky little weenified stomach.

Damn it!

Well, that plus Teddy's costly provocations, of course (not to mention his own fountainous contributions).

I guess I can take a little heart from the 'just desserts' that Teddy's got to be enjoying right about now, not only sick as a dog that's just licked up its first keg of spilled beer, but stuck on that stinking airplane as well, wearing and surrounded by his own puke. And all with that livid loadmaster glaring down on him, riding out the ship's slow growling descent into the airport at Moses Lake.

Hah! Laugh at that, *asshole!*

* * *

ONE AFTER ANOTHER AFTER another, my teammates before me settle to the ground, collapse and gather their chutes, and congregate between the two lonely vehicles. No doubt Skeeter and Monty are already getting an earful about the events on the plane from the first guys that touched down.

I sink closer and closer, praying all the way for a mammoth gust of hurricane-force winds to blow me far away from these guys and their accusing eyes, maybe even carry me into the Columbia River Gorge to be dashed upon the cliffs or drowned in its fast muddy waters. Anything but a re-introduction to my fellow co-workers right now.

But apparently my luck's not even *that* half-assed 'good.'

I slip past the pick-up truck in a quiet flutter, and crumple into the scrubby sand in its lee. I can hear laughter—manly 'guy laughter'—carried on the thin desert wind, and I know just exactly what the topic of discussion is: *the FNG ('Fucking New Guy'), Steve "The Vomit Comet" Stipp, the Wonder of Chunder, the Lunch Launcher, the team's newest problem child, a proven deficit after only one jump. More trouble than he'll ever be worth, most likely. Maybe we should let Pope have him after all.* Shit like that.

Hmmm.

Actually, I could live with that just fine, now that I think about it.

I unhorse my rig, and bundle it all away in my B-4 bag. Then I draw a deep breath of resignation, and troop around the truck to join my so-quickly-estranged teammates at the back of the pick-up's bed. Sgt. Sherrod—"Smoke"—waddles up to the truck at the same time, his own parachute and gear slung over his shoulders. Then he and I dump our loads together, and exchange an awkward smile. Miles Campbell separates from the rest of the laughing, shouting, smoking caucus and joins us.

"So how ya' feelin' there, Steve?" he asks.

Miles is probably the first person on the team to call me by my first name. Certainly the first of the higher ranking sergeants, anyway.

"Oh, I'm fine *now*," I answer with a beaming heartiness that I do not feel. "Just wish my debut could have been a little less *gross*, is all."

Smoke snorts, and pulls his ever-present pipe from his thigh pocket.

"Shit. I thought that was funny as hell," he says. "That's the stuff of legend, man."

I hardly ever see Smoke around the hangar. Not counting the Chief, Smoke, Manny and Miles are the three most senior enlisted guys, I believe. Five- and six-stripers... Tech and Master Sergeants all. Miles is the oldest and nicest, Manny the biggest and baddest, and Smoke the coolest and quietest. He's short, white-haired and blue-eyed, harmlessly Aryan in appearance. I like him for his easy smile and utter unflappability in the face of all chaos. So I listen when he speaks.

"Yeh, well...," I sigh, "Thanks, I guess." I glance over at the 'in-crowd' clustered around big old Manny Santos. "It's just not the legend I was hoping to be remembered for."

Smoke nods and finishes tamping down his tobacco. Then he looks at me with a placid warmth, and says, "Fuck it."

Miles chuckles as Smoke saunters off around the truck, looking for a windbreak to light up.

"Don't worry about it," says Miles. "It's all just... stories. You know? Shit to tell your grandkids about some day. And by then, it'll all be funny. Hell, even Borzinski—the loadmaster up there?—even *he'll* be laughing about it by tomorrow."

The congregation around Santos suddenly explodes with laughter. One voice shouts, "Spew! That's a great one!" And the group stumbles apart, roaring.

Great. Now I've got a nickname.

2
THE LEGACY

THE DRIVE INTO THE sun-baked town of Moses Lake takes a little over half an hour on ruler-straight dirt tracks and two-lane desert roads. Skeeter's driving the 'six-pack,' the hooded Dodge Ram pick-up truck. Drove it all the way over from Tacoma, apparently. And he clearly knows his way around this neck of the barbed wire and weeds.

He circumnavigates the treeless outskirts of town, following a dusty route past sun-baked silos, tumbledown tractor repair garages, a few tired looking aluminum-sided warehouses, and one big ugly canning factory, before entering the grounds of the Moses Lake Regional Airport.

And there, on a cracked and weedy parking apron, sits our C-130, its cargo ramp down and open—probably airing the damned thing out—with four or five men standing in its shadow.

Oh boy... here we go.

We pull up under its high left wing, and pile out onto the concrete.

Teddy is sitting on the edge of the cargo ramp, keeping himself propped up with his hands on his knees, staring hard at the ground, and looking thoroughly miserable and dejected. I feel for him, even though I can't imagine anyone who deserves it more right now. Because I know that, without at least three or four hours of motionless rest—or one good parachute jump—his nausea's not going to go away just because he discarded the contents of his stomach. And we've still got to fly back to McChord this afternoon... in that same airplane. So old Teddy-Boy's long day is still a long way from over.

The team splits up, senior echelons moving to consort and reconcile with the flight crew, I imagine, the more junior members swarming Teddy to console and torment, depending on the mood of the moment. I hang back, alone, only vaguely trailing Miles from a distance… a distance that feels a lot broader than the mere footage between us.

I've got to live with these guys, here in this far-flung corner of the country, so far from hearth and home. And here I've gone and started things off like this. Right now, they feel even more like strangers than they did on that first day in the hangar.

I watch as the loadmaster tromps down the ramp and is met by big and bullish Sgt. Santos, who seizes his hand and pumps it, and exchanges a few words and head nods. Then he wheels away to march on Teddy, who slowly creaks to his feet as Manny approaches.

"Spew!" shouts Manny, scattering the huddled crowd around him, "Welcome to the club, man!" And the whole team busts out laughing.

What? Teddy? Teddy is 'Spew?'

It's Teddy? Not me?

"Spew, man! Helluva' show!"

"The chocolate was a nice touch, man!"

"Way to go, Spew!"

So it's official then. Apparently, whatever Santos says goes. And Santos says Teddy's new handle is "Spew."

Teddy nods sheepishly, accepting the barbed congratulations with blushing grace (eating humble pie is one of Teddy's few positive traits).

So, the legend's going to be all about Teddy now, huh?

"Spew."

Hmmm.

Suddenly, I'm jealous.

STORY XXI

NEWBIE ZERO-ONE

1

LEARNING THE SECRET HANDSHAKE

October, 1977
Yakima Firing Range, Yakima, Washington

I MEET "MUTT"—that's Sgt. Helmut Siegel—on the long drive to Yakima (pronounced "*YACK-imma*"), Washington, just two days later. Mutt's a tall, wiry, bawdy brawler of a guy who doesn't look or talk even the least bit German (in fact, I think he's from St. Louis), with a thick awning of a moustache and a cigarette perpetually hanging from his lips. He's the last member of the McChord Combat Control Team that I haven't already met, and I've gotta' say, if nothing else, he at least knows how to make a boring drive interesting.

I'm riding shotgun in the unit's communications Jeep—an MRC-108 that everyone just calls "The Mark"—a top-heavy jury-rigged off-road vehicle loaded with racks of heavy radios of all types, and made all the more sluggish by the towing of a generator trailer. All that combined with a long winding crawl up through the Cascade Mountains, propelled with all the impetus of a gutless four-cylinder sewing machine of an engine. And I've got to say... *it's actually pretty goddamned embarrassing.*

But Mutt doesn't care.

We're bringing up the rear of a three-truck 'convoy' of CCT vehicles, the rest of which have already left us far behind as we've toiled up these switchbacks. This may be Interstate 90, but to watch us chugging our way uphill, you'd think we were the last car in a funeral procession.

Mutt's at the wheel, cigarette flaring in the cool breeze that's ruffling the canvas flaps, talking his ass off and laughing at every car that hurtles past us as if it's his pleasure to impede their high-speed travel in any way possible.

Every now and then, whenever the passing traffic warrants some 'special notice'—like a large breasted blonde whisking past us in her "Benz"—Mutt cheerfully calls ahead to the other team vehicles up the road on either HF or UHF (radio frequency ranges seldom, if ever, visited by civilians), and 'warns' them of her approach, using formal phraseology and official phonetics to mask the ribald nature of his words.

He might advise them, for instance—in his best 'air traffic control voice,' of course—of "*Traffic, a **M**ike **B**ravo three-five-zero with two, I say again TWO **F**oxtrot **O**scar **X**-rays and one **D**elta **I**ndia **L**ima **D**elta **O**scar, now passing **M**ike **M**ike niner-two. Over.*"

Translation: "An **MB** *350* (Mercedes Benz 350) with two **FOX**es (women) and one **DILDO** (a male) passing **M**ile **M**arker 92... over."

And that's a classy example. They get a whole lot raunchier.

The point is, he knows how to make the time pass.

Unfortunately, cresting the Cascades and starting down their eastern slopes does not allow us to travel any faster. For while the Mark's pathetic little engine might have labored to drag us *up* the mountains, the dangerously top-heavy radio stacks behind us preclude us from going *down* the mountains with any speed whatsoever. Cornering is just too delicate, its readiness to roll over too close to the edge. So, until the land flattens and the road straightens out in the middle of the state, we continue to putter along.

Dammit.

During the course of this long drawn-out easterly trek, however, our conversation naturally turns introductory. Still, I find myself answering a lot of personal questions that I wouldn't have expected from an initial dialogue—I mean, I've never met this guy before this moment—questions intended, I'm guessing, to help Mutt assess my character, determine the amount of 'heart' I possess, establish my willingness to fight alongside my brothers, and to delineate my long term objectives as a Combat Controller.

In other words, it's more like an audition.

And he seems genuinely shocked by some of my answers.

"You've *never* been in a fight *in your life?* In your *life?*"

"Not once," I answer. "Never taken—or *thrown*—a punch either. I wouldn't know how."

This he just cannot seem to fathom. But it's true.

Mutt, conversely—at least according to his reputation—*loves* to fight. And by that, I don't just mean he's better at it than most, or is merely easily provoked like Li'l Rocky. I mean he *enjoys* it. It's a sport to him, like playing racquetball or swimming. He'd fight his own mother if she'd be willing to exchange damaging blows with him. And none of this "cuffing each other around a bit" shit for Mutt either. He goes for knock-outs, blackened eyes and bloodied noses every time. You don't 'scrap' with Mutt. You either batter him to stillness, or he'll do it to you.

To listen to the others talk, it's both reassuring and a little unsettling to have someone like that on the team, knowing, on the one hand, that he's fearless and effective in a scrap, but at the same time knowing that you cannot afford for him to be mad *at you*.

Fortunately, Mutt is a very affable character. He's done it all, been everywhere, is checked out on everything, and he knows everybody in the friggin' business. So he's found his niche in life and is at peace with it. He may smoke like a chimney, drink like a fish, and brawl for a living, but for those very reasons, this job has proven to be the perfect outlet for his aggressive and cocksure nature.

It's all good. It's all fun for him. *Whew!*

* * *

STILL, AS THE MILES roll by, he keeps coming back to how amazed he is that anyone—especially any *male*, and even moreso, any male in *this* kind of work—would shy away from a physical conflict. And not just the lopsided or uneven contests, but *any* form of potentially violent confrontation. Which is exactly what I've repeatedly told him I do… avoid confrontations.

Yeh, I know, I know. It makes me *wonder what I'm doing here too.*

I mean, it's not like we're talking about military combat here. We're talking about bar fights and other 'peacetime' tussles… what I would consider 'stupid shit,' unnecessary complications, and self-inflicted wounds… the kind of bullshit you get *yourself* into, and so it's nobody else's problem but yours.

I'm still working on how to phrase *that* to a guy like Mutt, though.

In the meantime, he gets on a bit of a roll about the unwritten 'codes of the warrior,' and all that—*I've got your back, and you've got mine*: that kind of stuff—and finally gets around to informing me, point blank, that if I'm not up to that kind of mutual support and dependability in a fight, I might want to look for other work.

I reply then, perhaps a little defensively, that while it would not be my intention to let anybody down or leave them in the lurch, it's been my experience that most disputes of that nature can be resolved without resorting to savagery, and that I'd rather avoid the one if the other option is available.

Gawd, that sounds even weenier out loud than it did in my head.

Dangit!

That doesn't satisfy Mutt. Obviously.

"Are you trying to tell me," he asks, his brow skewed in genuine disbelief now, "that if your buddies were in trouble and needed your help, you wouldn't step in?"

"No, that's not what I'm saying *at all!*," I sigh. Again.

He just can't seem to get past this sticking point. But he's waiting for a longer answer than that.

"It would depend, I guess," I finally accede, looking for some middle ground between our polarities.

"Depend? On what?"

"On whether or not they brought it on themselves."

"Huh?"

"I mean, for instance, if *they* started it."—*and this I'm directing specifically at Mutt and his renowned propensity for starting fights just so that he can finish them*—"If they'd been *asking* for trouble and were only getting what they'd asked for, then why the hell would I want to get caught up in that? It's their problem. They wanted it, they got it, they can deal with it."

Traipsing along the ragged edge of disaster there, Stevie. Watch your step through that *minefield.*

But this, for the first time since the subject came up, seems to get through to him.

"Yeh, okay," he says, taking another deep drag off his cigarette and blowing it out the flap. "I guess I can see that."

He stares out the windshield for a long moment, watching the ass end of a semi that just blew by us, as it dwindles up the interstate.

"Yeh, I can live with that. It ain't exactly *my* code, but it's not unreasonable either." Then he turns and looks me square in the eye. "But with this job, and on this team, I and every one of the rest of your teammates need to *know*, with *confidence*, that we can count on you when the fur's a-flyin' and our backs are against the wall. We just have to. It's the only thing that makes small unit tactics survivable. You're there for us, we're there for you, or we're all dead. Always. It's that simple.

Uh-oh. I'm not sure I like where this is going, but I'm definitely feeling myself being cornered here.

"So here's the deal," he continues, as if he's the man with whom such covenants are struck. "I want your assurance, right here and now, that you'll be there in a pinch. I want you to *tell* me that if you ever see me or anybody else on this team in trouble—with the odds against us, or just in need of a show of solidarity—that you'll step up and get involved. Put your back up against mine, and do your part."

Damn! What kind of trouble is he expecting to get into here? And how often? Is this really a pressing issue with this group?

"You give me that assurance, and I'll assure *you* that I won't drag you into anything that I've brought down on myself. Okay? How's that? Deal?"

I can't believe what I'm hearing. *Is this really an ongoing problem? Does everyone get this 'deal'—this ultimatum—when they first meet Mutt Siegel? And does the need to circle the wagons really come up that often around here? If so, maybe I should go look for another job. I don't need this.*

Still, though it's not something I've ever had to ponder before—and Lord knows, with *my* fighting skills, I'm probably the *last* guy they'd want to depend on to 'cover their six'—this *is* a combat unit, that *is* how it works best, it's *not* too much to ask, and it really *doesn't* clash with my own personal ethics. I mean, if Mutt had never brought it up, I'd like to think that that's what I would have done anyway. I've just never had to think about it before, and certainly never had to take an oath to that effect. But then…

So what! Take the damned step and commit to it! Make it part of your personal evolution.

"Yeh, okay," I say. "I can do that."

"Say it."

"Say what?"

"Let me hear your assurance, Airman Stipp. Let me hear the words."

Jesus. "Alright, uhhh... I promise that I will step in and, uhh... help out with any... sorta'..."

"Just tell me that I can depend on you to be there in a fight."

"Well..."

"Any fight that I don't instigate myself, that is."

"Okay. I assure you that I will always do my part. I will be there beside you, should the need ever arise. How's that?"

Mutt watches my eyes for a moment (the demands of driving be damned), no doubt trying to decide just how half-hearted that was. Then that roguish smile splits his face again, and he kicks back in his seat.

"Good enough, man," he laughs. "Welcome to the team."

That was friggin' weird.

Now I'm wondering how *that's* gonna' come back to bite me in the ass.

2

A DAY WITH MY CRAZY INBRED TEAMMATES

AIR TRAFFIC CONTROL REALLY is different in the field.

Sitting up here on this scrubby ridgetop beside Mutt, with the Mark parked under a small copse of trees, its generator trailer chugging merrily along behind us, it resembles almost nothing I ever experienced during training.

Down at the bottom of this shallow high-mountain valley, there is an airstrip that looks about the size of a paper cut on my finger... Selah Creek LZ. Just a couple hundred feet of black asphalt with a teardrop-shaped loop at each end. Turnarounds, I presume. And parked just off the loop at the east end, idling in the deep grass, is a cluster of Army vehicles: a couple of pick-ups, the rest all 'deuce-and-a-halfs' (two-and-a-half ton transport trucks), waiting to carry off whatever is brought in by the C-130s that Mutt has been talking to on the Mark's UHF radio.

As I understand it, this morning the aircraft will be landing on that microscopic strip down there, off-loading supplies for the grunts that are scattered throughout these hills. That will also give the aircrews experience with combat approaches, short field landings and take-offs, and quick turnaround procedures. Then this afternoon we'll be getting in some training *for ourselves*, with Combat Controllers posted on hilltops all along this range, first learning how to direct inbound aircraft to remote locations, then ending up with several 'CDS' ("Container Delivery System") drops a little further up the valley.

Should be interesting.

"This is about as comfy as a field deployment can get," says Mutt, chewing his gum and adjusting the leg that he's got dangling out the open door. "In a covert or combat operation, you'd be laying out in the bushes somewhere, with sticks and weeds and shit stuffed down your collar and under your hat. You'd have one VHF radio only—one of those nasty-assed pricks"—(a PRC-77 portable radio, about the size of a briefcase, about the weight of a loaded tool chest)—"strapped to your back. You'd have to use your memory for things like callsigns, weather, and flight data information, and if it decided to rain, you'd get wet.

"But here..."—and he waves at the palatial accommodations of the Mark—"Here you've got a roof over your head, a heater if it gets cold, a whole array of radios from FM and HF to VHF and UHF, and high-speed mobility if you've suddenly got to bug out or something. This is the Ritz, baby, and don't you forget it. Appreciate it when you've got it."

I nod. *Sage words of wisdom indeed.*

One of the big radios in the rack behind our heads hisses to life and emits a tinny nasal voice.

"*Selah Creek, Rawley six-five is twelve miles southeast of the LZ, inbound to land.*"

Without looking back, Mutt tugs the mike off its little jury-rigged clothesline, and mashes the thumb button before he's even pulled it all the way around to his mouth. The radio whirs up to a turbine-like whine that peaks just as the handset reaches his lips, and he speaks.

"Rawley six-five, Selah Creek. You're cleared into the Range, number one for the field. Altimeter two-niner-eight-six. Report the airfield in sight."

As he waits for the pilot to reply, he snatches up a grease pencil and starts writing *on the Jeep's flat windshield!* He scribbles its callsign, aircraft type, and the time of initial contact, all small enough to leave space for any other aircraft that might soon be checking in. But the point is, *he writes it right on the windshield glass!*

I'm not sure why, but that just floors me.

The C-130 calls back while he's scribbling.

"*Rawley copies 'Cleared into the Range.' Airfield in sight.*"

"Roger that, Rawley," sighs Mutt once the radio has taken another second or two to whir back up to full power. "Check wheels down, wind calm, cleared to land."

"Rawley six-five is gear down, cleared to land."

Mutt hangs the handset from the clothesline again, spits his gum out in the tall grass beside the Mark, and taps out a fresh cigarette from the pack he pulls from his chest pocket.

He's been in an especially expansive mood today, spilling advice and war stories at a rate that implies he hasn't had a receptive audience in quite a while. But like everything else Mutt does, he's entertaining as he does it.

"So anyway, like I was saying, on this one exercise, about eight or nine months ago, we were the 'aggressors,' and the fuckin' SPs were the so-called 'good guys.' All they had to do was guard this 'prisoner'—a 'downed pilot,' supposedly—that *we* were supposed to snatch from them. They'd put a fake cast on his leg and everything, just to hobble him I guess. Keep him from running. They had a 'secure' base camp out in the woods on the eastern edge of McChord. It was on top of a small knoll, with a cleared perimeter between them and the trees, so they had a height advantage and a clear fire zone that we were gonna' have to cross. They had twice the number of men as we did, and they didn't have to move. *We* were coming to *them*. They even knew, to within an hour or so either side of midnight, *when* we were gonna' come and get that pilot."

Mutt chuckles wistfully, sucks a long hissing drag from his cigarette, and shakes his head.

"And we still kicked their sorry asses."—*(*sigh*)*—"God damn, those bastards are pathetic."

I've noticed that between Skeeter, "Monty" Montreaux, Manny Santos, and now Mutt—the *talkative* 'Old Heads' of the team—that not only are the stories all the same, with the exact same characters and identical endings, but the *moral* is always the same as well: *Air Force Security Police (and sometimes Army Rangers) are all professional-grade idiots. Combat Controllers ROCK.*

And it appears that today's bedtime story will be no different.

"I mean, we had Smoke all set up in the middle of their camp, just as an observer. A non-player. And he's sittin' there—right next to the 'downed pilot,' right—listening in on our secure channel, monitoring our approach maneuvers. All standard stuff. We weren't going for 'originality' or anything. Just '*hit 'em,*' you know? Test their readiness, coordination, fire discipline, shit like that. But the fuckin' SPs weren't even close to being ready for us, and Smoke could see this thing was going to be a rout, over in about ten seconds, if he didn't do *something* to at least make it interesting.

"So he unplugs his handset, goes to speaker, and cranks the volume up loud enough for everyone in the SP camp to hear it! Letting 'em all listen in on our comm! *He was giving us away to them*, the goofy son of a bitch! And they *still* didn't get it!"

Mutt giggles like a sleepy drunk, then points out the window towards the east end of the valley. Our C-130, Rawley 65, has just come into view, rolling out of a steep entry turn and settling onto final approach for the little sliver of a runway down to our left. From our ridgetop perch, we are looking down on the tops of its upturned wings.

Mutt grabs the mike again, mashes the button until the radio whirs up to speed, and sighs.

"Rawley six-five, got you in sight on two-mile final. You're still number one, the winds are still calm, and you're still cleared to land."

What the hell kind of phraseology was that?

"*Roger that, Selah Creek*," the radio replies. "*Understand we have* not been un*cleared to land.*"

What the...? Are you kidding me?

"So anyway," Mutt resumes, this time leaving the mike hanging over his shoulder, laying against his chest, "the Sock Puppets could hear Smoke's radio. They could hear every damned thing we were sayin' to each other while we were closing on their defenses. But—get this—not only did they not get the hint about how close we were, not only did they *not* pay any attention to the points we'd just said we were about to hit, but they all came a-wanderin' on in to the center of the camp where Smoke was sittin', *to listen in!* Yeh! They fuckin' abandoned their posts—which were already weakly disposed to begin with—and stood around in a circle, listening to Smoke's radio like it was playin' the Amos & Andy Show *while it broadcast our positions to 'em! Unbelievable!*"

I think I hear another fish story brewing here.

Mutt pauses to suck a little more life—or death—from his cigarette, and to watch Rawley 65 and its shadow pinch together over the end of the little landing strip. As soon as its main wheels touch down, its nose gear drops hard onto the asphalt. And even from clear up here on this ridgetop,

I can hear its four massive turboprops roaring in reverse thrust, trying to get it stopped on a dime.

Actually, that's what Mutt calls that landing strip: "The Dime."

Yeh, it's that damned tiny, even for a C-130 to land on.

We watch in silence as the little toy airplane rolls to the end of the little toy runway, and turns off onto the little toy turnaround loop.

"*Rawley six-five is clear of the active,*" says its pilot. "*Request taxi-back to the approach end for an engine-running offload.*"

"Roger that," Mutt replies into the microphone as he writes the downtime on the windshield. "Taxi to the approach end. I have no other traffic. Call me when you're ready to depart."

Damn! Am I going to have to unlearn everything they just taught me in school, just so that I can sound like that? Air traffic control phraseology is highly structured and rigidly enforced... normally. So I'm having a hard time wrapping my head around this flippant, almost *conversational* way of doing things.

"So anyway," he continues, as if his story had never broken stride even when *he* did, "by now we're getting so close to the camp's perimeter that *we* could hear Smoke's damned radio, it was so loud. I mean, I shut off *my own* radio, and I could still hear Monty announcing that our comm had been compromised, and to go radio silent. I could hear that coming from *Smoke's little speaker* up there in the clearing! And the dumbasses *still* didn't do anything! They just sorta' went, "*Awwww,*" you know—'cause their little radio show had been cut off—and moseyed right back out to their original positions as if nothing they'd just heard meant anything to them whatsoever!

"I couldn't believe it! It was unbelievable! Hell, it took 'em almost another ten goddamned minutes before they realized that while they'd been listening in on 'KCCT radio,' their captive—you know, 'the pilot?' The one with the cast on his leg?—had walked off on his own! Well, *limped* off, I guess you'd say. *He'd escaped!* Just got up and walked right out into our lines and turned himself over to us!

"Hell, we just turned around and left!," he chuckles. "Never did bother to attack 'em or tell 'em the exercise was over... that their prize had been captured. We were probably in bed, asleep, before they ever figured it out."

Mutt sighs, stubs his cigarette out on the door frame of the Jeep, and blows his last lungful of smoke into the breeze. His chuckling finally stops, and he shakes his head.

"Fuckin' pathetic," he says.

Then comes the inevitable closer... "And they're wearing the same damned berets that we are. Sorry-assed sons a' bitches."

Tah-dahhh! The underlying theme of every story.

Sounds an awful lot like the tale that Santos just recently told me, as a matter of fact, about another joint exercise they'd had with the SPs.

Again, the Security Police knew what, where, and when the Combat Controllers were going to attack. Again their troop dispositions were supposedly so ill-conceived that the CCT observer had felt compelled to discretely 'cheat' on their behalf. And again, despite all that, Santos, Siegel and company not only managed to reach their objective, according to them—a huge C-141 cargo jet transport parked out in the *middle* of an empty ramp—but they marked its tires with chalk, indicating that they'd been there and done blowed it up good, *and* left a handwritten note as well, thanking the SPs for having made it all so easy for them.

Apparently I'm going to have to start bringing a few grains of salt with me to these war story sessions, because they're all starting to taste the same.

* * *

DOWN ON 'THE DIME,' Rawley 65 has completed its turnaround on the little teardrop loop, and is back-taxiing down the runway to the approach end. Among the ranks of Army vehicles waiting for it at the other end, it looks like someone just kicked over an anthill. Little Army men are scurrying everywhere, diesel engines are gargling and whistling to life, tailgates are dropping open, and tarp canopies are being flung back to make way for whatever treasures this aircraft has brought for them. Mutt snorts again, evidently amused by all the frenetic industry down there. Not that there's anything 'wrong' with it. It just, well... looks funny from up here. Kinda' like a sped up old silent movie.

Then the radio chimes in again. "*Selah Creek, Rawley six-two.*"

Another customer.

On a whim, Mutt suddenly waves the microphone at *me*.

"Here. You take this one."

What?!

"No, that's okay," I simper. "I'm learning more from watching you."

"Just talk to the man. It's not like real air traffic control or anything."

I take the unwieldy field-mike—an ancient device that looks more like a clunky six-inch-tall 'periscope' than a microphone—swallow hard, and mash the thumb button.

The radio behind me wheezes up to speed again, and I wait until it peaks before speaking.

"Rawley six-two, Selah Creek LZ. Go ahead."

"Rawley six-two is eighteen miles south, inbound for the field."

I'm hesitant to reply. Mutt's 'technique' is just too instinctual and abstract for me to emulate after so little exposure to it. And *my* 'technique' is not only too new and untried to be professional, but it's also too inexperienced to allow for any kind of off-the-cuff improvisation. So I just don't know *what* the hell I should say.

Mutt sees my hesitancy, but still refuses to take the mike. Instead, he just fires off some quick questions.

"Look, do you have any relevant traffic in the area that he needs to know about?"

"No."

"Any weather issues?"

"No."

"Anything *at all* that would interfere with him just flying straight in here and landing?"

"Ummm... no?"

"No. So just clear him into the Range, give him the wind and altimeter, and have him report the airfield in sight. Then when he reports it, clear him to land. It's that simple."

All right. That does seem simple enough.

Except that I can't remember a thing that Mutt just said.

"Okay, uhhh..."

My thumb keys the mike on its own. And as the radio's fan spools up to speed, I stare wide-eyed at Mutt.

What?... I... but... tell me again what...

He flicks his hand back towards the skies to the south, waving vaguely toward Rawley 62's theoretical vicinity, and I follow his cue.

"Rawley six-two..." I say into the mike.

Mutt sweeps his hand back down toward the valley below us in a big old *Come on down!* kinda' gesture.

"... You're cleared into the Range..."

He pops one finger up.

"... number one for the field..."

He stabs that finger at the windshield next, where the word "*CALM*" is written in grease pencil.

"... wind calm..."

Then at the "*29.86*" written right next to it.

"... altimeter two-niner-eight-six..."

Then he holds up an imaginary handset to his mouth with *one* hand, while pointing back and forth between his eyes and the airfield with the other. It takes me an awkward second or two to figure that one out, all while the mike button stays hot, but it does finally dawn on me.

"... report the airfield in sight."

Then he slices his hand across his throat, and I unkey the mike.

The radio wheezes down to silence again.

"That's all there is to it," he says with a shrug.

Now if I could just remember whatever the hell it was I just said.

"*Cleared into the Range,*" the pilot repeats. "*We'll report the field in sight. Rawley six-two.*"

Wow. My first transmission as a real air traffic controller. Whew!

Thankfully, Mutt accepts the mike when I hand it back to him this time. Then he adds, "Like fallin' off a log, Chili Dog."

Whatever the hell that *means.*

Far below us, the first C-130 has stopped on the approach end teardrop loop with its cargo ramp half-opened, and the Army ants and their little toy trucks have all converged upon it. It looks like pallets, heaped high with boxed goodies, covered in clear plastic, and tied down with yellow netting, are being slid right out the back of the plane and onto the backs of the waiting deuces. Other *loose* gear is being tossed out by hand and relayed down a chain of grunts to a nearby six-pack.

Even without binoculars, the distant choreography is impressive. You'd almost think they'd done this before. And by the time Rawley 62 checks back in on approach, they're already done and dispersing into the nearest trees, with another wave of trucks swarming up to the airstrip for the next load to land. *Nice work!*

"*Rawley six-two is five miles straight out, field in sight,*" squawks the radio behind our shoulders.

"Roger that, six-two," Mutt answers with downright theatrical nonchalance. "Check wheels down, cleared to land."

It's all part of the show for the nervous rookie, I'm guessing.

He adds another line of grease pencil scribbling to the windshield, and fudges in an initial contact time. As he does, I look east and spot Rawley 62 droning down the valley, tracking its floor straight into the Selah Creek LZ.

I turn next to look at Rawley *65*, just in time to catch its cargo ramp sealing shut and its four turboprops stirring up a fresh plume of dust. The voice of its pilot hails us a moment later.

"*Selah Creek, Rawley six-five is holding short of the active, ready for take-off, VFR departure to the west.*"

Without stopping to think about it, or even pausing to look up, Mutt instantly responds with, "Rawley six-five, wind calm, cleared for take-off."

What? Wait! 'Cleared for take-off'? What about Rawley 62? You know, that big old four-engine transport that's on about a mile-and-a-half final right now? Even if you're confident that 65 can get onto the runway and airborne before 62 crosses the landing threshold—which I'm sure as hell not!—shouldn't you at least tell him about the other aircraft that's rapidly bearing down on his ass from point blank range?!

I look over at Mutt, and he's gazing calmly at the aircraft that's floating down the approach corridor. *So he knows it's there.*

I look down at the airfield, at the other aircraft that's just now wheeling out of the turnaround and taking its position on the runway... *right in front of Rawley 62! Shit!*

"Ummm... Sergeant Siegel..."

The radio spits out a familiar voice.

"*Selah Creek, Rawley six-two is one-mile final with traffic in sight taking the runway. Confirm we're cleared to land.*"

Mutt seems completely unfazed as he replies, "That's affirmative, six-two. You're cleared to land. That traffic will be holding in position. Overfly and touch down beyond that traffic."

What?!!! Is he crazy?!! He can't do that!

"*Roger that, Selah Creek. Copy, Rawley six-two is cleared to land beyond the company traffic.*"

Oh my God! This is going to be a disaster!

Mutt seems to read my mind, and winks at me.

"Watch this," he says. Then he puts the mike to his lips again, and keys it. "Rawley six-five, cancel take-off clearance and hold in position. Traffic will be a company one-thirty, short final, to land over you. Hold in position. Copy?"

"*Rawley six-five copies. Cancel take-off and hold in position. Roger.*"

Jesus Christ! That's even worse!!

This isn't just insanely dangerous and blatantly illegal, not to mention astonishingly reckless on Mutt's part *and* completely unnecessary—but I can't believe the friggin' pilots are going along with it! That little runway's absurdly narrow and short to begin with, but dropping onto it from *over the top* of a waiting C-130 is going to lop off half of *that* distance! Even if the landing pilot *doesn't* crash right through the roof of his departing squadron-mate, he'll never get it stopped in the few-hundred meager feet of remaining asphalt!

What the hell are they thinking?!

But I'll be damned if it doesn't all unfold exactly as they all agreed.

Rawley 62, settling onto its shadow on short final, kills its engines just as it slips over its brother's tail, then dives for the ground *right in front of its nose.* The last-second drop is precipitous as hell, but the machine flares perfectly, and without even a full second of floating, it settles onto its main landing gear with only one firm bounce. Then its nose wheel is jammed to the ground, its brakes dig in, and the whole valley roars with the echoing bellow of its four engines reversing pitch.

And I'll be diddled if that lunatic doesn't get that behemoth completely stopped in the short stretch of pavement remaining.

Amazing! Unbelievable!

Completely nuts! Unsafe! Illegal as hell!

"Rawley six-two is clear of the active," the landing pilot calmly states. But even from up here, I can see that he's nowhere *near* clear of the active runway. Hell, he hasn't even started turning into the departure end teardrop loop yet. But right now? Right here? What the hell difference could that possibly make?

Mutt answers with equal insouciance, "Roger that, six-two. Thanks for your help. Rawley six-*five*, that landing traffic is turning off at the departure end. Maintain visual, wind calm, cleared for take-off."

Are you friggin' kidding me?

"*Roger. Cleared for take-off, Rawley six-five.*"

Oh my gawd! What universe am I in?

It's bad enough that Mutt's so irresponsibly cavalier about all this, but the *pilots*... why aren't they declining his control instructions and complaining about his haphazard sequencing and separation standards? *Jeezy Pete!* It's not even *my* life he's endangering, and I want to swat that microphone right out of his hand!

I mean, I can understand following a somewhat more lax rulebook when we're talking about combat aircraft in a combat environment, with no other friendly aircraft in the area, *but this is a long way from that!* I could also understand it if the situation was such that there was just no other way to get the job done. But again, *this ain't that either!*

All Mutt had to do, to be safe, expeditious *and* legal about it, was to simply hold Rawley 65 (the outbound taxiing aircraft) short of the runway until Rawley 62 (the landing machine) had had a chance to touch down and roll past him. *Then* he could have entered the runway, held in place only as long as necessary for the other ship to roll-out and taxi off, then *boom!*, he'd have been cleared for take-off! That simple. Just as *quick* as his wildman solution, but *legal* and *safe*.

Good gravy! I'm a clue-free rookie, and that was obvious even to me!

Nobody says anything about it, though.

As Rawley 62 loops around the departure end teardrop, Rawley 65 powers up, charges down that ridiculously short little runway, and leaps into the air.

Bada-bing, bada-boom. Zip-zap-zoom, and dat's dat!

"Unbelievable," I mutter.

Mutt chuckles as he notes the departure time on the windshield.

"Pretty cool, huh?"

"Fucking insane, more like."

He's unfazed by the critique... at least at first. But then he drops the grease pencil into the ashtray, taps out another cigarette, lights up, kicks back, and blows out a small overcast layer against the canvas ceiling. Then he looks at me, a little more warily this time, draws a deep breath, and says, "Get used to it. That's how it's done around here."

3
NEWBIE ZERO-ONE

BY TWO-THIRTY IN THE afternoon, I'm alone atop the tallest 'mountain' in this range of rounded naked hillocks known as the Umtanum Ridge. And I mean almost literally *alone*. Just me and one of those damned thirty-pound 'pricks' (shorthand for the PRC-77 'portable' backpack radio). Honest.

After the morning's unnervingly *ad hoc* air traffic control operations, Mutt and I had rejoined the rest of the team for a little 'canned lunch.' It was during this sunny noon-time repast that I first paid notice to the markings on Mutt's uniform, in particular the badges etched into the leather 'stat patch' on his chest. And none too surprisingly—although plenty disconcertingly—he only had one badge there: his senior jump wings. The same jump wings that I have, except with a star on top indicating at least seven years on jump status.

But—and this is the whole point—*he had no tower wings.*

In other words, Mutt is *not* a rated air traffic controller, and that's just plain crazy.

His wretched technique aside then, he's not even legal to *talk* to an airplane—at least not without a fully certified trainer monitoring him—much less freewheel and improvise to the extent that I witnessed this morning. And crazier still, to be training someone else in his unsanctioned methodology.

But as the conversation among the elders soon revealed, his style is not only *typical* among the controllers on the team, but it's *applauded*.

Of the ten people congregated around the six-pack's tailgate—all but two of whom were from the air traffic control side of the team—only *three* had tower wings (ATC badges) on their uniforms... Sal Donado (a rookie like myself, but a fully rated controller from before his switch to CCT), Smoke Sherrod, and big old Manny Santos. Nobody else.

So why wasn't Smoke or Manny—or even Sal, for that matter—working the radios with me this morning instead of Mutt? I don't know, I don't like it, and in the end, it doesn't make a damned bit of difference either way. Because, as Mutt so ominously put it, "*This is how it's done around here.*" And I don't have to like it, I just have to *do* it.

'Nuff said.

I tamped down my cold spaghetti-and-meatballs, traded off everything else for two cans of fruit cocktail, washed it down with some tepid canteen water, and helped gather and bag our little cookout's clutter once we were done. Then I and everyone else piled into the front and back of the six-pack—the camouflaged Dodge Ram pick-up—and headed off on our next little hillbilly adventure.

It was a half-hour-long spleen-jolting off-road jaunt down *into* and across the valley, passing around the western end of the Selah Creek airstrip, followed by a roaring, clawing, four-wheel-spinning power climb up the dirt-and-gravel switchbacks of the opposite side. And the instant we crested the northern ridgeline, the truck had lurched to a stop, and out hopped Sgt. Santos with one of the three pricks, and a couple of bright orange vinyl panels rolled up under his arm. He got a quick radio check with Mutt, who was still sitting in the Jeep across the valley, then waved us off.

We left him standing there in the middle of that rutted summit trail, and continued our precarious traverse along the apex of the Umtanum Ridge, headed for the next fuzzy knuckle down the line.

Where they left... *me.*

I'd fumbled with the unfamiliar radio's dials and knobs until I got a crackling response from Mutt, then my thumbs-up sent the rest of them off on their merry way, headed further down the battlements to the other drop-off sites. And now here I stand.

* * *

THERE'S JUST ONE TREE, one scrawny, bedraggled, warped little specimen leaning away from the constant rush of air coursing over the ridge from the narrow channel of the valley below. Other than that though, there's *nothing* up here. Only dirt, some sparse patches of grass, and a big orange letter "**T**" that I just laid out with my own vinyl panels, weighted down with a couple of loose rocks. If it wasn't for the thickening greenery further down the fifteen-hundred, maybe two-thousand-foot slopes on either side of me, I could just as easily be standing alone atop the rim of a lunar crater.

Behind me, to the west, I can just barely make out the tiny (but hulking) silhouette of Manny Santos, pacing in circles about half a mile back along the line of promontories. And *ahead* of me—to the *east*—perhaps just a snoodge closer and a little lower in elevation, I can see Sal Donado at his own windswept station, down on one knee, and playing with his prick... er, *radio*. Beyond *him*, I can only see the likely high points among the sawteeth of the ridgeline where the others were probably dropped off. But I cannot see *them*.

Now this is *my* kind of deployment, where my only contact with my crazy inbred teammates is by radio, and with only long-range line-of-sight visuals between us.

So, by my count, there're now four VHF radios sprinkled down the length of this high hogback—Manny's, Sal's, Rocky's, and mine—plus Mutt's rack-mounted monster in the back of the Mark, which is still hidden among the trees over there where I was sitting with him this morning, across the valley, atop that lower rounded hillside.

We're all monitoring the same frequency here, and we're all about to get the same On-The-Job Training (OJT).

* * *

OUR FIRST CUSTOMER CALLS as I'm pissing on the trunk of my lonely skeletal little tree.

"*Selah Creek LZ, Rawley six-niner.*"

"*Rawley six-niner, Selah Creek,*" Mutt's disembodied voice answers. He's still the primary 'controller' here, and thereby the initial point of contact for the inbound aircraft.

I button up, grab my PRC by one of its top handles, and walk back up to the wind-whipped crest of the ridgeline again.

This first run will be Santos's. By his example, he'll show the rest of us how it's done *right*. Thereafter, each subsequent run will go to one of us rookies, so we'd best be listening up on this one.

"Rawley six-niner is one-five miles south of the LZ," says the pilot's mellifluent voice, still robust enough through the thin filter of the radio's speaker to sound like a TV anchorman. "*Inbound for sequential CDS drops.*"

"Roger that, six-niner," Mutt's voice answers without hesitation. "*You're cleared into the Range, direct to the Selah Creek LZ. Wind now two-eight-zero at ten, gusting to one-five. Altimeter two-niner-eight-niner. Report the airfield in sight.*"

"Copy altimeter eight-niner, and Rawley has the airfield in sight, sir."

He has that emaciated little strip in sight already? From fifteen miles out? Then why can't I see him?

"Roger that, six-niner," says Mutt, "*Stand-by this frequency for the Drop Site One controller, callsign FILO zero-one.*"

Sgt. Santos, by any other name.

It takes me a second, but... "*FILO zero-one.*" I get it now. *Cute.*

On these in-house training exercises, when there are no command-level observers or outside participants, these guys just love making up their own callsigns. And "FILO," I know, comes from the Combat Control motto—not the one on the flash that just says "*First There,*" but the one I've seen posted on photos, bulletin boards, and notebook binder covers everywhere—the one that says, "*First In, Last Out.*" F.I.L.O.

A new, coarser, more aggressive voice barks from the radio.

"*Rawley six-niner, FILO zero-one. Radio check.*"

Sgt. Santos on the air.

I look down the spine of the ridge, and spot him striking a bold profile atop his own private vertebra, as his arm lowers his microphone from his lips. It's a recruiting poster pose that deserves its own caption: "*Field Operative Uses Radio to Direct Air Traffic!*"

Or maybe something a little simpler and truer, like "*Huge Dude Looks for Airplane.*"

The pilot's thinned baritone returns.

"*FILO zero-one, Rawley six-niner has you loud and clear. We are currently one-four miles south-southeast of Selah Creek with the field in sight. Turning inbound at this time. Say your location.*"

"*Six-niner, FILO is one-point-five miles north-northwest of the strip on top of the east-west ridgeline. I have you in sight, in a left turn, southeast of my position. I will call your turns. Continue inbound to the airfield."*

He sees the C-130? Where?

Santos's arm is up again, this time pointing low on the horizon. I look back to the southeast, low this time, and… *there he is! Son of a biscuit-eater!*

I settle onto one haunch next to my radio, shield my eyes from the high sun, and in the snuffling silence of the mountaintop, I watch the scenario unfold before me.

Rawley 69 rolls out pointed straight at us. And I've gotta' tell ya', if I hadn't caught sight of him while his wings were turned up broadside to me, its top-planes glinting sunlight at me, I never would have found him at all in his current alignment. Looking like little more than a heat-rippled black dot sinking into the roils of the mountain currents, the distant transport just seems to hover there, waiting, for several minutes. Then its liquid shimmering form abruptly solidifies, and in an instant it is a whole, hale and hearty C-130 again, bearing down on us, head-on. I can even make out its shadow now, skiing over the knolls and hummocks below it.

"*Rawley six-niner is thirty seconds out from the airfield,*" says its pilot's filtered voice.

"Roger that, Rawley," Santos replies. "*You're pointed almost straight at my position now, sir. I should be just a little left of your present course at about your 11:30, just beyond the airfield at the top of the ridge. Report my DZ identifier in sight.*"

By "DZ identifier," I know he's referring to whatever letter he's formed with his international orange vinyl panels.

As I watch, the huge vulture-shape of the C-130 dips its left wing for just an instant, then straightens out again… pointed right at *me!* Maybe two, three miles out.

"*Rawley six-niner has your DZ in sight, FILO. Showing 'T' for 'Tango'.*"

Oops! He's spotted *me*! Or at least the "**T**" I made with my orange panels. Santos is quick to correct him, though.

"*Negative, six-niner. FILO zero-one is further left, a quarter-mile west of that marker.*" The C-130 banks immediately, even before Santos has finished addressing him. "*Report 'V' for 'Victor' in sight!*"

There's an uncomfortably pregnant pause as the looming aircraft swoops into its new last-second alignment. Then… "*FILO zero-one, Rawley six-niner has 'V' for 'Victor' in sight!*"

Its shadow slithers across the little runway on the floor of the valley, then charges up the nearside slope, converging—along with the giant aircraft itself—on Sgt. Santos's position.

"*Roger that, six-niner,*" Santos replies. "*You're cleared to drop!*"

I spare one quick glance down the ridgeline to where Manny's pacing right and left, radio in hand, watching the aircraft as if readying himself to dart in whatever direction Rawley's pallet *doesn't* go. Then my eyes are back on the big camouflaged warbird as it thunders overhead. Its rear cargo ramp is down, and as I watch, a streamer of silk wriggles out of it and into the slipstream, booming open into a larger green parachute. Instantly, it jerks its payload free of its internal moorings, and two seconds later, a tightly netted bundle of boxes is dragged out into space with it.

"*Load away!*" the radio announces, drowned out (unfinished) by the heavy brassy roar of the leviathan blowing past just over Manny's head.

For a moment, it looks like the pallet is going to arc right past its target like a meteor. But then the chute's grip on the air asserts itself, and the heavy bundle relaxes into a pendulum swing beneath its canopy. And in the light shuffling breeze, I can see that it's going to settle right into the little clearing beside Manny... and it does.

Wow! What a shot! Those guys are good!

I finally get a feel for the scale of the load when it thumps to the ground mere feet from Santos, punching a wreath of dust into the air, and disappearing under its own deflating parachute. And it's nothing to sneeze at! That's a heap of boxes stacked taller than a gorilla like Manny Santos, and strapped to a hefty steel pallet that's dropping out of the sky at something like *thirty vertical feet per second!* You'd definitely want to watch where you were standing!

Behind us now, the C-130 pitches over onto its left wing and races off towards the next ridge north. As I understand it, he'll be circling back around for another pass now, this time homing in on *me*, and it'll be *my* turn to practice directing and clearing him in.

Hoo-WEE! Time to concentrate! Get my shit together!

But the process doesn't look too tough—especially considering the casual and even flippant terminology that the Combat Controllers apparently use out here in the field—plus it ought to be pretty cool standing at ground zero when the next load drops in.

* * *

THERE'S A LONG, QUIET, downright serene gap in the activity that follows. Not a peep from the radio, not a rumble from the C-130, wherever it is... hell, even the breeze has died off to little more than a petulant snuffling. If I wasn't watching Manny Santos clambering all over his little 'gift from the sky,' unhooking the webbed tie-downs, and dragging off the plastic wrap, I'd have no reason to even suspect that what I'd just witnessed had actually happened.

It's pretty danged peaceful up here. I could get used to this.

I draw a deep steadying draft of clean mountain air. I stretch... I spin my arms, I swivel my back, I grab my elbows and pull my shoulder muscles apart. I 'rehearse my lines,' and scan the horizons. I kick up a little dust, resituate my field cap, and check my watch.

Still nothing, though.

Nothing but fucking peace and goddamned quiet.

What the hell?! Did he fly all the way back to McChord to pick up another load?

Then my radio squawks.

"Selah Creek, Rawley six-niner is one-zero miles out, inbound for the field for CDS drop number two."

There we go!

Mutt's still the initial point of contact for the entire Yakima Firing Range airspace though, so I let him answer the call while I try to exhale away my nerves.

"Rawley six-niner, Selah Creek," says Mutt's tiny pinched radio voice, *"You're number one for the field. Stand-by this frequency for the Drop Site Two controller, callsign Newbie zero-one."*

Hardy-har-har! I get it. Steve Stipp = rookie = 'Newbie.'

Good one, Mutt. It's definitely the Mutt Siegel Show today.

I clear my throat, take another calming breath, and key the mike.

"Rawley six-niner, Newbie zero-one. Radio check."

Whew! So far, so good.

"Nyoooo-bee zero-one," the radio answers, slowly distending and hyper-enunciating the words, with just a taste of a smirk to sour it for me, *"Rawley six-niner is now niner miles out, inbound to your location, with both the airfield and 'T' for 'Tango' in sight."*

What? He already has me in sight? Well... what do I say now?

He already has the wind and altimeter information: Mutt gave all that to him the first time around. And he doesn't *need* any steering or course change updates: he's already reported me in sight, and he's supposedly already pointed right at me... supposedly. I can't see *him*, so I'm having to take his word for it. So what's left? Do I clear him to drop when he's still nine miles out, with his position and alignment unconfirmed? *Shit!*

Gotta' say something, though. *Ummmm...*

Where the hell is he, anyway?

I scan the southern horizon in the vicinity of his previous appearance. *Nada.*

"Rawley six-niner, not in sight. Uhhh... continue inbound. Report five miles out." *Damn! What the hell was that?*

That was no worse than any of the amateur-hour crap that Mutt would have used. That's what that was.

I silence my inner panic alarms with that assurance, and go back to furiously scanning the horizons. *Where is this guy?!*

"*Uh, roger that, Newbie. We'll call again at five out.*"

Oo, that one was just dripping with smug condescension. Just "one of The Boys" snorting contemptuously at the neophyte's awkwardness.

Yeh, well, fuck you too.

Bravely uttered... in my head.

But I don't see this guy anywhere. *Anywhere!*

I spin in place, and search all three-hundred-and-sixty degrees of the horizon, both high and low. And... *nothing*. I look for that 'rippling mote' head-on silhouette that I saw the last time, and still... *nada! Nada ting!*

What direction did he say he was approaching from?

I don't believe he did.

I decide to wait until he checks in again at five miles before asking him for his direction from the DZ, just in case I manage to find him on my own before that.

But I never do.

"*Newbie zero-one,*" the radio chatters again (man, I just know Mutt's falling out of his Jeep laughing at that callsign), "*Rawley six-niner is now five miles out, 'T' for 'Tango' in sight. Ready to drop.*"

I still can't find him though. It's a clear blue sky, and he's the only airplane in it. I've got 20/10 vision in both eyes, and I know what I'm looking for. Hell, at five miles out, I should be able to *hear* him! But... *nothing!*

Where the hell is he?

More importantly though, *what do I say now?*

Do I clear him to drop, when he might not even be in the same county as me? For all I know, he could be lined up on the wrong target, and if I cleared him to drop, he could wind up putting that huge CDS pallet through the roof of a day care center or something. *Double-shit!*

But really, how likely is that? He already knows what my big orange "**T**" looks like—he already lined up on it, mistakenly, once before—so it *must* be me he's looking at, wherever the hell he is. But *procedurally—legally*—can I really clear him to unleash a couple thousand pounds of hurtling luggage at a target that I can't be certain is right? I... I just...

"*Newbie zero-one, did you copy Rawley six-niner?*"

Goddammit, I'm starting to hate *that friggin' callsign.*

I've got to say something, though.

"Roger, six-niner," I reply, somewhat hesitantly, dragging it out while my mind rockets through every option I can think of—both of them—and my eyes scour the horizons for any sign of the bastard. "I copy you five miles out and closing. Still not in sight. Uhhh..."

I unkey the mike.

Dammit! Take some friggin' control of the situation!

I key right back up before he can respond.

"Rawley six-niner, confirm you're approaching from the south."

He doesn't answer right away, for some reason, and when he finally does, it's an oddly cryptic—and a way too short—reply.

"*Negative, Newbie.*"

That's all he says.

Well what direction are *you coming from, asshole!*

Now I'm getting cranky. But I can finally hear the drone of an approaching aircraft now. Sounds awfully far away, though.

"Rawley six-niner, you're not in sight. Say your bearing and distance remaining to the DZ, please."

Did I just say "Please?"

He delays responding again, until, just as I'm getting ready to abort the drop altogether, his voice returns over the radio, still resonant and throaty, but sounding a little 'strained' this time.

"*Six-niner is one-and-a-half miles out, with 'Tango' in sight and confirmed...*" He pauses a beat, then with his mike still hot, he adds, "*... in from the west!*"

The WEST?!! What the...?!

I spin to my right and sweep the skies again. But still... *nothing!*

He's got to be right on friggin' top of me! He should be a huge, dark, looming, cruciform presence by now, bigger than any other land feature in sight! But...! Aaurgh! There's just nothing there! Anywhere!

"Abort the drop, six-niner!," I shout into the handset mike. "You are not in sight from my position! Abort the drop!"

I don't know what else to do. But I'm sure someone will educate me, and probably not too far off in the future either.

"*Roger that, Newbie!*" the pilot grunts, still sounding 'strained,' but oddly 'happy' to comply. "*Aborting the drop. Breaking out from the west.*"

Then... "*Hold on to your hat!*"

Huh?

BLAM!!!

A leaping *wall* of shadow and thunder blasts over my head! It startles me into a backward stumble, followed immediately by the *thump!* of a passing shockwave that blows my hat clean off!

I twirl, and follow the massive apparition as it soars skyward above and behind me, then rolls steeply onto its right wing and swoops away back to the south.

Rawley 69—a hundred-thousand pounds (give or take) of turbo-charged flying machine—just *strafed me!* Came up on me *from below*—from the *floor* of the valley, where I would never have thought to look, and where the reverberations of its four Rolls Royce engines were trapped—and then shot up the slopes like a ski jumper off a ramp. *Right in front of me!*

So, putting it clinically, *what the fuck was that?!!!*

Was that his *drop approach?* Had he *intended* to line up on my little DZ from a thousand feet *below it?* Or was that just some extreme break-out maneuver following the call to abort? I mean, maybe he was actually lined up to drop *on the airfield*, or something!

In either case though—seriously—*what the fuck was that?!!*

I've got no idea... not a trace of a clue.

Still, though, truth be told, *that was pretty damned cool!* Better than any airshow *I've* ever seen. I never knew a C-130 could do stuff like that.

The question now, I guess, is "*What did I do wrong?*"

But as the deep leonine grumble of the airplane drones away, I hear a new sound… an hysterical childlike w*hooping* coming from further down the ridgeline. From Sgt. Santos, I suddenly realize.

I look his way, and spot him hopping and dancing around his little clearing like a crazed hillbilly doing a jig. An occasional "*Yeh!*," and a fervent "*Got-DAY-yomm*" or two rises above the general yipping and hooting, just enough to make me think that maybe, just *maybe*, I might not be in any trouble after all. Still, *what does it mean?*

My radio—lying on its side in the dirt, where I apparently dropped it in my 'startlement'—begins to chatter again, starting with Mutt's tinny little voice saying, "*Thank you, Rawley. Appreciate the show.*"

Huh?

"*Roger that. My pleasure, Selah Creek.*"

What? That was supposed *to go like that?*

"*Six-niner, the Range is still clear,*" says Mutt. "*Go ahead and set up for a standard south entry into the LZ this time, for another CDS drop at Drop Site Two. Remain this frequency, and contact Newbie zero-one again at your turn-in, copy?*"

Son of a…

"*Copy all, Selah Creek. Six-niner is outbound to the perimeter.*"

Santos is still cheering and laughing like a full-on uncorked lunatic over on the next peak down.

I do believe I've just been had. And with nothing less than a multi-million dollar piece of military hardware, a crew of at least four put in frivolous peril, who knows how much fuel consumed and undue stress applied to that huge airframe, not to mention—*what?*—fifteen minutes of wasted time in the middle of this exercise? And all for what? So that Mutt could bust a gut laughing at me through his binoculars, and add yet another war story to his already outrageous legacy? So that some cowboy *fighter-jock-wannabe*, stuck driving an aerial *bus* for a living, could get a cookie off flying like a bush pilot for a few minutes? Is that what this was all about?

Really? We can do that kind of thing out here in the wilds? Really?

Actually, that's kinda' cool.

And that *was* some kick-ass flying.

It might take a while for me to adapt to the practical joking 'anything-for-a-laugh' lifestyle of these professional 'rapscallions,' but with toys this pricey and this high-tech, and with capabilities this thrilling, I think it just might be a madness whose methods I'm willing to try.

4

A LITTLE LARCENY WITH YOUR LINGUINI?

"**RAWLEY SIX-SIX, WIND** two-four-zero at eight, cleared to drop."

I lower the mike, and listen to the big radio's fans wheeze down.

"*Six-six, roger. Cleared to drop,*" it answers.

"Good," says Smoke from his shadowed position in the Jeep's shotgun seat. He's the soft-spoken pipe-smokin' Old Head of this little shindig, and this evening he's my 'mentor' as well, calmly answering my endless questions and nudging me through these final moments of my first field deployment. The bone-white meerschaum in his fist hisses as he draws two easy puffs from it.

"You can go ahead and erase your grease pencil shit now. This is the last run of the day."

"You don't transcribe any of this stuff onto paper for your records?," I ask.

The windshield is slathered in callsigns and inbound and outbound times from corner post to corner post, hasty scribblings that have been accumulating all day long like bug splatters, to the point that I can hardly even see out of it anymore. Not that it matters much right now, since the sun has gone down behind the western mountains, and the twilight is ebbing. The valley below is already immersed in long shadows.

"Records? Oh *hell* no," says Smoke. "Those are just notes for *your* sake, for controlling purposes only. You could have erased all of Mutt's shit as soon as you sat down."

Now he tells me.

I drag out the stolen hotel towel, and start scrubbing.

In the distance, droning out of the darker skies to the east, the last drop ship of the day comes winking and blinking down the valley. Smoke steps out of the Mark to watch, and I stop what I'm doing to join him.

It's not really all that dark of a dusk yet. It just *feels* like it, compared the cloudless blue scorcher of a day that preceded it. I can still see the little scratch of an airfield down there. I can still see the nearside dirt road that threads its way down to it. And parked under a lonely but leafy tree on the opposite side of the valley's crease, I can still see our six-pack loitering in the shadows... waiting for this last CDS drop—a "food drop," they said—to drift down and land in front of them.

Everything that our C-130s have dropped today, including this last one coming down the pike right now, has belonged to the Army. *Our* aircraft have been resupplying *their* troops all day long, and getting in training for our flight crews—and us—at the same time. So, aside from getting a little control and 'target' practice for ourselves, nothing that's reached the ground today has had anything to do with us. Naturally then, Mutt and Manny have decided to abscond with a token item or two from the Army for our efforts.

Let's just call it a 'toll.'

And of all the crap that's fallen from the sky today, the only load of interest to them is, what? The stuff on this *food pallet? Really?*

Unbelievable. How about a little larceny with your linguini?

Rawley 66, seared salmon and pumpkin by the lowering sun—which *it* can still see from up above the mountains, but we cannot—lumbers by overhead. And just before it passes our position up here at the control Jeep, one after another after another, three parachute-drawn bundles dribble out into the slipstream, and settle to the Earth in a pretty little chorus line of silk and bulk. *Boof, boof, boof!* Like giant square footfalls stomping down the valley. They land—one, two, three—starting about fifty meters west of the CCT truck, and continuing west from there.

Flinging a rooster-tail of dust behind it, the six-pack charges out from under the trees and races up to the closest pallet before its parachute has even fully deflated. Smoke lowers his binoculars and hands them to me (probably the same pair through which Mutt watched *me* getting blown onto my ass atop the far ridgeline earlier today), shaking his head and chuckling as he does.

"Crazy fuckers," he mutters, then turns back into the Mark to send off

Rawley. I put the eyepieces to my eyes, and zoom in on my nefarious colleagues.

Sure enough, they're doing it. *I can't believe it.*

I can clearly see Sergeants Siegel and Santos—Mutt and Wetback—prying up the webbing and the covering plastic, and tossing cases of C-Rats (supposedly) back to Sal and Rocky, who relay them straight into the truck bed. Then, in an almost comical scramble, they cinch everything down again, hurl themselves back into the truck, and patch out, headed for the proverbial hills. They're not quite out of sight yet, when I spot the bobbing sweeping headlights of the approaching Army retrieval convoy swinging back and forth along the nearside access road that trickles down to the valley floor.

We'd cleared the Army out of the valley just prior to this last series of open field drops "for safety's sake," of course. Now that the final aircraft has come and gone though, they're gamboling down to the littered drop zone to collect their deliveries... minus about half a dozen cases of Cs, it looks like, as well as just about anything else of value that Mutt could get his mitts on, I'd wager.

Hmmm... "Mutt's mitts." I must remember that one.

If there was any ammo on that pallet, I bet a sizable chunk of it is jingling around in the bed of our truck right now. And God help the grunts if they'd done anything so foolish as to package up a set of NightVision goggles, or laser sights, or a satcom rig, or anything exotic like that on that last pallet. Because if they did, well... they're ours now.

For that matter—having already experienced the extent to which these guys will go just to have a little fun—what if they somehow 'misrepresented' to me what was on that last CDS pallet when they explained what they were going to do? What if there wasn't any 'food' on there at all? I mean, really; what do we need C-Rats for? Not only do we have our own stockpile back at McChord, but we didn't need them on this deployment anyway, since we're staying in a hotel off the reservation! And it has a McDonalds across the street, and a Dennys across the parking lot.

And surely, now that I think about it, Mutt wouldn't waste his larcenous skills on anything so mundane as canned spaghetti-and-meatballs, not when there's likely to be more interesting stuff... like... *hmmm.*

I look at Smoke as we converge on the generator trailer at the back of the Mark. And as we shut it down and cover it up, it quickly becomes clear that he's been reading my mind.

Unless he *always* winks at confused rookies like that.

5

GOOD NEWS, BAD NEWS

October, 1977
McChord AFB, Tacoma, Washington

WHY IS IT ALWAYS Sgt. Santos who delivers bad news to me?

And why does he always think it's good news when he does?

First it was the news that I should have been sent to Pope AFB in North Carolina instead of here. And now... *this*.

"What?," I ask, praying desperately for either the universe to shift in a-whole-nother direction before he speaks again, or for the even greater unlikelihood that I might have just heard him wrong the first time.

"Yeh! Can you believe it?"

Santos is looming over the table where I've been toiling for the last three hours, trying to reassemble the thick FAA manual that I'd just finished *dis*assembling with the latest changes and updates inserted back into it. Impish glee has taken over his normally all-business scowl, though. Why? Because for *him* and for *the team*, this *is* good news. It rounds off the numbers, ties off some loose ends, and puts them ahead of the manpower curve for once.

I'm guessing.

"They just had a medical drop-out from the next CCS class," he repeats. "Some guy broke his leg or something, and ol' Skeeter—man, that boy's sharp, lemme' tell ya'—jumped right in there and submitted your name to fill the slot! Even though you're *way* short of the time-on-team minimums! And just like that, *BAM! They accepted you! You're in!*"

"Wow," I mumble, underwhelmed to the point of panic.

"You're in the next class, man!" he adds. As if the chilling truth wasn't already plain enough. "You'll be going down with Greg, Sal, and Rocky when they fly out of here this Sunday! All of you! *Together!*"

Another expectant pause.

"There'll be *four* of you instead of three!"

"Yep. Got it," I finally answer.

He's starting to sense my lack of enthusiasm though (he's very astute that way), so I hoist up a weak smile and start to rise to my feet.

"Cool... well... guess I'd better start getting my shit together then, shouldn't I."

Goddammit.

Whatever happened to that old 'six-months-with-your-team-before-you're-even-eligible-for-CCS' tradition? I'd been depending on that!

Ever since Randy, my absentee roommate, got back from Little Rock earlier this week, brand new dark blue beret molded over his right ear, that's all anybody has been able to talk about. Pogue's war stories. Pogue's warnings and recommendations. The questions and preparations of the other rookies, their extra training and study, the gathering of any additional equipment, the pumping up and steeling of nerves. They've been caught up in their own scary little whirlwind ever since, building themselves up for this huge next step that they're about to take, all with the support and encouragement of the rest of the team that's been helping them get ready, of course.

All but *me*, anyway.

I've been sitting on the sidelines—*gratefully*—observing the brewing ferment (so to speak), sharing their jittery nerves vicariously, and taking mental notes for that time—*half a year from now!*—when I'd theoretically have to face this same breathless anticipation myself.

And I've gotta' tell ya': I've been getting nervous *for* them.

To hear first the Old Heads, and then Randy reliving the trials and tribulations of Combat Control School—especially a dead-of-winter class like this one coming up—well, it's been giving me second thoughts and heebie-jeebies the size of garbage trucks.

And until just this moment, I was still *half a year away* from having to worry about it. So now...

Now, after only *a week-and-a-half* with my team (as opposed to the four to six *months* the rest of my 'fellow classmates' have already logged here locally), and with only *five days* until we ship out, I find myself not only woefully short on that all-important job-related experience (I've only jumped with my team *once*—a debacle of blown chunks all by itself—and my only deployment with the team was that little overnighter to the Yakima Firing Range two days ago, in which we ate at a Denny's, and slept at a Ramada), but on top of all *that*, I'm also laughably short on *equipment* as well. Still just two sets of cammies (everyone else has at least four, and as many as six), only one canteen and one ammo pouch for my web gear (as opposed to the *two* each that's standard issue), and a host of other essential shortages... like tent halves, poncho liners, air mattresses, sleeping bags, jungle boots, green undershirts, and *none* of the helpful little trinkety things like mosquito repellant, dog tag covers, and even camouflaged grease paint.

All the basics that everybody but me already has.

In other words, I've got squat, and no idea how to use *that*.

Hell, I don't even have a firm grasp of their *vocabulary* yet, for Criminey's sake! And they want to throw me into the crucible *now*, with these other fully prepared and accoutered hotshots, just so that they can balance the books and have a blue beanie on every head on the team? I'm going to be the rookiest rookie that ever stumbled through those doors down in Little Rock!

And if I was 'edgy' *before*, just watching what the other three were going through in these last days before leaving, I'm downright shaking now.

I'm not ready for this. *At all!* Not physically, not psychologically, and sure as *hell* not experientially! Not *gear*-wise, not knowledge-wise, not even *wisdom*-wise! Not even in friggin' *principle!* But that's not something you actually say to someone like Sgt. Santos.

Let him read it in my eyes, then... or my back, as I walk away.

I leave him behind at my table, looking a tad grumpy about my less-than-ebullient response, and I approach Skeeter at his desk.

Turns out Skeeter's just as happy for me as Manny was, though. And probably a whole lot *prouder* of his part in this minor miracle.

"Congratulations!," he says, as I get close enough to cast a shadow over him, "At this rate, you're gonna' set a new record for Phase III qualification. Faster than anyone *I* ever heard about anyway."

"Man, I don't even have a sleeping bag yet," I practically whisper.

"Oh, don't worry about that. Miles'll fix you right up. He's giving max priority to all the guys that are going out right now."

"He doesn't have anything *to* prioritize, Skeeter. His shelves are empty. I know! I've been checking in with him almost *daily* since I got here. I don't even have jungle boots, man!"

"He's got 'em on order, though. They'll be here any day."

"That's not the point," I sigh, no longer certain about how much further I should push this. This is an outfit in which a *can-do attitude* is at the crux of everything. Prepared or not, I should be *spiritually* up to the challenge, regardless of how daunting it might appear. So I draw a deep breath, and try to *look* ready, willing, and able, even while reciting my catalogue of reservations.

"Look... Skeeter..."

"Are you saying you want to decline the slot?"

He's got a guarded expression on his face now that tells me this would be tantamount to desertion in his book.

"No!," I answer without hesitation, as I'm thinking *Hell yes!*

"Then what's the problem?"

He honestly doesn't know, does he?

I sigh one more time.

"I'll go hit on Miles again."

Guess I'm going to Little Rock this weekend.

BOOK TWO
THE WANNABE

PART 2

Combat Control School (CCS)
Little Rock Air Force Base, Little Rock, Arkansas
November & December, 1977

STORY XXII

THE GATES OF HELL

1
THE BIG LEAGUES

November, 1977
Little Rock AFB, Little Rock, Arkansas

WELL, LIKE IT OR not, understand it or not... *ready* or not, here I am.
Little Rock Air Force Base. Combat Control School.
The Big Leagues.
What the hell am I doing here? I'm not ready for this!
Barely two weeks out of Jump School, and I'm already vying for my *beret* right alongside my far better prepared fellow rookies, standing here now at the very threshold of the Phase II gauntlet itself.
Combat Control School. CCS. *Jesus.* I still can't believe it.
Yet another Grand Anti-Climax though, as it turns out. At least that's what it looks like here at the beginning.
In my mind, I'd envisioned this place as a towering gothic fortress of cruelty and torment, a dark granite bastion under constant bombardment by lightning and thunder and wind-whipped rain, and wracked with the echoing cries of the tortured.
Instead, it turns out to be just another run-of-the-mill Air Force base, a bland cookie-cutter 'campus' of boxy 50s-vintage administrative and apartment buildings scattered over the knuckled countryside in accordance with the traditions and formulas of Air Force bases everywhere. And right now it's awash in the sunlight of a crisp Ozark autumn. To all outward

appearances, utterly nondescript and benign.

This might be a prematurely optimistic assessment on my part though.

* * *

DAY ONE: CHECK-IN at the BAQ ("Bachelor Airmen's Quarters," our on-base 'hotel' for the next two months). The sixteen of us are paired up with roommates from different teams. I get a guy from Pope. Formal in-processing, base orientation, and a late afternoon appearance at the Little Rock Combat Control *Team's* hangar, one end of which harbors the school's facilities. Some study and work-out supplies are dispensed, including our white gym shorts and OD-green T-shirts, each emblazoned with a huge CCT flash in the center of the chest. Then after a group dinner at the nearest chow hall, we close out the day with a big social 'shoe polishing party' in the BAQ's Day Room, preparation for showtime tomorrow morning. Then I call it an early night.

* * *

DAY TWO: IN OUR spiffy new PT togs, we start the day with a big physical entrance exam. Hitting the ground running, both figuratively and literally. We hammer through all the exercises in an unbroken stream: team sit-ups (with telephone poles), mixed with what feels like about a thousand *individual* sit-ups, fifty non-stop push-ups, plus scads of lesser endurance exercises, and culminating with a punishing five-mile run through the low rolling terrain of Little Rock's perimeter roads. All of it at a pitiless tempo, without a single pause or breather or even any second chances, for that matter. You either keep up, do it all, without a single rep missed, *or you fail. Everything! Period!* And if you fail, you go home. *Right now.* It's that simple, that merciless, and that real.

Count for count, it's not that bad. I could hit any of these targets easily, by themselves. But the relentless pace turns it into more of a battle of *stamina* than strength again, and that damn near sends me home before the end of my first thirty-six hours here. *Gawd!*

But not quite.

It does end the CCS aspirations for two of us, though.

And one of them is my brand new roomie from Pope, Hal.

* * *

I HESITATE AT THE door. *My* door.

My knuckles are poised to knock. But first I put my ear to the jamb, and listen.

Nothing.

Of course, that doesn't mean much. He might be in the attached bathroom, sitting on the toilet, brooding and depressed. Or he might be sitting on the edge of his bed beside his open suitcase, staring at his boots in disbelief. Or he might already be gone. I don't know, but I'm reluctant to enter if the guy's in there at all.

I know it's silly. I mean, *it's my room!* Well, mine and *his*, the late-great Harold Trefelden (pronounced "*TREE-feld'n*"... as in, "If a Trefelden the woods, would it make a sound?"). He prefers—or *preferred*—"Hal," though.

We were roommates until about two hours ago, when he failed the entrance "PT Evals"... by not being able to do fifty push-ups in a row.

That was it! That was all it took! They turned him around right there, and sent him right back out the door again, *done*. Headed back to Pope.

It's only Day Two of the School, and he's already been washed out!

Good gravy! How did he even get out of Keesler without being able to do fifty lousy push-ups?! Not to mention Army Jump School, and *half a year* with his team back in North Carolina?

Did no one point out to him that they wouldn't even let him *start* CCS without being able to meet some not-too-unreasonable minimum standards?

I don't mean to get all militant about this—fact is, I liked the guy!—but *come on!* You've got to know that the physical program here is going to kick your ass. So why would you even bother coming if you couldn't handle the basic exertions to which you'd already been exposed back at Keesler?

But Trefelden did... and he wasn't the only one.

Airman Mitch Kort also washed out today. *Amazing!* But at least in *his* case, it was because he was unable to finish our inaugural five-mile run. That run kicked *everybody's ass*, following so hot on the heels of that ruthless calisthenic marathon as it did. I barely remember crossing the finish line myself, in a state damned close to delirium. So I'm a little more sympathetic to his plight. But fifty push-ups? *Come on!*

I knock quietly. Nobody answers.

I slip my key into the lock and dart inside.

Sure enough, there's an open suitcase on the bed, surrounded by a bomb blast of barely unpacked clothes, personal items and toiletries, all waiting to go right back into the very bag they just came out of the day before yesterday. And from behind the closed bathroom door, the subdued hiss of a running shower. Hal's still in the house, apparently, and I imagine not much in the mood for a whole lot of awkward social banter. I know *I'm* not.

So I grab my wallet and sunglasses, snatch Trefelden's copy of the course itinerary off the desktop—*I'm presuming he's not going to miss it, nor even want to see it again, for that matter*—and scurry back out into the hallway. I already said all the goodbyes I had in me back at the gym. Now I just need to make myself scarce for another half hour or so, until the poor bastard's had a chance to bug out in peace.

* * *

AT A CONCRETE TABLE in the middle of the scalped grass courtyard between the BAQ buildings, I find a seat, doff my shades, and flip through the five pages of the syllabus. There's a crisp little November breeze funneling through the courtyard, and it keeps ruffling the pages... which only adds irritation to the absolute *incredulity* I'm already feeling just from my first brief scan of the list.

Holy crap!

This first week-and-a-half is *nothing*... just these first couple of days of in-processing and physical qualifiers, followed by a solid week of nothing but nighttime parachute packing classes. Night after night, *after* regular 'business hours' ('business hours' that contain no actual Combat Control '*business*' except for two brutal hours of PT around 1:00 every afternoon, the rest of the days being free to do with as we please). It's two back-to-back shifts at the rigging tables each night, eight students per shift. The classes last only five hours a shift—from 4:00 to 9:00, then 9:00 to 2:00 in the morning—and guess which one they assigned *me* to. That's right: the *through-midnight* shift. But that's only until the real schedule kicks in on that second Thursday. Then it's on to *everything else*, which accelerates it up to mach speeds.

With PT penciled in somewhere *every single day* (along with fifteen total hours of "silent kill" training, wherever it can be fit in), all the rest of the dawn-to-dusk hours are committed to intensive classroom time, covering a myriad, a multitude, *and* a plethora of subjects, skills, and equipment that fill all five pages of the curriculum.

Each week's study includes two "practical progress checks" (whatever that means), and culminates in a fifty-question pass-or-go-home written test every Friday. No do-overs.

So... weekly testing. *Great*.

And if you get through all that without failing a single test, botching a single 'progress check,' missing a single rep of the PT exercise regimen, or falling a single step short on any of the daily runs (my *other* Achilles Heel), *then* you've got ten straight days *in the field* (including five combat-load jumps, two of them at night) with which to put all that fancy book-learnin' to practical use. And sandwiched *in between* the six weeks of *desk* time and the week-and-a-half of *field* time, is that dreaded ball-busting rite of passage that Randy Pogue first mentioned to me upon his return to McChord... the *ten-mile run!* In uniform, in formation, and in *step*, chugging up and down through the rolling foothills of the Ozarks.

As we said in Basic, "*Fuck me. I can just go to hell.*"

I mean, just look at this list of subjects we'll be covering in the classroom...

Communications equipment, security and phraseology, map reading, and geographical coordinates... *and that's just the first Thursday and Friday* that follow the parachute packing classes!

After that, there's aerial photos and overlay studies, compass usage, artillery plotting, rappelling, navigational aids, and lots of weather-related shit. There's the criteria and formulas for setting up DZs, LZs, and EZs (that's Drop Zones, Landing Zones, and Extraction Zones, by the way), not to mention 'running gear' and rucksack packing, weapons training, mock war and maneuver principles. There are apparently five different infiltration techniques that we'll be learning, as well as three *ex*filtration methods, 'Escape and Evasion' (E&E) tactics, combat first-aid, and jumpmaster training.

And that's just the classroom stuff—the 'testable' stuff. The list goes on from there once (or *if*) we actually 'graduate' from the classroom phase with all its testing, *and* survive the ten-mile mountain run, and thereby get to continue on into the field portion.

There we'll deal with 'mechanical courses'—compass work, day and night overland navigation trials, small unit tactics, patrolling techniques, 'immediate action drills' (anti-ambush exercises), and 'hasty bivouacs'—then team, two-man, and individual cross-country deployments, and field fortifications. There will be tent classes in personal camouflage, first aid, team integrity, and demolitions... hands-on sessions with every single piece of navigational, weather, communications, weapons, and explosive ordinance in the friggin' inventory, not to mention a glorious afternoon-o-fun in a damned *gas chamber!* And every other day (and a couple of the nights), a full combat-load *parachute jump* to lead us into each of the five 'operational scenarios' that will pull all this mind-numbing data into context for us.

I say again, "*Holy shit!*"

A blue Ford van pulls up to the sidewalk at the end of our building, and its horn *parps* twice.

I fold up the syllabus, rub my aching eyes (and massage my aching *brain*), then don my shades again... to watch Airman Harold Trefelden, former student, roommate, and spec ops aspirant slump down the walkway, pitch his suitcase and duffel into the van's rear doors, then plop into the front passenger seat, and ride off to the Little Rock Regional Airport.

I almost envy him.

Hell, there ain't no 'almost' about it.

2
WEEK ONE: EATING DUST

GODDAMMIT! WHO THE HELL'S *idea was it to put Rocky at point?*

'Rocky'—a.k.a. Ricky Spradlin, from my very own McChord Team—is a running *fool*. Those of us from McChord know that, even if nobody else here does. That boy can *sprint* for longer than most cars can *drive*. And unfortunately, for today's mere three-mile run, the instructors have foolishly made him the point man, running all by himself up at the front of the pack, and thereby setting the pace for the rest of us.

As a result, today I think we're going for some kind of a land speed record… along with a new record for "number of simultaneous strokes and heart attacks occurring within a one-hundred-square-foot area." Because, thanks to Li'l Rocky, we are getting our collective asses *kicked*.

Even the instructors are starting to look a little less starchy this afternoon. And that's saying something.

As we stampede through a tight left turn at an intersection of two remote and empty roads along the base's perimeter, we spot Rocky already half way up the shallow incline of the next stretch of pavement.

Son of a bitch!

If he stopped dead in his tracks right where he is now, and stood there waiting for the rest of us, it would still take us a good two minutes just to catch up to him again.

Sgt. Stillman, the lead instructor on this run—whose job it is to run astride the point man and direct him where to make his turns—has lost so much ground on Rocky that the front rank of the pack is about to run over *his* ass. Off our right flank, the school's senior-most instructor, Sgt. Rabin—whom I'd just noticed starting to fade himself—shouts up to Sgt. Stillman.

"Hey, Still! Tell that little fucker to ease up! We've still got a mile-and-a-half to go here!"

I really didn't need to hear that either.

Sgt. Stillman is only too happy to oblige.

"Airman Spradlin!," he shouts.

But the tow-headed dot nearing the crest of the hill doesn't hear him.

"*Spradlin!*" he yells again.

Nothing.

Then one of the students flogging along just behind Stillman cuts loose a glass-shattering whistle, and Rocky's head finally snaps around. He seems genuinely shocked to find such a sprawling gap between himself and the rest of us. Must've been "in the zone" or something, and just forgot all about us.

In the meantime though, the damage has been done. Everybody—and I mean *everybody*, instructors marginally included, even our Olympic-class runners—every last one of us is sputtering along now, rubber-legged, heaving, sweating, gasping, and worst of all, *slowing*. And all because somebody had to go and put Rocky in the driver's seat.

Man! See if they ever do that again!

Rocky *never* has to slow down, or even stop for that matter. Maybe he's got some American Indian blood mixed in with all that Irish whiskey. I don't know. But now we're all so obliterated, there are some seriously concerned expressions on a lot of dripping bright-red faces, my own most prominently included.

I mean, just days into the program, and the herd has already been thinned by two for "inability to achieve minimum standards." Now here we all are, almost to the last man, disintegrating as a running formation, drooping in posture, slowing in pace, and being forced to apply downright heroic energies just to keep up with our withering peers. We're racing *ourselves* now, *anything* to avoid slipping back far enough to be classified as a straggler.

Me? I was *born* a straggler. My objective now is to convince these instructors otherwise.

Unfortunately, I have nothing left with which to dazzle them. Because churning up this spirit-killing little slope—which is probably only a block-and-a-half long, with barely a one degree uphill grade—has completely stripped the last of my gears. The running cramp that was just starting to form under my right shoulder blade has suddenly swollen and rammed all the way through to my chest like a javelin, stealing the last of my hysterical breath along the way. And struggling this hard just to drive myself up this pathetic little hill has all but de-boned my legs. My knees are gone, my muscles have turned liquid and are draining into my socks, and I have no energy reserves left to tap. I'm falling apart. And worse, despite all my grueling and devoted efforts, I'm starting to fall *back*.

No! No, no, no! I can't wash out this early! At least give me a chance to fuck up at the more challenging stuff before you write me off!

At least I'm in good company. Nobody here is alone in their struggles.

Then Airman Balzac backs into me.

Balzac's a big dude. Height-wise, at least, he's the biggest in the class. But for a spec ops wannabe, he's surprisingly unathletic. He's a lead-footed runner, always looking like he's stomping across a metal floor in magnetic boots, with a lot of soft flaccid meat shrugging up and down on his frame with every step. And today he started out right in front of me in the formation. Now he's reeling back into me, panting furiously, weaving drunkenly, and sagging like a big inflatable Balzac doll that's sprung a leak.

My first instinct is to block him from colliding with me. Hell, I'm barely staying upright myself. So I plant my hand between his shoulder blades, right in the middle of that sweat sponge of a T-shirt he's wearing, just to ward him off.

He lurches, his head rolls, and he nearly goes down—so do I—but for the moment at least, he's still in front of me, and not tumbling underfoot.

Then another hand lands just to the right of mine, followed by a third pushing against his left kidney.

There're three of us pushing him up the hill now. *Hmmm.*

During each of the last two days' PT runs, I've seen other guys doing this, first with Kort (who's no longer with us because of his poor showing on that first day's run), and then yesterday with Balzac again. And I've viewed it with mixed emotions.

On the one hand, that *"All for one, one for all"* kind of teamwork is pretty cool… in concept and in its place. It's reassuring to know that your teammates have selflessly "*got your six,*" even when they're suffering as much as you are.

On the other hand, this ain't exactly the time or place for that. This is a school, and it is as much a winnowing process as it is a learning environment. We are here to eliminate the weak links as much as we are here to strengthen the strong. And I can't believe that the instructors would consider Balzac, or anyone else for the matter, worthy of graduation if he'd been *pushed* across the finish line by others. Especially if it was obvious that he wouldn't have crossed it *without* their pushing.

In other words, I don't think we're helping anyone here when we keep them propped up like this... except maybe ourselves.

Is that what this is all about? Making ourselves look good in front of the instructors? "See what a team player I am, boss? Nobody gets left behind on my watch!"

No. As an ulterior motive, that might be buried down deep somewhere in the mix, but I don't believe it's the driving impetus here. These guys have all been with their teams for a while now—everyone but me, of course—so by now, I suspect, this is *just how it's done* for them. It's automatic. Inbred.

Irresistibly traditional.

Misguided though it may be then, it's noble enough that I can appreciate the sentiment.

I keep my hand where it is, and lean into this godforsaken trudge up this hill.

It just looks insurmountable, though. And despite all the heaving and panting and grunting going on around me, we just don't seem to be making any progress toward the top. But the instructors are no longer employing their usual haranguing techniques either, yapping for us to close it up and get it in step. Stuff like that. One look at them, and you can understand why: they're feeling it almost as much as we are.

Well, maybe not that *much.*

Oh sure, they're putting on a brave face of unfazed determination and all that, but you can't hide the uncharacteristically darkened T-shirts, the ferocious breathing through clenched teeth, or the heavy sluggish gait that makes them look like they're running through ankle-deep water. I'll take their grim silence as a small victory though, thank-you very much.

Balzac continues to swoon against my hand. I don't join the guys on either side of me with their coaxing banter though, urging him on. I haven't got the stamina, the air, or the desire. But I do keep my hand right where it is, and every last erg of my dwindling energy committed to ramming his fat ass up this fucking slope.

Why? I don't know.

It makes no sense. I can't afford to do this to myself, especially for so futile a cause. If I was running *alone* under these conditions, I'd practically be on my knees by now. So why am I throwing away what little endurance I've got left by making things harder on myself?

Because I *would* have been on my knees by now if I wasn't doing this.

Damn! Somehow, I suddenly realize, this seems to be actually *helping* me. Helping *me!*

As utterly astonishing and counterintuitive as that is, it seems to be a fact!

I can't believe it myself. But as our struggling pack labors over the top of the knoll and starts its way down the opposite side, I'm not only still with them, but I'm doing better than I was *at the bottom!*

I know it's crazy, but as Airman Balzac stumbles off downhill under his own steam again, I find myself strangely invigorated by my efforts on his behalf. I think I can actually *hear* my leg muscles whimpering, and I can hardly see through the sheets of sweat coursing down my face. But I've blundered into some kind of strange unaccustomed 'second wind' of sorts, and my heart has found new thunder as a result.

Wow!

If I'd only known about that before, I'd have been pushing *everybody* around me, whether they needed it or not!

Thank-you, Rodney Balzac!

And I'll see you tomorrow for another push around the base.

3

STOWING STRINGS, FOLDING SHEETS, AND BAGGING IT TO GO

I HATE PARACHUTE PACKING. But I *really* hate parachute packing *practice*.

For starters, regardless of how much I might enjoy being able to sleep in every morning, the fact is that I'm just not a 'night person.' And after four straight days of this nine-p.m.-to-two-a.m. shift, I'm

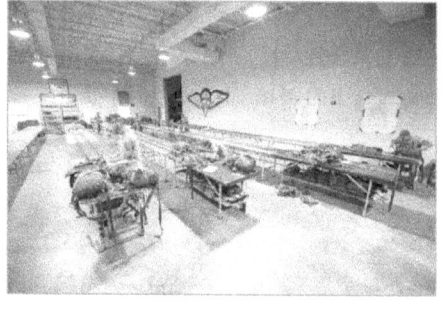

afraid this first block of training is going to friggin' kill me. Being awake *at all* after midnight is tough enough for me. Being awake after midnight while doing nothing but folding, fluffing, tucking, separating, stretching, jamming, and then folding some more, over and over and over again, well...

That's just bloody anesthetizing.

The process of packing a parachute, at least at our current level of expertise, takes more than an hour to complete. Hell, it took me more than *two* hours the first night. And it involves working your way through a lengthy, convoluted, and utterly inflexible sequence of steps. The checklist is three single-spaced pages long, and must be memorized in its entirety (good news for someone like me, whose brain doesn't *do* rote memory work). Each item is a tedious fiddling bore, but must be worked with precision and care in order for everything to function as advertised... the worst kind of task there is, in my opinion: work that's critical, but repetitious and achingly dull.

What could possibly go wrong?

For me at least then, nothing but sheer mind-numbing reiteration could ever hope to develop the level of mastery I'll need to become a safe packer of parachutes. Or perhaps more accurately, a packer of safe parachutes.

And so here I am again, at one in the morning, sorting tangled suspension lines, pleating acres of rumpled 'silk,' and stuffing it all into a bag that's too small to contain it... over and over and over and over again.

I mourn in advance for whatever hapless soul winds up having to jump with any chute I've packed.

Poor bastard.

On top of that, the procedures are different between the larger, flatter, backpack-shaped *main* chutes, and the smaller loaf-of-bread-shaped reserves, both of which we have to qualify on before the end of this block.

Thankfully, our first weekend here is upon us, and I am looking forward to the break. But by Wednesday of next week, I'd better be able to pack both a reserve and a main chute, back to back, without the aid of a checklist, in less than an hour and ten minutes, *total*, or I'm going home. It's just that simple.

No appeals, no second chances... just gone.

That's one point of which they've cheerily and regularly reminded us throughout this first week—that you cannot afford to fail at *anything* here; not a single PT run (and we run every day), not a single equipment proficiency test, not one written exam, nothing. No do-overs. You either *pass* everything, or you've *failed* everything. Period.

Needless to say, I can't wait for next Wednesday.

4

WEEK TWO: THE THINNING OF THE HERD

"ON YOUR FEET!," BELLOWS Sgt. Rabin.

And with the snappiest bound we can make, following yet another twenty-five set of four-count push-ups, all thirteen of us clop back to attention beneath the beams of the open-air shelter.

Yes. I said 'thirteen of us.' Another one bit the dust yesterday.

Sunday! Over the friggin' weekend, for Criminey's sake!
On his own friggin' time!

He wasn't even washed out for 'failure to complete,' or an inability to achieve any of the course's objectives. *He nuked himself!* Worse yet, it was Sgt. Cooper, a great guy and a born *chief*, our senior-ranking student, and thereby our *de facto* 'class leader.' And he went and took *himself* out!

Dangit!

Now, standing at the front of the formation next to Sgt. Rabin, facing us and calling off the counts in Coop's place, is our new class leader, none other than Sgt. Brad Haley.

I liked Coop. I *don't* like Sgt. Haley.

And the feeling's apparently mutual.

It seems that Bill Cooper wore contact lenses. He also liked to play racquetball. And he was playing racquetball yesterday… with his contacts *in*, and his sports goggles *off*. This is, of course, an elixir to the Gods of

Disaster. It invites Them in, it teases Them with opportunity, and it dares Them to do something about it.

And this time They did.

Sgt. Cooper took a 'line drive' straight into his unprotected right eye, and added his contact's dislodged presence to the list of other ocular damages. He spent last night in the hospital, and was 'medded' out of the school this morning. And at this very moment, even as we speak, he is no doubt sitting in a lounge at the Little Rock Regional Airport, with a bandage over one eye, and a dour look of pure self-loathing in the other, waiting for the next flight that will take him home... without his beret.

In the meantime, life here at CCS—with all its related miseries—pisseth on. And here we all are, back to the grind again, only this time in the form of an *extended* PT session. After a weekend off, with all its attendant neglect and misuse of body, heart, and will, the instructor cadre seems to feel that the best solution is a shorter run *preceded by* an extra-brutal battering on the exercise pad.

Damn! Another hundred-count of shoulder rotations?

As it is, I can hardly lift my arms high enough to smear the sweat dripping off my nose, much less hold my fists straight out at shoulder height and swivel them around until Sgt. Haley's counting reaches one-hundred.

But that's what we do. *Gah!*

And then twenty leg-thrusts... then windmills, mountain-climbers, and squat-thrusts. And as it turns out, they've even generously provided us with telephone poles for our sit-ups *here* as well, although the balance of the workload has been augmented by the losses of our three fellow lifting bodies. Just to even out the lifting load then, the manpower under each log had to be redistributed to accommodate the uneven numbers. And to that end, Sgt. Haley nobly volunteered to remain at the front of the class, calling out the counts. That way there's an even six men under each log.

How much more fair and even-handed can you get than that?

Sgt. Haley: always thinking of us.

* * *

IT'S COOLER TODAY THAN it was anytime last week—which isn't saying all that much, really—and today we have the added bonus of Rodney Balzac running at *point* this time… which, if nothing else, is at least better than trying to follow old 'Rocket Man' Rocky around the base. Throw in the fact that we're only doing a *two*-miler today (following that beating we just took back at the open-air shelter)—just running up and back alongside the runway on its perimeter road, where there's hardly a rise or fall in the entire length of the road—so this ought to be an 'easy one' for us.

Unfortunately, our freshly hammered and overused post-weekend muscles are hardly fit for an afternoon in a lounge chair, much less a brisk dash up and down the flightline. And as such, in no time at all, the storming herd is grunting, gasping, and hissing through its collective teeth again.

Added to that, my daily running cramp has introduced a friend today, a nagging little stitch that has pierced my right kidney and left me staggering.

Worse, for whatever insidious reason, they randomly chose to put me up in the front rank this time. So everybody in the formation gets to watch my bobbing, weaving, dripping performance without even turning their heads.

Ah, bliss.

I labor along, whipped and wiped out, grimacing and snorting around the two harpoons that are apparently jiggling in the middle of my back. And the thought crosses my mind, *You know, this would be a fine time for one of Rodney Balzac's patented fades.* He being the point man, the pace-setter this time around, I think if ever there was a time when he could afford to fall back and slow down a tad, this would be that time.

However, though he's definitely toiling, he's also apparently hellbent on showing some sign of improvement over last week's performances.

Bastard!

At a T-intersection abeam the end of the runway, the instructors lead Balzac through a slow shuffling right-180, and turn us back into the direction from which we just came. And as we roll out, facing back toward our distant hangar complex again, I find that my legs are simply no longer up to the task of pushing me back up to the pathetic limp I was doing before.

I'm slogging hard, driving for all I'm worth. But I can hardly even breathe anymore, so profound have my twin cramps become. My head—that one useless appendage that, so far, has just been along for the ride—starts to roll around its gimbals, tugging at the rest of my body, as if to say, *Come on, boys! Hang on! I'll get you there!* And it does help, marginally, but…

A hand lands in the middle of my back, and I find myself being pushed forward.

No! No! Don't put me in the same league as Balzac! No, I'll be good! I promise!

I throw out a weak wave-off, and manage to gasp out, "Thanks *(wheeze)*, I've got it." But I don't. And even if *I* won't admit it, it's plainly obvious to the guy behind me.

I try to outrun that hand, and I almost succeed, feeling it slip away with a light brush of fingertips, when good old Rodney Balzac—leading this disintegrating parade from right in front of me—suddenly wobbles backward, and nearly goes down under my feet.

I stumble and lurch half-around him, catching his right arm under the armpit, and hoisting him back to his feet, all without *quite* falling out of the run. And the hand that was in the middle of *my* back—Greg Dorn's, as it turns out—lunges forward and starts pushing Balzac instead.

Whew!

The three of us steady up and forge ahead. And again, for reasons I do not yet understand, the additional (and significant) burden of keeping Balzac hefted up somehow keeps *me* going as well.

I don't get it—it makes no sense to me whatsoever—but truth be told, it just doesn't matter. Pushing the Big B gives me what I apparently need to keep plodding along, whether it's *extra* energy, or just a more focused application of it. I don't know.

This time though, I join the others around me when they start verbally coaxing him onward, goading and encouraging him to just keep those heavy metal feet stomping along under him. Or maybe it's *me* I'm subconsciously talking to here. Maybe it's just a mindless mantra that keeps my attention away from my own body's distractions. But whatever it is, I finish the run along with everybody else.

Including Airman Rodney Balzac.

5
HURDLE NUMBER ONE

I REACH ACROSS THE parachute packing table, snatch up the rigging hook, and steal a quick glance over at Sgt. Stillman where he prowls the aisles between the tables. His stopwatch is still in his hand, but his hands are currently clasped behind his back while he's waiting for me to finish, and his attention is wandering among the other students at the other tables.

Good. Whatever I'm doing right or wrong here, it's apparently not severe enough to concern him too terribly. And that's good enough for me... for now.

I slip the T-handled hook through the top-right rubber band loop on the chute's outer flap, and leave it hanging there. Then I grab a fistful of suspension lines, bend a kink into them, and feed them into the crook of the rigging hook. Sgt. Stillman turns back around just in time to watch me pull the hook back out through the rubber band loop, creating the first 'switchback' out of twenty or so in the bundle of suspension lines. And from there, it's a fast sequence of hooking, pulling, stretching and threading my way down the little promenade of rubber bands until it looks like the back of the chute has been stitched together by a thick cord of bundled suspension lines.

Which it has.

Stillman's face shows no expression whatsoever—it never does—but he checks his stopwatch once more, and looks away without commenting.

I think that's a good sign.

I try to ignore him, and concentrate instead on pressing the drogue chute flat atop my freshly 'woven' panel, closing the outer flaps over it, and tying off the end of a yellow static line to the final grommet hole with a shoelace.

And the instant the last loop in the shoelace is tied, I toss my hands in the air and say, "Done!"

Sgt. Stillman turns his head only far enough to allow one eye to assess my handiwork, then looks away again.

"Now the reserve," says the back of his head.

I guess that means I did okay with the packing of the *main* parachute anyway. I prop my completed main against the wall, and march down to the end of the table where a large wad of green 'silk' and canvas spills over the edge of the neighboring table—the *unoccupied* neighboring table—the table that *used* to be, on these late night shifts, manned by Airman Rodney Balzac.

The *late-great* Rodney Balzac.

This afternoon's run was the third five-miler of the course so far... and Rodney's last. Because this afternoon, there was just no amount of pushing, propping, coaxing, or dragging that would carry Airman Balzac all the way to the end. He'd simply reached his limit.

He faded in his usual place (right around the two-mile mark), was goaded and shoved by his usual buddies for the usual amount of time and distance, and then he just surrendered. He finally gave up.

He quit running, weaved off the side of the road, and waved goodbye.

He was already out-processed from the barracks by the time I got back there myself.

I wasn't too surprised, then, when he didn't show up here at the rigging tables at nine o'clock this evening either. Just disappointed.

No, not even that.

Just... sad, I guess.

I liked ol' Rodney. I liked how helping *him* helped *me*. And I liked knowing that there was at least one other person in this class that was having a harder time with the physical stuff than me. Now *I'm* the weakest link.

Four down, twelve to go. We're not even two weeks into the program, and we ain't even gotten to the hard stuff yet.

Shit.

I throw the gutted reserve chute onto the table, untangle the jury-rigged 'belt' of suspension lines holding it all together, and spread the whole thing out down the length of the thirty-foot table, apex vent hooked at one end, harness flayed open at the other.

I pass another fleeting glance at Sgt. Stillman, who averts his own gaze by checking his stopwatch again, and I charge into the home stretch.

* * *

JUST BEFORE MIDNIGHT, I throw my hands up and shout, "Done!" for the second and final time.

Sgt. Stillman checks his stopwatch, takes his time ruminating over its results, then goes through the motions of 'examining' my finished reserve chute. No mysteries here; he watched what I was doing every step of the way. He milks the moment for all it's worth anyway, then he nods and says, "Two good chutes in fifty-three minutes." And he walks away.

That's all? That's it?
Fifty-three minutes, huh?
Well then... okay. Uhhh... I guess we're done with that then.
First big hurdle cleared.
Next!

STORY XXIII

BARELY HANGING ON

1
WEEK THREE: SETTING THE PACE

November, 1977
Little Rock AFB, Little Rock, Arkansas

WELL, SO MUCH FOR all the free time off.

Now that the parachute packing block of the course has passed—and I'm guessing its odd late-night hours were an accommodation for the Little Rock Combat Control *Team* (a small annex of which comprises the *school*), since they probably required unimpeded access to their rigging facilities during their normal business hours—now the schedule has reverted to a little more standard timeframe, with the school days starting just after sunrise, and ending just before sunset.

We took our first *written* test too. Took it last Friday. It covered all the parachute-related stuff (which was easy, considering the total immersion we'd just been through over the previous ten days), plus a sizable portion dedicated to all the radio equipment, security and phraseology stuff with which we'd *finished* the week. *That* was a bitch, for me at least. Too much memorization, too many things that we'd barely touched upon before being tested on it.

I passed it, with a score in the high eighties, but it's left me apprehensive about the rest of the written tests yet to come. Every day, new and varied subjects, all complex, detailed, and new to me (although probably not so much for the rest of the guys who've been using this gear for months already). Study, study, study, don't get anything mixed up in your head, then take a fifty-question test on Friday that you *cannot* fail. No do-overs, no re-tests, no second chances. You pass or you go home... period.

Yep; there was that inflexible mantra again. Obviously not the first time I'd heard it, and nor will it be the last, I'm certain.

Damn, I miss parachute packing.

* * *

I HAD A CRAMP *before* we started running today.

I've determined, though, that Sgt. Beaudry's pre-Phase I training back at Keesler was *not* intended to buff us up for the Army's Jump School. It was intended for *this place*. I see that now. And now that Balzac's gone, I think I've become the official 'Sorriest Physical Specimen in the Class.'

I'm still getting through everything they throw at me, but it ain't a pretty sight. There's not an inch of my work-out clothes that isn't drenched and heavy with sweat, my arms are dead and hanging off my shoulders like sandbags, and it doesn't take long before my breathing turns desperate and gasping, and then loud. And like I said, today I *started* the run with a thorny little stitch under my ribcage.

I'm holding on, though. I'm still up front, at *point* today, still "running" (quote-unquote), and, well... if nothing else, one thing I've learned about myself here (the hard way) is that just because no part of me *wants* to run— just because something aches, or is weak, or is seized up with cramps—that doesn't mean it *can't* run. A spike of pain embedded under my ribs doesn't keep my legs from pumping. Neither does breathlessness, nor blindness from the buckets of sweat sheeting into my eye sockets, and neither does a weakened neck that can't even hold my head up anymore.

I focus first on maintaining a metronomic breathing rhythm for as long as I can. But when that invariably succumbs to my tiny lungs and general weeniness, my focus next shifts to my legs, to just keeping them churning, one milepost at a time... then one *tree* at a time... and then, if things get that desperate, down to one *step* at a time.

They didn't tell us at the start of today's run how long it would be. But I know, from miserable experience, that a left turn at this empty intersection coming up, out here in the middle of nowhere (again), means a likely three-mile loop to get back to the PT shelter. Continuing on straight though, will take us *around* this little hill instead of *over* it, directly out to the flightline, to the relatively flat road that parallels the runway, for just *two* miles.

And that's what I'm praying for.

So naturally, Sgt. Rabin—who's jogging beside me in the lead instructor position today—trots up close and says, "Turn left up here."

Well, fudge.

Not only is that the beginning of an even longer ending, but the first thing it does is *go uphill!* Granted, not very steeply or for very long—it is, in fact, the same feeble little ascent that Ricky Spradlin nearly killed the entire class on a couple of weeks ago—but right now, with my breathing already so hopelessly out of control, and that red hot poker jostling under my ribs, I've got nothing left to give this hill.

We turn left anyway.

There's no hiding the physical distress I'm in right now. My stride is rubbery, my tread is heavy and stomping, and I'm making a lot of noise, wheezing, way too fast, and grunting with every footfall that jars my cramps. And Sgt. Rabin is right beside me... watching.

This one's gonna' kill me. I'm going to be forced to fall *back*, and then *out*, and then be left *behind* to quell my wildly flailing lungs, pulsing knots, and fibrillating heart... followed by a long slow limp back to the barracks, and the world's longest hot shower... an evening of packing, and a quiet solo commercial flight home tomorrow. And then what?

A transfer out of CCT, and back into regular old ATC. That's what.

Yes, that's what awaits me now.

Actually, that sounds pretty damned good!

What the hell am I fighting it for?

Still, for whatever internal and subconscious reasons, I throw myself at this little hill with a vengeance. I don't know why: probably just anger that this is all it will take to knock me out of this program for good. Or maybe it's just that this is the most conspicuous of all my Achilles heels, and I hate the thought of going down in flames right in front of my clearly physically superior classmates.

But whatever it is, I attack this pathetic little incline as if there were bullets nipping at my heels, as if the single most important thing I could ever do with my entire life would be to leave every one of my fellow students in the dust right now.

I don't, of course. I *can't*. But what I *do* is charge... and charge and charge and keep on motherfucking *charging!*

It's all I've got.

My wheezing devolves into whimpering, and then to a squeaky kind of 'barking.' My light 'jogging' gait shifts to *digging in*—writhing, twisting, and driving my way up this feckless little hill—and in turn, the poker jammed into my ribs flares white-hot and rams its way right out through my chest. If there was somebody running in front of me right now, my cramp would be stabbing *them* in the back! But the road slowly grinds past, Sgt. Rabin fades back behind me, and step by gnashing step, I storm the crest.

I stagger over the top—yes, against all odds, I make it that far—barely *crawling* upright, but upright nonetheless. And I start a drunken totter along the relatively level grade of the upper surface. Sgt. Rabin jogs up alongside almost immediately, and I can hear the chaotic thunder of a dozen pairs of boots drumming the pavement behind me, and closing fast.

So, yeh... I'd say it's pretty much over.

Even if all four of the frontrunners plant their hands in my back and push me, all that will happen is that they'll wind up pushing me *over*.

I'm slowing to a sloppy amble now, whether I want to or not. My lungs are in total hysterical spasm, clawing for air around the shaft of rebar that's buried under my scapula. My feet won't even clear the ground anymore. And here comes the rest of them. *Yes, it's all over now.*

"Flight!" shouts Sgt. Rabin. Then after four more synchronized steps, he adds, "*Halt!*"

What? Halt? Did he say 'halt?' Here?

But... why? Or... uhhh... Okay!

Two additional steps bring us to a sudden stop, and we are left standing there at a weaving, heaving form of attention. Everybody's gasping and snorting like race horses, of course, but beyond that, all our physical effort and mental concentration is focused on just holding our frenzied braces... heels together, fists at our sides, chins uplifted, pretending to be rigidly professional and unfazed, while every bodily function is failing, melting, and trying to collapse to the ground. I fight the urge to go reeling off into the grass, and instead force my posture to remain desperately erect, at least for the few more seconds it'll take for Sgt. Rabin to say...

"At ease!"

I sag, and blow my last gulp of air out in a gust. My chest immediately resumes its panicky gasping, and I pace in place with my hands on my hips, all the while maintaining a countenance of grim determination that hopefully has them all fooled.

I can't figure out *why* they've chosen to stop us way out here in the burbs of the toolies. They've never interrupted any of our runs before, even when Trefelden and Balzac were falling out of the formation. But lordy knows, *I ain't complainin'!*

Sgt. Rabin shouts, "All right, gentlemen! Take five and shake it off! We'll be starting up this next class right over here in this field in five minutes."

A 'class?' Out here? In this field? What class?

Who cares! At the very brink of collapse, just a couple of jelly-kneed steps away from falling back, then falling *out*, then *washing* out altogether, I've been granted this serendipitous reprieve.

I don't care if this is *"Home Ec 101: Sewing Doilies!" I'm in!*

And damned glad to still be here... for some stupid reason.

2
AN EXERCISE IN WALKING

AS IT TURNS OUT, this is where and this is *when* we've been scheduled to work out our individual 'pace counts.'

And as far as I'm concerned, it couldn't have happened at a better place or time.

Here atop this naked little knoll, just barely high enough to overlook the Little Rock AFB runway, they've marked off four ten-meter-long lanes in the scruffy grass using wooden stakes. And all that we each have to do is pick one of those lanes, and walk up and down it, maintaining a 'normal' cross-country stride and counting our steps, until we've established a reliable average. *And that's it!*

They stopped a run for this?

Why not? They had to get us out here some *way. Why not running?*

Short-legged runts like Spradlin and Hackett might take thirteen or fourteen steps to march the length of a lane, while *long*-legged lopers like Goebler or Matheson might take only nine.

Well, after five leisurely strolls up and back, I ascertain that I average *eleven steps* for every ten meters of distance. That's a hundred-and-ten paces for every hundred meters, or *eleven*-hundred for every thousand.

In other words, eleven-hundred steps for every kilometer, or "klick."

My new mental odometer.

An instructor writes that down. I commit it to memory for future use in the field. Then I yield my lane to someone else, and mosey off to unwind my shuddering muscles, stretch out my cramps, and nurse my breathing back down to the snorting of a lathered bull.

The whole process, cycling everyone through the lanes and recording their results, takes less than fifteen minutes; just enough time for my posture to straighten and my will to live to return. Then we're back on the road, in formation, with me in the lead again, jogging the rest of the way—*downhill*—to the PT shelter.

Saved—in the nick of time—by an exercise in walking.

Thank God I was qualified to do that much.

3
ON A ROPE AND A PRAYER

THIS SIX-STORY HIGHRISE on the far side of the airfield belongs to the Little Rock AFB Fire Department, they tell us. It has windows (open holes anyway, without glass) on three sides of the building and on all six floors. I presume they use it for, among other things, rappelling practice.

If not, it doesn't matter. That's what *we're* using it for today.

A dozen of us—all twelve of the remaining students, myself miraculously included—along with three of the instructors, are gathered on its roof, looking down at the asphalt parking lot sixty feet below. There, a fourth instructor, Sgt. Stillman, is standing, looking up at us and twiddling idly with both ends of a long green nylon rope, the center of which Sgt. Rabin has just finished anchoring up here at the top.

It didn't look this high from the ground when we first pulled up in the bus. Looking down from the top though, I feel like I'm back on the 250' tower at Fort Benning.

That is a long-ass way down there!

Our parked deuce-and-a-half looks like an OD-green Tonka truck, Sgt. Stillman looks like a G.I. Joe doll (*I'm sorry; I meant "action figure"*), and that parking lot looks extra hard from up here. It also feels like the Earth's gravity might be just a little bit stronger on this side of the base.

The only thing that *doesn't* look bigger, further, or stronger up here is that friggin' rope. That looks like a scrawny garden vine to me, or maybe a strand of thin green Christmas ribbon, but nothing that could possibly take on my full body weight.

Suck it up, hero! Sgt. Rabin's about to go over the side on it, just to show you how it's done. If it'll support his ass, it'll support yours. And if it doesn't, well, at least you'll have something soft and meaty to land on when you hit the ground.

Sergeants Myers and Hemingway circulate through the clutch of wide-eyed students, checking out the improvised 'rappelling harnesses' we've each got wrapped around our waists. These are jury-rigged 'seats' fashioned from the same kind of rope that's draped over the side of the building, threaded between our legs, and cinched together into a single frontal knot that has a mountaineer's carabiner ('biner, or "beaner" for short) embedded in it like a stylized chrome phallus (Sgt. Myers' adjustments are making me feel ridiculously self-conscious for that very reason). And as they move among us, Sgt. Rabin draws our collective attention back to himself where he stands boldly at the edge of the precipice.

"Alright, ladies. Listen up. 'Cause we don't want to have to keep repeating this every time one of you steps up here."

Trust me, Sarge. You've got my full attention.

"This is your '*control* hand'," he says, holding his gloved left hand out in front of his face, its palm turned inward like a Shakespearean actor contemplating the skull of poor Yoric. "And this is your '*brake* hand'," he adds, indicating his gloved *right* hand, which is hovering back beside his butt cheek like a gunslinger poised to make a quick-draw. "I don't care whether you're right- or left-handed. Here on *my* rappelling wall, your left hand is your control hand, and your right is your brake hand. And this is where they go. Got it?"

"*Oo-rah!*," we hoot in unison.

I look around, and everyone's already posing just like him, like students of the Lumberjack Ballet. I quickly join them... left glove aloft, right glove readied to spank myself.

Feeling pretty cool right about now. Yes, indeedy.

"Now for the important part," he continues. "Pay close attention to what I'm doing now." And he grabs the doubled rope with his left hand—his *control* hand, I remind myself—and draws it up to the 'biner that's hanging from the front of his own home-made 'rappelling harness.'

His carabiner, like all of ours, looks a lot like a plump oversized paperclip—roughly five inches long by three inches wide—with one of its long sides broken and hinged, creating a spring-loaded 'gate' of sorts. When we were cobbling together our own 'rappelling harnesses,' we'd all ensured that our carabiners were enmeshed with their 'gates' on their 'up' side. So, when Sgt. Rabin lays his paired ropes across the top of his 'biner, they easily push down through its gate, and *voila!*, the ropes now pass *through* it.

Tah-daahhh! Magic!

And the crowd goes, "*Ooooo*."

Now, as we watch, he loops the twin ropes around (under) the 'biner one more time, and again, when they pass over the top that second time, he pushes them through the gate again and, *voila!*, the ropes now not only pass *through* the 'biner, but they also coil once *around* the ungated side as well.

And the crowd goes, "*Aaahh*."

"And that's all there is to it," he says. "You're now ready to rappel."

Huh? That's it? But what keeps you from hurtling down the length of the ropes like a tethered anvil?

He steps up onto the ledge and turns, parking his heels out over the edge of space. He tugs the slack out of his lines, then his right hand—his '*brake*' hand—sweeps the ropes around to the small of his back and holds them there. He leans back, his ass out over the parking lot, seeming to settle against the fist behind his back, and he fixes his gaze upon us.

"Notice that I am not *grabbing* the rope at any point," he says.

Really?

I look closely, and sure enough, his left hand is *open*, the ropes merely passing across his palm. And the gloved fingers of his *right* hand, pinned at the small of his back, are formed in a loose "**O**" around the ropes.

What the...?

"It's not your *grip* on the rope that controls your rate of descent. It's the *angle* of the rope passing through the 'biner that does it. At this angle,"—*and with his left hand he traces the path of the ropes, where they round his right hip and stretch up into the 'biner at an angle that bunches them at its rounded tip*—"the rope gets bottled up and can't slide around itself anymore. And that's what stops you. That's what's allowing me to lean my weight back against my open fist without falling. That's how you brake, and that's why your right hand is called your *brake* hand. But watch closely what happens when I change that angle and loosen up the bottleneck."

And before we even understand what he's doing, he flicks his right arm out, as if flinging open the passenger door of a car, then snaps it right back behind his kidney an instant later. In that instant, though, with his boots still planted on the ledge, his 'brake' momentarily lets go, and everything between his ankles and his chest drops out of sight below the lip of the building. By the time his life-line goes taut again, all we can see are his head and shoulders—adorned with aviator shades and his blue beret—peeking up at us between the toes of his boots.

But I saw what he meant about the angle of the rope.

We crowd up against the rim of the roof and look down at him. And he's just suspended there, propped against the face of the wall like a capitol letter "**L**," held in place solely by that loosely 'guided' (not *gripped*) rope. Just an open ring of thumb and fingers for it to pass through, tucked against his lower lumbar region like he's plugging himself in to something. *And that's it!*

Son of a bitch!

"Do not grab onto the rope *ever*," he repeats blithely, as if there wasn't a sixty-foot death plunge licking its lips right under his ass. "These gloves will not stop you from getting a damned good rope burn. Just *move* the rope... out to the side to descend or drop, or behind your back to slow or stop (*aw, what a cute little rhyme*). That's all.

"And don't go trying to *bound* down the wall on your first try, at least not until you've got a lot more rope above you. Just *walk* it down a little ways first, maybe ten feet or more, before you start gettin' all frisky." And he backs his way down the wall a few steps just to illustrate.

"Watch the ground coming up. Don't let it catch you by surprise. Other than that, just relax and go with it. You've got Sgt. Stillman down there watching out for you on belay. *Isn't that right, Sgt. Stillman?!*"

"*Fuck no!*"

"Okay, then... *on rappel!*"

"*On belay!*," Sgt. Stillman yells back up to him, now taking a slightly more serious grip on his ends of the ropes.

And without another second's hesitation, Sgt. Rabin hops away from the wall, throws his brake hand out to the side, and drops away from us. Three increasingly larger vaults later, he drives himself *far* away from the building, and zips the last twenty feet or so to an exquisitely timed touchdown that is so light, he doesn't even have to bend his knees upon landing.

Applause erupts across the rooftop.

The tiny Rabin-figure—now at the *bottom* of the ropes—leans back and yells, "*Sgt. Myers! One stripe at a time, work your way up to the NCOs! Let's get 'em goin'!*"

And we're off... in more ways than one.

Starting with the one-stripers, as instructed, Sgt. Myers lines me up with Rocky and Greg (from the McChord Team), along with "PG" Padgitt and "Mex" Torrero (from the Dyess and Little Rocks teams respectively)—'skeeter-wings' one and all—and the rest of the class queues up in the order of ascending rank behind us.

All eyes are upon Sgt. Hemingway then, as he grabs Rocky by his 'chrome phallus' and starts manhandling him through the rope-loading process. Rocky is typically fearless though, and as soon as Hemingway clears him, he bounds down the face of the building as if the only gravity in the area was *inside* the edifice, pulling him toward it.

Mex is a little more circumspect, however, keeping his hops short and close to the wall, actually *walking* his way down the last ten feet or so.

Then it's *my* turn.

* * *

THE WORST PART OF the whole thing turns out to be that initial leaning-out-over-the-edge part.

For starters, it's just about the most *un*natural thing you can do when you're standing at the top of a six-story building.

So, when combined with my still undeveloped sense of confidence in the strength of the rope (or Sgt. Rabin's knot-tying skills, for that matter), it's a real act of faith and willpower to just keep tipping my ass out over the abyss like this, utterly dependent on not only the rope, but the intentionally loose grip on my brake hand as well.

Man, that is just... not... right!

It all holds as advertised, though. My body position might not be forming a perfect "**L**" shape—more like the hands of a watch at four or five o'clock, maybe—but it's close enough for a first effort. And once Sgt. Hemingway talks me through a couple of 'test tugs' with my brake hand (which drops my butt a little lower with each slip), a transition occurs in my head. And suddenly, going down the wall becomes the *most* natural thing I could do. I'm actually getting antsy for Hemingway to shut the hell up and let me go!

"All right, ya' ready?" he finally asks.

"*Oo-rah!*," I reply in ritual response, feeling twitchy and moronic at the same time.

"Let him know, then."

I nod and twist my head around to look down on Sgt. Stillman.

"*On rappel!*"

"*On belay!*," he shouts right back... although I still don't know exactly what that means.

And I go.

My first hop is more buck than bang, though... more like a little 'skip' than the 'power-drive' for 'max hang-time' that I was envisioning. But this is only because here at the top, as Sgt. Rabin had noted, there's barely four or five feet of rope above me between my 'biner and the edge of the roof. So I settle for a couple more diminutive bounces, with relatively frugal movements of my brake hand, until I'm a floor or two down from the edge—you know, the edge with all the goofy grinning faces of my nine brother students peering down at me—then I go for the big *heave-ho!*

On my fourth bounce off the wall, I decide to go for it. I kick hard out into space, and throw my brake hand all the way up to shoulder-level. The paired strands of rope thrum smoothly through my carabiner, and whiz painlessly through the loose loop of glove leather on my right hand. The ground rushes up—although nowhere near as fast as a freefall—and almost three floors of windows bolt past me before the energy of my push dwindles, and I start to swing back in towards the wall.

Automatically, my brake hand swoops around to the small of my back, the rope bogs to a stop (as does my plummet), and I am swept feet-first into the wall. My boots touch, my legs compress, and *foom!*, off I go again, as far away from the face of the building as my legs can drive me. My brake hand flies out to the side again, the ropes whir through gloves and 'biner alike, and *here comes the ground!*

The timing is simple, natural, and obvious though. And at just the right split second, I ease my brake hand down to about half-mast, which *slows* but doesn't completely *stop* my travel down the lines. And I alight—yes, I said "*alight*"—gently, and with confident *savoir faire*, at Sgt. Stillman's feet.

Hoo-HOO!!

How! Cool! Was! THAT?!!

I whisk the last of the paired ropes out of my 'biner, and with a satisfactory nod from each of the two instructors there on the ground, I go charging back into the building, and up the stairs once more.

I think I might like this even better than jumping!

* * *

WE GET A FINE exhibition of the role and function of the *Man on Belay* from none other than goofy-assed "PG" Padgitt barely ten minutes later.

On PG's second go—with only the limited experience of his single previous rappel—his irrepressible friskiness gets the better of him, and he leaps away from the building with all of his strength, and none of his brake hand, right from the ready position at the top of the wall. It's apparently his intent to rappel the entire height of the building in a single bound, something which Sgt. Stillman has told us he does "all the time." But for PG, it's only his second rappel. And considering Sgt. Rabin's specific admonishment about *not* attempting anything too extreme during these first fledgling efforts, it appears that PG also believes in Spew's *second* rule of outrageous behavior as well: "*Tis better to seek forgiveness than ask permission.*"

It's stupid, it's dangerous, and he's going to catch hell for it.

PG knows all this. And he does it anyway.

His initial push-off is instantly hamstrung by the short length of the rope between his 'biner and the top of the wall, just exactly as Sgt. Rabin had warned us, and as all of us, including PG, had already discovered for ourselves on our first attempts. So PG, having driven just as hard as he could, all wildly flying arms and kicking legs, is instantly yanked right back into the face of the building by the stunted rope... with his brake hand still fully extended (unfurling the rope like a broken elevator cable), and his feet still thrashing too boldly and dramatically to be brought back down in front of him in time.

He crashes back into the wall against his left side and butt cheek... which knocks his control hand loose... which causes him to immediately topple over backwards on the rebound, and start hurtling down the wall, *upside down!*

Everybody gasps. PG chokes out an airless, "Ah, Jesus," and all eyes plummet towards the ground along with him.

Out of a perfectly natural (albeit suicidal) human reflex then, PG lets go altogether and grapples for the rope as it zips past him... again, precisely what Sgt. Rabin had told us *not* to do. Of course, even if he somehow actually *succeeded* at grabbing it, all that would happen would be the addition of one extra line on the accident report that says, "*Plus two rope-burned hands.*"

Fortunately, it never gets that far.

Hardly have his arms begun to pinwheel than he's suddenly wrenched to a rubbery bouncing stop, about three floors up from the ground, suspended more or less in the middle of the lines... which are now drawn tight at an angle leading directly from the top of the roof to Sgt. Stillman down in the parking lot, whose outward leaning weight has stretched them taut.

So that's *what being "on belay" means!*

From the belay man's ground-based position, letting the ropes hang slack allows the rappeller to do whatever he wants, just as Sgt. Stillman had done at the start of every student's rappel. But if the belay man suddenly runs the slack out and *pulls them tight*—as Stillman did just now—he instead forces the rope through the *rappeller's carabiner* at the same angle the rappeller himself would have drawn it *if he'd been doing a normal braking adjustment!* And that stops the descent cold. Regardless of what the rappeller wants or is doing.

So Sgt. Stillman has just saved PG's life... *literally.*

And I bet the loony bastard didn't learn a goddamned thing from it.

* * *

ONCE EVERYONE HAS DONE the old 'vertical leapfrog' at least once, the 'instruction' eases off, and it turns into nothing but 'practice.'

Practice, practice, practice.

And it doesn't take very long doing *that* before we start acting like a bunch of kids on a playground, repeatedly shooting up and down the slide just as fast and as often as we can. Even the instructors get in on it, cycling students through the belay position as part of the rotation.

Sgt. Hemingway, second only to Sgt. Stillman when it comes to deadpan stoicism, even goes so far as to illustrate for PG, who has just stepped in to take his turn on belay, how utterly asinine he'd looked on that recent spastic rappel of his (with a minor embellishment or two).

After shrieking, "*On rappel!*" with a theatrical pubescent squeak, Hemingway shoves off, throwing all four arms and legs out into a full flapping spread eagle, and somehow manages to hold all *but* his brake hand in that configuration until the short rope smacks him back against the wall, face-first and still fully spread. *On purpose!*

Ouch!

He stays there too, blotted against the wall like a bug on a windshield, but only long enough to get everybody laughing. Then he abruptly flings himself off the face of the building again, this time with his *control hand* waving around wild and free... which causes him to topple over backwards (just like Mr. Padgitt), with his brake hand still planted firmly in his back, and swinging back into the wall again, this time reversed and *upside-down* (another familiar arrangement).

Everyone flinches at the impending disaster (much as we'd done with PG as well), but burst out laughing again when Sgt. Hemingway thumps harmlessly against the wall, inverted and dangling like a drunken spider.

Or an exaggerated Padgitt.

PG takes it well. Just like Spew back at McChord, it's what he does best: making a complete ass of himself, emblazoning himself indelibly in everyone's memory with glorious outrageousness, then wolfing down the humble pie with gusto.

I'll say this much for him: he takes as much shit as he dishes out, and he laughs at himself just as freely as everyone else... just like Spew.

Crazy fucker.

He's the first (and only) student to actually work a real-world belay though, because he has to help Sgt. Hemingway *undo* his comic handiwork by drawing the lines tight, thereby seizing his 'biner in place, and allowing the 'drunken spider' to let go of everything and turn himself back upright again.

Once back in a stable position though, Sgt. Hemingway looks down and shouts, "*On rappel!*" PG answers with "*On belay!*," and releases the slack back into the ropes. And Sgt. Hemingway finishes his rappel in two more grandly clownish bounces.

Well, that *was fun!*

* * *

I GET TO DO three more rappels before we break for lunch, each one bigger, bolder, and bawdier than the one before, as first caution turns to confidence, then fearlessness, then cockiness. It's the same for everyone else in the class as well, judging by all the broad toothy grins surrounding me.

I've decided that rappelling is *great!* It's simple, relatively safe, thrilling as hell, and surprisingly instinctual after only a round or two on the wall. I can't wait until next week when we get to do it again.

We're all standing around in the parking lot then, unraveling our 'crotch ropes' (dismantling our 'improvised rappelling harnesses'), when Sgt. Rabin calls us over to gather around Sgt. Stillman. He's got one more thing he wants to show us before we leave, he says, a little 'preview' of what's to come next week on this same bat-tower.

I join the others as they congregate around the four instructors, two of whom are assisting Sgt. Stillman *partially* dismantle, and then *reverse* his own jury-rigged harness. His carabiner now protrudes from the knot *above his tailbone.* And while they're doing this, Sgt. Rabin addresses the rest of us.

"What Sgt. Stillman is about to demonstrate for us here is called the Australian Rappel. I don't know why it's called that, and I don't care, so don't ask. And it is—in every way but *two*—*identical* to the standard rappelling technique that you just learned. The only differences are that (1) you go down the wall face-*down* instead of face-*up*, and (2) that, in turn, allows you to walk or even *run* straight down the wall without the need for a control hand to keep you stable."

*Huh? Run? Face-*down*? But... how?*

That's probably what Sgt. Stillman's going to show us.

The three sergeants tug and jerk on their reconfigured ropework, then pat Stillman on the back to signify that all is in order with his backward harness. He then strides over to the deuce-and-a-half that brought us out here, snatches a GAU-5 assault rifle from the cab, and marches off into the building.

What the hell?

Sgt. Rabin continues his little tour guide monologue while we wait for Sgt. Stillman to climb the stairs to the top of the building's six floors.

Apparently, as far as the relationship between the harness and the rope is concerned, everything's the same. The carabiner's still at the apex of the whole rig, and the rope is still fed through it the same way. Only the *human body* in the harness has changed, facing the 'wrong way,' as it were. Facing *down*. As such, since the 'braking angle' of the rope (entering and bunching up at the top of the carabiner) has to remain the same, the brake *hand* has to change. Instead of the *right hand* whipping the rope around to the small of your *back*, now your *left* hand has to draw it across your lower *abdomen*, like a belt-level Roman fist-salute. Same rope angle and activity, just different appendages used to move it that way.

No *jumping*, mind you... no pushing off from the wall. You've got no control hand to keep you upright anymore. So you've got to stick with walking, or even *running* down the wall. In other words, keeping your feet under you. But in the meantime, your right hand is free to do *whatever you need!* Like dropping grenades, or firing your weapon at enemy troops on the ground below you.

Well, isn't that special!

Sgt. Stillman appears at the edge of the roof, six stories up. He looks down at us for a moment, like an oracle upon his minions. Then his left hand sweeps the paired ropes across his diaphragm and clutches them there, while his right hefts his weapon into the crook of his arm. Stirring stagecraft indeed.

"*On rappel!,*" he finally shouts.

"*On belay!,*" answers Sgt. Rabin.

Then the crazy bastard just starts *leaning out over the abyss,* tilting forward like a statue being pulled off its pedestal. It's damned bizarre, and not a little unsettling, to watch this guy just 'hinging' outward like a drawbridge being lowered. But after only a few seconds, he's ready... standing out perpendicular to the vertical face of the building, his brake hand tucking the rope across his belly button, and his hard eyes glaring down at us with that patented expression of bored malevolence.

He waits there just long enough to get us all wondering what the hell he's doing, then his brake hand suddenly flings the rope out to his left, and he starts running.

Running!

Straight down! Storming the ground as if he's on a staircase in an Escher painting!

A second later, his GAU starts hammering away on full automatic, firing in the general vicinity of our truck. Then he starts *yelling! That's stony Sgt. Stillman I'm talking about here!* Just bellowing over the stutter of his weapon and charging the asphalt in great hurtling and heedless strides. It's a lunatic vision, wild and loud and freakishly unnatural... and the most noise that Sgt. Jack Stillman has probably ever made... *in his life!*

And I'm going to get to do that shit next week myself! Hoo-HOO!

He stops firing (or runs out of ammo, more likely), and slows his vertical sprint only once he's reached the first-floor windows. Then, with a minimal hop and the timely tucking of his brake hand, he alights on pointed toe in the parking lot, and whisks the last of the rope through his carabiner.

He's down—and breathing easily through his nose, by the way—and calmly popping a new mag into the GAU, before the class can even erupt in cheering applause. One side of that glacier-cold Grim Reaper mask of his buckles into a smirk.

Damn!

For Sgt. Stillman, that's practically an hysterically giddy outburst.

That must be a shitload of fun!

"And *that*, ladies," says Sgt. Rabin, as he tromps over from his belay position, tugging his gloves off, "is the Australian Rappel. It's extremely effective for maintaining an offensive posture during a descent—or just keeping your eyes on your target while you're sneaking up on them from above, or just a free hand for whatever it is you need to carry—but it is also extremely dangerous. Sgt. Stillman made it look easy, *but it's not*. Your balance is much more critical, and you've got no control hand to keep you upright. So don't expect to be *running* down any walls while you're here on *my* wall. You'll be walking it, and you'll be damned lucky if you get *that* right in the limited time you've got available. So no hot-doggin' it! Understood?!"

"*Oo-rah!*" we shout back in unison.

"Airman Padgitt? Did *you* hear that?"

Everyone chuckles, but ol' PG answers without hesitation or shyness.

"Oo-rah!"

Sgt. Rabin looks skeptical—perhaps even a little constipated, truth be told—but he finally nods, waves dismissively at the truck, and says, "Now get the fuck out of here."

4
CONSEQUENCES, CONSEQUENCES

GAWD, THAT'S A DEPRESSING prospect.

After an hour-and-a-half of dry clinical lecturing on the math, mechanics, and minutiae of accurate artillery plotting, they're now passing around these black-and-white photos of the results of *poor*—or at least *untimely*—artillery plotting.

The one I'm holding in my hand right now is a freeze-frame of a C-7 Caribou—an ungainly, twin-engine cargo plane—on final approach into some LZ in Vietnam. Its wheels are down, and it's apparently less than a hundred feet in the air, judging by the jungle terrain and the trashy Army outpost framing the bottom of the picture.

It's also in two pieces. Snapped in half like a Kit Kat bar… by a 'friendly' artillery round that was fired across the final approach corridor as it was coming in to land. The Caribou's front half has already started to tumble forward, and its severed tail is falling away behind it with the lazy swoops of a huge dead leaf.

It's a sickening thought to imagine the expressions on the faces of the men behind those cockpit windows right at that moment, men who, just *seconds* before, had been casually wrapping up an easy little cross-country jaunt with a leisurely drift down the glidepath, like they'd done a thousand times before, into some innocuous little dirt strip in the western foothills of Vietnam.

At this particular instant of frozen time, they have no idea what's happening to them. One second, it was just like any other day, the next, hell was upon them. They no doubt heard the *bang!*, felt the jarring kick in the side as the artillery round punched through, and most certainly noticed the jungle suddenly rearing up into their faces, even if they didn't understand *why*.

But, all other considerations aside, the most profound realization of the moment has got to be the sudden insight that they are about to die. They are struggling through the last seconds of their *lives* in this photo, as yet disbelieving of the fact that nothing they try will have any effect on their fates whatsoever. They are on an irreversible collision course with the ravaged jungle floor below, and those three to five seconds of somersaulting that remain between this instant and that one—between this plane of existence and the next—are all they have left. Not even enough time to remember the people they'll never see again. *Aaurgh!*

And all because some artillery coordinator—an Army radioman, they tell us, *not* a Combat Controller—dropped the ball, and either allowed an aircraft to fly into a hot fire zone, or allowed an artillery outpost to open fire without ensuring the airspace was clear of friendly aircraft first. Either way, it's heartbreaking.

Which is, of course, the whole point of showing us these pictures.

They say it all.

Consequences, consequences.

5

A GOOD SHELLACKING

LATE NOVEMBER, AND WINTER has finally arrived in Little Rock. Not just cold, not just windy, but wet too. And as far as the instructors are concerned, the worse it is, the better it is.

Not only does PT go on as scheduled, and outdoors, like always, but the uniform of the day remains unchanged: nothing but the usual CCT T-shirt, glossy black combat boots, and fucking shorts! No sweaters, no gloves, no wool caps. No sympathy whatsoever.

And as we jump up from our last set of rain-soaked push-ups, the drizzle begins to intensify, working its way up to a righteous little shower... of *freezing rain*. It lands on my skin and hardens instantly, which is, to put it delicately, an 'interesting sensation.' Given enough time, of course, it would ultimately melt. But today, it will not be given that time.

As we're trotting toward the street, it starts raining harder. And more 'liquid ice' means less melting time between strikes. So now the moisture already on my arms and legs is beginning to *re*-freeze.

I do a couple of stretchers and knee-bends on my way over to the starting line for the run, and when I do, I *crackle!* It feels like my skin is cracking and splitting as it stretches, but in reality, it's just the film of ice I'm now wearing.

Shit. We need to start running soon before we all wind up shellacked to the street!

We do, and I am blessedly nearer the back of the pack this time... less of an audience behind me watching me toil against my weaknesses, as well as a moving windbreak in front of me as we chug through the sleet.

That's the *good* news.

The *bad* news though, is that the wet chill sets off my automatic cramping mechanisms prematurely, before we've even rounded the second turn in the road, in fact.

Twang!

A tire iron wedges its way under my shoulder blade (again), and jiggles there in sharp breathtaking little stabs and jabs that coincide with my every stomping boot step… *for the entire three miles!*

Shit! Shit! Shit!

Now, I may have learned how to run with muscle spasms, knots, and seizures—hell, it's the only way I *can* run any distance—but I have not yet found a way to do it *quietly*. Clenched teeth, painful gunshot exhalations, hissing and grunting and gasping have all become personal trademarks of mine on these damned runs. I'm sure it's exasperating for the rest of these guys to have to listen to all the time, but, well… *so what?!* There's nothing I can do about it. It hurts, and it steals my air. And if I want to finish these friggin' things, it's *what I have to do* to forge ahead and tough it out to the end.

Sorry guys.

No I'm not! To hell with that!

This is hard enough without having to worry about how I'm uglying up the run for the rest of them. Maybe someday this miserable slogging will become second nature to me—maybe my body will eventually figure out what it needs to do to get through these things without knotting up like an over-wound rubber band—but until that time, I either make these unseemly noises, or I drop out and go home without my beret. It's that simple.

"Go home." Man, *that sounds pretty friggin' good right about now, actually.* So why am I fighting so hard to stay with this then?

I'll be damned if I know.

Maybe it's the idea of *surrendering* or something, you know? Of just 'giving up' because "*I can't take it anymore.*" I guess that just feels like I'd be adding a 'weakness of *character*' to my already growing catalogue of *physical* inadequacies. And that bothers me on a whole different level.

I mean, making the purely intellectual and *practical* choice to just stop doing something that I don't believe serves any real long-term purpose anymore, well, that's one thing. That would just be a 'preferential decision,' not a capitulation... and I'm not quite there yet. And being washed out? *Forced* out because the limits of my pampered physique had finally been exceeded? Well, that would just be something I couldn't help, right? Something beyond my control... sorta'. So I tell myself that *these* things I could live with, however begrudgingly.

But merely 'admitting defeat?' *Surrendering? 'Cause I'm tired?*
Never.
(idiot)
No. As stupid and self-destructive as it might be, something about that idea just keeps my rime-coated legs pumping, my ice-crusted brow scowling into the wind, and my flailing hammering lungs gasping for whatever air they can find... much to the annoyance of the closest guys around me, I'm sure.

Sorry, guys.
Oh, the HELL I am!

STORY XXIV

THE NITTY GRITTY

1
DIRTY WORK

November, 1977
Little Rock AFB, Little Rock, Arkansas

TODAY'S PT SESSION IS followed by what feels like an afterthought of a class called "Silent Kill techniques." This is the up-close-and-personal part of the program, the part where your hands, rather than a weapon, do the dirty work, where the choreography is intimate, where you *feel* the bones breaking under your blows and the warm blood spattering your arms.

I've awaited this class with mixed emotions: unsure of what to expect, curious but apprehensive, excited but wary, and now that the day is upon us, downright *scared*, truth be told.

One way or the other though, it's going to be different. It's interesting, it's hands-on, and it's, well… 'intriguingly grizzly.'

First they go over some hand-to-hand combat techniques—*jiu jitsu*, if you can believe that. And as it turns out, this is something for which I have absolutely no aptitude whatsoever. As I'd told Mutt when we first met, I've never been in a fight in my life, not even a half-assed schoolyard scrap, so my body doesn't even have the most rudimentary 'muscle memory' for how to throw a punch, or even *keep my balance* in a wrestling scenario. This is all so new, raw, and alien to me… and *oh gawd*, does it show!

I can grasp the *mechanics* of it, alright. I can understand the *principles* behind using my opponent's motions and energies against him, and I know what they're *going for* when they show me where my center of gravity should be, or the fulcrum of my leverage. But making them all flow together when they say, "*Go!*," just doesn't work. Not for me, anyway.

I think it's that damned 'over-thinking' thing again. It bites me every time. Or am I just over-thinking my tendency to over-think things? Again.

Hmmm, I don't know. Maybe I should think about that.

As we go through each maneuver, one frozen hyper-analyzed movement at a time, it's a perfectly logical straightforward process, an obvious step-by-step sequence that seems simple and natural, even *inevitable* in retrospect. At full speed, however, it's a spastic thrashing dance of the idiots.

That simple blocking move, for instance—that parrying swipe with my left arm that's supposed to deflect my opponent's incoming punch—it goes too far, and actually throws *me* off-balance. And that driving forward step—the one that's supposed to plant my calf right behind his—winds up kicking the guy in the shin instead, which in turn makes *me* stumble forward. Then the shove and the twist—that are supposed the throw the guy over the leg I just planted behind him—instead topples *both* of us onto the mat, except that *he* lands on his back, and *I* land on the side of my face.

This will obviously require some practice on my part.

Unfortunately (or maybe *fortunately*), we won't be practicing it today.

After only a few goofy and embarrassingly uncoordinated repeats of this block-and-flip drill, along with a few defensive maneuvers on how to fall and separate and reverse, *etcetera*, Sgt. Stillman takes the floor. And he's holding a huge green K-Bar combat knife in his hand.

So this must be the "kill" part of the "*Silent Kill*" title now.

***A little warning, here… if you're at all squeamish,
you might want to skip ahead past the next page. Seriously.
This gets nasty.***

***

ANYHOO… AS IT TURNS out, the classic Hollywood depiction of a knife-wielding attacker wrenching his victim's head back and doing a quick slash across the throat, opening them up from ear to ear, is *not* the preferred method for use in a tactical military situation. It's too easy to do improperly—too easy to cut rather than sever—accomplishing little more than slicing an ugly (but merely cosmetic) gash below the jaw line which, in addition to causing the victim to die slowly and painfully (if at all), also allows him to *continue breathing*, and thereby continue to make noise as he does so.

So 'we' don't do it that way in the real world.

No, what '*we*' do is far far worse.

And when I say "we," I apparently now mean "*I*."

Now, as Sgt. Stillman demonstrates, using the ever-ebullient PG Padgitt as his 'doomed sentry' model, the knife is driven, point-first, straight into the side of the neck (*oh gawd, I think I'm gonna' throw up*), plunging it through the carotid artery as it goes (*la-la-la-laaaaa! I can't hear you! La-la-la-la...!*), until, now sunk in all the  way up to the friggin' hilt (*baseball-baseball-baseball-baseball!*), it is then shoved *forward*, ripping straight out the *front* of the neck, thereby severing every pipe, vessel, and muscle it might have missed in the initial plunge (*AAURGH! Shut the fuck up! Shut the fuck up NOW!*). You *can't* cut too shallow with this technique, your victim's demise is assured, and even if the initial shock doesn't kill him, he still can't call for help while he awaits his expiration from blood loss.

Hence the method's preferential status.

Jesus Christ! And you expect me to do that?!

Just watching Stillman's cold, dispassionate, and horribly purposeful expression, as he pretends to saw PG's head half off, sends a shiver down my spine so hard it almost throws my back into spasm.

This clearly poses no moral dilemma whatsoever for the likes of Sgt. Stillman, though—and judging by the blithe, almost enrapt expressions of my fellow students, the 'likes of him' are all around me here on this training mat—but it poses a *severe* dilemma for *me*. Perhaps the first one I've encountered since choosing to pursue this line of work.

All of a sudden, a grotesque aspect of butchery has invaded all the glamour and romance, the heroics, and even the *fun stuff* that I've been aspiring to all this time. You know; all the jumping, and the rappelling, and the beret-wearing *braggadocio*... all the strutting play-hero exotica of being a 'professional jumper' and a presumed badass. Important stuff like that.

Of course, hard exhausting labor, misery, and drudgery has also intruded as well, but those I could live with. Those only affect *me*. *This*, however... this, to put it technically, is some *serious shit!* And I not only don't *like* it, but I honestly don't believe that I could ever do it. Nor would I want to change that much internally to even *try*.

Shoot somebody? Sure. That's abstract enough to be reduced to a mere test of steadiness and marksmanship, an almost surreal arcade-like challenge of one's skills. But *hack* them to death? To actually feel them squirming in my arms as I plunge a knife through the inner lattice of muscle, cartilage and organs beneath their skin? To feel their hot blood spill over my knuckles, to hear the gasp of gurgling air escape their severed windpipe... *oh God, I can feel that blade of tempered steel ramming through my own throat even as we speak! How the hell could I ever do that to someone else, when I can so clearly feel it being done to me just sitting here on this workout mat?*

Sgt. Stillman's ensuing demonstrations on PG's kidneys, along with one variant that involves the severing of his spinal cord, and another that opens up his intestinal cavity, are enough to put me off my food for a month.

Well, a week anyway.

Okay; at least until dinner tonight... maybe.

Everything he's describing now is etched in horror so acute, particularly to my elaborately visual brain, and especially with my empathetic tendency for putting myself in the victim's shoes as I'm eviscerating him—or her— that, well... I... I just won't...

How?

We appear, at last, to have reached the edge of my envelope here—*one* of its edges, anyway. So I guess the question now is, *Is this fairly profound limitation finally going to be sufficient to start my indecisive ass running for the proverbial hills?*

At present, I don't want it to, but... *so what?* Does my unwillingness to dispatch my enemies with a combat knife make me a liability to my teammates? Or would my *other* 'strengths' balance the scales enough? I mean, is that how a 'team' would function? Would the guy who's good with a knife—and loves the gruesome work—always get those kinds of jobs, while I might be, say, the guy they always put on the difficult air traffic control jobs, or the hairy high-platform rappelling jobs, or maybe the missions that involve playing a piano in front of a room full of strangers? I could *do* that. Or is it just a weakness that I would be expected to overcome (like my friggin' motion sensitivity)? And if so, do I really *want* to be able to overcome this particular reticence of mine? Do I really want to be that kind of guy?

Either way, it looks like 'play time' is now officially over. My little dalliance with exotic lifestyles—Sgt. Beaudry's little eighteen-month window for testing the waters of covert ops—has now officially become 'dirty, deadly, serious work.' Not just 'playing Army' to the extreme anymore, but *killing people*, up close and personal. Not exactly a surprise or a revelation—I understood the general nature of this job when I first signed up—but a rude slap to the face nonetheless.

Shit. Now what?

***

SGT. STILLMAN FINISHES HIS indelicate little demonstration on a slightly lighter note: namely, *how to silent kill a sentry with his own helmet. While he's wearing it!*

Yes, it turns out that the worst thing an unsuspecting sentinel can do is to don his helmet with his chin strap *attached*.

For this, Sgt. Stillman has Padgitt put on a basic steel-pot helmet that he just happened to bring along for this very demonstration (we don't have our own, since Combat Controllers would never have occasion to wear them), and makes sure he snaps the chin strap in place. Then, in step-by-step slow motion, he illustrates how, without using any other weapon, you can kill a man—silently—with his own helmet.

After sneaking up behind him (of course), he first claps one hand over PG's mouth—an applauded gesture all by itself—then with his other hand, he reaches around and seizes the front brim of the helmet. Moving carefully, so as not to actually cripple ol' PG in the process, he then pulls the helmet back over his head, all in slow motion. And as he does, the changing angle causes the chin strap to drop off PG's chin onto his Adam's Apple. And from there, it's just a simple but deadly application of leverage.

As the helmet's brim is pulled back past the crown of PG's head, its *rear* brim digs into the base of his neck, and suddenly becomes a lethal pivot point. Stillman has to stop there though—there's no simulating the next part—to show us how the final 'ratchet' works. Not that it's too tough to figure out. Assuming the chin strap doesn't let go, one good hard yank would not only break Mr. Padgitt's neck, but the strap would probably crush his larynx in the process. And that's how you apparently 'silent kill' a guy with his own helmet.

(*sigh*)

I think I'd rather just run over him with a deuce-and-a-half.

2
WEEK FOUR: ROAD TRIP!

November, 1977
Fort Polk, Alexandria, Louisiana

ROAD TRIP! HOO-HOO!

And it's big one too. An overnighter. And since it's going out of state, it starts with an early morning flight.

With our rucks packed for two days and a night in the wilds of Louisiana, we convene at the school's hangar in the pre-dawn darkness. Only *ten* of us appear though, since two more of my fellow inmates here—Jimson, from the Norton CC Team, and none other than good old fun-lovin' PG Padgitt, the only guy left from the Dyess Team—apparently succumbed to the cruel indifference of last Friday's written exam, and are now *gone*.

Damn! And I had gotten along so well with Jimson!

It *was* a tough test, though—all the nitnoy technicalities about the dozens of pieces of communications and navaid gear that we were only introduced to just last week, twenty-plus questions on the winds and weather alone, all kinds of computational problems on the setting up of DZs, LZs, and EZs, and of course, all that unsettling artillery plotting shit.

And that was just the stuff they'd taught us *that week*. It was brutal.

I managed to pass the damned thing, though—obviously; *I'm still here, ain't I?*—but it couldn't have been by much.

Jeezy Pete! They were serious when they said, "Fail one thing, and you fail everything."

Not quite halfway through the course, and almost half of the class has already been eliminated! *Six out of sixteen!* Kort, Trefelden, Cooper, Balzac, and now Jimson and Padgitt. *Damn!* We're averaging two wash-outs a week! If it keeps going at this rate, there won't be a single student left to attend the graduation banquet.

On the other hand, the mere fact that *I'm* one of the surviving ten just goes to prove that dumb luck and clean living *can* trump brilliance, natural aptitude, and worldly expertise occasionally.

In the meantime, those of us that remain now get to go on to Weapons School. It's another Army course, like Jump School, although this one is taught down at Fort Polk, a two-hour flight south of Little Rock, outside Alexandria, Louisiana. Right smack dab in the middle of the state, I believe.

They tell us the place is a real shit-hole, but that doesn't tell me much. Right now I'm not all that enamored of Little Rock Air Force Base either.

They bus us out to the flightline, and they pile us aboard a C-130 in the cold gray light and diffuse shadows of a foggy December sunrise. It tried to snow over the weekend, but it didn't stick, and yesterday's sun melted what few hardy patches had remained. So today it's just cold and wet... until we get above the clouds, that is. Then it turns *friggin' gorgeous!*

Crystal clear skies, radiant blue and floored with that foggy undercast deck which, as viewed from above, is awash in morning gold.

Just spectacular.

The plane might smell like an old oil-soaked jockstrap to me, and its gentle shuffles and jostles through the air might be settin' my guts a-sloshin' (like always), but that doesn't make the *outside* vista any less magnificent. And it *is* just bloody beautiful, in a painfully heartbreaking contradiction to the stinking windowless machine that's carrying me through it.

I can see how glorious it is out there because, as usual, I've posted myself at the jump door, where I can peer out its tiny porthole and maintain contact with the horizon, thereby keeping all the spinning gyros in my head on an even keel, as well as the heaving contents of my stomach

below the cork with which I've mentally plugged it.
Oh yeh. I was made for this kind of work.

* * *

WE LAND MID-MORNING at England AFB, a pleasant little Air Force installation on the outskirts of Alexandria, Louisiana.

We are met, right there on the parking ramp, by the very bus that then drives us straight off the base and down the forest-lined backroads for another hour or so, to the neighboring Army post of Fort Polk. Once through the gate there, we are directed to the 'post's' In-Processing Center—a sagging WWII-vintage edifice showing more naked splintering wood than white paint—and from there, directed on to our temporary overnight 'barracks.'

And here I feel I must pause for a moment to more thoroughly describe this setting in all its rich and wretched detail. Not just the rotting, tumbledown, wooden ghetto in which they've chosen to billet us, but, well, Fort Polk in general. Because, outside of a particularly gritty Hollywood western, I don't think I've ever seen anything like it.

Not in real life, anyway.

Not in twentieth-century America, anyway.

* * *

FORT POLK HAS THE look of a tired old nineteenth-century frontier town, an irregular muddy lesion scraped out of the lush rolling hills of central Louisiana. It's even laid out with all the thought-free creativity of the hardscrabble settlement in the movie *Shane*... a straight, rutted-mud main drag, lined with wooden 'storefronts' and wooden walkways, every structure a plain whitewashed two-story box, along with mud-splattered cars and trucks nosed up to the walkways like weary horses tied to their hitching posts. I'm sure there's some asphalt under all this schmutz—our bus hasn't bogged down yet (although the driver's probably pissed about the washing he's going to have to do once he gets back to England)—but since the mud *coating* is everywhere, the analogy holds true. And since the main drag rolls straight down an easy slope in front of us, we can see over the tarpaper roofs in the foreground to the patchy forests beyond, wherein all the firing ranges theoretically lie.

Ugly, primitive, and to all outward appearances, unchanged and unimproved since the last century. Then there's *our* building.

Another featureless two-story wooden box, weatherworn to the point that the only surviving scraps of ancient white paint are all clustered like freckles in the middle of its dead wood sides. Nothing but raw gray exposed wood at all four corners. It is also *literally* swaybacked. You can stand at one end, look down its length, and see the sagging arc of its slats.

But that's not the worst of it.

After jerking the sticky swollen door open, we are greeted with three new unpleasant realities. First is the moldering stench of old wood and wet carpet. Second, is the long, straight, uninterrupted flight of stairs leading up to the second floor... *which is missing the middle eighteen inches or so of every riser.* There's literally a chasm running right down the center of the staircase, as if the whole flight had been left 'unzipped,' exposing the dark dank basement beneath, worn right down to nothing by the millions of booted feet that must have thundered up and down these steps over the decades. And third, is the fact that we've been billeted *on* the second floor.

Shit. We have to climb that sorry mess.

How can they continue to bunk people in such a ramshackle heap of rotting wood? One that should have been condemned back in the Hoover administration. This place isn't fit to *provide shade*, much less protection against any real weather. But, at least the handrails are still in place.

Unbelievable.

In a slow, creeping, single-file then, we tippy-toe our way up what's left of the stairs, straddling the ragged maw beneath them, until we're all congregated at the head of our new 'living quarters,' and staring at the next appalling vision in this cavalcade of horrors... our bunk room.

The entire second floor is one huge open bay, with both its towering vaulted ceiling and its vast uncarpeted floor visibly bowing toward the center of the Earth. Big windows, no blinds or curtains. Exposed rafters, with cobwebs so thick, it makes the whole room look like one big canopied bed.

And speaking of beds, the twenty or so that are lined up on either side of the broad central aisle have got so much empty acreage between and around them, they look like ugly desolate islands. Scuffed metal frames, bare mattresses, wafer-thin pillows, and itchy green horse blankets folded at the foot of each bunk.

Gawd, the warmth and hospitality that just radiates from every board.

We pick out beds, and drop our rucksacks on our choices—*delicately*, of course, for fear that any sudden impacts might cause the beds to crash right through the floor into the bay below—then we head out for our busy day of shootin' shit down, and blowin' shit up.

3

WEAPONS SCHOOL: STEEL-JACKETED HAIL, AND INCENDIARY SLEET

BY THE TIME WE get to the M-60 firing range, it's already been a pretty good morning. I mean, we started off with the basics—the good old GAU-5 assault rifle, the chopped-down special forces variant of the venerable M-16, which is destined to become my full-time faithful sidekick once I get back up to McChord. We disassembled and reassembled it, reviewed its specs and zeroed it in, then shot for accuracy on a short twenty-five yard range. First single shots, then double-taps. *Cool.*

And then, once all the essentials had been covered, and with a thirty-round 'banana mag' of ammo left apiece, they let us try a little *full-auto* fire with our remaining rounds, ostensibly just to get a feel for how the weapons tend to pull when hammering away wide open.

But who cares why they had us do it?

The fact was that mashing that trigger, and holding it there for the three or four seconds it took for the clip to empty—casings arcing out of the ejector port, slugs splattering through the treetops, chewing the upper branches into a cloud of flying mulch—well, that was just plain orgasmic.

I'd like to be able to claim a nobler, more high-minded character than what that last sentence implied—I wouldn't want to reinforce the notion that testosterone equals a penchant for destruction and violence—but, like it or not, proud of it or not, wielding that kind of destructive power is just plain undeniably invigorating!

How could anyone stand before a man so armed?
(by being similarly, or better *armed, of course… that's how)*

* * *

BUT NOW WE'VE MOVED up, to the vaunted M-60, a bigger heavier weapon, firing bigger heavier ammunition, across bigger longer distances. And for those reasons, we've moved to a bigger broader firing range—a whole valley, this time—with firing positions located atop a ridgeline on one side, and the targets scattered across the floor of the valley and up its opposite slope, the furthest ones being atop the far ridge-top, *at fifteen-hundred yards away!*

Almost a mile distant! Hoo-WEE!

In reality, the targets are about the size of highway billboards. But it would require almost impossible marksmanship to actually *intentionally* hit one of them from this far away… at least with *this* weapon and *our* skills.

Still, how cool is it that I actually get to try?

Again though, our familiarization begins with a complete breakdown and reassembly of the weapon. And this one's got a lot more pieces than the smaller GAU-5. Barrels inside heat shields, recoil springs, carrying handles, and even a bipod. This a *belt-fed* weapon (meaning that its ammunition—hefty bronze missiles, each round about the size and weight of a roll of nickels—comes in belts that are accordion-folded into metal ammo boxes, which are themselves only slightly smaller, and only slightly less heavy, than car batteries), as well as being considered a 'crew-served' machine gun (meaning that optimally, it requires two men to operate: one to carry, set-up, and fire the *weapon*, and the other to carry and feed the *ammo*).

So, once we've all had a chance to strip, clean, and rebuild the damned things—from yet another 'picnic table' covered in hundreds of oily parts, back up to fully functional killing machines again—they pair the ten of us up into five two-man teams, and lead us to our firing stations.

And today, my randomly selected 'firing buddy' is none other than Rocky... McChord's own Li'l Ricky Spradlin.

We have to take turns at the trigger, and Rocky graciously allows me first dibs. He hauls the heavy cans of ammo, I haul the weapon itself, and we find ourselves a nice little patch of bald Earth to lie down upon. There, overlooking the shallow scrubby valley, I deploy the weapon's attached bipod, set it up like a sniper rifle, then lower myself into a prone firing position behind it.

In the meantime, Rocky drops his cans to my left, flips the feeder plate open on the top of the gun, and unfurls a bandoleer of 'sixty-mike-mike' between the can and the feeder. Then he slaps the plate closed again, and claps me on the shoulder, signifying the readiness of our "team."

The big shovel-jawed Army instructor has been talking the entire time, of course, strutting powerfully behind us, and belting out his oft-repeated schtick like an auctioneer. Preoccupied or not though, I *have* been listening.

Every fifth round in the belt is a 'tracer,' apparently, which will leave hot orange streaks in their wake, thereby etching our firestreams like laser bolts across the sky and against the backdrop of the lower terrain. And this is helpful, of course, for adjusting our aim. It is *not*, however, sufficient to fully counter the voluminous and all but *blinding* effect of the smoke that this weapon issues forth when firing.

For that reason then, the ammo handler has to pull double-duty as a "spotter"—that's actually his official title; not "ammo handler" or "bullet-carrying guy"—by which I mean he watches the flight of the tracer rounds from his position *beside* the shooter, outside most of the veil of smoke, and directing the shooter's fire onto the target.

Cool! The spotter gets to do something more than just feeding ammo belts and clearing jams! This could be fun!

* * *

"**READY ON THE LEFT?!**" shouts the lead instructor.

"Ready on the left!," his underling on the left returns.

"Ready on the right?!"

"Ready right!" answers his opposite.

"Ready on the firing line!"

"Ready!," they *both* shout.

What a quaint little ritual.

Then, "*FIRE!!*"

I pull the trigger at the same time as everyone else. All five M-60s cut loose at the same instant, and it feels like a noisy earthquake shuddering through the ridgeline.

These big guns *thud!* None of that girly "popping" or "rattling" like the lightweight GAU-5s and M-16s do. These suckers *hammer!* Slower but heavier—*thud-thud-thud-thud-thud-thud!*—like the metronomic ticking of the *60 Minutes* stopwatch... *on steroids...* with the treble turned down to zero, and the bass cranked to eleven.

Thud-thud-thud! Thud-thud-thud-thud!

It just wallops you, with the bucking that's punching your shoulder through the stock *also* being transmitted into the Earth through the bipod... which in turn makes the ground that you're lying on tremble. It wouldn't be that much with just one weapon, but *five* of them? In a row? In such close proximity? It's a minor earthquake.

Then there's the tracers: little flits of yellow-orange that bolt across the distance every so many "*thuds.*" It's amazing how fast they fly, how straight and fearless, until they smack into something half a mile away that's angled like a ridgeline's upslope, and skip off into space. And our five parallel firestreams are raking the valley floor and sweeping up the far pitches like fire hoses, splattering orange ricochets in all directions. *Wow!*

Still, they were right about the curtain of white smoke this thing throws up as it shoots. Though I *can* vaguely discern the hot orange streaks of my tracers going out, even through the boiling smoke screen, what I *can't* see any more are the targets at which I'm supposed to be shooting.

But that's where Rocky comes in handy.

Over the heavy juddering of the five-gun barrage—along with the distant exhortations of the instructors, bellowing something about 'picking our targets,' and 'actually trying to *hit* something' instead of spraying the hillsides like lunatics, *blah, blah, blah*—I can just make out Rocky's voice beside me, barking out corrections and adjustments.

"You're high and right of the five-hundred yarder! Come back *down* and *left!* Just a tick! *Down* and *left!*"

Either through the veil of smoke, or during the brief smokeless interludes between volleys, I can make out the big white rectangle with the "**500**" painted on it, just above the crease in the floor of the valley. I just keep losing it whenever I pull the trigger and unleash another smoke screen.

I adjust down-and-left, and let fly another burst.

Thud-thud! Thud-thud-thud-thud!

A couple more tracers dart across the void, but once again disappear behind the wall of smoke. Only Rocky knows the real score.

"*Hoo-WEE!*," he shouts. "High but centered! Pull it straight down!"

Apparently, pretty sparkly ricochets really tickle Rocky's G-spot.

I adjust once more, noting that my sights are already pointed left of the target—so the wind that's blowing the smoke away up here is also pushing my bullets to the right during their flight—as well as pointing well above the big white target.

Whatever.

Following Rocky's directions, I nudge the barrel a little lower, and squeeze again.

Thud-thud-thud…!

"That's it! Dead-on! Fire for effect! Kill that motherfucker!"

Yep; terminology straight out of the Army manual, I'm sure.

I hammer out a few more rounds, just to keep my one-man peanut gallery entertained, then let up just enough to let the smoke drift away. And I zero in on a different, more distant target—the thousand-yarder—and cut loose again.

Thud-thud-thud-thud-thud-thud! Thud-thud-thud!

"Oh yeh! Fuckin'-A Skippy!"

Nobody else's spotter is cheering obscenely. But then mine's also giving me some pretty good, sharp, succinct-yet-colorful corrections that are apparently putting my shots right on target.

"*Hoo-wee!* You are just flat beatin' that thing up!"

I take that to mean that my tracers are now punching through the "**1000**" marker—which is about halfway up the far slope of the valley—beating the dust off it, and tickling Rocky pink with each hot-orange ricochet that *spangs* off the rocks behind it. He's just a kid in a fireworks shop right now, getting more and more wound up, and if left to his own devices, in a minute he'll probably be playing with matches too.

"Tail of the belt!," he suddenly yells, and I look over to see the last bullets in my ammo belt laying across Rocky's open palms.

Just twenty more shots or so. My turn at the trigger is coming to an end... *dangit!*

So I decide to go for the gusto... the fifteen-hundred yard target.

Just under a *mile* away, the fifteen-hundred-yard target—essentially just a big white panel which, from here, is barely the size of one of my cuticles at arm's length—sits high atop the far slope just below the top of the ridgeline. I won't even pretend to have the skills necessary to *compute* such a long-range shot. I'm just going to start shooting, and let wildman Ricky talk my tracers onto it.

"Okay," I announce, as I squirm the stock more firmly into my shoulder, "This time I'm going to...!"

"Go for the fifteen-hundred, man! Let's see some fuckin' hair!"

"Um... okay." *Why didn't I think of that?*

I hold my slightly-left-of-target alignment, and mentally project the arc my shots ought to follow through space. Then I squeeze.

Thud-thud-thud-thud! Thud-thud! Thud-thud-thud!

"Holy shit!," Rocky Shouts. "That went clear over the ridge! *Hee-hee!* You didn't hit nothin', dude!"

Oh, I'm sure I hit something. *The question is 'what?' And 'where?'*

I adjust lower, and go after it again.

This time though, a ruffle of wind coils through my smoke screen just as I fire, and snatches it away. And as Rocky starts hooting and hollering again, I get to see it myself... the splatter of dirt geysers all around the target, right at the very rim of the escarpment, and the skipping off of tracers on both sides. It's beautiful... like fireworks.

"*Hoo-hoo!*"

"Nice shootin' there, Number Four!" one of the instructors hollers right behind me. "Try and concentrate it more, though! Don't throw your ammo away!"

What-the-hell-ever!

I brace myself a little sturdier, and once more let fly. And in less than five seconds, the last of my ammo belt rattles through the breach, and my weapon finally goes silent.

I am breathless. *What a rush!*

The other teams sputter out a few seconds later.

Rocky instantly leaps up, flips the feeder plate open, 'dusts' the breach clear of any remaining brass from the belt—just the last spindly chain links that jingle to the ground without any bullets for them to hold together—then kicks his way through the pile of spent casings to loom over me.

"All right, dude, let's switch out," he says. "Come on! Get your ass up and let *me* kill something!"

Personally, I don't see how that could benefit *anybody*, but, well, I guess I am out of ammunition. Might as well get up and crack open a fresh box for the daffy little bastard.

I lever myself up out of the dirt, slap off that portion of the firing ridge that rises with me, then go to work swapping out my empty for the box-o-bandoleers to which Rocky will now lay waste.

* * *

THUD-THUD-THUD-THUD-*thud-thud!*
"*BAH-hah ha-ha-ha-ha-haaa!*"
Thud-thud! Thud-thud-thud-thud-thud!
"*Hoo-WEE!* Eat that, motherfucker!"
"Um, Rocky?"
Thud-thud-thud-thud-thud-thud-thud!
"Hot damn!"
"*Rocky, goddammit!*," I'm really screaming now. "You're completely missing everything! All your shots are going over the hill!"
"I know!," he yells right back. "Ain't it cool?!"
Cool? He's doing that on purpose?
Thud-thud-thud-thud-thud! Thud-thud-thud!
"Fuckin'-A Skippy!"

Lying in the dirt beside him, with my unobstructed view of the high-flying arc of his tracers, it's like watching an endless stream of home runs being belted out of the park. And, untethered lunacy that it is, I have to admit it *is* pretty cool-lookin'... until I start thinking about where all those missiles might be landing.

I mean, who knows what's on the other side of that ridgeline?

Images of steel-jacketed hail splattering through an elementary school's crosswalk two miles away, go dancing through my head. Playgrounds sparkling with incendiary sleet, a mall parking lot somewhere, full of cars, clanging and banging and rattling under a deluge of invisible buckshot.

Stuff like that.

"*Rocky, man!*"

"Number Four!," the Army instructor barks from right behind me. "Check your shots! You're missing the whole goddamned mountain!"

Thank-you, Sergeant.

"And Spotter! Do your job, and tell him where his damned shots are going! Come on, gentlemen! Pay attention!"

Ah. Thank-you, Rocky. Thanks a lot.

He casts a mischievous grin my way—one that the instructor can't see—completely unrepentant, downright *proud* of his chastisement, in fact.

Damn. Spew must've gotten to him.

Then he snuggles back into the butt of the weapon, this time with the barrel deflected lower, and gets back to work emptying his ammo can.

4

EXPLODING CHRISTMAS ORNAMENTS

MODERN HAND GRENADES TURN out to be a bit of a disappointment.

Not only is their real-world *bang* so much less than their Hollywood *buck*—no deafening ragged blasts, no great fountains of fuel-fed flame or thumping sprays of dirt... just a puff of smoke, and a dull *poomp!*—but on top of that, they even *look* harmless and boring in your hand. Contrary to the classic World War II 'pineapples' (nasty little iron 'footballs'  cut with a cross-hatch of deep grooves, such that when they exploded, the segments would fly apart as shrapnel), the grenade that's sitting in my palm right now is a smooth, green, utterly benign-looking 'baseball,' perfectly spherical, and capped with a lever or 'paddle' with a cotter pin stuck through it to hold it in place. And that's it.

It's like holding a two- or three-pound Christmas ornament... an ornament full of shredded wire and enough explosive to blow my gutted carcass onto the roof of the neighboring bunker if I mishandle it.

And though the principles for using it seem simple enough—"grasp grenade with the paddle gripped against it, pull safety pin and *throw*"—this instructor just insists on making things complicated.

For one thing, he won't just let us *heave* it like a baseball.

Sure! Why let a guy who's been throwing balls with power and precision all his life just pitch it the way he knows how? Why keep it simple, and natural, and accurate, when you can instead make it awkward and slow and uncoordinated?

But that's how he wants it.

"That's how it's done," he says.

So, before I can even attempt the elementary task of just 'lobbing' this 'Christmas ornament' across the twenty or so yards between my trench and the bomb crater over there where it's supposed to go off—normally an easy and automatic 'given' for me—I will apparently have to re-learn how to throw an ornament first.

To begin with, I can't just use my elbow (doesn't *that* make sense?). Or my shoulder, for that matter. At least not in the conventional way an elbow and a shoulder are *designed* to operate. Instead, they want me to go through motions that more resemble a straight-arm cricket pitch than a 'throw,' basically turning myself into a human trebuchet. And as unwieldy as that is in the friendly trenches of Fort Polk, Louisiana, I can't imagine what a potentially *deadly* way this would be to show my ass in actual combat.

I mean, I have to stand up so high in the trench just to free up my fully extended throwing arm. And this, when combined with the extra second or two that it takes to complete this huge windmilling feat of acrobatics, leaves me far too exposed for far too long. And doing it with a five-second time-delayed ball of explosives in my hand, one that starts counting down the instant I let go of the grenade and allow that paddle to spring up? Then something as simple as tossing a ball sixty feet into a crater the size of a swimming pool suddenly becomes an exercise in flirting with death. And that's *without* any enemy sharpshooters trying to pick you off while you're going through your little cartwheeling 'Butterfly Ballet' across from them.

But our instructor, Sgt. Cornhall, seems uninterested in discussing the matter beyond the dictates of tradition and precedence.

Just do it, and shut the hell up.

Okay then. 'Nuff said.

So, after a couple of dry runs—practice flings that never feel right, much less 'comfortable,' but are sufficient to satisfy an impatient weapons instructor—it's time for the real thing. Sgt. Cornhall turns to the rest of the class, who are all waiting for their own turns back inside a sandbagged bunker behind us, and shouts, "Fire in the hole!"

And I pull the pin.

For a moment I pause, ostensibly to get my 'catapulting arm' set up just right. But in reality, I'm actually sorta' *frozen*, not with 'fear' so much as *amazement* at the thought that I'm now holding an armed explosive in my hand, an armed explosive that is only refraining from blasting me to bloody pieces because of the death-grip I've still got on that spring-loaded paddle.

It actually makes it tough to let go of it!

Then again, having the weight of extinction resting in your palm, in addition to its laxative effect, also tends to provide an incentive to just *get rid of the damned thing!* So, at long last... I do.

Unfortunately, I do it badly.

Very badly.

Dammit!

Too little experience with overhand bowling, I guess, combined with too *much* time spent fixated on the destructive potential in my hand, and I wind up releasing it way too early.

And by "way too early," I mean on the *upswing* of this ridiculous exaggerated 'shoulder sling' he's ordered me to do. And there's a reason that's considered 'doing it badly.' The grenade—the armed and *ticking* grenade—goes almost straight *up!* Not *out*... UP! And needless to say, ducking below the open walls of a trench is rendered somewhat moot when the detonation goes off directly overhead.

"*Airburst!*," screams the instructor as he throws himself on top of me, driving us both to the floor of the trench. Give him that much—he had the presence of mind to think of someone else before himself.

But as it turns out, the timed five-second delay is a lot longer than you'd think, and the verticality of my throw less 'straight up' than it looks.

As I hit the trench floor on my back, pile-driven into the dirt like a *tackle dummy*, I get one split second to look up... and I can actually still see the grenade hanging up there at the apex of its arc. It feels like it's already been up there for at least half an hour, just waiting for me to turn my gaze up to it. And I realize that if it goes off right now, I won't even have time to close my eyes before the concussion and the heat wave blows a fistful of shredded wire into my face. This flashes through my mind in an instant... one timeless, frozen, mortifyingly idiotic instant.

What an unbelievably stupid-assed way to die!

Then the grenade drops out of sight up there, hits the outer lip of the berm with a small *thump*—less than ten feet beyond the rim of the trench, it sounds like—and explodes.

Well... it '*pops*' anyway.

Poomp!

A little 'burp' of gray smoke boils past overhead, and it's all over.

A bit of an anti-climax, really. A humiliating one to be sure, but anti-climactic nonetheless.

Sgt. Cornhall is quick to bound back to his feet and slap the dirt off his fatigues. I scramble up beside him.

"That is *not* what I meant," he shouts into my face, "when I said *throw the damned thing downrange*, Mr. Stripp!"

His eyes dart from the scorch mark on the ground to the line of student heads that's only now rising above the sill of the bunker behind us.

"Gentlemen! For those of you who might not have been keeping up, AIRBURSTS ARE BAD!!!"

Discomfited chuckles ripple through the ranks of my fellow classmates, as well as a look or two of disgust, as if I'd just embarrassed the entire Air Force with that little blunder—which, I suppose, is just exactly what I did. I can feel my cheeks flush and my brow burn.

Dammit-dammit!

Whatever minimal progress I might have made squirreling my way back up the class's food chain from Tail-End Charlie, just crashed all the way back to the bottom again.

Good work there, Steve.

Fuck. Back to being the weak link again, I guess (if I'd ever risen above that station in the first place).

In the meantime, *lesson learned. Gotta' press on.*

Sgt. Cornhall hands me another grenade, admonishing me once more that my objective is to *lob* the damned thing into that well-worn blast crater over there (where, obviously, many many folks before me had managed to put *their* grenades without incident), *not* try to blow bird's nests out of the tree tops, or have it drop right back down into the trench between us.

I smile tolerantly—a little sarcasm is to be expected now, I suppose—but this next one, I promise myself, will go where it's supposed to, even if I have to resort to *throwing it like a normal human* in order to do it. In fact, with my newfound emphasis on *not releasing the grenade too early*, it's more likely that I'll hang on to it *too long* this time, and wind up spiking it straight into the dirt wall in front of me.

But it's all just so much wasted conjecture. My second 'toss,' despite its goofy-assed bowling technique, is perfect, and the Christmas ornament goes *poomp!* dead on target. The next student is rotated into my place in the trench, and I go shuffling back to the bunker with the others.

Which of my throws do you think they're going to remember, though?

5

MASTER OF THE BLUNDERBUSS

NEXT UP IS THE M-79 grenade *launcher*.

And this, as it turns out, is one toy I'm good at! I don't know why.

Who'da thunk that?

This thing is a short, plump, blunderbuss of a weapon, a cartoon shotgun with a three-inch-wide barrel. Essentially just a handheld mortar tube with a shoulder stock attached.

It cracks open like a hunting gun, and a single fat 'bullet'—a full-sized *grenade* stuffed into the top of an equally fat cartridge casing—is inserted into the tube. Then you snap it closed, point it towards the sky, and *poof!*, you're a one-man mortar team!

The 'acquired skill' here—the *artistry*, really—is in computing the *range* of your shot. Because there is no real 'gunsight' on this thing. Oh sure, there's this little flip-up doo-hicky thinga-ma-bobber about halfway down the barrel, and the instructor does go into a fairly lengthy little dissertation on how to use it to *not only* figure out the *distance* to your target, but the angle at which you should hold the weapon in order to fling a grenade *across* that distance.

It sounds complicated, however—not to mention horribly impractical, trying to do math under the pressure and time constraints of combat conditions—and his speech quickly becomes a southern-drawl-buzz in my ears that I just can't follow any more.

It doesn't help either that I'm still feeling stung by the humiliation of the grenade pits that we just came from, which has me hiding at the back of the pack trying to be invisible, unwilling to draw any more attention to myself by asking stupid questions. But the fact of the matter is, this is just going to be a tricky little sumbitch to get good at.

I think.

* * *

THE SAVING GRACE FOR me comes from watching the others that fire it before me.

Fortunately, unlike a typical rifle bullet, the grenade is so big, and its flight speed so slow, that you can *see* it in flight as it arcs up and out and back down again, dropping onto the far side of the blast-ravaged little gully there, and exploding upon contact with the ground. And for me (with my no-math, no-memorizing, but good pattern-recognizing and flightpath-projecting brain tracking each grenade's speed and arc), the relationship between the upward angle of the launcher, and the distance that that angle will cause the projectile to fly downrange quickly becomes apparent... to me, anyway.

The instructor pops off a round or two, just to show us how easy it is, calculations and all. But in the process, he *inadvertently* illustrates, in the most succinct shorthand possible, just exactly how $a + b$ can equal c without doing any of the math in between.

I don't know why—it's just something that comes naturally to me—but as soon as my brain sees how fast (or slow) the shell *thoops* out of that upturned barrel, it can tell instantly how far that velocity will carry it. And his second shot only confirms it. Before he even pulls the trigger, I can tell from the incline of the tube where that grenade's going to wind up hitting. And my estimate proves to be sufficiently correct.

Sgt. Haley—senior student, class leader, and asshole extraordinaire—is the first up. He shoulders the M-79, and starts to calculate his firing angle, using all of the instructor's parameters and cross-reference points. In my own head though, every little adjustment he makes with the angle of that thing just stretches and distorts an invisible parabolic line that my *mind's eye* can see quite clearly, arching between the wavering gun barrel and the far scrub across the gully. And that's when I realize…

We don' need no steenking computations!

Haley gets the last of it worked out in his skull, steadies himself, and fires. And, as if on rails, the lobbed shell traces my invisible parabolic track right to its predicted terminus, an old blast crater about ten yards uphill from a denuded tree, which is itself a good *twenty yards* beyond Haley's target area. Right where I knew it was going to land. He either miscalculated it, or misread the increments on that sight-like thingy in the middle of the barrel. But either way, it doesn't matter… because it went just exactly as far up the opposite hill as I knew it would.

I say not a word.

Too many ways *that* could backfire on me on a day like today.

I ain't no genius or grenade-launchin' prodigy. I just see trajectories and recognize patterns. That's it. Not much science to it really: just an obvious path that an object that small and that heavy, lofted up a gradient that steep, and with that much impetus behind it, would have to follow.

And it does… through shot after shot after shot, student after student, grenade after grenade, one missed target after the next.

Oh, Sal Donado does okay, nailing his third shot dead-on, and getting a 'close enough' on his fourth. But aside from those (plus Matheson's and Torrero's two near-ringers), nobody else can seem to 'master the blunderbuss.' Nobody really even comes terribly close.

I'm second-to-last in the line-up. But despite the last hour's little grenade-tossing debacle, by the time I step up to receive the smoking M-79 from the instructor, I'm smelling redemption (along with a lot of cordite) riding the breeze.

I can almost *hear* Sgt. Haley's grinding teeth behind me.

* * *

THE INSTRUCTOR AGAIN GOES through the motions of guiding another ignorant student (me) through the computational steps, and I go through the motions of pretending to follow him, step by mind-numbing step.

I can see how it's all supposed to add up. It just seems unnecessarily slow and complicated, since all it's doing is *mathematically* moving the barrel to where my own mental range-finder has already arrived and been long waiting. But right now? The *last* thing I'm going to do is act like I know more than the Army instructor out here. So I continue to play along.

The only thing that's proven to be a bit of an unexpected problem has been *the change of perspective*... from being a spectator, to being a shooter.

When I was standing off to the side watching the others, the angle of the weapon was always conspicuous and clear. I was looking right at it, *from the side*. But standing here now, holding it myself, it's a lot harder to tell.

It's enough to make you think there's a *reason* for mastering the calculations!

Firing the M-79 sounds a lot like popping a paper bag. I pull back on its big old clunky trigger, and it goes *bop!*, spitting the big old tubby projectile skyward atop a belch of thin smoke.

Tracking the soaring arc of the grenade is just as easy from behind the launcher as from beside it, too. It's still a very visible missile, much like a high flyball belted into the outfield. But as with any home run viewed from the batter's perspective, the depth of the shot—its *range*—is tougher to gauge from home plate, even when it's glaringly obvious to anyone sitting along the first base line. And such is the case here.

From where I'm standing, it almost looks like it's going straight *up* and straight *down*... until I hear a rising tumult from my classmates just before it hits the ground. Kind of like the anticipatory gasp from the crowd at a golf tournament, as a long curving putt rolls closer to the hole. *They* can see what *I* cannot, just like *I* could see when *they* were shooting.

My little bomb spears into the farside rim of the target crater, and *thumps* a splash of gray-brown dirt into the air. And for an M-79, from almost two-hundred feet away—two-thirds of a *football field!*—that's as good as a friggin' *bullseye*.

A couple of "*oo*'s" and "*ah*'s," along with a smattering of applause, trickles up from the peanut gallery, and Sal, no longer the only one of us with a dead-center hit, gets poked and prodded and generally harassed for his dethroning. But I ain't through yet apparently, whether I (or they) know it, or believe it, or not.

The instructor nods approvingly, and with my next shell in hand, points to a closer crater book-ended by two leafless trees down at the bottom of the little ravine.

"Try and drop this one on top of that North Korean command post down there between those trees," he says. Then he hands me the round.

I crack open the barrel, snatch out the smoking case, and pop in the new grenade. Then I snap the weapon closed again, and go through the motions of finding reference points through the flip-up sight thingy. I'm really only using it for left-right orientation though. The up-down part is once again just a matter of 'feel' and reading the invisible flight paths between me and that 'NK bunker' down there.

The trick in *this* case—since the target is at less than half the distance of the last one, and is *down*hill rather than up—is in how best to *put it there?* Pop-up or line drive? Shoot it more or less level (like a low-powered rifle), or near-*vertical* (like a mortar tube)?

On the one hand, having just witnessed how each of my predecessors dealt with this little conundrum before me—and to a man, every last one of them went with the 'line drive' or 'level trajectory' approach (and to a man, every last one of them missed, by a sizable margin I might add, even Sal)—I am leery of perpetuating that 'tradition' by doing the same thing myself.

On the other hand though, with the legacy of my recent 'airburst' still stinging my pride, I am loathe to risk a repeat of *that* humiliation by pointing the barrel *too vertically*, and forcing another Army instructor to throw himself on top of me... inspiring and educational as that was.

However, there are two significant differences between the 'baseball' grenades that I was *throwing* by hand on the last range, and the 'mortar round' grenades that I'm *firing* here.

Firstly, these rounds are 'spun' or 'rifled' as they leave the barrel (which is what makes them stable enough in flight to make them predictable, and thereby *aim-able*). As an added safety feature, they are also rigged to where it takes *five* of those revolutions just to *arm themselves*. In other words, they are 'inert'—duds—until they've spun at least five times, such that if you inadvertently drop or fire one straight into the ground, it won't explode at your feet and kill you. A handy little attribute, I've got to say.

And secondly, unlike the hand-tossed grenades, once armed, these rounds only explode *on contact* with something, like the ground, or a charging vehicle, or the wall of a building. In other words, you *can't* get an airburst from one of these.

So, contrary to the rest of my colleagues here, I opt for the *high*-angle 'pop-up' shot instead.

It'll be tricky, though. With that 'North Korean command bunker' being barely thirty-some-odd yards away, this is going to be a *very* vertical shot—a very *high* vertical shot, lobbed almost straight up and down—and with the M-79's stock planted in my shoulder, I find that I can't point the weapon skyward *and* still aim at a target that is straight ahead and *lower* than my line of sight. So (much to the instructor's chagrin), I pull the weapon down, and make it a *hip*-shot.

He starts to speak.

"Ummm... you're gonna' wanna'..."

But that invisible flight arc is still clearly visible to me. So I just keep angling the gun back until I 'see' the "splody" end of that parabola slide back into that crater. And before he can finish his sentence, I pull the trigger.

Bop!

The grenade bounds into the sky.

And my first impression, much like everyone else's apparently, is that I've done it again. The goddamned thing is going to hang there in space for a moment, and then, foiled by a headwind I didn't take into account, or following an errant trajectory I simply misjudged, or whatever—*something stupid*—it's going to fall right back at my feet and kill us all.

"*Jesus*," I hear the instructor mutter. And out of the corner of my eye, I catch him tensing to bolt... I think.

Or maybe not.

He doesn't move. Perhaps from his offset perspective, he has a sufficiently broadside view that he can tell where it's really going to wind up. And after a moment, as gravity takes its inevitable toll, the grenade begins to fall again... and everyone else suddenly catches on as well.

That collective anticipatory gasp goes up from the peanut gallery again, peaking just as my little projectile plunges into the heart of the crater and explodes.

Well, 'burps' anyway.

Boomp!

A bullseye! Dead center! Left-to-right, front-to-back, nothing but air! A perfect ringer!

The only member of my class to do so on this short-range target.

Somebody behind me starts to say, "Son of a bitch," but is drowned out by the cheer that goes up from everybody else... everybody but Sgt. Haley, I'm sure.

I look nervously at the instructor, who looks back with conflicting emotions rearranging his face. He looks like he's torn between chewing me a brand new squared-away asshole for scaring him like that, or congratulating me for hitting the one target that even *he* probably hasn't been able to nail himself. Or maybe he's just too stupefied to formulate an appropriately 'military' response right now. I don't know. And that makes me nervous.

Instead, he just stares hard at me for an extra moment or two, which I return with a timid, almost apologetic shrug of my shoulders. Then he hands me another round, and points to a distant tree-lined *sliver* of a ledge about halfway up the face of a larger berm, which is itself something like fifty or sixty yards beyond this nearer lower embankment, which rises slowly for, I'm guessing, fifteen or twenty yards past that crater I just blasted. All told? Probably over a hundred yards or more, maybe a hundred-and-twenty. Nowhere near its max range of four-hundred meters, but far enough out there that my mystical parabolas and flight arcs grow vague and dissolute.

Shit.

"Okay, hotshot," he says, "Do something about that column of Chinese trucks up there now."

Though slender, shallow, and far away, *left-to-right* the ledge is probably sixty or seventy yards long. A plenty wide target. So, keeping my tone as humble as possible, I ask, "You want me to put the shot in the *center* of the 'convoy?' Or should I take out the 'lead vehicle'?"

He looks at me as if he's not sure how much of a smart-ass he's got on his hands here. Then, without breaking eye contact with me, he points to the far left end of the scar and says, "The 'lead vehicle'... please."

There's a sad little sapling of a tree, alone, right about the point where the ledge peters out altogether, roughly in the area where he's pointing. But its far-left placement adds about another twenty yards to my already-strained mental math. *Uh-oh.* So what are we up to now? About a hundred-and-*forty* yards approximately? Almost a football field and a half? *Sheesh!*

Maybe I should've paid closer attention to all that 'southern-drawl-buzz' claptrap he was spittin' out earlier, about, you know, how to use this little flip-up sight thingy and all.

Nothing I can do about that now, though. Not after he just so recently repeated it all for me. So...

Again, as tactfully as possible, I ask, "*That* tree?"

He finally breaks eye contact and looks back at the tree. Then he turns back to me.

"Yes. That tree. Try to blow it up before it drives off around the corner. Okay?"

So I do... well, close enough, anyway.

The fact is, to the naked eye—and the confused brain, and the inattentive ear—the shot just doesn't look possible. At least not with any hope of *intentional* accuracy. It looks to be at or slightly *beyond* the ragged edge of the weapon's 'aim-able' envelope (which, of course, it's *not*, if you've actually paid attention to what the instructor has been saying all this time), right about where all my mental trajectories blur and fall short. And there's only one other blast crater anywhere near it, which implies that either no one else has ever *tried* for this target before, or if they have, no one has ever *achieved* it.

So I quickly change my entire estimation process. And while settling the stock into my shoulder and pretending to tighten down my sighting, I secretly attempt to 'reverse engineer' the process... in five seconds or less.

The M-79's max range is rated at 400 meters, or 430-something yards, achievable only by pointing it upward at a 45-degree angle. And this distance is roughly a third of that, max. Which means... what? Add or subtract two-thirds of that up-angle to compensate? I don't know.

Shit. That didn't help at all.

Back to the invisible parabola method again, I guess. *Quickly!*

It's true that the target-end of that mental arc is now too indistinct to be *certain*, but, much like the spread of a sprinkler's stream, I just try to put that lonely sapling within that general sweep area, and stop over-thinking the damned problem *right there*.

I eyeball the left-to-right, and pull the trigger.

Bop!

It's high! It's fast! It's outa' there! A little drift to the left, maybe—which is a good thing, since my half-assed aiming launched it a tad right of center to begin with. But it's going... and going... and going... and now dropping... and dropping... and dropping and dropping and dropping and accelerating straight down onto that poor doomed tree.

Dang! It's actually trying to hit it! It's really reaching!

"Damn," another voice from the peanut gallery mutters.

Then... *wh-boomp!*

My little missile, barely a streaked shadow against the sky in its last second, punches into the hillside probably fifteen or twenty *feet* above that tree—a pretty minor overshoot, all things considered—and it thumps another fan of dirt and smoke into the air. This, in turn, calves off a narrow wedge of the hillside just above the ledge, which then tumbles down around the base of the tree in a miniature avalanche.

I may not have *hit* the 'lead truck' in that Chinese convoy, but I half-buried it, and damn-sure blocked the road in front of it!

Someone *whoops* behind me, and a brief burst of applause smothers it.

Wow! Is this what redemption sounds like?

Another round from the instructor—my fourth, and thereby my last—and another target, this one back at a more reasonable distance.

Bop! Hang-time. *Ooo*'s and *aaah*'s rising in volume behind me as its flight path unfurls. Then... *whump!*

Another geyser of dirty smoke, another bullseye.

And the crowd goes wild!

Another round from the instructor—*another one?*—and another target, this one only the splintered top of a small shredded tree that's sticking up from behind a gouged berm. I can't see the actual point of impact from here though, just that ravaged stalk standing there like the pin on a concealed putting green.

I feel it out, coerce my intuitive arc up over the crest of that berm, then *bop!* Another one's in the air!

And again, *boomp!*

A black-fringed spray of soil erupts from behind that ridge, and that pathetic corpse of a tree cartwheels through the flying clods, and disappears.

"*Yeh, baby!,*" I hear Rocky shout.

Another round, my *sixth*—*man, what's this guy doing?*—and a new target. And *bop!*

Silence.

Then, in concert with its final plunge, another rising anticipatory yell swells from the peanut gallery. Another *boomf!* Another shower of dirt, this one just a hair right of a pure bullseye—my closest thing to a total miss so far!—and an almost *choral* "*Ooooo!*" from the gang behind me. And the instructor hands me a *seventh* round! *Wow!*

Thoop!

Arc, plummet, *whomp!*

"*Fuckin'-A damn, boy!*" Greg this time.

An *eighth* round, double the normal allotment per student. *Dang!*

The target this time though, is probably only twenty-five or thirty yards away, straight across this battered little gully against its vertical facing. Basically firing into a wall. But before I can start my usual 'feeling it out' ritual, the instructor waves for me to hold up, and says, "Let's try a *level* trajectory this time, shall we? We already know you can do a *high* one."

"Okay."

For this, I notch the stock into my shoulder again, and sight through the little flip-up reticule. But I find that the 'invisible rail' my previous shots had all ridden has once again turned broad, diffuse, and uncertain in my mind's eye. So, no clear indications or suggestions from my usual senses this time. No easy math, nothing I can do with my embarrassing ignorance of how to use the sight. Apparently I'm going to do as badly as everyone else this time.

So how did *they* shoot when they tried *their* low-trajectory shots? Or perhaps more importantly, how did they *miss?*

Well, almost to the last man, they all *overshot*. They aimed high, even if only slightly, probably in anticipation of the grenade's rapidly decaying flight arc, and wound up taking out a chunk of the hillside *beyond* the target. So apparently this thing's got more muzzle velocity than its high-looping mortar-like trajectories would suggest. It just *looks* slower than it really is, relatively speaking.

Guess I'll go with that, then.

I line it up with what feels like a decent ballpark angle, a reasonable if indefinite loft, then I toss that out, and lower it a few more degrees—almost to the same level that I'd have lowered a regular old GAU-5—and squeeze off the shot before I once again over-think it.

The M-79 kicks back against my shoulder, and the round spears straight into the bulwark of dirt across the way. Another belch of flying dirt and another miniature avalanche unleashed to tumble into the gully. And this time, the gang's clapping and whistling. *Wow!*

Who'da thunk I had that one in me? Does this mean I'm out of the doghouse now? Probably not.

"Okay, hotshot. That's enough," growls the instructor with a reluctant smirk. "Give somebody else a chance."

As if it was *my* choice to keep on shooting.

He takes the smoking launcher from my hands, and waves Goebler up, the last one of the group. I pass him on the path going the other way.

"Now how the hell am I supposed to top *that?*," he chuckles.

"Just don't ask me to *throw* it," I snigger back.

Goebler has a more 'standard' success rate with the M-79—which is to say, a lot of fun high-flying carnage, but little hit that he actually *aims* at—and the day finally draws to an end with his fourth shot.

We plod back to the crappy OD-green 'school bus' that brought us out here, and ride back in jostled silence to the mud and sagging structures of fabulous Fort Polk.

* * *

ONLY ONCE WE'VE DEBARKED at the curb of our Guest Shithouse, and have monkey-climbed our way back up the rotting shards of the 'unzipped' staircase that leads up to our cobwebbed 'loft,' does someone finally address me personally. And it's Rocky.

"Where'd you learn to shoot like that, man?"

You mean, where'd I take my secret lessons?

Guess I'm feeling a little cocky now.

"Fort Polk, Louisiana," I reply... stupidly.

I can barely hear it over all the clomping boots on creaking boards, but someone distinctly mutters, "*Asshole*" under his breath.

Good old Sgt. Haley. I bet he just loved witnessing my rise back up out of the dust this afternoon.

Well, if the old adage is true about it "*taking one to know one*," then I guess he's right.

I must be one absolutely *huge* unbelievable asshole, alright.

STORY XXV

OVER THE HUMP

1
THE DREADED "BIG ONE"

December, 1977
Back at Little Rock AFB, Little Rock, Arkansas

I CAN STILL REMEMBER dreading that killer one-and-a-half-mile graduation run back in Basic Training (not to mention how I barely survived it at the time). And I can oh-so-vividly recall my torturous rise up through the pre-Phase-I miles at Keesler AFB—three miles, four miles, and then five miles per run—seizing and cramping and wheezing and gasping and driving myself through a realm of pain from which I could not emerge until each run was over.

It *always* sucked. And I *never* got good at it.

All I ever really mastered—and only *just barely* at that—was the sheer mental perseverance to just keep on running *despite* the debilitating agonies and breathlessness. And that kind of sustained self-torture is never fun. I've always hated it, and I hate it still.

So, I'm really hating today.

I've hated today since before I even left McChord to come down here. I've feared it since the day that Randy Pogue returned from this school, crowned with his brand new beret... right from the instant that he dumped the contents of his duffel bag on his bed, and said, "Man, you wouldn't believe the mother-bitch of a qualifyin' run you gotta' do down there."

For today is that much-anticipated—perhaps I should say, "much *apprehended"*—ten-mile mountain qualifying run.

The dreaded 'Big One.'

Not just double the length of the longest run I've ever done in my life. Not just running in boots and uniform (*sans* cap and blouse), in step and in formation, but off-base, on a public road (in front of—and inconveniencing—*that very public*), chugging up and down the steeply rolling foothills of the Ozark Mountains.

The ones known locally as the Ouachitas... or "*What cheetahs?!*"

And as always, it's *finish with the group, or you're finished with the program*. Period.

No ifs, ands, or buts.

Son of a bitch.

After all the hurdles that I just barely managed to clear in order to get this far—sometimes grazing the obstacles so closely that I got my nuts thumped—I'm probably going to wind up throwing it all away right here. Today. And putting it technically, *that will suck.*

Then again, maybe not.

Rumor has it that two more guys—Torrero and Corbin—were supposed to have been washed out yesterday when they failed the final written test, but were *not* because their scores were apparently borderline (just a point or two under seventy). But most importantly, as the scuttlebutt implies, because they're the only two students from the Little Rock Combat Control *Team*, based right here in the same building as our classrooms. And heaving a couple of 'home boys' out on their asses, on their *home turf*, might be just a little too awkward.

Or something. *Who knows.*

I have no idea how much, if any, of the rumor is true. It seems pretty unlikely and uncharacteristically lenient of the instructor cadre. But both guys are still with us in the back of this truck as we rumble out the gate beneath brisk but sunny skies. And as much as I'd resent that kind of favoritism if it proved to be true, the fact is that right about now, I'm actually kinda' counting on a little uncharacteristic leniency myself.

Because this surely ain't gonna' be pretty.

The deuce-and-a-half pulls over onto the shoulder of an unremarkable stretch of backroad asphalt, a lightly travelled two-lane ribbon that looks like it rolls about half a mile downhill-ish before abruptly snapping left and beginning a series of right and left switchbacks up the near side of that first ridgeline up ahead. And I am instantly depressed... to the point of being near-nauseous with dread.

I am grim. I feel like I'm humping an extra thirty pounds on my back already—thirty pounds of pure oozing brown foreboding—weighing me down as they form us up into our exercise ranks, and start running us through some warm-ups.

Cars rush past—one even honks—while two of the instructors hang a bright yellow banner across the truck's tailgate that says, "*Slow—Runners Ahead.*"

Boy, could that *ever be taken in more ways than one.*

Then, before I know it—long before I'm *ready* for it, in fact—it's time. No warning, no cool-down, no ceremony. They just pull the deuce-and-a-half back onto the road with its flashers going. They assemble the students in front of the truck in three rows of three, plus a front-right point man (*thank God it's not Rocky*), surrounded by three of the instructors (who, amazingly enough, will be running the whole way with us), and call us to attention.

Then it's, "Forward! March!," for about four whole steps, followed by "Double-time, *HUH!*"

And we're off to the races.

* * *

I AM ON THE right end of the second (or middle) rank of runners. Good ol' Sgt. Haley is right smack dab in the middle of the whole pack, to my immediate left.

Oh joy of joys.

I manage to contain my usual chuffings and wheezings for the first half mile or so, sworn to a private blood oath with myself that I will, *at all costs*, keep my breathing locked on to a steady boot-synched rhythm. But as soon as we reach the first switchback and the road starts to climb, any semblance of discipline instantly dissolves.

Screw the oath!

Within seconds of the steepening of the grade, everyone's cadence disintegrates. Not just mine. *Thank gawd*, not just mine.

The rhythmic showcase clomping crumbles into a chaotic drumbeat of disorderly bootfalls. Everyone's breathing succumbs to the same gasping and grunting and hissing profanity, and the proud pace bogs down to a furious slog. Even first gear isn't slow enough to keep the deuce-and-a-half moving behind us, and the truck finally has to stop just to let us flail away at the hill for a minute or two ahead of it, and get a little distance between us again.

And oh lordy, is this a misery-and-a-half.

They ran us over a few small hills every now and then during the last five weeks on base, but they were *nothing* compared to this. Those were *anthills* compared to these *hangars*, *golf carts* compared to these *747s!* These hills are steep *and* tall (relatively speaking, anyway... I'm sure they're barely detectable when you're riding in a car).

It takes all the sheer grit and teeth-grinding perseverance I've got in my entire convulsing body just to keep gamely chugging along toward that little hairpin turn that I can see up ahead... only to finally get there, stagger around the turn, and discover that it's only one more switchback in an ever-climbing series of the bastards. Which means that I—*we*—get to start the next upward grade already helplessly winded and rubber-legged.

Everyone but little Rocky, of course. He's going crazy up there in the *left*-front position, practically trotting in place, just to stay with our melting formation.

The instructors keep shouting at us to shore up our ranks and get back in step. But that too is a cause so lost, I doubt anyone is even listening. Besides, the extent to which the *instructors* are gasping tells me that surely even they know how ludicrous a command that is. They may not be *dying* like the rest of us are, but they *do* still have to work at it.

So we dig, and we drive, and we thrust with all we've got, shoving the road downhill under our boots. I'm whimpering—*aloud*—by the time I sense the gradient easing, and I look up, for the first time, to see *sunlight* filtering through the trees ahead instead of just more trees and more mountainside.

Oh, thank the heavens! The summit of Mount Everest at last!

I shovel everything I've got into the furnace now; all my energy, all my heart, my soul... my firstborn child, for that matter. *Especially* my firstborn child. *Everything!*

Can't... drop... out... now! Must... keep... going...!

And at long last, I thrash my way around the turn at the crest of the ridge, and follow it to its descent down the other side.

OhGodOhGodOhGodOhGod! Son of a...!

The driver of the deuce-and-a-half taps his horn once... *once.*

We've apparently just completed our first mile. Our *first* one.

The first of *ten.*

Worse still, I make the mistake of lifting my dripping head and looking out over the trees along the downhill side of the road... where I can see the floor of the next valley a couple hundred feet below, and the next ridgeline rising steeply out of that. It's so close, I could throw a rock across the fold in the terrain and into the treetops on the opposite side... if I had a rock... or an arm... or the will to live.

And we'll be churning up that bitch as soon as we get to the bottom of this one.

Gentlemen, let us please PLEASE take our time limping down this hill. I need every second of recoop time I can get my hands on.

Fortunately, we all seem to be of like mind on this one issue. Our disheveled loping tightens up into a semblance of military rhythm again, and in no time, all that's left of our previous distress is the snorting and huffing of a herd of stampeded cattle. Everyone's breathing still needs to be reined in, to be sure, but aside from that, anyone driving past us in a car would no doubt be amazed by the uniformity of our stride, not to mention the relatively composed facial expressions of the thirteen men trotting through these mountains.

Like it t'weren't nothin' a'tall.

Oh, great googly-moogly.

The downhill feels great, though. I don't even have to lift my feet. My throbbing hamstrings and Achilles' tendons quiet down, my heart stops battering the inside of my ribcage, and my panting once more wheezes down to an even, plodding, boot-driven rhythm. And by the time the road bends to the right at the bottom of all those switchbacks, I'm even breathing through my nose again. Then we break out of the trees into that narrow little sun-filled defile, and the incline of the next ridgeline rears up before me.

And I almost swallow my tongue.

It looks so much higher and steeper from down here!

No! Please don't make me do that again! Please!

But they do. And so *I* do. And here we go again.

Of course, this one is so much worse than the last. It *had* to be. Not only do my weary leg muscles and panicky lungs rebel at this renewed assault, but the dispiriting psychological precedent of that last mountain just drains away all my energy and will before I even reach the first switchback.

Then the truck's horn hoots again... *twice.*

"That's two miles, gentlemen!," shouts Sgt. Rabin. "Almost done!"

Aw, Christ!

What the hell am I doing here again? What possible logic could there be for willingly putting myself through this shit?

Because I *said* I would, that's why.

I could drop out of this pack right here and now and put an end to this torment if I wanted to. *Today. Right this moment!* And then I could spend the rest of my life wondering what difference just a little more effort might have made. As Sgt. Beaudry once said, *"You can quit any time."* We already know what lies along that path, though. What I'm trying to find out now is what might lie along *this* route... what the world—and my *life*—might be like if I somehow manage to pull this one off.

Well, I've already made a career out of pushing myself through the pain and sweat and winded desperation every time I run. Let's just push it a little further than normal this time, shall we.

And I make a new pact with myself: if I am physically capable of planting one foot in front of the other, then I just quite simply *WILL.* Period. Lungs or no lungs, cramps or no cramps... torn ligaments, buckled knees, hopelessly out-of-control breathing, *whatever.* If my legs *can* move, I'm just going to *move them.* And that's all there is to it.

I think.

In the meantime, the infinite climb continues on and on, up and up, higher and further, and worst of all, *steeper. I swear!*

Our 'formation' is all over the place again, as is our obliterated rhythm. Everyone is grunting, growling, cursing. Everything in me is howling for me to stop... everything but that last stalwart alliance of brain and legs, that is. They're committed to their pact, even if it means running in a coma.

Weaving, whimpering, gasping like an asthmatic for whatever air I can catch—head bobbing, leaning so far into the uphill grade that my hands almost touch the ground—my mind just blacks out the rest of the world, and focuses every last erg of mental energy on the singleminded mantra of, "left, right, *left, right, lllefffft, rrrriight, llllllefffffft....!*"

And step by laborious step, the crest of the ridge finally hoves into view... which adds a slightly hysterical 'giggle' to my already desperate heaving and sniveling. And this, in turn, provides just enough of an inspiration to keep on fighting just that little bit longer, until somehow, despite all odds, I manage to flog my way over the top with the rest of these struggling cripples.

I can't believe it! I did it again! And somehow, I'm still here!

I may be sweating blood, wobbling atop flaccid legs, and dribbling benumbed body parts down the length of this god-forsaken highway to hell, but I'm in good company, and somehow holding my own alongside the comparably devastated Sgt. Haley and party. And that's worth a lot all by itself (*although, a lot of 'what,' I'm not sure*).

Again though, through the skeletal winter trees beside the road, I catch sight of the next ridge down the line... again. And I have to close my eyes.

I can't do another one of those. I just can't!

But apparently I'm gonna'.

Then the cramp hits (I was wondering what it was waiting for).

It just sorta' *twangs*.

One second I'm gulping in frantic chestfuls of air, the next, something under my right shoulder blade just seizes, and torques my entire body over to the right. Just like that. Like a tire iron driven between my two lowest ribs and levered upward, I spears into the back of my lungs and punches the air right out of them. I grunt—*loudly*—and stagger down the shoulder of the road, unable to even *hiccup* a little air back into my chest.

Oh, now this is what I need. Especially with another mountain looming in my immediate future.

Whatever! Breath or no breath, just keep putting one foot in front of the other. Just... don't... stop!

Shit on a stick.

I suck in one deep painful swig of air, and hold it, letting *that* hold the cramp at bay while I weave back onto the asphalt, and resume my hard-earned place in the formation (such as it is).

Never stop running. Just don't ever stop running... EVER!

And slowly but surely, as the downhill mile shuffles limply past, my throbbing leg muscles unknot, my liquefying glutes revive and firm up, my rampant breathing settles into an exhausted but stable rhythm again, and nearing the bottom of the grade, that damned cramp finally fades from my awareness.

I take some momentary heart, then, from the stabilization of all my red-lined bodily functions.

Whew! I'm still here! I'm still hangin' with the big dogs. I might be hanging by my fingernails, but the fact is I'M STILL HANGIN'!

What a MAN!

What a friggin' IDIOT!

The truck honks its horn again—three miles and counting—and I draw another cool recharging draught of Ozark Mountain air, in preparation for the next ridge assault.

We tromp across a tiny bridge that crosses an even tinier babbling brook. We clomp through a shadow-dappled vale, past a sun-drenched field of deep grass, then back into the tree-shrouded tunnel of the next big climb. All very scenic, and all of it moot. Of no help to me whatsoever.

I lean into this new slope. I focus, and visualize my lungs finding all the air they need, sustaining that all-important (and regularly lost) rhythm as my legs once again dig in and *drive*. I tell myself that the worst is now behind me, that compared to those last two battlements in our wake, this hill—and whatever others might lie beyond it—is as *nothing*. And I've just about got myself convinced.

Then that fucking cramp rams home again. And this time, it stays.

The slog up this third mountain—which turns out to be the last and the least of the obstacles along this miserable run—is a blurred repeat of the previous two, only with the added bonus of that damned cramp clenching at the meat above my right kidney. It feels like I'm towing a friggin' *skier* from a hook embedded in my lower ribs!

Funny thing about a 'blur,' though… it blurs *everything*. It blurs your *brains*. It blurs your memory. It even blurs *time*, enough to lose track of it anyway. It blurs everything *but* the pain and exhaustion, unfortunately, although even those eventually blur into a continuous dull roar of life-sapping misery all their own.

Here on this hillside, even the goddamned *pull of gravity* seems to have tripled. So, when I say I've finally 'settled into' this run, it's not because the suffering has lessened even one iota. It's just spread out and saturated *everything* now, to the extent that *nothing* stands out any more.

* * *

IT'S NOT THAT THE run's agonies have become more endurable. Not at all. They've just become... *everything*. They are *all there is*. And so I lose myself in it all. When every sensory organ is screaming at you, the din becomes almost self-canceling. Unintelligible, indecipherable... unremarkable. You just ride the shrieking wave. Your thoughts retreat to a single focused objective; a *resolution*, if you will. Your vision narrows, and everything else just sort of radiates away in a cacophony of anguish. Or something like that.

It sounds ridiculously overblown when I try to put it into words—and 'putting it into words' is the last thing on my mind right now—but there it is.

And here I am.

A few seconds later—or a lifetime, or an eternity, I can no longer tell—I hobble over this third hilltop, cramped, twisted, limping, completely breathless and keeping up only because no one else can go any faster.

Except for Rocky, of course, the miserable little bastard. He's jogging *backwards* for a spell, just to give his knees a break, I guess.

But this time, even the downhill can't save me. Oh yes, my hamstrings unbind, and my breathing flutters back to a steadier more strident heaving, but the cramp never lets go. And because it has a death-grip on my right lung, I can only calm my gasping so far and then I'm stuck, grunting around that damned jiggling harpoon that's wedged between my ribs again.

The hills are finally petering out, though. *Thank God!*

Yes, the land now flattens into a deeply forested 'plain' of low rolling hummocks, and I settle into my agonies as if they are the new standard of my life, forever and ever, amen. I will never know peace or painlessness again.

* * *

MILE FOUR LABORS PAST.

Then mile five. And that cramp's still there, still clamped to the back of my lungs like a fist, cutting every breath short, and spiking every inhalation with a sharp knife-point of pain.

Mile six. Nothing new, nothing changed. Nothing detected beyond my own raw, seething, desperate little sphere of distress, nothing that I'm even capable of thinking about other than *not stopping*. And, at absolutely all costs, *keeping up with the others!* Period. *Nothing else.*

The universe outside that sphere is simply *gone*.

Mile seven. Seven little raps on the truck's horn steadily unfogs my brain. I look around almost as if I don't know where I am. I *don't*. But this is the first time in quite a while that I've been coherent enough to even realize it. And that momentary coherence reveals something else as well… that my cramp has finally started to recede. After nearly *four miles* of its incessancy, it now feels more like an old bruise, rather than a drag-line hooked through the back of my ribs. It still stabs at me whenever I try to draw a deep breath, but at least I *can* draw a deep breath again.

Hallelujah!

I start nursing my breathing back down from its point of coiled retreat, actually *holding* my breath for short periods, trying to force it back into some kind of salvageable cadence again. And when the horn next honks eight times, I've once more got some regularity to my breathing.

The last two miles toil past in a blur all their own, although this time the blur is less a result of all-encompassing pain so much as just simple exhausted numbness. I've lost track of everything—well, all but the mental and spiritual *imperative* of *never dropping out of the formation*, anyway—and somehow lived long enough to witness the end of eternity.

At least that's how it feels when we round the last tree-shrouded corner, and we spot the Jeep parked off the side of the road at the far end of the straightaway.

Somebody whoops, and Sgt. Rabin shouts, "Looky there, boys! It's the ten-mile Jeep!"

And on that cue, as if released from bondage, Rocky splits off from the left side of the pack, and rockets off at a sprint—something he's probably been itching to do for about the last two-hundred miles or so—running right down the broken white line in the middle of the highway.

Goebler, then Sal, then Greg, all lunge to chase him down, which in turn spurs everyone else to accelerate up to a half-assed final sprint of their own. But all it really does is disintegrate the formation into a thinly strung-out stampede, most of which is still clotted around Sgt. Haley… and of course, me.

I put my head down, and hurl the last speck of my energy into my molten legs, eking an extra hiccup or two of speed from them before the easy downhill grade flattens out, and I plod to a stop beside the Jeep.

Oh my God! I made it!
Ten miles! Through the mountains! In boots, and in formation!

It surely wasn't pretty (as I knew it wouldn't be). But, as improbable as it may have seemed, *I friggin' made it!*

I honestly never believed I would. Truly.

But danged if I didn't!

Everyone else in the damned class did it too, of course, but for no one else was the outcome so much in doubt as it was for me. And judging by some of the odd furtive glances I'm getting from the instructors right now, I really don't think they saw this coming either. I just wish I knew whether they'd been *expecting* or *hoping* that I wouldn't make it.

Oh, well. At least I made it to Field Week, whether they like it or not.

Hoo-HOO!

Ew.

Damn.

Wait a minute.

I made it to Field Week.

What the hell was I thinking?

2

WEEK SIX: THE 'EASY PART'

WOW. ALL WEEKEND LONG I've been pinching myself, replaying the improbable skin-of-my-teeth 'victories' that have gotten me this far through all these challenges, personal shortcomings, obstacles, and even *barriers*, assessing and *re*-assessing my accomplishments of the last five weeks, and contemplating this evolution in my life. And I gotta' tell ya', regardless of what anyone else thinks, *I'm a-friggin'-mazed!*

I mean, despite the furious pace, the complexity, the wide variety of subjects, and the sheer inundation of facts, figures, minutia, and trivia—and despite the fact that I am, historically, a *terrible* test-taker—I managed to pass every one of those weekly written exams. A couple of others did not.

Despite some embarrassing setbacks, I actually accomplished every one of the *physical* feats they set before us as well, from rappelling down the face of a six-story building, to firing an M-79 grenade launcher *with accuracy*. And again, some did not.

And despite the desperate and often panicky measures I regularly had to take, I somehow completed every sit-up, push-up and jumping jack that they threw at me. More miraculous still, *I even finished every goddamned run*, including that mother of all max-stamina marathons, the ten-mile formation run through the mountains!

Sumbitch! Who'da thunk it?!

Not me. That's for sure.

In fact, as I consciously noticed for the first time only this morning, *all four* of us 'Boys from McChord' are still here: Sal, Greg, Rocky *and* me. No other team can make that claim. And with only ten students left in the entire class after the winnowing of the previous weeks, that means that nearly *half* of the survivors are from McChord, the rest representing all six of the other stateside CCT bases.

Of all the things I did or didn't accomplish over the past month, the most satisfying right now is that I didn't let my team down. The McChord Team is still intact and looking good here... despite me being part of it.

So now, according to the school's grand vision, having plowed through every obstacle, hurdled every hurdle, and slain every dragon that's risen in our paths, the ten of us have now all proven our mettle sufficiently to qualify for this final phase, 'Field Week,' where we'll be puttin' all that trainin' and sprainin' to good use.

No more tests. No more pushing of envelopes. No more fighting for survival. Now it's just time to *do it*.

* * *

SO I CAME TO the hangar this morning, loaded rucksack slung over one shoulder, ready to turn all this theory into reality. Then...

The first bad news came with the list they gave us last Friday, the one that inventoried all the crap we were going to have to cram into our rucksacks for this first jump into the field. Because we had to ensure that we had everything necessary to last *ten days* in the frozen winter woods of northern Arkansas. And, my undeveloped packing skills aside, I didn't even leave *McChord* with half the stuff I needed to pack.

I've only got two sets of camouflaged fatigues (or 'BDUs,' as they're officially called, for 'Battle-Dress Uniforms'). I've still only got one ammo pouch, *no* first aid kit, and my jungle boots are so new, they hurt my feet to wear them... so I *haven't* been.

But now I'm going to have to.

The instructors though, aware of the somewhat rushed and 'severe-rookie' last-second status of my enrollment here, were able to accommodate some of these shortages. They managed to rustle up another ammo pouch (no doubt procured from the Little Rock Team's supply lockers), along with two tent-halves and an air mattress. But the rest of my deficiencies I'm just going to have to live with.

The second bad news came when they handed out the parachutes this morning. Because it turns out that we *are* going to be jumping with the very chutes that we ourselves packed back during the parachute-packing block of the course. *Yep (*sigh*)... the same ones.* The four chutes that each of us learned on, plus the *fifth* chute that each of us time-tested on, including the reserves, had all been meticulously stored away in piles labeled with each student's name. And now they're coming back to haunt us.

I gotta' tell ya', it did my morale no good whatsoever to look into that storeroom this morning, and see that Steve-packed pile of parachutes sitting over against that wall, knowing that every one I'll be *using* over the next ten days will be coming from that pile. Because even if nobody else does, *I* know how clueless I was when I was packing those things. And I'll be damned if *I* want to jump with any of them.

But that's just exactly what I'm going to have to do. Starting today.

And the third piece of wonderful news came when Sgt. Haley was called to the front of the classroom to brief the first 'frag'—'Fragmentary Order'—of Field Week. *His* frag.

Shit.

They'd handed it to him sometime yesterday, I guess—Sunday—and he'd spent the rest of that day and most of last night working it up for this presentation today. And apparently, my continued presence in '*his*' CCS class still irks him a tad.

Our first 'mission' then (our opening 'scenario')—that he, as the class's official Senior Ranking Student, will be 'commanding'—will be to jump into 'enemy territory,' and set up a daylight EZ/LZ right there on our landing field.

In terms of their configurations, EZs and LZs—Extraction Zones and Landing Zones respectively—are virtually identical, differing only in how they are *used*. Both are set up as field-expedient landing strips, or improvised runways,' and in the case of an LZ, that's just how it's used:

aircraft land on it and take-off from it, just like a *prepared* airfield.

In the case of an *EZ,* however, the aircraft itself never lands; just its palletized *load*, which gets yanked ('extracted') out the back end by a huge drogue chute that booms open as the aircraft is floating along only a couple of feet off the deck. The pallet drops those few feet to the ground all by itself, then bounces, skids, and slides to a stop, while the aircraft flies off to other points unknown.

I can't wait to see *that* little spectacle play out in front of me.

But what makes it such a joy to contemplate is that Sgt. Haley has chosen, completely arbitrarily I'm sure, to not only have *me* carry the second 'prick' (radio) on my back, but he also assigned me as one of the guys who gets to run the markers out to the far corners of the usable field as well.

No matter how well or badly anything else goes, running across all that acreage with the equivalent of a loaded tool chest bouncing on my back, is not going to be pleasant. But then, neither is Sgt. Haley.

At least I'll have some torturously new jungle boots in which to do all that running.

Oh well. Let the games begin.

* * *

HERE'S SOMETHING NEW FOR me... jumping with a weapon (other than my knife). I've never done that before, not at Jump School, nor even with my team. My six total jumps-to-date have all been so-called 'Hollywood jumps.' Just me and a parachute or two going out the door. Nothing else.

Now I'm going out *armed*. For *war*.

And that's not all. I've never jumped with my web gear on before either. That's the belt-and-suspenders rig that carries all my ammo, my compass, my flashlight, my canteens, and other trinkety crap like that. Neither have I jumped with my gas mask, for that matter. And I've certainly never tried to take a loaded rucksack out the door with me either.

And since you can't carry *any* of those things in your *hands*, it all has to be *attached* to your rigging somehow and some*where*, which is an interesting little exercise in creativity all by itself.

The gas mask, in its holster, is worn like normal, strapped to your thigh like a six-shooter. The web gear too is worn normally, and then further secured to your body once your main and reserve chutes have been donned over the top of it. The rucksack, however, is tied to a twenty-foot coil of rope, then hooked to your parachute harness beneath your reserve chute—dangling against the front of your legs like a plump, heavy apron—with a wooden-knobbed pin release (called a 'Red Apple,' because of its shape, size, and color) holding it in place. This also comes with an ankle strap to keep the ruck from flying up into your face when you hit the slipstream.

And finally, the GAU-5 assault rifle. This is slung over one shoulder, muzzle down, with the barrel tied off to your leg with a shoestring.

The chutes go on last, of course, thereby trapping everything else against your body. And the whole kit and kaboodle is capped off with a pair of foam ear plugs and a jump helmet. *Tah-daaah!*

Jiminy Crickets! I look like a heap of luggage lumbering around the staging area.

They review the advanced jump sequence without actually practicing it. After all, everybody's already racked up a hundred or more combat-load jumps before they even came here, right?

Right?

Yep. Everybody but me, of course.

But it doesn't look too tough. Once you've completed the standard jump-clear-and-steer routine and are established under a healthy canopy tracking toward your IP, the only additional steps are (1) releasing that ankle strap, and (2) pulling on that old Red Apple, which drops your rucksack to the end of its twenty-foot tether.

And that's it. Everything else is the same.

I think I can handle that.

Sgt. Rabin claps his hands, and calls for this little tea party to adjourn to the aircraft waiting outside.

And with a comradely wink from my McChord Team buddy, good ol' Greg Dorn—along with a venomous scowl from my ever-lovin' class leader, Sgt. Brad Haley (who I can tell is just *galled* that I am still here, when so many clearly superior candidates have been washed out)—I unhook my rucksack from its harness rig, pitch it over my shoulder again, and join the procession waddling out the door.

Fuck Haley!

I damned well earned the right to be this miserable, scared, and skeptical of my own sanity.

STORY XXVI

INTO THE FIELD

1
OH YEH, THIS IS THE LIFE

December, 1977
In the field outside Little Rock AFB, Little Rock, Arkansas

OH, THE JUMP WAS painless enough.

Sure, there was the usual queasiness-threatening-to-become-vomitus thing again, percolating under my diaphragm like the tar pits of La Brea—my personal trademark these days whenever there's a military aircraft involved—but the flight to the drop zone was so ridiculously short, it never had the chance to evolve from mere 'bubblin' crude' to a full-blown 'gusher'… if you know what I mean.

And of course, you do.

Hell, it seemed like the C-130's wheels were barely in their wells when the red jump lights winked on, and the loadmaster was shouting, "*Two! Minutes!*" Then it was all, "*Stand up!*," and "*Hook up!*," and the port side jump door being heaved open. Sgt. Haley was then ushered into the bellowing vortex and parked in his official spot, so that Sgt. Rabin might pass on a few last-minute pointers on how to be a good jumpmaster, all before the lights went green.

Then the lights went green.

And while Haley stood there beside that doorway, leaning into the battering wind, hanging on to his static line with one hand while his other hand slapped each of us on the back as we passed, we'd chugged through the portal and into the howling skies of Arkansas like ten little Indians (or maybe ten little *lemmings*).

The air was bright, crisp, and cool, the handful of clouds were fluffy, friendly, and unobtrusive (mostly because they were higher than we were), and everything worked as advertised on the parachute I had personally packed almost five weeks ago. *Whew!* The DZ was huge—probably close to a mile long, and maybe a little over a quarter wide—a man-made clearing with long straight-cut edges on two sides holding back the dense forests, and a ten-foot-wide circle of pea gravel in the middle, designating our official Point of Impact, or 'PI'. The bullseye of the DZ.

That, in turn, was framed on one side by a quartet of idling vehicles: a communications Jeep (a 'Mark'), a capped pick-up truck (a 'six-pack'), a deuce-and-a-half (a 'deuce'), and an ambulance (or 'meat wagon') loitering at the end of the line like a big orange-and-white vulture.

I never like to contemplate the implications of a waiting ambulance.

But as I said, everything went great.

With only ten jumpers, the skies weren't exactly crowded. And once my combat load had jerked to a stop at the end of its tether, the only thing I'd had to concern myself with was trying to land as close to the PI as possible... not for purposes of showing off or anything like that, but simply to keep from being the last one to the Rally Point, or 'RP.'

A hundred push-ups is a lot worse than it sounds.

My touchdown was on-target, although a little jarring. But I wasted no time creaking my way back up to speed again. Too many other guys around me were madly scrambling to get their chutes stowed away and slung into the back of the deuce for me to do much dawdling.

And it paid off too. I was the fourth guy to the RP, and Goebler wound up doing all the push-ups while the rest of us watched.

Haley was quick to dispatch Hackett and I (his two least favorite subordinates) to our far-end-of-the-field duties, Hackett fussing and bitching the whole way (like always), and me with that damned prick jouncing against my shoulders like a lead cape (*and* cussing up a storm... only far less conspicuously).

But I really couldn't complain. As much as I hated the burdened run (as well as the spiteful intentions behind the order), I appreciated *not* having to hang around to witness Haley's 'leadership style' in action, flinging orders around like an unmanned fire hose. I'll take weariness and breathlessness and *silence* over that any day.

The only real 'down-side' was that I didn't learn anything from the process. I could look back there and see the core half-dozen or so of Haley and his favored minions commiserating with the instructors and acting all industrious… fingers pointing in every direction but *down*, heads occasionally coming together to recalculate their facts and figures, and every now and then, an enthusiastic dash by someone running an errand for him.

Dang. It's a shame I missed all that.

Eventually, the same aircraft that dropped us all off made a soul-stirring low approach over the field, the official sanctification of Sgt. Haley's LZ, I presume. And shortly after that, the five-ton radio on my back crackled with an impatient grunt from His Highness announcing that the scenario was over, and for Hackett and myself to pack it up and run back to the PI, where he and everyone else was forming up to begin the next lesson: the 'Team Overland Deployment."

And that's what we've been doing ever since… the 'TOD.'

* * *

TROMPING ALONG NARROW BACKWOOD dirt roads, in a long roundabout hike to the campsite that will be our home for the next ten days (which is actually only a few feet inside the DZ's bordering tree line back there), they've been hammering us with counter-ambush techniques. Switching us out between different positions in the column's marching order, getting us familiarized with the responsibilities of each position, and getting us used to scanning our assigned quadrants with a downright feral intensity. That's what we've been doing ever since we trooped off the DZ and into the woods.

Every now and then, one or a couple of the instructors will abruptly wheel on us, scream, "*Ambush!*," and start spraying us with blanks. And we get to practice diving off our respective sides of the road, and assuming our defensive positions among the dirt and leaves of the ditches there.

But the principles are not difficult to understand, and the attacks help break up the tedium of the long walk.

It's all easy common sense stuff. No real surprises or mysteries here. No, the problem for *me* is just that I can't seem to keep my mind on any of the tasks at hand. I'm just too busy dealing with all the parts of my body that are *hurting* right now.

For starters, I'm still toting this goddamned prick around!

As soon as the EZ/LZ scenario had ended, Sgt. Haley had handed off *his* radio to Sgt. Donado for this overland deployment dealy. But nobody came up to *me*—student, instructor, or otherwise—to relieve me of *my* burden. And since I couldn't think of an appropriate or professional way to bring the subject up myself, well... *guess what! That's right!* I get to carry it along for this second stretch of the program as well.

Unfortunately, its straps lay over the exact same parts of my shoulders as those of my rucksack, so the combined weight of both heavy items is starting to seriously dig into the meat over both collar bones.

That's not the worst of it, though.

With the radio resting on *top* of my ruck, it's been pushing the ruck down, not only contributing that much more dead weight to my shoulders, but forcing the pack's lower lumbar support even lower along my waist—below my belt line, in fact—to where it's started shoving the waist strap of my gas mask holster lower and lower on my hips.

Now, *that* wouldn't be so bad, except for the thinness of that canvas strap which the rucksack's pressure has been forcibly rolling into an even thinner 'cord' of tension, which *in turn* cuts across the tops of my butt cheeks like a strand of wire. Sort of a steadily tightening 'garrote' for my ass. Sharp and annoying, but still manageable.

But that's still not the most distracting ache or pain in this cumulative 'repertoire' of nuisances. No.

My *boots*—my brand new fucking jungle boots—are *killing* me.

They weren't bad earlier this morning when I was just walking around the shop and boarding the plane. Stuff like that. But once I'd run up and down the length of that friggin' DZ a couple of times, with a full ruck-and-radio combo adding another seventy, eighty pounds to my running load—not to mention about a half hour of squatting on my haunches, waiting for Haley to call me back into the fold—then those boots had time to clamp down on my feet like the jaws of a wolf. Particularly on my *heels*.

Jiminy Crickets, my heels feel like they're being ripped right off the back of my feet!

The air's comfortably nippy, but I'm sweating in sheets. And walking kinda' funny too, truth be told... sort of a light gliding 'tip-toe' (which, fortunately, fits in quite nicely with the covert nature of the moment, and so, is hopefully going unnoticed by everyone else).

The objective, though, is to minimize the stretching of my Achilles tendons, of course.

Unfortunately, I couldn't pack any other boots. Couldn't pack another thing into my damned rucksack. So this is it for footwear... for the next *week-and-a-half*.

Oh, yeh. This is the life.

This is going to be a great *little jamboree.*

I try not to think about the fact that this is only the *second hour* of the *first day* of the *ten*-day-long Field Week.

Because I really don't want to cry in front of these guys.

* * *

BY THE TIME WE reach the clearing that will be our 'home' for the next nine days and ten nights, we're all dead beat, I'm a virtual cripple, and we've all been 'killed' at least a dozen times a piece over the course of our multi-mile-long 'ambush gauntlet.'

Even little Rocky is showing actual signs of *fatigue* for the first time ever, as he shrugs off his rucksack and plops down on a log. Plops down so limply, in fact, that the butt of his GAU-5 clips the edge of the log, and fires a slugless round into the air.

BAM!

Everybody jumps, especially Rocky, who is back up on his feet again before the rest of us have even finished flinching.

For a moment, he looks stunned stupid, startled and disbelieving. Then, as the first instructors charge into the clearing looking for someone to kill, he regains his senses enough to snatch his weapon up and thumb its safety switch back on. Too late to fool the instructors, though.

And with that, Rocky becomes the first student to pay for his inattention with push-ups... fifty of them, to be precise.

With typical Spradlin aplomb, he pumps them out in less than a minute—one furious self-flagellating minute—then throws himself back onto the log, angry, burning, and making a big show of checking the *hell* out of his safety this time.

I decide that, whatever else I might bungle, I will not bungle *that*.

No way.

I mean, how hard could *not* squeezing the trigger be?

2

DAY 2: A WALK IN THE WOODS... IN ARKANSAS... IN HUNTING SEASON

AGAIN THEY PAIR US up into five little two-man teams. And this time I get Goebler. Far worse though, Goebler gets *me*... the mega-rookie.

Poor bastard.

Senior Airman (SrA) John Goebler is the last survivor here from the Norton AFB Combat Control Team. His buddy (and former teammate)

Airman Lenny Jimson was one of our last two wash-outs—right before our little roadtrip down to the Weapons School at Fort Polk—a victim of last week's written test.

So Goebler's been walking on eggshells ever since, trying to stay off the instructor's radar, ducking the spotlight, blending into the wallpaper, and any other metaphor I can think of along those lines. Anything to keep from being noticed, or worse, focused upon. Or worse still, *remembered*.

Because, in addition to being Norton's sole remaining representative here at CCS, he also wears the brand of being the only student in our class who's back here for a *second try!*

Goebler's already washed out of this course once before. A year ago.

In his case though, since his disqualification was not due to any scholastic or performance lapses, but was rather the result of a pretty horrific parachuting injury (*crippling*, actually), he was allowed to return and try again, starting from scratch, as soon as he'd completely recuperated.

And now here he is, experienced and worldly in the ways of this school—which has been a great help on many occasions for the rest of us first-timers—but also terrified of not only blowing it again, but of possibly even *repeating his previous injuries*.

Hell, considering the nature of those injuries, I'm nervous *for* him.

But that's another story, one better suited for telling at another time.

So, while he's a good guy and a knowledgeable fellow student, he's also been a little sullen, tentative, and quiet. And I don't blame him a bit.

* * *

TODAY IS OUR FIRST Overland Navigation course. Six miles of making our separate ways through the forests and brambles, across the fields and rivers, and over the fences and hills of backwood Arkansas... without the instructors... through multiple waypoints and changes of compass direction... to a rally point somewhere over there on that distant blue-gray horizon.

There, if all goes as planned, we will then reassemble back into our full ten-man formation, and review our line-of-march procedures again, as we hike all the way back to our campsite.

Aaurgh!

My bruised heels are throbbing just thinking about it.

Sgt. Rabin walks down the line handing out index cards, one to each team of two. Goebler accepts ours, and shares it with me as the rest are being passed out.

On it are just two numbers, handwritten in Magic Marker: a compass heading of three-hundred-and-forty-two degrees, and a distance of one-point-seven kilometers. And that's it.

342°/1.7

Even before Sgt. Rabin starts reviewing the rules, I'm doing the math in my head.

One-point-seven klicks—just over a mile—at my personal measured standard of eleven-hundred paces per klick, or a hundred-and-ten paces for every hundred meters. So that's eleven-hundred plus seven-seventy, which comes to eighteen-hundred-and-seventy paces to the next waypoint. That's one-thousand eight-hundred-and-seventy heel-crushing steps, starting with (I sneak a peek at my compass) a steep uphill climb right through that dense underbrush over there... *(*sigh*)*.

"Each waypoint along your route consists of a card," says Sgt. Rabin, "just like the ones in your hands there, with the coordinates for the next waypoints written on them. Just like those. They'll be in clear plastic sleeves, nailed to tree trunks or fence posts, or in some way posted near eye level. But *they won't be hidden*. They will be in plain sight. Obviously they're not very large though, so your land nav will have to be precise enough to at least put you within sight-range of a three-by-five index card. And that ain't as easy as it sounds."

Funny. It sounds *like it is.*

"Each team has completely different waypoints, so don't try to cheat by following someone else. They won't be going to the same landmarks. Besides, once you reach any given waypoint, you'll be removing that card from its sleeve, and using it to not only navigate to the next point, but *keeping it* to turn in to Sgt. Stillman later, when—or *if*—you finally finish the course. So forget about the other teams. They won't be any help to you at all. Besides, following somebody else is *not* a good way to keep from being the last one to the rally point, is it?"

"*Oo-rah!*"

"And remember: this is supposed to be a *covert* move. That's 'covert,' as in '*undetected.*' And that means *unseen by any civilians* whose paths you might cross along the way. It also means *unseen by your fellow students*. And that means, if your route crosses a public road, you cross it *unseen*. And we'll be watching. Is that understood?"

"*Oo-rah!*"

"And bear one more thing in mind: it's early December here in Arkansas, and that's still hunting season hereabouts. And that means you most likely won't be alone out there. There'll be real-world hunters in those hills, prowling the woods with you, and they'll *also* be trying to stay 'covert'… except that *their* guns will be loaded with live ammunition. And too damned many of them will shoot at anything that moves. So be careful."

What? "Be careful"? What the hell good is that gonna' do against a hair-trigger hillbilly with a deer rifle and a camouflaged Coors Lite hat?

"Pay attention to your surroundings, *think* about where they'd be most likely to hide, and what they'd be looking for. And most importantly…"

"Don't act like a deer," snorts Sgt. Corbin.

"… if you have a problem, fire off a short burst on full-auto."

Huh? Really?

"There aren't many deer that'd shoot back like that, so it'll definitely get the shooter's attention…"

"Probably take care of that pesky constipation problem too," says Matheson with a smirk in his tone. Corbin snickers along with him.

"Don't do it if you can avoid it, though," Sgt. Rabin continues, while holding his gaze on the two smart-asses, "You would be seriously fucking up someone's perfectly legal hunt. But don't allow yourselves to be endangered either. If you hear a shot nearby, squeeze off a quick burst—just enough to let 'em know you're there—but otherwise, stay covert. That's your *job*."

Well isn't that novel… not to mention 'inspiring.'

"All right, then. Any questions?"

No, I think that's pretty friggin' clear as it is, thank-you very much.

3

OVER THE RIVER AND THROUGH THE WOODS

NOT TWENTY MINUTES LATER...

Goebler and I are paused behind a pair of stout trees on the opposite side of the ridgeline from where we started. Before us, sprawling out beyond this last screen of trees, is a broad fallow plain. It's split by an overgrown fenceline and a two-lane road almost half a mile away, and then a creek maybe a hundred yards or so beyond that, invisible beneath its own leafy 'scar' of a canopy.

The two of us, still partially snagged in this final phalanx of armpit-deep brambles, are trying to guesstimate just how much further ahead our next navigational waypoint might be, since we both gave up counting our paces about halfway through that initial uphill slog through the forest undergrowth. It's been so *thick*, we haven't been able to take a step of more than a foot or two at a time, dragging entire thickets along with us, and constantly plucking the thorns from our clothing. I doubt if we've covered more than half a klick, all told, but who the hell can tell?

We're both breathing harder than normal. The backs of our hands, and even the sides of our *faces* look like we just pulled two battling cats apart. And my fucking heels are yodeling like they're *broken. Stupid new boots!*

Stupid Steve for not breaking them in before now!

Goebler's got a cool little 'monocular' up to one eye—basically a palm-sized telescope in a smooth, high-tech, camo-green case (nobody ever issued me one of those either)—and he's scanning the terrain for anything that might look like it has an index card tacked to it. Beside him, I'm fumbling with my compass, and waiting for my rampant breathing to calm enough to steady the floating needle and give me a good heading.

"It's gotta' be in those trees over there," he says between deep gulps of air. "By that little river, or whatever the hell it is."

"Yup," I reply. "That's what I was thinkin' too."

I haven't even looked up yet. I'm just trying to sound competent.

"Ain't nothin' but tall grass between here and there. Nothin' to nail a waypoint card to anyway."

I finally stabilize myself and my compass, and gasp, "Well, according to this, a three-four-two heading oughta' take us…"

The distant report of a heavy-gauge rifle *clops* across the valley, short and crisp and hanging on the breeze like dying thunder. A cloud of startled birds explodes into flight further down the ridgeline to our left.

We both freeze. *Hunters?*

Another *clop* cracks the air.

Goebler snatches up his GAU-5 and flips off the safety, ready to cut loose a dissuasive burst, as Sgt. Rabin had suggested. But barely a second later, the brittle rattle of a submachine gun, far off and clipped by the distance, chases away the larger gun's echo. Somebody else beat us to it.

Goebler lowers his own weapon, and turns to reveal a spreading grin.

"Who do you suppose that was?"

"I dunno," I answer. "Think they got 'im?"

We exchange a winded chuckle, then we relax, and I go back to my compass.

One thing I quickly figured out *all by myself* during our struggle through the brambles back there, was the uselessness of trying to follow a jiggling compass needle every step of the way, of trying to stay on course solely through a visual fixation on its dial, especially with so many other things our eyes needed to be looking for. Instead, I found that if I just identified some conspicuous terrain feature where the needle was pointing, I could put my compass away for a few minutes and *just walk*—or slog—toward *that feature*. Maybe even walk *around* some particularly inconvenient obstructions along the way, all without losing track of my objective.

As such, having followed a pretty straight and true connect-the-dots line comprised of oddly bent trees, mossy boulders, and notches in the ridge's crest, all of which were right off the tip of the compass needle when it was pointed at 342, I'm at least confident that we're still on-track. I just have no idea how far *along it* we are, that's all. And apparently, neither does Goebler.

But I steady my compass again, orient it toward 342 degrees, and once more lower my eye to its flip-up sight. And after a moment or two of scanning the landscape along that thin reticule wire, I find another distant anomaly that I can home in on for the rest of this leg.

"Well, it looks like we're headed for that low leaning tree over there, just above and to the left of that brown patch in the field."

"Sounds good then," says Goebler, without a second's hesitation. "So let's go."

Oh... well... okay then.

And with that, we tuck away our monoculars and compasses, rip the remaining bramble snags from our clothing, and scurry out of the trees into the high grass.

* * *

WE FIND OUR FIRST waypoint card by accident... mostly.

Oh, it's right where they said it would be, alright... right there at eye level, nailed to a tree in its plastic sleeve and everything. But they nailed it to the *opposite side* of the tree from our direction of approach.

Bastards,

We'd darted across the field, vaulted the overgrown fence, scampered across the highway between passing cars, ever mindful of our 'covert mandate,' and scooted the last couple dozen meters into the shadows of the shrouded creek. We still didn't know exactly how far we'd traveled, but we knew that it had to be more than a klick-and-a-half by then. And since there wasn't much more than hip-deep grass *beyond* the creek bed for at least another half klick leading up to the foot of the next forested ridgeline, we figured that it had to be somewhere in here among these densely cloistered canopy trees. Otherwise it couldn't have been stuck to anything close to eye level... we thought.

But... *nothing.*

We circled, and backtracked, and side-stepped—Goebler even hopped *across* the creek to check out the foliage on the other side—but neither of us could find anything that looked even remotely 'card-like' at *any* height above the ground. *Nada.*

Then we'd stopped and slumped against a couple of trees, facing each other across the creek.

Now what?

Goebler took out his canteen and spun off its cap.

"The same shit happened to me the last time, goddammit." He tossed back a swig, and lowered his eyes to mine. "I don't know what…"

Then he froze, staring at a point above my head.

"Son of a bitch."

"What?"

I twisted in place, and followed his gaze upward. And there it was… tacked to the *back* side of the very tree I was leaning against. *Bastards!*

"Son of a binge-drinker."

But at least we found it.

Now, with sore calves, stiff knees, and practically *crushed* heels, I grunt and lurch my way upright, slip the card from its sleeve, then limp down the tiny creek's bank, and hop painfully across to Goebler's side. He takes the card while I grapple my compass open again.

All that's written on the card is "$298°/.9K$"—a roughly northwesterly track for nine-hundred-and-ninety more crippling steps—a relatively short 'leisurely' stroll to our second waypoint. And as soon as I've steadied my compass with the **298** and the tip of the needle both pointing in the same direction, Goebler and I breathe a simultaneous sigh of relief… because my hand is aiming straight toward the saddle *between* the two hills ahead of us, rather than straight up the *face* of one of them. Which means a whole lot less climbing than we'd feared on this next leg.

Thank God for small favors.

In fact, through my flip-up sight, the lone coulee-hat-shaped tree that I can see rising above all else in the middle of that saddle— kind of like the flat head of a bird between its two upraised wings— is sitting right smack dab astride the extended 298° line. *Hell, it's*

probably the very tree to which our next waypoint card is attached.

I point it out to Goebler, who pauses only long enough to heft his rucksack a little more squarely on his shoulders, then he smiles, and starts trudging off toward that saddle.

* * *

WELL, LESSER CLIMB OR not, uphill is still uphill. And with both of my heels feeling like they've got spikes pounded through them… spikes that have chains hooked to them… chains that are dragging concrete blocks behind me… let's just say it's getting harder and harder to keep my grunts and whimpers quiet. I'm also feeling less and less inclined to *try*.

My newfound 'technique' of homing in on distant landmarks (as opposed to fixating on my bouncing, wobbling compass every step of the way) pays off, though, when we have to circumnavigate a 'machine graveyard' about a third of the way up the slope.

Completely invisible, until the tall grass and brambles abruptly and 'inexplicably' thicken before us, it appears first as a head-high thicket of dry dun colors and interwoven green weeds, then turns out to be a hummock of overgrowth smothering a decayed assemblage of what looks like ancient tractor parts. There's an engine block and body, minus the axles and wheels, plus a separate component of some kind, like maybe an old towed mower or a plow or something. They might once have been painted red. Now they're just a uniform rust.

We detour to the left, only to find ourselves wading into deeper and deeper snaggle-brush. The tops are deceptively level, but the bottom seems to drop into a shallow swale, like a dry creek bed or something. We're up to our armpits in thorns before we opt to divert our course yet again.

Then there's a small copse of exceptionally green trees to circle, followed by a second fording of that same dry creek bed, and then we're back out into the open again… and a long way off-track.

My first inclination is to wrestle out my compass again and take another heading. But I'm able to rein in that impulse when I look up between gasps to find that same 'coulee-hat tree' looking back down at me from the saddle. *No need to drag out a compass when a previously ascertained visual fix is in plain sight. All we gotta' do is keeping walking towards* that.

So I do.

Of course, we lost track of our steps again during our thorny little diversion, but apparently neither of us remembered to even start the damned count in the first place, so *that's* a moot point. And then, to top it all off, we both forgot to 'square off' our detour around that last thicket, *or* to count the number of sidesteps (to ensure a precise return to our original course line), so the overall pace count would have been obliterated by our deviation anyway.

Good thing we had a pre-sighted landmark to navigate off of at least, and not just our compasses. Because if we just resume a 298 degree heading again *now*, we'd only wind up *paralleling* our original course—about fifteen yards off to one side—and we'd probably never come within visual range of our next waypoint card. *I'm so friggin' smart.*

Well, let's just say I have my moments of lesser stupidity.

You'd think this rather obvious 'technique' would have been taught in the classroom part of the Overland Navigation lesson, but *nooOOOOooo...*

* * *

HALF AN HOUR LATER, the pain in my heels has grown and spread so far that I can't even feel them anymore. And truth be told, that's not an entirely unwelcome development.

Goebler and I find our second waypoint card without complication. And sure enough, it's tacked to the very tree we've been homing in on since the previous waypoint: none other than my so-called 'coulee-hat tree.' And now we're cutting across the western slope of the eastern hill, on a theoretical beeline for our third and final waypoint, which *should* be just around the bend up ahead, somewhere in the vicinity of the hill's northern face.

Again, my compass is packed away while we simply work our way toward the notch in the incline that I'd picked out earlier through the compass's wire sight.

In accordance with the teachings of our 'Infiltration Techniques' class, however, we're staying *out* of the riverbeds, *off* the roads and beaten paths, *well below* the crests of the hills and ridgelines, and just *inside* the lower tree line. So our walking, and thereby our *progress*, is being hampered somewhat by both the awkward angle of the slope and the straggling trees through which we're threading our way. But at least we're being good boys, and keeping it clandestine... which is more than can be said about some of the other two-man teams, apparently.

* * *

WE HEAR THEM BEFORE we see them. But regardless of which comes first, nobody could possibly *miss* them.

I mean, Goebler and I are down to the last klick of this little cross-country jaunt, toiling along in grim hobbling silence, and concentrating solely on the placement of each step, when, from somewhere below and behind us, a lone voice, thinned by distance, suddenly shouts.

"*I got it! Okay?!*"

The two of us freeze in mid-wheeze—just long enough to exchange a genuinely bemused look—then we both drop low and backpedal into the scrub at the base of a tree. But as we settle into stillness, so too does the mystery voice.

It's just us then, our stifled heavy breathing, and the wind again.

I can tell we both want to ask, "*Who was that?*" But I also know that neither of us has a clue, so the question would just be stupid. And so we sit. And we wait. And we watch the sunny slopes below us, just playing the covert game like they told us. Until...

"*... don't GIVE a shit!,*" burbles up from the lower saddle. And Goebler, still dutifully mindful of our stealthy guerilla role-playing orders, snicks his GAU-5's safety off, and raises it to the ready position... pressed to his cheek, and pointed downhill.

I do the same.

And again, we wait.

No more outbursts, though.

So what do we have here? A couple of bored farmboys maybe? Just strolling the empty fields with cane poles in their hands, lookin' for good fishin' cricks? Maybe moonshiners carrying empty jugs up to a hidden still somewhere? Or maybe just a dumbass city-slick 'hunter' storming back to his Beemer and screaming at his gun-caddy along the way. Or maybe it's just...

Hackett and Torrero.

They shamble into view a moment later, maybe seventy-five, eighty meters downhill from our hiding place—*less than a football field away*—

right out in the open sunshine and trudging uphill around the skirt of this low mountain, bound for the same final compass point as the rest of us.

I'd expected that our divergent courses would converge again once we all neared our shared objective: the 'finish line,' the end of this exercise, whatever. But I'd also presumed that, with everyone playing the 'commando game,' we wouldn't actually *see* each other until we practically collided at Sgt. Stillman's feet,

Seeing these two now—Hackett in the lead, his GAU-5 dangling wearily from one hand, its sights dragging through the high grass, and Torrero plodding along behind him, head down, but with his weapon held ready across his chest—I begin to wonder if Goebler and I have been foolish, acting all sneaky-like and 'professional' this whole time, compounding the difficulty of our hike by following a harder path through the environment than is really necessary. I mean, if all we had to do was shuffle along like these two, walking the clearest, least obstructed path, stealth be damned, we could have been at the rally point already, eating cold spaghetti from a can and waiting to see which team got to do all the push-ups for being last.

I can see Hackett's arms waving in limp exasperation, his boots dragging, his head lolling. I can't make out any specific words from this far away, but there's no mistaking the muffled petulance in his voice.

So Hackett is bitching... again.

Quelle suprise (that's French).

And judging by Torrero's defeated looking posture, I'd say he's been at it for a while. Probably right from his first step.

Yes, I can see now that Torrero's lowered head isn't bowed out of any weariness or boredom, but out of a boiling cumulative irritation. His teeth are grinding—I can see his jaw muscles clenching from clear up here—and I think I can see a little steam leaking from his ears as well.

That boy is stewing.

I look up from my sights, and turn to meet Goebler's grin.

Without removing his cheek from his rifle's stock, he mutters, "I got a feeling that if Hackett don't shut the hell up right quick, he's gonna' get his ass whooped."

I chuckle, and turn my attention back downhill... just in time to watch Torrero stop dead in his tracks, draw a deep shoulder-heaving sigh, throw his head back, and shout, "*Shut! The fuck! UP!*"

It's all Goebler and I can do to keep from laughing out loud.

Hackett barely reacts, though. He throws his arms up, and does go silent (I think), at least for the moment. But he doesn't stop slogging onward.

But now *Torrero* can't seem to stop fussin', cussin', spittin' and snortin', and at a volume that's too low to make out details from this far away. Every now and then though, a key point of emphasis blurts out loud enough to hear, and gets the two of us quietly snickering again.

"*Got-DAMN! Mumble-mumble-mumble WHINING little grumble-grumble-grumble like a damned PUSSY! Murmur-growl-rumble just shut the FUCK UP!*"

And then the grand finale, following an even longer stream of invective, "*Mumble-mumble Jesus CHRIST!*"

Goebler and I are openly snerking and sniggering by the time Torrero's diatribe finally cuts off and the hillside goes silent. We have to bite our lips just to keep from being heard.

But the show is apparently over now. The two of *them* lean back into their trudge up the steepening slope, unaware that the two of *us* have been watching them the whole time. Hackett's drooping to such an exaggerated degree, you'd think it was his fourth straight day without water, draggin'-ass across the Sahara. And for a while, there's nothing to do but watch their backs recede... until Hackett starts in again.

They're far off to our right now, almost at eye level and probably a little over a hundred yards away, maybe a minute or two from lumbering over this higher saddle and out of sight. But the steady rise of the terrain has sapped the last of Hackett's spent resolve. His every step is now a massive labor of misery, his entire body is thrown into every footfall, his hands are pushing on his knees for added thrust, and he finally staggers to a halt, breathing heavily, and weaving in place. We can see that even from here. We can't *hear* anything from this far back, but his flaccid arm gestures tell the whole story.

He's kvetching again, and doesn't give a damn who hears it.

Torrero's arms fly about angrily as well, Hackett's flail back weakly, and their pathetic pantomime twitches along for a good thirty seconds or so before Hackett begrudgingly surrenders, and resumes his uphill digging.

But even though we can't hear anything anymore, his arms are signaling that he's still bitching. And after a few more steps, it becomes abundantly clear that Mex Torrero's had enough.

For the second time, he stops dead in his tracks. He lets Hackett squirm a few steps higher, sputtering and whining every step, then he levels his assault rifle on him... *and pulls the trigger. From barely ten feet away!*

He hammers off a good twelve to fifteen rounds in a brief but sustained burst, probably half a magazine in a second-and-a-half on full auto. And if we didn't know that he was firing blanks, we would honestly believe, based on Hackett's explosive reaction, that Mex just blasted the little dumbass into the next life *for real*.

The instant the firecracker rattle of Torrero's weapon erupts, Hackett flings himself facedown against the hillside, so fast and spastic it looks like he's been smashed flat by some huge invisible club... or maybe pelted into the dirt by a salvo of point-blank-range submachine-gun fire. One or the other. He actually *bounces*, flops over on his back, and slides a couple of feet downhill, back towards Torrero and his smoking GAU, where all motion finally stops.

Goebler and I are on our feet, stunned speechless, as the last of the clattering racket echoes off through the hills,.

Hackett gets to squeal out about two-and-a-half words—"*What the fuh...!*"—before Torrero cuts loose a savage roar that actually chases the other echo out of range.

"*SHUT! THE FUCK! UP! NOW!!*"

Hackett mutters something unintelligible across the distance, but is interrupted by Torrero's bellowing again.

"*NOW! Shut the fuck up NOW! Not another goddamned word outa' your face! Is THAT clear enough for you, asshole!*"

I know it's clear enough for me.

And those are the last words we hear.

Without waiting for Hackett to even get back on his feet, Torrero stomps past him, and marches off over the limn of the hill, alone. Hackett, on the other hand, remains sprawled where his slide came to rest for most of another minute. Then he makes a slow, unbalanced lurch to his feet, dusts himself off, gathers up a few scattered trinkets (his sunglasses, field cap, and a flashlight that came off his web gear), and tromps off in Torrero's wake.

Not until everything but the top of his head has stepped down out of sight on the other side of the crest do we resume our own traverse, still threading our way through the trees the hard way, aiming toward that same notch that my compass pointed us toward so long ago. And since I just spent a good ten minutes frozen in an awkward crouch, my heels are really wailing now, as they shift back into 'uphill-marching' mode.

Son of a bitch!

Back on my tiptoes again. Back to clamping my lips shut, biting them to keep from walking off into the sunset muttering, "*Ouch, ooch, eech, arf, oof, ah-jeez, shit, ouch...*"

4

THE SHOT HEARD 'ROUND THE WOODS

WE ARE THE MIDDLE team, Goebler and I. The third team out of five to reach the rally point.

Rocky and Corbin came in first—pretty much a given whenever Rocky's on your team—scant seconds before Torrero blustered into the clearing, alone. Hackett wandered in a few minutes later (also alone), looking frazzled and scolded for some reason. And *he* was followed by the Goebler/Stipp team just five minutes after *that*. Which means that, if we hadn't stopped to watch the Hackett/Torrero Show back there, we would have come in *first*. Right? I mean, we stopped and took cover before those two had even rounded the bend below and behind us. Then we sat out most of ten minutes waiting for them to finish yelling, stalling, and shooting each other. Which means that, barring those delays, we'd have made it here a good ten minutes *ahead* of them, which would have put us ahead of even the Spradlin/Corbin duo, *And that's sayin' somethin', dammit!*

It says *I'm good—damned good—at cross-country nav, anyway.*

I hobble over to where Rocky's chugging down a whole canteen of warm water. I'm grinning from ear to ear, cocky, proud (exhausted, sore), and showing it with my half-crippled swagger. I can't wait to tell him all about the Laurel and Hardy Show that we just witnessed—which he no doubt *heard*—and to compare notes on our clearly superior point-to-point techniques.

I unsling my GAU, and switch hands with it while I creak around into a sitting position beside him on the dirt berm.

"Hey, man. Did you hear...?" *BAM!*

I look down in disbelief at my weapon—*my* weapon, the one I just took off my shoulder, the one I just carried for six klicks without a hiccup, the one that *just went off in my friggin' hand!*—and search it for clues as to how that could have possibly happened.

Maybe my finger being on the trigger had something to do with it.

What the hell is my finger doing on the trigger? I was in the process of setting it down and leaning it against the log beside me! My finger shouldn't have been anywhere near *the trigger!*

And maybe the fact that the damned safety was off played a pertinent role as well.

Why the hell was the damned safety off? I never flick the safety off! Except maybe... while... (*sigh*)...

... sitting behind cover, in a defensive stance, peering through my sights at a pair of Keystone Kops duking it out in the field below me.

Fuck.

Goddamn Hackett.

On the unlikely chance that maybe my little misfire went unnoticed by any instructors in the area, I discretely thumb the safety back on, and prop it against the berm.

"Did I hear *what?*," Rocky asks, as if a gunshot hadn't just gone off next to his ear.

I share a sheepish grin with the rest of the students around me.

"Well..."

Sgt. Stillman strolls out of the bushes across the clearing.

"Airman Stipp! I do believe you owe me about a hundred push-ups right now! Don't you agree?"

Well, it isn't like I didn't see it coming.

"Oo-rah, sergeant!"

Shit.

It takes me a couple of minutes to shuck all my combat paraphernalia—my ruck, gas mask, and web gear—then I drop straight into the ever-lovin' 'plank position,' and start pumping them out.

The Haley/Donado team saunters in while I'm flogging my way

through the forties. *Great.* The class leader (who already hates my guts), and the senior-ranking member of the McChord contingent (who is no doubt proudest of 'his guys' at moments like these), have to walk in right as I'm paying for my sins, and having most certainly *heard* the crime for which I'm paying right now.

Dammit!

My 'credibility' (such as it is), even my *acceptability* among my fellow inmates here, having just barely and so *recently* (as in *just now*) been hoisted back to the level of 'marginal,' has now taken yet another nosedive... back to the ass-end of the class food chain again.

Dammit! Dammit! Dammit!

Well, there are a couple of positives that come from this, though.

(1) Since I'm only the *second* idiot to discharge his weapon at an inopportune moment like this, I 'only' have to do a hundred push-ups... which is no more than my good buddy Greg Dorn and his cross-country teammate Sgt. Matheson are going to have to do whenever they finally get here, and pay their debt for being the last.

(2) I'm actually able to reclaim a *little* of my tarnished reputation when, in front of these seven peers of mine—including the president of my fan club, Sgt. Haley—I manage to slam my way through *eighty-two* straight push-ups without stopping! And that after just completing a six-kilometer uphill hike! I know *I'm* impressed. I just bested my old record, *and* exceeded the highest non-stop count I've seen *any* of these guys do since we've been here.

And finally, (3) I'm not even thinking about my throbbing heels anymore.

STORY XXVII

A SURVIVOR OF THE DAY

1
DAWN PATROL

December, 1977
In the field outside Little Rock AFB, Little Rock, Arkansas

YOU KNOW, I'M RAPIDLY discovering just how much of a natural at this 'outdoor business' I am *not*.

Every morning, bright and sparkling early—anywhere from 5:00 to 6:00am, depending on the whim of the human alarm clock that has the wake-up duty—one of the instructors blusters through our dank and muddy little camp shouting for everyone to *wake the hell up!* "Let's go! Let's go! Let's go!"

Yesterday it was Sgt. Rabin himself, and he came through banging the metal components of his mess kit together, in addition to all the yelling. He claims that, in the past, they've even fired weapons into the air! And on one occasion, back when *he* was but a neophyte, they set off a damned *grenade* a little ways back in the woods.

Boy, I bet that *made for some stinky sleeping bags.*

Personally, it doesn't matter to me what mode of 'inspiration' they choose: a rude awakening is a rude awakening, regardless of the medium. But what *does* matter to me is how utterly inept I appear to be at this field-living shit, which seems to be most succinctly illustrated at each morning's wake-up call. Take this morning, for example.

I was already pretty half-assed 'awake' when the youngest of the instructor cadre, Sgt. Myers, came bellowing through the camp, yelling for everyone to *wake the hell up right now!* And because I've been experimenting each night with different configurations of my 'sleeping attire' (trying to find that perfect combination, that ideal balance between warmth, cleanliness, and *readiness*)—which everyone else already seems to know from all their *months* with their teams prior to coming here—this morning I *flew* out of my sleeping bag in my latest variation: socks, pants and undershirt already on (my 'field pajamas'), just needing to tug on my boots and pull on a shirt as I exited my little one-man tent. How could it be any more streamlined?

Despite all this foresight and 'cheating' though, I was still barely halfway through the lacing of my first boot, when I looked outside to see several of my fellow students *already strolling around the campfire!* A campfire that somebody else had already found the time *to relight!* All of them fully dressed, accoutered, and ready for war.

How are they doing this?

I was ready! I'd thrown myself headlong into getting dressed as quickly as possible (bearing in mind that I was already half-dressed to begin with), starting the split second I'd first heard Sgt. Myers' voice. *I only had boots and a shirt to put on, fer Criminey's sakes! And I laced them babies up as fast as humanly possible!* And I was *still* the last one out of my tent—by friggin' *minutes!*—by the time I was done!

What the hell?!! Are these people sleeping in full uniform? Boots, hat, web gear and all?!

I mean, COME ON!!!

The only way they could possibly be up and out that quickly is if they had simply leapt to their feet and stepped out without a single diversion along the way.

So that means... *what?* That they never take their uniforms off *at all*, or even any portions thereof? Or are they actually just getting up *before* the wake-up call, taking their own sweet time getting ready, and then just stepping outside once they hear the instructor's voice? Something like that?

Really? Could it be that simple and obvious?

I guess I'm just going to have to flush my pride (again), and *ask* somebody. "*So, what do you wear when you're sleeping?*" Yeh; no way *that'll* raise any eyebrows. Or maybe just, "*How the hell are you getting dressed so friggin' fast?!*"

Damn, I'm tired of being such a clueless rookie.

But that's not all.

I woke up this morning to find that one corner of my tent had sagged inward, to within less than an inch of my forehead, actually, and had leaked (or 'sweated') water all over the right shoulder of my sleeping bag, as well as my rucksack.

Turned out that the tent peg in that corner had simply pulled out of the ground, and allowed part of that side to 'cave in.' *But how? Why?* The ground was just as firm there as anywhere else, it hasn't seriously rained enough to saturate or loosen up the dirt, and I'd hammered in the peg (using my miserable-assed 'entrenching tool' or 'collapsible shovel') the exact same way as all the others. So, you know... *what the hell?*

Or maybe I should be asking, *Who* the hell? *Hmmm.*

Who knows.

But it's the same thing with the damned fire. Using every technique they'd taught us in the classroom, along with a great deal of encouragement and advice from my more experienced 'buddies,' I'd stoked and I'd kindled... I lit and I blew and I shielded, and I did everything else that *any*one else would have done *with near-instantaneous success*, and... nothing. Never more than a mockingly thin little tendril of smoke. Never any flames, never any heat, never *anything* worth a tenth-of-a-shit.

So it would appear that I'm one of those guys for whom fires just don't light, tents just don't pitch, and knots just don't hold.

Or maybe there's actually a damned good *reason* for why they want you to spend a few *months* with your team before you come here.

Thank-you, Manny.

*And thank-*you*, Skeeter.*

2

DAY THREE: DUMB LUCK, CLEAN LIVING... AND JESUS

WHEN YOU JUMP WITH a full combat load—say, a seventy-five, maybe a *one-hundred* pound rucksack crammed to bursting with your survival gear, rations, a few smoke canisters, spare ammo and batteries, a sleeping bag and, of course, clean socks and undies—you can't go out the door with it *on your back*.  Your parachute has to go there. You can't carry it out in your *hands* either. A one-hundred-plus mile an hour slipstream will pretty much rip anything from your grip before you've even tumbled past the tail. So it has to go attached to your *front*, hooked to your harness *below* your reserve chute, so that it doesn't impede the *reserve's* operation either.

But even *that's* not really enough.

When you hurl yourself out the door into hurricane force winds with only the *top* of your ruck secured to your rigging, the *bottom* of it is going to fly up into your face like Marilyn Monroe's skirt in '*Seven Year Itch*'... if that skirt had been made of concrete. And don't even get me started about the affects of having the equivalent of a twenty-seven inch TV flailing around below your chest, battering everything between your chin and your knees, not to mention adding some pretty violent 'instability' to your personal aerodynamics. Just trust me when I say that it is unpleasant no matter how you look at it.

So, to *fully* secure your combat load, you must also tie off its bottom end to your right leg. To your *ankle*, specifically. It might make walking a tad cumbersome—you'll look like Frankenstein trying to carry a small refrigerator out the door—but it'll get you into the wind and under your canopy without catching a faceful of your own luggage.

This, however, leads to a couple of other complications once you're safely 'under silk.'

Number one: before you can pull on the so-called 'Red Apple' to release your combat load to drop to the end of its twenty-foot tether, you must first reach down to your right ankle, and *undo* that leg strap. Otherwise, your half-ton rucksack will just take your foot along with it as it falls away. And when you're hanging in a taut harness, suspended between the pull of gravity and the drag of your canopy, and with your leg held straight and stiff by the weight of your load, reaching your ankle is not as easy as it sounds. It's a long way down there, and you can't bend very far. Throw in the fact that you've got to do all this in the mere thirty seconds between your chute's opening and your body hitting the ground, and you've got, well… a 'challenge.'

And number two, your form exiting the aircraft becomes much more critical. With all that extra mass strapped to your leg, it *has* to go out first. It *has* to stay pointed down the whole time. If it doesn't—if somehow, your lurching Frankenstein-stagger should topple you out the door *head* first— your off-center ballast will flip you through your risers over and over and over again, like a big unbalanced propeller that's thrown a blade. And needless to say, this offers up a veritable cavalcade of opportunities for disaster.

Case in point… Amn. Goebler.

* * *

SENIOR AIRMAN JOHN GOEBLER is the only guy in our class who's been here before. This is his second time through Combat Control School, and for the worst of all possible reasons… a serious crippling injury that he incurred on one of the course's five jumps from his last time through. And it was a result of just this very issue. Merely hearing him tell his story is enough to make my eyes water and my knees buckle in sympathetic agony.

On that fateful jump, his heavy laboring stagger to the door, combined with the reeling and pitching of the aircraft itself, caused him to stumble into space—you guessed it—*headfirst*. And as his static line—which connected his parachute to the anchor cable inside the aircraft—dragged the chute from his backpack and pulled his harness's risers tight and vertical at his shoulders, he was tossed *through* them like a gymnast between his rings.

On his first passage betwixt his risers, he'd slipped through cleanly, but was snapped all the way around and flung through them *again* by the violent lopsided momentum of his first somersault. And his second time through was *not* a clean transition.

Still only a second or two out the door, his chute still deploying and the world twirling around him, his legs were thrown apart by his flipping. And as he whipped between his risers that second time, his *right* leg, burdened and bound to that ponderous combat load, flew all the way through.

His *left* leg did not.

It caught high on his left riser, and snarled there.

That effectively stopped his flipping, but did nothing to slow the impetus behind his other weighted leg, which continued on through and was yanked straight down by his own motion and the pull of gravity.

In an instant, he was ripped into an agonizing vertical leg split, his left leg forced up over his left *ear*, his right drawn heavily downward by his combat load, compounded by his chute's ferocious deceleration. For it was just booming open at that moment, hauling upward *hard* on his risers, dragging his falling speed down from a hundred miles an hour to practically *zero* in less than two seconds.

He'd screamed as every muscle, ligament, and tendon in his groin—along with the crotch of his pants—was torn or stretched far beyond its design specs. Every jumper in the air, and every instructor on the ground could hear his desperate shrieks. And worse, they could see his distorted silhouette dangling beneath his chute, one foot high over his head, pointing in the wrong direction, the other twitching *below* him under the weight of its unnatural load. And there was nothing that either he or anyone else could do about it.

Wailing and wracked with searing pain, he'd tried everything he could think of to free his skyward leg. But every tug on his risers only jolted his hyper-extended sinews even worse. He couldn't release his combat load until he'd unstrapped it from his ankle, and in his twisted condition, he couldn't even come close to reaching that strap in the first place.

In his frenzied search for relief then, he'd done the unthinkable: he snatched his K-Bar combat knife from its scabbard, and started *sawing through his suspension lines!*

Oh sure, he could have just popped his riser releases, and discarded his primary chute with one quick tug. But he was only a couple hundred feet off the ground by then, and that was nowhere near enough altitude to cut away and deploy his reserve before splattering his way into the history books.

No, he just wanted to sever the specific lines that were pinning his leg back over his shoulder. Just enough to release his foot. But there are something like thirty of the thin nylon suspension lines strung between a harness's risers and the 'silken' canopy overhead, and they are each not only very strong, but under a great deal of load at such a time.

Still he'd hacked at them, one at a time, in the area surrounding his pinioned left foot—and he claims to have cut through at least three of them in his struggles (which sounds about right... any more and it likely would have collapsed his parachute)—until the ground, rushing up unnoticed, reached him and clubbed him to stillness. The Meat Wagon then rushed him off to Little Rock General, unable to move his legs, and in excruciating 'groinal' pain.

Needless to say, he couldn't complete the class from his hospital bed, and had to wait more than a year for both his crotch to heal, and for this opportunity to repeat the course again.

* * *

WHY DO I BRING this up *now? Now* of all times?

Because right now, that's the only thing I *can* think of.

Right now, that horrific story is pulsing—no, more like pounding, *strobing* in my head like a loud, blindingly bright nuclear meltdown alarm going off right next to my temple. Because right now, I'm in kind of a similar situation myself. Close enough, anyway.

* * *

IT'S ONLY OUR SECOND jump of the final five, a simple 'day hop' into the lopsided DZ that borders our campsite, and we're carrying our first *simulated* combat loads with us. I'm the fourth braindead superhero in the stick today, and I'm struggling with the damned load just as strenuously as everybody else, apparently.

Simulated combat load, you ask?

Why, yes... *simulated*.

We do not have our bloated rucksacks with us today. But try not to think of that as good news... because it's not. The one and only convenience the simulated loads offer is that they allow us to skip the arduous pain-in-the-ass of packing and packing and *re*packing our rucks for each and every jump. In every *other* way though, the simulated loads are much *worse*.

For starters, the package is intended to simulate a 'worst case scenario' kind of load... larger, more rigid, and heavier than a typical overstuffed rucksack. It also needs to be durable, to last for hundreds of these nasty jumps (or, more accurately, hundreds of these brutal *landings*).

So, what does it consist of?

Well, basically, it looks like a large wooden *railroad tie*, wrapped in OD green canvas.

Yep. Starting with a roughly hewn, splintery, squared-off 'log,' roughly four feet in length, and about a foot square in cross-section, they wrap the tie in a customized canvas sheath (sewn together right there at the local parachute shop), which has all the straps, buckles, spring-loaded clips, rope anchors and carrying handles of a real combat load, intended to be hooked up to a parachute harness in the exact same way as our rucks. Then, when they hand these things out to us, they make sure to play up their value as 'convenience items'—"for our *benefit*"—because of how they obviate the need to completely repack every other day.

Yeh. Whatever.

Don't let 'em fool you. Unlike the swollen seventy-five pound rucksack with which I'd jumped into the DZ two days ago—carrying in everything I'd need to last the full ten days of this final field portion of the course—this monstrous chunk of a telephone pole weighs in at close to a *hundred freakin' pounds!* And yes, it's a noticeable difference.

It's also (again, unlike the stuffed rucksack) completely inflexible. It doesn't bend or allow itself to be reshaped in any way.

And finally, its nearly four-foot length, suspended from the hooks under my reserve chute, completely immobilizes the leg to which it is attached from ankle strap to belt buckle. You can't bend your leg *at all* (to help in reaching for that strap), and in order to walk with it, you have to grab it by its side handles and hoist it, at least a little bit, *off your foot*. Otherwise, that's exactly where it rests... on top of your foot.

It's cumbersome; roughly the size and shape of a set of golf clubs, heavy as an office safe, and, as far as I'm concerned (taking into account the way it forces your right leg to remain straight), it's dangerous as hell come landing time. After all, it was one of these *F'ing* logs that nearly tore Airman Goebler in half like a wishbone.

All the more reason to train with them. So sayeth the instructor cadre. You never know what your mission is going to require you to carry out the door. Best, then, to train for that dreaded 'worst case scenario.'

True enough, I suppose.

So, with Sgt. Matheson (the second of our four student NCOs) standing beside the instructor at the jump door shouting, "*Go! Go! Go! Go! Go!*" to each of his passing minions, I'd manhandled my 'simulated combat load' out into the ragged maelstrom, and rode the torrent through the heavy three-second deceleration of my parachute's deployment.

And up through that point, all had gone as well as could be expected.

For a moment there, as I was crossing the door's threshold, I'd felt a brief spike of terror as the wind had caught my load and yanked me out of the plane in a clumsy forward topple. I was afraid it was going to pull me into a headfirst somersault, just like with Airman Goebler. But it didn't.

Fortunately, the log *wants* to go out first, and it stayed below me the whole way. Kind of like jumping into the ocean with an anvil in your hands, I guess. No matter how you go over the edge, it's going to lead you all the way down... unless you somehow get underneath it at the start.

My chute opened nicely. There were no twists in my suspension lines, there were no tears in the silk, and I was in a good position relative to the DZ.

I took a couple of seconds to assess the wind direction and steer myself toward the tiny pea-gravel pit in the center of the drop zone... the PI, or Point of Impact (I've never liked that term). Then I released my toggle lines to go to work on my combat load... my *simulated* one. With less than thirty seconds until my reunion with good old *terra firma*, I didn't intend to arrive still coupled to this goddamned log.

The goddamned log, of course, had other plans.

First step: release the ankle strap that holds the log to my leg. A simple operation with a simple device: a canvas strap with a thickly waxed tip, slipped out of a basic friction buckle. *That's it!* Granted, it has to be done *with fingertips only*, since the strap's at the extreme limits of my reach—no 'grip,' no *thumb* involved, just a weak tweezer-like pinching between the tips of my two longest fingers—but that's okay. It doesn't offer a resistance significant enough to test my dainty chopsticks grip. There're no metal hasps or grommet holes like on a dress belt, no release button or lever clasp like on a car's seatbelt. Just a length of canvas fed through a typical (albeit 'industrial strength') over-and-under buckle, like on the back of a baseball cap.

Nothing to catch, nothing to snag, nothing requiring any tricky or prolonged maneuvering. *Nothing that could possibly go wrong.*

So naturally, something has gone wrong.

And here we are.

* * *

AFTER I TUG A loop of slack into the middle of the strap channel, the damned strap abruptly *stops dead*, and refuses to budge any further.

What the hell?

I tug harder. I tug faster. *Nothing.*

I tug hard *and* fast. *Nada.*

I tug right and left, up and down, in and out.

I tug angrily. I tug loudly. I tug with passion, vehemence, and then profanity. I put my whole body into it, which starts me thrashing in my harness… still without effect. And the delicate, overreached 'tweezer-like grip' of my fingertips just cannot find sufficient purchase to apply any more appreciable force to the effort. That strap is simply *not* going to let go.

I can't imagine how that's even possible. And I can't see my ankle down there, at least not well enough to spot, much less *resolve* the problem.

Which leads me to my *next* problem.

I've now burned up half of my extremely finite time in the air just wrestling with this unbelievably stupid little 'minor glitch.' And in the process, this trifling little annoyance has now bloomed into a full-blown *crisis*, with barely fifteen seconds left in which to solve it. For if I cannot release that strap, then I *cannot release the load.*

And that means *landing with it STILL ATTACHED TO MY LEG!!*

Perhaps I should expound upon one other niggling little detail here.

The standard round 'Commander' type parachute, like the one I'm wearing right now, lowers you to the ground at the fairly brisk rate of *twenty-two vertical feet per second.* This is faster than it sounds. In fact, hitting the ground under a fully inflated, perfectly healthy round parachute has the same impact velocity as jumping off the roof of a typical one-story house. This is an acknowledged fact, mentioned repeatedly throughout Jump School, and again here at CCS. Which is why a rather prominent aspect of our basic jump *training* had to do with 'PLFs,' or 'Parachute Landing Falls'... the proper way to avoid breaking bones in these jarring collisions with the Earth.

And the first and most fundamental part of a good PLF is touching down on your toes, with your legs bent loosely at the knees.

Now, knowing this, try to picture jumping off that same roof, only this time with a one-hundred pound log strapped to one leg like a massive splint, the bottom of it resting atop your boot, the top of it tucked snugly under your diaphragm. *Can you see the problem developing here?*

Of course, there's always the slim chance that I might be over-thinking this thing just a skosh. But... *naahhh...*

Come with me now, and let's mentally play out the sequence of events that will quite likely transpire in about thirteen seconds or so, shall we?

* * *

FIRST, FOOT CRUNCHES INTO ground, followed immediately by one-hundred pound log crunching down on top of foot, turning it into a meaty bag of bone mulch.

Second: knee, just above pulped foot, which is unable to bend because it is bound to the backside of a log, absorbs landing shock by exploding in its socket, most likely *sharing* that same crushing force with the bones directly above and below it at the same time.

Third: log is driven upward, scraping past pelvic girdle into the lower torso, and ramming into the bottom ribs.

Fourth: upper body, still plunging earthward at twenty-two vertical feet per second, folds over top of log like a big bag of crunchy bird seed, breaking more bones, bashing air out of lungs, and forcing one to say something terribly pithy like, "*Oof!*"

And fifth: log and crumpled body *together* topple slowly over to one side, while mouth gasps out the word "*Medic*," too quietly to be heard.

I can see every step of this crushing sequence as clearly as a scene from a big-screen movie, and all in only a fraction of a second.

It's not my *life* that's flashing before my eyes right now, but rather my *immediate future*, apparently.

And I've got to tell you, *it's looking a trifle bleak*.

* * *

NOW, WITH BARELY TEN seconds left before I pile-drive myself into the dirt—while my hand (or at least my desperately scissoring fingertips) continues to 'fumble *with*' and 'yank *at*' the recalcitrant ankle strap as if on autopilot—time stalls, events grind to a standstill around me, and my brain suddenly shifts into *High-Speed Survival Option* mode (*HS2O*), rocketing through *all* of my last-ditch options like a thumb riffling through the Yellow Pages. Both of them.

Option One: if I pull on the old 'Red Apple' and release my combat load without first releasing that damned ankle strap, the log, unable to fall away *straight down* as designed, will instead pivot *around* its connection to my ankle, ratcheting it tighter and tighter until the log has swung completely upside-down beneath my foot, at which point the damage that it could inflict becomes anybody's guess. It might tear itself free, possibly taking my boot, sock, and some skin with it, and most likely pranging up my ankle in the process. Or it might catch for a moment or two, maybe just twist in the wind, wrenching and torquing at my ankle with all its plunging mass, until it hits the ground... *first*... maybe a half-second or two before the rest of me, and completely demolishes the joint. Either way, my ankle is toast.

And all at the same time that it fucks up my all-important PLF.

So I don't like the '*Pull the Red Apple Anyway*' option, and set it aside for now.

But that only leaves Option Two: '*NOT-Pulling-the-Old-Red-Apple.*' And that means landing with this monstrous bastard still bound to my leg, with all the grisly repercussions and painful foreshadowing already discussed and so graphically envisioned above.

And that's it. There are no other Yellow Pages.

* * *

SIX SECONDS TILL IMPACT—just thirteen stories above the ground—with the landscape visibly accelerating up to smash me.

My mind flicks back to Option One, not so much because it senses any promising new possibilities there, but because it is rapidly resigning itself to the likelihood that pain and structural damage is about to be incurred... and Option One offers slightly less of both. A demolished ankle is decidedly 'better' than the smorgasbord of a crushed foot, shattered knee, broken leg, caved-in ribs, internal bleeding, and probably a lacerated organ or two, all very real prospects for anyone attempting to jump off their roof with a one-hundred-pound log splinted to their leg... or the equivalent thereof.

It's not a *good* choice by any means. The mind is resistant to it, even as it's signing off on the deal... sort of like spreading one's legs and nodding, giving the go-ahead for someone to give you a running kick in the balls, *in lieu of taking a baseball bat to the face*. It's the lesser of two mighty evils, and that's about the best that can be said for it.

* * *

FIVE SECONDS TO IMPACT—just over a hundred feet in the air—I seize the Red Apple with both hands, I swallow the choking bolus of dread in my throat...

... and *freeze*.

In my head, the mental re-runs of my impending foot-mangling collision with Mother Earth have suddenly acquired an unforeseen 'bonus feature:' *the uprushing ground itself!* Now each time the toppling log falls away from me (in my mind), it is interrupted by the *rising ground!*

All of a sudden I'm seeing—repeating itself faster and faster and faster on my internal screens—that because of my shrinking proximity to the ground, the log no longer has the *time* to swivel all the way around to wrench at my ankle before we all hit the dirt together! *A ray of hope!*

If I can time it just right, to where the log only has a second or two to pitch forward before we all crunch down in the same instant, then I could possibly land *straddling* the evil thing (as opposed to landing *on top of it* as it's bouncing and ripping my foot off at the ankle joint) *with no weight or grip on my ankle at all!* And wouldn't *that* be a happy ending! *If* I can time it right.

* * *

FOUR SECONDS TO ZERO—descending swiftly past the tops of the tallest trees surrounding me, with my shadow now visible at the edge of my vision, rushing across the ground to meet me—I hesitate for an extra second, feeling out the passing moments for that perfect window of opportunity when that instant of 'Immaculate Timing' might present itself... *then*...

* * *

THREE SECONDS BEFORE PLOWING into the scrubby field, I yank upward on the Red Apple with all my might.

And hallelujah! Praise Jesus! A sho'nuff bonafide 'miracle' unfurls in the hills north of Little Rock, Arkansas!

Not only do I touch down so lightly that I hardly have to flex my knees at all to remain standing... not only does that obstinate ankle strap magically let go all by itself, severing all contact between log and limb and allowing us to land separately... but I alight—*gently*—right smack dab in the *center* of the tiny ten-foot-wide pea-gravel pit that marks the *bullseye* of the DZ! The only one in the class to hit the mark *dead center!*

My softest, most painless, most *accurate* parachute landing *EVER!*

I'm standing here, *stupefied*, staring at the fallen log between my legs where it lays like an unrequited hard-on, impotent and harmless, stripped of its menace. Other jumpers are also landing around me, slamming to ground and rolling through their shock-absorbing PLFs, while I stand at the epicenter of an exultant, living, breathing universe in which all things turn out well, trying not to burst out laughing!

What the hell just happened?!

My chute flutters limp before me, like a sheet that's been pulled free of its clothesline. And I find myself wondering—no, *marveling*—at this strange implausible 'edit' in the film of my life.

Where did it come from? And why? And HOW? I mean, this wasn't even an option in the short list of possible endings I'd considered, so...

What the hell just happened here?

As I lurch into my post-jump routine—daisy-chaining my canopy and shroud lines, shucking my harness, and bagging the whole rig up, making sure I'm not the last one to the rally point—my mind races through all the evidence and clues, trying to figure out how and why this 'miracle' occurred.

And before I've even hefted my loaded B-4 bag onto my shoulders, I've got three of the four 'major components' of my 'miracle' all worked out.

But, to explain, I must first dissect the last two seconds of my descent into smaller bite-sized morsels.

* * *

FOR STARTERS, IT TURNS out the reason that stupid strap wouldn't let go was because of its thickly waxed tip. I discover this as I'm bundling up my onerous 'simulated combat load' for removal from the field.

Over the course of its many uses, that poor abused strap had been tugged and yanked and jerked around enough that the wax had been dented in along both of its outer edges. Sort of like a toothpaste tube that's been pinched near its top. Those indentations had created a kind of 'flange' at the very tip of the wax, a stubby variation on the front end of a hammerhead shark. And it was those two minimal little wax 'barbs' that had caught on the last part of the buckle as I was trying to pull it through.

If I'd had more than a mere fingertip pinch on that strap, I could easily have overcome those tiny wax snags in one or two quick tugs. But I didn't.

Secondly, once I did finally commit to releasing the load with the ankle strap still in place, two *more* unforeseen effects instantly occurred.

First, when the log was cut loose from my harness rigging, one-hundred pounds of dead weight tried to drop straight down. That's what gravity was compelling it to do anyway. And what two barely-brushing fingertips and an arm at full extension could *not* accomplish with that strap, that falling deadweight achieved with ease. As that one-hundred pound railroad tie fell past my ankle, it pulled the last of that waxed tip past its barbs, the strap was torn free of the buckle, and the log separated cleanly from my leg, *just like normal*. The strap offered no resistance at all.

And finally, as soon as the Red Apple had pulled the pins holding the log to my harness, my risers, suspension lines, and parachute canopy all suddenly lost a third of the weight that they'd been lowering to the ground. *Just like that!* The stretched lines naturally recoiled at the abrupt loss of tension, which in turn allowed the canopy, far overhead, to momentarily bloom open a little wider. As such, it fleetingly caught more air. And for just that brief second, the chute essentially *stopped* in the air—barely a foot or two off the ground, as it turned out—and I was able to just *step off* that freakish little perch as if alighting from the bottom step of a flight of stairs.

And I'm not just making that last part up.

That's an actual 'technique' (officially frowned upon by the safety-conscious military hierarchy) used by the more experienced veterans of combat jumping to do stand-up landings, which are generally ill-advised with a round *Commander* rig like this one.

You see, unlike a *square ram* parachute—which is essentially just an 'inflated wing,' an airfoil shape with the leading edge cut open to allow air to be rammed into its channels and thereby keep the wing semi-rigid—a *round* chute cannot be 'flared' for a gentle landing. It can only lower you more or less straight down, at a controlled rate, spilling trapped air out through its various openings. Like...

There's an 'apex vent' at the top-center of the canopy, right over the jumper's head (designed to keep the chute from swinging wildly from side to side as it spills its air in big sloppy belches), and a series of missing panels around the aft rim that *direct* the escaping air, in a weak 'jet,' out the back of the canopy, giving it its built-in ten knots of forward airspeed. So-called 'toggle lines,' attached to the outermost of those vent panels, give the 'chutist' the ability to close one or the other, pinching off some of the canopy and making the 'thrust' asymmetrical, thereby causing the chute to turn right or left as desired. This is what *steers* the parachute.

However, if *both* toggle lines are pulled at the same time (sort of 'bunching up' the chute's general 'cup shape'... definitely not an intended design feature), the chute, with its reduced 'aerial footprint,' drops at a slightly faster than normal rate.

And as bizarre as it may seem, *that's* what allows an experienced jumper to land *gently... if his timing is* perfect.

What happens is, in the last few seconds before touchdown, the jumper hauls down on both toggle lines simultaneously, which, as mentioned above, causes the chute to suddenly contract and accelerate towards the ground. Then, at the last possible second—at that intuitively perfect instant—the jumper *releases* both toggle lines simultaneously. They snap upward, which pops those vents open again, and allows the chute to *boom* to full size once more. It catches a big gulp of air, and momentarily 'stalls'—or *stops*—theoretically just inches above the ground, such that the jumper can just 'step off' onto dry land, once again "as if alighting from that proverbial flight of stairs." And this is much easier on the bones than your standard Parachute Landing Fall. *If* you do it right!

The danger is obvious, though. Release those toggles too *late*, and you crash to ground at an even faster rate than you would have had you done nothing. Fast enough to sprain ankles, and break bones.

Hence the military's decision to officially prohibit the practice.

So this phenomenon is no figment of my imagination. It's a very real idiosyncrasy of a round parachute. I've seen Smoke and Monty do it.

And I can see now the role that it just played in my salvation.

* * *

BASICALLY THEN, (1) THE tug of the released load *dropping* finished what I'd so feebly started with that stupid ankle strap, ripping it apart and allowing the log to fall away normally, and (2) the sudden loss of that much weight triggered the unique effect of bringing my round parachute to an abrupt stop in the air. The detached log then belly-flopped into the pea-gravel a split second before my feet touched down, and I found myself standing upright, unscathed, at the exact bullseye of the DZ.

Amazing!

In retrospect, I suppose only that last part actually qualifies as a 'miracle.' Considering that I hadn't *touched* my toggle lines throughout my entire descent—preoccupied as I was with that damned strap and the impending disaster it was about to create—the fact that my *first turn* towards the DZ was sufficient to guide my chute right to the heart of the PI, despite any effects of the wind on the way down, is *astonishing*.

Actually, now that I think about it, my joy is tempered somewhat by an embarrassing new realization... that with nothing but those minuscule wax 'barbs' hanging up my ankle strap, I could have just pulled the old Red Apple *at altitude! Like normal!* I could have ignored the snag's impasse altogether, and the log's falling weight would have pulled the strap from its buckle *for me*. Just as it ultimately did anyway, a mere thirty or so feet above the ground.

In other words, this could have been a completely routine jump.

Of course, I had no way of knowing that at the time. And maybe envisioning all the worst case scenarios and over-thinking my limited options didn't help as much as I'd thought.

Hard to believe, I know.

Oh well; at least it finished perfectly.

I look up at Sal Donado as he lumbers past me, burdened with all his chutes and logs and weapons.

"Did you see that?," I shout.

He returns a constipated grimace.

"What da' hell wa' youze yelling about up d'ere? You sounded like a fuckin' asshole."

I bust out laughing, and follow him back to the rally point, first, last, and foremost, a survivor of the day.

STORY XXVIII

SOUR NOTES

1
THE LITTLE SHED IN THE WOODS

December, 1977
In the field outside Little Rock AFB, Little Rock, Arkansas

THIS JUST CANNOT BE GOOD.

I mean, the name's bad enough—*the "Gas Chamber"*—but, having found it out here, alone and isolated in this little clearing in the Arkansas woods, its appearance does nothing to embolden the spirit either.

It's a corrugated steel shack, about the size of a one-car garage, with two doors (on the 'side' and on the 'end') and no windows. It's brown with rust, mold, age, and general forest filth, and looks like something into which things disappear and never come back.

That, or just a nasty old shit-stank two-holer outhouse.

Either way, I do not want to get a whiff of what's inside that shack.

Of course, that's just exactly what we're here to do today.

Sgt. Stillman, the ever-grim dirty-jobber of the instructor cadre, has already donned his gas mask, and is now drawing gas *canisters* from a box and tucking them into his leg pockets. The rest of us are just shuffling around in the grass, keeping an eye on him and chuckling nervously, like condemned men watching their executioner sharpen his axe.

He finishes collecting his 'stink bombs,' and vanishes—alone, and without preamble—into the ramshackle little structure. Sgt. Rabin struts into our midst as the metal door squeaks closed behind Stillman, and starts reviewing the mask-donning procedures one more time.

Chin tucked into its pocket first, straps pulled back over the skull, stretched and adjusted for a snug fit. Then one palm cupped under the chin of the mask (plugging the exhaust vent), and blowing *(which creates an overpressure that clears the mask of any residual gas), followed immediately by hands over the side filters (covering the inlet vents) and* inhaling *(either sucking the air* out *of the mask and creating a good vacuum seal, or letting air* in, *and thereby telling you in no uncertain terms that you* haven't *got a good seal). And in the event of the latter, you reseat, and repeat the sequence until you get it right. Finish by tugging all the straps tight for comfort and stability, and then sit back and enjoy sucking the good air out of the bad.*

Fortunately for me, step by step, everything works as advertised, and within seven or eight seconds, my mask is on and *doin' its thang*, filtering out all that nasty backwood oxygen and clean-smelling leafy air shit, and leaving me with the far more pleasant and healthy *eau du sweat un rubbair*.

Looking out through the mask's eyepieces is like looking out through heavy-gauge biker's goggles... *that cover your whole face*. Sorta' like a wetsuit for your head. Around me, the nine other black-headed goggle-eyed aliens are checking each other out with equal parts curiosity and trepidation.

Not for long, though.

"All right, gentlemen!" shouts Sgt. Rabin (the only creature in this clearing that's not mummified in rubber), "You're going to be making *two* passes through the chamber this afternoon. On this first one, you're going to go in with your masks already on—as you are now—and Sgt. Stillman will pop some teargas for you to sample. You'll spend a minute or two breathing normally and getting a feel for just how well your masks really work. Then we're going to have you *remove* your masks, so you can see what you were missing when they were on."

This gets everyone swallowing hard and swapping nervous glances.

"Take a breath or two, then we'll let you out the back door to air out. Use your canteens to wash out your eyes, and take some time getting cleared up and squared away. Then it's back into the chamber for Round Two.

"On this one, you'll be going in *without* your masks—they'll be holstered—and the room will already be filled with gas. Once everybody's in and has had a couple of seconds to take in the 'aromatic ambience,' we'll cue you to *mask up*, and you'll get to practice your rapid-donning-and-clearing techniques. And once everybody's done, you'll exit back out this door, you'll *air* out and *rinse* out, and we'll call it a day. Okay? Any questions?"

Nothing. Not a peep... for once.

"All right then, let's go."

* * *

HE PULLS THE DOOR open for us... and it's *dark* in there!

Well, not *completely* dark. There's a bare bulb swinging at the end of a long cord that's dangling from the apex of the roof. It casts a wan mustard pool of light over Sgt. Stillman where he stands—at parade rest, no less—astride his gathered gas grenades and an empty bucket, right smack dab in the dead center of the chamber.

There is no flooring. It's the same grass and dirt that's *outside* the shed, only a little deader. And there's absolutely nothing else inside it but us hooded chickens.

Hey! This building is nothing but a shell! A gas trap!

Well, duhhh!

The door finally closes behind us, leaving only that dim star floating in the middle of the room, top-lighting old 'Darth Vader in cammies' there. And while Sgt. Rabin squirms into his own mask, Sgt. Stillman's rubber-muffled voice shouts out, "*Check your seals one more time, gentlemen! We're about to begin!*"

Then he reaches down and snatches up one of the grenades. And I notice that he's wearing gloves.

I run through my clearing and sealing procedures again, reassuring myself that my mask has all but fused itself to my face, and turn back to Sgt. Stillman just in time to watch him pull the lanyard on the first grenade. It hisses and spits out some thin smoke, and he raises it to his filtered nose. He waves it back and forth there for a moment, looking like an alien wine connoisseur sniffing the smokey *odeur* of a rancid Bourdeaux, then he leans forward and drops the bomb in the bucket.

Probably getting a little warm, even for gloved fingertips, I imagine.

From there, he picks up the bucket and, starting with the last student to my right, he begins a lazy stroll down the line, pausing every few steps to more fully immerse each of us in the swirls of oily smoke.

And I have to admit that, throughout the three to five seconds that he stands in front of me, waving that bucket like a lantern under my rubber nose, I don't smell a thing... at least nothing beyond what I smelled when I first dragged this damned mask over my face. Just fresh rubber and old sweat.

Well, that's reassuring, at least. My filters work, and my seals seem to be holding. Or maybe that's just a regular old smoke bomb he's got in there.

We'll know in a moment, I guess.

Sgt. Stillman finishes with the last student to my *left*, strolls back out under the solitary light bulb, and sets the smoldering bucket down at his feet.

His voice sounds like he's shouting from inside a sleeping bag when he barks, "*Alright, gentlemen! Masks off! Let's go!*"

Sgt. Rabin steps out of the shadows, and joins him in urging us on.

"*Come on, let's go! Let's get this over with! You're not going to gain anything by puttin' this off! Let's get those masks off... now!*"

Damn, I don't want to do this, but... well... *here goes!*

I draw a deep breath, hold it, and clamp my eyes shut. Then I seize the edges of my mask along the jaw lines, and rip the whole thing off over the top of my head... and stand there, hunched and grimacing with my eyes squeezed shut, like a kid waiting for the next whack on his ass from his dad's paddle... except that *I'm* just waiting to hear Sgt. Stillman's call for us to get out of the chamber. That's all I want, I want it now, and I want it bad.

Any time now, boss! Before this shit starts to burn!

Someone coughs, explosively, down the row to my left, followed a second later by somebody else gagging out, "*Aw, jeez-z-greist!*" Then the entire student echelon collapses into hacking, weeping, retching chaos. I doggedly keep my eyes shut and my breath bottled, but the gas still manages to find the moist seams of my eyes and the mucus membranes in my nose, and *sets them afire*. A second later—still without

having drawn a breath of the stuff—my lungs somehow spasm, and yank in what feels like a throatful of flaming saltwater... and I'm off to the races with the rest of them, honking and coughing furiously, doubled over and jamming the heels of my palms into my sizzling eye sockets.

What the hell!

My eyelid muscles—already clenched about as tight as they could possibly be—now *convulse*, slamming so hard shut that it makes a roaring sound *in my ears!* I couldn't *pry* them open now if I wanted to (and I'm not convinced I *do*), not with fingers, popsicle sticks, or screwdrivers, much less with the paltry facial muscles surrounding them. Tears are spilling down my cheeks in hot sheets, and my nose is running like a snot-hose.

I am utterly blind, and coughing too helplessly to even stand upright. Yet somehow—and I know this because I've seen film footage of gassed rioters running with nothing but wet hankies clutched to their faces—somehow *some* people are still capable of functioning and forging ahead under such a searing and personal assault.

How? My face is on fire, my eyes are welded shut, the snot stringing from my nose is probably touching the ground right now, and I'm coughing like I just belched up a three-alarm jalapeno burp! How can you even function like this?

You're not supposed to.

That's kind of the whole friggin' point, actually.

Okay, guys! I can appreciate how effective my gas mask is already! How about letting me outa' here now? Okay? Guys?! Guys?!!!

Nothing. The instructors are silent. Or maybe I just can't hear them over my own hysterical coughing. I mean, this shed is filled with all the overlapping, echoing, barking bedlam of a dog kennel that just had a cat saunter down the center aisle. Nobody can even stop coughing long enough to beg to be let out. But when the call finally comes, even though it's muffled by mask rubber, I have no trouble hearing it or obeying it.

"Alright, gentlemen! *The door is open to your left! To your left! Let's go! Turn and move! Turn and move! To your left! That's it! Go, go, go!*"

I reel roughly ninety degrees to my left, collide with somebody else—at least our weaving arms do—and blunder after them.

Another instructor, his voice smothered by his mask and sounding like he's trying to scream through a pillow, shouts over the pandemonium, "*Come to my voice! Follow my voice! I'm standing next to the doorway! Come to my voice! That's it!*"

And now it's full-body billiards, as all ten blinded students converge on that voice at the same time.

I throw my head back, and with every muscle in my *head* concentrating on my eyelids, I manage to strain my left eye partially open—just a crack, and for just a split second—just enough to get a quick mental snapshot of the blurred and blinding white rectangle of the doorway before my lids crash shut again as if on powerful springs. I veer towards it, and bowl through the opening into clean air, caroming off my colleagues like a single aggie amid a spill of mixed marbles.

The 'burnt metal' smell of the gas vanishes once I'm outside, and the acoustics instantly 'dry up.' But the dire coughing, gasping, sniffing and snorting continues unabated. I stumble onward, as far away from that fucking shed as I can get in a flat-out drunken stagger. Then I lurch to a stop and start clawing at my web belt, trying frantically to tear my canteen free of its snaps.

Naturally, it chooses this moment to fight me, its simple post-and-hole snaps refusing to let go. And in my struggle, I wind up wrenching my web belt almost up to my armpits before they finally pop free.

Canteen in hand then, I spin off its top, lean back, and dump it all over my smoldering eyes... *with absolutely zero effect*. I can't open them enough to even let any water in!

"Ah, *fuck!*"

This epithet, shouted in harmony with several other comparable variations, is repeated all around me, spat and roared and yodeled atop the chorus of helpless coughing and retching, as apparently each of my fellow victims is having similar success with their canteens.

"*Use your fingers!*," an unidentifiable instructor yells through the snorkeling of his gas mask. "*Pull your eyes open with your fingers, if you have to, but wash 'em out! Come on, ladies, you can do it!*"

And I do. With a shaking thumb and forefinger, I pry my top and bottom eyelids apart—and it's a struggle, let me tell you—while my other hand floods my eyeball with canteen water. Normally I hate getting water in my eyes, but right now it borders on *orgasmic!* Not exactly 'instant relief,' it's still blessedly cool and soothing, like a big swig of something cold and wet after you've bitten into a white hot pepper... *with your eyes!*

I pour a little down my scalded throat as well.

My coughing slowly abates, as does the roaring in my ears (from my tightly clenched eyes), and I sag into a weary stoop, gasping and sputtering, hands on knees, empty canteen clattering to the ground. Around me, the cannonade of my classmates' desperate coughing also peters out into sporadic honks and hacks as well, interspersed with colorful blasphemies and imprecations, many of which imply some biologically unlikely origins of our instructor cadre.

After a minute or two of that, though, my five-thousandth attempt at opening my eyes finally succeeds.

"*Son of a BITCH!*"

Everyone appears to be in agreement with *that* sentiment as well.

Looking around, I see that everyone is sporting the same wild-eyed, *red*-eyed, red-*faced* expression that I am. Head and shoulders, we are all dripping wet, and most are still delicately plucking great ropes of snot and phlegmy drool from our noses and mouths.

For some reason, I don't recall seeing any slides of *this* during Sgt. Beaudry's grand sales pitch back at Keesler. Because I'm pretty sure it would have had a bit of a dampening effect on my interest in this career choice.

"Alright, ladies!" shouts Sgt. Rabin, his own mask now cocked back high on his head like a welder's shield between firings. "Take your masks, and wave 'em around for a minute or two! Get 'em aired out! Then holster them, and snap your holsters shut! You'll be going back into the chamber as soon as Sgt. Stillman is ready in there!"

As soon as he's "ready" in there? What the hell else does he need to do? Make it more toxic? What; is he popping all the rest of his grenades at the same time now?

My eyes burn and tear up just thinking about it.

I find my gas mask lying on the ground somewhere nearby. At least I presume it's mine. I don't even remember dropping it. Then like everyone else, I start walking around in circles, flapping it back and forth in my hands, as if drying out the pages of a wet book.

In the meantime, Sgt. Rabin slips his mask back down over his face, and steps back into the chamber to check on Stillman's progress. An ugly yellow cloud of noxious mist boils out through the door as he does, and all nine of my fearless classmates recoil from it as if a Doberman had just slipped out before the door could close again.

Oh man, I do not want to go back in there again... not without my gas mask on... not without being wheeled in inside a sealed and pressurized hyperbaric chamber, for that matter.

The door creaks open again, unleashing another belch of greasy, yellowish, *infected-looking* fog, and Sgt. Rabin steps out of the sickly mist, waving us over.

"*Holster your masks, gentlemen!,*" he yells, muffled and barely audible inside his gas mask again. "*Make sure your holsters are secured—both snaps closed—then get your asses in here! Come on! Hurry up!*"

Oh, yeh. Can't wait!

Is it okay if I run *to get back in there as soon as possible?*

But, along with everyone else, I draw a deep unwilling breath, and stuff my mask back into the holster on my right hip. Then I join the reluctant herd gathering around the door where Sgt. Rabin still stands, half obscured by that thin diseased mist that continues to ooze out of the opening.

"*Ready?*" he asks.

"Fuck no!" we shout back, almost in unison.

"*Alright, then! Come on in!*" And he steps aside.

* * *

I CAN'T HELP IT (and neither can anyone else, apparently): I turn around, suck in a deep draught of clean outside air before turning back, clamp my eyes shut again, and lunge into the chamber blind. It's stupid, I know, and of course it's completely ineffective, but I just can't help it.

This doesn't bother the instructors at all, naturally. What do they care about how long we try to hold our breaths? It doesn't make any difference whatsoever, obviously. As we've already quite convincingly established for ourselves, teargas does not require any actual inhalation in order to make your life miserable.

And sure enough, within only a couple of steps of re-entering the chamber, I am quickly reminded of its many alternative angles of attack. The damned stuff finds the moisture along the seams of my eyelids, and once again my eyes start to *scream!* All around me, the coughing kicks in again. So does the profanity, much of it directed pretty brazenly at the instructors themselves—their sexual proclivities, their reprehensible gene pool, all the usual stuff—though its impact is somewhat mitigated by all the hysterical flailing, coughing, gasping, and the hawking up of decorative phlegm that steals most of our air.

I continue to wander, half doubled over, toward the general vicinity of the middle of the room. But it's all on 'inertial navigation' now, since none of my 'external sensors' are even working anymore.

Jiminy Crickets! It feels like I've got a Fourth of July sparkler spittin' away inside my lungs, right behind my sternum, hot and scratchy, burning and triggering cough after cough after helpless cough. I can actually *feel* the flames licking the inside of my nose and curling outside my nostrils, and my eyelids have now been soldered completely shut, melting and fusing together with what feels like a bead of acid.

Seriously folks! What the hell good will it do to put my mask on now?!

"Alright, gentlemen!," a rubber-smothered voice shouts (with perfect timing), "Put 'em on! Now! Get 'em out and put 'em on! Go, go, go!"

I slap at my holster, and somehow manage to rip my mask out in just one deft motion—*why couldn't I do that earlier with the friggin' canteen?*—followed by several much longer seconds of fumbling and juggling the mask... trying to figure out which side is up (I have to find both eyepieces with both hands before I do), untangling the basket of straps, and planting my chin in the correct inner pocket before stretching it over the top of my head.

From there, though, it goes like clockwork. Desperate *frantic* clockwork. Palm plugging my chin exhaust vent and blowing the last of my lung's air into the mask, overpressurizing it and theoretically purging it of any trapped gas... covering the inlet filters on each cheek and sucking for all I'm worth to ensure a tight vacuum seal... then letting go, and taking my first untainted breaths since walking through that door... for all the good it does.

Needless to say, it doesn't help even a *damned* bit. The damage has already been done, and I can't *air* out or *wash* out my eyes with this friggin' mask on. I take some heart knowing that I can breathe normally now and not make things any worse than they already are, but in the meantime, my eyelids still cannot break the smoldering welds that bind them, my nose is still gushing snot down my chin and into the mask's exhaust vent, and I'm still coughing like an entire wing of an emphysema clinic. Throw in the hot rubber facial wetsuit that's now stuck to my burning skin—none of which I can relieve as long as I'm in this shed and in this mask—and I am full-on *hating this shit!*

Of course, the whole point of this re-entry into the chamber was not to show us how wonderfully comfortable we'd become the instant we donned a mask in a gaseous environment, but rather to let us actually *experience* the long slow clearing process of a mask worn over an 'already poisoned face.' To prove to us that ultimately the mask *will* set things right again.

It was also intended to show us the importance of mastering our quick-donning procedures, I imagine. And to that end, well, I suppose I did learn *something*. Like, "*I need to practice donning my mask with my eyes closed a whole lot more.*" But beyond that, the only things I've gotten out of all this are that (1) *teargas SUCKS*, and (2) *I didn't need to come back in here a second time to figure that out!*

They keep us in here anyway. No leaving just yet! Apparently there's something *else* to be learned from the miseries of continued immersion. Personally, I'm having a little trouble picking up on it, though. And through all the coughing and gagging and swearing, I can now hear somebody repeating, "*Walk it off! Walk it off! Walk it off!,*" then, "*Breathe deep, and blow it all out! Breathe deep and blow it all out!*"

I can do that outside! *With my mask* off!

Let's blow this popsicle stand!

But as the minutes crawl past—with my eyes gushing peppery tears that my fingers cannot reach, and my lungs scraped raw by that sputtering sparkler and the incessant coughing it's provoked—the mask's filters do their job and feed cleansed air into my nose and through my goggles. And slowly—achingly, frustratingly, impatiently slowly—my eyes unclench (although remaining unfocused and flooded with tears), my coughing subsides, and at last I can straighten up and look around the dark and foggy shed.

I can't actually *see* anything, of course, except for some stooped and blurry shadow-figures milling around that lonely pool of light in the middle of the chamber. But the fact that I can open my eyes at all feels like a minor miracle unto itself.

And that's the cue, apparently. Because once enough of us appear sufficiently recovered, they suddenly open the side door, and let us out!

Just like that!

* * *

OUT IN THE CLEAN Arkansas air again, I rip my mask off, douse my face with the contents of my second canteen, then plop down in the grass to catch my breath... along with severing the strings of snot that are stretching between my nose and the mask like melted pizza cheese.

Yeh, a photo of this *during Sgt. Beaudry's slide presentation would have painted an entirely different picture of this 'glamorous' and 'heroic' job for me.*

But after another minute or two of exhausted gasping (and dousing and spitting and clearing throats), the group falls back on its normal grab-ass nature, and the laughing and razzing and insulting resumes... especially once Sgt. Stillman finally strolls out of the shed, tendrils of that nasty jaundiced smoke sloughing off his arms and shoulders like dry ice, his bucket of spent canisters clutched in one fist like a severed head, and steps into a *sprawling* (as opposed to a *standing*) ovation of sarcastic applause.

He looks like some kind of sci-fi bounty hunter who's just stepped out of an airlock off the surface of a Jovian ice moon... or something.

Well, that's one way to be remembered, I suppose.

He doffs his mask with grand stoic showmanship, and stares us all down until the acclaim fizzles out, and the clearing in the woods goes quiet again. Then he waves us all towards the deuce-and-a-half for our ride back to the hangar.

And so ends our visit to the Little Shed in the Woods.

2

"LADIES AND GENTLEMEN, OUR INSPIRATIONAL CLASS LEADER!"

INSTEAD OF RETURNING US to our field camp though, this time the truck drives us all the way back to the BAQ, our accommodations at Little Rock Air Force Base. In the wake of our gassing, everyone needs to "shit, shower, and shave," as they say… and sanitize, and air out our clothing. And the timing is perfect, because our next 'frag'—and thereby the jump that goes with it—is scheduled to be a *night op*, our first, which requires a roadtrip back to base anyway just to catch our next flight.

So for now we're back in our rooms (*long time no see!*), just long enough to thoroughly delouse ourselves and air out our cammies. Then it's off to the hangar again to chute-up and jump into Sal Donado's Frag #3; the dreaded *Night DZ*.

Now, thanks to my ex-roomie, Harold Trefelden, who managed to wash out of the program on only its second day, I've had this room all to myself right from the very beginning. And that seems especially propitious at a time like this, when my deepening feelings of inferiority among my student 'peers,' including the alienation and ostracism that go along with it, make such a moment of solitude (and downright wondrous cleanliness) a respite of near-religious ecstasy.

So, of course, *that* can't last.

I'm pacing around the room in my skivvies, rubbing a towel through my hair, still damp from my shower, when two loud knocks bring me over to my door.

I shout, "Yeh?" by which I *obviously* mean, "*Who is it?*"

The door swings open without an answer, and there stands Sgt. Haley, fully shat, showered, and shaven, and dressed for war. He looks me over for a few seconds, then scans the room as if looking for witnesses.

"What's up?" I ask.

His eyes return to me, and his brow crimps into a strange mixture of vexation and disbelief.

Finally, through clenched teeth, he says, "Why are you here?"

What?

I have no idea what to say to that. So I stand there, in my underwear, in the middle of my own (theoretically 'private') room, gawping like a goldfish and trying to formulate some kind of a witty riposte, like, "*because this is the only place I can dress like this and not get arrested.*" Rim-shot. "*Hardy har-har-har!*"

But Haley doesn't wait for my snappy comeback.

"Seriously, man: what are you doing here? You're not right for this job, and you know it. So what *the fuck* are you doing here?"

I... no, uh... I'm... what?

"You suck at this shit."

I suck? You mean...

Then, for close to another ten seconds or so, he seems to fidget in place, not out of any nervousness or uncertainty—I don't think he's *ever* had to deal with that—but just from the sheer frustration of not being able to spew forth all the vitriol and anger that's apparently been building up since Day One, nor all the righteous speeches he's no doubt been practicing in his head that entire time, but which are now clogging his throat as they fight to come out all at the same time.

And through it all, I just stand there, rooted to my wet spot in the carpet, speechless and stupefied in my own way.

At last, with a snap of his head, as if shaking clear the bottleneck of hostile words, he gives up trying to salvage his carefully crafted little oratory, and instead grabs the door knob to leave. And as he backs out into the hallway, he adds, "You need to quit, man. You just need to quit."

And the door slams shut.

Ladies and gentlemen! Our inspirational class leader!

Thank you very much!

Well now… wasn't that helpful. Probably fixed everything *with that one stirring address.*

I know *I* feel better.

3
MANNA FROM HEAVEN

NO SIMULATED COMBAT LOADS tonight.

We're jumping in with lights, anemometers, weather balloons, and a whole passel of 'defensive ordinance.' We need our real *rucksacks* tonight.

In an effort to forestall my inevitable queasiness, however, I opt *not* to participate in the group C-rat 'buffet' that precedes the event. I'll just eat later, once we're on the ground and the DZ is up and running. Besides, after Haley's 'motivational sermon' in my room an hour ago, it doesn't really feel like I fit in well enough to partake in anything terribly 'social' right now. Instead, I take my box of Cs, and try to stuff it into my loaded rucksack among all the Elco lights, spare batteries, and my wadded up field jacket.

But it just doesn't fit. It's too big and boxy, and will have to sit *on top* of everything else rather than being tucked in *among* it. And I'm not convinced it would stay there through the parachute's opening shock anyway. So...

What to do?

Then, from out of the blue, it dawns on me that I don't *need* to take the whole box with me. I don't use half of what's in the damned thing anyway. Just the entree, the fruit cocktail, and maybe the canned crackers, if it's got 'em, but that's all.

And with that revelation, a whole new brilliantly 'clever' alternative crosses my mind... if I'm only going to be taking just the two or three cans that I have an actual interest in, why jam them in among all the clutter and junk in my *ruck* when I've got perfectly good—and perfectly *unused*—*leg pockets* on my pants? I can stow my spaghetti-and-meatballs, fruit cocktail, and maybe even unsalted crackers *in my thigh pockets*, and crack into them any time it's convenient, without having to hunt for them or find ways to dispose of the unwanted box and unused condiments!

I'm a friggin' genius!

I wonder why nobody's ever thought of this before?

So, while the rest of the gang consorts and consumes and communes along the Ready Room's back wall, clattering through their rations and bolstering their bravado with bullshit, I rip open my own box, select out my preferences, and set the rest aside. I just leave the rejects right there on the countertop, presuming someone else will find some use for them.

Then I slip the entree can into my left thigh pocket, the dessert can into my right, toss in a small peanut-butter-and-chocolate hockey puck (no crackers in this box, unfortunately), and a P-38 can opener, and button everything up.

Tah-daaahhh!

Everything in its place, ready for war.

* * *

JUMP #3 HERE AT Combat Control School is only the second night jump I've ever been on (the first one being at Jump School). In this, I am once again unique among my more experienced peers, who have all got a multitude of such drops tucked under their belts from their months spent with their teams prior to coming here to Little Rock.

But the main things I remember from my one and only Jump School night drop are (1) those surreal last steps as I charged out the door into the great black vortex, (2) the slow unsettling descent into the featureless pitch of the drop zone, and (3) the jarring impact with the unseen ground.

And, well... *here we go again.*

* * *

AS EXPECTED, THE FLIGHT has been short and painless, and in no time I'm lined up with the others, queued on the open (and thundering) portside jump door, waiting on the red jump light, and watching Sal—

tonight's 'leader' (and thereby its defacto 'jumpmaster-in-training')—as Sgt. Hemingway points out the timing and perimeter lights down on the ground to him, and screams into the side of his helmet. A moment later, the two of them rear back from the door together, Hemingway stepping several paces out of the way, while Sal waves Haley (the lead jumper in our stick) right up into the ready position in the door jamb.

The skies are cold and clear tonight, the air commensurately smooth. And before the rest of us have even finished compacting up behind him, the light goes a barely visible green (lost in the overall red wash of the plane's interior), and the stampede begins.

Like every jumpmaster before him, Sal stands in the pummeling slipstream, slapping each passing shoulder, and shouting "*Go! Go! Go! Go! Go!...*"

I shuffle forward along with the rest of the herd, left hand guiding my static line down the anchor cable, right hand clutching the end of my reserve chute, my rucksack banging against my knee, the butt of my GAU-5 jiggling under my armpit, and the cans of my cleverly cached C-rats clonking around loose in the thigh pockets of my pants.

As I near the doorway, I whip my static line into the loadmaster's hands, and turn into the roaring black maw, doing my best (under all my encumbrances) to *charge* the precipice. I feel the clap of Sgt. Donado's hand on my shoulder, I feel the plunge in temperature as I enter the wintry torrent, and I feel the icy bite of the C-130's outer skin as my thinly gloved fingers grab the doorframe. I ignore the panicky reflexive cave-in of my guts, as well as the jarring flash of adrenaline that instantly takes their place, and I hurl myself into bottomless space. The black avalanche of passing air seizes me in flight, and bundles me off to the rear, tumbling blind and close to giggling.

So far, so good.

Then comes the opening shock.

Oh, it's a perfectly normal, by-the-numbers, firm-but-smooth parachute opening and all that, and that makes me very happy. But just as the upward tugging of my risers hits its peak and my legs are flung downward, I feel a sharp 'unzipping' sensation down the outsides of both legs. And by the time my two pendulum swings have ended and I've finished bicycling a couple of twists out of my suspension lines, I realize an embarrassing new truth.

I've just blown out both of my pant legs.

On opening shock, those stupid C-rat cans *just kept right on going*, blasting out the bottoms of my pockets, and, as I shortly discover, flaying open my lower pant legs all the way down to the blousing rubbers. I can see the tattered halves flapping in the breeze, and my lovely *uncamouflaged* white long-johns winking up at me in the moonlight. So I've not only just trashed one of the *only two* sets of cammies I own—before even getting *halfway through Field Week*, by the way—but I just threw away my dinner as well.

What I *can't* see, though, are the three OD-green cans that are now hurtling Earthward like a meteor shower. They've plunged into the darkness beneath my feet.

Fist-sized hail.

Manna from Heaven.

Good work there, Steve... ya' dumbass.

STORY XXIX

NIGHT MOVES

1
DAY FIVE: MY LUCKY STARS

December, 1977
In the field outside Little Rock AFB, Little Rock, Arkansas

OKAY, NOW I'M TIRED. And the weird part is that we got to *sleep in* this morning. I was actually well rested for once. After last night's DZ work (and C-rat meteor shower), and considering today's drawn-out training agenda, they'd penciled in a morning rest period for us.

Quite the novelty here at CCS.

So I got to eat my canned ham-and-eggs *after 9:00am today* (instead of the usual 'sick-before-six' routine). Still cold, greasy, unidentifiable and borderline unpalatable, but at least filling and unhurried for once.

That was followed at ten by four hours of field classroom: ten students in folding chairs at one end of a twenty-man tent, with a freestanding blackboard, an easel with flipcharts, and an instructor or two at the other end.

They bludgeoned us (or at least *me*) into a near-coma with the procedures and mathematical formulae for rigging explosives to various disposable objects, as well as some night navigation stuff. But I spent all but the first few minutes of that time in a desperate struggle to just *not nod off* too conspicuously, while my aching frozen prune-feet twitched and stretched and ground and clocked against each other in a futile attempt to work out the kinks and knots. Because, though the torturous grip of these new boots on my bruised and battered heels has eased somewhat, the pain has also broadened into a *full-time* throbbing now, whether I'm walking at the time or not. So, when it comes to my feet at least, the misery just never ends any more.

It seemed I'd also under-dressed a tad for the weather today, which chilled and turned a little drippy overnight. So I also got to enjoy the bone-deep shivers and the rolling shudders that sank in so early, and then just never went away.

Livin' the dream, boys! Livin' the dream.

Then, when the tent-classes finally ended at around two in the afternoon, they loaded us all into the deuce-and-a-half again—the old "Wind Chill Express"—and drove us back to base for Frag #4 (and with it, *jump* #4), this time led by Sgt. Corbin, the youngest, the most junior in rank (of the sergeants), and the *last* of our four student NCOs.

The instructors still haven't divulged their plans yet for who will inherit the fifth and final frag some three days hence. But since we're plum out of untried sergeants now, it seems to be the general consensus that it will just have to befall good old Sgt. Haley again.

Good. I hope it's a nasty one.

The jump that followed this afternoon—our second one with a *simulated* combat load (*fucking railroad ties*), and my fourth one wearing one of the parachutes that *I* packed, under duress, a full *month* ago—well, that went just fine. For once.

It was almost 'fun.'

And the frag itself? Though it was pretty much just another straightforward daylight DZ scenario, it culminated with a live *multi*-ship CDS ("Container Delivery System") drop, which really illustrated just how critical precise wind-drift calculations are. Plus it was cool to watch. Maybe not as cool as the ridge-strafing drop I witnessed up at Yakima with the McChord guys, but still very cool for its own reasons... like the fact that there were *three* ships in today's formation versus the one-at-a-time at Yakima, and how they dropped a *skyful* of netted cargo with each pass, as opposed to Yakima's *one* pallet at a time. They also offset their runs—well off the obvious centerline of the DZ—in accordance with our wind-drift calculations. And it was cooler still watching the descending loads waft across the DZ with the wind, but then thump to ground in a straight line *right down the middle of the drop zone*, all thanks to *our good math!*

Then again, maybe I'm just more easily entertained these days.

Sunset settled in shortly after we wrapped that up, and that left us with barely an hour-and-a-half with which to make our way off the DZ—or, in *my* case, *limp*—into the woods to our camp, and there gather up the rucksacks that we *hadn't* brought along for the jump and the frag scenario, along with whatever 'dinner' we could throw down our necks in the time remaining... that being the 'time remaining' before the commencement of tonight's cross-country festivities.

That's right. After an already long and busy day of physical *and* mental exertion, tonight we've got another overland navigation marathon to get through! Only this time, it's in *the dark*.

Oh, and while I'm thinking about it: funny story here...

* * *

AS WE WERE SHUFFLING back into camp between our day and night taskings, Rocky, aware of his limited time, snatched a can of baked beans from his C-rat collection, and set it down next to our campfire on one of the half-burned logs that we use as a bench, while *he* went on to his tent to work on his rucksack preparations. It had seemed like a good idea at the time, too. He'd be one of the only ones to have an actual 'hot meal' before tromping off into the wilds of nighttime Arkansas. I can remember watching him and thinking, *You know, that's not a bad idea.*

Well, it probably *would* have been a good idea if he hadn't gotten all caught up with rigging his ruck and changing his sodden clothes (something I can't do, since my only other set of cammies now has both legs blown out). But he *did* get caught up with it. And on top of everything else, by the time he was done re-lacing his boots and was standing up to go retrieve his meal, other members of 'the team'—who hadn't noticed the lone can-o-beans sitting there on that log—had since stoked and rekindled the fire into a right fine little bone-warming clothes-drying blaze, and were standing around it, soaking up the heat... when the can exploded.

Rocky had anticipated neither the amount of time he was going to be tied up at his tent, nor the extent to which our feeble little campfire would be fed and fanned into a world-class bonfire by the other students, and so had not taken the time to punch any holes in the can to vent it. Inevitably then, once its contents had reached the boiling point, the building pressures finally ruptured the can's containment with a *POW!* that rivaled the grenades at the Army's Weapons School.

There was a brief patter of supersonic beans rattling through the nearest trees and against the sides of tents, along with a howl of startlement from the half-dozen or so guys within the immediate blast radius. Naturally! They were justifiably certain that they'd just been riddled with *metal shrapnel*.

Then as realization replaced consternation, the whole camp erupted in laughter. Everything within a broad circumference of the fire was plastered with baked beans, including—much to my great glee—the inimitable born-to-command uber-trooper himself, Sgt. Brad Haley, just freshly changed into a spankin'-sharp new set of cammies.

Everyone took it well, though. Even Sgt. Haley. Rocky even made a point of yelling at his fellow classmates for *stealing his food*. And when several of them offered to give it back to him, he took them up on it. With his plastic Spork, he walked around plucking individual beans off of other people's sleeves, shoulders, and hat brims. In no time at all then, everyone else got into it. And before we knew it, everyone—myself included—was eating beans off of tree trunks, fallen logs, and even scooping dollops of goop from the ashes and charcoal dust of the campfire.

Yes, indeeedy. A fine time was had by all.

Good and good for *ya'!*

* * *

AND NOW HERE WE ARE. Quarter till nine on a cold, clear, moonless Friday night. The deep woods—as well as every inch of our clothing—are wet from the off-and-on drizzliness of the day (plus there are a couple of guys whose fresh baked-bean-glaze of brown sugar and molasses is bound to make them popular with the little woodland creatures tonight). The trees are shadowy pillars crowded against the stars, but those damned thorny brambles are armpit-deep and *completely invisible* in the starlight. *Wonderful.*

Lordy, you just know I can't *wait* to march off into that stuff again, only this time in the dark, and without a flashlight (one of the ground rules of tonight's little covert exercise).

Tonight they've paired me up with Sgt. Sal Donado, and that's decent. He's been in a jocular mood ever since the Big Baked Bean Incident of '77. And since he's also a McChord guy like myself, he's always treated me more like a fellow inmate than just an annoying sub-par co-worker.

So I've got that much going for me anyway.

When they hand him the waypoint card, he turns to me and asks how good my night vision is (as in, *"How well can you read in the dim radium glow of your compass?"*). I assure him of my nocturnal capabilities, and relieve him of the card. And as he turns then to cinch up his weapon's shoulder strap—so that it hangs up high on his chest like a really wide bowtie, out of the reach of the brambles, and in the ready-fire position—I deploy my trusty compass and juice up its phosphorescence by pressing the head of my flashlight against its face and flicking it on for a few seconds.

When I'm done, the compass dial is glowing so brightly I can use it to illuminate the waypoint card and read its numbers: 087°/.62K. Almost due east, for a little over half a klick... six-hundred-and-eighty-two paces in... *that* direction. I peer over the fading yellow-green aura coming off the face of my compass, looking for a landmark along the zero-eight-seven-degree radial, and see... squat. I can't see dick... or jack, or shit, or even bupkis out there.

It's night, in the woods... *way out* in the woods. It's shadows layered upon shadows behind even more shadows out there. Darkness striped vertically by the even deeper darkness of the silhouetted trees. All part of a black-on-black world in which even profiles and outlines can't clearly exist.

Oh crap! What am I supposed to navigate off of this *time?*

Sounds? Smells?

Do they really expect me to just go crashing through the smothered clutter of the forest with my eyes locked on to my compass dial the whole way?

That's all that was suggested in the tent-classroom this morning: the critical need to follow that magnetic needle without deviation. But that can't be the best way to do this. There's got to be something out there that I can home in on, something true and anchored and just barely visible enough to allow me to keep my head up and my eyes dark-adapted.

Like...maybe the *treetops*. Or better yet, the stars *between* them!

Yeh! The stars!

I take my heading again, and this time carry my gaze straight up from the needle. And there, low on the barely implied horizon and peeking through the lattice of trees, is a pair of stars, one low and bright, the other one higher and dim. And the bright one is sitting right on the top of the sighting wire.

That's m'boy!

I can't tell what star it is, from which constellation—I can't see enough of its neighboring stars through the screen of foreground trees to put it in context—but it doesn't matter. I don't need to name it. As long as I can see it, tell it apart from its nearest stellar buddies, and hopefully keep it framed (but never occluded) by the trees that bracket it, it is a perfectly viable beacon for my purposes here tonight.

Yeh, but the stars move across the sky as the night rolls on. That beacon won't remain stationary enough for long *enough to follow it (and* only *it) for very far.*

True enough.

I think about that for a moment, while Sal wrestles his canteen out of his holster and takes a final swig.

We're heading east (at least initially), with the 'North Star', Polaris—around which all the rest of the stars of the northern hemisphere rotate like some grand cosmic Ferris wheel—off to our left. I can't see *that* right now, but it doesn't matter. That rotation means that those eastern stars in front of us will be drifting *upwards* (mostly)—rising more-or-less straight up from the horizon, give or take a little axial tilt—moreso than any left-to-right trend that might throw off my compass heading over time.

Still, to play it safe, I decide that at least every ten minutes, I'll need to take another sighting, maybe pick out a new star and re-orient on that, should the need arise, just to make sure I don't follow a course bent by the slow roll of the night sky.

I don't mention any of this to anyone. There are probably too many reasons why this tactic wasn't addressed by the instructors in the tent-class. Maybe it's too easy to wander off onto a parallel track when you're homing in on something so distant. Or maybe they just want us to master doing it the *hard way* first, so that we'll always have that compass-fixated method to fall back on whenever the stars are clouded over. I don't know. But whatever their reasoning, I just don't want to be talked out of it right now.

So, when Sal indicates that he's finally ready to go, I just turn into the deepest shadows and start marching toward my chosen star.

I even remember to keep track of my pace count this time.

* * *

IT WORKS SO WELL that when I spot our next waypoint card approaching, like a tiny rectangular ghost materializing out of the darkness, I start counting off my paces *out loud*, just so that Sal can hear it.

"Six-seventy-nine, six-eighty, six-eighty-*one*, six… eighty… *two*."

Then I stop dead in my tracks, the little white index card barely five feet in front of me, tacked to its midnight tree.

Sal thrashes through the last of the brambles behind me, and steps up to my shoulder.

"*Son of a bitch*," he whispers in that marble-mouthed Nu Yawk accent of his. I sense, from the way his voice seemed to shift, that he turned to look at me as he spoke. And I like to imagine there's a little 'awe' in his expression right now.

I grin.

"*You want the next one?*" I murmur.

"*Yeh. Wha'evuh.*"

And he marches up to the card, and snatches it from its sleeve.

* * *

NOT THAT THE GOING is ever easy. You can't see *anything* from the supposed horizon-line down. And the only thing you can see from the horizon-line *up* is the diamond-dusted sky peeking through the ranks of dark leafless trees. But at least my attention can be wholly dedicated to the placement of my feet and the scanning of my surroundings, and not constantly referring to the dimming dial of my compass.

Not that there's exactly a whole lot to be seen around my feet either, of course. It's weird because, with my eyes fully dark-adapted, the minimal starlight filtering down through the trees is sufficient to silver just about everything with a discernible glow—low-hanging boughs, the moving surface of a small trickling creek that we have to cross over, and even old Sal himself—everything limned with a pixie-dust of dim light.

Except for those damned chest-deep brambles.

For some reason, those are just *completely invisible*. And by that I mean, *to the point that* visually *they don't even exist*.

I can see Sal's legs all the way down to his knees. I can see the tree trunks all the way down to about three feet off the ground, where the pixie dust peters out and the pillars just blend into the blackness. But nothing else. For all intents and purposes, the forest floor appears to be clear. It *should* be an easy stroll through the wide open lanes between the pines and scrub oaks. And yet, holding my GAU-5 high over my head like a Civil War soldier fording a stream, I'm being clawed—constantly, from shins to pits—by a million '*non-existent*' thorns.

My one remaining set of cammies is going to be in tatters come the morning.

It seems odd to me that, despite all my exertions and frustrations draggin'-ass through this ghostly thicket, I still break out into a helpless chuckle watching Sal Donado's starlit silhouette twitching and staggering and snarling its way through... well... *nothing*. 'Nothing,' fought through to the accompaniment of invisible snapping twigs, invisible rustling brush, and the tugging and tearing of cloth by invisible claws. *Bizarre!*

But Sal is, as usual, undaunted by any of it. He just forges ahead, the strap of his weapon cinched up to his throat, and following the compass that he's holding out in front of himself like a one-handed divining rod.

He's good at it too. He's not watching the star that *I'm* watching, but he's tracking as straight and true as if he was. And when we finally plow through the last of the brambles, and find ourselves tromping down a sparsely foliated slope under the now-unimpeded stars, we also find the next waypoint card posted right where it should be... at eye level, on the edge of the next little copse of trees. Sal marches up to it, slips it out of its sleeve, and hands it back to me.

"*You take the point on dis one.*"

"*Okay*," I sigh, not a little breathlessly.

I take the card, unclip my red-lensed flashlight from my web belt, and give it another two seconds of shielded illumination. Then I stow the card, quietly repeating the numbers to myself, while I press the flashlight against the face of my compass, and fire up *its* luminescent face with about a ten-second blast of bottled light. The dial is glowing like a hot lava bed when I pull the flashlight away, and I put it to work immediately, hunting up the next star to follow.

Meanwhile, Sal is cussin' and fussin' away behind me, jostling various parts and pieces of his gear into newer more comfortable positions... until, just as I've picked out my next guiding light, I hear him mutter, *"Fuckin' t'orns."*

* * *

FORTUNATELY, THE HOME STRETCH is all but unencumbered... no more brambles to speak of, no more uphill grades, and only one split-rail fence to contort our way through, stuffed rucksacks and all. And almost before we know it, we spot the glow of headlights in the woods ahead, and pick-up the sound of an idling diesel engine.

The Finish Line.

Wow! That was three-and-a-half klicks already?

I pause in my club-footed hobbling to let Sal sidle past me, to take the lead and assess how best we should approach this potential ambush site. But he just marches past without a second thought... sidesteps over a small culvert at the edge of the clearing, bullies his way through a low fringe of bushes, and tramps right out into the wash of the deuce's high beams.

Well, I guess we're done playing 'stealthy operator' for the night, huh.

Fine by me.

I follow in his wake, trying not to limp too obviously in front of the instructors, and shrug my ruck off next to Sal's. Then I pull out the waypoint cards we'd collected, and hand them to Sgt. Myers where he sits behind the wheel of the truck, bundled up against the cold like a big old beret-wearing panda.

"Congratulations," he says. "You're the first team to finish the course."

Really? The first?

I'd figured for sure that, with all the nasty slogging we'd done through those neck-deep brambles back there, we had to be the *last* team to make it in.

But apparently not. *Wow.*

Man, those other guys must be having a really *bad night.*

2
DAY SIX: THE STILL MAN

WELL, AS SCRUMPDELI-ICIOUS as that was, I don't think I'm going to need seconds. There's just something about cold canned meatloaf that so completely resolves your appetite on so many levels.

Instead, I break out my trusty P-38 can opener again, ratchet open one of the two cans of fruit cocktail for which I'd bartered off everything else in my C-rats, and drink it straight from the can like a big old sweet carafe of 'lumpy juice.'

Aahhh. A drink, a dessert, and a second course all in one.

You gotta' love it.

From where I'm sitting, alone on this side of the crackling fire, I can see my pathetic sway-backed tent across the way on the other side. And it, much like myself, is also uncrowded by the presence of too many of its fellow tent-mates being too close by.

Arced around the campfire, in a crescent that starts about eight feet away from my right, are five of my fellow 'junior' classmates, all gabbing and laughing and clattering through their own dinners like Cub Scouts at a jamboree. They're not consciously avoiding me—nor I them—but the
natural order of things does seem to have evolved to this point on its own

now. And nobody seems to mind.

Including me.

It's been another long day, although not for the usual reasons this time.

Today we did almost nothing physical. It was all 'classroom,' starting with a thirty-yard stroll out of the woods and onto the nearby drop zone (to review LZ and EZ establishment criteria), followed by over four hours in the twenty-man tent going over High Frequency (HF) radio net operations, with a one-hour lunch break in the middle. After that, we finished up with an accounting of all our communications, demolitions, and support gear, and a complete breakdown, cleaning, and re-assembly of our weapons.

That wrapped up just before sunset, leading us into this inspirational dining experience, and now here we are.

* * *

YES... HERE I AM. And I feel like a giant bag of constipated weasels. Just beat-up, wrung-out, lumpy, wet, and stinky. And now, thanks to all those invisible brambles we fought our way through last night, my one and only remaining set of camouflaged fatigues looks like it barely survived a full frontal assault by a lunatic with a cheese grater.

But at least my heels have finally quit hurting! I first noticed it during our short hike out to the DZ this morning, and then in the walk-around that followed it. *No pain for once! No limping! What a concept! And after just six days of non-stop torture!*

My feet are still perpetually wet though (no amount of rotating my socks on the little 'clothesline' inside my tent has had any effect whatsoever on their constant dampness), and I'll probably *never* get my feet to 'un-prune' again. But, if nothing else, my heels have finally gotten past that *crushed* feeling. I can actually walk like I've evolved past the Cro-Magnon stage again.

So, I've got *that* much going for me anyway.

Everything else, on the other hand, *sucks*.

* * *

I TAP THE SIDE of my fruit cocktail can, dislodging the last cubes of peaches and pears that cling there, then tuck the empty can away in the large black plastic bag between Greg and myself. He pays me no mind, embroiled as he is in the frazzled and punch-drunk dialogue between himself and the others—Rocky, Mex, Goebler, and Hackett—and I turn back to the task of cracking open my second can of 'lumpy juice.'

In my effort to avoid making eye contact with the rest of them though—which I accomplish with ease by simply sweeping my gaze off through the dark woods behind my sagging tent instead—something catches my eye.

I don't know why. Nothing flickered, glinted, or moved, or anything like that. But for some reason, an odd, rounded, non-leafy shape among the shadows has seized my attention.

I pause, frozen like a slack-jawed mannequin, an unopened can of fruit cocktail in one hand, my P-38 can opener poised in the other, staring over the fire's low flame into the inky black forest beyond.

The ground over there behind my tent rises slightly, a half-assed little berm prickled with the last trees, logs, stumps, and bushes before the vast clearing of the DZ opens up on the other side. But there's something... what?... something '*wrong*' among all that scruffy randomness of the elevated treeline. Nothing 'off-color.' Just something '*smoothish*,' kind of 'rounded,' like a big wad of identically textured Silly Putty tucked in between the bases of two trees. And I squint, thinking *I don't remember seeing that there before.*

Like any trained modern warrior, of course, I've left my weapon propped against the end of the log upon which I'm sitting, ignored, and probably tilted far enough over now that it's pointed straight at my head. And by the time I snap out of my sudden fixation and turn my head to the right (to let my peripheral vision take over the scanning), Rocky—in the middle of the five guys seated around the fire across from me—has noticed my transfixed gaze, and is now staring hard... at *me*.

What the hell is *that up there?*

My peripheral vision doesn't reveal anything new, however. Without movement, an oddly-shaped green-and-black shadow is just an oddly-shaped green-and-black shadow. So it's back to staring straight at it again.

What in nature looks like a mottled green beachball? One pinched into a roughly ovoid shape by the two trees squashing it between them?

Nothing that I *know of.*

And whatever it is, what's it doing there? *How did it* get *there, if it wasn't there all along? And if it* was *there all along, how the hell did I manage to miss it until now? I mean, it's right behind my friggin' tent!*

Because it *wasn't* there before, and it's *not* natural. That's why.

That's a *person*, dressed in camouflage, hunched low and covering his face among the shadows cast by his boonie hat and his rumpled sleeves.

I realize that now.

Without breaking eye contact, I set my unopened fruit cocktail and its unused can opener down on the log beside me. But the surface there is not level, and they both immediately fall off.

I don't care. My right hand's already reaching blindly for my GAU-5.

This is a joke, of course, since it's loaded with blanks. But a stranger won't know that, and an instructor won't care. He'll just be impressed with my readiness and vigilance.

Somebody whispers, "*What's up?*" And that's the first I notice that my five campfire buddies have gone silent as well. I spare a quick glance to my right to find Rocky and Greg (the McChord Boys! *Good for us!*) already on their feet, their weapons rising in their hands to the ready positions, their postures bent and back-stepping away from their own logs. The other three guys, though they don't seem to know what's going on exactly, are taking the cues anyway, and doing the same.

Rocky points once at the strange shape in the woods, then signals right and left for everyone to fan out and encircle 'it.'

Hmm. What did I start here?

I'm not sure, but whatever it is, I'm glad Rocky's taken over.

This is weird. And I'm a trifle uncertain as to just how seriously I should take it. But I go left—weapon up and shouldered, safety thumbed off, playing the game full-tilt... *just in case*—side-stepping between Matheson's and Haley's tents into the darkness behind them. As far as I know, both of them are already asleep inside. Greg's right behind me too, matching my steps in a half-crouch, weapon sighted on that 'big wad of dappled Silly Putty' across the clearing.

And it occurs to me that this could wind up being even more embarrassing than it already is... or *might* be.

What if it's nothing? A mold-covered tree stump that I (and apparently everybody else) just never noticed before. Maybe somebody's misplaced rucksack left leaning against that tree for some reason. *That* would turn some exasperated eyes my way.

What if it's something perfectly normal? Something easily and obviously explained? Something that might be better left undisturbed?

Something like Sgt. Haley, hunched over, taking a dump?

Oh, lordy. As much as I'd relish the look on his face if he found himself in mid-squat, suddenly surrounded by leveled assault rifles, I'm not sure I could handle the hugely escalated misery that would likely follow.

Still, everyone else seems committed to seeing this all the way through. So I stick with it, tippy-toeing in loud snaps, crunches, and crashes through the dry winter detritus, negotiating my way around the 'intruder's' flank with Greg.

Whoever it is though—presuming that it is, in fact, a '*who*'—does not seem overly concerned by our oafish approach, for 'he' hasn't moved an inch since I first spotted 'him.'

Man, those old second thoughts are coming in an avalanche now.

Rocky's the first to reach and 'engage' the target.

Of course he is. Rocky's the first to do *anything*.

And the first words out of his mouth are, "Sgt. Stillman?"

Sgt. Stillman? Oh good gravy! Please tell me we didn't interrupt him taking a crap. But then, what would an instructor be doing pinching a loaf behind my tent?

I lower my weapon, and join the others converging on him (in a somewhat 'relieved' saunter now). And as I watch, Sgt. Stillman just seems to sort of 'unfurl' from his hunker. Apparently he'd been squatting, low—the way a Vietnamese peasant might squat to do his household ("*hut*hold?") chores—his ass low on his heels, but with his GAU-5 laid across his lap, his arms and gloved hands crossed over his knees, and his face tucked down into the hollow formed by his arms... like a big old camouflaged ball.

His head is *up* now, though, his eyes looking down on our campfire, ignoring the six of us. If his head had been up like that five minutes ago, I would have spotted *and recognized* him right away. Which is, of course, precisely why his head *wasn't* up until now. He probably had only his eyes peeking over the top of his arms, with the brim of his boonie hat pulled down low enough to shield them from the illumination of the firelight.

But why is he out here at all? Is he grading us? Stalking us? *Testing* us? Testing *himself?* Trying out different camouflage techniques?

And regardless of the purpose, if he'd wanted to remain unseen, why didn't he hide *behind* something? Why hunch down in the shadowed (but otherwise *open*) space *between* the trees, when he could have laid down more casually—and *comfortably*—*behind* one of them?

Then again, maybe he just wanted to make a point about our general inattentiveness while in camp... which he could only make once we'd actually spotted him up here, and then asked him why.

Oh hell, I don't know. Maybe we should *just 'ask him why.'*

Now that we're all standing in a loose semi-circle around him, Rocky speaks again.

"Sgt. Stillman?"

"Gentlemen," Stillman grunts in return. His gaze is still locked on our fire though, beside which Sal is now standing, his own weapon up and ready in both hands, looking up at us with an expression that clearly says, *What the hell is going on up there?*

"Not a bad response," Stillman continues, "Pretty damned slow on the uptake, and pretty fuckin' noisy in your approach, but at least you did spot and react to the threat. Most students never do."

'Threat?' 'Most students?' He's done this before?

"How long have you been up here?" asks Torrero.

"Since nightfall," he says. "Like always."

We all look at each other. *That's more than an hour.*

What the hell?

For an awkward moment, nobody really knows what to say to that. Finally, I just can't stand it anymore, and break the silence with, "Why?"

"Why do you *think*?" he growls, his eyebrow (on my side) raised. "To keep an eye on you children. Make sure you ain't misbehavin' whenever the instructors aren't around."

A couple of the guys chuckle. Hackett plops back against a tree, his GAU-5 dangling alongside his leg, perfectly positioned to blow his own foot off at a moment's notice. Then he starts swinging it, absentmindedly, as Sgt. Stillman continues.

"Plus, I like to see how much you're paying attention when you're not actively working an exercise, see how long it takes before someone figures out that you're never alone out here in the field Airman Hackett *safe that weapon*."

The flow of that last sentence is so seamless that it takes Hackett several more seconds to realize that he was just specifically addressed. And when it does finally dawn on him, it jolts him like a slap to the face.

"My safety *is* on, Sergeant," he splutters, twiddling the switch with his thumb. Then, "Aw, shit."—*click*—"Sorry about that."

The rest of us discretely brush our own safety switches, just to make sure. Mine's secured. I don't remember securing it, but it's secure nonetheless.

Another click comes from the other side of the circle, over where Goebler's standing. *Oops.*

Stillman continues to squat though, unfazed, his gaze still riveted on the middle of our camp for some reason.

How is he doing that? I'd be numb and *cramped from the hips down within the first thirty seconds of squatting like that. He must do this a lot.*

"So, you do this a lot?" I ask.

"Any time you clowns are in camp and off the clock," he replies.

Really? I hadn't expected that answer.

"You've been out here every time we've been in camp?" asks Rocky.

"Yep."

"Watching everything we do?"

"Yep."

Well, that's a tad disconcerting.

"Jesus Christ," mutters Hackett.

"Yeh," says Sgt. Stillman, "We told you not to wipe your ass with those leaves."

That busts us all up.

But Stillman still hasn't moved: still squatting, still staring straight ahead, not a muscle moved save for a small seldom-used one at the corner of his mouth that *looks like* it's thinking about 'smiling'. But that can't be right.

Greg Dorn slings his GAU across his back, and settles onto his own haunches beside the stoic instructor.

"You must have spent *some time* in Vietnam if you can squat like that for more than five minutes."

Stillman draws a deep sigh, and actually blinks for the first time.

"*All* the instructors here have done time in 'Nam. Just some more than others, is all."

"As Combat Controllers?" asks Torrero, as he lowers himself into the dead leaves on his other side. The rest of us stir up a wave of rustling noises as we find places to sit as well.

Stillman nods slowly. "All but Garner and Myers. They were F.A.G.s in the 'Nam."

"Fags?" Hackett giggles.

Goebler unleashes a contemptuous snort. "That's *Forward Air Guides*, you dumbass."

"Ground mobile liaisons for the Army," Stillman adds. "They call 'em 'ROMADs' nowadays."

So that's *what a 'ROMAD' is!*

"Sgt. Garner and Sgt. Myers switched to CCT once they got back Stateside," he adds.

"So, you've all... you know... you've done this shit *for real* then," says Greg a little self-consciously.

Stillman sighs. "Obviously."

And before we know it, we're all kicked back in the dead leaves and shadows—even Sgt. Donado now, with my abandoned can of fruit cocktail in hand—listening to Sgt. Stillman's grim tales like kids fetched up at the feet of Mother Goose herself (Mother *Mon*goose, more like).

Life in the Real World of Special Ops, by Sergeant Jack Stillman.

It's novel enough just getting five words in a row from the phlegmatic and stony-faced NCO, hearing him speak in something resembling a 'conversational tone' for the first time since meeting him a full month-and-a-half ago. But then, as his stories go deeper (in time *and* intimacy), I begin to detect the first traces of remorse and loss as well, something other than his typical monotone gravel. And, well... coming from him, that's almost too eerie to absorb.

And all without budging from that nasty peasant squat of his.

Not once.

My attention just keeps coming back to that, over and over and over again. I can't help it. It just looks too damned uncomfortable. But it seems to be perfectly natural for him, and he never so much as twists or stretches a limb even once. He never diverts his gaze from our campfire either.

At first, I attribute that to the fact that it's the only source of light within miles in this dark and dripping forest, and as such, its effect can be almost hypnotic. But as I watch him talking—answering our inane questions, and describing the Vietnamese firebases and old friends long gone that seem to have comprised the fulcrum of his entire life—I come to realize that it's not the fire that has him entranced... it's the *past*. His gaze is not *outward*, but *inward*. And it sees only emptiness and dust there.

Lordy, this is an unsettling side of an unsettling guy.

What I'd previously seen as merely a stoic affectation on his part—a theatrical 'lone wolf' aloofness intended solely to establish a personal and professional moat between himself and his students (*or maybe just to look all 'cool' and 'badass'... who knew?*)—now has the look and smell of a much deeper desolation. I mean, he actually seems uncharacteristically *eager* to talk to us here—or *someone*; maybe *anyone*—which is a side of him I would never have suspected, or even *believed*, at any point in the previous seven weeks.

His stories aren't pretty, the endings are seldom happy (although one of them is at least pretty *funny*), but grim as it all is, the craziest thing is that right now it's just him... and *us*. 'The guys.' His 'peers.' The only *kind* of 'friends' he seems to have ever known... 'brother soldiers,' if you will.

And that's so depressing, it makes my heart ache.

One of his tales meanders for a while, losing sight of its 'destination' several times before circling back to a retrospective of a couple of old buddies whose survival instincts (or luck, or fate) were apparently not quite as innate as his (since *he* lived, and they *didn't*). Then it winds down rather abruptly, without a clear ending—just wanders away from us and never comes back—leaving us *all* staring off into the campfire for most of thirty seconds, reluctant to do or say anything that might rupture the odd silence.

Until Percy Hackett sighs, loudly, and clears his throat.

"So," he says, "You've probably worked with them all. Who do *you* think are the best special forces in the world?"

Part of me wants to backhand him for interrupting a reverent moment with a question so stupid, childish and vapid. The other part of me can't wait to hear the answer.

"U.S. Navy SEALs," Stillman replies without a second's hesitation.

What? The friggin' Navy? Not Air Force Combat Controllers?

According to the tiresome litanies of Siegel, Santos and Montreaux back at McChord, Combat Controllers *rock*, and pretty much everybody else is a joke. And with all the Brits and Aussies and Germans and Koreans and Israelis that Sgt. Stillman's worked with at one time or another, surely *one of them* surpassed even the best the United States has to offer.

Nope.

"Really? The fockin' Navy?" Sal asks.

"Yep."

"The *best*? In the *world*?"

"Hands down."

And another ghost story unfurls in the chilly darkness.

* * *

IT SEEMS THAT ON Stillman's last deployment in-country—sometime in 1972, he says, right about the time that I was wrapping up junior high, probably, ignoring my pain-in-the-ass homework, and complaining about the *one whole mile* I had to walk to school—*he* was walking as an air liaison attached to a six-man Army 'Lurp' team (spelled 'LRRP,' for *Long-Range Reconnaissance Patrol*) through the highlands of Vietnam, near the Cambodian border.

Toting a PRC-*15*, an even heavier older model of the damned PRC radios that we've been carrying here at CCS, he was trooping along through enemy-held territory, close on the heels of the Lurp's team leader, when they were ambushed... from *above*. From the *trees*.

This, he says, was a tactic not often employed by the Vietcong, since (a) it took a while to set up, getting the men and weapons up into the treetops, (b) it left the ambushers fairly vulnerable themselves (not much cover among the thin upper branches), and (c) it made escape and retreat nearly impossible (since they would first have to clamber down *out* of the trees before they could bug out). Which meant that an enemy using such a technique was either supremely confident of success, suicidally brave, self-destructively stupid, or some combination of the three.

On the flip side of the coin—at least in a jungle environment, where top cover might obstruct vision, but does nothing to stop bullets—the high angle of attack was (a) unexpected, and as such, was seldom watched for, and (b) left your targets with nowhere to hide from your plunging fire.

And such was the case on this particular occasion.

Within seconds of the opening volley, as the sudden small arms fire pelted down from above and the Americans bolted in every direction looking for cover, Sgt. Stillman—then *Airman* Stillman—was smashed flat by a blow that felt like a baseball bat between his shoulder blades.

'Clubbed' to the ground by the impacts, he slid face-down under a low canopy of elephant ear ferns, stunned, breathless, and for the moment at least, *paralyzed*. As he would shortly discover, however, he was uninjured. It was his *radio*—that massive box of lead ballast on his back, now battered into junk—that had absorbed the bullet strikes, knocked his breath out, and essentially swatted him right out of the kill zone.

He pauses his growling monologue for a moment, and for the first time, he looks away from our guttering campfire to share a wry look with us, one that fairly screams, *Remember that, assholes, the next time you feel like complaining about how heavy and uncomfortable that damned prick is. It may not qualify as an 'honor' to have to carry the friggin' thing, but it might just save your sorry lives... in more ways than one.*

Then he *harrumphs*, and turns his attention back inward.

The ambush didn't last long. It didn't *have* to, so total and devastating was the surprise, and so deadly that first salvo. As he later found out, every last man on that LRRP was, in fact, killed—well, every man *but himself*, of course—if not under that initial barrage, then in the grisly mop-up that followed.

Once all the screaming and crashing and banging abruptly ended, the next thing he heard was the sound of men dropping out of the trees and the gabbling of peasant soldiers, followed by the individual *pops* and *pows* of single shots being fired into the heads of the downed men. And he knew that it was just a matter of seconds then, before one of the ambushers would find him, and end it all with a final spark of light, noise, and pain.

"Fact is," he says, his eyes momentarily diverted to the ground between his legs, "I had *no idea* what to do. I didn't know how much cover I was under, how much of my ass was hangin' out in the open—I didn't know if there was a gook standing over me right at that moment, if there was a smokin' gun pointed at the back of my head, if I could afford to even *take a breath*—and I was afraid to move or even open my eyes to find out."

In my mind's eye, I can 'see' him back then, frozen with fear and indecision, both terrified of his looming demise, and furious with the hesitancy that was immobilizing him while his killer strolled up behind him and casually blew his brains out.

Well, that's what *I* get from his far more succinct description, anyway.

Sgt. Stillman might be in an abnormally expansive mood right now, but he's still a man of few and simple words. And apparently he's tired of using even those now.

He sighs, props his GAU butt-first in the dirt like a walking stick, and rocks himself forward onto one knee, dusting off his pants as he does. And when he resumes speaking, kneeling there in that odd 'ready' pose, it's with a tone of finality... as in, *this is the* end *of the story now, so listen the hell up.*

"I did finally get my shit together enough to look around and assess my situation. And it wasn't good. But it wasn't beyond hope either. Only my feet were sticking out from under my cover, and for the moment, most of the damned Cong were over kicking their way through the growth on the other side of the trail. If I could move slowly and quietly enough, I might just be able to slither the rest of the way out of sight, maybe find some spidey-hole to disappear into or something, and then wait there until nightfall, or until they left, whichever came first. Something like that."

He sighs again and hoists himself to his feet. We all rise with him.

Then he takes a moment to look each one of us in the eye—taking some sort of mental roll-call, I guess—before wrapping it all up.

"I dragged myself, *slowly*, under deeper cover, for about ten seconds or so. And I was just pulling my feet in out of the sunlight, when this hand suddenly came outa' nowhere and clamped down on my mouth. Scared the livin' *fuck* outa' me, I'll tell you that. But it also kept me from shriekin' like a woman."

He's not looking for a chuckle from that, and he doesn't get one. We're too riveted to even break eye contact.

"Whoever had me though, didn't fight me, and when I rolled to face him, I swear to God, I was looking into the eyes of a U.S. Navy SEAL. *Two* of 'em, actually—boonie hats, face paint, Nomex gloves, the works—one of 'em hunkered down behind a tree with his weapon trained on the enemy, ignoring me, the other one pulling his hand back from my mouth and putting a finger to his lips... like this." And he makes a silent *sshhhh* gesture.

"Jesus," somebody whispers.

"No, it wasn't Jesus. Just two guys, deep in gomer country. They mighta' been tracking the ambush team, they might not. I never found out. But they were in the area, and they had the self-control and professionalism to keep their heads cool in the middle of superior enemy numbers, and they had the fuckin' *cojones* to step up and get involved when the shit went south. And I don't care *how* 'bad-ass' you are—how strong, or fast, or brave, or well-equipped, or how good a shot you are—*that's* as good as it gets."

Silence. Absolute forget-to-breathe total-vacuum *silence*.

"And *that's* what I'm trying to make *you* into," he concludes.

Nobody knows what to say to that either.

"Goodnight, gentlemen."

And he parts our little circle as blithely as if we'd just passed on a sidewalk, and evaporates into the darkness behind us.

Hell of a story.

Horrible sales pitch, though.

STORY XXX

TURNING POINT

1
DAY SEVEN: HASTY BIVOUAC

December, 1977
In the field outside Little Rock AFB, Little Rock, Arkansas

AT AN UNREMARKABLE AND completely nondescript spot in the dark pattering woods, our instructors finally bring the column to a halt.

I don't know where we are, I don't know how we got here, and I cannot imagine what made this one particular little hummock—this one particular *tree*, for that matter—stand out among all the anonymous others. I might be able to tell if I could actually *see* the friggin' tree, but it's one of those dark-on-dark nights, moonless and starless, thanks to the thick dripping sponge of an overcast deck that's been dragging its belly through the treetops since mid-afternoon. So nothing short of an intimate familiarity with these woods, or an incredibly fertile imagination, could even tell that there was a specific tree here at all.

However, since the instructor cadre marched us out here without a deviation or comment, I'm guessing they've probably been here before.

Sgt. Stillman (of all people) is the first person to speak in over an hour. And when he does, it's a dull growl, barely distinguishable above the gentle drumming of the rain on our ponchos.

"This is your 'hasty bivouac' site, gentlemen," he says. And he waves a hand across the sinkhole of darkness surrounding us. "This is where you'll encamp for the rest of the night, covert and ready to move on a moment's notice. That means *no unpacking*, ladies. No tents, no sleeping bags, no lights, and no fucking noise. Understood?"

A mumbled assent ripples through the 'team.' No '*oo-rahs*' this late at night, or this deep in 'enemy territory'... or with this little remaining energy.

"Just hunker down under some cover, with your weapon at the ready. Try to stay dry, and get some sleep any way you can. Sgt. Haley, establish a perimeter, and set your watches on two-hour shifts. We'll be moving out for the final half-klick to our objective at oh-five-thirty. Everybody got all that?"

"*Objective?*" *What 'objective?' I thought we were just practicing walking!*

And why Sgt. Haley again, goddammit? He doesn't need *another sharp stick to poke me with. Give somebody else a chance to screw me over.*

But we all grunt an acknowledgment, and Sgt. Stillman wheels away to be absorbed by the darkness. I mean he just friggin' vanishes.

I'm starting to get used to that, though.

I check my watch inside my poncho—coming up on 11:30—then I join the others as they encircle Sgt. Haley, my very own personal tormentor. Because I know, I *know* just exactly what he's going to say before he even starts to say it.

The first two most miserable watch shifts are going to go to...

"Hackett," he says. "You take the first watch."

"Fuck," says Hackett, also right on cue.

Then... *here it comes... wait for it... wait for it...*

"Stipp,"—*bingo!*—"you relieve Hackett at one-thirty."

"No kidding," I grunt before he's even finished speaking.

He pauses, no doubt pondering whether this is the best time or place for a lecture on attitude and insubordination, but presses on without further comment.

"Torrero, you relieve Stipp here at zero-three-thirty, and wake *me* up at oh-five-hundred. Copy?"

"Roger that," Mex sighs.

"Alright then. Let's do this by the book. We're supposed to be invisible and we're supposed to be quiet, people. So everybody take a whiz now, then pick a spot with some cover, get yourselves situated and comfortable for the long haul, and get some sleep. If the guy next to you starts snoring though, wake him up. And be ready for anything the instructors decide to pull out of their asses. If something happens, respond instantly and assertively.

Assume firing positions, weapons at the ready. Okay?"

I wonder... *is there anybody here who wasn't already going to do all those things* before *Haley's inspirational pep talk? Anybody? No?*

"And you guys on watch: that means *relief* is also silent. No talking. Just tap or shake your relief awake. You might want to set up positions close to each other for just those reasons. But whatever you do, do it quietly. Okay?"

"Yeh, okay," says Hackett, "But... so... what do you want us to do if somebody *does* come through the perimeter while we're on watch? You know? I mean, you want us to get loud enough to wake everybody up? Maybe..."

It's a stupid question (I think) since, in theory, nobody here could have survived this long at this school without having picked up at least a *little* of what they've been teaching us for the last six wretched weeks. But I'm glad it was asked... which is to say, *I'm glad that* he *asked it*. Because regardless of whether or not it *is* a stupid question, the fact is that I'm just not sure of the answer myself.

Haley looks at Hackett as if he'd just offered him a baloney-and-whipped-cream sandwich. "Don't be an idiot," is all he says.

Then he disperses everyone to their duties.

Well, that was helpful... as always.

I don't have to pee, though. So, while everyone else is off marking his territory for the night (so to speak), I lay claim to the first dark tree-like shadow I come to. It's embedded in a loose muffler of thorny shrubs (like everything else in these goddamned woods, apparently), which will have to suffice for my 'cover,' I guess. The ground has a slight slope to it, which means drainage, so I won't have to sit with my ass in a puddle. And Hackett, who brilliantly chose to piss right next to the very spot where he'll be sitting and sleeping for the rest of the night, is fussing through his preparations just one tree over... which means a short commute when it comes time to wake me up for my 'second watch.'

Fucking 'second watch.' It's only the worst watch there is.

The *first* watch might suck because, as tired as he is—as we *all* are—Hackett will have to stay awake for another two hours before succumbing to his exhaustion. But at least he's already awake, and once relieved, he'll have the rest of the night to sleep.

I, on the *second* watch, however, will have just two hours to try and catch some Zs, the first hour of which will no doubt be spent just trying to get 'comfortable'—propped up against this wet tree, with as much of me as possible tucked up under my poncho, out of the rain, trying to sleep in an essentially 'upright' position, with my chin on my chest—such that right about the time I finally cave in to my fatigue, Percy ought to be nudging me back awake again... at 1:30 in the morning. Then I'll have to *stay* awake for two *more* hours until I can wake up Torrero at *3*:30. And *then* it'll be just two *more* hours before I'm woken up *again*, at *5*:30, to start a whole new glorious day out here in the field at fabulous CCS.

Fucking second watch.
Fucking Haley.

* * *

I SPEND THE FIRST twenty minutes of my 'sleep time' just rigging up my 'poncho *liner*.' It's the first time I've ever tried to use it *as it was intended to be used*, rather than as just a nifty, high-tech, *stylish* camouflaged blanket... because the poncho liner really is nothing but a field-expedient *blanket*, ridiculously simple in concept and design, but surprisingly effective in dismal situations like this.

About the size of a typical one-man (or 'twin') bedspread—and I know this because I used mine as my sole bed cover for the two whole weeks that I was at McChord—it's just a 'coverlet' made of two layers of light, almost *silky* camouflaged material that sandwich a thin layer of insulation in the middle.

As I said, it's essentially just a lightweight high-tech *blanket*.

At six points around its periphery though—at its four corners, plus two places at the midpoints of its longer sides—it has pairs of strings, each about eight inches long, and the thickness of shoe laces. Up until this evening's 'hasty bivouac' briefing, I'd never known what those strings were for.

Now I do. And now I'm using them... correctly.

As it turns out, previously unbeknownst to me, there are three little loops of material built into our ponchos, on the *inside*, in a literal 'ring around the collar.' I'd never even noticed them until this evening, and nobody at McChord had ever said anything about them. But those loops were specifically installed so that our poncho *liners* (those awesome high-tech blankets) would have something to tie onto *inside our ponchos*, using those strings. That's right; hang your poncho-lining 'blanket' around your poncho's interior, like a plump insulated shower curtain encircling your body from a ring around your throat, and you're basically wearing *a walk-around sleeping bag! Pretty damned cool!*

Or 'warm,' I guess.

Of course I waste probably *ten minutes* just trying to wrestle it out of my rucksack in the pitch darkness, then fumbling it into position, and tying it off in three places. But once it's done, I'm actually surprisingly toasty and dry inside my little one-man 'poncho-tent.'

However, my sleep time is now down to just over an hour-and-a-half. And warm, dry, or not—even as ready as I am to just collapse into a coma out of sheer physical exhaustion—it's still not easy to 'sleep' sitting cross-legged against a wet tree, with a wet ass, a loaded GAU-5 laying across my lap, and the constant rain drumming on my poncho.

So I settle for just closing my eyes, and using this time to think.

* * *

SO... JUST WHAT THE HELL *was* I thinking? God forbid, but in his own guileless, tactless, and utterly *classless* way, Sgt. Haley just might have been right about one thing... I'm *not* a Combat Controller. I'm *not* right for this job, and I *do* know it now... *dammit!*

So, what *am* I doing here, really? And who do I think I'm fooling?

This might have *started off* as a game for me, as a personal test or a 'grand adventure' of sorts, a chance to 'play Army' to the max. But, not only has the novelty worn off (along with a lot of its exotic shine), but the hard-edged reality of it all has finally broken through. *And the Truth has set me free!* Or at least it's let me recognize this *shit sandwich* for what it really is!

And I say again, *What the hell was I thinking?!*

This is some mighty miserable, debilitatingly difficult, and genuinely *dangerous* shit here. This isn't a friggin' *sport* or a *challenge*, like running a marathon or doing a stint with the Peace Corps. And this isn't some weekend Fantasy Escape Package for bored yuppies. *This is the real thing!*

It's as real as it gets!

This is the bleeding edge of the nation's blade, the proverbial tip of the proverbial spear—*literally!*—not just the Big Leagues for thrill junkies. Everything they've taught me here comes with real life-or-death ramifications—again, *literally*—and not just for *me*, but for everyone who'll ever have to work with me, every mission planner who'll ever have to depend on me, and every 'enemy soldier' who'll ever find himself standing in my way.

This isn't a movie set here. The bullets will be real, as will the explosives, the airplanes, and the friggin' parachutes... not to mention the high winds, freezing temperatures, and pouring rain in which we'll be working... so too the unbreathably thin air of higher altitudes, the dark and crushing depths of the oceans, and the horribly asymmetrical ratios of bad guys to good guys in most of our scenarios. And those are just the conditions, realms, and tools of the trade. The *enemies* will be real too, as will their bullets and knives, *their* lethal training, and *their* lethal hatred for *me*.

All of it real. All of it vast, heavy, toxic, hazardous, and treacherous.

And too important to be playfully trifled with.

I'm sitting here right now, my ass wet, my feet soaked and frozen (which has at least taken my mind off the dimming throb of my Achilles tendons for a while), my shoulders aching from the weighty cut of my pack straps, and my neck killing me from all the times my head has fallen over on the verge of fitful sleep. I'm listening to the incessant tapping of the rain on the hood of my poncho, peering out through the deep forest night at the other huddled gray lumps around me, and aware that my bone-deep weariness will not be relieved tonight. Because even if I *could* fall asleep in an upright position (which I can't), I'll just be woken right back up again by Hackett before I've even noticed that my lights went out.

And all for what?

I mean, misery *with a purpose* is just a momentary low-point through which you can physically and psychologically push yourself, even if it takes more time and pain than you'd expected. But *misery for no good reason? What the hell is* that *all about?*

Really, folks! What's the point of all this? What's our ultimate objective here? Am I working toward achieving some sort of life-long dream here, and this is just the difficult 'home stretch' before crossing the finish line?

No. I'm pretty much just dabbling here.

Will all the pressures, stresses, trials and tribulations abruptly cease if I can just force my way through these last few merciless feet to victory?

No. In fact, from what I can tell, they will have only just begun. 'Winning' here—seeing this through, graduating, and actually walking away from this with a hard-earned beret—isn't like fighting my way to the top of Mount Everest. This barely qualifies as the 'hike to the base camp,' This isn't *The Big Game*. This is just the 'opening ceremonies,' the *start* of the gauntlet.

Hell, this is just the *ticket booth* you have to get past *to even be allowed to enter the arena!*

And that's really the bottom line here, isn't it?

Not that this is so insurmountably hard (although it comes damned close), but that it's just such an 'insignificant' *first step* on an endless and steepening *staircase* of struggle and privation and duress.

Well, maybe I shouldn't have said "*insignificant.*" CCS *is*, after all, the make-or-break prerequisite for everything else that will follow. Maybe I should have said "*elemental,*" as in "*All this that I'm killing myself to achieve here comprises just the bare-bones* elemental *minimums, the* basics *that I need to attain in order to even be capable of learning how to do the rest of this job on a daily basis for the rest of my career!*"

In other words, it's never going to get any easier than this.

It'll only get harder.

Then again... *maybe I'm just over-thinking this shit again.*

* * *

I ADJUST MY SITTING position once more.

I squirm my benumbed ass cheeks around to take the weight off my aching tailbone, unfold my stiffening legs for a moment... and a runnel of cold rain water spills from a crease in my rain gear, right above my shoulder, and runs down the inside of the poncho's collar.

Ahh, shit! This sucks!

I slap at my poncho from the inside, theoretically punching the accumulated water out of any *other* creases, then reseat my weapon so that it sticks straight out like a proudly exaggerated hard-on, trying to prop the poncho out a little further over my legs. But the poncho's not quite long enough for that, and instead slides back down the barrel of the GAU, exposing my legs to the rain again, from the knees down.

Dammit! It looks like it's going to be a long cross-legged night.

* * *

OBVIOUSLY, I WASN'T ASPIRING to *this* when I first signed up for this program. So what the hell was it that *did* sell me on this whole thing?

The glamour, of course. You know; the *important* stuff. Jumping out of airplanes, rappelling from high-rises, skiing glaciers, sniping the bad guys, skulking like a jungle cat through the shadows, and of course, strutting around base wearing the beret of an elite *Spec Ops Warrior*.

And that's it!

Well, you know what? It turns out that all of those things (*well, all but one, anyway*) are actually a hell of a lot of hard work, are dangerous as hell, will only earn me an extra fifty-five bucks a month in Hazardous Duty Pay, and I've already done enough of them to satisfy my curiosity. So I don't *need* to do any more to sate that curiosity—it's done *sated*—I don't *want* to have to push myself this hard *ever again, for the rest of my LIFE*, and it ain't exactly like I'm a 'natural' at it anyway.

Hell, the truth is, *I suck at this stuff.*

Granted, that suckiness is due in large part to my lack of preparedness in coming down here so green (through no fault of my own, I might add, and entirely against my own wishes), but that doesn't cover *all* of my inherent unsuitability here. Throw in my out-of-place social ineptitude—my complete inability to drink or dance or womanize, or just generally 'carouse'—the fact that I've never been in a fight *in my life* (so I don't even possess the most rudimentary *muscle memory* of how to do it, nor any memories of what it 'feels like' or what to expect) and I don't appear to be too terribly adroit at learning how. Hell, I don't even like playing contact sports. Include my recent epiphany about wielding a knife in close proximity to another human's throat, and, well... *who's kidding who here?*

I'm about as right for this job as a cat for a cattle rancher.

I might be *physically capable*, I might be *mentally trainable*, I might even be *'morally indoctrinatable'* (if I had the desire or personal fortitude to further pursue any of those goals), but I will never be *'right'* for the job. *Ever.* And I know that now, better than anyone.

Even Staff Sergeant Brad Haley.

Still, even *that's* not really the absolute bottom line here, is it.

Not really.

No, the *final* and truly *deciding* consideration in this lopsided weighing of micro-pros and macro-cons, is this: *I just flat don't wanna' do this shit anymore! Period!*

So...

There it is. 'Nuff said.

Hmmm.

Now what are we going to do about it?

My tired brain seems to stall on that question though, stuck and repeating it like a broken record.

Not that I notice it, mind you. Nor do I notice the thickening of the echoes in my head, nor the susurrus of muddy 'white noise' filling the gaps.

The last thing my consciousness registers before closing the curtains for the night, is the muted snuffling sounds of one of the other shadowy lumps across the way... snoring... with all the subtlety of a couch being dragged across a concrete floor... and nobody even trying to wake him up.

Including me.

* * *

SOMETHING SHOVES ME, AND I start to fall, a bottomless rush that arrests itself only once every muscle in my body has jolted in panic.

I come to in total darkness, my face just inches from the sodden ground, a rivulet of cold rainwater coursing over my face from the upturned creases around the neck of my poncho.

I bolt upright, and a large hand grips my shoulder, steadying me.

"*Ay, man,*" a Latino voice whispers, "*You forgot to wake me up.*"

Forgot? No, I... what? Torrero? But...

"*You fell asleep on your watch, man.*"

"No, I... I was never..."

I look up at the dripping hooded specter beside me—Torrero—then past him to the deflated lump crumpled against the next tree over.

Hackett.

"Son of a bitch," I spit, fighting to keep my voice below the audible. "Hackett never woke me up. He probably fell asleep as soon as he sat down."

"What? You mean we haven't had any security all night?"

"Apparently not." I start wrestling my arms out from under my poncho. "*Jesus, what time is it?*"

"*It's quarter to five, man.*"

"*Holy shit!*"

"*Tell me about it. I just happened to wake up, on my own, a couple of minutes ago, and I couldn't believe it when I checked the time. Fuck. I'm supposed to wake Haley up in fifteen more minutes, you know that? I'm gonna' kill that little rat-fuck Hackett.*"

I know he means it, too. I've seen him *shoot* Hackett before.

Point blank!

But what if Hackett *did* try to pass me the 'sentry baton', and maybe I stirred just enough to register my acceptance, then fell right back to sleep again? What if I *am* the one who dropped the ball here?

Oh lordy, how that would suck.

But no. I'd remember *something*. And the last thing embedded in my memory right now is the sound of somebody across the circle snoring. That's it. Everything's a black hole after that.

Now I've just got to hope that Hackett doesn't suggest such a scenario himself. In a battle of my word against his, I'm not sure which one of us would fare the worst in Haley's wrathful judgment. He doesn't like either of us—Hackett for his constant whining and petulance, me for my resilient mediocrity—and if he thinks that he's been made to look bad by either or both of us, life here in Little Rock is likely to reach new depths of unpleasantness.

Torrero turns toward Hackett's boneless form, coiled to pounce. But before I can reach the hem of his poncho to stop him, I catch the movement of another shadow at the periphery of my vision. And it's coming toward us.

I slap at Torrero's ankle, and whisper, "*Hey, man! One o'clock!*"

Torrero freezes for a moment, squinting in that general direction, then suddenly snatches his weapon up to the ready position and wheels on the intruder. The approaching figure raises its hand before Torrero can speak though, and hisses, "*Yo. Easy, easy, dude. It's me. Haley.*"

Fuck. That's just who we need right now.

"*Everything go okay last night?*" he murmurs as he moves in close.

I swallow hard enough to be heard over the dripping rain.

"*Yeh, yeh,*" Torrero whispers, nodding and turning to me for concurrence.

"*Yeh, no problem,*" I agree, rising to my feet.

"*I was just going to wake you up in about fifteen minutes,*" Torrero continues, gesturing to his watch for emphasis.

"*Yeh, well, don't worry about that now,*" sighs Haley. "*I woke up on my own a minute or two ago. But I could hear you guys whispering from clear over there. You need to keep it down.*"

Mex and I share a quick glance.

"*Sure, sure. Sorry.*"

"*Alright then. We'll rouse the rest of these guys at five-twenty. Make sure we're all up and ready when the instructors come through. Keep it down until then, okay?*"

"*Oo-rah,*" Torrero mutters.

A muttered "*oo-rah*" sounds even dumber than a shouted one though, and Haley pauses for a moment to stare at him. Then he trudges off to find himself another pissing-tree, no doubt.

Torrero and I watch the darkness absorb him, then turn back to each other to release our mutually held breaths.

Son of a businessman.

We both look at Hackett next, who, to all outward appearances, is utterly deceased. Torrero apparently feels like making that a certainty.

Still facing away from me, I can barely make out the words growling up from within his poncho.

"*I am gonna' kill that little rat-shit bastard.*"

Me? I'm actually not too terribly surprised to discover that I just don't friggin' care.

2

DAY EIGHT: THWARTED PLANS

WELL, I MIGHT NOT remember anything of last night between about midnight and quarter-to-five in the morning, but the way I'm feeling today, I don't believe that time lapse included anything similar to 'sleep' or even a little catnap. A *coma* maybe, but nothing restful.

Right now it feels like a five-hour chunk of my life has simply been 'edited out,' with *"Shivering in Rain-Soaked Misery"* spliced directly to *"Woken Up Confused and Exhausted Three-Hundred Minutes Later."*

Gawd; I just feel drugged. Stuporous.

Sitting here on this fragile little folding chair in this chilled and musty tent-classroom, even *without* my rucksack, my back and shoulders still ache with the muscle memory of its eternal weight. My pecked, frayed, and abraded uniform might also be wet, but my boots—and especially my friggin' *socks*—are *soaked*. My feet are cold—*frozen*, actually—and if I dared to expose them, I bet I'd find them to be pasty white and pruned into identically wadded knots. And  since I didn't have the energy this morning (or the stomach) to contend with unheated canned eggs again, I've also had no breakfast either.

As such, between the starvation and exhaustion, the sleep deprivation, the dampness and deep chills, not to mention the ongoing *social* exile, and all the aggravations and reservations that were still swirling through my muddled brain when I finally passed out last night, well...

I'm staring at my club feet now, where they're knocking together under the chair in front of me, and trying desperately to think of a single good reason for continuing with this program for even *one more hour*. And I can't think of a one! *Not one!*

I mean, *what's the point? What's left to do? To see? To try? On what is there left to test myself?* And why the hell would I need even one more minute of *'personal testing' anyway?*

As fried and oatmeal-brained as I'm feeling right now though, I still can't believe that it's finally come down to this. But apparently it has. My last justification for sticking with this shit any further just burned up, sometime last night.

So, if I've got no reason for sitting here anymore—if there's no longer a spec ops future toward which I should be aspiring, no function or purpose to putting up with even one more minute of privation here—if I just plain *don't need this shit anymore*, and all I've got to do to put an end to it is utter just two little words, then... well... *why am I still sitting here?*

* * *

AND THERE IT IS... the last boundary to cross.

Though I'm slumped in my seat, drooping and crushed and fighting off the rolling shivers, in my heart and mind I've just crossed that line.

For good.

I just did it. Just now! *I'm out!*

Wow.

Now I've just gotta' tell somebody else.

* * *

SERGEANT RABIN HIMSELF IS teaching this morning's class—alone, with no other instructors present to assist—so I guess he's the one I'll have to break the news to on our next break. And I suppose that's as it should be. He *is* the senior instructor, after all. Sooner or later, I'm going to have to face him anyway. Might as well be sooner.

When I raise my eyes to look at him though, I catch *his* eyes just looking away from *me*.

Hmmm.

But eleven o'clock does finally roll around, the end of another hour segment, and Sgt. Rabin announces it by collapsing his pointer down to the size of a ballpoint pen, popping it into his chest pocket, and saying, "Break time, gentlemen. Go smoke 'em if you got 'em, but have your asses back in those seats again in ten minutes."

Back on base, in the school's primary classroom, that announcement would have been followed by an orchestral eruption of desks and boots barking and chirping across the linoleum. But out here in the field, folding chairs on dirt make no noise at all. Instead, the first sounds that follow our official release are those of deep and long-bottled yawns, along with the grunts and longwinded sighs that attend a tent filled with spectacular full-body stretches.

At this point, the instructor(s) would normally be surrounded by a few students that either had questions about the preceding material, or just felt like being sociable, while a couple of the chain-smokers would dawdle on out the tent flap into the cold. I decide to be among the 'sociable' ones this time, to converge on Sgt. Rabin and then await the first opportunity to privately issue my verbal resignation.

But by the time I've sidestepped out into the center aisle, I look up to find him gone. And I never even saw him leave.

But the instructors never *leave.*

Alright, then. I guess I'll just have to go and catch him outside.

Hobbling stiffly on my shriveled club feet, I shoulder my way past the others, and out through the tent flap into the chilly morning air. Haley, Corbin and Goebler are already there, communing over freshly lit cigarettes. But, aside from a disinterested and desultory glance, they ignore me.

But far more importantly, Sgt. Rabin is nowhere in sight. *Jesus!*

I walk around the end of the tent, and peer down the path that leads back through the woods to the instructors' camp. *Nothing.*

What the hell?

I turn, and march back the other way, to the other end of the tent, from which you can see the clearing and circle of tents that composes the *students'* camp. And again… *nada!*

Where the hell did he go? I wasn't that far behind him leaving the tent. So he had to have either *bolted* the split second he was outside, or dove for cover immediately and was laying low by the time I'd stepped out myself, all under the curious eyes of the smoking club at the tent's opening. Either way though—and regardless of how evolved his 'vanishing skills' might be—it had to have been a conscious effort on his part to disappear like this. There's simply no way he could have casually 'moseyed' out of sight in that little time.

Okay. Well... he's got to return. So I guess I'll just wait.

It's a little awkward, pacing around in restless circles so close to Haley and his smoking buddies—especially when I'm alone, I'm not smoking, and I'm not even dressed for the cold (I left my jacket hanging on the back of my chair inside)—but, well, *fuck it! I don't work here anymore! What do I care about the discomfiture of strangers?*

I rehearse my opening lines while I wait. I run through a dozen different variations, but in the end decide to just stick with the basics.

Sergeant Rabin, I quit.

My mind runs on through expansive monologues about the value of the Teams, the 'nobility' of these men, the 'rightness' of the cause, *blah, blah, blah, etcetera, etcetera*. But I know that it's really just going to come down to *"I quit. Can I go home now?"*

Eventually, of course, the ten-minute break runs its course. Haley and company stub out their butts, sweep an irritated glower over me, and push back inside. And I am left alone, outside, still waiting for Sgt. Rabin to return.

Until I hear his voice inside.

"Alright, gentlemen. Who are we missing?"

What the hell?

"Stipp's just outside there," I hear Haley's voice reply. "I don't know what the hell he's doing."

I push back through the flap, and sure enough, there stands Sgt. Rabin in front of his blackboard and flipchart stand, looking as bored and impatient as ever—as if he hadn't just snuck back into the tent in an effort to avoid me—checking his watch.

"Ten after, Airman Stipp," he says, tapping its face.

He *had* to have re-entered the tent from the opposite side for me to have missed him. *I was standing in front of the only other access point!* But *nobody* goes through that farside flap, because that whole side of the tent is tucked right up against the trees and underbrush that line that edge of the clearing. You'd have to pick your way through the brambles and deadfall—slowly, 'snaggly,' and *loudly*—to come in from that side.

"Sorry," I say, looking at my watch as if *it* had betrayed me. "I thought I had another minute."

Then I head for my chair through the crossfire of everyone's gaze.

Well, wasn't that interesting.

Guess I'll just have to try again at the noon break.

* * *

WELL, BEFORE THE NOON break rolls around, three more instructors join the teaching line-up at the front of the tent, first lugging in several large and horrifically ungainly pieces of 'portable' equipment, then setting them each up while Sgt. Rabin talks us through the procedures.

We're supposed to jump *with those massive components between us? Are you kidding me?*

This runs the class segment past its originally scheduled break time. And then, once they can finally call it a wrap, it's for lunch, and the exodus from the tent, for students and instructors alike, is downright *explosive*.

Within seconds, I am alone in the tent.

Outside, the rain resumes—well, the *dripping*, anyway—and just the thought of following the others through that icy sprinkle, just so that I can squat, alone, beside the dead wet 'fire,' and pack another can of cold spaghetti down my throat, has so little appeal that, well… I do it anyway.

Maybe it's just as well that I couldn't find Sgt. Rabin an hour ago. As miserable as all this is, the fact is that in two more days this is all going to come to an end anyway. One way or another, I'll be either a wash-out or a graduate from this school.

So after all I've already been through, why not just buckle down and *finish* this shit. *What's two more days, you know?*

Well, it's two more days of something I don't ever want to do again.

That's what.

3
DEJA VU ALL OVER AGAIN

SO AS THE SUNSET, unseen above the endlessly leaking overcast, darkens our little circle of existence, I stumble back into our campsite, numbed as much from boredom as from the wet chill of mid-December in the Ozarks. The ten surviving members of my class just spent the last two stultifying hours huddled around a field-portable TACAN—that's a TACtical Air Navigation beacon—learning how to tote, assemble and operate the huge God be-damned monstrosity under a day-long freezing drizzle.

As for me, the only thing I think I've gotten out of the whole wasted exercise is about an hour-and-a-half of a standing nap. I'm just so friggin' exhausted and beaten down, I almost forgot to follow the rest of my classmates back to our camp once the TACAN thing finally ended.

Truth is, the only thing that's gotten me through this day at all is the fact that it's the eighth day out of the final ten that we have to spend in the field before graduation. And even that is something I couldn't possibly care less about anymore. My feet are wet and frozen into muddy popsicles. My camouflaged fatigues are crusted and torn and damp—both sets—which makes changing my sodden clothes a completely useless gesture. I'm hungry, sore, cold, wet and dead tired, and I've only taken a shit twice in the eight days we've been out here so far. All I want to do right now is get off my feet and slip off into blessed oblivion, mentally reciting the last of my desperate mantras: *"In three days this will all be a memory. In three days this will all be a memory. In three days..."*

But it is not to be.

As I shuffle up to the dead coals of our late great fire, Sergeant Hemingway marches into our circle of tents. His weapons and web gear, canteens and ammo pouches clank and clatter proudly, muffled only slightly by a few strategic strips of duct tape layered between them. His cammies still have their starched creases, for cryin' out loud. Mine don't look that good when I first pick them up at the dry cleaners.

Now, I'm about as low on the student food chain as you can get, and I am grateful for that anonymity at times like these. Apparently, one of our poor abused student NCOs is about to get him a Grand Atomic Wedgy for some trivial oversight—one of us lower ranking slobs probably has his socks on inside-out, or something critical like that—and as usual, it will be a public spectacle. I don't have the energy to pay it any attention though, and I begin the slow, groaning, creaking descent to my sitting spot on the log beside the charcoal mud that was once our campfire.

But Sgt. Hemingway grabs my elbow just as I'm reaching the half-stooped phase of my hunker, hoists me back upright, and announces, loudly enough for anyone within gunshot range to hear, "Airman Stipp! Your frag! The truck leaves in twenty minutes! Better hustle!"

Oh, that's right! Tonight's the final frag! But... hey... wait a minute...

He stuffs a piece of paper into my hand—*my* hand—*my* 'Fragmentary Order' or 'frag'—claps me hard on the back (everybody in gunshot range probably heard that too), and marches off into the mists again.

Wha'? Is this some kind of a joke? Did he not notice the one little measly stripe on my uniform, as opposed to the three or four stripes on all the sergeants' sleeves?

Do I really even look *like a leader of men?*

In the center of a slowly contracting circle of fellow students then, I stare dumbfounded at the dirty wad of Xerox paper in my hand. The dreaded Frag #5. *My* frag now. *Mine!* These are mission orders, the kind that high commanders hand to lower commanders, but *commanders all!* This is a clinical summary of a tactical situation that must be resolved immediately by a team of 'elite specialists'—the ten students of this class, apparently—led by...

Who? Me?

They're giving *me* the frag?

I look around as if they just dropped a dead rat into my palm.

What am I supposed to do with this? A lowly airman. The lowliest airman in the group, in fact. Yet still they've decided to hand this, the final and most difficult frag of the entire course, to me. *To me?!*

What about Sgt. Haley? No one deserves it more than him! Or any of the other sergeants for that matter! I'm not even an NCO!! And if it just has to be me, why'd you wait until JUST NOW to give it to me?!!!

"Well, what's it say?"

It's my buddy Greg, trying to goose me out of my stupor.

My brain stumbles back on track, my throat swallows dry, and I read from the paper.

"Uhhh... *Southeast Command advises; Green Beret team egressing from hostile territory with multiple prisoners and wounded. Will require mass evac at earliest possible time. Insert one ten-man CCT* (that's us) *to DZ Delta (see map insert 1), ingress overland five kilometers to RP Echo (see map insert 2), and make contact with friendlies. Establish a secure perimeter, and set up a 2,500 foot LZ with full lighting and VHF comm for night recovery ops. CCT will direct and protect the C-130 extraction aircraft through landing, loading and departure, then police up the area and egress on foot. Action to commence immediately.*"

I look up, my mouth hanging open. Most of the class—the other lowly airmen at least—are watching me, waiting for words to issue forth. The four student NCOs, on the other hand—Sergeants Haley, Matheson, Donado and Corbin—just scowl at me, as if this was some kind of scheme of mine to steal their moment of glory. I am fully prepared to hand it over to any one of them though, while I go trotting off into the woods to take my third crap of the week, which has suddenly become an urgent priority for me again. But that too, apparently, will not happen.

"Okay then," says Greg, trying once more to jump-start my brain, "Tell us what to do."

Oh yeh... like I *know.*

STORY XXXI

REDEMPTION

1

DAY NINE; THE MORNING AFTER THE NIGHT BEFORE

December, 1977
In the field outside Little Rock AFB, Little Rock, Arkansas

"GENTLEMEN!" SGT. RABIN BOOMS from the front of the twenty-man tent classroom. "How do you suppose you did last night?"

He's not exactly chipper, but neither is he angry, nor half as glum as the rest of us. As usual, his cammies are lethally starched and creased, his jaw is smoothly shaven (and it's a jaw that will have another five o'clock shadow by *ten* o'clock!), and his boots—standing right there in the slushy mud of the tent's floor—are spotless and shined like the hood of a black Cadillac. I hate him right now, and I know I'm *really* going to hate this debrief.

It doesn't help seeing Sergeants Hemingway and Stillman standing on both sides of us either, all stern-faced, at parade rest, like palace bouncers anticipating a spontaneous riot.

"We blew it," Sgt. Haley growls, in a voice that's clearly saying, "*Stipp* blew it."

Thank-you, Sgt. Haley.

And that whole wretched night comes back to me in a mudslide.

Despite all my feverish denial, despite all my desperate prayers that that miserable frag might have been just a really bad dream, the last hopeful voice in my head lets out a sigh of suicidal resignation, pulls out a rhetorical gun, and sticks it in its metaphorical mouth. The mental tapes in my head hit 'replay,' and last night rockets across my inner screens all over again.

All of it.

The cockpit fire in the first C-130, and the long drawn-out hammering flight of the second one... the airsickness, the multiple barf bags (two of which I had to carry out the door with me), and the near-weeping dry heaves... my dazed and dizzied moments standing in the jump door with the instructor, and then my stupendously idiotic leap into space in *front* of everybody else... the hard high-wind landings that wound up breaking the leg of one of my fellow students... Hackett's weapon going off, and then his bitching that *just wouldn't stop* until I finally had to 'fire' him and send him to the rear of the column... the slow progress through the woods that ultimately left us with too little time to complete the set-up of our 'runway'... the red lens caps that nobody could find until it was too late... the cold, the wet... the aching bones, the sullen tired eyes... the ridiculously short-notice impossibilities...

... the blown deadline... the failed frag... *ah, GAAHHHD!!*

So this is what it's like when your life flashes (or lynches itself) before your very eyes, huh. Does this mean I'm dead then?

God, I hope so.

"Yes, that's true," Sgt. Rabin agrees, nodding, "You did fail to achieve your mission in the time allotted. And I suspect that most of you have some pretty strong opinions on just how that happened. And that's what we're going to review here first. *Your* impressions, gentlemen. Then we're going to give you *ours*. And then, this evening, we're all going to go out, and we're going to do it all over again."

All nine of us groan and shuffle in place. I can feel every eye in the tent boring in on me.

"*All* of it, Sergeant?" Hackett asks timidly.

"Yep. All of it. All but the jump itself, that is." The class deflates with audible relief. "You did complete your fifth and final combat-load jump last night, so there's no need to repeat *that* to complete your course objectives. Besides, the weather genies are predicting a dense fog this evening that oughta' kill any chance of even attempting another jump. So you don't need to worry about going through *that* again."

"Who'll be getting the frag tonight, Sergeant Rabin?"

"Oh, it'll still be Airman Stipp's frag. It'll be the same identical mission you did last night, just minus the airborne insertion."

Wordlessly, the class fires the word "*shit*" at me. I hear it at the gut level. My eyes drop to the mud floor, then I let them close.

"So, Sgt. Haley, since you seem to have such a vested interest in seeing this mission done right, why don't you go first. Give us your assessment of the errors made last night."

Our valiant class leader hesitates only a moment, then he's out of the starting blocks and on a roll that only accelerates as he goes along.

For all of a minute, he gives cursory lip-service to the handicaps of the weather, and the setbacks of malfunctioning aircraft and injured teammates. But then his momentum carries him over that line, and the rest of his diatribe is now dedicated entirely to my shortcomings as a team leader, my shortsighted and amateurish 'battle plan,' my clumsy handling of events at the final LZ, and of course, my spectacularly *stupid* jump out of the airplane *in front* of my team.

If Haley hadn't already hated me half to death, I know he's there now. I expected nothing less from him.

Others that follow him have much the same things to say, though with significantly less vehemence. My fellow McChord team buddies—Greg, Rocky, and Sal—are thankfully tactful about focusing on those problems that were beyond my control. They know everyone else will have plenty to say about my mishandling of things, so they don't need to beat me over the head with those same issues. Besides, when this is all over, the four of us will have to fly back to McChord together.

Blessedly, Sgt. Rabin decides he's gotten the gist of it all before all eight guys have had their say. So he cuts the rest of them off, and turns to me.

"And Mister Stipp. What did *you* get out of all this?"

I'm just not in the mood for this. I take a quick look around the room, give my shoulders a weary shrug, and say, "I guess I learned about a dozen things *I'll* never do again."—*like spending even one more day at this fuckin' job, for one thing*—and I leave it at that.

Sgt. Rabin lets the silence seep in a little deeper before he speaks again. And when he does, his tone is strangely 'understanding,' and at least temporarily indulgent.

"Okay then. Now it's *our* turn. And we'll start with the basics.

"Yes, the weather sucked. It was freezing cold, pitch dark, and the winds were high. But they're going to be that way sometimes, and you're going to have to do the job anyway. And last night, *you did.* You all even made it to the DZ! *All* of you! Personally, I'd thought for sure that we were going to have to send out a search party into the next county for *somebody.* But you all made it to the target area. Even the late great Airman Torrero. So getting to the ground under unfavorable conditions was not an issue.

"And yes, Airman Stipp here made some errors and some 'interesting' judgment calls out there." He turns to face me directly. "For instance, leaving Mister Hackett behind to finish his push-ups—for *any* reason, for that matter, *including* life-or-death urgencies—could never happen in the real world, and it was *cheating* here at this school. So *that* was a definite no-no."

I can hear a couple of righteous *harrumphs* among the seats behind me. Probably Hackett and Haley. I just nod dully.

"Surprisingly, the biggest error *we* thought you made was one nobody here even thought to mention."

Oh good! I did something even worse than all the crap everyone just spent the last fifteen minutes bitching about. I can't wait to hear this.

"You didn't need to be quite *that* tactical on the overland portion."

Oh hell, I already figured that one out on my own. I'm way ahead of you on that one.

"You had limited time, and a lot of distance to cover. Under those circumstances, a little less stealth and a lot more speed would have better suited your mission. Had you just been a little faster, you would have had plenty of time to reach the LZ and still made your deadline, even with the fuck-ups with the lens covers. In other words, you would have achieved your mission's objectives, and we wouldn't be going back out there again tonight."

Ah, wonderful. Now my life's complete.

But then Sgt. Rabin breaks eye contact, straightens up, and abruptly sheds the last of his fatherly demeanor. He's suddenly all hard-edged business.

"Gentlemen, what we observed last night was that this mission failed for two primary reasons. And neither of them had anything to do with the weather, the aircraft, the loss of your secondary radioman, Mister Stipp's one or two minor misjudgments, or even Mister Hackett firing off his weapon in the middle of his teammates. You were able to overcome, and continued to operate, despite each of these issues and more. So you can put those things out of your minds right now. Forget 'em. They're not the real problems.

"No, what cost you this mission was (1) you took too long doing it—and we've already discussed the reasons for why *that* happened."

Uh-oh. I wonder if anyone else here is sensing a hurricane coming.

"And (2) —and this was the biggest issue *by far*—you *all*, almost to the last man, *let your team down last night.*"

As one, the entire class rears back in its seats, aghast. Even me.

"That's right, gentlemen. Last night, you guys *sucked* as a team—I mean, just about the worst we've ever seen at this school—and that had nothing to do with how Airman Stipp might have mishandled his duties as team leader. That was all about how *you* responded to Airman Stipp."

Uh-oh. Mixed emotions here. Mixed emotions.

"Sgt. Haley!" he continues, startling him out of a boiling fugue. "When you were handed *your* frag, how long did you have to prepare for it?"

Our class leader scowls heavily, knowing what's coming and wanting to qualify his answer. In the end though, he finally releases a sigh and says, "Twenty-four hours."

"And what was your frag?"

"I'm sorry?"

"What was your objective? Set up a DZ? LZ? EZ? What was your tasking for?"

"Uh, to jump in, set up an Extraction Zone, with lights and panels and within forty-five minutes."

"Did you have to go overland to get there?"

"No sir."

"Did you have to do it at night?"

"No sir."

"Did you seek any assistance or advice during the planning stages?"

"Uh, well... sure. Some."

"Sgt. Matheson! When you got *your* frag, how long did *you* have to prepare for it?"

Another reluctant sigh, then, "Twenty-four hours."

"And what was *your* mission?"

"We set up a DZ for a CDS drop, with timing points and wind corrections, sir."

"Have to travel far to get there?"

"No sir. We, uh… we set up right where we landed."
"Was it dark?"
"No sir."
"Consult with anybody during the planning for it?"
Another sigh. "Yessir. Of course."
"Sgt. Donado!"

Oh God! We get the point! Please don't rub their noses in it anymore.

But he does it anyway. And each NCO he homes in on finds himself under the three-way crossfire of Sergeants Rabin, Hemingway and Stillman glaring at them as the grilling goes on.

I'm looking at the floor, and rubbing my throbbing temples, when he finally gets back on track and continues.

"Do you all know why we gave this last frag to Airman Stipp?"

Silence.

"This is for *all* of you now. Do you think we just did it on a whim?"

I know *I* did. Now I'm shrinking down into my collar.

"We did it *not* to see how *he* handled it, but how the rest of *you* handled it. And I'm here to tell you, *you guys SUCKED! You just flat shit the bed on this one!* As a so-called 'team,' you people failed *yourselves*."

Damn. He seems genuinely outraged.

I can hear a lone cricket. I can see a lone tumbleweed blowing through the scene. This tent is 'OCQ': 'Old Cemetery Quiet.' And I'm just trying to get as small in my seat as I can. Sgt. Rabin is working up a righteous head of steam though, by the time he resumes.

"Every one of you NCOs had a full *twenty-four hours* to set up each of your missions. Airman Stipp had less than *half* an hour. Every one of you had others to consult with you and plan for every contingency. Airman Stipp wasn't given the *time* for all that. But did even *one* of you offer to assist him *in any way*? Offer any suggestions? Pass on even a little of your worldly experience? No. Not a word. In fact, in most cases, you didn't even lift a finger to help with the loading of the damned truck! They were tossing mission gear *onto your feet*, because you were already sitting in the truck bed, pouting!

"This was your opportunity to really *shine* as a team, gentlemen. *All of you!* This was a moment when all your *individual* experience could've been *combined* to achieve your objectives. You had a vitally important mission, involving the rescue of American forces in harm's way, you had almost no time to prepare, and you had inexperienced leadership trying to organize the whole thing. Can you think of a *better* time for a '*team*' to come together *as a team?* To work with each other and *contribute* towards a common goal? Isn't that the fucking *definition* of 'team?' You all needed to pull this one off right. And to do it, you *needed* to work together.

"So how do *you*, as a *TEAM*, think you handled this? Hmm? How do *you* think you came together as a unit?

"Let me answer that for you… you *blew it.*"

Man, he's really *seething* right now.

"Yes, Airman Stipp fucked up when he went out the door first instead of last. But, except for blowing procedure and making himself look stupid, did that really, in *any way*, have *anything whatsoever* to do with the success or failure of the mission? Did it impede or endanger your progress in any way?

"And as long as we're on that subject, just who the hell *was* it that landed *with* the wind and broke his damned leg? Was that Airman Stipp? Who *was* it that fired off a round in the middle of his own teammates? Was that Airman Stipp too? And just who the hell was it that didn't notice a six-deep stack of lens covers on top of one of his own lights? Was that Airman Stipp as well? No, gentlemen. You did plenty of screwing up on your own, and with a far greater impact on the success of the mission. You bitched and pouted and whined, showed no respect for your mission leadership, and acted like a bunch of punk-assed amateurs out there. I bet that imaginary Green Beret team was impressed as hell."

Sgt. Hemingway can't quite contain a little snicker at that one.

"Is that how you're going to handle things in the real world? Cooperate with the team leaders you *like*, fuck over the ones that you don't? 'Cause if it is, I'll fire you all *right now*. Save us from a few disasters further on down the line. The last letter in 'CCT' is a fucking *T!* Anybody here know what that stands for?"

Everybody's so hunkered down, absorbing the scolding, that nobody even notices that they've just been asked a question that actually begs an answer. Myself included.

"*Am I talking to a wall here? What does the damned T stand for?*"

We splutter for a couple of seconds, and a few of us mutter the word 'team.' Kind of pathetic, actually.

"*What?!*"

We're up and alert and *ready* for this one, though.

"*Team, Sergeant Rabin!*"

"You're damned right is stands for *team*. And don't you *ever* forget it! Not in *here*, and sure as *hell* not out *there!* Your mission objectives have priority over *any and all* relationship problems, petty rivalries, old grudges, childhood insults, *anything* like that. You are *all—together—*working for the success of the frag, or you are working *somewhere else! Period.*"

He pauses to steady his breathing, temper his fury, lower his volume.

"Now, maybe you think Airman Stipp was a little indecisive in places, lacked assertiveness in others, maybe acted a little rashly or didn't think things all the way through in some cases. But what the hell did he have to work with? His highly cooperative 'team?' His experienced and helpful NCOs? And why do you suppose it was that he felt compelled to *fire his pacer* and send him to the rear of the column? Airman Hackett? Any ideas?"

This time he *isn't* looking for an answer, and he doesn't wait for one.

Thank God he's finally gotten around to his conclusion, though.

"Airman Stipp, with no prior leadership experience, was given just twenty minutes to formulate a full battle plan that included a night jump, in bad weather, a five-klick overland march that required some pretty precise night navigation, and an extremely tight deadline for setting up a complete lighted runway... *and he damn near did it!* He damn near pulled it off even with his own errors and inexperience. Not only that, but he damned near did it *without your help!* He had that plan ready to go when we called for it. He briefed it thoroughly, he left no one unclear about the mission's objectives or their specific parts in it. He carried his load, he led from the front—*literally*, starting right at the door of the airplane, actually—he did what he had to do, and he did the best he could. He made his share of mistakes, but then so did just about everybody else here. And with only one or two exceptions, you people fought him every step of the way. Do you sense a theme coming through here yet?"

Heads are bobbing shamefully all around me.

Oh my God! How the hell am I going to be able to work with these guys after this? Stop it already!

"Alright then," and Sergeants Stillman and Hemingway apparently take the softening of his tone as their cue, drop their 'intimidating centurion' acts, and march out of the tent. "Tonight, at twenty-one hundred, fog or no fog, we will march from here directly out onto the DZ, to the exact same rally point as last night. Airman Stipp will still have the frag, and unless he alters anything between now and then, you'll all still have your same assignments as last night. We'll start the clock again at the same point, and you will repeat everything from the RP on, including the same full LZ set-up, and with the same deadlines. Understood?"

"*Oo-rah!*"

"Good. Now," and he turns to his flipcharts again. "Today's lesson is on trenchfoot."

Wow. Vilified and vindicated in the same speech.

How often does that happen?

2
A WALK IN THE PARK

FRIGGIN' FOG. SO MUCH for 'celestial navigation' tonight.

Forget the stars. Tonight it's not just a moonless Stygian pit, but the depths of a black hole smothered under a vast blanket of mist as well. You know? Nothing to look at, and no way to see that.

That's what we've got to work with tonight. No ghostly limn of pixie dust outlining everything like normal, nothing to glow with a faint iridescence that only the most dark-adapted eye can see. Tonight, *nothing* is detectable to the naked eye, *nothing*... unless it glows on its own, like the luminescent faces of watches or compass dials, the strips of glow-in-the-dark tape that some guys have stuck to the backs of their caps, or, in a couple of cases—like mine—the Cyalume sticks we've cracked and stuck down the backs of our T-shirts. Just enough of a shielded radiance to give the man behind us something to track through this 'ocean floor of darkness.'

I feel bad for Rocky too, up front walking point, breaking an invisible trail for the rest of us. He has to follow his own compass *and* let his feet (and battered shins) find the obstacles the hard way. The rest of us can follow the glowing bars of tape on the back of his cap. Truth be told though, knowing Rocky, I bet he's loving every second of walking point.

At least I was able to cancel the two flankers for this little do-over. They were a waste of manpower the first time around. But if I'd kept them out there again *this* time, paralleling our column like blind wingmen through this sinkhole of deep shadows, they probably wouldn't have shown up again until sometime next spring.

What a mess.

For all our readiness to streamline this scenario and get it over with quickly, we're actually moving slower than last night. We have to. We have to feel out every step—like walking in Braille—trying not to lose sight, or at least the *sound* of the man in front of us. I've lost Goebler a couple of times already, and I'd be lying if I claimed that wasn't just a little bit scary. But I picked him up again right away each time, just a few seconds later, whenever he'd either turn his head back forward (presenting to me the glowing bars on the back of his hat again), or I stepped past whatever invisible branch or screen of leaves had temporarily eclipsed my view of his head.

Still... *spooky.*

Surprisingly though, there are a couple of *positive* notes working in my favor tonight... sort of.

For one thing, *my heels no longer hurt!* Or maybe they're just permanently numb now, I don't know. And to tell you the truth, I don't really *care* what the reason is. I'm just enjoying the notable change.

For another, we've found that we don't need to bother with the petty annoyance of having to circumnavigate every clearing along the way, or darting one-by-one, 'covertly,' across every road or path we meet. The dense fog has made *every* move covert, and every clearing undetectable to anyone who might be trying to track us tonight. Or even to *ourselves*, for that matter. So we haven't had to waste any time diverting our course or delaying our crossings. *Yay!*

But the biggest improvement to the situation (mostly) has been the newfound cooperation of my 'team.' After this morning's lambasting by Sgt. Rabin, everyone has just been *ferociously* intent on making sure they are seen as *team players*, by God! Even Sgt. Haley's been unnaturally contrite tonight, checking frequently to see if there's anything else I need him to do, responding snappily to any signals that I give, and accepting any changes to his marching orders or duties without complaint or even hesitation. It's so unlike him (and his outspoken disdain for *me*)—so clearly a charade intended to curry the favor of the observing instructors, maybe even earn a few more brownie points toward Honor Grad—that I think I almost prefer the old spiteful Haley that I'd grown so accustomed to despising.

But he's not alone. *Everyone's* doing it. So eager to please, so desperate to atone, so willing to suck up, that I do believe, if I just had the balls to ask, I could probably get one of these guys to carry my rucksack and radio for me as well.

Of course, it's also possible that we all might have actually learned something about being a '*team*' from this morning's scolding. Who knows?

I *want* to like it. I *want* to revel in my exoneration, and enjoy the exaggerated cooperation. But I don't. It just feels too much like an act, like overcompensation. 'Collaboration overkill.' Or, more succinctly, like *lying*. An awkward and uncomfortable conspiracy of false decency. And all I want is for it to end, *now*, for this weird, ghostly, pandering night to just be over with.

Creeping through the darkness like this, though, is not helping to move things along.

But even with all our blind tippy-toeing, we still manage to reach the same spot on the same straightaway portion of the same road with a full thirty-five minutes left to kill this time.

Amazing what an undiverted beeline through the woods can do, even in slow motion.

Actually, although it would be hard to tell, I do believe we might have lost one or two of our trailing instructors back there somewhere. Not that I'd know, and not that it would matter much anyway. But between that likelihood, the all-consuming mists, the weariness of myself and my fellow students, plus the fact that I just flat *don't give a shit anymore*, I decide to march our little nine-man war party right down the *middle* of our socked-in dirt road LZ, dropping off Elco lights in sequence as we go, and saving ourselves the time-consuming, frustrating, and *noisy* effort of working our way through the underbrush off either side of the road.

I'd like to think that the gesture is appreciated by my still-penitent classmates, but *who friggin' knows*.

I just want to get this damned thing over with.

Ultimately though, I've got nothing to complain about.

Once on the hard-packed road, the deployment of the lights goes quickly and easily (*I guess*... at least I can't *hear* anything going wrong). And in a little over five minutes, Sal Donado and I once again find ourselves alone at the far end of the runway. Again, Sal and I run out our lines of green-capped approach-end lights, after which I drop off the edge of the road, and feel around in the shoulder brush for a depression that we can turn into a defensive position. I crack a fresh Cyalume, and drop it, glowing, among the leaves and detritus at my feet (something for Sal to home in on). Then I settle behind my weapon, snatch my radio's 'phone' receiver off the D-ring on my web gear, and, without actually touching the transmit key, I 'call' our 'inbound aircraft.'

"Coil Zero-One, this is Padlock Control on point-seven, over."

Nothing.

"Coil Zero-One, Padlock Control on one-two-five-point-seven, over."

Nada.

I hear Sal scuffling into my little hidey-hole behind me, rigging up his own defensive apparatus, and 'assuming the position' facing the opposite way.

I tear the velcro cover off my watch, and check our time—*still almost twenty-five minutes left on the clock*—then I return to the radio. I'm not really transmitting anything to anyone, of course, but I surely wish our pretend-pilot (whomever and wherever he might be) would hurry his ass up and answer my pretend-call, so that we can wrap this very-real-shit up, and call it a friggin' night already.

"Coil Zero-One, Padlock Control on point-seven. How do you read?"

Nothing. Again.

Where the hell is Sgt. Myers, damn it? He was the instructor who pretended to be the pilot last night. Why isn't he here now?

Unless…

Holy crap! What if we *did* lose some of the instructors in this smothering darkness! And if we did—and especially if Sgt. Myers is one of the lost ones—*what do we do now?* If they don't catch up to us in the next twenty minutes or so, does our deadline lapse and we fail this frag again? Or should we just declare *ourselves* winners right now, turn on our runway lights on our own, and call this one a done deal?

I know what *my* vote is.

"*Whaddaya' think, Sal?*" I whisper.

The darkness sighs.

"*Fucked if I know. You da' boss. You tell me.*"

Well, that wasn't quite the 'we're-all-in-this-together' response I was looking for. Apparently Sal has completed his acts of contrition, and is back to just being Sal again. But that doesn't change the fact that he's right. How *should* he know? And yes, I *am* 'da' boo-woss' now, aren't I.

I decide to give the instructors one more try. And this time, instead of *pretend*-transmitting into a dead microphone, I actually key my handset and transmit. At least Sgt. Corbin (on the other prick) will *hear* that I was trying to get this damned thing over with. Maybe earn me a few 'brownie points' of my own.

"Coil Zero-One, Padlock Control, over."

Nothing. Of course not.

Okay. Now what?

I'll tell you what. I'm going to give the instructors some lights to help bring them back into the fold, that's what.

Funny how much easier decisions are to make once you no longer give a corn-studded shit about the repercussions. Still, there's a moment of pause before my thumb actually presses the button, not out of any reluctance or hesitancy, you understand... just forming the words in my head. And in that one extra moment, I hear the handset's tiny earpiece squawk.

"Padlock Control, Coil Zero-One is three minutes out, inbound from the south."

What the...? That didn't sound like Sgt. Corbin—the only other guy with a 'prick' out here—and that wasn't on 125.7 either. That was Team Channel 5 (the frequency I'd chosen just so that Corbin could hear me *trying* to end this nightmare). Actually, it sounded more like *Sgt. Stillman!*

Who cares! Play this out, and get it over with!

"Coil Zero-One, this is Padlock Control. LZ and assets are in place. Runway zero-five in use. Wind calm, altimeter unknown. Ready for lights-on at your discretion. Over."

"Roger that, Padlock. Lights on. Lights on."

Dang! Somebody *wants to wrap this shit up right the hell* now.

Sal scrambles up out of our little 'foxhole' without waiting to be cued, leaving the dim green glow of the Cyalume stick I'd dropped between us, and starts clicking on our Elco lights.

Wow. I guess everybody's *ready to go home.*

I don't have to rechannelize the radio to pass the word on to Corbin—*hell, I don't really even have to give the command, do I? 'Coil 01' called from Sgt. Corbin's radio!*—but, as with everything else, I go through the motions like I'm supposed to.

"Lights on," I say into my handset. "Lights on."

And two-by-two, in the deep dark fog-shrouded woods of Arkansas, two parallel strings of light come to life, marching off into the mists like the airport scene from "*Casablanca.*" If someone came strolling out of the smokiness right now, backlit by our Elcos, hands plunged into the pockets of a full-length trench coat, a fedora cocked rakishly to one side of his  head, and an unlit cigarette dangling lazily from one lip, it wouldn't seem the least bit out of place.

I want to laugh at that, but I don't. Instead, I settle for a tired smile.

Sal, now a visible silhouette scurrying out of the green-and-white glowing fog, hops back into our hole beside me, and reassumes his defensive station. *Instructors will be coming soon. Gotta' look our best!*

And sure enough, barely a minute later, the squat profile of Sgt. Stillman tromps into our sphere of swaddled light, pauses to count our green approach array, then, without being able to actually see us, he shouts into the general gloom.

"Alright, gentlemen! That's it! Police this shit up, and get your asses on the truck! Let's go!"

I take that to mean, *Congratulations, Airman Stipp. Your mission is (finally) a success! You may return now to the palatial accommodations of your tent, and enjoy the sleep of the righteous, the vindicated, and the validated. For, the day after tomorrow, you will be a* graduate *of this school. And the day after that, you will leave this place with a beret on your head, a justifiably smug-ass smile on your face, and more pride than you've ever known in your life.*

I take it well, and key my radio one more time.

"Lights out, guys. Pack it up."

Sgt. Stillman turns, and is instantly swallowed by the smoky night.

I rise from my defensive position, and bound up out of our 'foxhole.'

Funny how much easier that is without the weight of failure on your back.

STORY XXXII

CULMINATIONS

1
DAY TEN: YE OLDE HOME STRETCH

December, 1977
Last day in the field outside Little Rock AFB, Little Rock, Arkansas

LAST TENT-CLASS IN the field.

Last class of *any* kind at this school, for that matter. *Thank gawd!*

And it's an easy one too: *"Day & Night Weather Alternatives,"* the syllabus says. Also known as *"Waste of Time 101."*

Sure could have used that during last night's 'frag replay.' You know?

Or maybe not. What could we have really done differently anyway?

Oh, and by the way, it turned out that the tag-along instructors on last night's forced march—Sergeants Stillman and Myers—*had* lost us in the depths of that inky blackness after all.

As the story trickled back to me (unembellished by all the retellings, I'm sure... from Corbin to Goebler, then through Hackett and Spradlin), the only reason Sgt. Stillman ever found us at all was because he just happened to be standing in the middle of our LZ road (no doubt wondering where the hell we were), when I made that last broadcast in the blind... and he heard it coming from *Corbin's radio*, somewhere in the invisible bushes off the side of the road. He'd homed in on the faint sound, collided with Corbin in the darkness, then snatched up his handset to answer me. Hence,

'Coil 01' (*he*) was able to respond to 'Padlock' (*me*) before our time ran out. *Whew!*

Sgt. Myers, on the other hand, was still out in the woods when the runway lights came on, and guided him into our fully operational LZ with their glow. At least that's how the legend goes (and how it will long be retold) by the time it gets to me.

And the fog that socked us in so solidly last night? Well, that hung on all the way through to this morning apparently. And that's kept the temperature down, and the soppiness up. My favorite combination.

Lordy, I am so sick to death of being clammy and cold... not to mention sore, dead-friggin'-tired, cramped, bruised, and constipated. Oh, and don't forget socially ostracized, out of my element, over my head, bored, scared, and just generally stupid.

But mostly just clammy and cold.

Man, I am so ready to be warm and dry again... and outa' here!

* * *

I AWOKE IN MY tent this morning, rumpled and damp in my soggy uniform, to find the world outside still drowned in milk, and with the mists still so thick that I couldn't even see all the guys who were already up, fully dressed, and making their C-rat coffee around the fire that they'd already re-stoked.

Show-offs.

But it's been slowly burning off as the day has progressed. It's gotten thinner and lighter each time I've stepped outside the 'classroom' on our hourly breaks, and it's even been getting warmer. In fact, it's supposed to get clear up into the upper-*fifties* today, maybe even the *sixties*, just in time for this afternoon's "*Map & Compass Qualifying Confidence Course,*" the school's culminating cross-country overland navigation run.

And today, it's a *solo* challenge. *Zoo-hah!*

The last event in these games. And fortunately, it's one that I'm actually *good* at.

But first we have to finish this last achingly dull, tediously redundant, and now utterly superfluous class on 'weather issues.' Then it's back to camp to throw down some lunch, smother the fire, strike our tents, and pack up all our gear... which we will then have to carry on our backs while we hike our six miles over open country—wintry central Arkansas country—on our final navigational trial, to our grand finale: an idling deuce-an-a-half, out in the middle of nowhere, waiting to take us 'home.'

Well, to Little Rock Air Force Base, anyway.

Pfft. Nothing to it.

* * *

PERFECT! NOT ONLY HAS the afternoon temperature warmed its way up into the lower sixties, without an ounce of chilly breeze to scamper down my collar, but the fog has all but melted away. Actually, it looks more like it was *pulled* away, like hair from a brush, leaving cobwebby strands tangled in the trees and pooled in some of the low spots.

And overhead, there's not a cloud in the sky. Not a trace, not a wisp. Even the blue looks deeper and more vivid than normal, despite the white hot lens of the sun blazing away just past its noon zenith.

As I lope down out of the brambly tree line, hunched low in the tall grass and angling toward a strand of trees with a barbed wire fence running through it, I can see clear across this low rolling glen with crystalline clarity. And down among the hummocks and river beds of the sprawling valley floor, there are still a few cotton candy shreds of the fog left for me to disappear into, pockets of privacy where I won't have to work so hard at remaining hidden in broad daylight.

But that's still not the *decisive* 'perfect touch.'

The best part is that I'm *alone. Finally!*

A little over a mile into this solo cross-country dash, and, with the exception of the dry crunch and rustle of the ground cover underfoot, accompanied by my own heavy breathing, it is exquisitely quiet out here. A thread of asphalt in the distance occasionally sighs with the passage of a single car, a bird might occasionally twitter, usually from afar, but otherwise it's just me and nature and a leisurely two-hour hike to freedom. No one looking over my shoulder, no averted glances, no whispered asides. No one training, grading, or assessing my every move, no one out-performing me at some supposedly simple task, not a single living soul around me that I need to please or impress. Just me, setting my own standard, and pushing myself to achieve it.

And for today, that 'standard' is *speed*. I intend to set a new class record for completing this course in minimal time. I know it's not what this final trial is about, but what do I care?

I *know* 'land nav.' What I *need* is a 'point of pride' to finish with.

How much speed can you muster though, with a fifty- or sixty-pound rucksack bouncing around on your back, shrugging heavily with every jostle, snagging tree limbs, getting wedged in every bottleneck, and shoving the holster strap of your gas mask halfway down your ass to where it starts digging into your hip and cheek hard enough to feel like a cramp?

But it just doesn't matter anymore.

Today I almost—*almost*—'enjoy' the pain, keeping my attention on it as if it was the last spoonful of a particularly nasty medicine that I'll never have to take again.

It's not pleasant, but it's a form of celebration in its own way.

There's a rotting old shed (or something similar)—maybe even an ancient outhouse—sunk up to its crescent moon in tall weeds, junk, and brambles about two-hundred yards beyond this fenceline. I marked it as a waypoint from higher up the slope. And with that as my target, I haven't had to keep referring to my compass. And without *that* distraction, it's been all about picking my cover, and moving as quickly as practicable between points.

In other words, *it's been fun* for once.

So after another dash through the high weeds, hunched over low enough that only my overstuffed rucksack should be visible above the grass-tops, like a really swollen dorsal fin cutting through sun-tinted water, I hustle into the treeline, and throw myself against the barbed wire fence. Just to bring my downhill scamper to a stop.

This is going to be a tough one to get over, though: too high to just push down and swing a leg over, too thin and spindly to *climb* with all this gear on, and with vertical wires threaded through the horizontal ones—presumably as spacers—that'll prevent me from *spreading* them and just sidestepping through. There are trees close enough to assist with the climb-over though, but not with this damned ruck on my back.

So, after only a moment's hesitation to contemplate the variables, I *shuck the ruck... happily.*

I unclip the chest strap and the lumbar support buckle, shrug it off both shoulders, then give it a good old two-handed heave over the fence and into the dry leaves on the other side.

Aaahhh. Nothing like shedding sixty pounds in an instant.

Man, I feel almost weightless.

From there, I sling my GAU over my shoulder, and do a quick shinny up a white-barked tree, where I hang for a moment before swinging my dangling feet over onto one of the fence posts. With one foot then, I settle my weight onto the top of the post, and using it like a tall skinny 'stepping stone,' I step over to the downhill side and hop off. I drop into the leaves beside my rucksack, and reluctantly heft it back onto my shoulders again.

But dang, that felt good while it lasted.

* * *

A LITTLE FURTHER ALONG, I crash across a tiny dribble of a stream, wet boots be damned. Any other time, I would have hopped across, taking care to keep my boots dry. But today?

How much wetter, muddier, or chewed up could my boots be? How much wetter my socks?

Squishing up to the edge of that lonely two-lane road I'd seen earlier then, I plop down against a tree, out of sight from the 'highway,' ostensibly to wait out the passage of several cars (this *is* supposed to be a 'covert move,' after all). But, long after the last three cars have whisked past, I'm still sitting here, quietly reveling in the motionlessness.

I'm a little over halfway through this final course—not quite four klicks yet, I do believe—but I've been pushing my speed and keeping up the tempo, and I could use the damned break... especially since, on the other side of the road, the terrain starts back uphill again.

Stupid terrain.

My spot here is good to the extent that no one driving this road will be able to see me until they've rounded that nearby corner and practically run me over. The downside though, is that I can't see *them* coming any better. I should move along the roadside a little distance until I'm in a position to see traffic coming sooner, but, well... I just *don't*. I've decided I'm just going to wait here until it's dead quiet again, and that will just have to do. This is *Ye Olde Home Stretch*, after all. The proverbial 'light at the end of the tunnel' is coming fast upon me, and even a diversion of that little is too much to put up with any longer. Because *I'm done.*

In my mind, I'm just walking *home* right now. And we don't need no stinkin' detours to delay that even one minute more than we already have.

So when the next car rolls out of sight down the grade to my right, taking the rush of its tires with it, I draw a deep (and resigned) breath, hoist myself to my feet with an old man's grunt, and ski down the leafy embankment to the roadside. There I pause to measure the silence once more. Then I lean into the weight of my pack, and start trotting across the pavement.

In the middle of the road though, something about this situation just slaps me upright again, and I stop, straddling the painted centerline.

Look at me! Look at where I am, and what I'm doing right now!

I'm standing, all by myself, in the middle of a lonely Arkansas back road, on a crisp winter afternoon. I'm holding a loaded GAU-5 assault rifle in my hands. My face is raked with green, brown, and black grease paint, my camouflaged fatigues are wet and tattered, my boots almost *tan* from both the mud and the shredded leather. I'm festooned with canteens and ammo pouches, along with a knife, my flashlight, and my gas mask holster, and there's a massive rucksack on my back big enough to carry an adult dwarf as a stowaway. To all outward appearances, every inch a battle-hardened modern warrior.

(*snork!*)

Me! I'm talking about me *here! Will you look at this?*

If a car came around that corner right now, what would that driver think of the apparition—of the weary 'legionnaire'—poised in the middle of the road before him? Or *her*. I know what *I'd* think.

I want to laugh... but I'm not sure why.

* * *

OTHER THAN TWO BIG-SOUNDING dogs that I never actually see—their baying seems to come from the vicinity of a rustic farmyard a couple hundred meters up the floor of the valley from me—I manage to pass 'unseen,' and for all intents and purposes, 'unsuspected' through the rural landscape.

I think. But what do *I* know? At least I *feel* alone.

I'm not sure about those damned dogs though. I mean, for fifteen or twenty minutes now, as I've been skirting around that farm and its widespread fences, I swear they've barked every time I've moved, and have fallen silent every time I've stopped, regardless of the distance between us, and of my own efforts at stealth. And that bothers me.

I've got the GAU's safety flicked off, though. I am ready to hammer right back at them if they get too curious or come too close.

But nothing comes of it. And once I get up into the higher trees again, they either lose interest, or lose my scent, or lose whatever mysterious connection they have with the universe that allows them to 'sense' the passage of suspicious characters moving through tall grass and bushes two football fields away. And the pastoral scene returns to postcard tranquility again.

Of course, for all I can tell, there might be fifty little unseen homesteads buried among the hollers or perched on the tree-blanketed hillsides all around me right now, each with a clear view of my crashing transition through their domain.

A picture forms in my mind of two old toothless hillbillies sitting in rocking chairs on a rickety front porch—one with a pipe and a jug, and the other with a shotgun laying across his lap—blithely watching this tiny little dark green alien slogging through the light winter tans and dusky grays of their valley, while they cackle their asses off.

"Think I could hit 'im from up here?" asks the one with the shotgun.

"Hell, Jeb," says the pipe-smoker, "You couldn't hit the broad side of a barn if'n you was inside of it."

"Screw you, ya' daffy ol' coot! I oughta' blow that hump right off'n his back just to show ya'!"

"Well go on then! I dare ya'!"

Yeh. A real 'Chamber of Commerce' moment there, played out in my head to the tune of "Dueling Banjos"... just waiting to hear that "POW!" in the distance, or the soul-stirring lilt of "Suey!" echoing down from the trees up ahead.

Yeh. Sometimes solitude ain't all that it's cracked up to be.

But the silence remains blessedly total, and I remain a virtual virgin for a little while longer.

So all is serene and unthreatening as I plunge into the home stretch of the course... of the whole *school, by God!*

The end of the tunnel. The finish line... in sight at last.

* * *

I FIND MY FIFTH and final waypoint card tacked to the tallest tree in this little hillside grove, the same one that I'd zoomed in on through my compass reticule some twenty minutes before, back at the previous waypoint... back when the dogs were still barking, and I was starting to feel my 'oneness with nature' tripping over its own two feet and falling on its ass.

I'll tell you what, though: my lack of natural 'outdoor skills' notwithstanding, I just flat *get* how to use a friggin' compass. Despite my detoured, evasive, and serpentine track across this valley, I still managed to home in on this copse of trees as if it was at the bottom of a funnel.

And now the last card is in my hand.

It actually feels 'heavier' than the others somehow.

My compass is hanging from an improvised lanyard around my neck, a loop of parachute cord actually, so it's in hand and flipped open in an instant. And with only a kilometer remaining to go, and the compass's sighting wire splitting a gap between trees at the visible edge of the far downslope, that means that the final stretch will be a *downhill sprint* down the other side of the hill and across the finish line. And man, does *downhill* ever sound good right about now. *You know?*

Enough with being covert. Let's get this the hell over with.

* * *

I SPOT THE IDLING deuce-and-a-half a couple hundred meters out. And with the exception of a silhouetted figure sitting behind the wheel, there doesn't appear to be anyone else around it. And that means *I'm number one!*

Hoo-HOO!

My grand finale.

I march down the rest of the incline, part the bushes and brambles, and step boldly onto the dirt road just in front of the deuce's front bumper. Sgt. Rabin himself, sitting in the driver's seat, nods and grins and does a two-fingered 'salute' with the gloved hand that's resting on the steering wheel. I nod back, fighting the urge to flaunt my victory, and instead start the process of doffing my three-ton rucksack.

I unbuckle the chest and lumbar straps, shrug the whole rig off, and toss it into the truck bed. Then as I'm re-shouldering my weapon, Rocky steps into view from around the opposite side of the truck. He's not wearing his ruck, though, and he's busily buttoning up his fly.

What?

"Ay, man," he says, fully engrossed in fiddling with his crotch. "You made good time!"

"How long have *you* been here?" I ask.

"Oh, I don't know... five, ten minutes maybe?"

Shit. The indefatigable little bastard probably sprinted the whole way from our base camp, non-stop, all the way to here. And he got here with enough time to shuck his ruck and take a piss before I came sauntering up to the deuce, all flushed with my non-existent triumph.

Shit, shit!

On the other hand, the *fastest and most unrelenting long distance runner in the class* barely beat me—barely beat *me!*—by a mere five or ten minutes on a six-mile cross-country race.

Hoo-HOO!

I'm number two!

2
LEAVING IT ALL BEHIND

THE 'WIND CHILL EXPRESS,' I call it. The final deuce-ride back to the base. It offers only a token nippiness this time. And even that is more a result of my sweat-soaked layers than any real bite to the wind. But again, like so much else today, *who... gives... a SHIT!*

We're done! We made it! Nine out of the original sixteen, anyway. But more importantly—hell, almost *impossibly*—*I'm* done! *I* made it!

I'm one of the *Final Nine!*

And better yet, I'm one of the *McChord Four!*

That still makes my head shake... that all four of the tenderfeet sent here from McChord AFB—against the averages, against all likelihood, and against all odds—stayed the course, survived the gauntlet, and will return home wearing brand spankin' new berets! *All four of them!* Even the rookiest rookie in history! *Moi!*

Oddly, the only words spoken the whole way back to Little Rock, by anyone in the back of this rolling deuce, are Goebler's.

"Does this mean I don't have to come back here again?"

* * *

FOR ONCE, IT'S A *pleasure* breaking down and cleaning my weapon.

It's also a pleasure tromping across the Little Rock Combat Control Team's pristine tile floors in my scuffed and muddy boots, to trudge past their spotless office windows in my damp and shredded cammies, to exchange silent congratulations and share a newly earned camaraderie with whatever showered, pressed, and immaculate members of their team happen to be present when the nine of us march in.

But that's a different *kind* of pleasure. That's more like... *pride*.

Standing here at this cleaning table right now—me and eight other filthy, stinking, exhausted, and proud finishers—this kind of pleasure comes from *relief*. After all that my weapon and I have been through over the last ten days, today it *deserves* these final ministrations of mine.

Heck, this is more of a finalizing gesture than tomorrow night's party will be. At least for me.

I scrub every last pin, spring, and flash suppressor with uncommon tenderness and attention. I run a cleaning rod through the barrel over and over without impatience or rancor. I reassemble the thing with uncharacteristic ease and satisfaction. I pull the charging handle and dry-fire the weapon before the eyes of Sgt. Stillman. Then I set it in place on the gun rack for the last time, and mentally close that book for good.

* * *

THE SUN IS SETTING when they lead us out to the wash rack. And again, it is my *pleasure* to join in the final vehicle-washing ritual.

The deuce-and-a-half and the Jeep are waiting, slathered in mud, and surrounded by buckets and brushes and sponges and hoses. And we attack those puppies with vigor.

Half an hour later, once both have been scrubbed completely mudless and dustless, we turn them back in to the local team, clean up our implements, stow them away, and just like that, our final exertions are over.

They're *all* over.

We get to sleep in tonight! We get to shower, relax, shower again, drink heavily, shower some more—however we want to do it—*then* we don't have to show up at The Section again until noon tomorrow. We'll have an afternoon of cleaning and surrendering more gear, tidying and straightening up the classroom (the one that we haven't even seen in ten fun-filled days), and handing in our manuals, training materials, and any other borrowed shit.

For me, that'll include the tent halves they loaned me, the air mattress that leaked faster than I could fall asleep, and that one extra ammo pouch that they could spare. And we'll have to do all this in our PT togs, since everyone's cammies were all but demolished in the field.

Fine by me.

Tomorrow night—*Thursday* night—will be our graduation party. A fancy banquet room in a downtown Little Rock hotel, our best civilian clothes, steaks and plenty of beer, berets handed out, and permission to be unabashedly irreverent with our instructors.

Well... I'll enjoy the steak and the beret, anyway.

Then on Friday, we fly away home.

But right now, the sweetest thing they could possibly say to me is, "You're released. Go get some sleep."

They make it even sweeter though, when they add, "Just leave your rucksacks here. We'll break them down tomorrow."

And I do.

Oh baby, I do.

3

A CORONATION OF SORTS, A KNIGHTING, IF YOU WILL

December, 1977
Downtown Little Rock, Arkansas

MEX TORRERO LOOKS GOOD. Well, as good as you *can* look anyway, with your leg in a cast from ankle to thigh, an overhead rig hoisting it up at a thirty-three degree angle, and only a couple of sponge baths to make a dent on the previous eight days of filth, sweat, and mud. His hair's been washed though, he's at least had that sponge bath I mentioned (I think), and he's shaved. But he still smells like a pile of burnt laundry to me.

We left the base a half hour early just so that we could stop in here at Little Rock General Hospital on the way to our banquet, to convey our best wishes to our fallen comrade and all that. He's taking it pretty well, too. He says he can't believe that everyone who went *into* the field with him came out the other end as graduates... *except* for him.

Gawd, that's gotta' suck! Three days left out of seven hellish weeks, on the very last jump of the course, on the very last frag, one untimely lapse of concentration—landing *with* the winds instead of against them, blind as he was in the middle of the night—and it's all thrown away.

You know that realization has got to be killing him. It would *me*.

But he keeps up a game face for us. He smiles, laughs at the ribald humor, and congratulates every one of us as we each step up to shake his hand and pass on our condolences, in whatever crude or heartless form those condolences might take. Goebler reassures him that the school doesn't get a damn bit easier the second time around... *and he oughta' know.*

The whole room erupts in coarse laughter. Then we're done.

We've got reservations to keep.

We each sign his cast, clap him on the shoulder for good luck, then we're headed out the door and out of his life... for good.

What can you say? Survival of the luckiest, and all that.

* * *

THE NICEST HOLIDAY INN in Little Rock, Arkansas.

That's where the ending finally begins.

The meal is profoundly adequate, an inspired afterthought for the hotel's top-flight cooking staff, I'm sure. But as far as I'm concerned, it's the nectar of the Gods.

No dry chewy steak ever tasted so sweet, no Dr. Pepper ever so exquisitely 'quenching,' no dollop of plain vanilla ice cream ever so satisfying. And judging by the ravenous assault on the food by everyone else in attendance, I'd have to say that this assessment is pretty much unanimous.

There are fifteen of us here—nine student graduates, and six instructors (*sans* wives)—seated unevenly around four circular banquet tables, which are themselves arranged in a half-hearted semi-circle around a fifth table that stands alone under the windows of the room's longest wall. The lights of nighttime Little Rock sparkle beyond those windows, an orderly spangling viewed through a veil of gauzy curtains. And since no music has been piped into this room, the background ambience consists entirely of the susurrus of traffic on the nearby expressway, accented by an occasional honking horn or the muted shriek of a low-flying aircraft.

However, as with the quality of the food, *who gives a shit!*

In this room, it's all flying elbows, heedless lunges for condiments, silverware clutched in fists, and steak sauce splashing on all sides. Clinking stemware, manly laughter, ferocious gnawing and guzzling sounds, occasional belching, and almost continuous profanity. A level of sophistication and decorum seldom seen outside a Viking family reunion. So I doubt that a little Muzak would have had much of an impact anyway.

All the tables are covered in basic white linen, now freckled with gravy, ketchup, and even a little Dr. Pepper. *Hey, Rocky made me laugh while I was drinking, okay! My nose* still *burns from that untimely little snort.*

But, under that lone display table's drapery, I can see the bottoms of boxes peeking out. Boxes of *berets*, I'll bet. The whole point of all this 'high-society elegance and finery.' And we finally get to it as the dessert is being served (single scoops of vanilla ice cream, no less... *yawn!*).

Sergeants Rabin and Hemingway—our lead instructor and his senior ranking deputy—stand up from their place settings, stroll up to that single table, and manhandle it away from the wall so that they can get behind it. For a moment, they tussle gracelessly with the boxes beneath. Nothing but class, I tell ya'. "*Class out the ass!*" But when Sgt. Rabin straightens up again, he has one of the coveted berets in his hands.

It looks like a dark blue cow flop in a baggy. But the room goes silent as he lifts it into the light.

There it is. The singular reward for all the hell we've just been through. Every last one of us damned well earned that shapeless blob of blue felt. Yet for all its simple plainness, it still leaves us speechless.

Or maybe that's just me.

Anyway, although the setting *is* pretty half-assed and rinky-tink, Sgt. Rabin does his level best to inject as much dignity as possible into the proceedings. This is, after all—in its own way—a 'coronation' of sorts, a 'knighting,' if you will, the admittance into this elite brotherhood, this fraternity of blood and fire, of nine new inductees. And as such, it deserves at least a *pretense* of reverence and politesse in the ceremonial ritual... before we get thrown out for stealing the cutlery, groping the waitress, and trashing the bathrooms, anyway.

He talks briefly about the historical significance of the beret—its role among the elite corps the world over, its symbolic impact as worn by French Foreign Legionnaires and partisans of the Resistance alike (not to mention a few Basque shepherds)—and he touches on the record of these particular *blue* berets, their evolution from the post-World War II days when the Army's unique *Pathfinders* went over to the newly independent 'Air Force,' and were renamed *Combat Controllers*. He speaks of the kind of men who've worn this beret before us, and of the diverse missions they fulfilled while wearing it. He speaks of the legions of men who've striven mightily for—but still failed to achieve—the right to wear this very beret.

And he speaks of the kind of men that *we* need to be, the honorable shoes that we need to fill, and the reputation that we need to perpetuate.

It's not a long speech. It might be a tad melodramatic and groping for heroic overstatement in a few places, but it doesn't last long enough to become completely overblown or oversold or anything like that. It's 'just about right,' I think. It still gets a little under my skin after a minute or two though, as if he might be trying harder to inspire than to acknowledge and reward.

And right now, I'm all about the latter.

And I don't think *that's* 'just me,' by the way.

He finally wraps up his amateur-hour soliloquy by announcing that this first beret will go to none other than our fearless class leader, Staff Sergeant Brad Haley.

Applause erupts as Haley stands (accompanied by shouts and whistles from the three guys in his fan club), and marches up to Sgt. Rabin's table. Right hands are shaken, left hands exchange the bagged cow pie (along with an extra set of jump wings to be affixed later), and Sgt. Rabin leans forward to say something private under the din of the cheering. Then Haley returns to his seat, where he accepts more handshakes.

Sgt. Matheson—the *second*-highest ranking student—is next, and the routine is much the same… except that this time *I* join in on the applause.

Sgt. Sal Donado—the highest ranking among those of us from McChord—receives the additional accolade of being named the class's official 'Honor Grad.' Having scored the highest on all the written tests, *and* having excelled at all the field applications of that knowledge as well, this was not a surprise award. The volume of the cheering jumps to a whole new level, and from there on, the proceedings just get rowdier.

Sgt. Corbin is the last of the student NCOs, then they're into the rest of us lowly enlisted slobs.

Goebler gets a little extra mention (and applause) in recognition of his stick-to-it-tiveness in forging through all this shit *twice*. Hackett gets as much laughter as acclaim, for some reason, when his beret and wings are handed to him. And then, from there to the end, it's all about The McChord Boys.

Greg Dorn's up first—everybody's buddy and helper—followed by the brash, unstoppable (not to mention short and feisty) Ricky Spradlin ('Rocky'). And finally, at the end (as always), Mr. Grand Finale'… *me*.

Tail-end Charlie. Ass-end of the food chain. Again.

I get a weird vibe from the sparser clapping I receive, though.

For one thing, the instructors seem extra enthusiastic this time, as if they hadn't been convinced of my capacity to finish the course, but approved of the unlikely success story when it actually happened. And for another, there's a strange sort of 'begrudging acceptance' in the clapping of my fellow grads. Nothing 'forced' or 'obligatory,' you understand, but more like a 'dawning recognition,' an unspoken acknowledgment that I did in fact *earn* this… that I not only passed every test, finished every run, completed every task, suffered every misery right along with the rest of them, but that I even *'led'* them once (well, *twice*, if do-overs count), against ridiculously lopsided odds. It just feels as if there's a surprised sort of "*damn*" mixed in with all the hooting and clapping.

Oh, hell. Who knows how much I'm just 'reading into it.'

But that's how it feels to me.

Once I'm back in my chair though, Sgt. Rabin raises a glass, and the instructors, as a single synchronized organism, rise to their feet together, glasses and beer bottles held high. The rest of us are just scrambling to join them, when he toasts… *us. Now isn't that nice?*

Glasses clink, congratulations are exchanged (there's at least one laudatory instructor at every table, making sure that everyone gets a personal nod), and every vessel is drained. And then… *it's party time!*

* * *

THE ROLL-IN BAR is opened, and for the rest of the night it does a brisk business. The conversation gets louder and raunchier, the laughter more wild and unchained, and everybody is everybody's pal tonight… even Staff Sergeant Fucking Haley.

And me? I slide right back into comfortable contented isolation again, savoring every boisterous moment from a serene remove, back behind my mental palisades, beaming and 'intoxicated' in my own teetotaling way.

Good times, the only way I know how.

As usual, I just don't fit into a party atmosphere. I never have. Without the ability to even tolerate the taste (or *smell*) of alcohol, in *any* form, without that helpful little catalyst to loosen me up, I've never felt uninhibited enough to plunge headlong into a celebratory affair like this, to abandon myself to the moment. So… *I don't*. And that's perfectly okay.

But everybody else does. Even the instructors. And that comes as a bit of a shock to me actually, seeing such professionally reserved people coming so publicly unhinged.

Like Sgt. Hemingway over there, loudly contributing to the whoops and cheers of a bunch of guys egging Goebler on (and *he's* been *extra* celebratory tonight for some reason) as he chugs down his entire beer in one prolonged guzzle. And the heretofore deathly stoic Sgt. Stillman, who's laughing so hard and loud that it sounds almost frantic.

Somehow—I don't know—somehow, it just doesn't seem 'right,' seeing this side of them, at least not while we're still here at their school, and they're still technically our 'mentors.' Something in me just feels that my last impression of these worldly and accomplished men ought to be one of some 'reverence.' You know? Like, I ought to remember them for their supreme competence, for the lethal and lifesaving principles they passed on to us, for their consummate proficiency and job-related wisdom, and for their measured self-restraint and professional composure… not their capacity for revelry.

But then maybe—*obviously*—that too is just me.

Even Sgt. Rabin seems to be carrying around a weirdly 'appreciative buzz' of his own, strolling among his carousing minions like a king, sated on mutton and mead, circulating and blessing each exchange with a genuinely pleasant nod and a tip of his ever-present beer. He just looks 'warm' and satisfied with the outcome of yet another grueling CCS class.

Still, when his wandering eye catches mine, and his wandering drift through the crowd bends my way, it strikes me as more unsettling than inclusive. I break off my conversation with my buddy Greg as Sgt. Rabin nears, and I rise to accept his proffered hand.

"Congratulations, Mister Stipp," he says, with just a smudge of bleariness and a wobbly posture that he stabilizes with the back of a chair.

"Thank-you, sir."

He doesn't let go of my hand though, and instead pulls me a little closer to him, into 'conspiracy range.'

"You surprised a lot of people, Mister Stipp. A lot of people."

"I surprised me too, Sergeant. Just probably not for the same reasons."

Har har hardy-har-har! Get it?

Thank-you, thank-you. I'll be here all week.

His drowsy smile doesn't change though, nor his grip lessen.

"You surprised a lot of people out there," he repeats, adding a slow-motion wink that looks like it almost puts him to sleep.

"Well... again... thank-you, sir."

"You really showed us somethin', ya' know?"

Okay, now this is getting weird.

"Well, hopefully it wasn't my ass," I reply. *Hah-hah-hah-hah-hah...*

He snorts, and finally releases my hand. I get a trademark 'tip of the beer' and a nod. Then he reaches across the table and gives Greg a token handshake and some muzzy congratulations as well.

I'm starting to think he might have had a beer or two before he even got here. As he turns to move on though, he adds one last aside to me.

"I was pullin' for ya', Mister Stipp,"—*huh?*—"And ya' did good."

And he walks off.

Okay. Now, I know a lot of that was just the beer talking, but how much? I mean, come on! The Lead Instructor was 'pulling for me?'

How seriously should I take that? How much 'pulling' was there? And when did it start?

I can't help it. My mind instantly snaps back to that moment out in the field, in the classroom tent, when I'd stood to confront him, to tell him I quit... *and he disappeared!* He *never*—*none* of the instructors *ever*—walked off during those breaks, not if there was a student who wanted to talk to them. But on that one occasion, he not only walked out, he *vanished*. He took conscious and extreme (though seemingly innocent) steps to avoid me just then... almost as if he'd known that I was breaking, that I was about to give up, and he didn't want to give me the chance to throw it all away so close to the end.

No! No way! Horseshit! Seven people—seven *good* people—had already been washed out of the program before that, and all with callous machine-like efficiency and an institutional disregard for wounded pride.

So a reluctance to 'do the hard thing' was not one of Sgt. Rabin's character flaws.

Granted, two of the wash-outs—Sgt. Turner in the beginning, and Amn. Torrero at the end—were *medded* out with injuries. And two others—my former roommate Amn. Trefelden and Amn. Kort—never qualified to even *start*. But the other three were cut without a single look back... Jimson and Padgitt fell to their failed written tests, and Balzac surrendered to his physical inadequacies.

So what would have made *me* stand out as any more worthy of 'saving' than them?

My written test scores were mediocre to marginal, and my physical shortcomings were daily apparent and *noisy*. I came to Little Rock grossly unprepared and ill-equipped, with almost no field experience and only two weeks of exposure to my new team. I'd never lit a fire nor pitched a tent before coming here, never jumped with a combat load or even a weapon in my possession, and hadn't even had time to *break in my friggin' jungle boots!* Compared to the rest of my classmates, with their four to six *months* of pre-CCS familiarization and experience, I was about one step above a random civilian, pulled off the street and thrown into the crucible cold. So it's hard to imagine anyone *less* qualified, or deserving, or even worthy of consideration—much less worthy of *saving*—than me.

Then again...

Maybe that was *precisely* my appeal: the hopelessly overmatched underdog. They were probably just *itching* to drive me out every day of the first five weeks of the course—probably all the way through the damned ten-mile run, I imagine—when I was just an unready irritant and a clueless wannabe. But then something changed.

Maybe it was that I just kept *barely clearing the bar*, no matter how high it was raised or secretly moved... that I kept dragging my ass across all the finish lines, kept passing all the damned tests, kept absorbing the abuse, and was still there at the end when so many others weren't. Or maybe he just empathized with someone so clearly out of his league, so over his head and shunted off as the runt of the litter, that the longer I hung on, the more he wanted to see me succeed.

I don't know. And I'm not sure how much weight or validity to even give such a statement anyway, considering the inebriated circumstances. But since I'm the only sober one here right now, you know I'm going to stew over it—in other words, *over-think* everything—for the rest of the damned night.

And, of course, that's just exactly what I do.

4

FUCKERS

Leaving Little Rock AFB, Little Rock, Arkansas

LITTLE ROCK AIR FORCE BASE trundles past the frosted windows of the bus, washed out by the silvers and grays of a sleety overcast morning. Everything is drippy and splashy, almost *chromed*, leeched of color and depressing... and *beautiful*.

Beautiful because it's 'going away'... because it's 'headed aft.'

It actually looks unfamiliar again, as unfamiliar and alien as it did when I first arrived almost two months ago. It might just be the icy lighting, but I don't know. Other than the BX complex, and the five-block walk between the BAQ and the school's hangar, I guess I never saw much of the base at all. Especially not over these last two weeks.

Inside the bus though, every*thing* and every*one* looks spotless and formal. In fact, it looks like everyone's going to a royal wedding.

Despite the fact that we're all flying out on different flights, on different airlines, and at different hours, we're all being bused to the airport at the same time. And because the school's last official act was to put us through a full inspection (a silly waste of time, as far as I was concerned... I mean, what were they going to do about any failures? Hold us back? Cancel our graduation? Take back our berets?), we're all dressed to the max: dress blues, including beribboned jackets and ties, spit-polished boots (or, in my case, cordovan-tipped jump boots), and of course, our brand new berets.

My boots are a brand new pair of Corcorans—tall, zipper-laced, and shaped from sexy curves—that I'd bought the weekend before Field Week. Completing that dreaded ten-mile run had really boosted my confidence, apparently. They were still in their box, stuffed with paper, when I pulled them out this morning.

And as for the beret, well...

As it came out of its bag, it was plump and symmetrical—it looked like the cap of a mushroom, in fact—overhanging evenly all the way around. Entirely inappropriate for a true warrior. At the very least, it must be molded into the proper shape, flattened and pulled down hard over the right ear. And at *worst*, it must be altered.

Its inner lining and plastic protective layer are often gutted by the hardcore elite, 'deflating' and thinning the beret and allowing it to hang flaccid any way they want. But it doesn't *last* as long that way. Without that inner lining, hair oils and scalp-sweat tend to soil its material. And though some consider the residual salt rings and spotty darkenings to be the veteran badges of work and struggle and sacrifice (not to mention machismo and a disdain for personal hygiene), most people in the business just think it's nasty. So they leave the inner lining and protective film in place, and instead concentrate on pressing and stretching the plumper beret into a more rakish and dashing shape. And that's what I did.

That's apparently what *everybody* here did. Because we're all looking damned sharp now.

I didn't bother wearing my two measly little ribbons though (for 'marksmanship' and, believe it or not, 'good behavior'), and my uniform still only has one stripe (or 'wing') on each sleeve. But there are jump wings on my chest, and now there are jump wings on my beret as well.

No more piss-cutter caps for Stevie.

I may be only a babe-in-the-woods when it comes to 'time in the military'—I may have only the trappings of a fresh-faced rookie stitched and pinned all over me—but now I'm also wearing a true emblem of achievement: the beret of an elite spec ops warrior. I'm a long way from being genuinely competent at even *half* of the specialties that that emblem infers, but I've now stepped above and beyond the general military population. And anybody who sees me in uniform from this point forward will know it.

Oh man, that is a thrilling—downright inspiring—notion.

Damned few people ever even *try* to enter the spec ops field. An even tinier fraction ever make it. And I've still got a *long* way to go before *I've* 'made it' all the way. Once 'made' though, it will be into a *minuscule fraternity* compared to the military population at large. And in the Air Force, spec ops types are even more rare than they are in other services. In fact, Combat Controllers are *it*, actually... seven teams of roughly twenty-four people each in the States, and another three or four teams scattered elsewhere around the world. And that's it!

So being recognized as a member of so unique and difficult and *bold* a brotherhood as this is truly an honor, felt right down to the marrow. And wearing this badge of honor, this royal blue '*crown*' of sorts, is a source of downright searing pride for me...

... until the bus rolls out the gate, past the two SPs working the ID check lanes... *both of whom are wearing the exact same berets as we are!*

At that's just WRONG!

Everyone on my side of the bus utters the same word at the same time. "Fuckers."

It's good to be part of a team.

BOOK TWO
THE WANNABE

PART 3

Back with the McChord CC Team
McChord Air Force Base, Tacoma, Washington
January, 1978

STORY XXXIII

PEAKS AND VALLEYS

1
MIXED EMOTIONS

January, 1978
Returning from leave to McChord AFB, Tacoma, Washington

I STILL CAN'T BELIEVE IT! *Look at me! I'm a friggin' Phase II Combat Controller now!*
— Yep. Still. Just like you were yesterday... and the day before that... and the day before that. Just like you were two weeks ago when you graduated.
What? Am I boring you?
— Nah. I love having something obvious repeated to me five-hundred times a day.
Hey! This is nothing short of a friggin' miracle, man!
— Hey! You're right about that, man!
No, I mean it! I'm not just Phase II! I made Phase II in record time!
— Good news.
Damn right it is! That's a huge accomplishment!
— So you're saying you're *happy you're on your way back to McChord again now?*
Well, no. Not necessarily 'happy.' *But* 'proud?' *Hell yes!*
— Does it matter at all that you hate this shit?
No. Well... yeh. But that's just because I'm going through all the worst of it now. It'll get better once I get all these damned training schools behind me, and I can settle into the normal daily routines of the Team.

— Why? Are the temperatures going to be warmer up at McChord—up near the friggin' Canadian border—than they were in Arkansas?

No, but...

— And I suppose you think you'll sleep better on an overnight bivouac in the Rockies than you did in the Ozarks?

Look, I'm not saying...

— Are you suddenly going to start enjoying five-mile runs, or ten-mile hikes in full combat gear?

Hey, it's not like that's something they do every day.

— And how about that weenie-assed stomach of yours? Think you'll suddenly start to enjoy a career that has you throwing up every time your workplace moves?

They said that'll get better with time, the more I fly.

* * *

AND THAT'S TRUE. They did say that. In fact, that's the whole reason I didn't take any Dramamine before this flight. Just working on 'toughening up' the old 'puke chute' a little.

My brain's been running this schizophrenic argument for hours now. For pretty much the entire duration of the flight, in fact. I mean, *what the hell else have I had to pass the damned time?* The in-flight movie *sucked*, those cheap plastic stethoscope 'earphones' were murder, and I still fell asleep with the damned things in my ears.

Flying from Miami to Seattle is just about as far as you *can* fly and still be in the continental United States the whole way. It's almost six hours in the air, non-stop! And though this big old beautiful jumbo jet—this Eastern Airlines L-1011—is a sweet *sweet* ride, I've got just about the shittiest *shittiest* seat there is onboard. Because I'm right in the middle *seat* of the middle *row*, right smack dab in the middle of the *whole airplane*.

The L-1011 wide-body, which has two parallel aisles, has five seats in the middle *between* those aisles (at least here in *this* section). And I'm in the dead center of those five seats, surrounded by seatbacks and tightly pressed travelers on all sides, with no easy access to either aisle, and no window within twenty feet of me. And I need my horizon. That's what my stupid tummy always tells me anyway.

Gawd, this flight has just gone on and on and on and on..!

With about forty-five minutes of the trip left to go though, everybody—and I do mean *everybody... but me*—is out cold. Sound asleep. As far as the eye can see in all directions around this vast plush cattle-car, every head is canted, lolling around on those tiny airline pillows, or propped up atop benumbed arms. Most of the window shades are down, and no overhead lights are on *anywhere*. I feel like I'm riding in the back of the world's largest hearse on an especially busy day.

Actually, I've spent most of this eternal flight in and out of a coma myself. Never comfortably '*asleep*,' mind you. Just intermittently collapsing from exhaustion. And after five-some hours of that kind of fitful fidgeting narcolepsy, I just can't sit still anymore.

For everyone else, apparently, it's exactly the opposite.

So I'm sitting here, staring at the ceiling—or the seatback in front of me, or the fairly spectacular bosom of the plump lady snoring in the aisle seat two down from me—and letting the voices inside my head run wild. And while two of those voices fuss and argue over my love/hate relationship with Combat Control, another one reflects longingly upon the glorious two-week leave that I just left behind.

Oh man, was that nice.

From the frozen mud, icy mists, and the extreme physical torments of Combat Control School in winter, to the dry sunny mid-seventies and carefree lightheartedness of Christmas in Miami. From the chilly, friendless, forest encampments, to the warm embrace of lifelong friends, and the bracing sanctuary of Home. *Plus Christmas!*

Lordy, it was enough to make me contemplate desertion.

* * *

I'D ARRIVED AT HOME still dapper in my dress blues and beret, to a storm of hugs, handshakes, and flashing cameras. My old bed in my old room was mine again. And every last one of my high school friends was there, all but one of them fresh back from their assorted colleges around the country (the one exception being Eldon, the youngest of our eclectic tribe, who was still in town, and halfway through his last year in high school), and all of them in that most festive of moods, the 'Christmas Spirit!' Even me.

Especially me.

For my youngest brother Gavin, I'd gotten a couple of model airplane kits while I was still in Little Rock—one a C-141 Starlifter, the other a C-130 Hercules (two of the three airplanes from which I have thus far jumped)—and had to scramble to hide them until they could be wrapped. But it didn't take long back among my old home clan before I realized what a stupid gift that was for him. He'd never built a model in his life, and had no interest in the military *or* aviation, for that matter, outside of a minor (and seriously misplaced) appreciation for *my* involvement in them.

I guess I was still trying to impress upon him the wisdom and nobility of my new calling, or something like that. You know... *for that job that I hate.*

Or maybe I was just trying to impress *me.*

So, since I still had to get something for everybody else, I went ahead and did some shopping over the next few days, and got the *family* something that *everybody* could use and enjoy, including Gavin... a brand new state-of-the-art *turntable* for the household stereo system.

Hoo-WEE! A gift just dripping with heartfelt sentiment.

But the days that unfurled there, from the week before Christmas right up to today, New Year's Eve, were lazy, languorous, and luxurious for me. I ate, I relaxed, I played in a huge volleyball tournament in the Sherman's sprawling backyard, and I completely forgot about Combat Control. Because, none too surprisingly, once those first moments of curiosity had passed—fresh off the plane, and still sparkling and proud in a uniform bedecked with achievements—nobody ever asked about CCT again.

All my baubles, badges and beanies meant nothing in their world. And the gauntlet I'd just fought my way through for so long and so hard, well, *they just had no idea.* To them, it was just sort of 'advanced ROTC.' More fancy marchin' and salutin' and bein' a good little soldier boy. *Whatever!* So I don't think it even crossed their minds (or piqued their interest, for that matter) to *ask* about the trials or the tribulations or the personal sacrifices I might have endured just to earn the *right* to wear that beret. To them it was just a new hat.

They'd even seen the short haircut before. Nothing new there either.

So, for everyone else, friends and family alike, it was just regular old 'home again'—pre-enlistment, pre-university, pre-'war' *home*—just as it always had been. In fact, they all had far more curiosity about each other's college experiences, since that was something they all shared in common. My little freak show was just a flash-in-the-pan novelty that barely held their interest for as long as it took for me to put my luggage down, and then it was all but forgotten.

One would expect that I would be disappointed by that—heck, *I* would have expected that too—but the fact is, I wasn't.

I'd come home. I'd come *running* home. I was *rolling* in 'home' like a dog on freshly mown grass, and there was no 'military' in that world called 'home.' And as it turned out, that was exactly how I wanted it. I didn't miss it one bit.

So we all went to the movies, and we visited each others' homes. We ate a lot, those who *could* drink *drank* a lot. We re-visited our still-warm childhoods and adolescences, we exchanged gifts, and we watched 1977 breathe its last. And then it was time to abandon the womb all over again.

I couldn't believe it. Hell, I could barely *handle* it.

Just last night, as I was leaving my friend Gene's house in my Dad's dorky Pacer, I had to stop. And I sat in that car at the end of his street, and almost wept at the thought of having to leave it all behind again, of having to return to miserable socked-in drizzly-cold Seattle, and to that huge soulless room in 'the Castle' that I shared with Randy Pogue.

Gawd! Back to Combat Control again. Long workouts and longer runs every other day, come rain or come shine... *and I still suck at running.* Long bumpy flights in windowless cargo holds, constantly battling my fluttering gorge, *because I'm still so damned motion sensitive.* Long hikes, endless training. More schools, more gear, more facts and figures and formulas for maximum destruction to cram into the dribble-glass of my brain. More cold, more wet, more heat, more sweat.

Merry friggin' Christmas, there Stevie. What the hell am I doing?

* * *

AND WITH THAT REMEMBRANCE, those two old familiar voices float back to the forefront of my consciousness again, still arguing from both sides of the same psyche.

— *You see what I'm saying here? This is so not worth it, dude.*

What are you talking about? This is exactly what we thought it would be… tough, challenging, and often miserable, but exciting and exotic too! And all the more rewarding because of it.

— *Sgt. Beaudry? Is that you?*

Oh shut-up. You know you're feeling damned good about yourself right now.

— *You know what also feels good? When you stop hitting yourself in the head with a hammer. Of course, you could also just GET RID OF THE DAMNED HAMMER!*

I can think of one place that hammer could go right now.

— *Nah. You can't fit your head* and *a hammer up there at the same time. Or* can *you?*

And so it goes, round and round and round in my head.

It would probably be a pretty even draw—up and down, left and right, pro and con, black and white—if I hadn't just left *Home*, at *Christmas*, in *Miami*, among *lifelong friends*, to spend my last day of leave—the leave that I'd been so assiduously saving up since graduating from Basic Training—wedged in tight in the middle of this flying amphitheater full of zombies. And all just so that I can spend New Year's *night* sitting alone in that desolate Day Room down the hall—the one that always reminds me of the sterile 'communal room' in "*One Flew Over the Cuckoo's Nest*"—watching the ball drop on that shitty little TV, and knowing that less than thirty-six hours after that, I'll be picking up right where I left off, getting the shit beaten out of me for a living.

— *See! You're dreading being here just as much as I am.*

No. It's just that I wasn't ready to leave Miami so soon.

— *I wonder why.*

Oh, why don't you go blow some chunks or something.

And so I do.

In the roaring, jostling, cataleptic silence of this huge flying bus, I quietly slip a barf bag out of the seatback pocket, and ralph up my in-flight meal.

And then my breakfast.

No one notices.

2
LET THE ROLLER COASTER RIDE BEGIN

McChord AFB, Tacoma, Washington
January, 1978

ACTUALLY, 1977 ENDS ABOUT as well as could be hoped.
The unveiling of 1978, on the other hand… *not so much.*

* * *

THERE IS NO EVENING TWILIGHT in Seattle on New Year's night when we land, not under leaden skies choked with chilled and oozing mists, and everything glistening with puddle water. There *was* some gold and orange *above* the clouds, but not down here below.
Just one more foul ingredient in this bitter stew.
It gets better though, when I come up the jetway to find my old Keesler buddy, Mike Dumbass, waiting for me in the gate area, his pesky little brother Chris on one side, and his brand new girlfriend Cheryl on the other, tucked under his arm like a lifetime achievement award. Mike and Cheryl break out in heart-melting smiles. Little Chris Dumas couldn't give a shit.
I show off my new beret while we're waiting for my duffel bag to appear

on the baggage carousel, and our introductory conversation is at least momentarily uplifting. But in its own strangely backfiring way, watching Mike and Cheryl together—she being breathtakingly gorgeous, with eyes that could melt reinforced concrete, and he being, well... *home* here in Seattle, with his family so close by—well, it actually makes me feel all the more separate from the rest of the blissful world. And that, in turn, makes me miss everyone back at *my* home in Miami even more than I already was.

Everyone *there* is still on vacation. *Bastards!*

I was the only one who had to pack up and leave *before* New Years. *Dammit!*

Mike drives us in his big old purple-ish GTO (*what* is *that color anyway? Mauve?*) to a Pizza Hut in Tacoma, just across the interstate from the base. And he pays for it all too, since I am utterly penniless.

Then, sensing my waning spirits as the holiday evening winds down, we all pile back into his car, and he drives us further south to Fort Lewis, to Army post housing where his retired military family (and little Chris) still live. We pitch his brother out there, then press on further south still—clear down to Olympia, in fact—to drop Cheryl off at her apartment. Then Mike and I turn back toward Tacoma, to go 'cruising' for something 'fun' to do with the rest of New Year's Eve.

Oddly enough, we wind up at a *roller skating rink*, of all places, just a block or two down the street from the same Pizza Hut where we'd had our dinner. And there we spend the next two hours publicly humiliating ourselves. Me especially, since, if I've been on skates more than twice *in my life*, I don't remember when that was. Plus, *I'm still in uniform.*

Well, I guess if you're going to do something *so* stupid *so* badly that there's not even a point to being embarrassed, you might as well be thorough. And tonight, I think we've raised the bar on mortifying ineptitude. Or did we *lower* it? I guess it depends on whether you consider ice skating to be a sport, a pastime, an art form, or a hazing ritual.

Either way though, it works. He has me laughing again in no time, and my mind's fixation on the depressing consequences of my choices gets pulled out by the roots.

Unfortunately, by 10:30, he announces that he has to get back to base to prepare for his graveyard shift in the control tower. And by 10:45, I find myself standing in the doorway of my old room again, bags dumped at my feet, staring at the rearranged furniture that my roommate apparently can't stop playing with when he's alone.

Gone is the open S-shaped path through the lockers, dressers, desks and beds that Randy had concocted the last time I was here. Instead, the two diagonally opposed corners of the room are now 'walled in' by the taller pieces, like the lockers and chests of drawers, hiding the beds from each other, and essentially creating two smaller 'semi-private rooms' within the larger one.

I wonder if he's trying to tell me something.

Well, I guess it's still generally S-shaped. You still have to slalom back and forth between the furniture clusters to get to *my* little nook in the back. And he's still graciously 'allowed me' the window, beneath which is my bed, shielded now by the large, free-standing, K-Mart-quality 'closet' that blocks the view from the door. So... *no problem there*, I guess.

But in the end, the main thing that hits me is that *I'm really back here again*... which naturally comes with the predictable postscript: "*Fuck*."

So, three hours after the ball drops for my friends celebrating on the east coast, the ball finally drops here in the west. But I don't see it.

Because I'm busy, flipping through a backlog of unopened mail, unpacking my bags, and smothering myself to sleep.

* * *

1978 STARTS WITH A whimper (literally)... followed shortly thereafter by the flush of a toilet (also literally). But then it gets up to speed with all the impetus, inconvenience, and even the *symbolism* of an avalanche of *shit* (figuratively speaking).

I'm standing here in the hallway now, at 7:30 in the morning of 1978, in my 'Airborne' shorts, a rumpled T-shirt, and my bare feet, staring in disbelief... at the *outside* of my *locked door.*

This is not happening. And it's just too stupid to be Hell.

I was awoken by the bladder that I had so mercilessly neglected last night, which felt like it was threatening to blow my twinkie clean off. Outside my window, the gray-white overcast seemed to have settled right down on the rooftops. Across the street, the triangular 'quad' was flecked with the last melting clumps of old snow, the trees were skeletal, and everything else was dripping squishy wet. Even the American flag looked shriveled and stuck to its pole. *Lovely.*

Happy fucking New Year.

So, at the urging of my bladder, I threw on the bare minimum clothing needed to be 'decent' for my dash through the corridors, grabbed my key, and scurried off to the common bathroom down at the bend in the hall.

Only, as it turned out, it wasn't my *room* key that I'd grabbed.

I don't believe this. I mean, I just can't friggin' believe this!

Now what?

* * *

MY ROOMMATE, RANDY POGUE, wasn't in the room when I got in last night, and he wasn't in his bed when I got up this morning.

I don't know where he is. He might have spent the night with a girlfriend, he might be out of town on leave, or he might have spent the night in a gutter, for all I know. He might even have been sent off to another school while I was gone to Little Rock. So I have no idea when, if ever, to expect him back. And isn't *that* helpful?

I know for a fact that there is no ledge on the outside of the building, so even if I felt like braving the ice and the twenty-two degree temperatures out there, there's still no way to sneak in through my second-floor window. And it's just too early on New Year's Day to be waking up any of my CCT buddies on this floor... that's if they're even in their rooms to begin with, and it also presumes that there's something they could do to help me anyway.

So I pad barefoot down the stairs to the first floor administrative wing, hoping to find someone at their desk with access to a master key of some sort. What I find though, is no one working on a Sunday and a holiday.

So much for Plan A.

From there then, I dash back up to the Day Room on my floor, flip through the Base Directory lying on the endtable next to the communal phone, and with a deep and disgusted sigh, I call the friggin' cops.

You know; the Security Police. The 'SPs'... the *Sock Puppets*.

The bastards that'll show up wearing the same beret that I now wear.

But it turns out that they don't have any master keys either, nor the tools for cleanly breaking into apartments. So, at their recommendation, I call the Base Fire Department instead. But their answer is much the same: short of putting an axe through the door, they have no way of getting in either.

Civil Engineering is next. But even their switchboard operator says that they have no master keys, and would have no choice but to practically demolish the door, for which I would then have to reimburse the Air Force.

So much for Plan B.

Does 'people-getting-locked-out-of-their-rooms' happen so rarely around here that nobody has a contingency plan for how to deal with it?

I finally give up. I turn on the damned TV, and plop down to watch it while I wait for Randy to come home... if he ever does. But what other choice do I have?

Gawd! Look at how I'm spending New Year's Day!

Last year, our whole Miami amateur movie-making gang spent the end of 1976 in the Sherman's den, *most* of us drunk, but *all* of us laughing hysterically as we watched that stupid disco ball descend the pole in Times Square. And *this* year, they all had plans to go to the Miami Planetarium, where Eldon once again works (and where I used to work in my last days as a civilian), to watch him run "*UFO Alert!*" for the hundreds of goofy-assed fans dressed as aliens. Sort of a 'local tradition' down there. And then they were going to spend today at the beach. *At the friggin' beach, people!*

Then I think about how *I* spent last night... folding underwear, hanging up my dress blues and tattered cammies next to each other in my big stand-up locker, hiding fully loaded machine-gun magazines (filled with blanks) in my desk drawer under stiff rappelling gloves, and slipping pictures of my ex-girlfriend Nita (that had come in that stack of mail) into my photo albums... and knowing exactly when midnight fell, because a cheer went up from this very Day Room, and echoed down these empty halls.

Jeezy Pete! Am I pathetic or what?!

* * *

FOUR HOURS LATER, AND a couple dozen fruitless trips back and forth to my room to see if Pogue has ever returned, and it's time to try something else.

I haven't heard a peep from this entire floor all morning long—not one slamming door, not one voice, not one flushing toilet—and it's now almost noon. *Holy crap! Did* everybody *stay out all night last night?*

Finally, entirely against my will, and with nothing but sheer raw open contempt for myself, I am forced to call Mike Dumas in his barracks across the base. It makes me sick with guilt, since he not only picked me up at the airport last night, *and* fed me, *and* entertained me till all hours, but then he worked a six-hour overnight shift in the tower, and only got off at six o'clock this morning. But at least I know he's home.

As usual, I have to wait until some fried, pissed-off barracks rat answers the hallway phone over there, then wait for him to trudge off to Mike's room, bang on his door until he wakes up, then direct him to the phone.

Lordy, I can't apologize enough, nor call myself enough derogatory names. But once I finally get around to describing my situation to him, Mike is quick to say, "No problem," and "I'll be right over."

Bless his little pea-pickin' heart.

He even calls Cheryl first, to tell her he's going to be late for whatever it was they'd planned to do today. *Dammit!*

And I don't even have the money to buy him lunch or anything.

* * *

HE SHOWS UP AROUND 12:30 in the afternoon with two different sized screwdrivers, and a butter knife. The consummate locksmith.

Unfortunately, since the door opens inward, its hinges are on the inside, and inaccessible to his screwdrivers. So much for popping the hinge pins and removing the door altogether. So much for doing it the easy, painless, non-destructive way. Plan C down the toilet.

As such, just as the SPs, the Fire Department, and the Civil Engineers had told me earlier this morning, Mike has no choice now but to attack the door frontally.

He jams a screwdriver in between the metal plates next to the knob, and pries at the metal just enough to wedge it *open* just enough to slip in the butter knife, and work on the deadbolt that way. He pulls, and he levers, and he digs, and he scrapes at the components, until, sure enough, despite his precautions, the wood starts to splinter around the locking mechanism.

Damn!

Well, the line's been crossed now. Might as well just get it over with.

Helping in the only way I know how then, while he continues to dig and root around and drag the deadbolt that one little extra micrometer it needs to clear the hole, I press my fingers against the bulging fracturing wood surrounding it, trying just to keep it from blowing out altogether. And amazingly, *it works!*

After something like ten or fifteen minutes of sweatin' and cussin' and coercin' the moving parts, he finally gets the butter knife *behind* the end of the deadbolt, and jimmies it out of the way. The door swings open, and at last, we're in. *I'm* in, for the first time in five-and-a-half hours. And without a single living soul in the building to witness our desecration.

I thank Mike profusely, let him know how much I owe him, and send him on his way to be with his girlfriend.

Fortunately, thanks to my efforts at preventing the wood from fraying, I'm able to press its flayed edges back into position, leaving it virtually unscarred to all but the most meticulous close-up inspection.

But does the day get any better after that?

Not a bit.

I'm dead broke, the banks are all closed, and until I can get my meal card reinstated *tomorrow*, I've got nothing to use at the chow hall either. I've got no car, it's sub-freezing and drizzling outside (not that there's anywhere for me to go without money anyway), and there doesn't appear to be anybody else in this entire building from whom to beg assistance. So, *thank the gods that Pogue left some* "Heavy Metal" *comic books strewn across the top of his desk!* They're not something I would have spent any time reading before now, but under the current circumstances, it's either spend the day going through back-to-back issues, or see if I can't just sleep for eighteen hours straight.

I gather them up, lock the door again (from the *inside*), and settle back to read Randy's magazines all... friggin'... day... long. And I do mean *all* day.

There is one other thing that I opt to do with this endless and desolate day, though. I decide that, considering what a wretched start 1978 has gotten off to, I really need to get a diary going.

And so I do.

Starting with my depressingly mundane activities at the time the Midnight Cheer went up from the Day Room—specifically, hanging shredded uniforms and hiding ammunition—I catch my readers-to-be up to the present, right up to these riveting moments spent reading comic books, skipping meals, and watching the day expire and rot unused.

Who knows! Thirty years from now, this might actually be more interesting than it is right now.

By 10:30 though, I just can't take it anymore, and I finally cave in for the night.

* * *

AT ONE O'CLOCK IN the morning, a light but intense rapping on my door rattles me from sleep.

I answer it in my underwear (always ready for action, that's me). It turns out to be Mike Dumas, giggly and hyper and definitely 'friskied up' by what was apparently a very good day (and evening) with Cheryl.

All he wants to know though, is *would I be interested in coming along with the two of them tomorrow... er, 'today'... later today—whatever—when they go to Mount Rainier?*

I surely don't want to, at least not 'today'—*that's like cold and far away and stuff*—but, lordy knows, I do owe this boy. So, if he wants me to go, I'm going.

I agree.

We settle on 10:00am, then we say goodnight, and let my tattered door close again between us.

3

SNOW THERAPY

Mount Rainier, Washington

1978 STOPS BEING STUPID, lonely, depressing, and useless on its second day.

However, the weather is still socked-in heavy and gray. And though nothing notable is falling from the sky, the air is still fat with sleety mists that are just pervasive enough to keep the windshield wipers busy.

This is actually the first chance I've had to get out to Mount Rainier in the three months that I've been officially stationed at McChord AFB. And I might not have been terribly interested in this drive yesterday... *er, last night... earlier this morning—whatever*—but today I'm damned glad I agreed to go. Plus I get to do the driving! I haven't had a car of my own in more than a year now. And here, the first time I'm able to get behind the wheel again, I'm zig-zagging through the back-country and mountain roads of Washington state in Mike's big old mauve GTO. *Pretty cool.*

And great therapy, too!

Once Mike picked me up at The Castle this morning, we stopped by the Airmen's Club to cash a $10.74 check that I'd found in my mail my first night back. We used it to top off his tank. Then we drove all the way down to Olympia to pick up Cheryl (*after all, what's a little gut-wrenching jealousy between friends?*). And it was there that he decided that with another driver in the car, he could devote more of his attention to Cheryl if *I* drove instead of him. So he handed me his keys, and now they're both back there in the rear seat, snugglin' and neckin' and being nauseatingly intimate, with Mike only occasionally dispensing directions whenever a pertinent intersection nears.

And me? I get to play *chauffeur* for a day.

And to finally feel human again.

* * *

EVEN IN THE MURK, the scenery up here is gorgeous. And once we get through the park's main gate, it only gets more spectacular as the switchbacks work their way up the flank of the mountain... and then up into the clouds themselves. Soon, snow starts to appear on the sides of the road, first in little strips and piles, then in denser and more frequent patches. Climbing up through the still-green evergreens, it becomes a solid carpet, and then a deeper *blanket* of pristine white fluffiness. It isn't long then, until the branches have snow heaped upon them, looking like weighty dollops of whipped cream. But the road itself remains clear—wet, and a little slushy, but otherwise user-friendly—while *beside* the road, the cushion of snow deepens.

And after about twenty minutes of this, not only have the banks of snow on both sides piled up to depths exceeding the height of the car, but the mists have finally begun to thin a bit. Apparently we've climbed up through the cloud deck almost to its top. A little more, and we should break out into the clear skies *above* the overcast, to find ourselves about half way up the snow-draped margin of the massive volcano.

Or not.

I'm from Florida. What do I know from mountains and snow clouds?

But before the misty veil can dissolve altogether, we arrive at the Paradise Lodge, the Visitor's Center and chalet at the end—or the top—of the long and winding road. We slip into the high parking lot between towering ten-to-fifteen-foot cliffs of packed snow, and squish into a spot amid a surprisingly large number of cars.

Apparently we aren't the only ones with this idea today.

Having come all this way though, *what do we do now?* There's nothing to *see* from here. Aside from the fortress walls of snow that surround this car lot on all sides, the swirling fog of the cloud tops in which we're still so deeply immersed preclude any chance of seeing anything beyond about a quarter-mile in any direction anyway. No view *of* the mountain, no view *off* the mountain. So... *what now?*

A distant *yip* of glee, and an acoustically deadened volley of cheers and laughter answers that for us.

Tubing.

Atop the uphill precipice of snow, on a long plummeting slope that bottoms out at the chalet, several dozen people are busily trudging *up* or sliding *down* what looks like a well-polished toboggan run. Several of them are doing so on inner tubes that range in size from truck to tractor tires, but the rest are brandishing what I would call 'platters': red plastic disks only slightly larger than trashcan lids. And as I track the stream of platters downhill, I find that they're all being purchased right there at the lodge's gift shop.

Cool.

Mike and I look at each other and smile.

* * *

I'M THE FIRST TO try out our brand new, top-of-the-line, state-of-the-art, six-dollar, piece-of-shit, cheap-assed plastic platter. And, hero that I am, I start with a timid hop onto the 'bunny run.'

For about fifteen seconds, I skitter down the shallow slope like a rock skipping across a pond... intermittent contact with the ground, no control whatsoever over which way I'm going, and pirouetting in disorienting circles the whole way. And it's amazing how much faster the ride *is* than it looks from the sidelines. Or maybe I'm the only one who actually *does* manage to hit two-hundred miles an hour as I rocket the fifty or sixty yards to the bottom.

Then I hit the untrampled snow at the finish line, and even my desperate grip on the platters two little handles isn't enough to keep me from parting ways with it.

Together, platter and rider hit the loose stuff like a collision with a buried curb, sending up a bomb burst of flying snow. *Separately*, we cartwheel off in two different directions, to the cheers, laughter, and applause of the sideline crowd. I land ass-first in a pillow of the loose stuff, facing uphill and looking between my wet sneakers as if I'm kicked back in a recliner.

Hoo-WEE! Wicked!

So... no reason to do that *again.*

I stagger to my feet, pound the snow off my jeans and jacket, then tromp over to where the platter is embedded in the snow, edge-on, like a ninja-star. Mike meets me there and snatches the platter up before I can reach it.

"*My* turn," he says, way too eagerly.

"Damned right it is," I answer, just as readily.

I've decided that, when it comes to tubing or tobogganing or plattering your way down an icy slope, this Florida boy is far better suited to the role of 'spectator' than 'participant.' So Mike can have it.

I follow him and Cheryl uphill about half way—and they're headed all the way to the top of the bigger, taller, steeper *main* run—then I stop at a perfectly lovely viewing spot, and zip my jacket up to the throat to wait.

It takes the two of them most of another ten minutes to chug their way all the way to the top. And in the meantime, I get to enjoy the violent passage of one tubin'/platterin' lunatic after the next.

Folks riding those huge inner tubes get a much smoother ride for the most part, as well as a convenient 'air bag' to buffer them against the stiffer impacts. But because there's so much recoil and rebound built into them, these guys whoosh by me looking like they're lying on a trampoline *that other people are jumping on!* Their slams and bounces might be cushioned by the rubbery mushiness of the tubes, but the riders seem to spend most of their time being flung into the air and trying desperately just to hang on to the danged things. The 'platter jockeys,' on the other hand, seem to be *all or nothing.* They're either whisking and skittering across the snow like the plastic puck on an air-hockey table, or they're slamming *hard* into moguls and berms that bash them into discombobulated flight. Nothing in between. They either make it all the way with most of their teeth still in their sockets, or they're 'blasted to smithereens' somewhere along the way.

Either way, tube or disk, the wipe-outs are spectacular, supremely entertaining. and the crowd lining the course almost never stops cheering. At any given moment, somebody somewhere is either getting creamed or is leaping to their feet and celebrating a victory over the lopsided odds.

And either way, I've got to admit, *this is damned fun.*

And I needed that.

Then it's Mike and Cheryl's turn.

* * *

FAR UP THE INCLINE, I spot them fumbling their way into a train of platter jockeys, Cheryl between Mike's legs, a complete stranger on another platter enwrapped in hers. Then, with the assistance of some others around them, the entire eight-platter train gets a helpful little push over the edge, *and here they come!*

They gather speed quickly, and as usual, between the minimal friction of the hard plastic disks on the packed snow and the steepness of the slope's initial plunge, they slip just as quickly *out* of control. Despite the efforts of the guy on the lead platter to 'steer' by digging his heels in wherever it seems helpful, all that he actually accomplishes is the slowing of the *front* of the pack. As such, behind him, the 'caboose' of the train begins to pass the rest of the group, and the folks in the middle begin to topple over from the torque.

And Mike and Cheryl are in the middle.

Hurtling along now at what looks like more than forty miles an hour, and writhing kinda' half sideways—more like a charging skirmish line than a single-file parade now—the train hits the deep scoop where the slope flattens out, and enters the knobby mogul field, eight-wide and *flyin'.*

Wham! The guy second-from-the-end hits a nub of snow square-on, and is slammed into flight as if he'd slid over a land mine. This severs the *last* guy from the rest of the train, and *he* hurtles the rest of the way to the bottom solo and twirling and dragging his hands in an unrequited bid for control. He loses a glove in the process.

From there, the six remaining platters begin to peel away in a steady but violent disintegration, like shingles torn from the roof of a house in a tornado. Platters flutter through the air, mittens and even a shoe fly off like shrapnel, and hapless bodies tumble into the snow drifts.

It's painful, riveting, and hilarious to watch, all at the same time.

Cheryl and Mike, on the other hand, along with the guy in front of them—around whom Cheryl has wrapped those long sinewy legs of hers—make it all the way to the bottom, still upright and connected, but battered and breathless... and laughing like tickled children. I join the rest of the sideline crowd in cheering, laughing, hooting, and applauding them all.

The survivors are still barely struggling to their feet though, when the next lunatic flings himself off the precipice, and rockets toward the debris field alone.

And so it goes, over and over and over again, for the rest of the afternoon.

* * *

MIKE AND CHERYL MAKE the exhausting ten-minute hike to the top two more times, each time waiting there until another train can be assembled, then joining them for the launch over the edge.

The climb doesn't take quite as long on the third ascent though, because they start the climb so much closer to the top. And this is because they'd spilled *out* of the train so much sooner after starting the time before *that*. Unhorsed and skidding downhill on their asses, they never even made it down to where I was standing (around the midway point). So for once, the climb back up was only half the time and work.

This third run, though... this is the one that convinces them it's time to take a break.

I don't know what they were thinking. Maybe the members of this new train made some sort of a pact before interlocking their platters, promising to never let go of each other, *no matter what*, or something like that. But when, roughly a third of the way down the chute, Cheryl gets jostled out of Mike's grasp and tumbles out of the train, Mike lunges for her, and actually manages to snag the shoulder of her sweater before she somersaults out of reach... *and then he doesn't let go!*... even though she's now flat on her back *beside* the train, plowing up her own rooster-tail of powder. *He's* still part of the train, and the train's still flying down the hill. She's *separate* from the train... *but he never lets go of her.*

At first, I don't recognize who the 'draggee' is, until the disheveled conga line swooshes past me, everyone aboard either giggling hysterically or shrieking in terror, with one stand-out female voice *screaming in fury for Mike to let-the-hell go!* Recognizing the insistent voice, that's when I identify the sleek jeans, the demure hiking boots, and Cheryl's ridiculously stretched white cowl-neck sweater *with her still in it*, flopping and flailing alongside the others like a half-unbolted motorcycle sidecar.

Naturally, this time they last all the way to the bottom, having lost only two of their riders, one of them flung free at the exact same spot as the first one, the other being Cheryl (who technically finished the ride with the rest of them, only 'a little off to the right'). She's the slowest getting back on her feet afterward, and requires a good five minutes—plus the assistance of several nearby 'Good Samaritans'—to dig all the snow out of her collar, shake the snow out of her distorted sweater, dust the snow off her back and shoulders, and help comb the snow out of her hair.

But *boy*, did the crowd ever love *that* run.

Still, *why the hell didn't Mike just let her go?* Why did he feel compelled to drag her the whole way down the mountain once she'd fallen overboard? I know that if *I* was her, I'd be damned pissed right about now.

And that she is.

It takes them most of another ten minutes to slog their way back up to where I'm standing, and Cheryl does not look up once. She's scowling pretty ferociously, truth be told... until she looks up and sees me. Then all those perfect teeth break out in a tired smile again.

Mike hands me the dented platter, and gasps, "Enough. Your turn."

Surprisingly, especially to *me*, I agree, and start trudging to the distant top of the run, alone, and carrying that stupid platter over my upper arm like a Spartan shield.

* * *

BY THE TIME I finally reach the crest, I am spent. The last thing in the world I ever want to do again is lift one foot higher than the other one, *ever*, for the rest of my life.

My breathing (by which I mean "*my frantic heaving*") is all over the friggin' place. I convince myself it's not so much the exertion as the altitude. We're somewhere between five- and six-thousand feet in elevation here, and my supposedly fit body—*the same one that just conquered the rigors of Combat Control School*—is only acclimated to *zero* feet (give or take).

That's my story, and I'm stickin' to it.

I turn around and look back down the slope—I'm sorry; I meant to say, "*I gape at the sheer vertical drop-off at my feet*"—and utter my first words since leaving Mike Dumbass's side.

"*No... fuckin'... way.*"

I feel like I'm looking down an Olympic ski-jump ramp. Going down this thing on a scuffed and dinged-up plastic disk would be like greasing my ass and sliding down the angled side of the TransAmerica building in San Francisco. I might as well skydive without a parachute.

I watch two people go over the edge while I recover my breathing.

Sitting cross-legged on their platters and clutching their flimsy little handles with foolhardy faith, they either scooch themselves up to the brink, or enlist the aid of a bystander to give them a push. Then gravity grabs hold of the front lip of their platter, and *yanks* them over the edge. Literally. Their heads actually whip backwards as they go.

Right from the start though, they have absolutely no control over their saucers. The instant they recover from their initial plummet, they begin to twirl around backwards. Their track might then veer toward the spectators along the side, or they might be thrown back so far that the rim of their disk threatens to dig in and vault them into inverted flight. But *whatever* it does, it's through no influence of their own. They're at the mercy of random physics and the mischievous whims of motion, especially the laws about rapid and seemingly *endless* acceleration.

Though I knew the odds and miserable success ratios before I came up here, I'm still amazed at the horrendous attrition rates among the folks that willingly topple themselves over the abyss. I think fully two-thirds of those taking the leap are obliterated before they even reach the 'big swoop' in the middle. And of those that *do* survive beyond that point, half of *them* are bashed into helpless disarray as soon as they skitter into the mogul field below. So, I mean... *what the hell?*

There seems to be no commonality among the rare few that actually make it all the way either. Athletes fare no better than skinny shrieking little girls, sometimes older doughy bald guys outlast their younger counterparts, and one gangly gooberish teenager makes it all the way to the end despite having been launched from his platter several times along the way, and having slid into the final powder ridges sprawled half out of his disk and dragging all four limbs in the snow.

So, since 'luck' seems to be the prevailing dynamic here, I conclude that I am therefore doomed, and opt not to test the Fates any further.

Now... *how to head back down again without looking chicken enough to lay an egg.*

While I'm mulling this over, a guy who had been following me the whole way up the ascent, finally reaches the top and collapses beside me. It took him extra time, and he arrives here extra bushed, because he's been manhandling the huge (and *heavy*) inner tube of a *tractor tire* the whole way up the mountain.

He flops onto his back, as if to make an exhausted snow angel, gasping for air, and chuffing great geysers of steam from his mouth. And after several more melodramatic gulps for air, he finally splutters, "Anybody want an inner tube?"

"Sure," I chuckle. "How much you asking for it?"

"It's yours. If you're willing to drag it back up here again when you're done, go ahead and take it. I'm gonna' be here a while."

Really? I think I could probably handle this suicide plunge if I could do it wrapped in a 360-degree air-bag!

"You're serious?" I ask, as much of myself as of him.

"Hell, I don't even wanna' *look* at that thing for another hour."

He coughs, wheezes, and swallows hard. Then adds, "I'm getting too old for this shit."

"Okay then," I say. "Guard this with your life." And I hand him my flimsy dented platter.

When I grab that inner tube though, I quickly discover what depleted him so. *This bitch is heavy!* It's big, and it's soft, and it's bound to be more stable than my cheap-assed plastic disk, but I can also see that regardless of how well this thing might 'handle' on this downhill run, the trek back to the top afterward, lugging (or dragging, or rolling) this behemoth the whole way, is going to be a bitch-and-a-half.

Fuck it. I'm here, I'm not going to tackle this course on my ridiculous little plastic trashcan lid, I don't want to walk *back down, and riding this tire is the only way I'm going over that edge, so...*

"Be back in a minute."

"Take your time."

I roll it over to 'the brink,' lay it flat, and nudge about a third of it out over space. Then I nurse myself into position atop it, chest down and leading with my face, the way a surfer would paddle out to meet the waves. From there, with my chin resting on the leading edge, where it protrudes over the lip of the drop, I draw a deep and steadying breath, snigger momentarily at my own insanity, then turn to ask the big dude behind me for 'a little boost.'

He responds with a leisurely kick to the back of the tube. The rubber, and the air contained therein, absorb the kick easily, but the rebound *launches* me over the edge like a friggin' *catapult*. And the next thing I know, I'm slapping flat on the downslope, and rocketing toward that tiny Visitor's Lodge way down there.

Holy shit!

The adrenaline rush is downright explosive in my chest. The acceleration is ferocious, feeling more like a runaway elevator than a slide. My panicked howling converts to childlike war whoops, my chin patters against the fluttering rubber beneath it, and the hard-packed and corrugated snow rumbles under me, faster and faster and impossibly faster. Freezing wind carves around my face, clawing tears from my eyes. *Wow!*

Just before I barrel into the 'Big Scoop' though—where the plummet flattens out into a shallower but bumpier grade—the tube begins to rotate to the left, swinging my legs around to the right. Out of reflex, I stick my right foot out and drag the toe of my sneaker, hoping to hook the rotation back the other way. The best it's able to do though is halt the counter-clockwise trend and keep things from spinning any further. But I'm still half-sideways when I swoop into the lower mogul field, and the steady hammering turns into a slower (but heavier) battering.

Now the tube is *punching* me in the chest and throat, as I careen broadside into the knobbed and pitted lower slope. The 'impacts' themselves don't hurt, of course, absorbed as they are by the mammoth 'air bag.' But they do start an intensifying series of bounces, bounds, and *re*bounds that hurl me into the air higher and higher (not to mention more skewed, twisted, and flailing) each time. I grapple with my bucking bronco, my hands often being my only point of contact with the beast, and somehow manage to keep it within reach as we repeatedly part ways and come back together again, over and over and over again.

After about the fourth return to Earth, I find the tube and myself rejoined and sliding relatively smoothly again, except that we're now skidding along *backwards*. I can feel the snow spray founting up the leg of my jeans.

I stick my gloved left hand out, and drag its fingertips across the furrowed hard-pack, just enough to get the hurtling tube rotating back into the direction of travel again. But when I look back over my shoulder, I get about one-and-a-half seconds of jarring clarity in which to panic, before a wide crater—a literal *crater*, with a nasty deepening lower rim, exacerbated by the repeated impacts of repeated tubers—flashes under my tube... *and the rocketing world explodes.*

For a tiny sliver of a second, I am airborne again—not from being 'launched' this time, but from having *the bottom drop out from under me*—then I hit the crater's opposite rim. And I 'exacerbate' it one more time.

The tube caroms off that battered edge, and just *bashes me* into low Earth orbit.

For a moment I am sailing through the air, propellering through a blast of snowy shrapnel, and cartwheeling over the blurred terrain, until my feet clip the ground and *whump!*, I smack into a bank of loose snow on my side, and it's all over. Clubbed to a dead stop in an instant.

I lay there, stunned stupid and refusing to breathe while the bomb blast of flying snow rains down on me. And even once that ends, I don't get up. I don't know why. I just don't. I'm not injured. The wind hasn't been knocked out of me or anything. But... I guess I'm just... *dazed*. I feel like I just survived the longest heart attack in history.

Wow. That'll wake you right the hell up. Or kill you. One of the two.

I sit up giggling, flip the snow out of my hair, and try to knock the snow out of my ears. This apparently reassures a couple of guys who were tromping their way over to see if I was alright.

We all laugh, exchange waves, and they point toward the parking lot off the side of the slope... where the inner tube has finally come to rest.

Oh Lordy. I hope that massive doughnut didn't hit anybody's car.

Well, if I wasn't done before, I'm sure as hell done *now*. I think that's about all the sheer raw terror anybody needs in one day.

Well, maybe not 'terror,' so much as 'heart-stopping thrills.'
How about that?

I guess the only real difference between the two is how much you're able to laugh afterwards. And right now, I can't *stop* laughing.

All the way down to the parking lot, I've got a big old goofy-assed red-faced grin scrawled across my face, and every little slip and stumble just gets me sniggering again.

Well, say what you will, but considering how I was doing yesterday, today I am fully alive! I'm actually awake, excited, and yes, even happy again.

They ought to call this 'snow therapy.'

* * *

THOUGH CHERYL AND I never run either course again, Mike runs the big one two more times before calling it quits.

First he runs it on that same humongous inner tube, which he and several other bemused passersby help me wrestle up out of the parking lot and back onto the upper snow field again (I guess the guy who gave it to *me* really meant it when he said he didn't even want to look at it for another hour).

Then he runs the chute one last time... by himself... on that stupid little plastic platter of ours.

While he's making his multiple hikes to the top of the hill, and doing his multiple runs to the *bottom*, Cheryl and I, observing from the sidelines, watch with some concern as the carnage begins to mount at one particular point about midway through the lower 'mogul field.' Right about where *my* spectacular wipe-out occurred, as a matter of fact.

More and more frequently, and then more and more *consistently*, we watch different riders—and then *every* rider, on *any* mode of conveyance, who makes it as far as the moguls—hit that same 'crater' that I hit, and just get *blown to pieces*. Because each one that hits it *worsens* it. They deepen it, they pound back and reshape its 'lower lip' (its '*launching* lip'), they heap up more blasted snow below it, and they sharpen its edges... which makes it that much worse for the *next* guy that hits it... who then wipes out even more violently than the one before, and worsens the crater even further.

Over and over and over again, that same crater clobbers every platter-jockey and tube-runner that reaches it, just flat nuking them every time.

No matter how fast or slow, smooth or rough, in or out of control anyone approaches it, if they hit that crater at all, it's as if a mortar round dropped on them. *Whammo!* Rider and vehicle just get detonated into flying chaos. Vicious cartwheels, neck-snapping impacts, and everything from shoes to watches to wallets being flung in all directions. Every time.

What used to make the onlookers "*oo*" and "*ah*" and erupt in cheering laughter, now has them wincing and murmuring and watching for serious injuries. Soon people are talking about shutting this slope down altogether before somebody gets killed.

And at the absolute apex of this butchery, Mike makes his final run.

And it's on that damned platter.

* * *

AT FIRST, IT LOOKS like his hard-jouncing flight down the slope is going to shoot him wide, *past* the crater. But as he skitters sideways into the lower mogul field, one of the snowy knobs slams him into a furious spin, and between that and his flailing arms and legs, his track gets deflected into a whole new direction... twirling straight toward 'The Crater.'

And he hits it *hard*.

Cheryl's hand seizes mine just as he sails over the pit with his feet flying over his head. A split second later though, when he hits that lethal downhill lip *with his back*, separate from his tumbling platter, the whole crowd "*oofs!*" and groans as if they'd all been gut-punched at the same time. Because Mike gets bashed into *such* a wild freefall, he looks 'broken.' His pinwheeling form just looks *boneless*, like a rag doll flung out from under a lawn mower. And even once he hits the snow again, he continues to bounce and tumble and somersault for another fifty or sixty feet down the slope.

It's *The Agony of Defeat* all over again.

A bunch of people converge on him before he's even finished sliding. And I have to run to catch up with Cheryl, who's bounding recklessly across the kill zone with panic in her eyes.

But Mike sits up immediately, powdered and tussled and wobbly, and spitting bloody snow from his mouth. His jacket is torqued around halfway backwards, and the seam of his jeans has been split open at his right hip.

He chuckles at his disheveled appearance, and sends a ripple of relieved laughter and scattered applause back up through the crowd. He's bitten his tongue though, and gashed the side of his hand, neither all that badly, but apparently enough to finally get him to say, "Let's call it a day."

We all agree.

But what a day it's been.

* * *

I CHAUFFEUR THE TWO battered lovebirds back down the mountain, out the bottom of the darkening lower overcast, and into a light but freezing mid-afternoon sprinkle. And at my suggestion, I drive us all the sixty-plus miles straight back to McChord first.

There, I drop my own ass off at the Base Theater, thank Mike and Cheryl for a hell of a good time (which I needed badly), and watch the two of them drive off through the drizzle to Olympia. And for just a moment or two (I don't want to get too rain-soaked here), I pause to look around at my surroundings.

The base's movie theater and the Airmen's Club sit across from each other on opposite sides of the street. And half a block away, veiled by the mists, and framed by the rain-streaked streetlights at the intersection, is the 'Quad' and 'The Castle.' My home.

It's not a bad arrangement, as bachelor situations go. I've got a decent room up there on the second floor—*and I see the light is on, so Pogue must finally be home*—with one of the base's main chow halls right there in its rear wing. There's free TV in the Day Room, and free laundering facilities right across the hall. And within a short walking distance, I've also got this movie theater and that Airmen's Club, with its piano room and snack bar, just for a little variety. The flight line is only three blocks further past The Castle, and on a clear day (something I have not yet seen since I got back from Miami), you can see the sprawling snow-capped volcano on which I just spent the day.

It's beautiful, it's green, it's convenient, and it's cheap, and apparently life goes on here even when I'm gone or just having a bad day.

I could do a whole lot worse than living and working here. And when I'm not all wrapped up in my private dramas, personal setbacks, or professional miseries, the good things about this place are actually pretty obvious. And numerous.

(*sigh*)

Well, enough with the frivolity and introspection. Tomorrow it's back to work (in my last surviving set of shredded cammies, no less). And now I guess we'll see if it makes any difference whatsoever that I finally have a few clues about what I'm doing.

4
AND THE ROLLER COASTER SWOOPS BACK UP

January, 1978
McChord AFB, Tacoma, Washington

MUCH TO MY AMAZEMENT, the McChord Combat Control Team actually turns out to be a pretty good place to come back to.
 Now who'da thunk that?

For one thing, the four of us that just got back from Little Rock have been very well received. Welcomed, cheered, patted on the back even. And repeatedly congratulated, believe it or not. And not just by our 'peers' either, but by everyone of every rank, including the much revered Chief Roswell himself, our Team Commander Captain Forth, and even Spew! Legitimate heartfelt accolades from both the rough-and-tumble Sgt. Santos, and the grimly stoic Sgt. Cole Mabry as well.

Everyone seems to be genuinely impressed, pleasantly surprised, and all-round *happy* about the outcome.

Because we didn't just *survive* the damned school. It's not even that all four of us came through the brutal process of elimination intact, *as a team*. Nor is it just that one of us came out of it as the class's Honor Grad, nor that another one of us managed to get through the whole thing without any preparation, equipment, or even a spare *clue*, each remarkable feats in and of themselves.

No, I think it has more to do with the *expectations that were exceeded*.

Anytime you send people to a place with a thirty-three to fifty percent attrition rate, you expect the worst. And the more you send, the more you expect to fail. Statistically speaking then, sending four greenies to Little Rock—especially when one of them was, well... *me*—all but *assured* that at least one, if not *two* of us should have been winnowed out by the process.

But no! Every damn last one of us came home with a beret on his head. And that makes the whole McChord *team* look good.

In fact, now *no one* on the McChord Combat Control Team is less than Phase II qualified. Not even me. And that, according to the Old Heads, is fairly unique. *Every* team has at least one fledgling, at least one newbie standing out from the pack by virtue of his lack of a beret.

But not at McChord!

When our class started at the beginning of November, with candidates representing just about every stateside team there is, a quarter of the first-day students were from McChord. But when it ended, a week before Christmas, almost *half* of the remaining class was from McChord.

Considering how little 'connection' I had with this team before I left for CCS (and how 'poisoned' that minimal connection had been by my first jump with them), it seems strange that the greatest satisfaction I would draw from this whole thing now is the fact that I held up my end of the deal. I pulled my weight, I held my part of the line, and I didn't let my team down. Having graduated *at all* is a major source of pride and amazement for me, of course. But having made my *team* look good? That's more gratifying than I would have ever suspected.

Stranger still, it turns out that my beret actually *is* ample reward for all my trials and tribulations pursuing it. And that makes absolutely no sense to me at all.

But, almost as good as all the appreciation and recognition—the welcoming into this extremely exclusive club, and the acceptance into a rather guarded circle of camaraderie—is the fact that our first day back is wide open for us to do whatever it is that we've got to do to hit the ground running, and get ourselves right back up to speed again. We have no responsibilities today, and all the time we need to just take care of our chores and errands.

And I take full advantage of that.

* * *

DESPITE THE SKY'S SULLENNESS and constant leaking, and despite having to wear the only set of camouflaged fatigues that I have left—clawed and shredded (but dry cleaned and pressed) as they are—I spend the morning making the rounds. I return my medical records to the Flight Surgeon (a 'doctor' by any other name), I visit the squadron offices to get my meal card back, and I celebrate *that* by enjoying my *first breakfast since leaving Miami.*

Man, nothing brings a guy back to life better than free food!

Well, almost *nothing.*

So, following a downright *orgasmic* ham, cheese, and mushroom omelet (with hash browns, toast, and three glasses of fake orange juice), I step out into a rain that has kicked up just a little too much for me to *walk* across base without getting drenched. Instead then, I catch the base shuttle bus over to the BX complex, and visit the bank. There I find over six-hundred dollars in my account that had accumulated while I was at CCS not spending anything. I take forty with me in cash, and revel in the fleeting pleasure of actually tucking money *into* that dusty cavity in my wallet for once.

At the Accounting & Finance office, I gather, fill-out, and submit my travel vouchers for the roundtrip to and from Little Rock—another little chunk of change I can expect to collect in a couple of days—then I stop by the tailor to drop off the four sets of fresh *new* cammies that Miles just gave me this morning for alterations and the sewing on of insignia.

One of the odd things about camouflaged fatigues though, is that they don't want them all slathered in patches and badges and nametags and rank like normal uniforms (although the Army seems to be perfectly okay with it). For one thing, such orderly symmetrical shapes defeat the entire purpose of the *dis*orderly jungle pattern of the camouflage. And for another, in the event of capture, the less information that you make readily available to your captors the better.

So what they do instead is sew on a single rectangle of velcro, on the left breast where your specialty badges would normally be affixed, and to *that* you can then stick a custom-made, velcro-backed, black, *faux*-leather patch that has all that regular uniform information printed on it in that one little rectangle: name, rank, and badges, all artfully etched in silver-on-black. That way, you're fully identifiable while on base, but in the event of capture, that patch can be torn off and thrown away, leaving you anonymous.

On the one hand, that's kinda' cool: an elegantly simple solution that even looks good. On the other hand, it's a little disconcerting to realize that such a contingency even needs to be considered.

I've already got the customized patch though. I wore it on the cammies that I demolished down at CCS, and I'm wearing it now. So in a couple of days, once the tailoring is done, I'm going to be fully up to speed, at least uniform-wise... and that feels good too.

* * *

BACK OUT ON THE curb, waiting in the thinning drizzle for the shuttle bus to take me back to 'The Shop,' I cannot help but smile.

Look at me!

I'm standing here among these other mere mortals, some in their civilian clothes, others in their regular old standard-issue uniforms, wearing my 'battle-scarred' cammies, with the pant legs bloused over spit-polished jump boots, jump wings on my chest and on the facing of my fashionably canted beret. My *beret*, people!

I am fucking standing out!

I'm full of food, I've got money in my pocket and more on the way, and for all my newness and awkwardness in this weird and exotic field (thanks to my premature passage through Combat Control School), I'm further ahead than just about anybody else at this stage of the game. *Less than three months out of Jump School, and already Phase II! I could be Phase III by friggin' Thanksgiving, fer criminey's sake!* Five months *ahead of schedule!*

Dang! Am I 'Sierra-Hotel' or what?

('Sierra-hotel,' by the way, is phonetic for 'SH,' which stands for "Shit Hot"... obviously)

What can I say? The roller-coaster's peaking, and I'm just feeling good right now.

And just like a roller coaster, well... how long can *that* last?

STORY XXXIV

THE LONGEST NIGHT... EVER

1
THERE MAY NOT BE AN 'I' IN 'TEAM,' BUT THERE'S A 'ME'

January, 1978
McChord Air Force Base, Tacoma, Washington

OVER THE PAST TWO months while I've been gone, Sgt. Miles Campbell, the team's unofficial 'Supply Sergeant,' has been busy acquiring and stockpiling all the paraphernalia that I could've used *two friggin' months ago!*

You know, *before* they sent me off to CCS.

But hey, that's water under the bridge now. No hard feelings.

It wasn't Miles's fault that I showed up unannounced back in October, an extra body that he suddenly and unexpectedly had to equip with whatever he had on the shelves. And it surely wasn't his doing that they turned around and shot me off to Little Rock before he'd even had a chance to order what I needed. Hell, they practically had me out the door again before I'd finished unpacking from Jump School. So I could hardly blame Miles for my lack of preparedness… at least not *all* of it.

Besides, I scurried off to CCS and I 'conquered' it *despite* my notable shortcomings. So, as much of a pain-in-the-ass as it might have been, it surely didn't hurt my reputation any.

Damn! I'm just feeling so friggin' cocky these days!

Regardless though, when I finally get back to 'The Section' later in the morning—just before noon, actually—Miles is waiting for me with open arms and an apologetic grimace on his face.

He's set up a locker for me—with a padlock on it and everything (although he had to leave it open, because he couldn't find the key for it)—and it's packed to the rafters with all the goodies I could've used nine weeks ago.

Christmas at the Front!

There's a brand new sleeping bag, tightly rolled and tied off in its very own waterproof pouch. I got a new and improved rucksack, I got a fresh pair of Nomex gloves (the kind pilots wear), extra thermal underwear, extra-thick socks, four pairs of camouflaged pants (the matching shirts for which I just dropped off at the tailors earlier this morning), a new camouflaged field jacket (I've never seen one of those before), new jungle boots, and even two extra blue berets. Apparently the only thing I'm missing now is my *heavy* cold weather gear—a parka—which is still on back-order for *most* of the guys.

Dang! So this is what it's like to be an actual part of a team, *rather than a fifth wheel and a surprise tag-along wannabe who doesn't even speak the language.* So this is what Sgt. Beaudry was talking about.

In addition, I (along with everyone else in the unit, apparently) have been issued a voucher for a pair of absolute top-of-the-line 'field boots' (hiking boots on steroids, as only the free market can produce) that we have to go to Tacoma's biggest sporting goods store to pick up. Definitely not standard military-issue gear. Spew already has his, and I have to admit, they look danged cool. And comfy. He says they're light but unbelievably sturdy, warm and exquisitely cushioned (although Spew's never used the word 'exquisitely' in his life). I can't wait to pick up my own.

Then, to cap off all the rest of the good news, my roommate Randy tells me that he's off to HALO School next week (that's "High Altitude, Low Opening," or 'skydiving' school... freefalling versus static-line jumping) all the way over in Fort Bragg, North Carolina. So, starting Sunday, when he flies out, I'll have the room all to myself again. *Wow!*

You know, technically, I've been a resident of The Castle since last October. Almost three months now. But, except for a one-week overlap at the end of that month—between Pogue's *return* from CCS, and my departure *to* it—plus this week right now, we've never been in that room at the same time. After a quarter of a year as 'roommates,' I really don't even know the guy. And apparently that won't be changing anytime soon.

Fine by me. I can live with it.

He seems decent enough, I guess... from what I can tell... although we've barely exchanged the most basic pleasantries so far. But he's got the dull 'slab-face' of an adolescent bully... or at least he bears an unfortunate resemblance to a couple of guys of that ilk that I remember from my youth. And from what I've seen, he really only smiles at dirty jokes, or when he's shooting stuff. He's certainly never said or done anything wrong with me, but still, I really don't see us getting all that close anytime soon.

Speaking of roommates, though: there were three new faces on the team when I got back from Little Rock. Two of them—Doug Belkin and Leo Roth—are neophytes fresh out of Keesler's Radio Maintenance School and the Army's Jump School. They're both single, both younger than me, and they're both of even lower rank than myself (meaning no stripes at all), if that's possible to imagine.

Holy patoots! I (and my beret) am actually 'worldlier' than someone else on this team now!

They were moving into the room across the hallway from mine when I got back from the Mount Rainier trip with Mike and Cheryl.

Doug has the friendly, toothy, *hopeful* face of a kid barely out of high school. Kind of like me... new to adulthood, and still trying to stay on the world's good side. Leo, on the other hand, looks like he just graduated from the Superhero Academy... strong-chinned, square-jawed, with steely close-set eyes, all posted atop a solidly muscled mid-sized body. If first impressions hold true, I should get along famously with both of them. But Leo seems to offer a little *extra* promise, in that he also plays the acoustic guitar (which reminds me that I need to get Mom to ship me *my* guitar right quick), *and* he's an excellent pencil artist as well!

My God, we might be able to share something other than ammunition and war stories.

The third New Guy on the team is a married three-striper and a recently converted *air traffic controller* named 'Trey' (short for 'William the *third*,' I'm told). Trey and his wife have taken up residence *off*-base, so there hasn't been quite the same 'instant connection' with him.

At the same time, Connor Duncan ("Aussie") was *gone* from the team when I got back. Moved *on*, or maybe moved all the way back to *Australia*, for all I know. Nobody's deigned to explain it yet, and I ain't asking.

Big changes everywhere I look.

***

LUNCH IS ANOTHER JOYOUSLY filling meal at the Castle's chow hall (after two days of being broke and starving, everything there just looks, smells, and tastes so *five star* now), and the afternoon is a light and lazy distraction of sporadic busywork, familiarizing myself with all the cool new stuff in my cool new locker, and flitting from one congratulatory conversation to the next. No actual duties or deadlines, no physical labor or pressing chores. And by 2:30, they release us for the day with an off-handed reminder about an evening 'mission' the team has slated for tomorrow night… a jump, followed by a short cross-country, the setting up of a night EZ, and the directing and grading of a cargo drop. And that's it.

It sounds like a simple little problem, especially now with all my worldly expertise. And it ought to be easy (and comfortable) with all the new gear I've got now.

I head back to my room without giving it a second thought.

***

MIKE DUMAS SHOWS UP at my door after dinner, with no particular plan in mind, but hoping to do *something* fun with the remainder of the evening. And I'm amenable to that. It's been a damned good day—a damned good *couple* of days, actually—and I'm starting to think that life here at McChord might not be so bad after all.

So hell yeh, let's go have some fun.

As it turns out though, for a non-drinker like myself, who's already eaten and doesn't have the social skills to get a date at a women's prison, the 'fun' options are actually pretty limited. No clubs, no bars, no restaurants, and not that godawful skating rink again. We check the movie listings, and quickly write that off as well.

In the end, we wind up just cruising the ugly sodium-lit commercial streets of Tacoma, talking about anything that comes to mind—like Cheryl (the lucky bastard)—and looking for anything that might catch our eyes.

And what finally catches *my* eye is a used car dealership.

I haven't had a car for most of a year now. And yesterday's little adventure in high-mountain chauffeuring reminded me all over again just how much I miss it.

So... *let's go look at some cars!*

2
BUZZ KILL

Fort Lewis, Tacoma, Washington

ALRIGHT, WHAT WOULD *YOU* think they meant if someone told you that the next day (today) (a) you were going to make a twilight jump into an Army reservation, followed by (b) a night overland hike, which would finally culminate with (c) the setting up of an EZ in the middle of nowhere, and (d) the grading of some exciting pallet extractions? Doesn't that sound like it's basically just some jumping, hiking, rigging, grading, tearing down, and going home? *It did to me.*

Doesn't it sound like a simple, straightforward—albeit somewhat drawn-out—single evening's worth of work? *It did to me.*

And doesn't it sound sorta' *familiar?* Kinda' like the last frag at CCS? *Been there. Led that. Twice.*

A shiver rockets down my spine.

Oh, it sounds bloody dismal, alright. Our first deployment of the new year, and it's going to be cold, and wet, and endless, as long as this stalled, dripping, and refrigerated weather system continues to sit on top of us like a big sopping wet blanket, as it has ever since I got back from Miami five days ago. But it *also* sounds—to *me*, anyway—like four, maybe *five* hours of squishy shivering torment... *and then it's over! Period! Home by midnight or shortly thereafter*. Hot shower, warm bed, the sleep of the righteous and all that. *Done.*

That kind of wishful thinking *used* to be regarded as 'cute' and 'naive.' Now at my new level of recently acquired expertise, it just sounds stupid.

I should know better.

In preparation for tonight's 'short high-energy mission' then, I pack accordingly... according to that very miscalculation.

I pack light (who needs heavy cold-weather gear when you're only going to be gone for a couple of very physically active hours? Right?), I dress in layers (including my brand new camouflaged field jacket), and I don't eat anything ahead of time, as a precaution against the unsettling influences of the flight over to the drop zone. Then I step out under the drizzling afternoon overcast to await the bus ride out to our plane. Our 'jump ship.'

I look up at the low and leaking cloud bellies overhead.

Oh, it's going to be fun trying to jump in this *stuff.*

Well, a bus does show up, a standard, dark blue, Air Force issue 'school bus,' the kind that has no interior temperature controls, and so cannot stop its windows from fogging any time there are breathing passengers on board. But it turns out it's *not* a 'shuttle' out to our jump ship. No, this is our ride all the way over to the drop *zone* over at Fort Lewis. Because, sure enough, the weather's just a little too shitty to be putting jumpers out over forests they can't even see from the air.

(*sigh*)

Well, this is off to a great start.

So, for the first fifteen minutes of what has now become a *road trip*—while we *drive* off-base, loop down onto I-5, and head south for a few exits to the sprawling Army installation next door—I just stare out through the smeared fog of my window at the rain-streaked suburbs rolling past, and think, *Man, I could've had a late lunch after all! You know?*

Now I'm going to be starving all night.

Oh, if only that was the worst of my problems.

* * *

ONCE THROUGH FORT LEWIS'S main gate, it's another half hour of splashing past Gray Army Airfield—the post's aptly named landing strip—and out onto the dirt roads of its vast operational ranges.

Off-roading in a bus.

Eventually, deep in the woods, at a nondescript intersection of muddy tank trails, Sgt. Santos signals the driver, and the bus jounces to a stop. I have no idea where we are, and I can't imagine how the driver's ever going to find his way back out of here again. But then, that's not my problem, is it?

No, *my* problem begins with the gathering of all my gear from the overhead racks and under the seats, then sidling off the bus with all that junk in my arms… like my brand new jam-packed rucksack (with a sleeping bag attached to the bottom of the rig, tied off inside its own waterproof pouch, something that *should* have been a clue, I suppose, that this was an *over*night deployment, and not just a romantic evening stroll through the woods), plus my web gear, my gas mask holster, and my very own newly issued GAU-5.

The scenario only worsens though, as the bus completes its three-point turnaround and chugs off out of sight again. Because then, and only *just* then, does Sgt. Santos finally reveal the full agenda for tonight's festivities. And it's only *then* that I finally comprehend all of the intentions, objectives, tactics and targets—as well as the *duration*—of tonight's little 'mission.' And it's that little 'duration' thingy that really slaps the naïveté out of me for good.

Namely, *all friggin' night long!*

The EZ we'll be setting up *tonight* won't be going operational until sometime tomorrow *morning!*

Aw, you gotta' be shittin' me!

It's almost 4:30 on a colorless winter afternoon. The temperatures have barely reached the lower fifties today, and by now they're on their way back down again. I've had no dinner, I've got a mountain of equipment heaped at my feet—gear that I'm going to have to lug around on my back for the next *fourteen hours now*—and with the exception of my Nomex gloves, my long johns, and the ratty brown sweater I'm wearing under my cammies, my only cold weather gear is the light field jacket I just rolled up and stuffed under the top flap of my ruck.

Great. I guess I must have been enjoying life a little too much for a while there, and now it's time to balance the karmic scales again.

First things first, though.

3

AND THE ROLLER-COASTER PLUMMETS TO THE BOTTOM AGAIN

THE REASON NOBODY'S DONNING all their gear just yet is because, per Manny's master plan, we've apparently got to run some 'immediate action drills' first—ambush response exercises—right here, and right now.

Good news. Just what I wanted.

On a forest road like this—as opposed to a narrow trail or footpath—you never walk single-file, and you never walk close together. You split up, half the team walking down the left side of the road, the other half taking the right. And whatever side you're walking on, you keep your eyes *and your weapon* trained on a relatively narrow wedge of the surrounding environment *on that side of the road only*. Leave the other side to the guys walking along that shoulder. Trust them, as they must trust you, to scan and defend that portion of the passing scenery that you cannot. And you keep your distance from each other, never less than six meters apart, preferably *ten* meters or more between each trailing teammate... unless, of course, it's foggy or it's night (both of which it's about to become here), in which case you do whatever you've got to do to keep the guy in front of you in sight.

The obvious objective with these rules is to stay spread out and avoid 'clumping' (giving the enemy a lot of targets in a small or concentrated area), and to keep all three-hundred-and-sixty degrees of the surrounding terrain under constant focused surveillance with a minimum amount of overlapping redundancy. The guys bringing up the rear actually spend a sizable percentage of their time walking *backwards*.

The bottom line though, is that you are responsible for both the scrutiny and the protection of your individual 'sector' alone. And that goes for your reaction to an attack as well. Just guard *your part*, and count on the others to do the same with theirs.

I'm in the right column, just two forward of Sal Donado, who's playing Tail-End Charlie this time, at least on this side of the road. And I'm playing the game to the hilt. *All* of my attention is on my slender window of passing scenery, a window that has *already* been scanned by each of the seven guys ahead of me, theoretically, as *their* wedges of scrutiny swept over it. And I am just flat *looking* for those ambushing bastards.

I mean, *how hard could it be to spot a couple of the biggest, oldest, most out of shape, creakiest old coots on the team?* We're talking about Sergeants Blake Burley ("BB") and Miles Campbell here. Even if their camouflage is *superb* (which is hard enough to conceive, considering the jungle green of their cammies versus the dead gray and brown winter foliage and the pale naked trunks of the trees), the swaths of destruction they had to have left just crashing their way out *into* that foliage ought to be glaringly conspicuous.

But, much like the guys in front of me, I see nothing.

Obviously then, our would-be attackers must have taken their position on the other side of the road from me. Either that, or they're still up ahead somewhere, further up the road. So, naturally...

Two GAU-5s open fire at the same time—from the woods on *both* sides of the road, and from just *aft* of our columns (which means we *all* walked right past them, and *nobody* noticed them)—rattling dryly like castanets in the deadening gloom. I catch one quick blink of a burst of stuttering light, less than thirty yards back in the scrub, before my dive off the side of the road drops me at the base of a tree, and I lose sight of it.

The 'cover' here is lousy though. There's a wet leafy 'mulch' of winter deadfall all over the ground, which softens my landing but provides little other assistance. Beside me is a lacy screen of dead bushes, and the trunk of a small denuded tree barely a foot in diameter... and that's it. The 'trench' next to the road is so shallow as to be no trench at all, and the only way my ass could hang out in the open *more* would be if I was also wearing that pregnant rucksack as well. Because, if that thing was on my back right now, even if I was pressed into the ground as flat as roadkill, that heap of gear would be humped up two-and-a-half feet high, and marking my position no matter where I moved. Kinda' like a camel trying to hide behind a log.

So, note to self: *in the event of a real ambush—one in which we're pinned down by* real *enemy fire—consider shucking the ruck. Leave it next to some kind of obvious cover, and maybe it'll serve as a decoy.*

They never taught us that, though—maybe even for several really good reasons that I haven't yet considered—but lying here now, imagining the air above my head zipping and whistling with bullets, each one seeking whatever bundles of jiggling dark green they can find, it doesn't sound like such a bad idea at all.

In the meantime, the guys have started returning fire, and I join in. It's little more than a token gesture, of course; just going through the motions, playing the game, since I not only don't have a visible target in my sights, but I'm also firing blanks, *and* I'm probably officially dead right now anyway. But it's a fun release nonetheless.

We clatter and rattle away at each other for a few more seconds, while at the front of our columns, I spot Rocky and Mutt scampering low through the trees, presumably using our little firefight as a distraction while they try to dash around and flank our attackers. They don't get far though.

BB's voice rises above the fireworks, coming from the scrub on the opposite side of the road behind me, and I turn to see him standing there, waving his arms and weapon, shouting, "*Cease fire! Cease fire!*"

The toy-like pattering of our assault rifles cuts off, and one by one, everybody rises to their feet. I notice then, as I'm side-stepping through the brush and migrating back toward the road, that the front of Spew's uniform looks like he dove into a pile of elephant shit. It's just mud, but once the biggest wet clods slough off, he looks a bit like he did on that airplane during our one flight together back in October… when he earned his nickname.

A couple of the guys are really razzing him for it, too (I still don't feel 'credible' or *worthy* enough to razz *anybody* in this outfit yet), the closest to him being Randy Pogue, my roommate back at The Castle. Soon, *everybody's* laughing—which is, of course, precisely what Teddy lives for—until he, and then Randy, step out of the weeds and onto the hard-packed surface of the road. Then he abruptly wheels around, and seizes Randy in a big bearhug, a full-body buddy-buddy embrace.

"I love you, man!" he shouts in his best surfer-dude voice, pounding him on the back. Then he separates and walks off without looking back, leaving Randy standing there, his mouth hanging open, and the front of *his* uniform now slathered in shi... *er*, mud.

Miles announces, though, that we were all slaughtered in that attack anyway. Too inattentive as we walked right past our ambushers (who really shouldn't have been that hard to spot), too slow responding, too little effective use of the limited ground cover, and too little suppressive return fire to keep those ambushers from either escaping or decimating Mutt's little counter-attack.

What? How could he tell how ineffective my return fire was? I might have killed him with my first blind and utterly random shot into the bushes. What does he *know?*

"Let's do it again," he says. And without a moment's hesitation, he and BB march off down the road again, disappearing around the next bend to hunt up another ambush site. *Oh, boy. This is gonna' be a long night.*

* * *

WE DO IT TWO more times. According to Miles, we get massacred both of those times too. Mom would be thrilled to hear that news.

Killed three times in one night, Ma!

Great career choice there, Hon. Glad we had that little talk on your last birthday. Yes, I said your last *birthday.*

On the second ambush, I'm in the *left* column, up near the front this time... and both of our attackers open up from that side. In fact, they're both in my zone of surveillance at the time.

I actually thought that I'd seen something out there right before they started shooting. But, in addition to being unsure about that, I was also undecided about what exactly I should do about it if I was right. And that's something I've mentally wrestled with ever since CCS, where I felt it was also 'under-explained' and left dangerously unclear.

Should I point and shout? Or should I whisper? Or maybe rap my weapon like we did at CCS, and then point it out to whatever teammates respond to my signal. Should I dive headlong into the weeds, hoping that everyone else takes the hint from that? Or should I just start *blazing away* into the friggin' shadows? That might get the jump on our would-be ambushers, but what if I'm wrong? What if it's just a wild pig rooting around in the bushes, or something like that? We might not care about the impact on the local fauna, but I think we might care *a lot* about blowing our silent cover. And is it really a good idea to leave the initiation of a full-blown firefight up to *me?*

Either way, I spend just enough time stewing (and no doubt *overthinking*) my way into a paralyzed state of indecision, all while staring hard into the watchful eyes of our attackers, as it turned out, such that they wind up getting the jump on us, and *poof!*, dead again.

Nobody else knows that I saw anything, of course—except for maybe Miles and BB—and our post-attack scolding includes everyone in the forward-left quadrant of the team (who also failed to thwart the assault), not just me. But that does not make me feel any better. On top of that, since 'all' of the attackers were on that one side, it is decided that (a) *everyone* in my immediate vicinity, myself obviously included—having taken the brunt of the opening salvo and all—was killed outright. And (b) everyone *else* reacted so awkwardly to the one-sided surprise that our attackers had plenty of time to hose the lot of them before they could rally a credible response.

Wonderful. I feel so much better prepared now.

The third time (being 'the charm' and all), it's *my* turn as Tail-End Charlie, bringing up the rear of the rightside column. And apparently, Miles and BB walked a long way this time before finding the perfect ambush site, because we walk a long way before walking into their next ambush... long enough to get myself fretting over what I've gotten myself into with this crew.

The evening shadows have been thickening for a while now, so it takes no great stretch of the imagination for me to picture this as an actual Vietnamese jungle road... or a winter woodland near the Fulda Gap in eastern Europe... or an Andean foot trail outside Medellin, Colombia, or even a Nigerian coastal forest, with real enemy troops combing the woods for us. And with me walking *backwards* most of the time, I begin running scenarios in my mind. *What do I do if I see this or that?* That sort of thing.

I mean, what's more important? Staying silent and covert (on the presumption that, just because I've seen or heard some 'bad guys,' that doesn't mean they've seen or heard *us* yet), or opening fire and getting the jump on them before they can get the jump on *us*, and thereby blowing our invisibility for a one-time shot at ridding ourselves of our pursuers? Both options have their pros and cons. And I'm confident of neither.

What if I just lay low for a moment or two—kind of using the rest of my team as 'bait'—while I watch and wait for a clear shot on an enemy I haven't seen clearly yet? Oh, but what if I lose contact with the rest of my team in the darkness? How often are they keeping track of me back here anyway? And how will I *know*, one way or the other?

I'm still mulling over all the unpleasant possibilities when Miles and BB cut loose again, from both sides of the road this time, and from *close range* too!

Shit!

Assault rifles clatter and flash all over the place. Guys are shouting and throwing themselves flat alongside the one stretch of road that has absolutely no ground cover whatsoever. No wonder Miles chose this spot for his ambush.

Me? I just dash off the road and keep on running until I reach the nearest skeletal trees, spraying untargeted cover fire as I run.

I think Miles and BB go through two whole thirty-round mags of ammo apiece before calling it quits. But that's just for fun. Even I can tell we've all been wiped out long before that. Hard to believe these are the same guys who supposedly outclassed the SPs every time they ever played together. Or is it possible those stories were just a tad one-sided and exaggerated?

Again we shuffle back onto the road. Again, *while* we shuffle, Miles dispenses a cranky lecture on all that we did wrong... which was apparently *everything*. And this includes another repeat of his previous assessments.

Namely, that we were butchered every time.

Miles is repeating those all too familiar words when Mutt Siegel, who's been extra slow dawdling his way back this time, steps up onto the road. He turns to face Miles, who's about twenty feet away from him and still criticizing our shoddy efforts. And without warning, *Mutt opens fire on him! On full automatic!*

For like three solid seconds, he hammers off a whole thirty-round banana clip worth of blanks. Then the clip runs dry, and the deep gray woods crash back to silence again.

Miles is stunned, and suddenly speechless. Everybody is. But Mutt just turns to face the rest of us, raises his arms (and his steaming weapon), and with one of his patented cheesy grins, shouts, "*Got him!*"

And the woods erupt with laughter.

Thus ends our 'Immediate Action Drills' for the night.

4
THE LONGEST NIGHT... EVER

"TEAM THREE," SGT. 'MONTY' Montreaux barks as he stares at his wristwatch, "*Go!*"

I sigh, lean against the weight of my rucksack, and start walking.

I'm 'Team Three.' Me and, believe it or not, the very same Miles and BB who just spent the last half hour repeatedly killing me. Is that Fate, Karma, or Irony at work there? And with the day dying in gray all around us—the low and saturated overcast darkening the trees into a shadowy, almost '*underwater*' tableau—the three of us march off the road and straight into the murky woods on a 076-degree heading.

I'm in the lead. But, short of carrying my teammates' gear as well, I think I've been tasked with just about every job an entire column of men would normally share. I'm point man, radio man (toting the fucking prick again), navigator (we're following *my* compass), and pacer (counting *my* footsteps), not to mention left *and* right forward defense, and 'trailblazer' all rolled into one. Miles and BB? Well, I guess they're both just 'bringing up the rear' on this one. I think they're also the official 'Figures of Authority,' 'Voices of Experience,' 'Tag-Along Evaluators,' and 'Inconvenienced Old Timers' of my 'team.' They're sure as hell not doing anything else.

It's not exactly a balanced dissemination of duties, but from what I gathered back at the starting line, it's the standard for all six of the three-man teams tonight. A recently beanied rookie leading a pair of older, 'wiser,' more experienced characters into the nighttime wilds of Fort Lewis.

For instance, Rocky led off 'Team One' half an hour ago, consisting of himself, Smoke, and Skeeter, while Greg Dorn's 'Team Two' saw him at the front of Mutt and our new second-in-command, Lieutenant Kostas. Miles, BB and I followed fifteen minutes behind *them*, leaving Sal breaking trail for 'Team Four' (along with Howdy and Manny) another quarter-hour behind *us*. Teams Five and Six were fronted by Randy and Spew respectively, with Gino, Jamie, Reb, and even Captain Forth fleshing out their ranks. Quite a gaggle.

This feels more like an assessment of the team's fledglings than a real 'exercise.' Then again, I suppose that's pretty much what an 'exercise' *is*.

Nobody mentioned, though, with whom Cole and Monty were supposed to be teamed. In fact, I didn't even see Cole back there at the assembly point at all. *Where the hell did* he *go?*

* * *

THE FIRST THING I forget to keep track of is my pace count. Between the frequency of my compass checks, the attention paid to my careful and even semi-silent foot placement, plus my eagle-eyed surveillance of the deepening shadows—not to mention my mental fixation on all the worst-case ambush scenarios I can imagine, along with the myriad and uncertain ways they ought to be handled—I'm just too preoccupied to think about counting footsteps as well. It's not until BB specifically *asks* how far we've gone already that it even occurs to me to think about it.

Pretending not to have heard him, I keep walking in silence, and extend my slow (and highly professional) visual scan back past my left shoulder. In reality, of course, *I'm cheating*, looking back to quickly *estimate* how far we've traveled.

In the distance, meandering like a faint ribbon through the trees, I spot the road from which we started.

"*Pssst! Steve!,*" BB whispers again.

I do a fast guesstimate.

Looks like two-and-a-half, maybe three football fields. A little less than three-hundred yards, I'm thinking.

"Yo," I whisper back, still pretending not to have heard him the first time. An Oscar-worthy performance, I'm sure.

"*How far have we gone so far?*"

I'm still doing the fudged math in my head as I whisper back, *"Call it two-hundred-and-eighty paces. Maybe two-hundred-and-fifty meters?"*

"Copy that."

Good. He bought it... I think.

But, with all due respect, this early in the game, *what the hell difference does it make?* I mean, *come on!* We're going to be at this for *hours* tonight. We've got miles and miles of tippy-toeing to do, ninety-eight percent of which *is still ahead of us!* So why fret over our walking distance after only the first ten minutes of walking? Is he just checking up on *me*, making sure that I *remember* to count? Or is something else going on here? Maybe something that the Old Heads on each team already know about, but that us newbies are doomed to find out the hard way? *Hmmm.*

Well, at least all this 'ambush preparation' hasn't made me paranoid or anything.

The three of us have been plodding through this chilly forest for not quite a dozen minutes now—just long enough for the guys back at the starting line to finally slip beyond earshot—and *man*, this is a quiet place once the shadows and silence take over. If a tree fell over right now, I don't think it *could* make a sound.

I'm more concerned though, with how friggin' *dark* it's going to get out here once the night has fully descended. I can remember all too well how impenetrably black the star-swallowing overcast turned the world back at Little Rock. And the low dripping ceiling over our heads right now is just as bad as *that* ever was.

Oy. This is going to be a long fucking night.

* * *

UP AHEAD, A LIGHT patch in the gloom catches my attention. It's just a little clearing in the woods, a small space without the brittle winter 'canopy' overhead to contribute its shadow to the darkness. But because of that, it has a misty sort of 'glow' to it, like a streetlight dimmed by the foggy night around it. So my focus is on that when, peeking through the silhouetted scrub on the near side of that clearing, I spot the roof of a camouflaged pick-up truck. It looks a lot like one of *our* six-packs, as a matter of fact.

I freeze, take an extra moment to confirm it, then tap the side of my weapon and drop to one knee, just like we did at CCS. I hear Miles and BB doing the same behind me.

After a few breathless seconds, BB squat-walks up to me and whispers, *"Whatcha' got, man?"*

"Looks like a six-pack," I mutter back, *"Up there in that clearing."*

"So? What are you gonna' do about it?" he asks.

He didn't even look, he didn't question my assessment, and he was quick to inquire as to my intentions... as if I really *was* the 'leader' of this team or something... as if this whole thing was a test for *me*, right from the start, one that he knew about and was expecting all along.

Great. So this is how it's gonna' be all night long then, is it?

I think about it for a second or two, but the only thing that comes to mind (based on all my worldly experience) is an evasive box-pattern *around* the threat. I don't know if that's what they're looking for, but it's all I've got.

I flick a thumb over my shoulder and whisper, *"I'm thinking about fifty meters left, then about a hundred meters or so past 'em, then fifty meters back to the right, and we're back on course."*

"Sounds good to me," he hisses back. *"Let's do it."*

Well, okay then.

I rise to half-mast for about ten seconds, scanning the lacy silhouettes of the trees and the chest-high scrub surrounding that haloed pick-up truck over there, watching for movement—bobbing heads, darting figures, whatever—but, *nothing*. To all outward appearances, the truck has simply been parked and abandoned there. *But why? And by whom?*

Maybe I should over-think it some more. You know; keep on kneeling here, pondering all the infinite possibilities until the sun comes up again. That ought to be a fruitful strategy, don'cha' think?

Enough. I'll fret over it later. For now, it's time to move.

I do some fast mental math—subtracting ninety degrees from our current compass bearing—then take off at a 'hurried skulk' along our new 346º heading. Fifty-five mostly-silent steps later, I flip my compass open again, site on a target shadow in the distance along the original 076 radial, and resume our line of march.

We're now *bypassing* that mystery truck and its clearing on a wide parallel track, offset from it by about half a football field's length, and working our way through the last of the shriveling light toward a low rise in the terrain up ahead. As I figure it, once we scamper over that rise, it should be safe to sidestep back over to our original line again. But until then, we're moving low and slow, light-footed, swift, and quiet as a...

BAM!

Jesus! Scared the crap out of me!

An angry voice snaps out of the distance, "*Shit! Shit! Son of a bitch!*"

Instantly, all three of us drop to our bellies and turn to face the clearing from which the noises (and the cursing) came. But, this low in the underbrush, there's nothing to be seen through the overlapping screens of foreground shadows... except for a tiny cotton-puff of dissipating white smoke that wafts up into the light.

"*What the hell was that?*" I spit. "*Was that somebody shooting at us?*"

"*Not sure,*" whispers BB with a grunt, "*It sounded kinda' like...*"

"*Sounded like his weapon blew up,*" says Miles from further back in the darkness.

"*Yeh, that's what I was thinkin'.*" says BB. "*Sounded like he blew the bottom out of his magazine.*" And the two of them start to snicker.

I've never heard of such a thing, and I'm not sure what to do with it now. All I can say then, is, "*Sooo...*"

"*So let's get the fuck outa' here while the fuck-gettin's good.*"

What?

And before I can react, Miles and BB scramble to their feet, and start bulling their way forward.

I lurch my way upright (*goddamned deadweight ruck! fucking two-ton prick!*), and stumble for a step or two, clocking my shin on something buried in the undergrowth. Then it's a strange high-stepping half-ducking dash through the tangled shadows toward that rise I'd pegged in the distance, with BB's big old paw intermittently shoving me forward, and his voice spitting, "*Go! Go-go-go!*"

Silence is the first casualty of this wild thrashing charge. Within only *seconds*, we've discarded all pretense of stealth, and are just crashing pell-mell up the incline, putting the clearing as *far* and as *fast* behind us as possible. But not quickly enough, apparently.

As my breathing control once again starts slipping away, the rattle of a GAU-5 on full-auto suddenly erupts from the clearing.

My first impulse is to dive for cover again. But not only is BB still pushing me from behind, but he and Miles open fire themselves, one-handed hip-shots at a full flailing sprint. I join them, my own wobbling GAU spraying blindly in my right hand, while my left fends off the invisible twigs and leaves rushing at my face.

Is this really the way we'd handle this in a real-world situation? If we'd really been skirting a real-world enemy position, and they'd really opened fire on us like this, would we really just, you know... run away like this? Would we really throw away precious (and limited) ammunition shooting one-handed and unaimed through close-passing trees like this?

Doesn't seem likely.

The barrel of my weapon *whacks* against the side of a passing tree, which very nearly deflects my fire back into my following teammates.

This is stupid! It's wasteful, it's unrealistic, and if nothing else, it gives our position away, making it easier to locate, chase, and trap us. So why are we doing it?

A second weapon opens up on us from the same vicinity as the first, and now it's an all-out full-auto firefight tattering and strobing the night, with the three of us barreling right through the middle of it like idiots. In my mind, bullets flit and whicker all around me. Ricochets skip, whistle, and whine past my ears, and wood chips and shredded leaves burst into flight on all sides. And in the corner of my brain that's been keeping a running tab, I've just been killed for the fourth time tonight.

Hi, Mom! Guess what just happened to me... again!

I wonder how the other teams are reacting to all this racket.

But the fire from the clearing finally peters out (*ooo... that's* realistic), followed closely by the three of us running our own clips dry. Then the crest of the rise is upon us, and with a desperate gasping lunge, we flog our way over the top and out of sight from the clearing.

We lope a little way down the shallow back-slope, stumbling once or twice among the hidden complexities underfoot, until we find an extra-dark pocket of shadow, and all go to ground to just listen for a minute or two.

The first thing BB says once we're all huddled together is, "*Reload.*"

Good idea.

But it's my first time trying to switch magazines blind, or with gloves on, or while I'm breathing like a runaway furnace, for that matter. I can't see anything below eye-level, and my Nomex gloves, while thin and even fairly touch-sensitive, are not *that* dexterous. Ejecting my empty mag is simple enough—*good old gravity*—and extricating a fresh one from my ammo pouch, though a little fumble-fingered, goes mostly without a hitch. I even manage to insert the new clip into the weapon after only two tries, feeling it snick into place and lock there. I 'charge' the weapon (chamber a round), and flick the safety back in place. Then I start looking for the ejected empty amid all the ground clutter.

And after thirty seconds or so of padding around the roots and mulch with my fingertips, I come to the conclusion that it is gone.

Dammit! Where the hell did it go?

"*Okay, Steve*," says BB in a low panting whisper, "*Where to now?*"

I abandon my futile search for my ammo clip, and attempt to look (or at least *sound*) competent instead.

"*Well, fifty meters or so on a 166 heading ought to get us back on our original track, and we can pick up where we left off from there.*"

I think.

"*Okay then. Let's do it.*" And without another second wasted on contemplation, the two of them hoist themselves back to their feet.

Wait a minute! Who's in charge here?

I take an extra second or two anyway, ostensibly shrugging my rucksack into a better position on my back. But in reality, I'm doing one last furious (and unrequited) pat-down of the ground clutter, looking for my discarded magazine. Then I give it up, and heave myself upright.

Hell, I had too many damned ammo clips anyway.

* * *

NIGHT IS FULL UPON us by the time we reach what my hopelessly jumbled pace count says should be our first waypoint. I opt, however, not to convey my personal lack of confidence in the precision of my navigation to my senior teammates. Instead, I simply signal them and take a knee beside a wet and mossy tree, which is itself barely a dozen steps short of yet another forest road.

Who knows? Maybe this is exactly *where we're supposed to be.*

BB shuffles forward, and settles beside me

"*This it?*" he whispers.

"*By my count,*" I whisper back, somewhat evasively.

"*Radio,*" he says, holding out an all-but-invisible gloved hand.

I unclip the prick's handset from the D-ring on my web gear, and hand it to him. I feel some tugging at my back as he checks the settings, then hear the muted murmurings of a man talking quietly into his cupped hand. He pauses and mumbles, pause and mumbles, for most of another minute. Then he nudges my arm and hands the thing back to me. Miles has now joined us.

"*We're a little early,*" whispers BB, "*So we need to standby here until they call us back with our new waypoint data.*"

"*Great,*" says Miles.

"*Fuck,*" say I.

"*So let's find some good cover, and make ourselves comfortable. It could be anywhere from fifteen to thirty minutes or so.*"

'Comfortable?'

"*Rog.*"

"*Roger that.*"

Wonderful. Not even back a *week* yet, and I'm already doing another hasty goddamned bivouac.

I hate hasty goddamned bivouacs.

* * *

AN HOUR-AND-A-HALF LATER, and I'm still shivering in place.

Even with the extra added layer of my field jacket now, the chill has sunk all the way into my bones, and wave after wave of the rolling shudders just keeps hammering through my body.

The main problem is my wet *inner* layers. That mad dash through that firefight a klick or two back apparently generated just enough sweat to dampen the layers of clothing closest to my skin. And this had gone unnoticed throughout the rest of the hike simply because the continued physical exertion had kept my body temperature up. But once we'd stopped, after the first half hour of motionlessness hunkered down at the base of this tree, my body heat had melted away, and the deepening cold found those moist inner layers.

That was when I dragged out my new field jacket and put it on... to almost no avail. It was just too lightweight.

Great!

Right now, with my knees tucked up against my chest, I've got my jacket draped *over* me like a feeble little blanket. I've taken my arms out of its sleeves and snuggled them in tight within the cocoon, but again without effect. *I am friggin' freezing!* And it is taking every ounce of self-control and restraint that I can muster just to keep from screaming, "*What the fuck are we waiting for?! Let's go!!!*"

But if the two old coots bundled beside me can remain quiet and motionless for all this time, then by-God, *so can I! Dammit!*

I take my mind off my miseries by imagining all the other grunts that could be out here in these woods with us tonight. Air Force *and* Army. Who knows? There could be a couple dozen of the sorry bastards curled up in silent suffering right now—maybe right over there, across that scrawny little road, for all I know—believing themselves to be alone and forgotten in the world, just like me.

Or maybe I'm the only one in the business who's just too stupid or insufficiently trained to know how to get through these moments 'comfortably'. Or at least *patiently*.

Gawd, I hate this shit!

Come on! Come on! Come on!! COME ON!!

The handset for my prick, clipped to my web gear right beside my head, mutters something, and I snatch it up to my ear. *Damned if I'm waiting for BB to waddle over here.*

I draw a deep and steadying breath, and key the mike.

"*Team Three, go.*"

"*Team Three,*" says the unrecognizable little voice inside the handset, "*Advise when ready to copy your new coordinates.*"

"*Team Three is ready,*" I whisper back, trying my best to sound bored and even nonchalant.

A quiet rustle and the brush of a displaced twig tells me that BB has heard my whispers, and has moved close to investigate. But I pay him no heed. The only thing in the *world* that I care about now is the much anticipated call to *move*, and to where. And I am listening for that with all my might.

"*Roger that, Command,*" I say, "*Team Three copies all.*" Then I shrug off my pathetic little 'blanket-jacket', and turn to face the BB-shaped shadow beside me. "*We're moving. Now.*"

Yes, General Steve has decided that we're moving, now. *So let's go!*

I don and button up my jacket correctly, heft my ruck back onto my shoulders, then take my red-lensed flashlight, press it against the face of the compass, and burn it for a good five seconds or so. And when I pull the flashlight away, the phosphorescent compass dial glows bright enough to illuminate BB's face.

I rise to my aching feet (my heels have started hurting again, the same way they did down at Little Rock), take my new heading, then close up my compass and let it drop to the end of the parachute cord lanyard I'd jury-rigged around my neck. Miles and BB are standing next to me in the darkness once I've finished.

"*Ready when you are,*" whispers BB.

I don't even bother answering him. I just start walking.

* * *

DAMN! IN THE DAYLIGHT, the ground clutter in these woods hadn't looked anywhere near this tangled and convoluted and uneven. But right now, I can't seem to find a single square meter of surface cover that's firm or flat enough to step into with any confidence. Every step is a fishing trip, dipping a frozen toe into the gnarled void and feeling around for stable purchase. I go from balancing on slime-slick roots, to ripping my feet out of the mud and brambles, to clocking my shin on a low tree stump, to feeling my way down the steep embankment of some dry debris-filled creek bed. And after half an hour of tippy-toeing blindly through this snarling black labyrinth, I can't believe how *low* my pace count still is. It's like we haven't covered any distance *at all!*

If somebody threw the lights on right now, I bet I could turn around, and with some lucky aiming and a decent wind-up, I could still throw a rock back to the spot where I just sat frozen for the previous hour-and-a-half.

No stars, no moon, and only the faintest hint of a cobalt glow seeping through the treetops, seemingly emanating from everywhere. That's kept my face constantly buried in my compass tonight. No other way to tell where we're going.

Glad I listened to Skeeter's recommendation about tying off a big loop of parachute cord to my compass, and hanging it around my neck like a two-foot-long medallion. It's come in damned handy more times than I can count.

The effort, the strain, and the struggle have brought back my body heat too. The chills and shivers have subsided, unnoticed until just now. The endless creeping and stretching and balancing and sidestepping must have thrown my muscles into overdrive or something because, despite the biting wet cold, I am once again 'comfortable' (temperature-wise, anyway), although still a little damp in the long johns. Deep under all these insulating layers, my body is once again moistening my thermal undies with sweat.

Dammit!

Well, as long as we don't have to do any more of those long silent 'intermissions' again, I should be alright. Continuous movement seems to be the antidote to those seeping chills.

* * *

AMONG THE SMOKY BLUE pixie dust outlining the forest clutter (*where is that dim glow coming from anyway?*), a long horizontal line now crosses my path like a lowered railroad crossing gate. A bead of slightly lesser shadow limned in weak blue. A fallen tree, as it turns out. A log barrier about waist-high.

I feel it out with my hands, shove against it, checking it for stability and rottenness. Then, having ascertained its solidity, strength, and permanence in its place, I straddle it, just like a horse.

BB bumps into me just then, and spits out a hissing apology as only a Combat Controller knows how.

"*Jesus H. Christ on a fuckin' pogo stick! You scared the sideways fuck outa' me!*"

I don't understand it either, but it cracks me up.

"*Just making my way over this log, man,*" I mutter in return. "*Keep your damned panty hose on.*"

Though it wasn't that high to mount in the first place, now that I'm astride the downed tree, for some reason my foot is just not finding the ground on its other side. And as my weight slips further and further over the 'saddle,' I realize two more things: (1) for whatever reason, the ground *is* lower on the other side here, and if I don't back off *right now*, my dismount is not going to be pretty. And (2) regardless of whatever choices I make now—regardless of what I hang onto, or what I pull toward—I'm *going* the rest of the way over, right the hell now, whether I'm ready or not, and whether I *fight* it or not. My top-heavy ruck-and-prick combo, now tilted beyond the point of no return, has assured that.

And before my grappling can find a better handhold, gravity tips the scales, and over I go.

Now, toppling out of sight and landing on my ass in the wet mulch would be embarrassing enough even without my usual embellishments. *You'd think.* But I don't believe in doing anything halfway. No, I believe in going that extra mile, and actually trying to *kill* myself. And on this particular occasion, to choose to do so with my *compass.*

Unbeknownst to me, somewhere in mid-crossing, my compass—dangling from that long lanyard and trailing behind me as I slither over the log—drags through a sturdy fork of old branch stubs. And as I tumble the rest of the way over now, all *but* the compass zips past, over, or *through* that fork unfettered. All *but* the compass. *That* bottles up *between* the stubs, and slams to a stop… which instantly snaps the slack out of the lanyard… which, in turn, stops my *neck* from traveling any further… even though my ass still hasn't found the ground yet. And, just as advertised, it takes a lot more than that to break parachute cord.

Suddenly, in the near-total darkness, I am *lynched*. My head gets wrenched sideways, my tongue pops out, my arms flail, and my arrested descent now swings me laterally, into the *side* of the fallen tree. My shoulders and head bang off its flank, and my legs flop into the muddy leaves below.

For another five seconds or so, I thrash against the choking—groping at the lanyard with both hands and digging with both feet to get them back under me, anything to get the weight off my throat—until at last I'm on one knee, and ripping my head out of the noose. I gasp, and fall back on my heels, feeling around my neck for the rope burns.

Oh my gawd! What a stupid way to go!

Looky, Ma! The fifth time in one night that I was killed!

Only this time, FOR REAL!

After another full minute of awkward silence, a whisper from BB floats over the top of the log.

"*We good to go there, Steve?*"

I stand up, straighten up, and steady my strangled breathing enough to inject a little nonchalance into my whispered reply.

"Nah. Got a little drop-off here. You might wanna' go to the right about *five or ten meters, and try to cross over there.*"

"*Roger that.*"

I hear the rustle of their movement, the snapping of the odd twig or two, and the muttered curses of two old, fat and flustered phantoms.

Who's kidding whom about this 'silent-but-deadly' shit?

* * *

FORTY MINUTES LATER, I once again reach the end of my pace count.

This *should* be where 'Command' said the Jeep ('the Mark') would be.

Theoretically, at least, this is where all the divergent three-man teams will *re*converge (assuming that everyone's compass and pace-counting skills were better than mine tonight). But I'm still neck-deep in the thickest part of the forest here, nary a road nor clearing anywhere within sight in this inky blue-tinged darkness. And that's embarrassing.

Between running firefights and lynching logs, starless skies and awkward irregular footing, my night nav was bound to be a little more 'off' than normal anyway. But standing here, looking around at the uniform density of the woods on all sides of me, I wouldn't be surprised if we weren't even in the same *county* as that Mark. This time, I've got no confidence whatsoever that I've gotten us anywhere close to our target.

Miles and BB huff up beside me, and pause to take in our unlikely surroundings themselves.

Okay. Who's going to be the first to admit that we're lost?

"*So,*" mutters BB, "*This it?*"

I sigh. "*Yeh. Supposedly. This is where the numbers run out, anyway.*"

We stand there, looking around as if something might suddenly change into something useful (or at least recognizable), but seeing nothing different from what we've been slogging through for the last couple of hours... shadows smothered in darkness, trees crowded among trees, backed up by ever more trees, surrounded by an eternity of trees... but nothing that even distantly resembles a 'landmark' of any kind.

(*sigh*)

My heading was good. I'm absolutely certain of that. But my pace count? That was probably off by miles.

This is pathetic.

So... what do we do now?

Miles is the next to chime in. "*Okay then. Let's just give it a couple more minutes.*"

What? 'A couple more minutes?' Why? How is time spent sitting around doing nothing going to help?

But wait we do.

After a few seconds, I hear BB rummaging around in his thigh pockets, then quietly unscrewing the lid on something.

His friggin' spittin' t'backy, fer criminey's sake! Oy! Gag a maggot!

A moment or two later though, and all is absolutely quiet again.

I don't get this. What are we doing here? Shouldn't we be 'probing' or 'bracketing' or calling on the radio for directions, or *something* productive?

"*Um... Sgt. Burley...*" I whisper.

"*Sshhh,*" he interrupts. "*Quiet. Listen.*"

Huh? 'Quiet?' How much more quiet could it get? And 'listen?'

For what?

I sigh—quietly, of course—shrug my ruck a little more squarely on my shoulders, and lean against the nearest tree.

"*Sshhh.*" Miles this time.

Alright. Somebody needs to explain to me just what...

From somewhere far off in the woods, the distant chittering of a radio scratches the silence. Desperately soft—we would have missed it entirely if I'd so much as changed the hand holding my weapon—but there it is nonetheless.

There's no way to tell what's being said—it probably wouldn't have even registered as the faint squawk of a radio to a lesser trained ear—but everybody here recognizes it. Even me. And even *I* know that if I can hear it *at all*, then it's not coming from the handset of a shoulder-mounted PRC-77. It's coming from a *speaker*. And the only place you'd find a radio *speaker* out here in the deep primeval would be in the back of a communications Jeep.

Which means that somewhere fairly close by is our target... the mythical MRC-108... 'the Mark.'

I'm turning my head, trying to triangulate on the sound, when a supernova of light flares to life in the trees off to our right, painfully blinding to my dark-adapted eyes. It's the Mark's headlights, spearing through the lattice of the forest ahead of us, originating about thirty meters off to our right.

Damn! My navigation actually came pretty danged close to it!

The headlights flash on and off for about five seconds, then disappear again, plunging the woods back into pitch darkness.

Apparently, one of the other teams called in for a little help finding the Jeep. *Well, at least it wasn't us.*

BB sighs as he hoists himself to his feet.

"*I'm guessin' the Mark's over that-a-way.*"

5
NOT EVEN HALF WAY THERE

OKAY, NOW I REMEMBER why I wanted to quit so badly.

And now that I think about it, that's exactly how I *did* quit.

Once again I'm huddled in the darkness, shivering hard from the inside out. Sweat-dampened *inner* layers have let the *outer* chill back in—again—and there's not a damned thing I can do about it. I can't get up, or move around to re-stoke my body heat. I sure as hell can't afford to take anything *off*. And, short of dragging my sleeping bag out of its containment, I've got nothing else to layer *on*, not even the poncho liner that served me so well at Little Rock.

No, that's back on my bed again, in my room, in *The Castle*... right where it's the least helpful to me right now.

It took most of an hour for all six teams to rendezvous at the Jeep. Miles, BB and I (Team Three) were actually the *second* trio in, right behind Team One, the Rocky, Skeeter and Smoke party, who'd done us the favor of calling ahead to have the Jeep flash its headlights (apparently I wasn't the worst compass man in the team's history after all).

But at least while we'd waited *there*, I could pace in furious circles, rub my arms, and pound the cold off me. Not *here* though, hiding in this dry ditch, just off the side of this new dirt road. Here I've got to be as quiet and still—and professional—as everybody else... *dammit!*

How the hell can they not *be cold? They're wearing the same stuff I am, carrying the same gear, moving through the same woods. Why aren't* their *thermal undies cold with refrigerated sweat like mine? What the hell are they doing different? Why am I the only one shivering and fidgeting out here?!*

Or am I?

I mean, once everybody had formed up into a single eighteen-man formation again back there at the Jeep, we'd set out marching on this road at a fairly brisk clip, once more spread and spaced and tromping down the opposing shoulders in silence and darkness. And once again, just like before, my body heat had steadily returned, even warmed my spongy inner layers back up, and I was 'comfortable' again (if you didn't count my aching shoulders and heels, or my half-garroted ass) for most of that next hour-long march... to here.

We had one lighter moment though, when, out in the woods on our right—where Rocky had been paralleling us as a flanker (*and man, I still don't see the point or the 'advantage' of having men walking off to either side of the column like that, having to navigate and break trail on their own, alone and vulnerable, just itching to get lost or killed*)—we heard a couple of loud snaps, followed by a much louder *crash!* and a subdued "*Shit!*" The rest of us bolted off into the trees and took up defensive stations there, waiting to find out what that noise was.

More snapping, crunching, and a couple more minor crashes followed, all riding atop a steady undertow of muttered profanity, and then... silence.

We waited... until a lonely little voice wafted out of the darkness.

Rocky's.

"*Um... guys?*"

Sniggering rippled through the underbrush on either side of the road.

Then, from back near the rear of my column, a couple of murmuring voices leaked forward, followed by an assertive grunt, and the crackling footsteps of another teammate being sent off into the woods.

As it turned out, it was Spew, dispatched by Smoke to offer whatever assistance was necessary for Rocky. A minute later though, an identical volley of snaps, with an identical *crash*, ended Spew's tippy-toed approach. This, of course, ended a few seconds later with his patented giggle, trickling through the trees like the sound of a happy drunk. And *that* triggered a *wave* of hushed laughter among the rest of us.

Yep, folks. That's how the professionals do it... laughing in the pitch black bushes, on either side of a dirt road, in the middle of the night, in the middle of friggin' nowhere.

It seemed that Spew had found the same abandoned foxhole that Rocky had found, in exactly the same way, and had landed on top of him. Together though, they managed to extricate themselves from the entanglement and resumed the march.

Most of another twenty minutes then passed before our fearless leadership finally stopped us, right here in this little clearing off the side of the road (where I've been shivering ever since), looking out across that huge open field over there. They told us to hunker down and hold this spot, while Manny, Mutt, and the 'LT' (the team's new second-in-command, Lieutenant Kostas) scouted ahead for a new hasty bivouac site for the night.

Naturally, as soon as I'd finished adjusting my little hidey-hole, and had settled in to wait, I could feel the night chills running their fingers over me again. My radiated heat began to dwindle away to nothing, and despite my pre-emptive efforts to prevent the cool-down, after half an hour, maybe forty-five minutes, I was shivering again.

This sucks!

And where the hell did the Three Musketeers go? How long does it take to sniff out a decent hidey-hole in a friggin' forest? And come to think of it, what the hell's wrong with these trees right here?

Once again, after estimating a ten to fifteen minute wait, they've now been gone for more than an *hour*. And *nothing!* Neither a peep nor a peek from our 'valiant scouts' in all this time… and I am *fucking freezing!*

But, if everyone else can somehow huddle out here in stillness and in silence for hours in these temperatures, then I guess I have to too.

Dammit!

* * *

MY WATCHBAND IS A clever/stupid contrivance that had seemed merely *clever* at the time I'd bought it… *clever* because of the cover flap that lays over the watch's face, thereby masking its luminescent glow and hiding it from lurking enemies, but *stupid* because of the velcro they used to secure that same flap, which *announces* your presence to those same lurking enemies every time you rip it open to check the time… which I do now.

RIP! 11:12pm.

Fuck.

* * *

IT'S AFTER 11:30 BY the time our trusty 'scouts' finally stroll back into our dark little cordon—*an hour-and-a-half* since they headed out on their 'fifteen-minute' mission—and they call us together in the middle of the road with a couple of light raps on their weapons.

I roll out from under the ridiculous leaves I'd piled on top of myself for warmth (another wasted effort, since it not only didn't make me any warmer, but the jackhammering of all my quivering muscles made the leaves rustle), and step up to join the huddle. Manny, as usual, does all the talking... or in this case, all the murmuring.

"Okay, we're a little over half an hour's straight march from the EZ, maybe an *hour* covert."—*Great! Then let's get moving! Please God, let me get moving again!*—"Unfortunately, there's very little cover between here and there, so there's no secure place to set up a bivouac."

Without looking back, he waves one of his huge gloved paws toward the open field beyond the treeline, which is completely visible, oddly *illuminated*, actually, bathed in that strange cool blue light that has dimly blanketed everything... the nighttime glow of Tacoma, as it turns out, just over the horizon and reflecting off the belly of the low overcast.

"So," Manny concludes, "We checked out just about every dark spot between here and there... and we think *this* is probably as good a bivouac site as we're going to find tonight."

Oh... no! No-no-no-no! Not here! I just spent the last hour-and-a half frozen to the ground here, clinging desperately to the notion that any minute now we were going to get up and MOVE to our final staging point, a move that would relight my body's pilot light, and end with me being able to pull out my damned sleeping bag, and sustain that heat for the rest of the night!

Now you're suggesting that I sit back down and just settle into my icy undergarments again for another five hours instead?! No! No-no-no-no-no!

"All-righty then," says Captain Forth, "Let's find ourselves some cover over here at the edge of the clearing, and finish this night out."

But...!

"Since we've got the manpower to cover one-hour watches tonight," adds Manny as we start to walk, "Spew, why don't you take the first hour?"

"Roger that," he answers without hesitating.

Aw shit. Not again! Should I even bother guessing who's going to get the dreaded 'second watch?'

"Airman Stipp,"—*shocked, I am!*—"You relieve him around 12:30 or so, okay?"

No kidding? An hour from now? Imagine my surprise.

"Copy that," I sigh.

What-the-hell-ever. If your life is going to suck, you might as well be thorough about it.

About the only thing missing from this experience right now, is a freezing rain.

Don't... even... think it.

* * *

OH GOD, I AM *going to have to kill something.*

Nothing is where I left it when I packed this damned rucksack. I can't get to anything without unloading a mountain of crap that I cleverly packed on top of it first. And in this darkness, every search is a blind grope. Of course, every knot is also an impenetrable granny knot as well. Gloves on or off makes no difference whatsoever. *Nothing* on this rig will open, untie, or let go.

Fuck!

I was surprised enough when everyone started unhorsing their rucks and unfurling their sleeping gear like they were just camping out in their own backyards. That's a little different from how we did 'hasty bivouacs' at CCS, where we slept in our full regalia, our backs against our rucks against our trees, ready to bolt at a moment's notice. Then again, at CCS it was raining at the time, and we had to keep everything under our ponchos anyway.

Not here, though. Here they're treating it more like a regular old 'camp-out'... everything but the tents, the fire, and the gabby bullshit.

Not that I'm complaining, mind you. Without any other options for keeping warm, I'd been trying to figure out some way to employ my new sleeping bag without defeating the whole point of a hasty bivouac. As it turns out though, that's apparently not an issue with this group. *Everybody's* unpacking *everything*, and making themselves comfortable here.

Except for me, of course.

In no time, the entire tribe is bedded down and squirreling in deeper for the night... while I'm still fumbling around, dropping and kicking and stumbling over all the junk in my own little private disaster area, unpacking and repacking all the irrelevant clutter I'd brought along—*because I didn't know any better!*—and tussling mightily with the cords tying off my sleep-roll to the frame of the rucksack.

Everything is fighting me. *Nothing* is letting go easily.

And to top it all off, right now—at a moment when I'm brewing up a righteous little fury, intense enough to blow both temples right off the sides of my head, heave my fucking rucksack into the trees, and cut loose a furious roar of frustration—I am compelled by the circumstances to be *excruciatingly quiet!* Covert. *Stealthy*, even. *Aagh!*

And so I continue to fiddle with the damned tie-downs. An empty canteen clatters off a tree root. My gas mask makes a funny flatulent sound when my weight, settling onto one wet knee, settles instead onto the invisible holster. And though I'm doing my *utmost* to control it, little grunts and hisses and whispered profanity continue to sputter from me in the darkness and silence.

This is embarrassing. Although I can't see anything or any*one* around me in their shadowy nests, in my mind's eye, I can quite *clearly* 'see' all the faces turning my way in bemusement as I flog and flail my way through my oafish ministrations.

This is pathetic!

I finally give up—*screw the damned knots!*—and just wrestle the bagged sleepsack out of the loops of parachute cord without untying them. It'll be a bitch-and-a-half trying to stuff it back *into* those same loops later, but that's just something I'll have to worry about *then*.

Then the knot at the throat of the waterproof bag refuses to let go.

Aw, you gotta' be shittin' me!

I'm about one hiccup away from ripping out my combat knife and *cutting* the damned cord, when one of the gnarls in the knot finally succumbs to my thumbnail, and I untangle the rest of it in a flurry. I turn the damned pouch over, and shake my sleeping bag out on the ground.

Gawd, how am I ever going to gather all this shit up again in the dark? I mean... GAH!

Then, as I'm unrolling the bag and hunting for its zipper, another thought occurs to me... *How should I climb into this thing? With my muddy boots on? How did everyone else do it? Surely they didn't take their boots off, did they? But what about all the mud and leaves and shit?*

What's the correct way to do this?

NOBODY TELLS ME NOTHIN' AROUND HERE!!!

Fuck it! I throw myself on the ground, and yank the damned sleeping bag over me, *still zipped closed*, like a plump blanket.

I hate this shit!

6
GAS! GAS! GAS!

MY MISERIES ARE JUST starting to blur out, as I cave in to my exhaustion and aggravation, when I hear a *pop!* and a *hiss!*, then the sound of the hiss passing overhead. Whatever-it-is thumps to ground behind me somewhere. I stick my head up, confused. *What the...?*

Suddenly, the woods straight out from me explode in stuttering light and the chattering of assault rifles.

Holy shit-on-a-stick! We're under attack now?!!!

I throw my sleeping bag off me, and start pawing through my little landfill. My first befuddled 'instinct' is to grab my GAU-5 and return fire, while I backpedal behind better cover. But just as I snatch it up, I hear someone cough, then the voice of the LT—coming from back where the 'hissing' landed—yelling, "*Gas! Gas-gas-gas! Get your masks on quick!*"

Oh gawd, tell me it ain't so.

Another weapon starts rattling away *behind* me. *One of 'my' guys returning fire, or another attacker opening up on our flank?*

I throw my weapon down, and instead begin a mad scramble for my gas mask. I'd rather be pretend-riddled to death in a simulated crossfire than draw even one whiff of that very real fucking gas.

Going for a record, Ma! My sixth time killed in one mission!

Naturally then, in accordance with how well everything else has gone this night, I cannot, *for the life of me*, find that damned gas mask *anywhere*. In fact, I'm still padding around blindly—my eyes clamped uselessly shut, my lips pursed in desperate futility, my cheeks inflated, my breath held—when all the clattering weapons abruptly cut off, and the woods go silent again.

Well, 'silent' except for all the coughing and struggling and swearing that's still going on all around me... except for that.

Everybody appears to be a little too preoccupied to even notice that they've all just been machine-gunned to death. Right now, it's all about escaping that dreaded gas.

I finally locate the damned holster—it must have been knocked off the top of my filleted rucksack when I'd first gone for my weapon—and despite the resistance of its snaps (*of course they resisted! What else could I expect on a night like this?*), I rip the thing open and slap the mask over my face in an instant. I do the old blow-and-clear, suck-and-seal routine as fast as I can... *and a wet farting sound blats along the rightside jaw-line of the mask!*

Air is slurping in! I don't have a good seal!

Are you friggin' kidding me?!!!

I wrench the whole thing into a new alignment, pat it down all the way around its seams, then try it again... *and that farting sound is still there!*

Oh great googly-moogly! I do NOT want any of that gas to get in!

Without a moment's hesitation then (but with plenty of post-sleep bewilderment), I grab my sleeping bag and plunge my head into it, gas mask and all, bundling it up tight around my neck.

— What the hell are you doing?

I don't know! But I've gotta' do something!

This, however, has the decidedly *unhelpful* side-effect of smothering my inlet vents—the silver-dollar-sized filters on both cheeks of the mask—making it damned near impossible to breathe. So I loosen the wrap of the sleeping bag around my *head*, but tighten it around my *throat*.

Even *I* don't really believe this is the best thing to do, though. And if I *look* half as stupid as I *feel* right now—and I don't see how that's possible (although the darkness surely helps)—the *rest of the team* would be too mortified to even allow me to continue living. They'd *have* to put me out of my misery, for *their* sake.

Gawd. Imagine what they'd see if the lights came on right now... some idiot, squirming around out in the open, *in the middle of an active battlefield, no less*, half consumed by his sleeping bag, and looking like he's being swallowed and digested by a big fat dirty-green snake.

Forget about taking cover from the enemy's fire, or even bothering to return it. Just stick your head in a bag, hold your breath, and close your eyes. That'll make it all go away.

Oh my gaahhhd!

But nobody's saying anything. Nobody's shouting any commands, no one's organizing a defensive perimeter or even a tactical retreat, and no one—on *either side*—is shooting at anyone else anymore. Or at least I can't hear them if they are.

What kind of firefight is this?

Fact is, the only noise I can hear at all now, aside from the loud sucking sounds of my own breathing, is the mask-muffled coughing of a couple of guys somewhere back in the woods behind me.

Is this even real? Shouldn't somebody be doing something?

Look who's asking.

After a couple more minutes of stalled time then—everything in a sort of limbo, as if *no one* knows what to do next—it finally dawns on me that if my hands just have to clutch *something* against the sides of my face, *it doesn't need to include a sleeping bag!* If my gas mask can't get a good seal along the jaw-line on its own, I can still dump the sleeping bag, and instead use my hands to manually press the rubber in place *directly*, sealing it airtight.

A-duuhhhh!

And so, at long last, I pull my head out of my bag (and my ass as well, simultaneously), look around at the surrounding gloom, and with one hand clapped under my chin (such that my thumb and forefinger can pin the mask tight to both sides of my jaw), I start a low crawl over to my GAU-5, and one-arm it into a defensive position over the top of my rucksack.

Oh, much better. I'm all-pro now, for sure, hiding behind my own luggage like a childhood fort.

But still, nothing else happens. Even the sporadic coughing steadily fades away until the night is once again silent.

So... now what?

Without all the coughing and cussing, not to mention any form of command directives, it's becoming easier and easier to fret over where the hell everybody *went*. Did they pull back to somewhere else, and I just missed the call? Am I laying out here in the open all by myself, a shivering dumbass huddled among the litter of his scattered kit, while everyone else is off in the woods somewhere, regrouping for a tactical counterstrike or something? Right about now, that seems entirely believable. And it's starting to worry me.

Fortunately, just five or six feet behind me and smothered in rubber, the muffled voice of Lt. Kostas breaks the stillness.

"Alright, guys. The gas should be clear. So, masks off."

Hmmm. *Why wasn't* his *mask off when he said that?*

I am not convinced, and opt to wait an extra moment or two, just to see how everyone else fares. *Nothing like using your own teammates as human guinea pigs, ay Stevie?* But, for the first time tonight, one of my damned choices actually pays off.

Within five seconds of the LT's command, I hear a rustle in the dry leaves behind me... followed immediately by someone's voice gagging out, "*Jesus Christ!,*" before collapsing into another fit of coughing. The coughing is quickly smothered again, as their gas mask is hurriedly slapped back in place... it sounds like.

I hear another voice—one that sounds an awful lot like Spew—choke out a throttled "*Fuck!*" And somewhere further back, I hear a strangled "*Ack!,*" some more gagged coughing, and then the LT's muffled voice shouting, "*Disregard! Disregard! Keep your masks on!*"

Which I do. Obviously, I'm a natural at this shit.

Now what?

It's tough to hear clearly through the muzzle of his gas mask, but I think the next voice—almost a minute later—is that of Captain Forth.

"*Well, gentlemen,*" he sighs, as if through a pillow, "*Might as well make yourselves comfortable. We'll be pulling out at oh-three-hundred, and this is where we'll be waiting, so... get what sleep you can.*"

What? *We're sleeping* here? *And we're sleeping in our gas masks?*

We've just been assaulted and gassed by an 'enemy' that obviously *knows right where we are*. And since I'm pretty sure we didn't get any of *them*, and since they could attack us again any time they want to, shouldn't we at least, you know... *move?* Or *hide?* Or at least act like we would if we were actually operating under these conditions in the real world? I mean, isn't that the whole point of us being out here tonight? To practice doing things the right way? Otherwise, *why are we even out here at all?*

I can ignore procedure and common sense from a warm bed at home.

But, nope. Nothing to do now, I guess, but 'get comfortable' in my gas mask, my frozen feet, and my unopened sleeping bag, and settle in for three or four more hours of shivering misery.

And that's just what I do.

7
THE NIGHT THAT TIME STOOD STILL

I COLLAPSE INTO A COMA, only to splutter awake again, seemingly seconds later, chilled to the bone, and smothering in my damned gas mask. I kick my way a little deeper into my sleeping bag, forcing the zipper down with my filthy boots, and wrench the opened portion around my shoulders like a soggy comforter.

I contemplate removing my gas mask. But the snoring I can hear around me still sounds snorkeled by mask rubber, and well... if *they're* still wearing them, I guess I'd better stick with it myself.

I fidget, and bundle myself tighter.

I tuck my empty gas mask holster under my neck, as a pillow.

I shiver in jarring waves, and I check my watch for the elapsed time.

Barely twenty minutes since I last checked. Gah!

And somewhere in the middle of stewing over this whole situation, unbeknownst to me, I fade into oblivion again... for about thirty-five more minutes of flickering consciousness. Then I jolt awake... again... and repeat the cycle all over... *again*... over and over and over again, all night friggin' long. In and out, back and forth... jostled awake, smothered to death, lurching back to awareness, surrendering to the darkness.

11:45, 12:22, 12:56, 1:19, 1:33, 2:04... *oh, my freakin' gourd!*

* * *

MY BODY FINALLY JUST quits *trying* to sleep. No matter how tightly clamped my eyes might be, or how tightly bundled my quivering form... no matter how much (or how little) attention I pay to my general exhaustion, or to the cutting cold, or to the metronomic sucking of air through my filters... no matter how much mental exertion I put toward draining away my consciousness, nothing changes. Nothing. And time just bogs down to a crawl.

I tremble and squirm.

I tuck and tighten.

I shuffle and bundle, ruffle and writhe...

And then I just give up. I've apparently gotten all the sleep I'm going to get tonight.

Dammit! I HATE this shit!

I wrestle my digital watch up in front of my eyepiece... 2:41.

Enough! Wake-up is in twenty more minutes anyway. It's going to take approximately forever to pack all my junk up again, and I'll be warmer tussling through that process *now* than laying here, counting the glacial passage of the remaining minutes. So I'm done huddling.

First things first: I break the unreliable seal of my gas mask, and sniff the air. It's been something like four hours since the gas attack, so it's gotta' be cleared up by now. Right? Still, once again, this ain't the best way to do this.

No stinging sensations, though. No watering or burning eyes, no burnt metal smells—*hell, we've probably had clean fresh air for hours now*—so it's time to retire the damned gas mask.

Damned straight, it is.

Next, I untangle myself from the half-opened sleeping bag. Then I attempt to fold and roll it up as tightly as possible, all in the deep and frigid darkness, not to mention the deep and total *silence*.

Once the thing is bundled as compactly as I can manage then, I pad my hand around in the shadows, groping for the waterproof bag it came in—wherever the hell it wound up after I ripped it off—then follow that with a grunting struggle to stuff one bag into the other, and tie off its top.

Now comes the tough part.

Now I've got to re-tie the bagged bundle to the bottom of my rucksack's frame, the main problem being that I never *un*tied it in the first place. In my earlier frustration—after numerous failed attempts to untie the damned thing in the dark—I had finally succumbed to my impatience, and simply *ripped* the bag out of its mooring lines, leaving the loops of cord *still tied* but empty. Now I've got to either stuff the bag back *into* those empty loops, or, if that winds up being as awkward as it *sounds* like it will, I'll have to untie those cords *now* just so that I can *re*-tie them again around this stupid waterproof bundle.

Aaugh!

With a teeth-grinding sigh then, I set about attempting Option One.

Blindfolded by the night and shivering in the cold, I drag all the components together, and start recombining my scattered 'luggage.' I think I detect other shadowy figures moving around me now, but I find that I no longer actually give a yodeling damn.

Ignoring them, I mash my sleeping bag flat under one knee. Then, after tussling with the ruck's strings and straps until I think I've found the correct cord, I wrestle the loop around the end of the bag. I think. At least I *try* to. But the damned thing just *will not go*, or stay where I put it, and I squirm and stretch and tug with all my might until, on the verge of screaming my guts out and stomping the whole fucking rig into a muddy wad, I finally stop and freeze there, clutching the ruck's lumbar support while I fight down the fury and its attendant shakes and heavy breathing.

Now though, I can definitely tell that the woods are stirring with silent airmen, sergeants and officers, so pausing to regain my elusive composure now seems to be appropriate. Another deep breath, and I bore back into my labors with renewed vigor... and *loathing*.

Five minutes later, my fully accoutered teammates are all up and milling around my tree, done with their preparations, and ready to march... and I'm still thrashing away on the ground with my rucksack and this stinkin' hateful sleeping bag.

Thank God they can't see my face right now—or read my seething mind—because if they could, they'd be breaking out the "**Jacket, Straight, Field Expedient, One Each**," and wrapping me up for the ride to the loony bin. Because I am friggin' *beside myself* with exasperation. If I didn't have an audience, I'd probably be whimpering right now.

Fuck it. I'll just hand-carry *the stinkin' sleeping bag back to McChord.*

And as the rest of the team gathers around Sgt. Santos for their marching orders, I do just that: I kick the damned sleeping bag aside, and start donning everything else.

Maybe I'll just leave the frappin' thing right here, and buy *a new one once* we get back to base. And why not? As far as I'm concerned, I'm officially DONE with this shit, as of right... the hell... NOW.

These guys may love this elemental lifestyle, but, more obviously than ever, *I am not one of them.*

In boiling silence then, I wrench my gas mask holster back onto my hips, cinch up my web gear, collect my weapon, and lurch over to the circle, still hefting the damned prick up onto my aching shoulders. And when I get within earshot of their low murmurs and chuckles, I find them quietly razzing Spew for failing to wake up his relief on watch. Namely, *me*.

Jeezy Pete! I forgot all about my turn on watch! And I was awake the whole damned night anyway!

I decide not to share that particular little tidbit of information. Besides, Spew seems perfectly comfortable eating their shit. So I let him.

* * *

IT'S 3:00AM NOW. Time to move out. And what am I doing?

I'm back at the base of 'my tree' again, knife in hand, going after my miserable sleeping bag one last time. No more pussyfooting around. This time *I mean business.*

While the rest of the troupe is assembling itself and making final adjustments, I shrug out of my rucksack again, and take my K-Bar to both of the recalcitrant lanyard loops hanging off its lumbar support. Two quick cuts, and both cords are severed. Then I seize that bitch of a bag, lay it between the loose ends and, with my full body weight kneeling on it, I re-tie those severed cords around the pouch as tightly as humanly possible.

Done! Finally!

Manny hisses for me to get my ass in line. I'm his radioman for this next stretch, and I'm supposed to be right in front of him in the column. I acknowledge him with a winded apology, heave everything back onto my shoulders, and tromp over into my place in line.

Everything about this *sucks*, including—perhaps *especially*—me. But if what we're about to do gets me closer to home, then I'm in. I'm cold and sore, and shivering as much from frustration as the soaking chill. But my attitude warms to the task ahead, to this final leg of this endless journey, and I settle in to the march.

Then it starts to rain.

* * *

ANOTHER HOUR LATER, AT *four o'clock* in the morning now, our column is brought to another halt, this time on the back side of a barn-sized knoll, the *front* side of which overlooks a broad and empty field. The field glows with that same dull cold blue from the reflected radiance of Tacoma's city lights, enough that I can just make out the dark bead of a road running along its far border, seemingly holding back the ocean of trees beyond.

According to Manny's map-reading, this field is our EZ... or it *will* be in another two-and-a-half hours anyway, once we've finished setting it up and declared it operational.

Between now and then, though—*surprise, sur-fucking-prise*—there's nothing to do but *wait. Again.*

Gaahhh!

Even the last hour's forced march wasn't enough to restore my body heat to full flower this time, what with the steady drizzle of chilled rain soaking everything that my poncho *would* have covered *if I'd thought to bring the damned thing along with me.*

And now? Now I get to sit down—again—and *wait—again—*for my uniform to re-freeze to my body, for my tolerance for misery to reach the end of its fuse, and for my will to live to shudder right out through my pores, and flutter off into the night. Whatever 'happy thoughts' I might have amassed during my first few days back from Miami have definitely evaporated now, obliterated by this wretched night-long exercise in discomfort, privation, and ineptitude.

I am just *so done*. I do believe I'd quit *right here* and *right now*, in this very field, if I thought I could march across to that road over there and thumb a ride home at four in the morning. But obviously, I can't. And as long as I'm going to have to cold-soak it out here for another two-and-a-half hours anyway, regardless of which way I go, I might as well sit here in shivering stoicism along with the rest of 'my team.' Make a final noble gesture for the cause, and all that... *then say goodbye to this shit for good. For ever! Period!*

Enough vacillating.

I dump my ruck and radio at the base of a tree as unceremoniously as I can, prop my GAU against the side of the pile, shrug off my web gear, and untangle myself from my gas mask holster. I kick the whole pile into a roughly U-shaped configuration, like a shallow OD-green 'nest.' Then I rip my arms out of my field jacket's sleeves, toss it over my head and shoulders like a blanket, and tuck myself into my nest of wet gear, curling up as tight and tiny as I can underneath the jacket.

I can hear others unpacking their sleeping bags once more. But as far as I'm concerned, I'd rather *die* tonight, frozen to the ground, than even touch that damned sleeping bag again.

And so—again—that's just exactly what I do.

* * *

4:22, 4:35, 4:48, 5:01—(**sigh**)—5:16, 5:22, 5:29... *Oh, come on!*
Can't sleep. Can't lie still. Can't get up and walk. Can't even stretch. *Can't friggin' stand it!*

And so, eternity passes... tectonically slow, maddeningly heedless and uncaring. Clocks and watches stop, cobwebs form, heavy with chilly dew. Generations rise and fall.

But when, at long *long* last—somewhere after six in the goddamned morning—the dense, low, saturated, and constantly leaking overcast finally begins to lighten, I am already on my feet (ostensibly to pee), but in reality, it's because I'm simply no longer *physically capable* of remaining fetal and shuddering anymore. I'd rather be up and pacing and potentially shot down by an enemy sniper, than huddling and freaking and screaming hysterically... which is what I'm about down to now.

A couple of the older, more established guys break out their morning C-Rats (*I didn't even think to bring any along... because it never crossed my mind that we'd be out here this long*), and for the first time, I witness that mysterious can of 'Sterno' in action. I'd always understood that its function was to heat whatever needed heating, but I'd never understood *how*. Now, after just a few seconds of scooping dirt into the lid of the can, tamping, soaking, and lighting it, Smoke has a presentable low blue flame licking at the base of his mess kit, coercing his canteen water to a boil... enough to provide hot water for everybody's coffee.

How quaint.

I don't drink coffee, though. Not that it matters much, since I didn't think to bring any anyway.

So I continue to pace around the chatty little gathering, rubbing my upper arms, dipping and bobbing as if to some unheard music in my head, and silently cursing everything and every*body* that led me to this moment, my own naively adventurous ass right at the top of the list.

On my second lap of our little enclave, I come upon a silhouetted figure standing on the limn of the knoll, his back to me, dark and striking against the dripping gray of the morning. It's Mutt, a PRC dangling from one hand, its handset in the other, pressing it against his ear. He's talking quietly with somebody while he looks out over the misty field, our soon-to-be all-important EZ.

Damn. That wildman just looks like he belongs here, as natural and primal as a puma watching over its domain. There's just something so, I don't know... something almost 'mythological' about the guy. The Vigilant Sentry. The Guardian on the Wall. The Warrior. Until his head drops and turns, and I see the cigarette ember dancing before his lips.

A second later, I hear him mutter, "*Aw, fuck me.*" Then he cuts loose a long and rolling fart, his microphone hand drops to his side in exasperation, and he adds, "*Son of a bitch.*"

Scratch one noble visage.

Good news?

With a disgusted grunt—and an extra *toot* from his other end—he throws the handset into its canvas pocket, sucks one last mighty drag from his cigarette and flicks it into the darkness. Then he wheels back toward the others without seeing (or at least *looking at*) me. I don't move as he passes.

Several crashing steps later, I hear his announcement behind me.

"EZ's canceled, gents!"

"What?"

"Figures."

"How come?"

"It's this damned overcast deck. Too thick to do anything with it *here*, too dense and low back at McChord. They said they can't even take-off in this shit, much less drop through it into a forest clearing they can't even see from above. So, we're done here, folks... unless you've got something else for us while we're out here, Cap'n Forth."

Aw, don't ask for more shit to do! That's like telling the teacher she forgot to hand out homework.

A long sigh rolls out through all the cursing. Captain Forth's, I presume.

Then his 'little kid' voice answers, "No, Sergeant. Nothing else from me. Let's just call it a night."

Oh, now *we're going to call it a night? Now that it's friggin'* daylight!

Mutt goes back to the radio, and calls for Cole to hustle up a bus to come out and get us. Everyone else drops their last pretense of mission dedication, sloughs off their gear, and settles in to enjoy a complete C-Rat breakfast while they wait out the hour or two it's going to take Sgt. Mabry to get out here with the bus.

Me? I stomp back to my disheveled nest, cobble together all my junk in a petulant huff, then march up to Greg and Rocky where they're busily divvying up each other's Cs.

"I'm going over to the road, if anyone asks," I growl. "I'll flag down the truck when it gets here."

Then I tramp out of the circle without waiting for a response. I march out of the shadowed woods, through the early dawn drizzle, and across the useless field to the road on the other side.

Nobody stops me. Or follows me. Or joins me.

STORY XXXV

AND LIFE GOES ON

1

AND THE ROLLER-COASTER SWOOPS BACK UP AGAIN... A LITTLE

January, 1978
McChord Air Force Base, Tacoma, Washington

"NICE JOB, MAN," SAYS the C-130's loadmaster.

I set the Mark's parking brake, kill the engine, and climb out into the aircraft's cargo hold to look over my handiwork.

Sure enough, by an absolute biblically miraculous stroke of good luck, I have somehow managed—*accidentally* managed—to park our Jeep, *with* its generator trailer in tow, in a perfectly straight line, *right down the center* of the plane's interior... after *backing it in!* Up a pair of precarious tire ramps!

On my first try! *Ever!*

I've never driven a vehicle with a trailer attached in my life. I've sure as hell never attempted to maneuver up a pair of steeply inclined '*planks*' before either. And *backwards*, to boot! But damned if I didn't do it! And all at the same time too!

Refraining from leaping up and down and shouting, "*Yoo-HOO! I fuckin' did it!*," I instead nod to the loadmaster with a smoldering professional disdain, snatch my rucksack off the Mark's sagging canvas roof, and march around the trailer to where Sgt. Donado—Sal—has set up 'camp' among the starboard troop seats.

Sal looks disgusted.

Or maybe that's just his look of 'serious professionalism.'

This is *his* mission after all, *his* frag. It was *his* job to get that Jeep-and-trailer situated aboard this C-130. He opted to 'delegate' it—as is entirely appropriate and common—to his subordinate. Me. He delegated it because he has no more experience backing a rig like that into an aircraft than I do, and most likely had no desire to look stupid when he (even *more* likely) *screwed it up* and had to re-attempt it over and over again. Handing it off to the 'one-winger-pinger' under his 'command' then was the logical solution. *I* could bungle the effort repeatedly, as everyone (including me) expected, and no one would be surprised or pissed off.

Plus Sal could yell at me for it, if he was so inclined.

Thankfully, though, he isn't the type.

All of this went unspoken, of course, as did my own bowel-loosening terror at the prospect. And had there been anyone of even lesser rank to whom *I* might have fobbed it off, *they* would have inherited the task instead. But there wasn't... so I took the wheel.

And danged if I didn't do it! Whew!

The worst part was just getting the wheels of that short little desk-sized trailer lined up with those individual ramps. But that was the part that went accidentally perfect! I was basically screwing it all up when everything went just right on its own!

Like all short-wheelbase trailers (I've been told), as soon as I started backing it up, it immediately cocked over to one side and threatened to jack-knife up against the side of the Mark. I counter-steered like crazy, over-correcting too much and way too fast, just in time for its *next* veer to roll it right up the ramps as if that was my plan all along. Thereafter, the ramps' little siderails might have been the only things that *kept* it straight, rubber squealing against metal the whole way, but they prevented the trailer from taking a header off the edge and wrecking everything. And that was just fine by me.

Leaning half out the door and craning my neck around to look back, I then swung the *Mark's* rear wheels onto the ramps, and straightened out the fronts to match. And everything rolled up into the aircraft in a perfectly straight line from that point on. As God intended.

For the moment then, Sal and I are at least *looking* and *acting* sublimely competent. We're both wearing brand new freshly tailored cammies, along with our brand new freshly earned berets, and our brand new high-tech hunter's boots as well. I just picked up *my* boots from that off-base store this afternoon, as a matter of fact. So they even *smell* new.

We were lethally punctual for our 4:15 spot time—to the *minute*, actually—and slipped right into the loading routine as smoothly and expertly as if we'd done this sort of thing a million times before. Sal *has* participated in these load-outs a few times, but I've never even *seen* a vehicle being loaded into a C-130 before. So right now, despite our deficiencies, inexperience, and untested incompetence, we're representing the Team about as well as it *could* be represented, for all this aircraft's crew can tell. And that makes me feel damned good.

But if they only knew...

* * *

HALF AN HOUR AGO, no one in our shop was aware—or at least *remembered*, anyway—that we even had this deployment this evening. In fact, all but a half dozen of us had already gone home for the day. And of those six that remained, two of them were off-base at the time, supposedly gone to Fort Lewis for something or other. Who knows where these guys really go on these little day jaunts. So that just left four of us still in the shop, three of them NCOs—Sergeants Burley, Murton, and Donado (BB, Skeeter, and Sal, by any other names)—and *me*. And we were all busily wrapping up whatever it was that we were each doing so that we could go home 'early' too.

It was actually quite pleasant, all things considered: peaceful, unhurried, even *private* in our individual labors... until, from BB's corner of the office space came, "*Fuck me!*"

This was immediately followed by increasingly louder renditions of, "*Shit on a stick!*," and "*Oh, you've gotta' be fuckin' shittin' me!*," and of course, that most eloquent of all BB-isms, "*Jesus H. Christ on a fuckin' pogo stick!*"

I've never understood that last one, but it cracks me up every time.

A moment later, he'd stormed into the little clutch of hand-me-down desks where Sal and I were immersed in our busywork, and shouted, "We've got a tasking in thirty minutes! And I just realized that *nobody's on it!*"

The first thought that crossed my mind was, *And what does that have to do with me?* But I made sure that never crossed my lips.

For something like ten seconds then, we all just stared at each other, eyes darting back and forth and swapping vapid gazes, waiting to see which one of us was going to step forward and singlehandedly resolve the situation, I guess. Skeeter wandered into this impasse shortly after it began, arms full of files, and immediately joined in the indecision.

BB whirled on him. But before he could even utter a plea, Skeeter shook his head and sidestepped over to his desk.

"Don't look at me, man. I'm up to my eyebrows in shit as it is. I'm already gonna' be here until seven tonight."

BB turned back to Sal and I, counted the heads again (both of them), and finally made a decision.

"I need an NCO, and I need him now," he said, looking at Sal. "And right now, *you're it*."

"Sure," Sal answered (pronouncing it *"shuwa"*), rising from his chair. "Whatcha' need?"

"Have you ever controlled and graded CDS drops before?"

"Yeh, a couple of times. But..."

"*Good!* 'Cause that's what you're gonna' be doing again tonight." And he handed over the crumpled frag.

To this, Sgt. Donado responded with a heartfelt, "*Huh?*"

"Take the Mark and the generator trailer, grab a few Elcos for DZ lighting... uhhh... take a couple of weather balloons, and I'll throw a tank of helium on the trailer for ya'. Oh, and cold weather gear! It's gonna' be colder than an Eskimo's bed pan out there tonight, so bring your parka."

Huh? Parka? Bed pan?

"Check the frag for the freqs," he added, "And hurry the frig up! You're supposed to be at the ship in thirty minutes."

Freqs? Frag? Frig? Really?

"The 'ship'?" Sal asked.

"The aircraft. Your C-130. Right out there on the ramp. Spot fifty-one, I think."

"A *C-130?* Wha'... wait... where am I...?"

"The drops are at Moses Lake tonight, Sal. Now go!"

"*Moses Lake?* But that's..."—*about two-hundred-and-fifty miles east of here*—"Uh... well... *okay.*"

I couldn't stand it. Sal was good—the best in our CCS class, actually: our Honor Grad—and not the type to shy away from any challenge. But, Honor Grad or not, he was still plenty green around the ears (and to look at his face just then, more than a little green around the *gills* as well). Valiant can-do attitude or not though, he was about to get run over by unaccustomed duties and responsibilities here, something to which I could most definitely relate.

And so, in keeping with my consistent inability to not volunteer for stuff, I cleared my throat and asked, "Need any help? I'm not doing anything else tonight."

This seemed to physically jolt Sal, and he wheeled toward me as if in a daze. BB was not so hesitant or uncertain.

"Yes! Yes!," he shouted, jabbing one of those huge bratwurst-sized fingers at me, "Airman Stipp, you are now Number Two on the team. Grab your cold weather gear, and help him throw this shit together."

"Um, the only cold weather gear I've *got* is this field jacket," I replied.

"And I don't even have *that*," added Sal.

"Well, that's just fuckin' great," BB huffed. "Okay, I'll go see what I can dig up. But in the meantime, start getting your load-out ready. I'll bring the Mark around back."

And before the echoes could die down, he was gone.

* * *

SO NOW, HERE WE SIT, Sal and I, the consummate spec ops warriors to all outward appearances, dressed to the nines in all-new pressed and starched regalia, state-of-the-art footwear, and dark blue virgin berets, punctual to the minute, stirringly capable, and ably hurried. You'd never suspect that we'd just hurtled through the last half hour in a panicky whirlwind with only one parka between us (borrowed from Skeeter and granted to Sal, since I at least had my anorexic field jacket handy), and with our last-second lunge onto the flightline done in such frantic haste that Sal was very nearly driven to the aircraft plastered across the hood.

All moot points. All that matters now is that we're here. We look good, we're at least *acting* cool, *looking* stoic, unflappable, and professional, and we whipped our Jeep-and-trailer combo into the cargo hold in one swift smooth motion, easier and more casually than this loadmaster has probably ever seen it done. That's what I tell myself, anyway.

So I'm feeling pretty good about things right at this moment.

* * *

YEH, YEH, I KNOW.

Three days ago—well, three *nights* ago, anyway—in the depths of that frozen, sleepless, *endless* overnight deployment, the choice to get the fuck out of this miserable job had been all but carved in stone. Why the hell would I ever want to inflict that kind of torment on myself again? I was done! I'd told myself that at least a dozen times throughout the course of that night.

But then...

Then we limped back onto base at around nine o'clock that morning, looking thoroughly scuffed, dinged, trampled, and run through the proverbial wringer. Our cammies and boots were soaked and muddy, our face paint smeared and clawed, and with a mountain of gear and weapons dangling and jangling from every hook, hand, and harness. And, as much of a stomped and frozen turd as I felt like at that moment—as bloodshot, aching, and bone-weary as I was—at the same time, I just felt... well... '*cool.*'

To me, we all looked 'battle-tested.' 'Bloodied' even. Survivors of a Carthaginian victory... 'winners' of a barely-escaped disaster.

It didn't matter that everything we'd done the night before had been screwed up, mismanaged, or outright *failed*... that I'd mortified myself with unrivaled incompetence and ineptitude, and suffered miserably because of it. No, what *mattered* was that right then and right there, sitting on that bus, we *looked* like warriors. And that's what counted for me... at the time.

When the SP at McChord's entry gate climbed aboard the bus to check our IDs, our berets and our war-weariness definitely caught his eye. Of course, as soon as he'd exited and the doors had closed, we'd all recited a unanimous "Fucker." But then, what do you expect?

Tradition, I guess.

And when we finally unloaded at the Shop—or 'the Section,' as it's more commonly known—heads turned. Heads in passing cars, heads in the parking lot, heads popping up from behind cubicles. When you look like a tip-of-the-spear kinda' trooper who's clearly been earning his pay, people notice. And at least in the military, they can appreciate it.

Beaten down, exhausted, pissed off, fed up, or not, it turns out that *I like that kind of recognition. Dangit!*

Even though all that we did with the rest of that day was clean weapons, sweep floors, move furniture around (they're getting ready to move the entire operation over to a whole different building, right there at the base of the control tower), and then went home early, by the time I shuffled back into my barracks, I might have been whipped, but I was *proud* whipped.

I went to bed confused by this dichotomy of contradictory feelings: the pride and the exasperation, the curiosity *for* and the revulsion *against* ever doing it again, and the frustration with myself for once again having said *nothing* about it once we'd gotten back to the Section.

Was I never going to act on my resolve?

Well, I decided, what I need to do is avoid committing myself, one way or the other, during such moments of emotional extremes. Announcing my desire to quit after a really horrible night would be just as much regretted the day after as *missing* an opportunity to quit after an especially *good* day. So, I nodded to myself, I need to wait, and make my decision during 'an emotionally *neutral* interlude'.

And yes, this is what *professional grade* 'over-thinking' sounds like.

Unfortunately, I haven't had one of those 'neutral interludes' since I got back from Miami. It's been a roller coaster of nothing but highs and lows since I stepped off that plane at SeaTac... so *depressed* spending New Year's Night alone in my room, and New Year's *Day* locked out of it... so *happy* playing on the upper slopes of Mount Rainier with Mike and Cheryl, and basking in the glow of my triumphal return to the Team the next day... then so *wretchedly miserable* again on that long overnight deployment.

And now?

Tough to tell. Probably best to wait and see... again... I guess.

So I went with the 'hold-off-a-little-longer' plan, and fell into bed, spending the rest of that day and night in a depleted coma.

And the next day *really was better.*

* * *

THE FIRST THING THEY did was send us young'uns, fresh back from CCS, up to The Castle, to the squadron's admin office, to pick up our CDCs— our 'Career Development Courses'—the next stepping stone along the path of our long slow career progressions. These are fairly large textbook-size packages filled with questions, answers, explanations, and reviews that pertain specifically to one's particular career field, the completion of which is mandatory in one's quest for '5-Level' (or, in Combat Control, '*Phase III*') qualification. *Oh great. Study and testing materials* in addition to *all our real world tests and training and performance evaluations.*

At first, I'd feared that this would add a whole new level of *suck* to the equation. But as it turns out, the CDCs are actually okay.

For one thing, they're simple, written in layman's (or at least *rookie's*) language. For another, the questions are immediately followed by their correct answers and clarifications, so they're not designed to trip you up, threaten you with failure, or even go into too much mind-numbing detail. And they read really quickly and comfortably, so the 'study grind' is not the chore that I'd thought it would be. Plus, when it's a dead slow day at The Section, and the team leaders are just looking for menial tasks to keep us occupied, the CDCs help pass the time and exempt us from the slave labor pool... usually.

And finally, tracking my progress through its pages—and steadily outpacing my peers as I do so, I might add—has shone a light on the distant end of this Phase III upgrade tunnel. And it actually feels like my CCT flash might not be so far off after all. *So* that's *a good thing too, right?*

Then two days ago, as the roller coaster was once more peaking, I added mobility, access, and personal freedom to my growing list of life improvements.

I bought a car.

* * *

I CHECK MY WATCH. Coming up on six o'clock.

Outside the open cargo ramp, the sun is setting over Puget Sound. And it's gotten dark enough now to warrant firing up a half dozen light stands around the aircraft... which is still parked. They still haven't cranked the engines yet.

Why not? What the hell are they waiting for?

I haven't seen Sal's frag myself, so I don't know what our up-and-operating time is supposed to be out in the desert west of Moses Lake. But I have a hard time believing that they wanted us out at the aircraft by 4:15

if we weren't scheduled to take off for *two more friggin' hours*. But... who knows.

Sal, his Puerto Rican blood apparently overriding his New York upbringing, is no longer able to hide his shivering, and finally bundles himself up in Skeeter's parka. I don't *have* a parka. But then somehow, I don't seem to be as susceptible to the cold tonight. And for whatever indecipherable reason, that just makes this all so... suddenly... *perfect*.

I don't know what it is—and I surely wouldn't have believed it three nights ago—but I find I'm actually *excited* about this mad little scramble. I'm picturing where we'll be in about an hour-and-a-half, maybe two hours, if this plane ever gets off the ground. And I'm amazed to discover its lack of appeal *strangely appealing*.

I mean, this Jeep—with its chugging generator trailer, its idling engine, and its roaring heater—is about to be the only speck of civilization within a roughly fifteen-mile radius of its lonely and dimly lit little spot in the middle of absolutely *nowhere*, looking like the glow of a wristwatch that's sunk to the bottom of the deepest darkest vault of the ocean. Nothing but black featureless desert in all directions, a sprawling amphitheater of stars overhead, and a crystalline winter chill filling the space in between. And huddled inside the flimsy canvas shell of the Mark, venting steam with every breath, and writing with gloved hands, with penlights in our teeth, will be Sal and I. One talks to the inbound aircraft, the other keeps the records, and both keep their eyes out for heavy loads floating down out of the stars, ready to score their accuracy *and* move the Mark the hell out of the way at a moment's notice just to keep from being squashed.

We're it!

Tonight, *we'll* be the beacon of familiarity and reassurance in the wilderness, the lone and tiny voice among all those empty airwaves. *We'll* be the guidance and control, *we'll* be the lonesome signal from the dark side of the moon, waiting in the bullseye of the target zone for the multi-ton pallets that will be raining down from the sky.

Those pilots—all of whom will also be missing *Happy Days* and *Three's Company* just like Sal and I—will be circling in the emptiness out there, navigating to the drop zone outlined by *our* little red Elco lights, and aiming for *our* voices in the darkness. *We'll* be the target. *We'll* be the judges and the referees tonight. *And how cool is that?*

I find that I am surprisingly ready. Maybe it's just the jitters from the chill that's starting to fill this open cargo compartment. Or maybe it's this unaccustomed feeling of 'relevance,' that in a moment of 'crisis,' it was Staff Sergeant Salvador J. Donado and Airman First Class Steven D. Stipp that stepped up and made the whole team look good. Or maybe it's just how unbelievably comfortable these new boots are... they're sturdy and tough, but somehow still lightweight and stylish at the same time... plus, they're so soft and warm on the *inside*, that it feels like I'm wearing a couple of little sleeping bags on my feet. But whatever it is, *I am just flat* liking *this stuff tonight!*

Then again, the *whole day's* been a good one: easy duty going through my CDCs, picking up these great new boots off-base, *and driving my brand new used car to go and get 'em.*

* * *

YEP. IT FINALLY HAPPENED last night. I got myself a new car.

A new *used* car. Twenty-eight-hundred bucks worth!

After several days of yanking Mike Dumas back and forth to that used car dealership that we 'discovered' a week or so ago—plus a couple of busy afternoons trying to schmooze the base credit union for the funds—it all came together yesterday, and wound up with me driving my 'brand new' '72 Datsun B-210 hatchback home to The Castle last night.

I've got wheels again! Hoo-HOO!

I've got wheels (and my very first payment schedule). I've got fresh threads and brand new treads, I've got my new blue beanie, I'm ripping through my training syllabus like a man possessed, and now I'm half of an elite two-man team that will be directing and grading senior officers flying real by-God multi-million dollar aircraft tonight.

And well... *what's not to like?*

I can do this—I *am* doing this—and you know, *it ain't so bad at all*.

I mean, when it comes right down to it, what was it that made the other night's overnighter so bloody godawful for me? Distilled down to its essences, what *was* it that made me so damned miserable?

Bottom line? I was cold. And I was tired. *That's it.*

Big whoop.

Big wuss.

And all that awkwardness and discomfort, well... that's just something I'll eventually conquer with *time*, right? Just like everybody else here. It's easy to forget that every one of my 'peers' already had *months* of experience under their belts before I even got here... *months* of stumbling through the woods like a rodeo clown, fumbling with *their* compasses and weapons and ammo, wrestling with *their* rucksacks and gas masks and sleeping bags until they'd become second nature... tussling with recalcitrant tents that wouldn't pitch, and fires that wouldn't light, working out the tricks of the trade that allowed *them* to sweat while in action, but *not* freeze to death in their own chilled juices once they'd stopped.

There *are* ways to do this stuff—*obviously*—and the only difference between me and them is that all-important Time and Experience. *Right?* My being months ahead of the normal training curve might be statistically cool, but it comes with all the *practical* problems that I encountered the other night. Give me that good old 'T&E,' and all the craziness and frustration should go away... or at least *ease off* a little. Right?

So yeh, I'm in the mood to kick some serious midnight-desert-drop-zone ass tonight!

* * *

BUT BY SIX-TWENTY, we're still sitting on the ground in this dark, silent, wide-open, and now *fucking freezing* C-130.

Are we even in the right aircraft? Is our loadmaster—who's been outside on the tarmac for the last forty-five minutes or so, getting all friendly with the restless ground crew—actually trying to figure out why two Combat Controllers suddenly showed up out of the blue just as they were shutting down for the night? I mean, come on! We've been sitting here for more than two hours now, and ... *nothing!* Not even a verbal update, or an estimated time of departure, or even a simple *Who the hell are you? And why are you on my aircraft?* kinda' thing. Nothing.

Sal and I have run over our procedures and protocols and rapid deployment sequences several times. We've divvied up the duties (Sal will talk to the airplanes, he being the only certified air traffic controller between us, and I'll do all the grunt work). We've laid out the choreography of our steps (I run out the DZ's boundary lights, Sal rigs and launches the weather balloon, and does the wind calculations, *etcetera, etcetera*), scripted the most streamlined set-up schedule we can muster with our limited resources, and verbally rehearsed it all the way through a couple of times now. So there's really nothing else we can do now, except keep sitting and waiting.

Only I can't sit. This lightweight little field jacket is simply no longer up to the task of fending off the chill anymore.

So I pace—inside *and* outside the aircraft—anything to keep the warmer juices warmer.

Out under the starboard wing, his every breath and spoken word jetting steam into the crossfire of the floodlights, I catch up to the loadmaster nodding and plotting with someone on his headset. Most likely the pilot. His head bobs one last time, then he wheels around toward the aft ramp, almost colliding with me head-on.

"*Whoa!*," he yelps, startled by the 'ghostly apparition' that just materialized out of the shadows in front of him—*no doubt reinforcing any first impressions he might have had about my innate 'covert mystique' in the process*—then gathering up his headset cord with a *'harrumph.'*

"The pilot says the mission's a cancel. You guys are released."

"Canceled?" I reply, doing my best to convey a look of minor league disappointment for a major league kind of player. "How come?"

"Well," he says, as he drifts back toward the cargo door, coiling his headset cord around his left forearm, "considering how all the aircraft you were going to be controlling tonight have already been gone for something like forty-five minutes now, and we're still sitting here on the ground at McChord… even if we took off *right now*, they'd be circling for two more hours just waiting for us to land at Moses Lake, offload you guys, then for you to drive out to your desert site and set up your DZ. And that's *if* we could take-off right now. But we can't. Fuel fumes in the wing, and a 'Hydraulics-2' light in the cockpit, the pilot says. Something like that."

Well, shit. That's a tad anti-climactic.

Then again, I'm cold now.

And bored. And tired. And now that my initial buzz has burned off, I'm ready to go home.

"Good enough for me," I sigh. "We'll get the Jeep unchained." And I trot off ahead.

I probably didn't hide my eagerness too well.

Or am I actually disappointed here? Tough to tell.

***

SAL DECIDES TO DRIVE the Mark out of the cargo hold himself this time. *What a hero! Driving forward, straight down the ramps to the ground.* Once on the apron, we whisk back to The Section with the dash heater roaring away at full blast. There we find the office blacked-out and empty (so much for Skeeter's claim that he had enough work to keep him busy through seven o'clock).

It takes us about fifteen minutes to get everything packed away again, the lights turned off, the doors locked, and the Mark secured in its little chicken-wire cage. Then we're headed back out into the icy black night, homeward bound.

I offer to drive Sal up to base housing in my cool new clatter-trap car, and Sal offers to buy me dinner. I make mention of the fact that I can eat at the chow hall for free, and he counters with the fact that his street is less than six blocks away, and his house is almost visible from where we're standing, so he doesn't need the ride.

We both compromise. I drive us to the Rec Center, and we eat on his dime. Not exactly the 'glory' of a come-from-behind victory over lopsided odds, but a decent ending to a decent day anyway.

I could get used to this.
I think.

2
BAD NEWS BEARERS

Late January, 1978

"SURVIVAL SCHOOL?" I STAMMER. Out loud. I think.

Looking up from my CDCs, disassembled and scattered across my borrowed desktop like a spilled newspaper, I can't believe that *once again* Sergeant Santos has come to me bearing the latest round of bad news. And once again, he's smiling and using a congratulatory tone of voice as he does so, in much the same way, I imagine, that a clothespin for the nose might be erroneously considered the same as *shit that don't stink*.

Skeeter struts up beside him, once again beaming with pride at what was no doubt a masterpiece of clerical sleight of hand on his part. He hands Manny a sheaf of printed orders. Santos casts his gaze over the top sheet, arches his eyebrows high, then turns to acknowledge Skeeter's work with an appreciative nod.

"Damn. Not bad, Skeeter-Peter. You wrangled *four* slots this time?"

"To *Survival School?*" I repeat.

"Yep," says Skeeter. "You, Spew, Rocky and Greg."

For some reason, the same as with me, nicknames just do not seem to stick to Greg.

"All in the same class," Manny adds superfluously.

"But... *Survival School?*"

"Yup."

"In February?"

"You betcha'." And Manny's smile turns sinister. "Trust me; you wouldn't like a summer class any better."

I decide not to mention the obvious… that I *just graduated* from the *last* school they sent me to *barely a month ago!* Plus, I'm just starting to build up a head of steam with my CDCs now. *Dangit!*

"Survival School," I repeat with a sigh. And I start policing up my study materials.

"*Basic* Survival School," says Skeeter.

"Basic? You mean there's more than one?"

"'More than one'?" Manny snorts. "There's gotta' be at least *six* that you'll be going through in just your first year with the Team, man."

"*Six? Six Survival Schools?*"

"Sure," says Skeeter, flipping his fingers up one by one as he calls them off. "You've got Jungle Survival, Desert Survival…"

"Arctic Survival," Manny interjects.

"Yep. Then there's Water Survival. *Two different kinds!* One for 'parachuting,' and one for '*non*-parachuting.' Basically ejecting—or freefalling—versus ditching."

"Jesus."

Skeeter turns to Manny next, and asks, "Would the Altitude Chamber count as a 'survival school,' do you think?"

Sgt. Santos pooches out his lower lip for a second, then nods.

"Sure. The Altitude Chamber too."

"*Holy shit!*" I say.

Santos's 'mad bandito' grin suddenly erupts in teeth.

"Not counting the SCUBA and HALO Schools, *muchacho*, pretty much *every* school you've got left is gonna' be some kind of survival school. Might as well get used to it."

I catch my mouth hanging open several seconds later, and actually flip my head back and forth to snap out of it.

"Well, damn," I mutter. "With all those *other* survival schools, what the hell's left to teach at *Basic* Survival School? '*Remembering To Eat And Breathe 101*'?"

"It's just two work-weeks, man," Skeeter chuckles. "You'll have the weekend *off* in between. One week of classroom, and a week in and out of the field putting everything you learned in class to good use. It ain't that bad."

"And don't forget *POW School*," adds Santos.

"Oh yeh. And POW School."

"*POW School?*" I gasp. "*Another* Survival School?"

"No, man," Skeeter giggles, "It's part of the *Basic* Survival School you're about to go to. The *last* part. You're gonna' love it."

Both of them break out in evil chortles, and turn to walk away. But Manny tosses one last 'reassurance' over his shoulder as he goes.

"Don't worry about it, man. There'll be four of you going. You won't be there alone."

I rock back in my chair, stunned stupid.

There were four of us that went to Combat Control School too! And that didn't make it one little bit easier!

Son of a bitch!

BOOK TWO
THE WANNABE

PART 4

BASIC SURVIVAL SCHOOL
Fairchild Air Force Base, Spokane, Washington
February, 1978

STORY XXXVI

WELCOME TO SURVIVAL SCHOOL

1
A COLD DAY IN HELL

February, 1978
On a mountain road outside Spokane, Washington

THE BUS GRINDS ITS way up through snowy mountain switchbacks, a big ugly box on slush-gray wheels—an Air Force 'school bus'—filled with parka-clad airmen and officers, men and women both, staring out through the smeared fog of its windows. And I am among them. A second bus is following right behind us, each vehicle carrying half of the class's students, bound for the same deep snows at the higher elevations. And all without heat.

Oh, the buses are perfectly capable of venting a modicum of engine heat into the passenger compartment, but what's the point? The driver's already having a bitch of a time just keeping his windshield clear from all the warm breathing and hot air being outgassed by the gabbier passengers. And besides, considering where we're headed, we're all wearing parkas and thermal underwear anyway, so turning the heat up would only turn this into a full-blown rolling sauna for us.

No, the driver can just crank the heat up later if he wants, once he's headed back down the mountain, *empty*.

For me, gazing out at the passing pines and firs as they drift past my window like an expectant crowd watching concert tour buses arrive—each tree poking up through the six-foot-deep swaddling of snow that's blanketed everything up here—spiders of dread just keep skittering up and down my spine. Maybe it's flashbacks to that first spooky bus ride from San Antonio's airport to the Basic Training base at Lackland or something… to that feeling that nothing but pure suck-ass misery is looming up ahead. I don't know. But it's real, it's dismal, and it makes me wish I'd come down with the measles again, just like I'd done back in Basic.

It's Monday. The *second* Monday, or the first *day* of the second *week* of Survival School. And it still amazes me, not only how fast that first week in the classroom flew past, but how much faster this second week *in the field* rushed up to fill its place.

And that just BLOWS!

I already knew how much I'd grown to despise field work. CCS beat any curiosity I might have possessed for that right out of me. But after five straight days of sitting at a desk in a heated classroom, listening to instructors, reading books, and watching their films, slides, overhead projections, and blackboard scribblings depicting all the myriad ways that Mother Nature conspires to poison, bludgeon, drown, and freeze my ass to death, I gotta' tell ya', I am in no mood whatsoever to step out into Her domain now, and test my abilities to defy Her efforts.

Truth be told, I *hate* that Bitch.

According to these guys though, that feeling is apparently mutual.

At least it's not snowing today. The ceiling is still the same low, gray, fuzzy lid that's been smothering the Pacific Northwest for the last week-and-a-half. But, unlike the six previous days, the heavy and constant *snow* has finally stopped falling. So it's just a regular old black-and-white (and icy stainless steel) day outside. The kind of day for which you normally wouldn't leave the comforts of home… only there's no 'home' where we're going today.

As the hummocks of passing snow deepen along the roadside, thrown up by the snowplows and mud-spackled by everyone else that's passed, they embrace and bury everything for as far as the eye can see, up to a depth of almost eight feet. And my mind harkens back to a similar scene from a week ago, when I first pulled into the Survival School's campus along the far periphery of Fairchild Air Force Base in my little mud-winged Datsun.

2
"WHERE THE FUGGARWE?"

February, 1978
Basic Survival School, Fairchild AFB, Spokane, Washington

THE SKY WAS JUST as low and slate-gray *then* as it still is now, the daylight just as dimmed. The trees were dead, the buildings dreary and frosted, and the roads little more than slushy trenches furrowing through the equally gray and rolling snowfields.
Inspirational indeed.
Though Fairchild AFB is a large and thriving installation, between the weather and the Survival School's isolation from the rest of the base, the campus had the look of a bleak and desolate outpost somewhere above the Arctic Circle.

I found the gathering of ugly, uninspired, shoebox-shaped buildings—looking like they'd been dragged straight out of some low-rent Russian apartment complex—arranged around a snow-choked rectangular 'quad' like pickets. An administrative edifice blocked off one end of the quad, looking squashed into the snow like a huge brick that had been dropped from the sky. A couple of classroom and equipment storage structures bracketed the near sides, and the rest of the space was ringed by barracks buildings. Our quarters for the next two weeks was among them, presumably. And framing the entire compound was a perimeter of parking spaces, themselves contained within a four-foot-high prison of snow.

Rocky and Spew had driven over in Spew's Jeep—on their own schedule and itinerary, so we never saw them—and Greg Dorn had ridden along as my passenger in my new-used little green B-210. He even hooked up his own CB radio under my dash, so that we could keep tabs on the cops during our six-hour crossing of the state.

And as we squished through the ice slurry that coated every horizontal surface at Fairchild, looking for a parking space close to the headquarters' front door, I just couldn't believe that this was where I'd come to... *now*. *'Voluntarily!'* Of all places, and of all times.

We parked, got out, and clomped into the building's main lobby, stomping the mud-Slurpee off our brand new boots and all over their welcome mat. And the first thing I saw once I looked back up, was a framed poster mounted prominently beside a pair of double-doors that opened into an empty auditorium. It was a painting of an Indian scout, a 'noble savage' standing on a rocky outcropping, staring off into the sunset with one hand shading his eyes. And at the bottom of the picture, in large bold type, was what I took to be the Survival School's motto: **"WHERE THE FUGGARWE?"**

Apparently long-lost tribal descendents of the *HECKawees*.

You know; the ones on "*F-Troop*."

Well, if nothing else, it certainly summed up *my* feelings at the time.

3
A MOUNTAIN OF FACTS, AN AVALANCHE OF RETENTION

THE SNOW RESUMED FALLING again that very first night. And with one half-assed exception three afternoons later, it never let up again for the rest of the week. Nor half of the week*end* that followed. The dense snow-bloated ceiling drooped low and swollen the entire time—seemingly just above the rooftops—sloughing off fat flakes, and floating atop a constant gauzy mist that reduced visibility down to maybe half a mile at most. That, in turn, veiled us off from the rest of the base, visually, physically and psychologically. For all we could tell, we might just as well have been marooned on an ice floe off the coast of Siberia... or the far side of one of Saturn's moons, for that matter.

It was depressing. Cold, dim, wet, windy, and perpetually flurried with snow. For six days straight! I never went anywhere outdoors without being bundled up for a deep-space EVA, my head down, and one thickly gloved hand pulling the fur-lined hood of my parka almost down to my nose.

That was outside. But *in*side, it was bright, warm, dry, and convivial. A-whole-nuther world.

And it was busy, too. Every instructor seemed to have a 'specialty,' and there were *lots* of specialties. For every good or reassuring thing that they taught, they immediately countered it with something else that was brutal, nasty, or just plain terrifying. Just to keep things balanced, I guess.

Here are all the plants that you can eat. But here are all the ones that'll kill you.

Here are all the bugs, beasts, and in-between critters that you can find, trap, and eat. But here too are all the ones that can bite, poison, eat, gore, or stomp your ass to death.

Melted snow can keep you hydrated and alive, but eaten *snow is worse than no food at all.*

You can use the sun as both a clock and a compass, but here are all the different circumstances under which it can burn or blind you.

A stream of mountain run-off can mean water with which to clean wounds and keep yourself hydrated. But falling into it can mean hypothermia and death, and following *it puts you on the most obvious path for enemy pursuers to track.*

Here's how to build weapons, traps, and shelters out of sticks, rocks, mud, snow, and dissected parachute parts. But here are all the ways that these too can backfire on you, injure you, waste precious escape time, or give your position away to the enemy.

Then there's all the specialized survival *equipment* with which you're expected to be proficient, or at least familiar. Handheld radios and beacons, flashlights and K-rats. *HELP* messages written in several different languages, printed on paper or sewn into the inner lining of your jacket. Maps, and foreign currency, and of course, the tools of rescue themselves… sling harnesses, tree penetrators, and retrieval baskets, all lowered from helicopters. Flares and colored smoke and strobes and signaling mirrors… and the list goes on and on and on. *And just so damned much of it.*

And all this before they even got into the plot twists of dealing with an enemy force that's trying its level best to catch you at the same time that you're trying to survive your injuries *and* the elements *and* your disconnection from the rest of your life. Covering tracks, camouflaging campsites and yourself, discreet movement, observing and taking notes on the enemy's assets and locations, plus hiding, evading, and escaping from a pursuing adversary.

And finally—worst case scenario—dealing with capture, abuse, interrogation, and that most dreaded of all possibilities, *torture*. They're putting that off until the end, though (making it part of the 'POW School' segment), so we've got *that* to look forward to at the end of this week.

The downside was that it all blurred together. Always interesting, but neverending... which turned it all into a blur.

The *up*side though, was that we were never *tested* on anything. And this was because, as we were told, the course wasn't so much a 'school' as an 'experience.' We were there to meet, touch, taste, feel and do—in other words, 'experience'—all those things that we might one day encounter, engage, or use in the event the normal technology, support networks, and/or best-laid plans ever failed us. *Oy*.

Certainly good and helpful information to have at one's fingertips in a moment of crisis, but depressing and unnerving having to spend so much time contemplating such exigencies. Especially the interrogation and torture part.

I say again for emphasis, "*Oy*."

4

LEARNING HOW TO FALL DOWN... AGAIN

SINCE, IN THE AIR FORCE at least, the aircrews (the folks that do all the actual *flying*) tend to be the folks most often and most likely to find themselves in survival situations, the Survival School's itinerary, language, and general orientation is biased quite heavily to *their* needs and perspectives. And I suppose that's only appropriate.

As such, most of the scenarios discussed in the classroom rightly began with those instances that would typically put a flightcrew member in peril in the first place... like stepping out of an aircraft that, for whatever reason, was no longer doing its job, whether it's still in the air and falling, or bobbing in the ocean and sinking, or scattered across the ground in little smoking pieces. And since wading out of a debris field apparently doesn't require all that much specialized training, the initial emphasis instead focused on surviving a *jump* from a failing aircraft, the descent under a parachute, and of course, a parachute *landing* in hostile environs.

Surprisingly—especially among the veteran *fighter* pilots in our group, who have theoretically been donning a parachute every time they've ever strapped on an aircraft—almost *none* of my fellow classmates had ever received training on how to do a basic PLF, or Parachute Landing Fall.

So, on that first Wednesday—Day Three of Week One—they led us through the eternal blizzard to the building at the front corner of the quad.

Once out of the smothering white-out, we were herded down the building's long central corridor, and into an odd little room that had apparently been set aside for just that purpose... practicing PLFs in bad weather.

It was all the way at the end of that long corridor. In fact, the corridor ended at its door, capping off the first floor's layout like a capital T. In other words, when we stepped into that end chamber, the far wall of that room, straight ahead of us, was barely fifteen feet away, but it ran some thirty to forty feet to right and left. Very strange. A long, narrow, rectangular space, open and uninterrupted to all three walls of the building's outer shell at that end. But that wasn't the strangest part.

Once inside the room, my classmates and I found ourselves standing atop a five-foot-wide 'ledge,' or 'stage,' if you will, like a subway platform that ran the length of the long near wall. And it was overlooking a three-foot drop-off into a *room-length sawdust pit!*

The building had its own skinny little 'indoor swimming pool' of wood chips! Not your standard Air Force office building accommodation.

Well, needless to say, I, plus the three other guys wearing camouflage, had *plenty* of experience with jumping, not to mention some finely honed falling-down skills. So when the call went out for volunteers who could demonstrate the correct PLF form, we got the nod. And while the *official* instructors called off the positions and movements, we—like the mermaids in an Esther Williams aqua-musical—peeled off in sequence, and dropped into the sawdust in perfect form and spacing.

The procedure was pretty elementary stuff, of course. So, in no time, the 'indoor shavings pool' was full of leaping, flopping, and tumbling pilots, navigators, loadmasters, and a loose assortment of other related specialists. Including me.

I was so proud.

But it was the first *physical* challenge we'd encountered in the course up to that point, even though several 'outdoor activities' had been *scheduled*... and then canceled. The weather had just been too consistently lousy. It hadn't stopped snowing *for even five minutes* since we'd gotten there on Monday. The ceiling was just too low for helicopters to fly, the visibility almost whited out with mists and dense flurries, and, with the snow mounded up to four and five feet deep everywhere, there were no show-and-tell excursions outside to look for medicinal or edible flora or fauna either. But thanks to that strange little sawdusty chamber, those folks who were not regular jumpers could at least practice their PLFs during those canceled time slots.

And there were some pretty senior-ranking types among our student body too: a couple of master sergeants, a major or two, and even a full-bird *colonel*. I could understand how a colonel could still be an active pilot, but I *didn't* understand how he could be so far into his career without having already gone through this course at a much earlier point.

There were also a few folks among the rank and file whose job specialties weren't exactly 'front line' positions—mostly aircraft or radio maintenance people—whose career progression checklists you wouldn't think would have included Survival School. But there they were, women, administrative types, and one gangly stork-like goober named Spiegelman.

Or, as I preferred to call him, *Spazman*.

* * *

AIRMAN SPIEGELMAN FIRST CAME to my attention during that PLF training session in the sawdust pit.

Notable for both his clumsiness and hesitancy when attempting *anything* physical, Spiegelman—or 'Spazman'—managed to achieve even greater notoriety when he became the first student in our class to *injure* himself... in a *sawdust pit*... hopping off a ledge barely *three feet* above it.

I know!

On his very first PLF attempt, after what seemed like several *minutes* of tentative stutter-stepping and indecision at the pit's edge, he finally overcame his diffidence by mustering all of his deskbound willpower and *hurling* himself off the platform. And when I say "hurling," I mean friggin' *launching!* As in "*a massively overpowered leap into space*," rather than a simple tidy little *hop* like everyone else was doing.

Well, as I might have mentioned before, the sawdust pit was barely ten feet wide—hell, the *ceiling* was barely ten feet over our heads, and he almost hit that too!—so Airman Spiegelman flew almost completely *over* the landing area, kicking and flailing most of the way, until his boots dug in barely a foot or two short of the pit's far side, and smacked everything else from the waist up against the wall. His head bounced off it, leaving a mark and a *dent* in the sheet rock. His shoulder crumpled, and he landed face-down in the wood shavings.

I couldn't believe it. Did he really have *that* little control over his body? *That* little coordination? *That* little ability to judge distances?

Apparently so.

The course instructors jumped in and rushed to his side. His hand was pressed to his bleeding forehead as they helped him to his feet, his shoulder hunched and immobilized, and his mouth uttering a steady (and nasal) stream of, "*Ow. Ow-ow-ow. Ow. OW!*"

Once the door closed behind them, the rest of us stopped to look at each other, then busted out laughing.

What the hell was that?

5

THE SPAZMAN COMETH

Back up in the mountains east of Spokane, Washington

AND NOW HERE WE are, the road rising up into the bellies of the scuddy clouds and slaloming through the mists like an uphill bobsled chute. Only a couple of ranks of snow-smothered trees are even visible from the road-cut anymore. And as we round another climbing hairpin turn, a graded pull-over area comes into view, and both buses turn off onto it.

This is apparently the end of the line. This is where we get off.

The four instructors on my bus bound to their feet, and storm out the door onto the packed snow outside, shouting, "Everybody off!"

"My group! Form up on me!"

"All my guys! Over here!"

Behind us, the second bus disgorges an identical quartet of yodeling instructors, and the exodus doubles.

Kee-reist-amighty! I do NOT want to spend the next three days out here in this frozen shit.

But much like everybody else, I sigh resignedly, hoist my 'improvised backpack' off the floor, gather my 'improvised snowshoes' from the overhead rack, and bumble down the aisle to the door with the rest of the parade.

Before we left Fairchild, we were each assigned—in eight-man 'field classes'—to particular instructors. So as I step off the bus, I angle over to where Sgt. Goodwin is waving and shouting for his eight designated students to join him.

Like him, I jam the 'heels' of my snowshoes (the handgrip-like 'stems' of the tennis-racket-shaped devices) into the deeper snow rimming the plowed turn-out, and dump my backpack beside them. Then I turn around... just in time to hear a yelp and the clatter of spilled utensils clanking and tinkling from the second bus.

As I watch, a disintegrating bundle of loose gear—clothing, cups, canteens, and compasses, along with the unraveling twine that had bound them all together—comes cartwheeling down the bus's steps, and bursts fully apart on the ground. Airman Spazman scurries down the steps right behind them, fretting and cursing and apologizing to all around him. And as he goes about gathering it all back up again, it reminds me of another one of his 'escapades' from last week, back on the school's grounds.

* * *

AFTER THREE STRAIGHT DAYS of unrelenting dark skies, weighty lumbering clouds dragging across the rooftops, and air so filled with swirling snow that it was almost hard to breathe, they'd been forced to cancel almost every outdoor activity on the schedule for that week. But by late morning on Thursday—the fourth day—the snow mysteriously abated, the clouds thinned and retreated slightly, and the wind died off altogether. So the instructors, looking at only a brief window of opportunity, had to choose which of the many canceled activities they wanted to attempt during the lull.

Flora and fauna identification, animal and human tracking, and solar navigation (*did you know you can use your* watch *as a compass?*) were still off the table, on account of the chest-deep snow banks and the still-occluded sun. And we'd already done our PLF training in that little indoor sawdust pit.

So that left... the Tree Penetrator.

I was surprised to learn that they didn't have a simulator for the Tree Penetrator. I mean, it couldn't have been simpler to make... run a rope up through an overhead pulley, and hang a Tree Penetrator from it! *Tah-dah!* But the fact was that they *didn't* have one, which meant that the only way to train on an actual Tree Penetrator was to use a *real one*, hanging from an actual flying helicopter... which was why they needed the weather to be at least a little bit clearer.

And on that Thursday afternoon, *it was just clear enough*.

At least for a little while.

So, much to my amazement, they bundled us up in our parkas and mukluks and extra-thick gloves, and marched us out across the ice-crunchy parking lot, split us into two groups, and had us wait beneath the gloomy skies... until we could hear the acoustically deadened *wop-wop-wopping* of a helicopter hammering its way toward us.

Although the solid charcoal-gray ceiling had 'risen' to a slightly loftier height, it was still low enough that the helicopter had to skim the treetops just to remain under it, and it was still *thick* enough to dim the afternoon light down to late evening hues. The streetlights had even come on. But still, they'd somehow managed to find a lunatic chopper pilot (who probably needed—or at least *wanted*—some flight time under those challenging conditions), one that was willing to try flying in these unfriendly skies just so that *we* could play with the Tree Penetrator for a half hour or so.

The helicopter, a stock Bell UH-1 "Huey," came *thwopping* over the school's classroom building, bent its course toward the two clusters of shivering students at the edge of the cleared area, and flared to a hover above us. A splash of loose snow was flung skyward as the rotor's downwash battered its way over the plowed edge of the parking lot, and filled the air with slush and ice shrapnel. And while that rained and pelted down on us, propelled by the same rotor wash that had launched it, the helicopter centered itself above the group opposite mine, and began to lower the Tree Penetrator.

As it was being lowered, the dangling Tree Penetrator looked like a large, heavy, metal 'arrow,' pointing straight down. It was a little over four feet tall, with a thick, blunt, conical 'point' at the bottom. In this configuration, I could easily see how it could penetrate a jungle canopy, punching through the leaves and branches all the way to the jungle floor unimpeded.

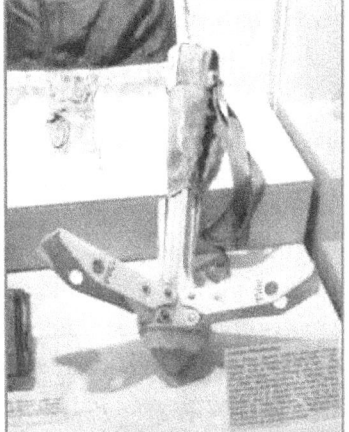

Once down though, the cone-shaped point—which was actually segmented into three separate 'plates' closed together—could be folded down into three separate 'seats' which stuck out from the core, flat, like the blades of a propeller.

Or the points of an anchor.

Up to three rescuees could then climb onto the Penetrator at one time, each straddling one of those folded-down 'seats' and hugging the center post, with their arms slipped through one of three hanging safety straps. And from there, all the helicopter had to do was winch their ass(es) back up through the treetops, twigs, leaves and branches be damned.

Simple.

So naturally, Airman Spazman managed to fuck it up... *and* hurt himself... *and* get the whole session cut short for the rest of us. All at the same time.

* * *

THERE WERE NO TREES for the Tree Penetrator to penetrate this time, obviously. We were in a parking lot, after all. But that wasn't the point. No, the plan was simply to dip the Penetrator into one group, load up three students, hoist them over to the other group, drop them off, then load up three more to be hoisted back the other way. Back and forth until everyone had gotten a chance to ride it, and the two groups had switched positions. *That's it!*

At least that was the *plan*.

Despite the threatening clouds above, and the whirling ice and snow below, the helicopter managed to pluck three students out of the first group, side-hover over to *my* group, and drop them at our feet amid a gale of ice-flecked rotor wash that made it damned hard to face the action with your eyes open. Then three of *our* guys climbed on, and were hoisted back across to the first group. Nice and easy. Just like clockwork. And that's how it should have gone for the rest of the exercise: roughly twenty-five people in each group, being shuttled back and forth, three at a time, for a total of approximately eight round-trips. That's how it *should* have gone... except that the next three riders from the other group included Airman Spazman.

I didn't get to see all of it, *dangit!* Most of my group was standing between me and the scene (and I'd placed myself that way on purpose, using my fellow students as blast deflectors against the wind-whipped ice chips). But, from what I could tell, it started when the rotor wash blew the Spazman's hat off.

Everyone else had already removed and stowed their hats. *Who needs a hat when you've got a parka hood covering your head?* The Spazman, however, had kept his hat on, and had chosen to simply pin it to his head with one hand. *Brilliant!* So, shortly after straddling the paddle on his side of the Penetrator, and slithering his head and shoulders up through the safety strap, his hat was suddenly (and inevitably) blown off his head.

His first reaction was to whip around and see where it went... which either dislodged his glasses, or more likely snapped his head back in such a way that the angle allowed the helicopter's downdraft to batter them sideways across his face.

Either way though, what immediately ensued was pure slapstick, a fumble-fingered juggling act in the middle of a hurricane.

First, he 'caught' his glasses by essentially *pinning* them against the side of his face with one hunched shoulder. He couldn't easily get his hand over to grab them though, not as long as the safety strap was hiking upward under his armpits. So, without really thinking it through (I'm guessing), he pulled one arm and shoulder *out* of the safety strap, and reached across to seize the errant glasses with his fingers... all while still twisted around half-backwards (keeping cheek to shoulder)... and just in time for the helicopter pilot to take the last of the slack out of the line and begin the lift.

For anyone else, having only one hand still gripping the Penetrator's center post would have been more than adequate to hang on.

But not for the Spazman.

Combined with the twist in his body, the odd angle of the one arm that was still looped through the safety strap, and the sudden upward motion of the hoist, his head slipped out from under the strap, he reflexively *let go* of the center post for some reason, and he toppled over backwards. Doing a complete ass-over-teakettle back-flip in the air, he fell the four or five feet to the scoured parking lot, where he landed face-down... and immediately curled into a fetal ball in the middle of the blast zone.

A flurry of hand signals drove the helicopter back, as the instructors converged on Spazman. And while the two remaining students on the Tree Penetrator were gently deposited on the far side of the parking lot, Airman Spiegelman was assisted to his feet—again—and escorted back to the building—*again*—to await another ambulance—*AGAIN!*—all the while reciting his personal mantra, "*Ow! Ow-ow-ow-ow-ow! OW!*"

You know, I'm starting to detect a theme with that boy.

I never did get to ride the Tree Penetrator myself. And I was looking forward to that too.

They waved the helicopter off, calling it a lost cause (the conditions really were too nasty for a helicopter and crew to be out in that weather anyway, just to give rides to a bunch of huddled students who'd already gotten the gist of the system the first time they'd seen it used), and they bundled the rest of us back into the classroom for the day.

Thanks, Spaz!

* * *

AND NOW LOOK AT what we've got here again today. Airman Spiegelman on his hands and knees, half *under* the bus and blocking its doorway (and everyone still inside trying to get out), as he scrambles to gather up the scattered detritus that used to be his 'improvised backpack.'

You know, you don't *want* to be angry with a guy who is, by nature, nice, quiet, shy, and unassuming (and covered with more and more bandages every day). But man, it's tough to empathize with that little coordination, that little common sense, and that much disruption of the class. And as a result, everyone's impatience is starting to show.

I look away once the passengers that are still on the bus begin stepping *over* him.

My condolences to the rest of the guys in Spiegelman's 'field class,' whoever they are (*thankfully, I'm not one of them*). This is going to be a long three days for them.

Then again, it's going to be a long three days for the folks in *my* field class as well. I'm the guy for whom fires just don't light, tents just don't stay pitched, and knots just don't hold. Remember? But at least my group has Greg Dorn in it too. I do believe he could build his own rescue helicopter out of sticks, mud, and weasel pelts if he had to. And for whatever bonus reason, he also gets along well *with me!* And that's a good combination.

So we might just survive this after all.

STORY XXXVII

SURVIVAL SCHOOL: IN THE RAW

1
DAY ONE: STRANDED

February, 1978
In the field, east of Fairchild Air Force Base, Spokane, Washington

BY MID-AFTERNOON, I'M the only one in my group still working on his 'parachute shelter.' It's constructed mostly from pre-dissected parachute parts, which also served as the key components of the 'improvised backpack' that lugged them all out here. But it's finally starting to look pretty good, all things considered.

It took me forever to find a suitable configuration of ground clutter upon which to begin construction. And in the end, my final selection really wasn't all that ideal, since it wasn't very well hidden from the eyes of any potential enemy pursuers. But by the time I finally settled on a spot and started picking through my gear for the materials I'd need, even the exasperated instructor no longer cared about the lack of subterfuge. I just needed to get something up before nightfall.

The spot I'd chosen would have been *ideal* for emergency shelter building if it just hadn't been out in the *middle* of our little forest clearing. Everyone else had been quick to find good locations back among the surrounding trees (although it seemed a bit of a moot point to me, considering the bony and leafless condition of those trees, the unblemished blanket of snow between them, and of course, the *deafening* 'international orange' color of the parachute material). No matter where you set up, you were going to be plenty visible.

Naturally, that wasn't the point of the exercise. I was supposed to be learning *what to look for*, and *where best to find it*, even if there wasn't any of 'it' in the immediate vicinity.

Still I'd wandered aimlessly among the potential shelter sites, rejecting everything I came to on account of one shortcoming or another, usually based on 'coziness' and 'ease of access' (and '*construction*'). After all, I was going to have to *sleep* in my creation in this weather. So 'style points' and 'adherence to tradition' had ranked pretty low on my scale of priorities. 'Comfort' and 'protection (from the elements)' wound up being more important to me than any half-assed camouflage against fictitious enemy hunting parties (or 'instructor disapproval").

I understand the principles here just fine. It's their relevance *among these naked trees, in this snow-smothered forest of sticks that makes me want to shrug it all off... until tomorrow, at least.*

I guess I should be glad this stuff *isn't* testable, that it's an '*experience*' rather than a graded analysis of my information retention. Gives me a little breathing room when it comes to following instructions to the letter... I hope.

So here I am now, squatting atop my miserable pain-in-the-ass snow-shoes, flipping through the bright orange folds of parachute material that I've got draped over this fallen tree trunk (*yeh,* screamin' *orange... a good upfront justification for not being too concerned about camouflage right at this moment*), and tussling with my very first 'acorn anchor' that will hopefully aid in getting this one edge of my 'tent' tied off and squared away finally.

Thankfully, Greg—who finished his shelter a long time ago (of course)—is helping me with my struggles.

An 'acorn anchor' (or, as *I* call it, an '*ancorn*') is nothing more than an acorn—*literally*—or a small stone, or a large button, or just about anything that size, that you press against the inside of your shelter material (in this case, the rip-stop nylon of my parachute canopy), making a lump around which you can then loop an anchor line from the *outside* (using a severed suspension line from that same pre-dissected parachute). And *voila!* A simple, quick, secure, easily adjustable, and *abundant* solution to a fundamental problem.

Pretty slick, if you ask me.

And amazingly, despite the armpit-deep snow burying everything in sight around here, I discovered a *pile* of acorns pooled at the bottom of this relatively snow-free depression at the base of this three-tree cluster.

Man, I've got enough 'ancorns' to tie off a damned revival tent!

I took my gloves off, though—in order to do fiddly little things like tying parachute cord around ancorns; stuff like that—and now my fingers are almost completely numb. It's also surprisingly difficult to *see* small finite details through the perpetual veil of steam jetting from my nose and mouth. So I regularly have to *stop breathing* for the duration of the shorter tasks. All very inconvenient, annoying, and worse, *unavoidable*.

In the distance, from somewhere back in 'the woods' beyond the far side of the clearing, somebody suddenly belts out, "*Fucking snow-fucking-shoes!*" And I can relate. I've grown to hate the damned things myself.

Greg chuckles.

All this bending and squatting and climbing and plodding around our campsite has repeatedly stretched and loosened my snowshoe's jury-rigged 'bindings' (improvised from more dissected parachute harness components), and now they are once again barely hanging on to my boots. So once I'm done tying off this latest anchor line to that little stub of a branch over there, I'm going to have to once again *re*-tie everything on my friggin' snowshoes... *again!* And I too am dead sick of it.

Greg, naturally, doesn't appear to be having *any* problems with *his* snowshoes. Of course.

However, despite my innate tendency to tie consistently slipshod knots, *this* ancorn manages to hold strong and true, and my shelter finally takes on the reassuring shape of a small 'saggy-roofed' house. *Tah-dahhh!*

Of the three lifeless trees poking up out of this dimple in the snow—two naked oaks (or maybe *one* with two *trunks*), and some white-barked thing (maybe a birch) that snapped about five feet about ground level and now lays across the snow bowl like a drawbridge—I've used the downed 'birch' as the 'ridge pole' of my shelter. The orange folds of my parachute are draped over it (and thereby over the snow bowl as well) as my ancorns, and the suspension lines pulling on them, draw the material tight.

My little crooked orange house in the woods.

Greg finally leaves me to my labors, and heads over to the communal fire pit, where I see a couple of other students dumping armloads of gathered kindling and firewood, preparing for the group's evening meal, I guess.

I take a little more time tidying up my little domicile, though. Excess parachute material—and *most* of it is excess—I tuck inside the hole, and pack snow atop it, 'sealing' it against the ruffling of the wind. I wrestle the remnants of my improvised backpack under the canopy, and dig a little 'shelf' for it out of the snow bowl's inner rim. Then I unfurl my sleeping bag, lay it out across the bottom of that bowl like a carpet, and—once again—stop to re-tighten all the knots and buckles and straps of my *goddamned snowshoes!*

Man, these things are a friggin' pain-in-the-ass!

And when, at last, I squirrel my way up and out of my little 'snow hutch,' I'm surprised to find that it's suddenly dark enough to be almost night! My watch says it's barely after five, but the low clouds, still dense and crawling through the treetops, say it's closer to *eight*.

I take only a moment to appraise my shelter rigging before finally tromping off to join my fellow campmates. And I've gotta' tell ya', *it came out pretty danged cool!*

The spread of orange 'silk' doesn't rise very high above the ground, since the felled tree over which it's draped snapped at a height barely a foot-and-a-half above the crest of the snow. So, thanks to its low profile, it's really not all that visible to begin with.

I suppose that if I was feeling really industrious (or maybe just *anal*), I could probably round up a few sprigs from some of the still-green pine and fir trees sprinkled throughout this forest of sticks, and mask that orange sheet a little better. But then... *naaahh.*

Besides, considering the riot of snowshoe prints already encircling my little fortress (which makes it look more like the lair of a very socially active Sasquatch), a half-assed and glaringly out-of-place little screen of pine boughs would probably prove to be more of an eye-*catcher* then a blind, which would kind of defeat the whole purpose of the camouflage in the first place.

I close the entry flap against a flurry of wind-whipped ice dust that suddenly tickles my neck, kick a shovelful of snow off the top of my right snowshoe, and tromp off to the central campfire to see what's for dinner.

* * *

MOOSE JERKY AND K-RATIONS, as it turns out. *Mm-mm, good!*

Actually, all sarcasm aside, it tastes *damned* good. The jerky's only slightly more leathery than the store-bought stuff (*although somehow I missed the moose hunt that garnered us this 'kill'*), and the K-Rats, well...

those are a whole new dining experience in themselves.

Unlike C-Rats, which are full-fledged field-portable *meals*, K-Rats are strictly *survival* rations. Compact, nutritionally dense, and sized and shaped to fit the limited confines of a survival kit (like the ones built in to a fighter's ejection seat), they are handier to carry, easier (and quicker) to eat, and are made to last despite their smaller dimensions.

They come in what look like little sardine cans… flat, rounded, rectangular tins with roll-back tops. Most of them would not appeal to me at all outside of a survival situation. Too much chocolate, or too much salt, or too much grease… too much *something*. But I quickly discover that there's one that I *love*. The "Lemon Bar."

I could live off that alone, I do believe.

Basically it's a sardine-can-shaped ingot of compressed corn flakes that's been soaked in some kind of lemony juice. It tastes sort of like a hard, brittle, lemon meringue pie. And even though it's barely the size of a large harmonica, I find that I can stretch out its consumption to last for most of a half hour.

And while we eat, our instructor, Sgt. Goodwin, regales us with tales of trap-setting, snow-boiling, and ways to urinate in the snow that make it virtually undetectable (*hint: work on your marksmanship*). He even pulls a thin metal wire out of a parachute harness's chest strap, and shows us how a simple wire slip-knot and a piece of K-Rat 'bait' can nab you a fine squirrel banquet.

And I'll tell you what: thanks to that little seminar, I think I'm starting to *appreciate* the constant but fitful blizzard conditions, as well as the neck-deep blanket of snow it's left for us to waddle through. It's buried all the foul tasting plants and leaves and berries we would have had to pick and eat, not to mention the innocent little woodland creatures we'd have had to lure to their deaths, then gut, clean, cook, and eat. And that's a worthy trade-off, I do believe. I might not get the chance to learn everything the survival gurus want to teach me, but that's okay.

The conversation becomes more social and giggly, the darkness swallows the world outside our campfire's glow, and finally, somewhere around 8:30, I do my awkward little snowshoe slog-waddle back to my shelter, and cave in for the night.

2

DAY TWO: SNOWSHOE APPRECIATION DAY

WE AWAKEN TO THE first clear sky we've seen in more than a week.

Actually, it's only clear *above* us. *Below* us—as viewed from our mountain's 'bare shoulder,' just a hundred yards or so downhill from our clearing—we discover the boiling cloud-*tops* of that same old overcast deck, still scouring the lower world with a heavy wet ruthlessness that we're perfectly happy to have missed. *Beautiful.*

The sudden appearance of the sun even gives us a chance to try out some of our signaling and navigation techniques that its previous absence had denied us. But we've got to hurry. The clouds will be deepening again soon, swelling upward to enshroud us like before, and we'll be back in the murk once more.

So, following a scrumptious K-Rat Lemon Bar breakfast, I join the others as they *ka-flop* their way out into the clearing as if they were walking in flippers, fussin' and cussin' the whole way, of course, about how their stupid snowshoes feel like they're tromping around in a field of frozen elephant turds, and now they're stuck to their boots in uneven lumps.

Then, with our requisite *kvetching* out of the way, we set about locating north, south, east and west using our watches and the sun.

Shortly after *that*, we're flashing each other—*with the sun and our survival kit mirrors... what did you* think *I meant?*—learning how to sight through the mirrors' little eyeholes, and signaling high-flying aircraft with them. Neither of these takes very long, and they're even kinda' fun. But after about twenty minutes of blinding each other with science, at least half the group is down on one knee again, tugging and tightening and adjusting their goddamned snowshoes for the umpty-eighth time, and exchanging cranky barbs about their unending inconvenience.

Sgt. Goodwin brings the exercise to an end with a single shout.

"Okay, gentlemen! Come and join me over here!"

It takes a minute or two to struggle back together again, converging from all corners of the snowbound clearing, padding along and doing our painstaking little penguin-waddles, as we try not to step on our own twenty-inch-wide 'feet' in the process. Sgt. Goodwin waits patiently, his tolerant smile barely visible through the steam leaking from his mouth and nose.

Once we're all finally assembled around him—not far from my inappropriately-located shelter, actually—he claps his gloved hands together and announces, "Good news, gentlemen! It's Snowshoe Appreciation Day! You can take those damned annoying things off now."

Oh thank gawd! And everybody hops off, giggling.

I plod the seven or eight steps over to my shelter, kneel to remove one snowshoe, then plop back on my ass in the snow to remove the other.

Man, this does *feel like I just pried a couple of frozen elephant turds off my feet.*

I jam their heel-stems into the snow, posting them there like a couple of cold tiki torches, and then stand up.

Well, I *try* to stand up anyway.

What actually happens though, is that my left leg plunges into the snow clear up to my crotch. I try to heft it back out by rocking my weight over onto my right knee... which, naturally, follows suit by punching through the thin crusty surface itself, and dropping my balls into the ice as well.

Hoo-HOO!

My automatic reflex? Palms down on the snow to *press* my way out.

Result? Both hands break through, collapse all the way up to the armpits, and my face hits the powder next.

I rock my way back upright, spitting snow and slapping it out of the fur of my parka's hood, and noticing for the first time that pretty much everyone around me is doing the same thing. My ass drops lower when I re-settle myself back onto that cheek. But with enough sustained straining and delicately applied leverage, I am finally able to suck one leg up out of its hole.

"Come on, guys!" shouts the instructor. "We've still got to make the rounds of all your shelters! Come on! Let's go! Get on your feet, and *get your asses over here!*"

I jerk my leg the rest of the way up, and with only a minor collapse on the other side, I wind up tentatively spread wide across the snow on hands and knees. *Okay then. Next... step...*

Placing all my extremities in those foot-, hand-, and ass-prints in front of me, where the snow has already been compressed and packed down a little, I heave myself upright... and immediately fall forward into another underfoot cave-in... only this time I attempt to sort of 'stumble-run' *through* it... which only ploughs me in up to be ribcage. My chest folds over the top, making me say "*Oof!,*" and I end up submerged clear up to my pits again, with only my arms, shoulders, and head still above the surface.

I look like I just fell through ice, and I'm clinging to the edge of the hole for dear life.

"Son of a bitch," say I.

"*Hey gentlemen! Dudes! Come on!,*" the instructor chides. "We haven't got all day here. You got what you wanted. You don't have to wear those stupid godawful snowshoes anymore. So let's get a move-on here! We've got places to be, people to see, things to do. Let's go!"

You know, I'm starting to think there might just be a 'lesson' in here somewhere.

I squirm and tug for purchase, but now *nothing* can find traction. *Any* downward pressure by *any* appendage only results in a further collapse.

Is this snow? Or quicksand?

I look around at my fellow classmates, and find them all in varying degrees of snow immersion themselves, all of them sharing embarrassed grins.

"*Now,* folks! I'm not kidding!" Sgt. Goodwin continues. "Get over here!" And points to the very spot where we'd all just been standing not five minutes before, the snow still chewed and compacted by all our overlapping snowshoe prints. *Okay, okay. I get the point. Now can we please...*

"Don't you touch those snowshoes!"

I look over to where he's pointing, to where Captain Cavanaugh—an annoyingly cocksure and infamously vocal F-4 pilot out of California—is sprawled across the snow, trying to slide his snowshoes under his *hands* for leverage. Pretty clever, actually.

"This is Snowshoe Appreciation Day! You won't need 'em! And we've got a lot of ground to cover, so *get over here! All of you!*"

I shove and dig... and slip and crash... and claw and drive... and plunge in even deeper. *Goddammit! There's got to be a way to do this!*

Yeh, there is. But it probably involves using snowshoes.

Down at the bottoms of my latest leg-holes, I squirrel the toes of my boots into the snow, essentially digging toe-holds as I go, trying to stair-step my way up and out. But that only goes so high, and then the more lightly compacted snow gives way, and I drop back in up to my chest again. *Shit!*

This only makes me crankier and more determined though, which, in turn, only makes my next attempt all the more aggressive. And I throw myself into it with an amped-up fervor.

Off to my left, I catch sight of my buddy Greg as he suddenly rises to his feet, and teeters there for a second as if balanced on a rolling log. He's only about ankle-deep in the snow somehow—probably packed down a small area in front of him where he could find some solidity—and is now steeling himself to make a lunge for the instructor. At least that's what it looks like.

And he does! He gets three whole steps into a staggering charge, one *shin*-deep, one *knee*-deep, and one *groin*-deep that then caves in up to his belt line. He doesn't quit, though. He just throws his arms out wide, and rolls hard left and right until first one and then the other leg flops back out onto the surface. He then half-swims, half-crawls another five feet forward, until he somehow magically hoists himself the rest of the way up onto his feet again... right in front of the instructor.

He's now standing, roughly knee-deep, on the pre-compacted snow where we'd all been milling around earlier.

Back *before* 'Snowshoe Appreciation Day.'

"Okay, that's one!," shouts Sgt. Goodwin.

A couple of the guys breakdown into helpless laughter, managing to rouse just enough energy for some exhausted applause.

Ah, jeez!

With another mighty heave, I bully my way forward again. *Enough of this 'trying to get on top' stuff. I'm too big and heavy for that.* Instead, I think I'm just going to *batter* my way forward, 'brute force' it, bashing my way through like an ice-breaker (or like Bugs Bunny burrowing his way through to Albakoiky). Let's see how far *that* gets me.

Turns out, not very far.

I throw everything I've got into it—legs stomping and driving and digging, hands clawing and scooping, arms pushing *up* or pulling *forward* as the moment demands, feet tripped up and hobbled by the funnel-like confines of my trench—and the goddamned snow just absorbs it all. My breathing flies hopelessly out of control, of course, worsened by the higher elevation of our campsite, I'm sure, and forced into arrhythmia by the herky-jerkiness of my thrashing. I grunt and heave and growl—I gasp and swear and gulp for air—and I assault the yielding battlements with an almost obsessive fury... until, at long last, I finally surrender.

I flop, breathless and deboned, over the lip of my trough. The bare side of my face is lying in the snow, and I'm sweating in sheets inside my parka... and I can't stop giggling... at myself. I must look pathetic.

I look up at Sgt. Goodwin... and he's still a mile away! Well, twenty feet, anyway. *The bastard must have been backing up!*

I rock up onto one elbow—which once again drops through the crust of the snow, sinking me up to my armpit—and look back at the trail I just 'blazed.' And I doubt if the channel I carved is even *fifteen feet long!* I could probably take *three steps* back down the rut, and reach my snowshoes where I left them, what... half an hour ago?

"Are you fucking kidding me?"

Did I just say that out loud?

I look back toward the instructor, plus the *three* students that are now standing or kneeling there beside him, slap the hood of my parka back out of the way, and nod my head.

"Okay," I gasp. "I get it. I get your point."

"Well, that's just fine," says Sgt. Goodwin, "But I still need you to get your ass over here so we can get this thing started. Come on! Let's go!"

Oh gawd. 'Get this thing started?' Seriously?

He's really going to push this, isn't he.

Well then, enough of that damned 'ice-breaker' technique. That about t'killed me.

Following a deep lung-steadying sigh, I scoop a couple of armfuls of snow *into* my hole, and on my elbows and knees, I inch my way up over it, and onto the surface. From there then, it's back to my original *one-caving-in-slipping-buckling-step-at-a-time* method, slogging my way oafishly across the chest-deep snow pack, toward where the rest of the gang is also struggling to converge.

Hours later, it seems, I slither the last of the distance up to Goodwin's tapping toes, and flop over onto my back, the second-to-the-last student to make it. And if it weren't for my heaving chest, I'm sure it would look like I'd been shot dead in the middle of making a snow angel.

Sgt. Dobbs, the portlier one of the two C-141 loadmasters in our group, is the last one to stagger into the circle, aided in his final push by none other than Cpt. Cavanaugh... who drops into the snow almost crotch-deep as a result of his helpful gesture. We all concede to weary laughter, and applaud our own sorry asses.

"Okay, gentlemen," says Sgt. Goodwin with an exasperated shove away from the tree that he's been leaning against for the last half hour. "Step One of Snowshoe Appreciation Day: choose between walking around *with* or *without* your snowshoes. If you'd rather have your snowshoes *on*, go ahead and put them on again."

Huh? But...

"Um," says Sgt. Dobbs, "You mean...?"

"We still have to do a walk-around inspection of your shelters," says Sgt. Goodwin, "So, if you think you'd rather be wearing your snowshoes for that walk-around, I would seriously recommend that you go and put them back on again before we leave."

We are hesitant, however, stooped, sitting, or kneeling where we are at the ends of our respective Trenches o' Torture.

Is he serious? After all this crap, we're just supposed to turn around and go back to our snowshoes now?

"So then," he continues after a long, silent, and immobile pause, "I gather you'd rather *not* have your snowshoes for the walk-around. Well, that's just fine with me. So..."

"*No, no, no!*," we interrupt, almost in harmony. And we each turn around to begin our slogs back through our outward radiating snow ditches.

Miserable son of a bitch.

Two hours later—okay, *fifteen minutes* later... okay, maybe *five* minutes later, five minutes that *felt* like two friggin' hours… five brutal and utterly debilitating minutes of fighting my way right back down the same mulched-up snow channel that I just finished battling going the other way, looking like an escaped prisoner fording waist-deep rapids at a clumsy stumbling sprint—I finally flop into my old butt-prints in the snow. And I lie there, puffing and panting beside my snowshoes… my beautiful *beautiful* snowshoes.

They just look so wonderful now, so sleek, stylish, functional. Actually, they look downright *ethereal*, standing there against the sun like lacy, teardrop-shaped sculptures. Like sparkly dreamcatchers. The light is not only glinting off the snow-dust lining every strand and edge, but the jury-rigged webbing has splintered the light into fans and beams of heavenly radiance.

Yes, I am that tired.

I release an epic sigh, then roll over and pluck them from the snow bank. Their donning goes quickly and easily (relatively speaking), especially considering the flaccid burn of my limbs, until finally, with one last mighty heave, I am able to heft myself back up onto my feet.

Yes, I said *on my feet!*

Holy crap! I'm standing *on the* snow! *Atop it even! What a miracle!*

True, I'd also been standing atop the snow *before* Snowshoe Appreciation Day, but for some reason, it just wasn't the same wondrously emotional experience then.

Turns out, I LOVE my snowshoes!

3

DAY TWO: WINTER WONDERLAND

SOMEWHERE JUST AFTER ONE in the afternoon, we finally hike up out of the *tops* of the clouds. They've been slithering over the mountains all day long, frequently eliciting the rather disconcerting sensation that the *mountains underfoot* were moving through *them*.

But now, as we trudge the last few hundred feet uphill toward the absolute apex of this one little snowy-naked peak, tromping carefully up the slope in our snowshoes—moving out of the silent stampede of cloud-shadows, and into pure dazzling unfiltered sunlight... past the last lonely whistling tree, and into vibrant blue skies so intense they look polished and buffed to a rich sapphire luster—the world above the weather unfurls around us. And even without a signal to do so, we all stop, in unison, to take in the broadening tableau.

Magnificent.

Below us, on all sides, the clouds are combing through the mountain range like milky water through shallow rapids. Hardly a handful of trees visible across all these snow cone mountaintops, hardly a wisp of cloud to mar the indigo dome above, and not a trace, not a nick, not a *ding* of civilization anywhere to be found. Just white-on-white capped by blue-on-blue.

For all that we can tell from up here, we could just as easily be atop the Himalayas right now.

The cold scours my nose red, the wind snuffles through the fur of my parka's hood, and the vista is almost too bright to look at. *Breathtaking.*

This, of course, is countered—*in its totality*—by the shaking of my exhausted legs, the deep, raw, and hollow scratchiness of my heaving lungs, the throbbing ache beneath my tongue, and the frozen snot bridging the gap between nostrils and lips. I'm also gasping so hard, it makes me laugh.

My so-called 'improvised backpack'—nothing more than a disheveled wad of loose components by now, bundled up in a lopsided poncho and some leftover parachute material, and bound together by a sloppy web of parachute suspension lines—has been steadily disintegrating as the march has gone on, requiring the occasional backtrack to pick up a dribbled sock or two, a canteen cup, or maybe a mess kit spoon.

Thank gawd I haven't dribbled any underwear along the way... yet.

And then, of course, there are my friggin' snowshoes…

I'm sorry! I meant my BELOVED snowshoes, whose helpful and crucial role in keeping me functional and on top *of this head-deep snow mass I can fully appreciate now, thank-you very much!*

But they absolutely will *not* stay tight for more than about fifty steps or so. They've been slapping at the soles of my boots and dragging their tennis-racket-handgrip 'heels' through this crusted powder for the last several minutes now... *again*. And as appreciative as I may be for their assistance, by now I am dead fucking sick and tired of these jury-rigged monstrosities.

Sheesh!

We've still got close to another half mile to go though, according to Sgt. Goodwin

As a group, we gasp and snort and swallow hard, trying desperately to lubricate our chilled-dry throats, and slowly congregate around our instructor. *He* looks like he was just dropped off, right in front of us, by a luxury helicopter. *We* look like turn-of-the-century polar explorers, bearded and chap-lipped and unkempt, and one step from Death's Door, gazing hopefully into his face, and waiting for him to give us meat or something.

At least *I* do. Greg *never* looks mussed.

Sgt. Goodwin points ahead to the next heaped vanilla spire before us. There's a lazy swoop of a saddle connecting our peak to that one, almost like a snow-draped suspension bridge, so the walk from here to there shouldn't be too long, too hard, or too vertical. And there's a broad 'ledge' on the *side* of the summit, as if a huge dollop had been scooped out of the ice cream. Goodwin's finger points to that ledge.

"That's where we're going to bivouac tonight," he says.

I pour the last of one canteen's water down my throat, and stare at that divot of pure snow in the distance there.

Are you kidding me? We won't be rigging improvised shelters out here tonight like we did *last* night. We'll just be making do with whatever we can find on-site, we were told. But... *there's nothing there! Not a tree, not a rock, not a bush!* Just a wide concavity of snow lopped out of the side of another snow-smothered mountaintop. *Home sweet home, my ass!*

I hate this shit.

* * *

BY LATE AFTERNOON, WE'RE still slogging our way across that damned saddle. Apparently it's just a little bigger and longer than it looked.

Nine tiny, hunched, insignificant little figures—a parade of fleas against the vast, surreal, and pristine white backdrop—plodding along in awkward, cautious, tentative little steps that still fail to keep our snowshoes from clacking *against*, and stepping *on top of* each other. Between the eight students, there's so much stumbling and dropping to knees and falling over on hips rippling up and down the line that, from any distance, we must look like target ducks getting repeatedly shot flat as we chug across a carney shooting gallery.

For a while, it was funny, in a giddy, bone-tired, oxygen-deprived kinda' way. But by now, with the sun settling lower on our cotton candy horizon and blazing straight into our eyes like a massive searchlight, every little slip and stagger just hits us as more and more exasperating.

I'm beginning to see the wisdom, though, in having us hike so far before crashing for the night under whatever rock or bush or fallen tree we can find. Because right now I am fairly certain that pickiness will not be an issue with me tonight. I could topple over right where I'm standing, right now, *face down in the snow*, and sleep like a baby. A *dead* baby.

I've got to say though, all miseries and inconveniences aside, this really is an unbelievable panorama up here, especially now that the lowering sun has made a sun*dial* out of every pinnacle, hummock, and ridgeline that pierces the solid cloud deck below us. This may be what Heaven looks like (on TV, at least), but it's probably closer to what Hell *feels* like.

A *frozen* Hell, anyway.

At the front of our little weaving, staggering, lurching high-mountain procession, Sgt. Goodwin suddenly steps aside and stops. The rest of us have to practically pile into each other before we look up from our snowshoes, and come to a stop ourselves.

"Okay, gentlemen," he chirps breathlessly, "This is it." And he sweeps a gloved hand across the field of snow as if sprinkling it with holy water.

We look around at the plain of unblemished glaring white powder.

"This is *what?*" Captain Cavanaugh blurts on our behalf.

The rest of us chuckle weakly.

"This is your home for the night. Make the best of it. You've got about an hour-and-a-half until nightfall, so I wouldn't waste any time."

"Doing what? There's nothing here!"

"There's *plenty* here. And by now, you should know just where to look to find it."

A few more loose helpless giggles spill out through the steam jetting from all eight mouths, saying, in no uncertain terms, *You have got to be kidding me.* Then, as a group, we just… surrender, I guess. We sigh, shrug, and disperse toward the perimeter of this broad snowy ledge, our snowshoes dragging dejectedly. Too mentally numbed to argue, too weary to resist, and too depleted to care… too ready to crumple into a coma at the first sign of a place to rest, so… yeh… might as well look.

As for me? For the moment, I've opted to just stand right here, right where I am, and watch what the rest of the gang does first. As much of a 'natural survivalist' as I am—as adept as I am in the wild, as gifted as I am with improvised or hand-fashioned tools, and as 'intuitive' as I've proven to be when confronted with no available flora, fauna, helpful ground features, or, most optimally, an *RV*—standing here right now, staring at all this unspoiled desolation, and trying to imagine what I should do with all this nothingness, turns out to be just a little too daunting for my morale.

Let's see: should I jury-rig my overnight shelter over there, where the snow is really flat, and there's not a stone or a log to start from? Or maybe I should assemble my all-natural lean-to over there, *where the snow is really REALLY flat, and there's not a twig or a stump anywhere to be seen.*

Decisions, decisions, decisions.

Turns out, though, this snow is actually covering stuff! *Usable* stuff!

And who'da thunk that?

I don't know how this Florida boy managed to miss that simple little Truth, but there it is.

Once one of the guys finally resigns himself to just digging a snow cave out of the mountain's powdery coat, he quickly discovers that just beneath the rolling surface are all the things that *made* it roll... like rocks, and logs, and bushes. Stuff like that. His excavation burrows right into a submerged bush, beneath which there is an air pocket, a small patch of dry grass and pine needles untouched by the snow *because* of the protective umbrella of the bush.

Perfect! A ready-made cubby hole! He need dig no more.

Greg, on the other hand, strikes rock with almost his first scoop of snow, a small tumbled-down heap of mini-boulders which, though not 'sheltering' enough to create an air pocket, are still *close* enough, *vertical* enough, and *stacked-against-each-other* enough that Greg can dig out his own little cubby hole, and it should maintain its structural integrity.

And suddenly, this starts to look almost '*fun.*'

So I start padding around the snowfield, looking for new angles on the sun's long shadows that might reveal a promising swell or undulation that no one else has yet seen, beneath which might lie the underpinnings of a viable overnight shelter... preferably one with electricity, indoor plumbing, and a fireplace. But I'll take whatever I can get.

As usual though, having waited to see how the others did first, I've now waited too long. The criss-crossing trails that they've mulched through the snow as they've gone about their own scavenging have all but obliterated the smooth and subtle rises and falls in the snow cover. I have to slog my way over, almost to the very brink of our shelf's downslope, where it abruptly plunges uninterrupted all the way down into the cloudy rapids filling the valley below, before I detect a ripple in the snow so faint that a second look almost convinces me it doesn't really exist. But it *is* there, like an ancient speed bump eroded down to almost nothing, or like the fine knuckling of a woman's spine beneath her skin. A ghost of a suggestion, but it's there.

I scuff at the surface powder with the tip of my snowshoe, and lo and behold, right there, not even five inches down, I hit pay-dirt.

Well, I hit pay-*bark* anyway.

Yes, I said *bark*. A small tree, with a trunk barely eight inches thick, lies horizontal just below the surface, snapped several feet above ground level and fallen to one side like a lowered gate. In fact, it seems to have dammed up a fairly large drift of snow which would otherwise have just sloughed off down the mountainside.

I chip away at the snowy rise leading up to it, and almost immediately it caves in, revealing an immaculate little man-sized pocket directly beneath the fallen tree. *Tah-daahh!*

Are you kidding me?

That was so easy, it's almost embarrassing. My 'search for shelter' turned out to be about as challenging as unwrapping a Christmas gift.

The collapsed opening is little more than a narrow mail slot though, running left to right under the log. I drop to

my knees (which once again sink into the snow up to my crotch), and stick my head into the slot.

Awesome! The spindly branches of this toppled tree, still flocked with dead leaves and bent by the weight of the snow atop them, arch over the hollow like ribs, providing a dry and well-supported ceiling overhead. And though the space is shallow and pinched off at both ends, it looks to be the perfect dimensions for me.

It's actually a little spooky, truth be told.

It looks more like a cocoon from which I've just *emerged*, than just a convenient little air bubble in the snow into which I'm about to be *sub*merged.

Well, no reason to look any further. *Honey! I'm home!*

I don't even bother calling Sgt. Goodwin over to get his approval first, like everyone else has been doing. I just thrash my makeshift 'backpack' off my back, wrench the sleeping bag from its disheveled guts, lay it down the length of the trough, then stuff the rest of the disintegrating 'pack' into the hole after it, bundling it up at the 'head of the bed' like a pillow. And the instant everything's in place, without hesitating even a heartbeat, I rip my snowshoes off, toss them inside as well, then roll in after it all. And I am *GONE!* I'm just a bundle of green insulation and steamy breath wadded into a nearly invisible little slit in the snow… and I pass out instantly.

* * *

SGT. GOODWIN STARTLES ME awake again—*Jeezy Pete! I must have conked out as soon as my head hit the pillow!*—and behind him, I see that the sky has turned a much darker smoky-blue color while I wasn't looking.

The sun has apparently *set* since I rolled into my little cubby-hole, what… *an hour ago?! Seriously? Man, I must've been wasted!*

I notice though that I am comfortably warm and snug, even though I've been lying *on top* of my sleeping-bag-bed the whole time. I guess the natural insulation in here is pretty good.

"So," says Sgt. Goodwin, "Are we all safe and comfy in there?"

I don't sit up—I can't, not without stuffing my head into my low twiggy ceiling—but I roll to face him more squarely, and I smile.

"Why, yes, Sgt. Goodwin. And it was a lot easier than I thought it was gonna' be."

"Yeh, I noticed. You look like you just laid down, and your body heat *melted* you into the snow."

"It's a gift, Sergeant. Like being naturally gassy."

He chuckles at that. "Well that's just excellent. You've got a great spot here, I see… good cover, good protection, good camouflage. I had a hard time finding you, actually. And it looks right toasty in there, too."

"That it is, Sergeant. That it is." I yawn, and 'lengthen' a little (there isn't enough room to actually *stretch*). "Didn't think I'd fall asleep like that, though. Sorry about that. Must've been more tired than I thought. Did I miss anything?"

"Not yet. But why don't you grab your snowshoes, and come join us over here. No fires tonight, but I hear the K-Rats and squirrel jerky are top notch."

"You talked me into it, Sarge. I'll be right there."

"Excellent." And Sgt. Goodwin hoists himself back up onto his feet, turns, and tromps away.

Getting *out* of my little 'snow womb' though, proves to be a tad more difficult than tumbling *into* it was. Trying to slither out between my thick tree-trunk roof—with its fragile little rib cage of snow-covered branches just looking for an excuse to dump their burden all over me—and the crumbling lip of snow at the edge of my slot, all without *collapsing* that lip of snow, rakes my neck with bark, fills my collar with snow, and forces me to do a one-armed push-up off the floor of my shelter.

Finally! A use for that unappreciated skill!

But once I'm up and out and manhandling my snowshoes back onto my boots, I take a moment to assess my shelter-rigging handiwork.

Damned sweet! More homey and cozy and warm than the shelter I'd spent half an afternoon assembling out of parachute parts at our last site.

So… apparently I make a danged good shelter, as long as I don't have to actually *make* a shelter. I do better at *finding* good shelters, I guess.

Know thine limitations.

STORY XXXVIII

DOWN FROM THE MOUNTAINS

1

DAY THREE: ESCAPE AND EVASION

February, 1978
In the field, east of Fairchild Air Force Base, Spokane, Washington

AT JUST A LITTLE after 9:30 in the morning, the rendezvous site comes into view.

Despite the fact that we've been plodding our way downhill since before sunrise, we're still above the soupy undercast of clouds—*just barely*—when our track arcs us around the end of the neighboring ridgeline, and reveals the gathering of other student groups who also spent the morning hours marching down to here.

In addition, there's about half a dozen large pick-up trucks and a small army of additional instructors that they brought up to join us, all convening over steaming cups of coffee at this little wide spot on this long forgotten logging road.

More instructors, huh? That can't be good.

Fortunately, the snow here is thin, muddied, and compacted enough by all the vehicles that we can take our friggin' snowshoes off and just mill around among our 'long lost buddies' for a bit, while we wait for the remainder of the scattered student groups to arrive. If I could tolerate coffee, I'd have a cup. But I can't, so I don't ('old radiator water,' as far as I'm concerned). Instead, I peel open my last K-Rat Lemon Bar—acquired only this morning by bartering off two nasty chocolate granola bars for it—and park my ass on the rear bumper of one of the trucks.

The bright unfiltered sunlight has me squinting hard, but it is heatless. The cold lays on everything up here, and plumes of steam flutter from every mouth, nose, coffee cup, and exhaust pipe around me.

I hear a bawdy and all-too-familiar eruption of laughter, and look up in time to catch a glimpse of *Spew*, his hair tweaked and tousled by three days and two nights without a shower, peeking out from under his field cap in matted flicks. He grabs an exaggerated handful of his crotch, and hefts it, as part of some 'hilarious' punchline apparently. The three or four guys standing around him burst into extra-manly *haws* and *hardy-hars* themselves, regardless of whether they *liked* or even *got* the joke, I suspect.

Gotta' make sure everybody knows you're just as macho as the rest of them are acting.

I turn away to avoid any possible recognition.

Instead, I stroll to the edge of the road, and look out over the drop-off into the plunging forest below. I feel like an ant, standing on the center knuckle of a large hand... a hand splayed flat in a pool of milk. The three middle 'fingers' radiate out away from me, sinking into the pooled clouds between them as they go. Trees—sparse along the *tops* of the ridgelines—thicken the further down the sides they grow. But they too vanish into the clouds that fill the valleys.

I wonder what this place looks like when it's not swimming in this soup of low and settling clouds.

Behind me, a cheer goes up, and I look back to see the long-awaited Last Student Group slog-waddling their way down to us from the upper slope and waving in response to the applause. I see 'Spazman' Spiegelman is among them. He's probably the reason they're the last.

At the same time, I notice the cadre of extra instructors tossing out the last of their coffee now, nodding to each other, then piling aboard all those pick-up trucks. Their engines roar to life, they back and jostle and maneuver around each other, then drive off in both directions down the logging road. And by the time those Last Students plod into the clearing, no vehicles remain, and the mountains are silent again.

Hmmm. Interesting.

The newest arrivals are given the chance to shuck their reviled snowshoes for a few minutes, and to rustle up something hot to drink. But then the remaining group instructors, like our own Sgt. Goodwin, herd everybody together again, this time into a single crowded knot arced around the lead instructor, Sgt. Chaffee.

"Alright, folks! Listen up!," he shouts. "It's E-and-E time! 'Escape and Evasion,' in case you didn't know that already!"

I *did* already know that. And I was already dreading it.

"This is the home stretch, ladies and gentlemen! *Finally!* But, if you think you're tired *now?* Well..."

He sweeps his hand back and forth between the two nearest gullies behind us, where they drop into the clouds between the finger-like ridgelines.

"Down there," he continues, "a little over a mile down those lower creek beds, are the buses that will take you back to base! All you've got to do is walk to them! And that's it! That's all there is to it!"

Of course, by that, what he really means is, '*There's a LOT more to it than that!*'

"The only problem is...!"—and he pauses here to make sure we all get a good look at his spreading grin—"that's all enemy territory down there! Starting right here, at the edge of this road, and going that-a-way all the way to the buses, The Enemy will be looking for you! And it's your job to make your way *out* of enemy territory safely... undetected, and uncaptured! In other words, you've already 'escaped.' Now you must '*evade!*'"

Great. I can't wait to see how I'm supposed to elude a party of experienced hunters and trackers that already knows exactly *when* and *where* I'm going, when I'm running through neck-deep snow in loose snowshoes and a disintegrating 'improvised backpack,' plowing a ragged scar through the snow, and dribbling unmentionables in my wake.

Seriously... how could they not *find me?*

Maybe if I tuck my hands under my armpits and flap my arms like a bird, honking a bicycle horn as I run, I can keep my pursuers laughing too hard to catch me.

They pair us up into two-man teams. No particular selection process this time; just whomever happens to be standing next to you when an instructor walks by. I turn and introduce myself to my new 'survival partner.'

He says his name is Maither. Lieutenant Tom Maither.

He's a helicopter pilot, in training... or he's *going* to be... or something like that. Sort of like how *I'm* an air traffic controller... to be... currently working my way through an extremely roundabout detour to that destination.

What a team.

Wait a minute... 'Tom Maither?' Ta'maither? Ta'mater? Really? My cross-country E&E buddy is named 'Ta'mater?' Lord, gimme' strength.

He seems a decent sort, though. Friendly, prone to smiling. Polite... maybe even a little 'timid,' even *'deferential'*. *To me? An airman?* Then again, he might be reading a little too much competence and confidence into my camouflaged fatigues, my smart-assed sarcasm, and my snowshoes being on backwards (*just kidding... about the snowshoes*). Perfect officer material.

They tell us we can head out whenever we're ready, taking whatever route we choose, as long as it follows the grain of those ridges and valleys dipping down into the clouds below us, bound for the buses at the other end. And since Lt. Ta'mater and I were quick to wrestle our snowshoes back onto our feet, we are among the first six or seven teams to step off the edge of the logging road, and forge our way down into the gullies.

* * *

WITH ME IN THE LEAD—I don't know whether ol' Ta'mater Man is being 'deferential' again, or if he's just being a typical officer and letting *me* break trail for *him*—I angle across to the right, first to the top of the rightmost 'finger' ridge, then side-step down its left flank into the misted pines where they're shrouded by the uppermost tendrils of clouds.

Remembering everything they taught us about covert cross-country movement, I'm staying *off* the ridgetops (where we'd cast conspicuous silhouettes against the sky), staying well *above* the creek bed (where our pursuers would most likely expect to find us), and, thanks to today's weather, staying *within* the thick soupy fog of the clouds (anything to help mask our glaringly obvious tracks through the snow).

Of course, even though the mists might white-out the posse's view of our snowshoe-mangled trail (at least as viewed from the creek bed looking up), if they ever do come upon our trail, anywhere along its length, there'll be no more 'hiding' after that. I pause for a moment to look back.

Jeezy Pete, the track we're leaving behind us looks more like a herd of moose (or is it *"meese?"*) passed this way. Or maybe a derailed locomotive.

It's like a big fat arrow of mulched snow pointing after us. *"They went that-a-way!"*

How could they not *find us?*

While I wait for Lt. Tomater to catch up, I lean my back against a tree and wrestle with my damned snowshoe straps again.

The lieutenant's really having some balance issues though, trying to walk *across* this steep incline atop loose and sloppy tennis rackets like this, top-heavy with his improvised backpack, and somehow even more breathless than I am. And when he finally gets close again, he swivels to twist his butt up against a neighboring tree—like me—but instead gets torqued completely *off* his feet when (a) his snowshoes don't pivot along *with* him, and (b) the weight of his backpack just keeps on going. He flops into the snow on his *side*, as if he intended to make a 'snow angel' in *profile*. Then he just stays there, spent and giggling.

It's a light, airy, slightly phlegmy snigger—kind of a helpless *'kee-hee-hee-hee'* sound—and it's infectious. It makes me chuckle and snort a little myself, and I slide down my tree and sit down beside him.

I like the old Tomater-Man. And his harmlessness is smoothing off some of the stressful edges of this forced march quite nicely.

Finally, he sniffs and gulps down a little extra air, then shoves himself up onto one elbow.

"I don't know about you," he gasps, "but I haven't seen anybody *else's* trails since we started. Have you?"

"No. Not that I've been looking, though."

"But we weren't the first to come this way, were we?"

What are you getting at there, Mister Tomater?

"No. I'm pretty sure a couple of other teams already came this way first. Why?"

"Hmm," he says, dabbing at his dripping red nose with a well-used hanky, "Guess I'm just hoping we're still going the right way, is all. Can't see shit in this fog."

"Well," I chuckle, keeping it 'light,' "that's kinda' the whole point... staying outa' sight. If *we* can't see shit, neither can *they*. Theoretically. But we're definitely going the right way. There's only one way *to* go, as long as we stay with this ridge."

"Okay then," he answers with a nod, jerking himself upright into a sitting position, and pulling up his stupid snowshoe for readjustment.

"That's good enough for me."

Well, I huff in my head, *it damned well oughta' be. I mean, who's the pilot here, and who's the air traffic controller?*

Or will *be... someday... eventually. Hopefully.*

I wrench and tug and tighten up my own snowshoe straps again. Then, before pulling myself back up onto my feet, I take a moment to scan the ghostly forest surrounding me, looking for traps or curious instructors peeking around trees, and confirming our continued route of travel at the same time. And in so doing, I discover, much to my chagrin, that *I'm actually having fun right now! And who'da thunk that?*

I'm busy 'outfoxing The Man' here... 'threading the enemy's needle,' 'slipping through his noose,' 'ducking his swing,' and 'trumping his hand.' And as long as we're headed for those buses up there, I'm also *running for home.*

Getting the hell out of here.

The flank of this ridgeline is pretty danged steep, though—at least thirty-five, maybe forty degrees—plunging from its crest above the clouds, down to the meandering creek bed about thirty meters below us. And we are edging *across* it, remaining fairly equidistant between the top and bottom... maybe a little lower than higher, just to stay within the murkiness of the mists.

To transverse the slope like this, however, requires some cautious trickery with these damned snowshoes, especially for the idiot who has to break trail. And naturally, that would be me. I've got to essentially swing my foot *sideways* into the snow, dig it in edge-on, then press down to flatten out a level footprint each time. Lt. Tomater just has to plant *his* snowshoes in *my* snowshoe *prints*. It's the same old officer-versus-peon story.

Looking back the way we came, I am mesmerized by the crumbling rut we've carved, as it swoops across the slope from tree to tree like Christmas bunting. It wouldn't take a whole lot of squinting to pick that out against the otherwise immaculate blanket of snow.

Yet another reason to keep trekking along up here in the mists.

I cling to the tree as I heft myself back onto my feet, then press on from there.

* * *

ANOTHER TEN MINUTES PASS in grunting gasping 'silence,' as we chip our way across the flank of the ridgeline in tottering half-steps. We see no one, above or below us, and I get the feeling that old Lt. Tomater is beginning to question the torturous and hobbling course I've chosen.

I mean, we seem to be all alone up here: no other students, no detectable instructors, and no other comparably inconvenienced snowshoe trails crossing our path through the snow.

So what are we beating ourselves up like this for?

It's taking us for-bloody-ever to trek this measly little mile-and-a-half to the buses. What if everybody else has already *finished* this damned thing? What if everybody else took more sensible 'streamlined' routes, and we're just thrashing our way along like this for nothing? Those are the 'whiny waves' I think I'm starting to sense from the officer who is my survival partner slogging along behind me. He doesn't actually *say* any of those things, of course—at least not *out loud*—but I know he's *thinkin' it!*

Until we suddenly hear voices below us.

* * *

WE FREEZE IN OUR TRACKS, and look down to spot two other students—*finally, other people!*—picking their way among the relatively 'flat-ish' snow-covered stones lining the edge of the creek.

Right where they were specifically told *not* to go.

I don't recognize either of them, but the Tomater Man seems to. They're talking to each other in subdued tones. I can't actually make out any specific words from up here, but even their low chuckling and jostled murmuring sounds downright riotous in this otherwise muffled silence.

"*What the hell are they doing?*" I whisper.

Tomater answers distractedly without taking his eyes off them.

"*They're being Posse Magnets.*"

I turn my gaze to the top of Tomater's head where he's lying low in the snow behind me... and I chuckle. *Good one, Mater Man.* Then he starts looking around at the woods that surround us, as if looking for other observers... or instructors... the 'posse' that those two dumbasses down there are working so hard to attract.

Hmm. Another good point, Mister Mater. Perhaps we'd best find ourselves some better cover before one of those chase teams finds us *in the process of homing in on* them.

I had been tracking a little uphill before we'd gone to ground, angling toward some scruffy leafless bushes that I'd planned to pass above (in order to mask at least a *little* of our trail from below). I scramble the rest of the way up to those bushes now, low and scuffing my way through the snow on my ass and elbows. Lt. Tomater is right there behind me, following in my wake.

Once we're both hunkered down behind our little screen of shrubs, though—thinly flecked with only a few dead leaves—I realize that we're going to have to do better than this. We're dressed in basic green, but the bushes are a lacy crosshatch of browns and grays, and everything else around here is a friggin' *radiant white*.

I start squirming my way deeper into the snow, driving one way with my butt and gloved hands, and bulldozing the other way with my snowshoes, heaping up a low berm of pretty white snow against the back of the bushes. A little something to semi-hide behind. Mater Man catches on quick, and is right there with me. We haven't been at it for even thirty seconds though, when another much louder 'authority voice' suddenly booms through the dry acoustics, freezing us in mid-burrow.

"You two! Right there!"—*uh-oh*—"Walking beside the stream!"

Oh, whew! Looks like we ducked low just in the nick of time.

I lay over on my right side—can't duck any lower with this ridiculous 'improvised backpack' draped across my shoulders like a deer carcass—and peek over my freshly piled battlements down to the creek below. Through the shield of twiggy bushes, I spot the two students in question, rising from their half-squats as if they'd been caught in mid-duck themselves. They're both looking over their shoulders, back up the creek bed.

Then one of them points to his own chest, and with wide-eyed innocence, shouts, "Us?"

"Yes! You!," the authority voice shouts in a jovial tone, more suited for a game show announcement. Sort of like, "*Come on down!*" Only *he* says, "*You! Are! Captured!*"

Down to my extreme lower-left, a squat barrel-chested figure, plumped even more by the parka he's wearing, emerges from a clot of trees that bow steeply out over the creek. *Lordy, those two must have practically walked right under him. And we* above *him, for that matter.* Then he skitters down the embankment to the creek's edge. The students shuffle resignedly back toward him.

"I guess you missed the part about *not* following streams and rivers, huh," the instructor continues.

Their response is quieter and humbler—not to mention unintelligible from up here—but I get the gist of it easily enough. They *had* been slogging along further up the slope, they insist, but the terrain conditions just kept corralling them lower and lower until, without really even noticing it, they'd wound up on the embankment just above the water's edge.

Uh-huh. Yeh. The instructor's head nods constantly as they plod up to each other. This is no doubt the first time he's *ever* heard that one.

"Yeh, well. See, that's just *one* of the many reasons why hunter and capture teams concentrate on the streams when they're looking for ya'. They know they're easier and faster for a fugitive to follow. Plus they're a source of clean water, they provide noise cover, and they usually show up on maps, so you know right where you're going... which means *so do the capture teams*. Stuff like that." They stop right in front of each other. "So that's why *you don't go there!*" And he hands them each a slip of yellow paper.

"Give those to the first instructor you see at the buses when you get there, and let him know you were caught."

The students slump with dejection. Then one of them asks the instructor a question that I cannot hear from up here. Fortunately, the instructor doesn't seem to believe in speaking quietly, and I have no trouble hearing his reply.

"Oh definitely. Keep on heading that way. You can even continue following the creek bed now if you want, since avoiding capture is a bit of a moot point for you two now. Go ahead. The buses are probably only a hundred yards or so further down that way."

They mutter something, to which the instructor says, "You're welcome!" Then the two of them trudge off along the stream's edge.

In the meantime, the instructor makes a note on a tiny pad of paper, and engages in a short dialogue over a walkie-talkie that he pulls out from under his parka. Then he turns and ambles back to his little hide-out among the trees.

Lt. Tomater and I remain immobile throughout the entire exchange, even breathing into our gloved hands to mask the steam coming from our mouths... until that instructor suddenly looks up at us and shouts, "You guys up there! Behind the bushes! Nice work! Good cover! Good technique! You can press on now too!"

Damn! He knew we were here the whole time! That's disappointing.
Not unforeseen. But disappointing, nonetheless.

I guess that applying the correct tactics, even ineffectively, is all they're really looking for here. And that *should* be good enough for me too.

But it's not.

Dammit! I really thought we'd pulled this off.

We struggle and thrash our way back up onto our tennis-racket feet again, pound the snow off each other, and forge ahead along the side of the ridgeline.

* * *

SOMEWHERE AROUND SIXTY OR SEVENTY meters further down the line, the 'finger' that we've been tracking the whole way abruptly peters out. Its crest shrivels down out of the clouds, and dwindles away to nothing right at the creek's edge. It forces a bend into the water's flow, but otherwise it just ends, as if cut off by the stream itself.

The ridge on the *other* side of the creek continues on though, marching off into the mists in both directions, with the brook hugging its base like a crooked little moat. But, as *our* ridgeline steadily erodes down to nothing, its shrinkage forces us further and further down to the water's edge, until, well... *here we are...* hopping across to the other side at a point where the water almost seems to disappear under the close-set roots and snow. And as we step off onto the opposite bank, we find ourselves standing in the middle of an apparently well-traveled traffic route.

Several snowshoe trails converge here, tracks coming down off the ridge, following the stream, and even fording the little creek in several places close to where we stepped across. We also hear voices coming from just up ahead, convivial, lighthearted, and way too loud for covert conversation, but definitely student voices.

Hmmm. Maybe we've finally reached the end of the gauntlet here.

Tomater and I pick our way along the mulched-up path, wary of its deceptive 'levelness' (a fiction composed of compacted snow squashed over rounded streambed rocks), and stabilize ourselves beneath our top-heavy backpacks by grabbing every trunk and tree branch we pass. And no more than twenty meters further on, where we break out of the trees, the banks abruptly flatten and widen, and the trail veers away from the precarious rocks and onto more solid level ground. *Now that's more like it.*

Up ahead—maybe a hundred meters beyond and uphill of the stream that I see we're going to have to *re*-cross again—atop an ugly and artificially leveled 'plateau' that's barely visible through the veil of moving clouds, sits a ghostly pair of buses, and three times that many pick-up trucks.

The end of the line, dude! Hoo-HOO! We made it!
Me and the Mater Man even did it without getting caught!
Officially.

The voices we'd heard from back there though, were apparently those of the four students we're now approaching, all loudly engaged in trying to traverse the stream at a log bridge spanning this much wider chokepoint. One of them is already on the far side, and I gather from the tenor of their exchange, that his was a pretty hairy transition. Now he and the nearside folks are shouting and gesticulating back and forth, coaxing and encouraging, balking and harassing each other, trying to get the next person across.

I look up and down the waterway, and notice that, once free of the tree-cluttered gully, our little creek finally had the freedom to broaden and straighten. And accelerate.

So it did.

In fact, were it not for the downed tree bridging the five-foot-wide bottleneck over there where those students are still so vociferously haggling with each other, there would be nowhere down here to cross it at all. At least not within sight... or without wading through knee-deep ice water.

I don't like the looks of it, and I turn to Lt. Tomater to see what he's thinking about all this.

"I don't know about you," I say, smearing my parka's sleeve across my raw and running nose, "but I'm thinking seriously about backtracking to where we just crossed over—back there in the trees—then just picking our way along that *other* shore back to here. What do *you* think?"

He crunches to a stop beside me, sniffing and shrugging his backpack into a better alignment, and looking the scene over. And he doesn't take long.

"Well, it looks to me like a *bunch* of snowshoe tracks all come together here. And over *there*, at the other end of that log, it's looking pretty well traveled also. So I'm thinkin' that, since a lot of other folks have already come this way and made it across right here, and since *we're* standing here already, well... this'll probably do just fine."

I knew he was going to say that.

"Okay then," I sigh. "Your call."

I hike the crumbling discombobulation of my 'backpack' higher up onto my shoulders, take another hit from my canteen, then turn toward the gaggle at the 'bridge' crossing... just in time to watch the next guy in the group make the mental commitment, heave himself up onto the log, and start his own traverse to the other side. And several things happen in rapid succession.

First of all, I recognize the guy. It's none other than Airman Spiegelman himself. The "Spazman." The same guy who didn't possess the physical coordination to hop into a pool of sawdust without hurting himself. That, all by itself, does not bode well.

And second, I notice that he's *still wearing his friggin' snowshoes!*

He's sidestepping along the rounded and snow-covered crest of a log, which is two feet in diameter and three feet above a fast-moving stream of freezing water, *with tennis rackets on his feet!*

That, and a giant wad of personal gear heaped on his shoulders like a load of junk being hoisted by a really disorganized Sherpa.

And did I mention, *it's Spazman Spiegelman!*

What happens next is anything *but* a surprise.

In fact, it's absolutely pre-ordained.

* * *

BARELY TWO STEPS AFTER releasing his grip on the upturned roots of the tree, his arms begin to pinwheel. *Frantically*. His feet attempt to backpedal, but in his snowshoes, he not only has no traction whatsoever, but they keep overlapping and stepping on each other. And after only a couple of clattering high-kicking dance steps, over he goes.

He smacks into the water, flat on his back, his feet scissoring in the air. And for the next several seconds, as the Mater Man and I hobble-trot in our own snowshoes toward the scene, all that we can see of the Spazman are his thrashing feet beating against the log, his snowshoes still attached. The rest of him is apparently underwater, weighted down and anchored there by his backpack.

He is drowning, in a foot-and-a-half of frigid water.

The two remaining guys on the nearside bank are stutter-stepping hesitantly along the creek's edge, no doubt trying to figure out how best to wade into a brisk current wearing their own snowshoes. But the lone guy on the *far* side of the stream—who at least had the common sense to *remove* his snowshoes before making the crossing—waffles only a moment or two before wading into the icy flow himself, and storming through the knee-deep water over to the Spazman.

In parka and gloves then, he plunges his arms into the water. And after one failed heave that very nearly topples him face-first into the drink, on the second try he manages to haul the Spaz out by the shoulder straps of his improvised backpack... one of which immediately breaks, and dumps him right back under the surface again.

Spazman's flailing hands seize on his rescuer's sleeve though, and between the two of them—and a fistful of his lapels—they are able to drag him back upright once more, against the current, and despite both of his feet still sticking straight up in the air, the heels of his snowshoes hooked over the top of the log and unable to free themselves.

Lt. Tomater and I clomp up to the scene, ungainly and oafish in our awkward footwear, and immediately join the two other guys in the furious act of ripping off our snowshoes. I catch a flicker of movement off to my distant left, and look over to see an instructor bounding our way, hopping sideways down the snowy slope and shouting into a walkie-talkie. Seconds later, another one magically appears off to my *right*, leaving his cover to rush to the stream's edge *without* snowshoes.

In the middle of the stream though, the Spazman and his rescuer are making just about as much noise as it's possible for two humans to make; Spazman spluttering and shrieking about the freezing water, his buddy growling from the strain of holding him upright, and barking at him to pull his legs down... Spazman screaming that he *caaaan't* because the heels of his snowshoes are snagged on the log, his 'buddy' yelling, "*Then get your arms behind you and prop yourself up! I can't hold you up like this much longer!*" More splashing and thrashing and roaring and yelping about the cold. Then his buddy shouts out, "*We could use a little help here!*"

One of the original two guys on the near bank finally frees his last snowshoe—he thinks—and leaps into the fray with it still dangling and flailing along behind him... until it comes off as he enters the water, and starts to float away with the current. He detours to lunge after the drifting snowshoe, then flings it up on the shore.

On the opposite bank, the first instructor on the scene, who had barreled down out of the woods without his snowshoes, now charges straight into the little river without breaking stride, and now there's four of them out there, frothing up the water as if they'd just waded into a piranha feeding frenzy. And rising above the rest of the tumult, I hear Spazman's copyrighted mantra: "*Ow! Ow-ow-ow-ow!*", followed by, "*You're bending my legs too far!*"

And that gives me an idea.

With my own stupid snowshoes still doggedly hanging on, flapping loose against the soles of my mukluks, I get up and sidestep around the root bole of the tree to the opposite side of the log from the others. Then, without actually stepping into the water, I lay across the top of the log and reach down its length to Spazman's squirming feet.

"Roll him onto his side!," I shout, "Just for a second!"

The instructor looks back over his shoulder, sees what I'm going for, and repeats the command.

"Roll him over! *That* way!"

"What? Huh?" Spazman splutters, "But... wait, I...!"

Ignoring his protests, along with another shriek about the icy water, they force him to roll toward the near bank. Up on the log 'bridge,' his snowshoes roll with him, and their tennis-racket-handgrip heels swing up and very nearly *over* the log all by themselves. I just reach across and finish the job, pushing his heels the rest of the way over.

His legs finally drop into the water with a couple of splashes. And the Spazman says, "*Ow!*"

"Okay, let's get him out of this damned water!," shouts the instructor, taking charge of the situation now. "Over here! On *this* side!," he adds, shrugging towards the shore with a trio of additional instructors bulling across it... the shore with the buses in the distance... the shore on the other side of the 'bridge' from me.

"All of you guys that got wet, you need to get up to those buses too! ASAP! And see the medic there! Come on! You've finished the course already anyway!"

The foursome splashes their way across to the opposite shore, and manhandle the Spazman up onto dry land. He's *still* wearing his friggin' snowshoes though, and he's making loud jittery whining noises, splintered by his chattering teeth.

Two of the other instructors unfurl dark green horse blankets as they converge on the party, and swoop them over Spazman's shoulders, while the first instructor rips his sodden backpack off, and dumps it on the ground with a soggy "*splat!*"

And again, Spazman says, "*Ow!*" He seems to say that a lot.

Somebody else wrestles his snowshoes off as well. Then they charge up the slope toward the buses, dragging the shivering Spazman between them.

I turn to Lieutenant Tom Maither, my survival buddy, and release a giddy sigh.

"That boy needs to seriously consider a career change. Maybe to accounting, or something."

"Or folding bandages."

I snort, and cock a '*good one*' finger at him.

Lt. Tomater. My kind of officer.

2

OUT OF THE BLIZZARD, AND INTO THE FRIDGE

BACK ON THE BUS again—*gawbless the bus!*—and chugging back downhill. Out of the damned mountains, *finally*, and headed back to fabulous friggin' Fairchild Air Force Base again. *Yee-hah!* But despite all my hopes to the contrary, the *in*side of the bus turns out to be just as cold as it was *out*side.

No heat! *Again! Dammit!* And for all the same reasons as those for our uphill trip.

As we descend through the clouds, winding our way down out of the mountains and their snow-laden forests, we emerge onto the slushy highways bracketing Spokane, and the universe closes down on us again. The sky is once again lidded off by that all too familiar dark, swollen, and oozing overcast that seems to have decapitated Spokane's tallest buildings. All color has been leached away, and suddenly the dark dirge-gray weather reminds me of just what's waiting for me up ahead...

... the last day-and-a-half of Survival School.

POW School.

It's coming up on noon now. They'll be closing the facility's chow hall in another hour, so we need to be getting back there *mui pronto*. Because I am *ravenous*... hungry enough to "eat the south end of a northbound water buffalo," as Mutt taught me to say.

Unfortunately, even though we've finally finished running the outdoor survival gauntlet, this week—Week Two—is far from over. Even worse, this third day of the last week *has only just begun.* And the final thirty-two hours of it were *designed* to suck.

Once we've finished lunch, we'll be headed right back into the classroom again, without having shat, showered, shaved, changed clothes, slept, or even brushed teeth… still with snarled and matted hair, dried mud up to our knees, and breaths smelling like a butcher shop with failed AC. And there we'll be spending the rest of the afternoon getting final instructions and counseling, in preparation for the course's grand finale', the hellish twenty-four hours of POW School… which begins tonight at eight o'clock, and runs straight through to sunset tomorrow… *Thursday* night. So we'll be *starting* it already scruffy, smelly, and ready to fall asleep on our feet.

Wondermous.

There is one up-side to all this, though. As it turns out—as it was just announced on this bus, in fact—this afternoon's classroom sessions will not be taught by any of our regular course instructors. Instead, we will be entirely under the tutelage of *real living breathing former POWs,* who'll be sharing their real-life personal stories, as well as their wisdom, worldly perspectives, and recommendations on how best to get through the home stretch of this school.

How cool is that?

3

VOICES OF EXPERIENCE

COLONEL OBERLUND, U.S. AIR FORCE RETIRED, slumps on his stool at the front of the auditorium like a bluesy bar singer, handheld mike hanging limp between his knees whenever he's not speaking. And even when he *is* speaking, the mike rises only as high as his wrist alone can heft it. He lowers his *head* to bring his lips within speaking range.

The years have not been kind to the former colonel, nor to any of the other ex-POWs that preceded him to the stage, either. Not time, and certainly not his North Vietnamese captors, for that matter. His sedentary weight hangs from him in bags—under his eyes, under his jaw, under his ribs—and his psychological baggage hangs from every sentence.

I can't decide if he's bored, bor*ing*, or just reluctant to be here.

And if it's the latter, is it because public speaking in general makes him uncomfortable, or because he's just sick to death of re-opening these wounds every time a Survival School class enters its last days?

But he holds nothing back. After growling his way through a dreary—or maybe just a personally discomfiting—recitation of some of the horrific and agonizing ordeals to which he was subjected at the infamous 'Hanoi Hilton,' he just as dully recounts the 'weaknesses' in his own character that ultimately led to his being 'broken' by his captors.

If he really does consider his 'capitulation' to be the result of some 'weakness' in his character though, rather than the inevitable conclusion of months and even *years* of beatings, starvation, broken (and un-reset) bones, and dislocated joints, then coming here every few weeks as a 'guest' to profess that 'weakness' over and over and over again has got to be like returning to a neverending AA meeting. The wounds would *never* heal, I'd think. And this lackluster performance could then be attributed to that torturous repetition.

Or maybe he's just a really bad public speaker.

It happens.

As he growls and mumbles his way through his presentation though, a large black-and-white photo, left on the overhead projector by the previous lecturer, continues to illuminate the broad screen behind him. It was taken by an American reconnaissance jet in Vietnam as it hurtled over a prisoner of war camp north of the DMZ. And in it, plainly and *amazingly*, you can clearly see how, like a discreet halftime marching band, the American prisoners milling around in the yard somehow managed to form themselves up into 'random clumps' that spelled out the letters "**P O W S**."

It's an awesome picture, depicting not only the creativity, but the courage it must have taken for a hundred-or-so beaten, broken, starved, and abused prisoners to defy their captors so brazenly. And right under the noses of the guards in their towers, no less, whose inability to read or recognize English letters had to have been a critical and desperate part of the plan for them. All that, plus the *readiness* to act whenever such a rare opportunity presented itself, the *adaptability* and the *speed* needed to form up and align themselves in accordance with the direction from which the jet approached, and the *resolve* it took to assemble and hold their ground at least through the aircraft's second pass, even while their overlords were trying to drive them back to their cages.

Incredible.

Proclaiming to the world *who* they were, *where* they were, and perhaps most importantly, *where not to bomb!*

Awesome work, guys.

In the meantime, Col. Oberlund's tedious narrative finally reaches its point, and it turns out to be more than just a protracted admission of his own human frailty. *A lot more.* For when the endless torture had at last reached the unbearable stage for him—as it does for everyone, at some point or another—after untold weeks and months of being blinded by battered eyes swollen shut, aching from electric shocks, his broken ankle still un-set, his shoulders in agony from the days spent suspended by his arms, which had been hoisted up behind him... when at long last, he could simply take no more, he was still able to deny them their ultimate victory after all.

Two massive shadow-hands switch out the acetate on the overhead projector. The photo of the prisoners disappears, and in its place, a copy of a formal 'confession' now fills the screen. *His* 'confession,' apparently.

He remains silent for a couple of minutes, allowing us the time to read it through from top to bottom. And it *is* remarkable, not to mention *bizarre.*

To think of the hideous and sadistic extremes to which his interrogators went just to coerce this 'admission' from him. Declarations of his supposed disbelief in the American cause, disgust with its leaders and their motivations, and his general revulsion over the 'war crimes' his country had led him to commit against the innocent people of Vietnam. To read this dogmatic dreck is to consider an alien sort of madness.

Did they really think that such a 'confession,' even if made public in the United States, would make any difference to the war effort *at all?* And even if it did, for Col. Oberlund, was it really worth the months of searing agony, crippling injuries, and possibly even *death*, just to resist writing something as politically and militarily impotent as that? As *that?*

Musta' been.

The colonel's amplified voice shatters the stillness.

"Did you notice anything unusual about that so-called 'confession'?"

Huh? How the hell would I know? It's not like I've seen a whole lot of other confessions to compare it to. Everything *about it is unusual to me.*

I give it another fast visual scan—and to me, it bears a striking resemblance to just about every piece of military paperwork ever produced—then I join the rest of my fellow students in shrugging my shoulders. A lone unmiked female voice though, from somewhere down front, chimes in hesitantly.

"Is it the address block?"

The colonel smiles for the first time. "Why yes, it is."

Okay. I look up to the top-left corner of the form, and re-read the name of the addressee. And the first line of it says;

"*TO: Gen. Garba Gefollows*"

It takes me a second, but after a moment or two, I do finally get it.

"*General Garbage Follows.*"

Awesome.

The rest of the room 'gets it' at about the same time, apparently, because the phrase begins to ripple around the auditorium in hushed tones, then builds to an appreciative buzz... then to sporadic clapping, which in turn blurs into a crescendo of applause... then cheering... then a full-on standing ovation. And by the time Col. Oberlund next leans down to his microphone to say, "Thank-you," he can hardly be heard at all.

Resistance in the guise of submission. Victory in the wake of defeat. Redemption from surrender.

You know, there's probably a lesson in there somewhere.

* * *

IT'S ALMOST SIX P.M. by the time they finally release us for a belated dinner... knowing full well that we'll have to be on the bus to POW School by 8:00. So we have a choice: food, maybe a shower, and/or a change of clothes, maybe even a quick 'combat nap,' but time for no more than two of the four.

I choose food and a short nap... involuntarily.

I eat. I sit down for a second. I pass out.

Then somebody bangs on my door at 7:45, and ruins everything.

BOOK TWO
THE WANNABE

PART 5

POW SCHOOL
Fairchild Air Force Base, Spokane, Washington
February, 1978

STORY XXXIX

PRISONER OF WAR

1
CAPTURE

February, 1978
Air Force POW School, Fairchild Air Force Base, Spokane, Washington

I STUMBLE ACROSS THE icy ditch, and thump flat against the levee on its opposite side.

I can hear, but can't *see*, others around me in the thickening darkness. I hear the squeaky crunching of boots breaking through puddle ice, the *whump* of breathless bodies landing on the shadowed side of the levee to my right and left, and from the far side of the embankment, the shouts and taunts of our common enemy braying over bullhorns.

Searchlights sizzle across the crown of the levee in swipes. And as they sweep past, I catch sight of people scrambling over the top in the light's wake. It's the only time I can actually see anyone clearly, as they pop up into the crossfire of the beams from the other side and vanish. I decide to wait, lying here against the frozen embankment, to see what comes of their actions.

Overhead, gauzy sheets of overcast veil the winter stars. You'd think that would only darken the scene all the more. Instead, the criss-crossing spotlights seem to *ignite* the low clouds, which, in turn, cast a dull pulsing radiance over everything. It's pitch black on my side only because I'm lying within the shadow well of the dike.

From the other side, machine gun fire suddenly erupts, choppy little firecracker pops mixed with shouting. It's intermittent, but it keeps recurring.

I guess the round-up has begun.

Gawd, is this cool, or what?

I scrape my way cautiously to the lip of the berm, and peek over. The levee drops into another ditch on the other side, a mirror image of *this* side. But beyond that is what looks like an unmarked football field, filled with running, dodging, yelling people, chattering AK-47s firing skyward, and dueling spotlights strumming the chaos. I can't tell what lies beyond that, since the glare of the searchlights has reduced the background to featureless pitch.

But that's where I'm supposed to go.

Well, that's the direction I'm supposed to *travel*, anyway. Truth is, getting to the other side is pretty much irrelevant. The whole point of all this overly dramatic stagecraft is really just to, well... *get captured!*

This is *POW School*, after all. And one prerequisite for imprisonment is, of course, *capture*.

Another wave of my fellow students charges over the ramparts, and joins the clamor on the field below. There's only a handful of us left now, hugging the backside of this levee, and, for whatever reason, trying to judge the most opportune moment to cross over ourselves.

As if it could possibly make any difference at all.

It crosses my mind that I'm wasting my time even attempting to evade the instructors. Not only is it a wide open brightly illuminated field, with absolutely no form of cover or even dark spots anywhere, and probably a dozen armed 'aggressors' running around 'capturing' people, but, bottom line, I'm *supposed* to get caught.

Still, wouldn't it be cool if...

* * *

NOW THAT ALL BUT a six-pack of us are embroiled in the melee over there, I start to notice a trend. Those that have been captured are being lined up along the distant right-side boundary of the field, facing away from me. The rest—and I imagine that by now, the instructors are probably thinking that that's about all of us—are being generally herded in the direction of that lengthening queue, maneuvered in a steadily tightening corral from the near-left corner to the far-right. So the aggressors' backs are more or less turned to this near-left quadrant now, with the searchlights concentrating their sweeps on those areas of the field in front of them.

In other words, it's getting darker at this end of the battlefield.

Some student-lieutenant beside me seems to have noticed this as well. And when he rolls over the top of the levee, angling toward that darker near-left zone, I go with him.

We slide down the embankment, and land in the other lit-up ditch undetected—that's what I choose to believe, anyway—and take one more assessment of the capture field before going any further.

This low to the ground, the searchlight beams fanning past us have already been broken up by their passage through the free-for-all out there in the open, like a car's headlights swinging through a picket fence. Lots of shadows—*moving* shadows—in which to take cover. And I start thinking crazy things, like… I should be able to stay out of the searchlight's line of fire if I can just keep low, and dart with the movements of the shadows, as long as none of the aggressors closest to my end of the field actually, you know, turn around and look this direction. Even then though, if I can see them starting to turn towards me in time, and I can drop and go inert in the penumbra of some of that mayhem out there, their eyes just might not be able to, you know… 'adapt'… maybe. *I don't know!*

The lieutenant and two of the guys beside me suddenly bolt up out of the trench and take off running, angling toward the seemingly 'ignored' left-side boundary of the field. I catch myself starting to follow them—some kind of 'subordinate reflex,' I'm sure—but I stop, and instead decide to dash, *alone*, down the length of the ditch in the opposite direction.

About halfway across this 'end zone' though, it finally dawns on me just how ridiculous all this scheming is. I *have* to be caught, you know, one way or the other. *To hell with this.*

Without any further consideration then, I slow, straighten up, then vault up onto the plain of the field. Steam jets from my mouth with every breath. It's damned cold out here on the high desert west of Spokane in the middle of February, and the frozen ground *thunks* beneath my boots like the wooden planking of a theater stage. The gunfire is winding down—most of the class has been apprehended by now, I'm sure—and the flitting shadows have become sparser and slower moving.

In the distance, the megaphones resume shouting instructions at the newest batch of prisoners that have been added to the end of the line. Yet I continue to sprint between the lonelier shadows, ducking and dropping and darting, and trying to follow the steady migration of my cover… sort of like a ninja trying to hide behind a moving car. Or maybe just an idiot.

Off to my far left, a sudden commotion breaks out; the rattle of machine gun fire, and more shouting voices. They've just caught the lieutenant and his two buddies skulking up the other boundary of the field.

Hah! That makes me one of the last ones caught! Hah!

So what! If that was so damned important, I could have assured it by just waiting to be the last one over the levee. Besides, even if no one *ever* caught me, I'd still have to turn myself in. The whole point of this school is to learn how to deal with incarceration as a Prisoner Of War (a "POW"), not how to evade capture. We already went through that in the brief "E&E" ("Escape and Evasion") part of the program earlier this morning, as we came down out of the mountains.

Surprisingly though, despite my waning efforts to avoid capture, I continue to go unnoticed (or at least 'unappreciated') for several more minutes. No weapon has been fired since that last lieutenant was taken down, most of the aggressors now being tied up with the management and supervision of the growing column of captives. Even the searchlights are now concentrating all their candlepower on that one corner of the field.

So I allow my hunkered posture to straighten up, my scampering to slow to a leisurely jog, and then to a brisk walk. And *still* no sign that anybody even knows that I exist.

Damn I'm good! Apparently as good as invisible!

But now I'm getting bored with trying to stay that way. I resume a light trot, and bee-line straight up the middle of the field, cutting right across the grain of the aggressors' little skirmish line. *Better hurry up, or they'll march off without you!*

And amazingly, I am finally caught!

* * *

"POOT YOUR PAWS ON the animal in front of you!"

The grip that's clenching the collar of my jacket shoves me forward. My own arms are out in front of me, waving with the blind groping of a sleepwalker. Or a zombie.

Because I've got a bag over my head. A small, shoulder-length, burlap bag with no eye-holes.

My Dad would enjoy the minor irony in this, I'm sure. He's always felt that the single most important piece in any 'ensemble' I've ever worn should have been a bag over my head. Preferably paper, plastic if nothing else was available, but burlap would do just fine.

I can tell, using my razor-sharp deductive skills, that I'm being led to the top of another levee (the steep climb kinda' gives it away). And with my inbred 'internal compass,' I can tell that this levee is in the far-right corner of the capture field... right where the prisoner queue was when I last could see.

My hands bump into someone else's back, and my captor—still chewing gamely on his half-baked pseudo-Soviet accent—repeats the same detailed instructions he'd issued earlier.

"Poot your paws on the animal's shoulders in front of you! Stand still and shut up!"

I plop my hands onto the epaulets of the last man in line. And magically, the grip on my collar releases.

And here I am! The new 'Last Man' in a long line of American prisoners. My uniform is mud-caked and filthy, my pathetic little field jacket insufficient against this cold, and my ungloved fingers are frozen. I'm standing atop a wind-whipped berm in the middle of a frigid winter night, surrounded by pretend-Commies wielding authentic Russian-made submachine guns.

HOT DAMN! Is this fun? Or what?

* * *

DOWN TO ONE SIDE of the levee, bullying over all the shootin' and shoutin', I can clearly make out the commotion of an 'actual interrogation' going on. I can't believe they're doing it *right here*, outdoors, on this hard snow-patched ground, in the middle of all this pandemonium. But then again, *why not?* They've got a lot of new inmates to process.

I can't quite hear the exact questions they're asking. I hear tone, volume, attitude. I hear fury and mangled bullshit Slovakian inflections, and I recognize a few key 'watchwords,' like *unit*, *strength*, and *plans*. But the terror in the voice of the man being questioned sounds unnervingly real.

Why? He's a student, isn't he?
We're all *students, essentially 'untouchable' by the instructors. Right?*
I mean, 'aggressors.'

For all their hype and bluster and posturing, they're hamstrung by all the rules and regulations that won't permit any actual physical abuse of their charges. *Right?* And to me, that's the best part of all this insanity.

They can play as dirty and menacing as they like, and I can play as self-destructively 'courageous' as I want, and no matter how close to a violent collision our excesses might carry us, *I cannot be hurt! Right?*

Right?

Just like playing 'Army' in the dirt of my old backyard.

So, either this kid I'm listening to is a truly sublime wuss, a terrified mental child, or just incredibly clueless.

Or maybe he's part of the school cadre, perhaps an instructor himself, just role-playing for the benefit of us cowled chickens up here on the levee.

Yeh, I'll go with that.

Then the interrogator's voice abruptly jumps in anger and impatience, and turns to some form of indecipherable fictional 'swearing.' I hear what sounds like a chair being kicked over. Then three or four fast whacks from something that has the aural weight of a riot control baton hitting a side of beef, each accompanied by a shriek of pain. The 'student' is wailing, blubbering, begging. The interrogator is badgering, bellowing, barking. More stomps, kicks, crashes. Another stinging *whack!*

Jesus! What acting! I think.

I hope.

No. Surely the school doesn't employ 'actors' of that caliber. Not for 'live performances' in the snow. Not before a blinded audience, anyway.

No. That's a tape. Yeh, it has to be. That's just a recording, played over a really good outdoor sound system. A good one-time gig in a recording studio, that's all. *Yeh, I'll buy that.*

Whew! Is this fun?

Or what?

* * *

WHILE THE 'INTERROGATION' BELOW me storms into another phase of begging and battery, footsteps scuffle up behind me, and a familiar command is issued once more.

"Poot your paws on the animal in front of you!"

"Wha'?" a stunned voice replies.

I hear a meaty thump, and a body stumbles into me, shoving me into the next animal in line. I manage to hang on to someone's field jacket and thereby stay on my feet, but the guy behind me tumbles down the back of my legs all the way to the ground.

"*Shtand up!*," is spat through clenched teeth, followed by the sounds of wrestling, or perhaps just a clumsy scuffle. Then the new guy is back behind me, and apparently just as confused as ever.

"Now poot your paws on the ani...!"

"I don't know what you mean by..."

"POOT YOUR DAMNED HANDS ON THE SHOULDERS OF THE MAN IN FRONT OF YOU, IDIOT!"

Jesus! How dense is this guy?

Then I find out. Only one hand lands on my left shoulder.

Come on, guy. Wake up.

"POOT YOUR OTHER HAND ON HIS SHOULDER!"

His right hand finds my other shoulder. His left hand disappears.

Oh shit.

Whump! Both hands are snatched away, and I cringe as I listen to him somersaulting down the side of the berm, grunting and yelping all the way. In hot pursuit, the rumble of a small aggressor posse thunders down the slope after him, converging with him at the bottom. Then comes the kicking and punching—or at least the noises I'd associate with them—accompanied by yowls of pain. *What the hell!* That's *definitely not a recording!*

Maybe they *do* have on-site actors. And maybe even some 'stunt men.' I sure hope so, anyway. Or maybe those official restrictions just don't apply in a place like this.

Another megaphone squawks.

"*Prisoners in the line! Prepare to move forward on my command! Step off with your left foot, and keep your paws on the animal in front of you!*"

Behind me, I hear that last guy being hustled back up the slope again, bundled along by, well... *who knows* how many guards. Probably *all* of them. And they're all breathing heavily.

He's snorting, and keeps repeating, "*Okay, okay, okay, okay...*" Then his hands slap down on my shoulders again—both of them, this time—and with the exception of his panting, the sounds of winded struggle at last recede.

In the background, the 'interrogation' is still going on.

That's got *to be a recording. And this beat-up moron behind me has to be a plant.*

Yeh. That's what they are.
"*Forward!*," shouts the megaphone way up front. "*March!*"

* * *

'HOME' FOR THE NIGHT is apparently going to be some kind of concrete blockhouse, with a big open central chamber, and what I interpret as a corrugated steel roof, based on the ringy play of the acoustics in this room.

We are marched in blind, our heads still bagged, clomping across a cement floor to the tune of an entire battalion of shouting guards. A lot of "*Come here!*," and "*Get in there!*," and "*Hurry up!*," mixed with chaotic boot steps, some loud woody thumps, and the bangs of slamming doors. And in between, the voice of a guard with a clumsy dialect yelling at a prisoner.

"Stand in the middle of your cell, hands at your sides! Face forward! Do not touch any of the walls! Do not remove the bag! And don't let me catch you sitting or sleeping!"

This is followed by the slam of another door, sometimes a kick.

Interesting.

The line accelerates slightly, then bunches up again. The shouting gets closer, more intimate. Then 'the animal' in front of me is snatched from my grip, and I can hear the rustle and bluster of another guard manhandling him into his 'suite.' I'm still trying to decipher as many details as I can from all the clamor, when the lapel of my own jacket is abruptly seized, and I am yanked to the right.

"Get in there!," someone barks.

A firm shove at my back, and I go stumbling forward. The diffuse light leaking in through the weave of my bag darkens, and a wooden wall collides with me, bouncing off my face and chest, and straightening me right up. I totter there for a moment, not sure what to do next.

"Stand in the middle of your cell, hands at your sides! Face this way!"

I'm spun around, facing back the way I came in.

"Keep that bag on your head at all times, and *stand there!* Don't touch or lean against any of the walls, and don't let me catch you sleeping!"

CRASH! The door slams shut in front of me, and the darkness ratchets down another notch, to pure pitch black.

Outside, the ritual repeats one last time, right next door—theoretically for that same dumbass who marched into this place behind me—ending with a stumbling crash against the wall of my cell. There's some more yelling, then the finality of another slammed door.

"Jesus," I hear my idiot neighbor blurt.

"*AND NO TALKING!*"

And just like that, the last of the racket dies. It's not *completely* silent. The 'lobby' out there still thrums with pacing guards, circling like Dobermans, just itching for someone to test the lock of his door, or say something stupid. But it seems that the last of the prisoners have finally been secured, and it's time now to move on to the next phase of this scenario... the psychological torment, the sleep deprivation, the isolation.

Solitary confinement.

2
SOLITARY

IT APPEARS THAT MY cell is a five-by-five-by-six-foot wooden closet. I can tell, because I can press the heels of my palms against the opposing walls at the same time. And if I lock my knees and crane my neck just a little bit, I find that I can wedge my head against the low ceiling. And I'm six feet tall.

It takes me a few minutes to muster the courage to peek out from under my bag, expecting some hidden camera somewhere to give me away and bring down a full gorilla cavity search on my ass. But after a little more time (and a little deep breathing), I do finally discover some momentary heroism, and quickly examine every pitch-black inch of my little booth.

There is no door on this cell. The entire front wall basically just swings outward. There's a low rectangular notch cut out of the bottom of it—the 'feeding hole,' presumably—and a pair of circular holes, half-dollar size, right at eye-level, covered by an outside flap of some kind. What little ambient glow there is in the room is just the aftereffect of the fan of light spilling in through the low food hole. And apparently, the walls are painted black.

I pull the bag back down over my eyes.

* * *

WITH THEIR ERRANT CHILDREN packed away for the night, the guards go and crank up an ancient stereo system somewhere—one with pre-blown speakers that add their own rattle and crackle to the cacophony—and a near-deafening assault of classical music starts to batter at my eardrums. A three-second snippet of busy strings jumping into a burst of horns, chopping off and repeating itself over and over and over again on an endless loop.

It's painfully loud and annoying as hell, but after about twenty minutes of this blistering dissonance, I finally settle into its rhythm, and put it mostly out of mind. So naturally, *that* can't be allowed to continue.

With the shriek of a phonograph needle being ripped across the face of a record, it suddenly derails onto a whole new track.

Now it's a *seven*-second loop, without a lick of music in it. Just a man screaming angrily, unintelligibly, while another one wails in terror and pain. Then the sound of a punch, an anguished warble, a kick, and the crash of a man and his stool hitting the ground. Before the clatter and howling can even ring out though, it abruptly cuts off and repeats again. And again. And again.

Scream! Wail! Smack! Shriek! Kick! Crash!
Scream! Wail! Smack! Shriek! Kick! Crash!
Scream! Wail! Smack! Shriek! Kick! Crash!

Over and over and over and over and over again.

And *Christ!*, it's echoing around this concrete shithole like the smashes and screams of a man bouncing his way down into the depths of a very deep canyon.

Maybe the guards hate this racket as much as we do. Maybe they're nowhere near this acoustic bombardment chamber right now. Maybe this is the best opportunity, then, for me to sneak a peek outside my little pigeonhole. We're supposed to be exhibiting some form of resistance the whole way through this thing anyway. So... *okay then*.

Here goes.

Carefully, I roll the front of the bag back over my head, ready to be snatched back down over my face at a moment's notice, and lean toward the eye holes. First, I press an ear to the door, listening for any sign of a loitering guard—which, considering the barrage of 'music' assaulting this room right now, is a lot like listening for someone sitting on a toilet while a hurricane is tearing the roof off the house—and surprisingly, I hear nothing incriminating. So I *slooowwwly... ever* so slowly... stick one finger through the eye hole, and lift the cover flap just the tiniest fraction of an inch away from the other hole.

Across the central chamber's broad floor, I can see a long row of green-painted wooden doors lining the far wall with food and eye holes cut into them, just like mine. The floor itself is strangely 'polished'—or maybe painted—concrete, and the one light bulb that I can make out through my tiny sliver of a crack here, is dangling from a ceiling too high for me to see, and is caged in wire mesh. My internal compass tells me that I entered this place from the left, which means that the...

WHAM!

The flap smashes down on my fingers. As fast as I can yank them back inside, I rip the bag back down over my eyes again, and snap back to attention.

A bolt is loudly thrown outside, and the door is nearly torn off its hinges before I can finish my panicky scramble. I can't *see* the guard, but the timbre, direction, and proximity of his voice implies that his last name might just be "Bunyon."

"*DO THAT AGAIN, AND I'LL BREAK YOUR FINGERS OFF!*"

He sounds like his nose is about three inches from mine, and like he might be big enough to snap off all my appendages like a little gingerbread prisoner. There's also a strong olfactory impression that he might have had cheese on his Filet-o-Fish. I'd probably take him more seriously though, if it weren't for that ludicrous high-school-play pseudo-Slavic accent of his.

The door crashes shut again to the tune of another one being jerked open further down the line.

* * *

WELL, AT LEAST THEY'RE BACK to playing 'music' again.

After giving us twenty minutes or so to slowly adapt to the sounds of screaming and bludgeoning repeating on an endless loop, they've just changed tracks again. And now it's a snippet of a fairly lush classical orchestration. Unfortunately, they've tortured that too, cranking the *speed* of the recording up and down in blasphemous sine waves. One moment it's accelerating up to the mincing chatter of a band of chipmunks arguing through kazoos, the next it's bogging down to the groans and yawns of a giant's all-tuba symphony. Up it goes, down it goes, up it goes, down it goes. Faster, slower, faster, slower. And then, about every ten seconds or so, it skips back to the beginning, and starts all over again. Repetition and sacrilege, chasing each other around the same nauseating circuit. *This one just might break me.*

It's been a while since the finger-smashing episode, though. And the loud surging-fading music is a pretty profound distraction. Maybe it's time for another adventure in resistance.

In the classroom, they taught us a real simple alphabetic tapping code, a knuckle-dragger's Morse code, intended to allow communication between prisoners separated by walls. Just like these. I haven't heard a peep from anyone but our demented 'DJ' since we got here though, so...

Turning to the wall to my *left*—there being a known *moron* in the cell to my *right*—I start quietly rapping the shortest ice-breaker message I can think of.

W-H-O-R-U. "*Who are you?*"

Hey, what can I say? I'm just trying to start up a dialogue here.

Amazingly, a discrete thumping returns in seconds, delicate enough to be barely audible to two people with their ears almost pressed against the wall, hopefully too subtle to be heard over the speeding-slowing-speeding-slowing music out in the central chamber. And I quickly discover just how much easier it is to *send* than it is to *receive*—or at least to *decipher*—someone else's string of thumps.

R- (or at least I think it's an *R*), *O-V-* (or is that an *S*? Yeh, I'm going with *S*. And there's another one), *S*. "*ROSS?*" *L-T-*. Then a pause, and *U*.

"*ROSSLTU?*"

"*ROSS-LT-U?*"

Ah! "**Ross. Lieutenant. You?**" Got it.

An answer followed by a question. Cool. We've got us a conversation!

Now, was that a first name or a last name?

Who the hell cares! It's not like I'm going to recognize the guy, one way or the other. But which one of my *names should I reply with? How about the shorter one. Shit, they're both five letters long.*

I go back to knuckling the wall.

S-T-I-P-P.

Hell, he won't know what to make of those letters.

So I cleverly add, **A-M-N**, for "**Airman**."

"**Stipp, Airman**."

I hear some more jumbled thumps. But this time they're muddled even more by a faint and contradictory knocking coming from my *other* wall.

Oh great. I've inspired the dingleberry who couldn't figure out how to put both of his hands on my shoulders.

Now, in the conflict of sporadic knocks and bonks drumming from both sides, I can't make out *anything* from either one of them. Not that it really matters any more, though.

Suddenly, this entire end of the hall seems to have caught on to this idea of proactively playing the game. Suddenly the whole place is *filled* with an escalating barrage of overlapping knock-knock messages. And it's getting progressively louder, as each new entrant tries to make himself heard over the building din.

This is getting ridiculous. In fact, it's laughable!

Do none of these people know what '*discreet*' means? Do they really think the guards are just going to sit back and listen to our clumsy knock-knock dialogues? If so, why not just *yell?*

BAM!

A door bangs open several cells down the row, and the drumbeat of knuckles goes abruptly silent.

"Vott do you t'ink you are do-ink?!"

Oh yeh. Time for some more cartoon-Russian.

More doors slam open. There must be half a dozen yelling guards storming through the outer echo chamber now. And I'm back at attention, bag down and in place, listening to the carnage I have wrought.

I guess this little challenge to *The Man's* authority is over now.

* * *

RATHER THAN CONFISCATE OUR personal stuff on-site, as would have happened in a real POW environment, they had us just leave everything but the clothes on our backs in our school billets. So I've got no wallet, no rings, and most importantly now, no *watch*.

You have no idea how pivotal the concept of *Time* is to someone who is miserable, who knows he is going to *remain* miserable for a long time, and who has nothing else to do but to *focus* on the glacial passage of Time throughout his misery. And I am now officially miserable.

I wasn't when I first came in. It was still a pretty cool, pretty elaborate *game* when it all started. But now, however many unknown hours have passed since then, I am dead tired… and miserable.

I've been standing the entire time, only rarely daring to lean against a wall, or even close my eyes. That repetitious 'music' has never let up even once, though it's never stayed the same for longer than twenty minutes either. Right now, it's a baby shrieking its guts out, the same grating little snippet playing over and over and over again.

And I can't stand the sound of shrieking babies. Never could.

They have occasionally peered into my cell through those eye holes—well, at least two times that I've been aware of—and fortunately, both times I was right where I was supposed to be: center of the room, hands at my sides, head-bag in place. But I've heard the commotion of others getting caught elsewhere in this cell block, doors rattling and slamming, angry 'Soviet' voices yelling, the thumps and bumps of people grappling.

It feels like I've been in here forever. I have no way of knowing for sure, but I figure it has to at least be after midnight by now. And all I want to do is lie down somewhere, and go to sleep. I can walk forever, but there are limits on how long I can tolerate just standing.

I did manage to show a little spine—*about, what, an hour or so ago?*—when, as one of those peephole inspections was ending and I heard the guard moving on, I'd stepped back, leaned against the rear wall, and slid to the floor. I figured it'd be at least fifteen, maybe twenty minutes before the next cell check—about the length of one of those obnoxious 'music' segments, the changing of which I could actually use as an alarm clock—and just those few minutes of shut-eye ought to be enough to keep me propped up like they wanted for maybe another hour or more. And I did actually nod off there for a minute or two. Who knows? It might have been longer.

I hate not having a watch.

But I was rudely re-awoken with a crashing start—actually it was more like a *'splashing'* start—when one of my incarcerated neighbors apparently got caught doing the exact same thing... sleeping. I heard a door bang open, followed almost immediately by a huge splash of water. Like a *bucketful!* A voice wailed and spluttered, bawling that the water was *freezing!* But he was interrupted by a far louder, more authoritative voice, bellowing at him for doing what he had specifically been told *not* to do.

I was scrambling dizzily to my feet, to a chorus of numerous other doors being ripped open at the same time all around me, and had barely tugged my bag back down over my face, when my own door was flung roughly aside, and an explosion of light barged into the cell. I could make out two amorphous human shapes through the weave of my bag, looming in the light before me like angry parents. Then the door slammed shut again, and I was left in the dark. Down the hall, I could hear the soaked prisoner bitching as they dragged him away.

He was the first to be taken to interrogation. And there've been several others since him. But since they seem to be pulling people out in 'cell order,' working their way down the rows, then it's going to be a long time before they ever get to me, all the way down here in the second-to-last cell. And as much as the prospect of matching my bleary wits against those of a trained interrogator makes me nervous, at least it would be a break in the monotony.

Something to listen to other than that *damned screaming baby!*
Something to *look* at besides the inside of this *damned ratty bag.*
And now they've gone and changed the 'music' again. *Shit!*
Now it sounds like a five-second sound byte of someone sawing through a steel pipe—that spine-shearing, raspy, back-and-forth *screeching*—followed by a mumbled curse, the painfully sharp clatter of metal on concrete, and the bright tinkling crash of shattering glass. Then cut. Then repeat.

Screechy-screechy-screechy! Snap! Curse! Clangity-bang! SMASH!
Screechy-screechy-screechy! Snap! Curse! Clangity-bang! SMASH!
Screechy-screechy-screechy! Snap! Curse! Clangity-bang! SMASH!
Fuck!

* * *

WELL, I'VE FINALLY FOUND a way to get some sleep and not get caught... sort of.

The top of my head-bag has been brushing against the damned ceiling *all night long!* That's been a source of annoyance all by itself. But, as I discovered when I first entered this cell, if I lock my knees and crane my neck just a little bit, I can essentially *wedge* myself between the floor and the low ceiling, and sustain it with almost no effort at all. *And* it passes a cursory peephole inspection. It's hardly optimal, it doesn't survive unconsciousness, but it's *something*. I may not be exactly 'asleep,' *per se*, but it does allow me to at least 'zone out' for short periods. Only when my little 'fades' *deepen* do my neck muscles tend to relax, and my 'wedges' buckle.

So I keep popping awake just as I'm starting to topple (*this must be what it's like to be a cow jolting awake in the middle of a 'cow-tipping'*), and that's pretty damned rude. But in between, I'm tuning out the cacophony, resting my eyes, and slipping partway into oblivion.

I'm doing that now, immersed in my own inner darkness, when the door to my cell rattles open, and the light yawns in over me.

"Animal! Step forward!"

Gawd, these guys really need a dialect coach.

Still muzzy with severed sleep then, I lurch toward the voice. Hands seize the shoulders of my field jacket on both sides, and I am hustled out into the middle of the lighted concourse.

And from there to my first interrogation.

STORY XL

TORTURE AVOIDANCE

1
INTERROGATION

February, 1978
Air Force POW School, Fairchild Air Force Base, Spokane, Washington

"HAVE A SEAT, MISTER, *aaahhh...*"

The cigarette in my interrogator's hand does a languid wave over his head as he looks down at my file, which is fanned open across the top of his desk like a deck of cards.

"... *Shtipe*. Airman Shtipe." He looks back up at me through his smoke screen. "Shteven."

He sounds more like Sean Connery than a Russki interrogator, if you ask me. Luckily, I like Sean Connery.

The guard who escorted me into this tiny shitty little office—the same one who manhandled me out of the cell block and into the chilly night... who guided me, blind, across the snow-dappled yard between buildings... who shoved me, stumbling, up the front steps and down the narrow wooden corridor, past other sealed offices leaking light and voices, to this room... who yanked me to a stop by my collar, and snatched the bag off my head, blinding me in a whole new way—that same guard now gestures accommodatingly to the lone chair in front of the desk.

I take a couple of steps around it, and sit down. Warily.

Below my inquisitor's cloud deck of spent tobacco, I can see him better, and I take a moment to study his face while he's engrossed in my 'dossier.'

He looks huge and imposing. And bored. His hair is buzz-cut blond—or maybe bleached white—and his square jaw and bloodshot watercolor blue eyes make him look like a mean drunk who's trying to act 'civilized' for a cop who's just pulled him over.

Either that, or an icy Soviet villain in a James Bond movie.

A dark blue fur-lined waistcoat hangs over the back of his chair, and he's wearing a black beret with a red star on it. The room and the furniture are minimalist and bare, to say the least. In fact, with the exception of a framed picture of Lenin on the wall to my left, and a poster full of indecipherable Cyrillic writing to my right, there's nothing here but thin wooden walls, an ugly, scuffed, gunmetal-gray desk, and us two chickens. *Cool.*

I'm as ready as I'll ever be. Bring it on!

* * *

I'VE BEEN MENTALLY REVIEWING everything they taught us in the classroom (or at least everything I actually retained), plotting my strategies, steeling myself for whatever curve balls they might throw my way. I mean, the main gist of all this role-playing is just to show us how to keep from revealing any pertinent military information, while at the same time not inciting their wrath to the point of torture. For torture is not only extremely unpleasant, frequently crippling, and often *fatal* to the prisoner in question, but it is also very persuasive in getting a prisoner to hand over said critical military information. As such, avoiding torture is also the best way to avoid handing over secrets.

But the tactics employed by the 'interview*ee*' need to be tailored to the approaches employed by his 'interview*ers*.' The John Wayne technique of telling them to go stuff themselves—"*You ain't a-gettin' shit outa' me!*"—only invites more persuasive modalities of questioning. Better to read the interrogator's mood, and play to that. Ready yourself to meet 'nice' with 'civil,' 'concerned' with 'grateful,' and 'polite curiosity' with 'apologetic ignorance.' That kind of thing.

Never be antagonistic, *always* be thankful for the tiniest courtesy. When they're insistent—and they're *always* insistent—try deflecting their pursuit. Pretend to be hazed with pain, either from injuries suffered during your capture or from the battle preceding it, or from the pharmaceuticals used to aid in your healing. Maybe pretend to be sick, about to ralph all over the interrogator's shoes. Lie only if you have to, preferably without straying *far from the truth*, with repeated references to the unreliability of your limited sources. And if all else fails, politely recite Geneva Convention passages, before contributing only your name, rank, birth date, and 'serial number.'

At all costs though, *TRY NOT TO PISS THEM OFF!*

I'm as ready as I'm ever going to be.

* * *

BEHIND THE INTERROGATOR, another door opens, and a second blue-clad thug marches in.

Okay. So, they're going with the 'gang-intimidation' technique here. Alright. So... ummm... I... no, wait a minute! There's a glass of tea in his hand!

What the hell kind of technique is that?

He swoops around the hulk behind the desk, and sets the drink down beside him. This seems to disrupt my host's perusal of my 'records,' and he looks up with a start.

"Oh! Thank-you, Karl."

He takes an overly dramatic gulp or two, swallows loudly, and sets the glass down.

"Shteven," he says, looking at *me* now, with eyebrows arched high over sleepy eyes, "Would you like some tea?"

Uck. Puddle water. But remember: 'Thankful for the tiniest courtesy.'

"No. But thank-you... sir."

"Some water perhaps? We may be here a while."

Okay. So it's the 'nice guy' approach.

"Uh, no... I... well, actually... now that I think about it, maybe that would be a good idea. A little water, please, if you don't mind."

"Certainly. Karl?" And Thug 2 scurries out the back door again.

"So. Mister... Shtipe..."

A thin smile flickers across his face without quite reaching his eyes. Then he rocks back in his chair.

Mine doesn't rock.

Alright. Here it comes. The grilling for sensitive information.

"How's your Datsun B-210 running?"

Huh? My car? How...?

"Probably a little better with that CB radio in it now, I'll bet."

The CB? Now how could he possibly know about that? The car's one thing. That's bad enough. I don't remember filling out any paperwork that included information about my car when I signed in at the school. But the CB radio? I don't *have* a CB. My crappy little Datsun B-210 hatchback doesn't even have an *AM* radio. But on this one particular trip, since my teammate Greg Dorn was riding with me, we'd brought along *his* CB radio for the drive from Seattle to Spokane. And I know I never told anyone at the school about that. I am stupefied... which is, of course, just exactly what he wants me to be.

It's got to be something like one or two in the damned morning. I haven't gotten any sleep, and I've been standing with a bag over my head all night long. I am frazzled. Now my very first interrogator has shown me, in no uncertain terms, just how much they *already know about me* before he even starts asking any serious questions. And the message is frighteningly clear... *I CAN'T LIE TO THESE PEOPLE!* They already know! *Everything!*

So much for Shrewd Counter-Strategy Number one (whatever it was going to be).

"Um... it's fine," I stammer, knowing I've already failed the Poker Face test. "It's just for... it just... it doesn't... you know..."

Smooth move, Ex Lax. Just keep on talking.

"How about your mother, Shteven? 'Edythe,' is it?"

Actually, she prefers to be called by her middle name, Lori.

He lifts a sheet of paper and looks it over, as if it's all right there.

"Is there anything in particular you'd like us to tell her? Other than letting her know you're here, of course."

"Oh, uh... no... thanks. She... uhhh..."

Now how the f...?

"I'm quite sure that, even from here, our mail will make it to Miami in America."

Oh my God! I KNOW I never filled out anything with her name on it or where she lived. How could they possibly...?

"Um, how's that water coming? I am really parched."

Cunning, there Stevie. The old Delaying Tactic. He'll never see through that one (unless he's awake). Cheesy, amateurish, and obvious, yet stupid and pointless at the same time.

"Oh, it'll be here shortly."

"It's just that..." and I start to gasp, swallowing hard and clawing at my throat, "... it's making it tough to talk. You know?"

"Certainly. Of course. I understand. *Karl?*"

Seconds later, old Karl the Thug enters the room again with a tall beaded glass of water in his hand, tinkling with ice, and sets it down in front of me. So much for *that* brilliant tap dance.

I guzzle it down like a hydroholic falling off the wagon. And there goes my excuse for delay.

'Major Meatneck'—or whatever my interrogator's real name is—just sits there staring placidly at me, as the last of my pretense goes down my throat. No need to rush me. I'm doing all his work for him, batting a thousand here, I'm sure.

"Could I get some more?" I ask timidly, once the silence has grown sufficiently uncomfortable.

"In a moment," he replies, rocking casually forward again. "But first I need to understand something. What is your unit doing up here? What is it? The..." And again he rummages through the spray of paperwork on his desk, as if, once again, he has the answer to anything he wants to know right there at his fingertips, but it would be so much easier if I'd just volunteer it myself.

This time though, I don't take the bait. This time I actually keep my mouth *shut*, innocently craning my neck to look at those same papers, only upside-down. And always making sure that I'm coming across as *not resisting him! Heaven forefend.*

After a moment though, he stops, and looks up at me, his smile darkening and hardening.

"You're Air Force Special Operations, aren't you? A so-called 'Combat Controller' with the Sixty-Second Military Airlift Wing, based out of McChord Air Force Base, near Seattle, Washington. A highly specialized unit, I believe, trained for clandestine operations behind enemy lines."

Oh, shit.

My heart plummets, dropping through the ice in my chest, and taking my lungs with it. Not only does he already know everything about me—which means he won't be very tolerant of any lying at which he catches me—but, based on his badly accented tone and his stiffening posture, he obviously doesn't think very highly of spec ops troops either.

"You're trained to be assassins," he growls, "Kidnappers, thieves, and arsonists... and spies."

Oh God. There it is. The dreaded 'S-word.' The Geneva Convention goes right out the window when it comes to the handling of spies. Captors tend to skip right past the all-night black-and-blue sessions, and just go straight to the *executions* of spies.

"I'm no spy," I counter lamely, tugging at the front of my uniform, "I'm just a line-grunt, *in uniform*. See? Just following orders."

Good. Give him something honest but empty, with little promise of anything better ahead.

"Uh-huh. So just how many of you 'line grunts' are there on the McChord Combat Control Team?"

Okay. Here's the first big test. He's already let me know that he knows everything about my personal life and my unit. So he almost certainly knows just how many men are in my outfit. Hell, he probably knows more about them than *I* do. Lying, then, would probably prove futile, *and* would only serve to 'disappoint' him. Maybe get my scrawny ass bounced around the walls a few times.

But that kind of information is just exactly the kind of thing I'm *not* supposed to be giving out, that I'm supposed to be learning how to keep to myself. So, do I resist on principle, give him misinformation (or a genuinely *stupid* answer, because I *don't* know), get caught (because he *does* know the answer), and get the shit beaten out of me (figuratively speaking)? Or do I do the unthinkable and hand over some semi-sensitive information? Information that he almost certainly already has, could care less about, but could save me an ass-whoopin'?

Man, there is just not enough time to do all the impotent over-thinking I want to do! But, really... what the hell.

This is a school. I'm sure they'll correct me if I'm wrong.

I go for Door Number Two.

"I think there's about sixteen, maybe eighteen of us. Something like that. I'm not sure."

At least that last part's true.

He glares at me with thinly veiled surprise. Or maybe that's contempt. *Is that the look of a disgusted fellow American soldier, or a simulated enemy who's been momentarily disarmed? Who knows.*

He rallies. "Really? Sixteen, huh?"

"Or maybe eighteen. Yessir. I think so. I've never really counted them before." *Again, at least that last element is true.*

I really am unsure about just how many are on my team. So many have come and gone in just the short time I've been there, some I've still never met, and there are a couple whose relationship with the team is yet undefined in my head, whether they're actual teammates, or some kind of 'support,' or whatever. But I bet I'm about to find out.

"So, not the full complement of twenty-four, like a normal full-strength unit?"

I think quickly.

"Could be. Maybe. If you include the officers. But you asked how many '*line grunts*,' low-ranking guys like me, and that's like sixteen or eighteen... I think."

Oo, I think I might have actually tripped him up there.

"I see," he smirks. He seems pleased with something. But is it himself, or me? He writes something on a loose scrap of paper, left-handed, I notice. "And just what exactly is it that you and your fifteen—or *seventeen*—fellow 'line grunts' are doing here?"

Oh shit. Delay! Deflect! Misdirect! Do something! It's getting deeper.

"Well..."

I can't look like I'm concocting fabrications. But at the same time, I can't look like I'm perfectly willing to tell him everything he wants to know. He wouldn't buy that either. I also can't afford to just come right out and say, "*Screw you!*" That'll just get simulated bones simulated broken, and weaken my resistance to later more pressing questions. Right?

So where do I draw the line?

I try to stick with the most harmless partial truths I can come up with on the spot. Just enough to satisfy him, not enough to make him suspicious. Not an overt lie in which he can trap me, nothing sensitive enough to cause any damage... I hope. Of course, I have absolutely no idea where that perfect line is that I can't cross.

"Well, we were deployed with our parent unit, the 62nd MAW,"— *which he already mentioned himself*—"like we always do whenever *they're* deployed somewhere. And so far, we've just been 'perimeter defense' for their advance airfield."

Oops. I may have gone too far there. That's what 'winging it' gets you. But at least it's a defensible fiction that reveals no grander strategy... I think.

He's smiling again though, wearily, but with an edge of 'gloating.'

"So, you were on 'perimeter defense' when you were captured?"

Uh-oh. That does seem a little unlikely, doesn't it. Do I detect the first tangles in my little web of deceit?

"No… it was more like a… a 'patrol'."

"Oh! A *'patrol'!*"

Karl snerks over in the corner.

This is actually getting kinda' silly. Four, five, six hours ago, I was climbing off a damned bus full of Survival School students. Then, after 'getting caught' and spending a few hours trying not to fall asleep while standing, I was brought here. My home unit has nothing to do with any of this. All this crap about 'deployments' and 'perimeter defense' are just storylines I've made up on the spot, complete fictions intended solely to give me something to say other than name, rank, and serial number. And surely, not everyone else in this class is putting all this cerebral energy into their stories, if they're ginning up any stories *at all*. Surely they're just going through the motions, resisting or playing possum or whatever far simpler variations the average guy can concoct. *So what the hell am I doing?*

I'm beginning to think that this 'interrogator'—this *instructor*—is inwardly chuckling at all my struggles making up this ludicrous and irrelevant backstory.

Damn. I'm wishing now that earlier on I'd just said something like, "*What B-210? I drive a Chevy pick-up!*" Or, even more embarrassing and discomfiting for him, "*What are you talking about my mother for? She's been dead for three years!*" I bet *that* would have thrown a monkey wrench or two into his smug-ass cross-examination.

Damn. Why couldn't I think of that before?

Instead, I just say, "My name is Steven D. Stipp," making sure to pronounce the last name better than he did. I tap the paired stripes on my sleeve that proclaim my measly rank of Airman First Class, and rattle off my Social Security number (officially my 'serial number'). "And I believe that's all that I am obligated to tell you under the terms of the Geneva Convention, sir."

Gawd, did that ever sound hokey.

And now he's glaring at me. *Shit.*

Karl the Thug fidgets behind him, as though this is just that moment of stupidity that he's been waiting for all night long. But Major Meatneck only sits there glowering.

After a studiously pregnant pause, however, he suddenly rocks forward onto his elbows, and says, "Break."

* * *

BEHIND HIM, THE CURRENT of aggression abruptly switches off in Karl, and he relaxes into his corner of the wall like a bored yuppie waiting on a commuter train. The casualness of the transition is just a little bit freaky. And when my interrogator next speaks, his pseudo-Slavic accent is gone, replaced by something flavorless and neutral.

Something from Blandsville, USA.

"You were doing pretty good there… for a while," says the new All-American behind the desk. "But you need to commit to your lies a little more."

Hmmm. Not your typical words of advice from a military instructor.

"Yeh. Okay," I nod earnestly. "I just wasn't sure where to go from there. I felt like I was kinda' painting myself into a corner with that story I was having to make up."

"Yeh, you were. But part of that was just the fact that you were making up an entire military deployment scenario on the fly. And you definitely don't want to get yourself started down *that* road. I know that was just so you could give me *something*—something 'harmless'—when my questions started getting specific. I could see what you were doing: trying to be accommodating to an interrogator who was using the 'friendly approach,' right? Trying to stay on my good side?"

"Right," I reply cautiously, unsure about whether to feel relieved or embarrassed.

"Well, that's good… to a point. That's what you *should* have done, at least in principle. But you didn't stick with your basic lie. You got nervous, started expanding on the theme, and then you had to try to back out of it."

"Well, I mean, I…"

"Maybe I shouldn't have said 'stick with your *lie.*' Maybe I should have said, 'stick with the *role* you're trying to play.' Even if *that's* a lie."

"I'm not sure I know wh…"

"You were doing good with that innocent bottom-of-the-totem-pole line-grunt angle. You weren't trying to antagonize me. You were being *about* as 'helpful' as military regulations and your limited knowledge would allow. You came across as at least working *with* me, if not *for* me. And that improves your chances of walking out of this room untortured."

"Yeh, but what about giving you the number of men in my unit? Wasn't that going too far? I wasn't sure about that one."

"Normally, yes. That would have been going too far. But in this particular case, when the interrogator has made it quite clear that he already knows everything about you and your unit, a question like that is nothing but bait. A fishing trip to see whether or not you're going to lie to him."

I knew it!

"And answering like you did, with plausible uncertainty, maintaining that act of lower echelon ignorance,"—*there was no 'act' about it*—"can be enough to convince your interrogator that you're a dead-end, information-wise, without getting your fingernails torn off."

"Oh good. I was…"

"*But!* You didn't stick with that line. You started making shit up, being *too* helpful, *unrealistically* and *unnecessarily* helpful, at least for a front-line spec ops guy, still untouched and perfectly healthy, in the first minutes of his first interrogation. I hadn't even given you a *reason* to be afraid yet. Then your lies became too detailed and elaborate. Then too tangled. Then too obvious."

"So, what should I…?"

"*Commit* to your lie. Well, commit to your *role*, anyway."

"Like…"

"Well," and he rocks back in his chair again, staring up at the ceiling, as if searching it for inspiration. "For example, you just picture yourself as the most clueless, uninformed, cannon fodder kind of guy in your outfit, and then answer the questions like that guy would. When I ask you why your unit is even here, don't look like you're trying to think about it. That'll just look like you're either thinking up a lie, or at least trying to wriggle out of this, which I'll just *presume* means you're lying anyway. Then I won't trust the answers you give me from then on out. No, instead, just try looking confused… sorta' like this."

His face cramps into a painful expression that looks like old Karl the Thug might've just lit off a nice eye-watering burrito-fart right beside him.

"You know. Make it look like I'm *hurting your brain* with a question like that. Then say something like, uh, you know… like, '*Jeez, I have no idea. They never let me in on stuff like that.*' You see? Something like that. Something that just reeks of innocence and genuinely hopeless ignorance."

"Yeh, okay," I answer, actually excited about trying that one out. Maybe next time. "I can do that."

"Alright, then. You ready to get back to work here?"
"Yes sir."
"All right, Karl?"
"Ready on you," says Karl the Thug, his first uttered words sounding surprisingly effeminate.
"Okay, then. Let's... *resume*."

* * *

SUDDENLY, BOTH MEN STIFFEN. Karl comes off the wall, quivering like a defensive lineman just waiting for me to say, "*Hike!*" Major Meatneck scowls at me, inexplicably furious, then barks, once again in that pathetic junior high school Russian accent, "*Shtand up!*"

I hesitate just a second too long though, uncertain and stumbling as I wade into this new and volatile scenario, and Maj. Meatneck leaps to his feet so explosively that his rolling chair bolts for the back wall.

"*I said SHTAND UP! NOW!*"

Before I can even push myself upright, Karl is charging around the end of the desk, and Meatneck is bellowing someone else's name. I jump back, reflexively nudging my chair into Karl's path.

This is a mistake.

Karl has pulled a battered wooden shaft from out of somewhere, and so has only one hand available with which to fling my chair into the far corner as he charges toward me. Training environment or not though, either way, that is still an intimidating gesture, and I find myself backing toward the door through which I first came in, shouting, "*Okay! Okay! Okay!*"

Then the back door crashes open, and two more blue-clad goons, wearing the same black berets with red stars barge into the room. They take less than a second to assess the situation—apparently coming to the conclusion that I am an enraged psychopath hopped up on angel dust or something—then storm across the room to assist Karl in slamming me up against the wall. Both of my arms are pinioned in a posture of crucifixion. The collar of my field jacket is seized by two huge fists, and Karl's 'baton' is across my throat driving my chin upward, and the rest of me up onto my tiptoes. Not *too* hard, I notice.

All part of the game, I assure myself. *All part of the game... I hope.*

I smell *Cheez-its* on somebody's breath.

"You were told to *shtand up*," Maj. Meatneck's disembodied voice growls from somewhere beyond the forest of no-necked heads in the foreground. I can't see him, but I can sense the movement as he strolls around to the front of his desk. His 'Cruel Inquisitor' tone slips a little though, taking on more of a 'Major-Hochstetter-sitcom-Gestapo-agent' flavor as he continues. "If you ever fail to do as you are commanded again, you will be immediately and severely punished. *Severely*. Do you understand me, Mister Shtipp?"

"Yes sir," I manage to choke out over the baton.

"Good."

He pauses, solely for the sake of the drama, then... "Gentlemen?"

Instantly, and with the discipline of a single organism, all three of his stooges step back, releasing me, all without averting their uniformly ferocious gaze for a second. Or even blinking, for that matter. I can see Maj. Meatneck now, leaning casually on the front edge of his desk, arms and ankles crossed, looking at his spit-polished boots as if it pains him to have to go to such lengths.

"Shtep away from the wall," he says calmly.

And I do... without hesitation this time.

None of his boys moves though, until the moment I take a step forward. Then suddenly, two of them are behind me, and I am surrounded.

Shit.

Okay. So now they're throwing the 'high threat' approach at me. Okay. Okay, so... how did they say I should handle that in the classroom?

Damned if I can remember.

"Now... Shteven..."

Quick! Think of something! Quick!

Blank. Dead fucking blank. My mind is a slate so clean you could do open-heart surgery on it. Shit!

"... tell me again where your Combat Control Team is based."

Oo! That one I can handle.

"Uh, McChord Air Force Base, in Tacoma, Washington," I mutter circumspectly, keenly aware of the three pairs of glaring eyes boring into me at point blank range.

"No," says Meatneck without lifting his gaze, a menacing grin now chilling his voice, "Not your *home* base. Your *field* base—here, in *this* country, in *my* country—your deployed forward base *here*."

There is, of course, no way that I can answer this. Not even academically. I have no idea what 'country' we're supposedly in—none of us has this background data, not even the interrogators—and I sure as hell don't know the names of any 'towns' or 'installations' in this fictitious setting. Forget the moral, ethical, and professional issues. Forget even whether you would *choose* to tell or *not* tell them what they want to hear. We, as students, have simply not been given this information. There is no prepared backstory. This is clearly intended to be one of those questions that you just cannot answer, whether you'd want to or not. This is the point at which, in a real-world scenario, I would simply have no choice but to draw the line.

Sorry, Hoss, but this is one card you ain't a-gonna' see.

Still, I do my best to keep his hungry minions off of me for a few more seconds.

"I have no idea," I mince pathetically, digging one last nugget of improvised fiction out of my ass. "My orders just said 'Firebase 5', sir. No city names or anything. And I just went where the airplane took me."

'Firebase 5.' What a happy load of horsh.

Not bad though, I tell myself... for all the good it'll do me.

Maj. Meatneck is chuckling when I finish. And it's contagious apparently, spreading in a sinister tide through the bouncers surrounding me.

Uh-oh.

"'Firebase Five', huh? That's pretty funny, Airman Shtipp. Pretty funny indeed. Would you like to try again? Just one more try?"

His eyes finally lift from his feet, and I can tell he really *wants* me to lie some more. I try to swallow, but everything's dry.

"No sir. That's all I know. That's all I *needed* to know, and that's all they told me. I have no idea where in this country 'Firebase 5' is though, sir. Only that..."

"Are you a hero, Shteven?"

The three stooges laugh out loud at that one.

"Am I a... ?"

"You must be quite a hero, Airman Shtipp. Maybe even a *super*hero!"

Meatneck pushes himself off the edge of the desk, and saunters over toward me. The borscht in his accent is thickening as he speaks.

"To be so brave in the face of such danger. You must be a real superhero... like *Superman*, I think."

More laughter from the sphincter gallery.

Oh, I'm not liking this at all. I've decided that words have served me as well as they're ever going to, so there's no need to utter any more.

"I've always wanted to meet a superhero," Meatneck continues. "I've always wondered what made them so... *super!*" His eyes go instantly cold, and his malevolent smile crashes back into a sneer. "So let's just see what a 'superman' really looks like. Shall we? *Strip!*"

Now that *I didn't see coming.*

"I'm sorry. Did you say... ?"

"*SHTRIP!*"

Four hands seize the arms and shoulders of my field jacket, and rip it right off my back in one swift motion. Almost as if they've done this before.

Oh. Fuck.

2
BACK IN THE DARK

SO, I'M STANDING IN my darkened cell again with my bag over my head, weaving in gentle circles like one of those inflatable punching clowns.

I just want to sleep.

I want to *die* sleeping... right now.

But the latest thundering soundtrack they've got pumping through this echo chamber is from some bass guitar riff that's been edited into tightly chopped fragments. In fact, the sound of it is blundering around the cell block with the same random arrhythmia of feet heard from the basement beneath a basketball court, only amplified about ninety times. Forget the length of the day—and the night—and the complete lack of sleep. Forget the total physical exhaustion of three days in the mountains, knee-deep in snow and mud, and battling the cold. Oh, and the snowshoes. This subsonic racket alone is enough to beat the life out of you.

But the guards are still slamming their way around the chamber, ripping open doors and screaming at prisoners caught slumping in the corners of their cells, occasionally heaving in a bucketful of ice water. Or two. They're also still circulating prisoners in and out of more interrogations. So I don't dare allow myself to succumb to the fatigue.

They're right outside the door, and they seem a trifle cranky.

A few minutes ago, I started hearing something different in their taunts. Something about *food*.

"Here! You've got five minutes to finish it!"

"Take it quick, or I'll give it to someone else."

And I can make out what sounds like little sliding doors being whisked aside. Food doors, I'm guessing.

Another reason to stay awake a little longer.

I try to point my mind at something else though, something more relevant and a lot less deafening to pass the time until my 'server' works his way down to my door.

Like my most recent interrogation sessions.

* * *

OFFICIALLY, I 'PASSED' TWO out of the three, and 'failed' only one, although technically, there's no such thing as 'passing' or 'failing' in this course. Only finishing. This is an 'experience,' not a 'pass-or-fail' certification process.

I'd 'passed' the first one—the one with the 'nice guy' approach, and Karl serving me the water—not because I hadn't screwed up at all, but because I had at least applied the appropriate counter-tactic to Meatneck's specific approach.

And I'd 'passed' the *last* one, which had involved them trying to get me to sign several forms. We're not supposed to sign anything but a Red Cross form—which lets the rest of the world know that we're alive and enjoying the delicate ministrations of our hosts—and he'd laid out several papers, none of which I'd recognized. Fortunately, by sheer dumb luck, as we'd returned to the scenario from the brief critiquing interlude, I'd arbitrarily chosen to try out that *I'm-too-sick-to-know-what-the-hell-is-going-on* defense. And it had proven to be exactly the right ploy for that particular approach.

Not to mention being a lot of fun.

I'd let my eyelids droop shut, my mouth sag open, my shoulders slump, and my head roll forward until it almost touched the desktop. And whenever he'd ask me anything, I'd just slur my speech and moan and let my head swivel loosely around its mounts. I also made a point of being very 'repetitive' with my answers, never actually addressing his issues, always saying stuff like, "*I need medicine,*" or "*I'm gonna' be sick,*" or "*I can't feel my hands.*" And I think he enjoyed that as much as I did.

No, it was the *second* interrogation—the one in the middle, the one with the Three Stooges, the high threat level, and the surprise strip search—that I'd 'failed.' And not because I'd applied an inappropriate counter-tactic. There's not much you *can* do in a high threat situation, except try your best not to piss them off any more than they already are. Rather, I'd failed because, after a certain point, well... they pissed *me* off. And I told them what they could do with their little scenario.

Sort of.

* * *

RATHER THAN HAVE THEM shred my uniform and tear both my arms off in the process, I'd voluntarily removed my own boots, belt, fatigue shirt and pants, leaving me standing there in my ancient and well-used long johns. They were aged and yellowed in certain places—*no, not there!*—tattered around the collar, and droopy in the caboose. Plus, at the point at which Major Meatneck told me to stop, my thick white thermal socks had been pulled halfway off my feet by the removal of my boots, which made each foot look about *two* feet long.

Yeh, I was lookin' pretty cool, alright.

Karl and the other two stooges had busted out in great exaggerated hardy-hars at the sight of that, and Meatneck seemed to have an endless wellspring of witticisms from which to draw one belittling comment after another. *And that was okay!* Laughter I could handle. I even encouraged it by trying to look as humbled and embarrassed and stigmatized as I could. But that didn't slow down old Meatneck.

He tugged at my stretched out long john top, wondering at what kind of a 'superhero's outfit' that was, then had me remove *that* so that he could see my 'superhero's *chest*.'

The pasty white hairless chicken breast that greeted them only tripled the volume of the laughter, of course. But again, that was just fine with me. The problem was, that despite all my efforts at acting cowed and wounded by the abuse, I guess old Meatneck wasn't buying it, and decided to push it one step further.

After asking me where the "**S**" was on my chest, he offered to make one *for* me. He went back to his desk, brought out a fat black *El Marko* (good to know they have those in Communist countries too), then proceeded to draw—*in indelible ink, no less!*—a huge "**S**" on my torso and chest, all to the bawdy laughter of his three goons.

I couldn't believe it. Standing here *now* in this cell, I *still* can't believe it... that he would actually draw *on my skin, in indelible ink!* That's just... so... *goddamned outrageous!*

I guessed they sensed the shift in my mood, for the laughter abruptly died. And with the demise of the harassment, came the return of the questions. Only *this* time—just like they wanted, unfortunately—I was *pissed*.

So, when Meatneck asked me again where my unit was stationed, this time I abandoned the whole lame-assed 'Firebase 5' detour. I stared right back at him with tired defiant eyes—*and floppy socks, and a droopy ass, and a big old black S on my chest*—and told him to pack it up his ass. Yes, I was *that* friggin' fried, my friends. Then I hammered off my name, rank, date of birth, and Social Security number, crossed my arms (no doubt *pouting* like an obnoxious little brat child), and dared him to say or do something else.

This taught us all where the limits were... except that *I* was the only one that had to spend the next ten minutes in a "Torture Position."

* * *

SINCE THE AIR FORCE cannot legally beat the shit out of its personnel, even in a school that's supposed to teach them how to survive such abuse, they had to come up with an alternative that would still produce the desired submissive effects without the *un*desirable physical damage. And to that end, they created 'Torture Positions.'

A 'Torture Position' is just what it sounds like: a very uncomfortable posture in which you must remain for at least ten minutes. It's that simple. But it's actually worse than it sounds. And therein lies its effectiveness.

For instance, one of the Torture Positions that was described for us back in the classroom was a sustained back arch, in which only your feet and the flats of your palms were allowed to touch the floor. Your ass is high off the ground, and your belt buckle is arched toward the ceiling.

Bearable for a minute or two, but painful, grueling, and exhausting for the rest of the endless time spent holding it. No damage, though. No injury, no trauma, no scarring, but you surely get the message... *this is what you want to avoid! This is where a* real *enemy can cripple you for life!*

For *my* torture though, I had to turn and face the front wall of the interrogation room, my feet spread apart, standing roughly four feet back from the wall. Then I had to reach forward with both hands, allowing my leaning weight to be supported against the wall by just *one fingertip* from each hand.

And that's it! Sounds simple enough, doesn't it?

Try it. See how long you can sustain it. See how long you *enjoy* it.

See just how long ten minutes really is.

I can tell you this: within thirty seconds, the first knuckle on each of those two fingers was screaming! After two minutes, it felt like those two fingers had been folded back *ninety degrees*. I was grunting and gasping, sweating and gritting my teeth long before my time was halfway up.

Fortunately, old Meatneck called "*break*" as soon as I was released from the Torture Position, and we did the critique while I climbed back into my clothes, and tried to snap the feeling back into my fingers.

The third and final interrogation of the session—the one in which I feigned delirium, and managed to avoid signing any paperwork—was spent with the constant awareness that there was a huge black "**S**" on my chest, and that neither of my pointer fingers would ever be the same again. Then he wrapped it all up, gave me my 'grades,' called "Resume," and an escort-guard clomped into the room behind me with my head-bag.

At least he let me pee in the snow on the way back to the cellblock.

* * *

NOW A RASPY CLACK sounds at the foot of my door. And through the bottom of my bag, I see a spill of light washing over my boots.

My food door is open.

"Here's your soup, animal!," another bad accent announces, as a fist beats heavily on my door. "You've got five minutes to get this bowl back out here, then I'm coming in to get it!"

I shed my bag, bend down, and reach out through the floor-level hole to the canteen cup waiting outside. It's metal, and conducts the soup's heat very well, thank-you very much. But that's not a problem. What *is* a problem is that the canteen cup is taller than the food door through which it must be retracted.

Bastards!

You know, I could almost believe they did that on purpose.

The seconds tick by as I fiddle with the damned soup, realigning it with the opening every which way I can think of. And of course, every little bump and jostle sloshes more hot broth over my hand and onto the floor. I try cautiously tipping it—only as far as it'll go without spilling any more than it already has—but it still won't fit under the low frame. I'm becoming audibly agitated now, and very aware of the passing time.

Finally, I just can't stand it anymore—*if they really want to play this game, they can just clean up the mess themselves*—and I tip it back a full forty-five degrees to let it slide through. Hot broth splashes across the floor, but the damned cup is at least on the *inside* now. Unfortunately, so is the spilled soup. I guess if I would have been thinking, I would have tipped the cup forty-five degrees *outward*, and let the guards do all the slipping and sliding... and mopping.

Instead, *I'm* the one left standing in my own private little Hot Springs.

The soup is great though—one step short of scalding—just what I need. But I have no spoon, so I have to just drink it, like hot coffee. And that's also just fine by me.

I leave the drained canteen cup outside my door with time to spare.

* * *

ABOUT AN HOUR AGO, when they changed that damned exasperating soundtrack again, I thought it sounded familiar... a short frantic riot of strings and horns from the middle of some busy classical piece, skipping over and over again on a tight three-second loop. *Now* I realize, two more familiar changes later, that they've re-started the entire cycle of nerve-jangling audio beat-downs all over again. I recognized the *seven*-second repeating excerpt from that nasty little real-world interrogation when it kicked in about a half hour later. And now they're back to that damned faster-slower-faster-slower, surging-dying-surging-dying orchestral piece that almost broke me the *first* time around. *Shit!*

I'm pacing around my cell now, head-bag in my hand, slapping it against the side of my leg.

Fuck them! If they really want a piece of me, they can just have it!

I am so fucking tired—so completely out-of-my-mind *obliterated*—that I can't even sleep. Can't even stand being still. *So I'm just not going to!*

How 'bout them *apples, you assholes!*

The first part of this little mini-rebellion of mine took the form of an overt attempt at a nap. I just shouted some terribly poignant expletive into the din of that 'music,' ripped the damned bag off my head, and plopped down into a comfy little fetal position in the corner of my cell (just beyond the shoreline of my slowly drying Soup Lake). All to no avail. Not only could I *not* fall asleep, or even stop fidgeting for that matter, but no one even cared enough to stop by and witness (and thereby become duly outraged by) my private bitchy little insurrection. And that was rather disappointing.

In the meantime, of course, that infuriating, lurching, skipping, shrieking, soundtrack went and shifted gears again, once more disrupting the rhythm into which my mind had just settled out of self-defense, *and I just couldn't stand it anymore!*

I leapt up off the floor, spitting venom, went straight to the eye-holes in the door, rammed the cover flap out of the way—just *daring* them to do the finger-smashing thing again—and peered out at the rest of the cellblock.

Nothing.

Nobody.

Not a single prowling guard, not one son-of-a-bitch poised to slap the flap back down, not even another pair of eyes peeking out through another pair of eye-holes across the way. It was almost as if I was alone in the cellblock. Just me and that fucking out-of-control soundtrack.

I've been circling in the darkness of my cell ever since, agitated and impotent, acting up, mentally screaming for attention, and being completely and utterly ignored... leaning my head against each wall... audibly cursing my captors... unashamedly peering out into the central chamber... twirling my head-bag, slapping my thighs, and... *goddammit, when the hell is this thing going to...!*

BANG!

A door, just a few cells down from mine, crashes open. A guard starts to bark instructions. I'm still trying to pick out the words, when the cell door right next to mine—the one with the idiot inside—explodes open.

"You! Animal! Step forward!"

I suddenly remember that I'm not wearing my prescribed headgear, and start tussling it back into place. Latches clatter, hinges squeal, and my door is abruptly torn open, even as I'm tugging the fringe of my bag down to my shoulders. The guard doesn't seem to care, though.

"Step forward, animal!"

I move toward him. And as the anteroom light floods in through the weave of my burlap bag, hands grab the shoulders of my field jacket on both sides, and I am bustled out into the center of the chamber where a queue of prisoners is being assembled.

"Poot your paws on the animal in front of you!"

Ah, here we go again.

3
THE WAITING ROOM

GAWD, IT'S STILL DARK OUTSIDE.

After what feels like twelve, fifteen, maybe *forty* straight hours in that cacophonous shithole back there, *it's still night out here! I don't believe it!*

This is simply never going to end.

Once again, I'm bringing up the rear of the column. Well, me and that clueless zombie from the last cell beside mine, anyway. Everyone's in lockstep, just to keep from stepping on each other's heels. Then the front of the line clomps up a short flight of wooden steps, and the line stretches and slows as each man tries to avoid tripping on the risers. We all manage to get up the stairs and through the door though, without incident. And now we're trooping down another hollow-sounding wooden corridor.

What's this going to be? A mass *interrogation? Everybody at once?*

The hallway eventually dumps us into a larger room, and our little blindfolded parade is dispersed by more guards. From all sides I hear clotted amateurish accents belting out instructions, though this time with more subdued volume. No less blunt or unfriendly, but not as loud either.

The animal in front of me is snatched from my grip, and almost immediately a pair of hands grabs *my* arms from behind, and yanks me to the right. I trip over my own feet, causing my 'handler' to jerk me back upright.

"Poot your feet together, animal, and bend forward, ninety degrees at the waist!"

Oh yeh. That's a posture I want to present to these guys, alright.
Naturally, I do it anyway.
"Now, take one step forward—*one!*—and stay bent at the waist. Go!"
What the hell?
I take one awkward bowed step, and my knees and toes bump up against a low wall. I know it's low because my *head* would have hit it first otherwise.
"Now lift your *right leg*, and climb up onto that ledge on your knees. Keep your head down."
I do.
"Crawl forward."
I do this too, until my bagged head bumps against another wall. Reflexively, I jerk my head up and back, and it clonks against a low ceiling, just inches overhead. Then a small door slams shut behind me, punching against the soles of my boots. I try to turn around, but hit walls on either side of me as well, pressed right up against my shoulders.
I'm in a box! On a shelf! And a little one at that!
I hear a heavy-metal clunking behind me, outside the box, like the sound of a loose locking wheel being spun on a submarine's watertight hatch, and suddenly my walls are closing in even tighter. They stop only once my shoulders have been forcibly hunched. A similar clunking sound *above* me crimps the ceiling down on top of my head. It finally stops, just a micrometer short of compressing me into a molded chicken loaf.
Strangely enough, I find this wonderfully comfortable.
I not only possess not a single claustrophobic bone in my body, but I am probably the ultimate *anti-*claustrophobe. I've always loved tight snug places, and this one, in addition to being tight and snug, is also *warm.* Warmed by my own overdressed wadded-up ass, *but who cares! It just feels so good!* It's also the first chance I've had to 'legally' fold up and collapse into sleep. Hell, it feels great just being *off my feet* for the first time in how many hours.
I have to bite back the urge to giggle like a six-year-old hiding from his favorite uncle.
Instead, I let my weight settle into the square embrace of this box, and I am out like a light.

* * *

THERE'S NO TELLING HOW long I've been out. Still no watch. But I've just been awoken by a whiny petulant voice coming from somewhere just outside my box, close by. To my left.

"*Come on, guys. I'm not kidding! I've really got to go!*"

Really? That's it? Somebody's gotta' tinkle?

My desperately needed sleep's been interrupted for that?

A rumble of bawdy fake-Russian laughter erupts from behind me. I guess that's where our guards are cloistered, hunched over some crappy little folding table, I imagine, playing the Eastern Bloc equivalent of *Go Fish*, and passing around a filthy bottle of vodka. Or something like that. In my slow-stirring mind, I see them all as bald—*shiny* bald, like billiard cue balls—with one long eyebrow per man, and each with at least one badly healed scar from some ancient saber duel or something, slicing across each forehead, brow and cheek. Something Hollywood like that.

Everything else here is a cliché. Why not these guys too?

"*Look, I don't want to cause any trouble here, but...*"

"Then shut up!"

Now *I* want to laugh.

"*No, I'm serious, guys. I have really... got... to... pee!*"

Chairs groan across concrete.

A sharper higher voice moves as it speaks. "Shut your mouth, *now!*"

"*Hey, look. Don't make me... !*"

"If you don't shut up, right *now*, you will be taken out and punished."

"*Fine! As long as I'm taken out!*"

BAM! The thunderclap of an open palm slamming down on a hollow wooden box top.

"You are going *nowhere!* And I will not tell you again to *SHUT UP!*"

For a moment, the weenie-in-question seems to have grasped the concept being expressed by the guard. But only for a moment.

"*If I don't get out of here, and real soon, I'm going to piss myself, right here in your damned box!*"

"Go ahead. Piss your pants. But if you make a mess in my box, it will be *you* cleaning it up yourself!"

The other guards apparently find this to be tremendously humorous.

Well, isn't this a quaint little drama. I can see both sides of the argument, though. Everyone's doing what they have to. And I can't wait to hear how it all plays out.

"*All right, you asked for it,*" hisses the bottled and grunting prisoner. Then just like that, he utters the unmentionable.

"*Flight surgeon!*"

Oh, Jeezy Pete! I can't believe he did that!

I don't think anyone saw that coming.

* * *

NEEDLESS TO SAY, IN a simulated environment like this—where the prisoner population is always aware that they're really only *students* in a safe and ultimately non-threatening setting—it's important that the continuity not be broken, that everyone remains in-character, and that the stress level, pressure, and duress of the situation be maintained to the maximum degree of realism. And that means that the students cannot be allowed to divorce themselves from the scenario whenever the whim strikes them. They must remain fully immersed—the whole way through, if possible—if they are to reap the full benefit of the experience. And to that end, the course's creators permitted only three ways for exiting out of 'The Situation.'

The first—and optimally the *only*—method that should *ever* be used to interrupt the flow, is for an *instructor* to say, "*Break.*" Only an instructor can say it, and it is recognized as authentic only when it comes from an instructor's lips. My interrogator used it three times during my sessions to separate his three different questioning techniques. And that was okay.

But in the event of some overwhelming circumstances—and by that I mean only the most *dire* of circumstances—there are two ways that a *student* can force his way back to reality on his own.

One is to say the words, "*Student Situation.*" This is to be used only for those occasions when the student simply can't handle it anymore… some phobia has kicked in and is about to boil over, or the student has gotten so angry (as a result of the scenario) that he's about to twang, possibly hurting himself or endangering somebody else, and putting a permanent black mark on his military records. Something like that.

The other is to call for, "*Flight Surgeon!*" And this is exclusively for medical emergencies, when you're about to hurl, you've strained a nad, or you've somehow broken something. Whatever. Since the bulk of the class roster is comprised of flight crew members—pilots, co-pilots, navigators, and loadmasters—who are specifically tended to by "flight surgeons" (as opposed to regular old ordinary "doctors"), the phrase is geared toward *them*. In other words, when you call "*Flight Surgeon!*," you're basically saying, "*Doctor!*"

So those are the only two ways for a student to stop the game-playing for a moment. But *damn*, you'd sure better have one hell of a spectacular reason for disrupting the proceedings like that.

Using 'Student Situation,' for instance, just to stop the dialogue long enough to scratch your back on a vacant door jamb, or to complain about your food slot being too small for your soup cup to fit through, would be enough to get your sorry ass thrown out of the school altogether, with an "incomplete." *Just that one inappropriate and untimely utterance!* And in the military—especially with a course like this, which is a critical step in a flight officer's career checklist—that could prove disastrous. At the very least, their eligibility for promotion would be affected. And at worst, especially among the flight crews, it could mean the end of their military flying careers. *So you just don't do it… except, perhaps, to stave off death.*

And having to pee—*even really badly*—is just not as life- (or career-) threatening as it sounds.

* * *

JESUS! IT SOUNDS LIKE there's a dozen furious Russian lumberjacks over there, ripping the whiner's box to pieces with their bare hands, trying to get at him. They're slamming and jerking and banging and dragging it around, every last one of them cursing in cartoon-Siberian. And beneath the surface mayhem, I can hear the troublemaker's stunned voice shouting.

"*Ho! Ho! Take it easy! Whoa! Come on! Easy!*"

With a final loud crash, they apparently get the box open, and now the noises all revert to the scuffles and bumps of a tag-team wrestling match.

"*Alright! Alright! I'm comin'! Take it easy!*"

"Get out here *now!*"

Then the thumping and kicking sounds downshift one more time to the squeaking and skidding and stomping of a tight clot of men all pushing and shoving and driving against each other like a rugby scrum.

I guess he's out of the damned box now.

I hear the thunder of their little stampede churning past my own box now, headed in the direction of the doorway through which we first entered. Strained voices skirmish as they recede.

"You wanted out? You *got* out!"

"Look, I told you I really had to go! What did you want me to do?"

"Yeh, you told us alright, and now you're getting your wish."

"What's the big deal here?"

Then the door slams shut, and the Box Chamber is quiet once more.

Fine. Whatever.

I adjust a couple of stiffening knees and elbows, and drop right back to sleep again.

4
BREAKING... BAD

"STAND RIGHT THERE, ANIMAL."

The hands that guided me into this room now tug me to a stop, and snatch the bag off my head. I flinch only slightly at the sudden light. The loose burlap lattice of the bag had let in enough light beforehand to jumpstart the adapting of my eyes, so it wasn't so bad. Besides, my eyes are mostly closed right now anyway. I'm so sleepy. I just feel drugged, stuporous.

For all the general good my happy little coma in The Box produced, waking me up again, to get me to this next interrogation session, was made far worse than normal by my having nodded off.

Like trying to revive a drowning victim, I just can't seem to rouse myself from the dead.

Now I'm swaying in place, drowsy, heavy-lidded, my mind sinking into its own little pool of cerebral quicksand.

I pass a bleary eye around the room. Same general decor—probably the same damned *room* as my last session, for all I know—but a different inquisitor behind the desk. And a new variant on the Karl-the-Thug thing too.

I think I'll call this guy 'Number Two.' For all the obvious reasons.

The guy behind the desk this time—a guy so 'middle-of-the-road-average-American-male' that he'd make a crime scene investigator weep for the sheer hopelessness of his description—rocks back in his squeaky chair, and steeples his fingers in front of his lips. And because he looks so much like the kind of guy you'd expect to see managing a McDonalds in central Iowa, the forced Slavic inflection in his voice just seems all the more out of place.

Ironically, it's the best—most authentic—accent I've heard all night.

"Are you aware of the rules against the smuggling of contraband into this prison?," he asks through a deep sigh.

"Yeh. Sure," I nod, as nonchalantly as would any good zombie in my current state of lethargy.

In the classroom phase of the course, the instructors had actually encouraged us to try smuggling stuff into the POW scenario. It's what 'real' prisoners would do, they'd said, particularly snack foods and cigarettes, since those were what we'd be craving the most after only a few hours in Solitary. And they were right about that. I've never wanted a *Snickers* so bad in all my life. If caught, of course, we would be punished—something 'real prisoners' would also get to enjoy as well—so we'd better be damned clever about it. But *trying* it was still recommended, since it could only enhance the overall POW experience for us.

However, not trusting my finely honed street cunning, I'd opted to come here contraband-free. Theoretically then, I have nothing to worry about.

Theoretically.

"You are aware then, of the punishment for smuggling?"

"No," I shrug, still sleepily nonchalant. "Since I didn't smuggle anything, it didn't matter to me what the punishments were."

He snorts a sinister chuckle, and nods appreciatively, as if to say, *Uh-huh. Yeh, right*. Then he sighs, "That's funny."

He drops his hands across his midriff, turns his head to look longingly at the wall beside him—a deep gaze, as if through a window overlooking a vast Alpine meadow, or something—then he sighs, and looks back at me.

"You know, every single American I've interrogated so far has said exactly the same thing. And every single one of them was *lying* to me... every... single... one. Do you know how sick to *DEATH I am of being LIED TO!?!*" The sudden jump in volume jolts me out of my haze.

"I'm not lying, though," I stammer unconvincingly.

Shit! I sure hope there's nothing illicit squirreled away in my jacket pockets somewhere, something ancient I haven't thought about in months. That's suddenly an unnerving possibility. But, no. I don't think so.

"Are you actually going to stick with that story? That... that *not only* have you *not* snuck anything in through those gates, but that you are the ONLY ONE *in this entire CAMP that HASN'T!?! Seriously?* Are you actually going to stick with that story, right here, right now? Are you actually going to tell *me* that? After all the lying capitalist thieves and pirates I've had to deal with today? *Really?*"

He's practically levitating out of his seat now, like some wiry jungle cat coiling for the pounce. Number Two starts strolling my way as well, his balled fists swinging casually into view from behind his back.

"Yeh, that's what I'm telling you!," I snap right back, a little too irritably actually, considering the dark storm clouds gathering in this room. I unsnap a few pocket flaps on my field jacket, so that he can see how empty they are, and flip my collar up, all with loose-wristed—hell, downright *exhausted*—movements. *I'm just not in the mood for this shit anymore.*

My interrogator—*I think I'll call him Colonel Jakinov*—uncoils slightly as he rounds the end of his desk, a jackal's smile creeping back onto his face.

"I think you're lying."

I sigh, and let my arms flop to my sides.

"Hey, whatever."

"I think you're lying. And because I've had all the lying I can stomach for one day—and because I've already warned you about the consequences of lying, to *me*, NOW—your punishment will be far worse than it was for anyone else before you. I'll make an example of you, an example about the far greater cost of lying to me from here on out. What do you think of that?"

I'm trying not to bust out laughing. That's what I think about that.

"I'm not lying," I answer crankily, "And I'm not smuggling anything."

He stops right in front of me, smiles, and cocks his head in mock curiosity.

"We'll see. Give me your field jacket."

"Fine. Here."

I rip the buttons open, and unzip it in one weary motion. Halfway through shucking it off my shoulders though, old Number Two grabs ahold of it, and tears it the rest of the way off. Then he hands it to Col. Jakinov, all the while glaring into my eyes.

Jakinov makes a few token rummages through a couple of the pockets. Those are too obvious as 'hiding places' though, and he knows it. So he starts feeling his way around the jacket's seams and edges. His mischievous gaze rises to meet mine as he does so.

"I think you've hidden cigarettes in here."

I sigh again, and roll my eyes. "I don't smoke," I say.

Of course, you don't have to be a smoker to profit from the bargaining power of cigarettes in a prison's black market economy, but I'm not thinking about that right now."

"Probably matches then."

"If I don't smoke, what would I need matches for?"

More half-logic.

Number Two fidgets with that '*Oo-boss-just-let-me-at-him*' energy.

Jakinov only snickers, and keeps crimping his way around the coat's periphery.

"You know what could also be hidden in a bulky coat like this?"

"A bag of hammers?," I answer, stupidly, without thinking.

"A... what?"

"Nothing."

He glances at Number Two, who never relinquishes his sizzling glare into my eyes. Then Jakinov shakes his head clear, goes back to crimping, and picks up right where he left off.

"A camera."

I look at him with bloodshot disbelief. He looks at me as if that's just exactly the reaction he'd expect from an arrogant American gunrunner.

"Yes, yes, yes. A camera. A small spy camera."

I don't even know what to say to that. It's just too ridiculous. So, in a burst of four-in-the-morning originality, I close my eyes, let my head droop and swing, and I mumble, "Yeh, right. There's a camera in there."

"Oh, yes, indeed. Sewn right into the lining, I'll bet."

His fondling becomes more intense.

"There's no camera in that damned jacket!," I suddenly bark. "There's nothing in that jacket because I didn't smuggle anything in here in the first place! I didn't have anything *to* smuggle!"

"Oh, I agree. You're no mere smuggler," he answers, almost gleefully. "You're a damned *spy*."

"*What?!*"

"I do believe we've caught us a spy here, Igor"—*so* that's *Number Two's play-name*—"If there's a camera in this coat, then this man is a spy."

The dreaded S-word again.

"I'm no spy!," I shout now. "And there's nothing in that goddamned jacket but lint, *and you know it!*"

"I think there is," he hisses right back.

Then he pauses, staring at me for a long hard moment, before tilting his head as if something new just occurred to him. He throws the jacket on the floor, and kicks it wide open.

"I believe that there is a small micro-camera sewn into the lining of this jacket, and I intend to find it."

He starts stomping around the hems and zipper lines with his spit-polished boots, all the while watching my face for a reaction.

I can't help it. I succumb to a hiccup of appalled laughter.

He freezes. "You think this is a joke." It's not a question.

The moment dies, and I shake my head with another bone-weary sigh. "No."

He continues to stare at me. And after a long uncomfortable silence, he finally speaks again.

"If there's nothing here, as you say, prove it. *You* step on it."

"Fine," I shrug, and I step forward.

I pad around the jacket's edges, disinterested and half-assed, just going through the motions with as much blatant tedium as possible.

"No, no. Since there's nothing there, as you say, I'm sure you won't mind doing some serious stomping."

"Fine."

"Hard enough to break that camera when you find it."

"*Fine!*"

"And not just around the edges either. I want to see you cover every inch of that jacket. Go on. Get all of it."

"*FINE!*," I snap through clenched teeth.

I stomp; right, left, right, left. *Fuck it!* I jump up and *drive* both feet down hard. *There! How's that, mother fucker?!*

"Get the collar too!," he chides. And I do. I stomp and kick and scuff at the material, pawing at it like a bull lathering up before a matador. "What about that chest pocket there?"

That's when I notice it. His voice is suddenly coming from further away. In fact, neither one of them is anywhere near me now.

I am alone, in the middle of the floor, dancing like a lunatic...

... on my field jacket. On my *uniform*.

I am stomping on the American uniform... *holy shit!*

I am desecrating an American... military... uniform.

I might as well be wiping my ass with the stars and stripes.

I stop, immobilized by this revelation.

I don't know what to do, or what to say. I find myself hoping that maybe *they* haven't noticed the greater implications here, and I step back tenderly, head down, terrified of meeting their eyes.

"I don't have to do this," I mumble.

No one says a word. The silence stretches out, with me shriveling, alone, in the spotlight.

I have failed... *miserably*. And not just this interrogation. Not just this scenario. I have failed *myself*. I have failed my brothers at arms. And I have failed my *country*. They led me into this trap like a rat to cheese, and I scurried right after them, faster and faster, until my neck was under the clapper. And *SNAP!*, they got me. I got *myself*.

Oh, God.

"Airman Stipp," says Jakinov with a gentle consoling tone this time. "Airman Stipp, look at me. *Look* at me."

I look up. He's rocked back in his chair again. And I never heard him move away from me. I never heard his squeaky chair squeak when his weight settled back into it. Nothing.

He's not exactly smiling right now, but there's a subdued glow of victory in his face... which is mortifying, infuriating, well earned, and absolutely deserved, all at the same time. *Dammit!*

"Do you see what's up in that corner there?"

Without looking himself, he lifts one finger to point back over his shoulder. I follow it up into the corner, where the walls and roof meet above the rear door, over Number Two's head. And there it is: a closed circuit TV camera. A little black box with a lens on the front—pointed right at me—and a tiny red pinlight telling me it got everything.

I'm dead.

I look back at my feet, and the silence descends once more.

Col. Jakinov lets it play out for a few more seconds before speaking.

"Do you know what your fellow prisoners are going to think when they see that tape?"

Oh God. There's not a sinew or synapse in my body that even remembers that I'm in a shed right now, on the outskirts of Fairchild Air Force Base, outside Spokane, Washington, in a simple training environment, surrounded by other Air Force people. No, I am standing here before a *real* enemy interrogator, and he has beaten me. The rest of the 'prison population' is going to be shown that tape—with me leaping and stomping and wiping up the floors with my American uniform—and I will be the pariah of the camp.

I have let them down. All of them.

I have broken, and I deserve their wrath.

My lower lip comes unhinged.

"And don't think that we'll stop at that. Oh no. I can make sure a copy of this gets into the hands of the Red Cross, and from there to your American commanders."

My face buckles and crumbles. My chin starts to quiver.

He rocks forward, and rests his weight on his elbows.

"You are an exile now. I have only to dispense that tape—to *whom*ever, *where*ver, *how*ever—and you are lost. An outcast. Even if no one kills you for it, you will be shunned. You know that, don't you."

I don't move. I'm too busy fighting back a sudden welling of tears.

"But of course," he continues, "that doesn't have to happen. Does it?"

I'm staring fiercely at my shoes right now, trying to mentally lock him out. But he's already in.

"It might be possible to convince me to just... put that tape away somewhere. Lock it away in some drawer. Right? I don't have to show this to anybody, do I? Because I can count on *you*... to help *me*... to make *my* superiors happy. Right? After all, all it takes is a couple of signatures on some forms, and we're..."

"Fuck you," I spit, pouting, with a sudden hitch in my breathing.

Right now, I think I want *to be tortured.*

I sniff, and a single tear tumbles out onto my cheek. *Dammit!*

He waits for a moment, perhaps gauging the depths of this new defiance, perhaps just thinking up a whole new Evil Inquisitor speech to shove down my throat. *Whatever.*

Instead, he simply says, "Break."

* * *

JAKINOV'S POST-DEBACLE REASSURANCES failed to assuage anything more than my most basic scholastic concerns.

"*Most* people take the bait," he'd said, "realizing only too late what they'd been lured into."—"Don't worry; technically it's not a violation of military law to tread on an American uniform. A flag, yes. A uniform, no."—"Don't let it break you. The whole point of this exercise is to expose you to the widest possible gamut of resolve-breaking techniques, so that you'll recognize them in the future, should the occasion ever arise."—"Remember, you can't '*fail*' this course."—"You haven't done badly. You've just discovered one of your limits." Crap like that. Enough to reassure me that I'm still a student in good standing, even if such an unthinking reactionary response in the *real* world might have brought the entire U.S. fighting machine to its collective knees... approximately.

But not enough to make me feel any better about *myself*.

I've been thinking about that one performance ever since. In fact, it's been the *only* thing on my mind since they brought me back to my lovely five-by-five-by-six-foot overnight suite. Hell, I can hardly even remember anything about the other two interrogations that followed it.

I know I 'passed' them both, though.

One of them was little more than a speech by Col. Jakinov, extolling the glorious virtues of communism, and pointing out every flaw, lie, and lapse of capitalism. Presumably, considering the well-practiced (but entirely theoretical) 'logic' and 'appeal' of his arguments, the point of this tactic was simply to persuade me towards sympathy for his 'cause.'

I guess they felt compelled to throw in at least one no-brainer for us to conquer with ease.

The other *final* session was an awkward attempt on their part to threaten me with *another* prisoner's torture—a fairly common approach, we were taught—essentially foisting the responsibility for someone else's suffering onto me. But I blew this off with disinterested ease. They gave me the name of one of the women in the class, who I did not know beyond the recognition of her name, and tried to convince me that, even as we spoke, she was standing outside in the snow, barefoot and stripped down to her long johns, her life in my hands, held there at gunpoint until I answered the same damned questions they'd already asked me a hundred times before.

I just shook my head with disgust, told them I'd never heard of her, that she knew what she was getting herself into when she signed up, *blah-blah-blah, what-the-hell-ever*. I just didn't want to play anymore. I loathed myself too much to care.

But I wasn't acting when it came to playing like I was stunned too stupid to cooperate. I could barely lift my head by then, so heavy was the shame. Even worse, *it was still dark outside* when they led me back across the compound.

Goddammit! Did I miss a whole day here, or what?
This night is absolutely never-ending!

Now, back in my cell, the weight of this endless night and all its experiences is sitting on me like a beached manatee.

Intellectually, I know that every point the good colonel made was valid. And I'm sure that with all the thousands of people that must go through this school every year, the odds are that I'm not the first person to be lured along by his fried instincts into doing something reactionary and self-defeating. I also know myself well enough to know that, thirty-six hours from now, with this damned school behind me, and six hours of interstate ahead of me, this is going to morph into yet another funny story, based once again on more of my profound ineptitude, and easily swept away into the vaults of old and musty memories that will never be shared with anyone… because it's all just so unrelateable to normal humans.

But right now—right this moment—I feel like I just backed the family station wagon over my own kids.

* * *

AT LEAST THEY FINALLY killed that damned mind-curdling soundtrack.

I returned to find the entire cellblock resting in blessed quietude, for the first time in all the *years* it feels like I've been incarcerated here. Naturally though, like everything else in this place, it's a mixed blessing, and it comes at a price.

On the one hand, my nerves are no longer being scraped raw by the constant clashing tumult.

On the other hand, now I can't even cut the cheese without bringing down a full-blown Speznaz storm-trooper assault right through my door. And God help you if your boot leather should creak, or some atrophied knee cartilage pop.

Lord, it's getting to where all I want to do is scream.

I'm jammed into my vertical 'sleep' posture again—zoning in and out of consciousness while wedged between the floor and ceiling like a totem pole—when a commotion out in the antechamber startles me from my doze, unlocks all my joints, and leaves me teetering at a rubbery attention.

What NOW?!

Door after door after rickety cell door is exploding open, in sequence, like big, loud, really slow firecrackers. And they're marching my way.

I don't move. I don't adjust anything. I don't even bother opening my eyes. Because I just don't care.

BAM! "You! Step forward!"

BAM! "Out!"

BAM! "Animal! Step out!"

BAM! Then...

Rattle, BAM! My door vanishes in a dam-burst of light.

"Animal! Step forward!"

Again with the 'animal' thing. Again with the 'paws' and the shoulders and the awkward parade of blind simians. Again we're marching. Again we're tromping out into the winter night. Again we're... no... *wait a minute!*

There's sunlight filtering through my head-bag!

It's morning! Daylight! Sunrise! It's dawn!

It's... the next friggin' day! That eternal night is finally over! No more solitary confinement!

Which means...

... now it's time for the Concentration Camp.

STORY XLI

CONCENTRATION CAMP

1
CAPTAIN LICKSPITTLE

February, 1978
Air Force POW School, Fairchild Air Force Base, Spokane, Washington

SO THIS IS HOME NOW.

An acre, acre-and-a-half of frozen treeless mud and heaped rock, dappled with snow, surrounded by paired fence lines, and crowned with concertina wire. Guard towers soar from all four corners, each one sporting a gimbaled searchlight the size of a Volkswagen, and an armed sentry brandishing a Soviet AK-47 assault rifle with a banana clip curving out the bottom of its stock. As if they mean business or something.

An ugly weather-streaked double-wide is huddled under the only tree in the area, outside the wire, right next to the main gate. I guess that's the Camp Commandant's 'office.'

I don't see any 'barracks' for the prisoners, though.

We're approaching the camp in a long strung-out line, shuffling lethargically along the dirt road that connects the two compounds. They had us doff our head-bags just outside the fences of the previous compound, and then allowed us to relinquish our grips on the 'animals in front of us.' We've been enjoying this chilly morning stroll between sites ever since.

The column bunches and slows as it enters the camp's main gate. Teams of shouting guards are dissecting the prisoners into groups—or 'houses' as they call them—eight to ten inmates per 'house.' Then a pair of guards escorts each newly formed 'house' off to... *where?*

It *looks* like they're being marched off toward the various scattered 'rock piles.'

Great. Right to work making little rocks out of big rocks, apparently.

Because I'm back among the rearmost echelons of the column—*again (apparently 'bringing up the rear' is just my 'thing')*—this time without a head-bag occluding my vision, I'm able to take a few mental notes before reaching the gate myself.

For instance, I notice that, about six or seven people ahead of me, the two senior ranking prisoners—Colonel Swanson, and some big doughy bald-headed major—have been discreetly consorting with each other the whole way down the road. This, I'm sure, is the first opportunity those two senior officers have *had* to 'consort' since the POW scenario began.

But as the trailing ranks of the procession begin to pass through the gate to the 'concentration camp,' a tight little cadre of enemy muscle suddenly homes in on the colonel, swarms him, then hustles him off to the double-wide without a word of explanation, or even a kiss goodnight. *Foom!* And just like that, *he's gone!* The one guy we've all been expecting, since the academic phase of the class, to take charge and organize whatever 'unified resistance' we're going to be able to muster, is now out of the picture.

The major is left standing in the middle of the road, arms out in disbelief, as if his prom date had just been swept off by the school's bronzed-god quarterback. In fact, the guards have to turn on *him* next, shoving him into forward motion again, just to keep the line moving.

Well, there's *a lumpy little plot twist we didn't see coming.*

Now, as the wrought iron arch of the gate passes over me, some pseudo-Russian slogan welded in Cyrillic characters riding the arch—*maybe the equivalent of "Arbeit Macht Frei" perhaps?*—up ahead, two more guards cut off the latest 'houseful' of prisoners, and march them off. And it quickly becomes apparent that the next 'house' will include *me*. Me and like seven or eight others. We're herded off to the side, and I can tell right away that this is going to be an 'eclectic' group.

Among my new 'housemates' are two paramedics ("parajumpers," or "PJs"), along with one of the only six women in the class. That, plus that same stunned major. He's still looking around, lost, as if he can't find his car in a crowded parking lot or something. I think he's just figured out that he's now the Senior Ranking (American) Officer (SRO) of the whole camp, and I suspect that the revelation has probably taken care of any constipation problems he might have had.

Once there's nine of us in our group—in our *'house'*—two enormous guards, beefed up even more by their thickly insulated blue waist coats, and topped with the requisite black berets with red stars, bully us down the gravel aisle between the rock piles, headed to... *where?*

"Here!," the lead one barks, stopping and pointing to a hole in the ground. "Go!"

I still don't see what he's pointing at, but the front of our little queue abruptly turns right and starts stepping *down... into the ground! Into the rock pile!* Under *the damned rock pile!*

What the hell?!

It turns out that those heaps of big beige and gray boulders that line both sides of the narrow walkways *are* our 'houses!' They're not actually 'heaps' either. They're arched 'roofs,' mortared shells hunched low over these long rectangular pits. They remind me of some of the tackier souvenirs my family used to pick up in the various foreign lands we visited... like cheap jewelry boxes plastered with so many glued-on stones and shells and chips of glass that they look dangerous to touch, only these are blown up to the size of a garage, and buried in the frozen mud up to the roofline. It's dank and dark inside our 'house,' and barely warmed at all by the embers throbbing in the black pot-bellied stove at the far end. Not a stick of furniture anywhere, of any kind. Not even a half-assed bench to sit on. Not one light bulb... not a window, not a rug, not a blanket, not even a *door*. Just a floor and four walls of dirt, with a low vaulted ceiling of heavy stones levitating over our heads.

Are you kidding me?

Gawd, it just keeps on coming.

But that's okay. I can endure.

We're scheduled to be back in our school barracks by six this evening, or thereabouts. Hot showers and sleep, followed by a graduation debrief in the morning, equipment (and parka) turn-in, student check-*out*, and a half-day's drive back to Seattle tomorrow. And back in my great little car again.

Go ahead. Do your worst.

Bring it on.

* * *

IT IS 'BROUGHT ON' barely forty-five minutes later (I'm guessing).

My 'house' is ordered up out of its frozen rat hole, and goosed back down the walkway to the main gate, which is closed now.

Set up just inside the gate, in the open and raked by the cutting breeze, is a row of collapsible tables lined up end-to-end, with eight pieces of paper laid out down their collective length, weighted to the tables with fist-sized chunks of rock. The same kind of rock doming all of our 'houses.' Two dour guards stand behind the tables, their weapons at port-arms. A third (and substantially less imposing) figure is posted at the end of the tables at parade rest, waiting for us.

Our escort jostles us into a single file facing the tables and the guards beyond them, and prods us to attention. Then the little guy at the end draws a deep and melodramatic breath, and begins a slow saunter down the length of our line, looking every bit the sinister weasel that he evidently aspires to be.

He introduces himself as the Deputy Commandant—*I cannot help but think of him as 'Captain Lickspittle'*—whose duty it is, at this time, to acquaint us with the camp rules. And this he does with all the *ennui* of a speech too often repeated, and too seldom appreciated.

We are not to leave our 'house' without a specific (and *authorized*) destination in mind, and a damned good reason for going there. If any guard should ask us where we're going, we'd better be able to provide those specifics, or expect punishment. Taking a casual sunset stroll does not qualify. Our 'sanitary facilities' consist of a nasty rank of wooden one-holers shouldered up against the right-rear corner of the fenceline, one end of which is at the foot of the corner guard tower.

Boy, that's got to be some pungent sentry duty.

We are not to encroach within so many feet of said fenceline, or face, at the very least, the ever-popular 'severe punishment,' and at worst, the possibility of being mowed down by a crossfire from the guard towers.

Blah, blah, blah. Yadi-yada-yada.

"We're the Rulers of the Universe, you're the shit on our shoes."

"You do work, do what you're told, obey the rules, and you might get fed twice a day."

Yeh, yeh, yeh. Where's my bread and water?

The one that gets me though—the one with which I see myself having the hardest time—is the one about the genuflection we must regularly perform for our captors.

Any time we so much as cross the path of a guard or camp official, we must snap to attention, lock our knees, *bow ninety degrees at the waist*, like one of those toy 'dipping birds,' and, while looking at the ground in front of our toes, recite the following: "*Bikon, Herr Commandant.*"

No, seriously.
What the hell is that?

That's "Bikon (*rhymes with "Nikon"*), Herr (*rhymes with "Hair"*) Commandant (regardless of their actual rank)."

What kind of half-baked goo is that? A little 'Hogan's Heroes' German, a little ginned-up faux-Russian shit?

But it's either that, or *spin the punishment wheel!*

This little pep-talk and all its tributaries lasts about ten minutes, while the wind chill scampers through us, and thin bands of fast-moving cirrus rake the ice-silver sky. Then he finally gets to his grand finale, the part that involves those papers rattling there under their limestone paperweights.

* * *

HE SOUNDS EXTRA-BORED and put-out as he discourses at length about the sheer *mountain* of paperwork that he must endure, all in order to officially register us as Prisoners of War with the various international agencies that insist on being kept apprised of such matters. And for the sake of making life easier on himself—and thereby, for *us*, of course—he's decided to just get it all out of the way at the same time. One big mass-signing.

So here they all are, all the forms that would normally be signed, piecemeal, over the ensuing weeks, after various briefings, indoctrinations, interrogations and visitations had been completed. Only this time we're skipping ahead, *past* all those standard exchanges and ceremonies, and going straight to the signatures. The ones we're going to eventually sign anyway.

He makes it all sound so reasonable, so perfectly sensible, in fact—all customary; mandatory, but tedious, repetitious, and superfluous, best gotten out of the way by the most streamlined method(s) possible… in other words, *compressed*—that I find myself not only empathizing with him, but questioning my own understanding of the terms of the Geneva Convention as well. Because I could've sworn they'd said that the only form we should *ever* sign is a clearly labeled International Red Cross form. Period. And I don't see one of those anywhere.

I'm standing right smack dab in the middle of our row of nine—at number five—and with only a tiny discreet tilt of my head, I am able to sneak a peek at the rest of my 'housemates' on both sides of me, while Ol' Lickspittle continues to ramble. And every one of them looks like he—or she—is mentally wrestling with how best to handle this.

Good. I feel better. It's not just me.

"Alright then," Lickspittle concludes with a clap and a brisk rubbing of his hands, "We'll begin at this end. You!" And he points to a PJ at the far left end of the line.

But the PJ only stiffens to an even more rigid form of attention, and growls through clenched teeth. "No sir."

The Deputy Commandant freezes in his tracks, and turns one ear toward the PJ as if he just can't believe what he's heard. On the other side of the tables, the guards tense.

"What did you say?"

"I said, 'No sir. I will not sign any of those forms,'... sir."

Lickspittle pads slowly towards him, his hands behind his back, looking an awful lot like a whooping crane tippy-toeing through the shallows stalking a nice plump toad to eat.

"That was not a request, animal. These papers are official, legal, internationally recognized forms that *require* your signature, as a normal part of a normal in-processing procedure. And you *will* sign them, or face severe punishment. Now step forward and sign these papers."

"No sir. I will not."

Lickspittle snaps his finger at one of the guards and shouts, "Take him to the doghouse. *Now!*"

Before the guard has even rounded the table though, the Deputy Commandant is already standing in front of the next man in line—which, coincidentally, happens to be the other paramedic—and sweeps an angry finger between his chest and the table.

"You! *You* will start instead. Step forward and sign."

None too surprisingly, there is a distinct lack of forward-steppage and form-signage from this guy as well.

"No sir," PJ Number Two asserts quietly but firmly. "With all due respect, I will not…"

"Take him with you!," Lickspittle snaps at the converging guards.

No second chance for Number Two, I guess.

Then the Deputy Commandant wheels around to face the rest of us.

As one—and it's just a jumpy reflex, I can assure you… it has nothing to do with training or discipline—we all tauten, and stare hard at the horizon. He apparently interprets this as an indication of unified resistance, though. And he sighs, shaking his head in melodramatic disappointment.

"Is this how it's going to be with all of you then? Resistance? So soon after arriving in my camp? And over something so trivial as this? *This?*"

No one says a word. Not a muscle flinches, not a breath is drawn. And I'm starting to like this shit all over again.

Lickspittle sighs, and starts another theatrical stroll back to the other end of the line—the end with The Major, our 'fearless leader'—shaking his head the whole way, as if he just can't understand this. The world is silent, save for the petulant wind snuffling through those eight unsigned papers, and the seven remaining members of our house.

When at last he reaches the far end of our rank, he stops and turns to face The Major. The Major, his comb-over blowing in the wind and built like a six-and-a-half foot pear, is a full head taller than the DC. But I can see, out of the corner of my eye, that he's about one "*Boo!*" away from squirting sweat like a sprinkler, then passing out. Standing at such a rigid (and puckered) brace, he is still somehow able to cringe away from his antagonist, his head drawn back far enough to double the number of his chins.

"Major?," says Lickspittle with another exaggerated sigh, "You are the Senior Ranking Officer here now, are you not?"

Jesus, I can hear the big guy swallowing clear over here.

"No sir. I believe that Colonel Swa…"

"Colonel Swanson is gone, Major, and you won't be seeing him again anytime soon. So… I believe that makes *you* the Senior Ranking Officer for the camp now. Yes?"

The Major does not answer. He only gulps again, which makes Lickspittle chuckle.

"Fine. I believe that American military law requires that every prisoner here follow your orders while they are incarcerated here. Is that not also correct? So it is *you* who will order these people to sign these papers—*now!*—or face the most dire of consequences. Do you understand, Major?"

"No... uh, no *sir*."

The smile drops from Lickspittle's face with a crash.

"Then allow me to make this simple for you," he growls. "If you don't order every one of these animals to sign these papers—and *right now!*—I will throw them *all* into the doghouse. *Together! At the same time!* Do you understand *that*, Major?"

"Sir, according to the Geneva Convention, I'm not..."

"*DON'T TELL me about the Geneva Convention, Major!* I know more about the damned Geneva Accords than any of you will ever know! Not that it should matter, since your country never signed the damned things anyway! But they say nothing about what *types* or *how many* different forms you may or may not sign! But now my patience has run out. Tell these animals, *now*, to sign these forms, or *every one of them*—every one *but YOU*, Major—is going into that doghouse!"

I don't think any of us has a clue about what the hell "The Doghouse" even *is*. But somehow, it just doesn't sound all that bad. So our stalwart and hard-swallowing 'leader' is holding out. *Good for him.* That's as it should be. For the moment then, he just says nothing at all. And the wiry little 'Russki' is not taking it very well.

Now visibly enraged, Lickspittle storms down our line.

"Perhaps you are not aware of just what a stretch in The Doghouse really means! Alright, then! *Look! All of you! Over there!*"

We turn to look in the direction to which his quivering finger is pointing, behind us and to the left, to the place, about twenty yards away, where the guards are busily packing the two naughty PJs into what looks like a big wooden capsule. And instantly, I am confident that all these threats of his have been just a big fat bluff. Because *there's no way in hell you could possibly cram eight people into that thing. You'd be lucky to fit half that.*

Basically, 'The Doghouse' is just an oversized rain barrel. Upright, it would probably stand about six feet tall, maybe a little more. But it's been laid on its side, and sunk halfway into the ground, so instead, it looks more like a miniature wooden Quonset Hut. And that's it. That's the whole thing.

It was designed to hold a couple of large dogs, like Dobermans,

Rotweilers, or German Shepherds. It might fit *four* adult Homo Sapiens, maybe five, if you used a shoe horn and a tamping rod. *Maybe*.

I face forward again, trying my best not to smile.

Old Lickspittle is bluffing.

"If you think I'm bluffing," he says, "try me. Refuse one more time, Major, and you'll be the only one left standing here. Everyone else will be packed inside that doghouse… along with those first two animals I already put in there. Now… *order your people to sign these papers!*"

Surprisingly, the major hesitates for several seconds.

What's to think about? You know he can't really fit us all in there!

Then, "Sir, I will not give any such order. We are required only to…"

"*GUARDS! Every one of these animals! Into the Doghouse! NOW!*"

The clatter and jingle of weapons and web gear bouncing on large running bodies suddenly converges on us. Apparently there were a few more guards involved here than just the handful that were plainly visible.

We are surrounded in an instant, and hustled along at a stumbling trot toward The Doghouse. The major remains behind, two guards dedicated just to him, along with old Lickspittle, who's now looking downright pleased with himself. And he's not looking at all like a man whose bluff has just been called.

Ruh-roh.

2
THE DOGHOUSE

ON THE PREMISE THAT if there's any chance whatsoever that this might still be a bluff, one that might yet be confessed and surrendered… on the premise that I'd rather not have to squirm all the way in there, only to squirm right back out again, I hang back. I loiter, always looking 'ready' to step up next, but 'willing' to allow ladies, or seniors, or 'age before beauty,' or *whatever* form of fake chivalry I can offer… *anybody*, really, to go first.

But as, one after the other, five, six, then *seven* people are squashed into that little half-barrel of a 'doghouse'—all without that hoped-for shout from Captain Lickspittle admitting defeat—it finally becomes apparent that I *am* going to have to join the rest of my group inside that nasty little horizontal phone booth after all. Only now, I'm the last one in. Again. And the circle of guards can now focus all their attention on me. *Why do I do this to myself?*

As I mentioned before, I am not the least bit claustrophobic. But as I crouch down to the little door, I see that it is filled to bursting with wads of straining humanity. A bundle of green fatigue material, a single boot, and the crumpled hem of somebody's field jacket—I think it's someone's ass, with one foot tangled in an uncomfortable position—is bloating out the tiny doorway like a big green hernia. I couldn't even slip my *hand* in there, much less pack my entire body through that opening.

"Move it!," one of the guards bellows, his AK-47 held up in a menacing head-club position.

I wave at the butt cheeks poking out of the hole.

"But... there's no way... I..."

"Get in there ! *NOW!*"

Another guard shoves at the offending ass with his boot, pressing it further inward... maybe a whole inch.

"Move in! All of you! There's one more coming!"

A muffled bleat of protest leaks out of the stuffed hutch, but the foreground body wriggles—just enough to untangle its own foot, which disappears into the darkness—and another boot connects with *my* ass.

"Now go! Get in there, animal!"

Yeh, that'll do it. That'll help me defy the laws of physics, alright.

With a disbelieving chuckle, I nudge at the barrier of green-clad meat. But there's just no way. That damned doghouse is packed solid, probably *waayyy* beyond the legal fire codes, I'm thinking.

I turn back to the looming circle of guards, and throw my hands up.

"Look, there's just no..."

The biggest guy kicks my feet sideways, unhorsing me from my kneeling posture. I land with my hip in the gravel, one hand in the snow.

"*Poot your feet in RIGHT THERE, animal! Then PUSH your way in! Do NOT make me tell you again!*"

Jesus!

I steal a quick glance back to the major. He's watching everything from a distance with the sort of distraught expression you'd find on the face of a man, stuck on the wrong side of town, watching his Porsche being stripped right down to its axles. Then I wheel around, and make a show of jamming my boots around the inside corner of the door, and shove hard.

My legs disappear up to the knees. I have to pry the wedged body in the door away from the other side of the jamb—the same way I'd force a balky elevator door to open—then I shoot one arm into the sliver of a gap. Inside, I can feel and hear the others writhing and fidgeting their ways into newer, more tightly compacted arrangements. But here on the outside, I'm still tugging at the doorframe with my one free hand, trying to jerk my way in closer. And 'closer' is about the best I can do here. Not 'further in.' Just 'closer.' There's clearly no way my body will ever fit all the way in. But I can put on a show for the crowd of angry guards still glaring down at me.

Then, after about thirty seconds of my phony 'struggle,' I suddenly feel the door *against my back*, pressing hard! *And then harder!* Seventy-five percent of me is still humped outside the opening, but the guards are trying to pack me in the rest of the way by ramming the door closed behind me.

"*Wait! Fuck! I'm not...!*"

Whump! Whump!

Jeez, they're really putting the shoulder to it!

Our lone female's voice makes a stifled squeak from somewhere back in the compressed darkness.

Damn! Apparently it's not her I'm spooning with here at the front of the doghouse.

Ewwww.

After several more seconds of being forcibly squashed into the hole, the light is snuffed, and the *clack!* of a heavy metal deadbolt slams home.

Son of a bitch! Damned if they didn't *actually manage to cram all eight of us into this doghouse! You know, I'm starting to think they might have done this before.*

For a few moments, we just lay in silence. Smothering pressure, rising warmth, and stunned incredulity all fill the tiny space along with our eight grunting bodies. Then the adjustments for comfort begin in earnest.

"Sorry... I..."

"Excuse me. I just... need to..."

"There."

"*Ouch! That's my hair!*"

"Sorry. There's just..."

"*Oof!*"

The minutes pass. I grind my hip through the crushed rock that lines the floor, trying to back my nose out of somebody's hair, and my Twinkie out from between someone else's buns. But for me at least, after only a few seconds, I'm comfortable *enough* to relax and take advantage of the warmth and the prone position for the first time in hours.

I close my eyes, and try to slip away.

The squirming continues around me though, and I have to settle for 'pretending to meditate' instead, 'slipping away' (in my little crease of space) with the equivalent of a heavy-breathing Sumo wrestler sitting on my chest.

Yeh, if it wasn't for that little breathing issue, I'd be doing just fine.

But... the girl's muted voice leaks back to me through all the pressed meat, sounding an awful lot like that guy who had to pee so bad back in the Box Chamber, only with an edge of *panic* to it.

"I... don't know... if I can take... much more of this."

Silence again. And, blessedly, stillness.

There's still a lot of desperate snorting noises, some wheezing and a few gasps, but otherwise you'd think we were all just cabin mates—locked in a really small cabin—at summer camp, after lights out. And we lay here quietly for several more minutes, just waiting for the time to pass... waiting for old Lickspittle to realize that our 'fearless leader' is never going to crack over something as meaningless and irrelevant as a few peasants stuffed into a space the size of a desk drawer... and willing ourselves to be thinner.

But the temperature's still rising, the air's getting stale, and I imagine a few limbs are going to sleep.

Then that lone female voice chimes in again, squeaky and sounding on the verge of tears.

"I can't... breathe..."

More valiant—and of course, futile—attempts to give her space fail almost before they're begun. But then another voice rises from the far end of this sardine can. One of the PJs, this time.

"So there's this kid," he says, as casually as if we were all just cloistered around the office water cooler. "He's a newspaper delivery boy, and it's Christmas." He grunts and shuffles for a moment, then continues. "And *because* it's Christmas, at every one of his stops people are slipping him a little something extra. You know, like a bonus. Ten bucks here, twenty bucks there, like that."

I don't believe it. This guy is telling a *joke*, right here, and right now, crammed into this wooden hole like a wad of cotton in a pill bottle. He's probably smooshed against the back wall, his nose buried in someone else's armpit. But everybody's listening. Including me.

"Then he gets to this one house. And when he tosses the paper up onto the porch, the front door opens, and there's this sexy blonde housewife wearing nothing but a silk robe opened all the way down to the belt line."

Even our panicky little lady's breathing calms and goes quiet now. I think I've heard this one before, but I've never wanted to hear a punchline more desperately than this one right now.

"So she's leaning up against the doorframe all slinky-like—you know, twirling her sash and shit—and she says, 'If you come on in, I'll give you your Christmas bonus in person'."

A strained male voice gasps out a feeble "*Hoo-HOO*" at that, and somebody else snickers.

"So he goes in, right? And she takes him upstairs, lays him out on the bed, drops her robe, and proceeds to throw him a hump like he ain't never had. Pops his cherry like a cork, and leaves him all sweaty and smilin'. Then she lights up a cigarette, sits on the edge of the bed, and hands him a one-dollar bill."

Total silence in The Doghouse.

You'd think this was a sermon by the Pope himself.

"He can't figure this shit out, though. I mean, you know... what? A dollar? So he asks her, 'What's with the sex and a buck?' And she explains to him, 'I told my husband we needed to give the paper boy something for a Christmas bonus. And he said, *Fuck him. Give him a dollar.*'"

Our little casket-for-eight *explodes* with laughter. Even 'the girl' is shrieking her guts out. The whole clot of compacted bodies heaves and jiggles against itself. Someone's hand starts thumping against the low ceiling. And I'm right there with them. Right now, I think I can honestly say that's just about the most hilarious joke I've ever heard in my life!

Around me, the laughter just goes ballistic, sailing off the top of the chart. But it's not the kind of uninhibited release you'd expect to hear at, say, an all-night kegger or something. No, it's more like a screaming desperate outburst, giddy, borderline hysterical, and we're all caught up in the current.

I go breathless, wailing like a loon and crying my eyes out. The whole doghouse is rocking to the jostling of its contents. And it just goes on and on. We're all pitching and bucking against each other, exacerbating the problem with all the tight, almost *ticklish* contact. I can't stop laughing! I just *can't! Minutes* pass, and we're still cackling like a pack of hyenas. The joke itself isn't even relevant anymore. Right now, I think we're just feeding off each other's insanity, uproarious with the absurdity of the whole situation.

Every little helpless giggle just sends ripples through the whole pile of us. And a big part of it, I think, is the girl's Carol-Burnett-style snorts and guffaws. Just as the rest of us are starting to get our collective breath back, she *snerks* and belts out another round, and we're all off to the races again.

But *damn*, I needed this. I'm weak and weepy and hard-pressed to draw a deep breath, but this was just such a spectacular release of so much pent-up emotion. I feel like I'm ready now to *take on the world!*

***

AS IF IN ANSWER to my cockiness, the door suddenly clatters open behind me, and the outward pressure of the group pops my ass out the door like the blunt tip of a ballpoint pen. I imagine a small cloud of steam boiled out with it.

"*Out! Everybody out! Now!*"

Well, that wasn't so bad. How long were we in there anyway? Probably not even ten minutes. But who knows.

I writhe and push… and apologize. I wrestle one arm out the door, and use it, pushing against the top of the doorframe, to pry myself the rest of the way out. Then I roll, limply, through the gravel and onto my knees, where a towering guard 'assists' me to my feet with a hefty yank.

Oops! Forgot to say 'Bikon, Herr Commandant.'

Fudge. Oh well.

Instead, I just stand there sniffing, wiping my swollen eyes, and trying to stifle the last of my giggles.

(*'Fuck him. Give him a dollar.' That's awesome.*)

One after the other, the rest of the sardines unfold themselves from the can, backing out into the chilly air. All of them are still teary-eyed. All look rumpled, pasty-faced, and sweaty (easily misinterpreted as traumatized and run through the wringer, I imagine), and because of that, I can see how we might look like we've been through hell. But, of course, we haven't.

Well, maybe 'the girl'… a little bit.

I attempt to offer my hand to one of the more 'sore-acting' ones, but a guard orders me back. *Well, okay then.*

The young lady—the fifth one out—stays on her knees for a moment to catch her breath, to dab at her still-moist eyes, and then assist the sixth man out. But she too is snatched to her feet by a guard, and ordered roughly to march back to the tables.

"Come on! Let's go!," Lickspittle shouts from twenty yards away, still standing beside the distressed looking major. "Let's get this over with!"

Again, I loiter for a moment while the others mosey off, just to get a good look at the two PJs when they come out last. But another guard barks at me, and I have to turn to follow the rest of the straggling line.

Looking around at the bright, fresh, nippy day—which feels absolutely *delicious* now after the time spent stewing in that tiny half-barrel—I notice that the entrance to every 'house' is crowded with faces, wide-eyed and watching as the first punished prisoners pile out of The Doghouse like midgets from a clown car. I want to laugh at that too.

Capt. Lickspittle seems to be in much better spirits this time as well, smirking as we scuffle to a stop in front of him and his tables. Most of us are still sniffling and drawing great deep draughts of the chilled winter air, so I take his pleasure as a gloating response to what he believes is the eight of us having been 'broken.' Or having at least 'learned our lesson.' Or something.

Well, I'm happy as hell to disappoint you, sir.

"You can thank the Major here, for getting your punishment cut as short as it was," he announces proudly, as the last of us—meaning myself and the two PJs—saunter blearily into place.

What? Cut short? What's he talking about?

"You have a good commander here, one who feels your pain, and cannot stand to see his men suffering needlessly."

What?!!

"Only because he agreed to have you sign these papers, I have, in turn, agreed to have you all released from The Doghouse before your time was up. And so now we will get this nasty business over with, yes? Major?"

The big doughy major turns to look at us, but freezes when he sees the shock in our red-rimmed eyes and gaping mouths. His own expression collapses into the feral gaze of a cornered rodent.

"Well, I couldn't just leave you in there. Jesus Christ! Eight people crammed into that tiny space? I could hear the noises clear over here, and I..."

"Yes, yes, yes, Major. You can tell them all about that later on," says Lickspittle. "But for now? Please, give them the order."

I can't imagine what's going through the major's mind right now, but if he's psychically sensitive at all, he's got to be fearing for his life. Because as soon as we get back to our 'house,' we're going to kill him.

He looks panicked and flustered for another moment. I'd like to think he's weighing the odds of reneging on his promise to Lickspittle, but right now I'm just not seeing that much spine in this guy. Then he blinks, hardens his resolve, and addresses us directly, head-on.

"In order to gain your release, I assured the captain that you... that *we* would all sign these papers as instructed. I take full responsibility, so..."

"Well *I* sure as hell didn't agree to that!,″ shouts the first PJ. "You can throw me back in the damned doghouse if you want, but I ain't signin' *nothin'* on that table!"

"Sergeant! Do not forget your place! You're still in the military, and while you're here, you're under my command! Now just sign the damned papers! And that's an order!"

The PJ bites his tongue, and pivots to face back forward. But he doesn't move. *Nobody* moves. Nobody *breathes*. Nobody in the entire damned camp! Not even Lickspittle.

"Sergeant," the major repeats, this time with a low but laughable 'warning tone' in his voice. "Make no mistake: that was an *order*. Real, official, and legally binding. Do not make me repeat it."

I don't believe this guy! I can't believe this limp-dicked 'officer' has the unmitigated *gall* to get all starchy and officious *now*, after caving in to something this stupid, this *weightless*, this *quickly!* Knuckling under to so little pressure under *any* circumstances would have been appalling enough. But to fold like this in a *simulated* environment—where he *knows* we can't be hurt!—is just too stunning to comprehend! Not to mention the fact that, thanks to his cowardice, we endured that time in the doghouse *for nothing!* We're going to wind up signing those damned papers anyway!

How could he choke like that? How could he crumble so easily under so little coercion? Even if old Lickspittle had pointed to a friggin' guillotine, threatened to have us gutted like fish, then have our heads lopped off if we didn't sign those stupid papers, *it still wouldn't have meant a damned thing!*

They can't touch us here (more or less)! Even if we *hadn't* been laughing so hard inside that little wooden bunghole... even if we *had* been screaming and begging to be let out... his cowardly surrender could never have been justified.

This bastard has got to be the biggest tower of tapioca I've ever seen!

The PJ steps up to the table, snatches up the pen angrily, and starts scribbling. Hard enough for the scratching to be heard across the yard.

What? What are you doing?! You may not be able to tell that mother-fucker off, but in this 'learning environment,' you can still play *like you're defying unsound orders! Stop signing things!*

He finishes it anyway.

"Keep going," chimes Capt. Lickspittle. "Sign all of them."

The PJ, who looks like he might once have spent some time as a linebacker for the Nebraska Cornhuskers, hurls a withering glare at the little commie shithead—one that tightens the cordon of equally beefy guards around him out of trained reflex—then sends that same glare straight at our 'fearless commander,' the "Milquetoast Major." But then he stomps over to the next piece of fluttering paper, and resumes his scribbling.

"Next!," says Lickspittle, pointing to the second PJ, the one who's standing right next to me.

NO!, I scream in my head. *Screw these clowns! Don't move!*

But he moves anyway. *Dammit!*

After only a second's hesitation, just enough to make a half-assed point I guess, he storms up to the table and starts writing as well.

I can't believe these *guys are knuckling under too! These PJs!*

These are some bad-ass dudes! I thought! How could they do this? Here, at this school?!

Well, I ain't signin' nuttin'! Fuck this! I'll do a left-face, and march myself *back to the doghouse before I lower myself* and my country—*again!*—to that level!

Once, in interrogation, was bad enough.

Doesn't anybody here understand? *This is a SCHOOL!*

This sniveling *faux*-Russian weasel is going to go home tonight to his house *in fucking Spokane!—not Smolensk, or Saigon, or Shanghai!*—without having bent a hair on a gnat's ass! *He can't!* And if he can't, then what can he possibly inflict on us that we can't resist? With *what* can he threaten, or coerce, or even *sway?* I want to storm down this line, *deck* that asshole major, then march back to my place, slapping every face along the way.

These PJs, though… *they're just letting me down.*

"Come on! Keep going! *You! Next!* Get up there!"

Now he's talking to *me*.

Well, to hell with that! I ain't doin' it! I ain't signin' shit! I'm not moving a goddamned muscle! Let that cum-bubble major rant and rave all he wants! Go ahead, Lickspittle! Threaten me with something interesting!

My feet step forward of their own volition.

What the…?!!! TRAITORS!!

Okay, well… I'll at least look *at the damned forms. Maybe the ones the PJs already signed really are Red Cross forms.*

I look down at the first sheet, snapping and crackling in the breeze.

Not only is it *not* a Red Cross or Red Crescent form, it's not even written in English.

How? HOW could they have willingly signed this?
I look down at the two signatures.

Mickey Mouse.

Donald Duck.

I love these guys.
I have to bite down to strangle a blurt of laughter.
Instead, I hold my angry glower, grab the pen left behind by the PJs, and sign my own damned name.

Hugh G. Rection.

"Come on! Next! Get up there!"
Lickspittle has no clue, but how long will that last? Eventually, once the first PJ reaches the last form, he'll be signing right next to our junior-despot Deputy Commandante. Then what? Even a ratty little shitheel from the wrong side of the Iron Curtain—*and especially a fake one*—is bound to be familiar with the more prominent Disney icons.
Oh well.
The next guy in line—Lieutenant Rayburn, as he introduced himself back in our 'house,' the same lieutenant I almost followed onto the capture field back at the beginning of all this, believe it or not—sidles up to the table beside me, and looks over the first form while I'm busy signing the second. I slap the pen down with righteous indignation (an Oscar-worthy performance, I'm sure), and move on to the next form… just as the lieutenant lets slip a single snicker. He's seen the first three signatures.
All eyes, including mine—and Lickspittle's—lock onto him. He's quick to clap a stern mask of 'insulted honor' over his face though, clearing his throat and 'glaring' at the first three of us as if *appalled* by our capitulation (or something like that). But the proverbial horse has long since fled the proverbial barn on this one.
Lickspittle charges down the line of tables, and shoulders him out of the way in mid-signature. He yanks the paper out from under its limestone paperweight, and glowers at the names. Without speaking, he seizes the second sheet, and then the third, right out from under my pen. His eyes

flash over the writing like scanning lasers.

Oh shit.

He glares at me, then at the two PJs beyond. And he does not relinquish that gaze, even as he crumples up the papers and addresses the major off to his distant left.

"If this is how you Americans honor your promises, Major, then the price for you is going to be very high."

"What?," he snivels.

GAWD, I want to drive my fist right through his teeth, clear up to the elbow. Adrenaline splashes through my chest in a wave, just thinking about it.

"What did they do?," he whines.

What did 'they' do? What did 'they' DO? They "resisted," you great flaming tubesteak! Just like you *were supposed to!*

Lickspittle just chuckles, and tosses the wad of paper over his shoulder. A guard automatically catches it.

"Since I must now go get new forms, you and the rest of these animals—except for *these* four, of course—will now return to your house *and stay there.* You are all restricted to quarters as of this moment. And that means no food, no wood gathering, and no toilet runs. *Nothing!* I don't even want to see your faces in the doorway. Is that clear, Major?"

"Yessir."

"Now *get out of my sight! GO!*"

I hear the gang scrambling away behind me.

"As for you four," he continues, his gaze riveted on each face in turn, "Since you seem to love the doghouse so much, please... *be my guests. Guards!*"

A storm of heavily booted feet crunches through gravel, and swarms around us from all sides. And we are led back to 'The Spa.'

Hah! Only four of us? In a structure built for two German Shepherds? Luxury!

3
MAJOR CHICKENSHIT

"HUGH G. RECTION?," snorts Captain Hammond. "Seriously?"

"Yeh," Lt. Rayburn answers, still mortified by his slip at the tables. "It just caught me by surprise, is all. What can I say? *It was funny*. And I laughed before I knew what I was doing."

More laughter ripples around our dark little cave. But I stay out of it. I'm more embarrassed than proud of that stupid pseudonym, since that's what caused Rayburn to cause *us* to revisit the doghouse, making *me* more culpable than him. *Whatever.*

We're back in our 'house' again now... and it is *fucking cold!*

Somebody oughta' close the damned door!

Of course, there is no door. We are, after all, living in a hole in the ground... under the *snow* on the ground... just south of the *Canadian border... in the dead of friggin' winter.* So yeh, being cold is kind of a 'given,' given the circumstances. And since, as a 'house,' we are restricted to quarters still, and unable to gather wood, my fellow 'housemates' have been unable to stoke the fire. And while the four of us were gone, the last feeble embers in the stove went and died.

God, I miss the doghouse!

I shuffle aimlessly around our frozen little dirt-floored cave now, hands in pockets, eyes on my boots as they kick their way through the soil. Nothing to look at. Nowhere to sit. And our fifteen minutes of fame for 'Defying the Man' having long since lapsed. We might have been greeted as 'heroes' upon our release from the doghouse, but our novelty has quickly worn out again in the chill of this muddy icebox.

Basically then, there's nothing to do now until they release us from our restriction to quarters. And there are two very large guards, AK-47s cradled in their crossed arms, standing right outside the portal, just to make sure we're not even peeking out.

I'm getting impatient (*I know, that's so hard to believe*). I hate this feeling of listlessness, of timelessness, and of wasted opportunities (or at least *missed* ones). But I take begrudging comfort from the knowledge that we're down to single-digit hours now—we *must* be—maybe eight or nine of them remaining in this muddy landfill. And miserable, fidgeting, grumpy or not, I can ride that out. It's time to quit making waves, and see if I can't just vanish completely into anonymity for the rest of the 'experience.'

* * *

MAJOR CHICKENSHIT HAD BEEN absent at the time of our 'triumphal return.' Just as well, I guess, since, even in a *simulated* prison camp, there are probably rules about clubbing the Senior Ranking Officer into a big yellow sniveling puddle of, well... *chickenshit*. And while I think I can safely say that he has not been missed, we *are* starting to wonder where they've taken him, how much longer he'll be gone, and whether the esteemed office of SRO will have to befall another unwilling candidate. And if so, *whom?*

Just as I'm resigning myself to copping a cold damp squat against a randomly selected wall, I hear a tired voice outside the 'door' addressing the guards. Then...

"Bikon, Herr Commandant."

Ah, the Prodigal Coward has returned.

A subdued conversation follows, which culminates shortly with the departure of the guards, and the big doughy major stepping down out of the light and into the shadows of our little underground leper colony.

He sighs, and tells us the restriction to quarters has been lifted. So if anyone needs to go to the bathroom, now would be the time to go.

We are up and prancing through the door before he's even through speaking.

I wonder what he promised them this time.

* * *

KAREN IS CLEARLY UPSET.

Karen is the 'token female' in our house, that 'Girl' in the doghouse. She'd be pretty enough with a little make-up and something other than fatigues, combat boots, and an oversized field jacket to flatter her slightly pudgy figure. But here, huddled in this frozen mud cave, that's all that's available. So instead, she kinda' looks like Dorothy Hamill, the Olympic ice skater, about a week after giving birth to a fifteen-pound baby... a little chubby and 'used-looking,' but vaguely cute despite it all.

She's a 'Life Support Specialist,' meaning she works on the oxygen masks that fighter pilots wear, which in turn means that she can be deployed to any forward operations bases to which her fighter squadron is assigned, which thereby means that she could be captured in the line of duty. And for that reason, according to recent changes in military regulations, she has to attend this school now as part of her normal career progression.

But a 'front line trooper' she is not.

Look who's talking.

And right now, she is pacing nervously, as if she can't decide whether to be outraged, terrified, or just submissively polite. She has the major's ear though, and because of her volume and agitation, she has *our* ears as well.

It seems that, on her way to the 'lady's room,' she'd found herself being tailed by some guards. Just a few steps beyond the 'door' of our 'house,' she'd been confronted by a trio of armed 'Russkies,' for whom she'd immediately performed the required ritual of obeisance... bowing at the waist, and reciting their ridiculous "Bikon" mumbo-jumbo. But, upon receiving their permission to continue on, as she'd turned to hurry off down the path, one of them had swatted her ass.

Out of reflex, she'd wheeled on the perpetrator, only to find two of the three men grunting and giggling lasciviously, making smooching sounds, and grabbing at their crotches, while the third was flashing her a fiery warning scowl, and dropping his shotgun into a ready posture.

Clearly they were just playing their roles as antagonists—bullies in a position of dominating power (i.e.; 'the enemy')—but to Karen, such acts of 'groping' and 'fondling' exceeded the bounds of even a simulated prison environment... just like they'd warned us would happen.

"Sons of bitches," the major growls through grinding teeth.

Oh yeh, now *he's a tough guy.*

On the other hand, I sorta' kinda' agree with him.

In the classroom phase preceding this exercise, the instructors had informed us that ours was one of the first POW School classes in the history of the Air Force to *include women.* And that, as such, there was bound to be a bit of a clumsy transition period until the school's structure and 'script' could be fully adapted to these new conditions.

However, bearing in mind that in a *real* POW situation, women would most definitely find themselves enduring a sexual component not heretofore considered relevant in this all-male venue, certain allowances were going to have to be made while they worked out how to *simulate* such psychologically influential tactics without getting the school closed down for breach of decorum. Because that component was going to be significant to both the women who would have to face it, *and* the men who were likely to become irrationally protective over it.

And looky here now!

As if in fulfillment of the prophecy, with the first smack of the first feminine derriere, Karen's almost on the verge of tears, the major's already ruminating over how to get these bastards hung from the nearest yardarm, and both PJs are circling the beleaguered lady, clenching their fists and glaring out the door with knives flying from their eyes.

Me too, I notice.

What a joke! Especially *from the likes of me.*

Part of me wants to walk up and assure her that *I'll go with you next time. That's right; I'll protect you!* As if my presence would have even the slightest deterrent effect on an armed prison guard. The rest of me is laughing at myself, and listening to the others with wonder.

My, what a powerful tool the enemy has acquired with these women.

4
ODD JOBS

MY FIRST WORK DETAIL has me joining about a dozen of my fellow inmates in the vitally important task of lifting wooden pallets off of one pile (near the front gate), carrying them, one at a time, to another pile (in the middle of the camp), then breaking them up into smaller wedges and slivers, to be disseminated as firewood among the various houses. It's dull, stupid, inefficient work, but for obvious reasons—at least in a prison camp—maximum efficiency and peak productivity (not to mention 'employee satisfaction') are not relevant factors. Keeping the prisoners preoccupied and breaking their spirit is what it's all about.

I don't care. It's gotten me 'out of the house,' it's given me something to do, and it's eating away the empty hours until we can get this shit over with.

It's also brought me back together with 'Rocky,' little Ricky Spradlin, my friend and fellow teammate from the McChord Combat Control Team. He and Teddy Heywood had driven over in one car, Greg and myself in another. But this is the first that any of the four of us has been able to link up since the start of the POW scenario.

He and I talk as we break boards with our boot heels, and wrench their splintered ends free of their nails with our gloves.

First and foremost on our minds, of course, are the interrogations from last night. *How was it for you? What did they do to you? Did they break ya?*

I start off telling him about the ones I handled *well*, like swooning my way through the one where they tried to get me to sign those papers. And the one that got me 'tortured.' I stretch out the collar of my T-shirt, and show him the big indelible "**S**" on my chest.

He has similar tales, including a familiar one in which they tried to convince him that there was a poor beleaguered female out shivering barefoot in the snow in her long johns, her life depending on him answering their questions.

"Yeh, they tried the same one on me too," I chuckle quietly.

Then I sigh and tell him about my bad one. The one that broke me. I tell him how they got me tired enough and pissed enough to stomp on my own uniform, and how the realization of what I was doing somehow made me fall apart. Right now, looking back on it, I'm having a hard time remembering what it was that had choked me up so bad. Then again, right now I'm not fried, cranky, sleep deprived, or dazedly incoherent either.

"Yeh, pretty much everybody in my house said they did the same thing," he answers, "And most of them didn't even know what they'd done until the debrief."

"Really? I thought I was the biggest stupidest loser in the class."

"Oh hell no," Rocky sighs. "You definitely weren't alone on that one."

"Really?" I'm trying to read his sudden change in humor. "Does that mean they got to you too?"

"Yeh, but in a little different way." He's speaking through a strange sort of 'introspective smirk' now, as he drives his boot through the wood of the pallet, and rips the splintered pieces free by hand. And he adds, "'Cause I called *Student Situation* on 'em."

That stops me dead in my tracks. "You did *what?*"

He pauses with a shiv of riven wood clenched in his fist, and grins.

"I called *Student Situation* on 'em."

"And what'd they do to you?"

"Well, the interrogator jumped up at yelled at me. *'What the hell do you think you're doing, Airman?! Why'd you say that?!'* And I jumped right back at him—grabbed the edge of his desk like I was gonna' flip it and everything—and I said, *'Cause I'm about to beat the livin' shit outa' you, sir! That's why!"*

My mouth drops open as if my best friend's mom just flashed me.

"Wha...? Are you insane?"

"Why? I wasn't lyin'. I was fuckin' pissed. I was about to come over that damned desk and separate his jaw for him. I was doin' him a favor, declaring *Student Situation* when I did."

Jesus! I'd always known that Li'l Rocky had a volatile temper, along with a 'short guy's' willingness to plunge into a fight at the drop of a hat. But *this... wow!*

"Damn, boy," I chuckle. "What'd they do then?"

Rocky's smile has become one big Evil Grin.

"It was kinda' funny, actually. The guy's face just drops, you know. Red-eyed fury one second, white as a sheet the next. Like this..." He does a comical little facial contortion that gets me laughing right along with him. "And he goes, *'Okay, okay. Let's just take a minute to calm down here, okay? Take a seat. Take a few deep breaths,'* you know? *'You want some water?'* Man, all of a sudden they couldn't do enough for me."

We both laugh out loud, until a passing guard stops in mid-patrol to glare at us. Back to breaking boards, tossing shards onto the growing pile, and *not* having a good time doing it. Once the guard moves on, though, I whisper to Rocky, "So did they finish the interrogation, or what?"

He looks up and grins again. "Yeh. But as soon as he said *Resume*, they threw my ass straight into a Torture Position. Said that in a real POW situation, if I'd gotten pissed enough to attack my interrogator, they'da sic'd half the army on my ass. And if they didn't kill me outright, I'd probably have spent a week gettin' the shit beat outa' me. So..."

"*Damn*, boy."

"Yeh. It was okay, though. By then I was fine. Just watchin' all the fire and guts drain outa' that guy just made my fuckin' day."

We both laugh, until that same guard returns, and yells at us to get back to work.

* * *

LUNCH WAS A SCRUMPTIOUS soup and bread affair, served on fine tin, while sitting on a stack of unbroken pallets next to the bonfire in the middle of the camp. No conversation, and no dessert, but otherwise not too unpleasant.

As I'm strolling back to 'House Three' though, I see my favorite major come busting up out of our little hole in the ground, and commence a fast blustery march toward the front gate. He's forced to skid to a halt in the gravel though, when a pair of guards crosses his path.

He does a fast, cantankerous, head-rolling rendition of the "Bikon, Herr Commandant" routine. But I swear I think those guards almost *ran* to get in his way, just to watch him throw up his hands, roll his eyes back in his head, and vent his exasperation with a loud gusty sigh that included the word "*gawd!*" Now they're keeping him standing there at attention, explaining where the hell he thinks he's going—*To see the Commandant about an important camp-related issue!*—and delaying him even further by arguing that the commandant has no intention of seeing *him.*

I walk a wide detour around them, and slip into my house, just as Karen escorts another teary-eyed female up out of the hole.

It's the girl who looks like Benjamin Franklin.

Karen flashes me an angry glare that fairly screams, "*Men! You're all alike!,*" and then they're past.

I recover, confused, and step down into the chilly gloom below.

A handful of the house's males, including both PJs, are huddled in the middle looking guardedly at me, as if I just interrupted a private bong party that was already starting to fall apart.

"What's up?," I ask, as I pound the cold off my hands.

Apparently they decide I'm not a threat, and go back to whatever it was they weren't doing beforehand. The largest and most bored-looking PJ sniffs and resumes scuffing at the dirt.

"The major's gone to ream the head instructor a new asshole."

The other PJ snorts at that one, which sets off a wave of contemptuous sniggering among the rest of the room's occupants.

"Oo, I bet the commandant's just a dumpin' in his jammies right about now," Cpt. Hammond comments.

"*Oh no! Not The Major!,*" Lt. Rayburn adds in a distressed falsetto.

The sniggering notches up to a short hushed burble of laughter.

"Really?," I reply. I am intrigued. "What set him off this time?"

"Karen's little friend there," the first PJ answers, thumbing toward the door. "Karen brought her in to see the SRO about a little run-in she'd had with a couple of the guards. Said they'd followed her all the way to the Shit Shack, but then wouldn't let her close the door when she went inside. So she had to 'hold it,' I guess. Something like that."

"Really."

They chose the Benjamin Franklin look-alike to follow to the john?

"Yep. Major says he's had enough. Says the camp cadre's gone too far this time, and he's gonna' set 'em right."

"Gonna' lay down the law," someone else chimes in.

"Shit."

More chuckling and head-shaking.

"Well," I interject, "I don't think he's gonna' get any further than he did any other time."

"Oh no!" the second PJ insists, his face taking on a comical mien of 'grim determination.' "He's gonna' by-God give that commandant a thing-or-two, even if'n it's the last by-God thing he does. He ain't-a lettin' no flunky sergeants, playin' "Bad Guy dress-up" and a-carryin' fake guns and play-actin' like guards, keep him from addressin' a fellow officer of the United States Air Force on a matter of important official business, *by-God!*"

"Yeh. Now *there's* a force to contend with!," says another voice from somewhere back in the darkness.

More cautious laughter ripples through the huddle.

"Well," I add, "when I was coming in here, there was a bunch of 'em had him cornered over by the doghouse, doing his Bikons and practicing his bows, just like every other time."

"No shit?"

The pack breaks up and heads toward the door—*going to go see for themselves, I suppose*—but they stop in their tracks when the major suddenly storms back into the house, still bald and pear-shaped, but somehow bigger and more menacing for all his outrage.

"The bastards will *not* let me anywhere *near* the Head Instructor, no matter *what* I say or do!"

His angry momentum carries him all the way back to the deepest corner of our little cave, where he dispels the sharpest edges of his fury with a good swift kick to the dirt wall.

"*Son-of-a-bitch!*"

Nobody moves or makes a sound while he paces among the shadows, clenching and unclenching his fists, and breathing heavily through his nose.

"We've gotta' do something about this," he finally mutters to himself.

The rest of us look at each other.

We?

* * *

THE AFTERNOON HAS DRUG on way too long.

At least I *think* it's the afternoon. I still don't have a watch, the overcast has been dense and constant, so the sun still hasn't made an appearance. But I know what the general dimming light and lowering temperatures mean. *It's getting nigh on sundown, and I am ready to blow this popsicle stand.*

This last 'job' they've given me, though—moving an entire pile of snow, one shovelful at a time, from one place to another, barely forty feet apart, when I just watched another guy move it the other direction less than an hour before—has dragged on far too long. Not just in terms of how much time and effort I've had to put into it, but rather how close we are to missing that six o'clock bus outa' here… which should be *any friggin' time now!*

There ought to be some kind of 'wrapping-up' ritual going on right about now, some kind of acknowledgment that 'we've paid our dues' and it's about time to start pulling up stakes. So to speak.

But… *nada.*

I'm still shoveling, another couple of guys nearby are still breaking up wooden pallets for firewood, and the guards are still prowling silently among us. *Come on!*

A little while ago, I overheard some of the conversation between two of the guys stripping the pallets. They'd somehow gotten the word that the class's official 'Escape Committee' had done it! They'd slipped out of the camp undetected by the guards, and successfully escaped. Rumor had it that they were now kicked back in the commandant's office, sipping hot chocolate, sharing their clever strategies, and waiting out the last hours of the class in comfort. *But who really knows? How* could *they know?*

I mean, I'd have liked to escape too, you know. But in the interest of maintaining *some* control over the simulated prison environment, it had been determined that they couldn't let every person in the class keep making break-out attempts. They'd never quit chasing down all the would-be jail-breakers, and the bi-weekly cost of repairs on all that snipped barbed wire would be astronomical, I imagine. Besides, it's not the intention of this class to teach escape techniques, but rather survival tactics within the confines of a prison.

So the rule, as stated in the classroom phase of the course, was that five volunteers (and surprisingly, not everyone *wanted* to try to escape) would be picked by lottery, and those five—and those five *only*—would be permitted, during this concentration camp phase, to attempt an escape.

Needless to say, I wasn't one of the 'Lucky Five.'

I never understood that logic anyway. I mean, what were the other forty-five people in the class (the other *un*designated 90% of the class) going to learn from it? How would it enhance, or change in any way, *our* POW experience?

It wouldn't. Hell, we couldn't even be certain that the rumors of the *attempt* were true, much less the likelihood of their success. It should have been either *every*body or *no*body, not just a randomly selected few.

But in the meantime, well… *it's sunset!* The escapees have all escaped, the women have all been sufficiently harassed, we've all mastered submissive bowing, and this pile of snow has been moved enough times to qualify for frequent flyer miles. *So what the hell are we waiting for?*

I don't know. But it's apparently gotten dark enough now to warrant turning on the floodlights that tower around the camp's periphery, adding harsh brightness and sudden high-contrast shadows to the stark little snow-and-mud tableau around me. *Lovely.*

What the hell's going on here?
Where the hell's the damned bus?!

* * *

DINNER? THEY'RE SERVING DINNER out here now?

A couple of zombie prisoners have just come shuffling around the fire, each with a heavy steaming bucket and a ladle, doling out sloppy splashes of hot broth to anyone who presents their mess kit to them. My own kit is sitting right over there, on top of the pile of splintered pallet boards. But I ignore it as the two soup dudes grumble past me.

I don't get it. The sky overhead, overcast with plump snow-sodden clouds, is now *dark*. As in *black*. Only the searing light of the perimeter floods, ricocheting off everything from the muddy-white ground cover to the frosted trees, reaches the bellies of the clouds with enough afterglow to illuminate the scene below. But the point is, *it's friggin' night out here, man! And a damned cold one at that! We're supposed to be home by now!*

By this time in the evening, I had expected to have already taken a nice hot shower, and been sidestepping through the serving line at the chow hall. In another half hour or so, I would have been in bed! So why the hell am I still standing out here in this shithole, steam boiling from my gaping mouth, watching two equally stunned airmen wade through the shivering crowd with buckets of *Swill du Armpit* for our dining pleasure?

I'm still staring at them, when a voice, soiled with a bad made-for-TV 'Slovassian' accent (or whatever it's supposed to be) barks at me from behind, making me jump.

"If you're not going to eat, animal, then get back to work!"

Out of sheer subservient habit, I snap my knees back into lock, bow ninety degrees at the waist, and shout, "Bikon, Herr Commandant."

I've barely picked my shovel back up though, when another guard barges through the milling crowd shouting.

"You! You and you! And you! Come here!"

I turn to see his pointing finger flitting from face to face, then suddenly land on mine.

"You too! Over here! Let's go!"

I spear my shovel into the snow mountain I've just spent the last hour moving, and plod wearily over to join the other 'selectees.' And it doesn't take me long to recognize the criteria by which we've been chosen… since none of us is carrying a mess kit steaming with hot soup.

In fact, once I look around at everyone else in the crowd, I see that we're the *only* ones not burdened with dinner.

In other words, my slow reflexes just screwed me *out of* food, and *into* another friggin' work detail.

Nice work there, Stevie.

"Follow!," the guard bellows in cartoon-Russian, and he turns to lead us toward the front gate, his shotgun resting lazily atop his collarbone. *These guys are getting lazy, and sloppy.* We follow, like grumpy pouting sheep.

Up ahead, clustered around the guard shack at the gate, is what looks like a posse forming up. About a half-dozen rumpled looking dudes with shotguns crooked against their hips, barrels pointing skyward. Surrounding them is a broader cordon of camp guards—only four or five, weapons dangling toward the ground—looking sharp in their dark blue cold weather gear, polished boots, and black berets.

It's only once I start to consciously compare their appearances though, that I realize the *inner* tier—the rumpled looking 'posse'—is actually comprised of *prisoners*.

They've given guns to some of my fellow inmates?
For what? Do I get one too?

Our escort stops and steps aside, ushering us past him with a wave of his shotgun, and addresses a clearly senior guard who's just stepped out of the commandant's trailer.

"Your work detail, Herr Kapitan!"

Man, I wish they'd just pick a language and stick with it.

The 'kapitan' nods grimly. And silently. Then he turns a puzzled gaze on the rest of us.

For a moment, nothing happens. Nobody moves, no one fidgets, no one clears their throat, no one seems to know what the hell is going on at all. Not even the damned 'kapitan.'

Then from just behind me, our 'escort guard' suddenly barks.

"*Bow, animals!*"

Oh shit. Forgot our 'Bikons.'

In startled semi-unison then, we all fold forward as a group, rippling like tall grass before a gust of wind. The tightly packed guys in the middle bump and jostle each other in the process, faces brushing asses, shotguns clanking against each other, multiple disasters just itching to happen.

"Bikon, Herr Commandant," we mutter lifelessly, until everybody's said it and straightened back up again.

Damn, that was stupid. Unnecessary, uninspired, meaningless, and damn near *deadly*. But the 'kapitan' doesn't seem to have noticed—or at least to have *cared*—that six shotguns were just leveled and colliding in the middle of a tight clot of unsuspecting dumbasses.

"There is a stack of wooden pallets out there," he says, shrugging in the general direction of the exit road, where it rolls like a white carpet out into the darkened forest. The only thing that I can *see* out there though, is a suspicious mound of snow heaped at the edge of the road. Presumably that's where his pallets are buried.

"You will gather up those pallets, and bring them in here, stacking them up over there by the fire to be burned. However, they will almost certainly not be enough to keep the fire going *all night*, so..."

Whoa, whoa, whoa, whoa... WHOA! All night? Wait a minute! What the hell are we talking about 'all night' for? We've got graduation ceremonies in what, ten?... eleven?... twelve hours from now? We're supposed to be back in our rooms *RIGHT NOW,* getting showered and packed and drunk and sleeping, and not necessarily in that order! This is a designated twelve-day course—two five-day work weeks, and one weekend in between—and this is *Day Eleven!*

One way or the other, we're outa' here tonight, Binky!

"So," he continues, "once you've brought all the pallets in, you will have to go back out there to gather deadfall from the woods, to supplement the handful of pallets—fallen branches and logs and so on—to keep the fire burning all night. Do you understand?"

No! Of course not!

We all nod anyway—someone even groans a quiet "*Yessir*"—and a cloud of dour resignation settles over us like mustard gas.

Shit! This is getting out of control!

"These men here will be going out with you," he adds, prowling around the shivering 'posse,' and nodding to each of them as he passes. "And you will obey their every command as if theirs was the voice of the Commandant himself. Is that also clear?"

Again, the muttered and begrudging assent.

Wait a minute here. Prisoners guarding prisoners? With loaded weapons? Outside the fences? At night? In the forest?

What the hell am I missing here?

"Carry on then, Sergeant." And the 'Kapitan' wheels around and marches back to the doublewide, alone, his hands still clasped behind his back.

"Yessir!," answers our escort. "Alright then! Animals on detail! Let's go! Open the gates!"

Two of the 'real' guards unlatch the gate, and walk them open, while the covey of 'trustee guards' scatters in confusion to let us pass between them.

Damn. Does anybody here have a clue about what's going on?

I mean, is any of this still following the school's actual syllabus anymore? Or are we just making this all up as we go along now?

And if we're making all this up, then... why?

STORY XLII

INSURRECTION

1
THE ASYLUM'S POSTER CHILD

February, 1978
Air Force POW School, Fairchild Air Force Base, Spokane, Washington

IT STARTS TO SNOW again as I'm chuffing back through the gate for the second time, a heavy wet pallet under each arm like a pair of soggy wooden wings. A sullen prisoner/guard sulks at me as I pass, shotgun cradled in his arms as if for warmth.

Man, I just don't get this. The finish line is well behind us now, yet time is still passing, and I'm still out here in the friggin' woods.

Did I somehow misunderstand how many days this Survival School / POW School combo was supposed to last? Did I miscount how many have *already* passed? *What the hell's going on here?!*

As I near the bonfire in the center of the compound, sidling my way through the throng of the living dead, it slowly dawns on me that it's starting to get crowded around here. I'm just a little too beaten down to pay it much more than a cursory notice, but somewhere back behind my frontal lobe—sort of 'subliminally'—I'm sensing the change.

I pitch my 'wings,' one at a time, up onto the mounting stack, and turn to tromp back to the gate again. But before I've gone even a few steps, a hand grabs my arm and pulls me aside.

It's Ricky Spradlin again. And he seems kinda' keyed up.

"Stay here," he says under his breath.

"Wha...?" I reply, as if slapped out of a drug-induced stupor. "But I'm on a... a thing... I can't..."

"Don't go back out there. Major's orders." And he tosses his head over his shoulder in the direction from which we just came.

I turn to look, and spot Major Chickenshit himself standing there on the far side of the bonfire, his arms crossed over his chest, his legs braced shoulder-width apart, his back to me, and staring defiantly toward the commandant's doublewide. A circle of junior officers has also assumed similar poses all around him, and every few seconds, I see one or another of them reach out to a passing airman and relay some kind of instructions. That's when I pull back my focus, and take in the larger scene.

No one is working. *No one* is in their 'house' either. No one is doing *anything* except bunching around the fire, and consorting with each other in conspiratorial whispers.

What's all this now? We got us a little insurrection here, have we?

"What's going on here, Rocky?"

"Major says we're not doing any more work until they let him see the Commandant. Says they've been jerking him off all day long, and he's had enough." An excited giggle slips out between Rocky's last words, a clear sign that he's enjoying this just a little bit too much. "I bet they didn't see this coming when they woke up this morning."

"No shit," I whisper back.

"Pretty cool, huh?"

I hadn't noticed it at first, because of the firelight bathing him from behind, but there's a searchlight anchored on the major, spearing down from one of the guard towers like a fat white laser beam.

I'm watching the snow flit through the beam, when an amplified 'Sortarussian' voice squawks from a bullhorn.

"Prisoners in the yard! You are ordered to disperse! Return to your work details immediately!"

Two more searchlights, and then a third, swing toward the major from their respective corners, setting him ablaze in a crossfire of searing white light.

Boy, now would be a good time to make a break for the shadows along the fenceline, wouldn't it? I bet there isn't a single guard looking anywhere but right here right now.

The major, looking like a big knock-kneed pear (albeit a disobedient one), turns his face up to the source of the amplified voice, and shouts into the snuffling wind.

"Nobody's moving until I speak with the Commandant!"

Wow! We've got the sweeping spotlights, the blowing snow, the squawling megaphone, the battle of wills between commanders. All we need is the thundering clatter and downwash of a low-hovering helicopter, and we've got us a full-blown prison riot movie.

The megaphone squawks down from on high again.

"*Prisoners in the yard! By order of the Camp Commandant, you are ordered to disperse immediately and return to your houses! Move now, or you will be severely punished! There will be no other warnings!*"

Oh, it's back to our 'houses' now... forget the work details, I guess.

A phalanx of heavily armed guards comes storming through the gate, spreading out rapidly to surround us. The major—our official 'Senior Ranking Officer' now—wheels on us, shouting angrily.

"Nobody moves! *Nobody!* And that's an order!"

A couple of his junior officers push in close to the fire, beckoning us in tighter.

"Close it up, guys! Keep it tight! Let's get the women on the inside, men on the outside, facing out! Come on, let's go!"

Everybody scurries to comply. I take a spot along the outer rim of the circle opposite the major, excited to be doing something interesting for once, and emboldened by my new role as a frontline *Protector of the Womenfolk.*

What the hell is that anyway? 'Women on the inside, men on the outside?' Like, what... the armed guards won't be able to reach the women as long as they're behind a thin cordon of shivering *un*armed males? Like any of us would even *try* to stop them if they dared?

Still, it feels good when that protective instinct rears up its ancient, blind, *stupid* head, and asserts itself anyway.

Again though, *why are we doing it?*

I twist to look back at the major and his little cadre of sycophants.

"We're done playing this game of yours!," he's yelling. "I want to speak to whoever's in charge here, *now!* And I..."

"*You are in no position to make any demands!,*" the megaphone interrupts, still remaining unflappably in character and in dialect. "*You will disperse this group immediately, or we will turn the hose on you! It's that simple! Move now, or get wet!*"

Ah. So *that's* what we're protecting our soft, chewy, feminine core from… blasting water, on a snowy-cold night.

Sure enough, beyond the major and his centerstage spotlight, I can now make out a hose crew shouldering their way through the skirmish line of guards. And that ain't no garden hose either. That's a friggin' professional-grade industrial-strength *fire* hose they got there.

The major's temper explodes. He takes two huge strides forward, and jabs his finger at the lowly peasant holding the head of the hose.

"Don't you even *think* about it, Airman!"

'Airman?' He's calling a Russian prison guard 'Airman?' Oo! I'd say the major's well past the point of calling a Student Situation now.

And speaking of *Student Situations*… why *doesn't* he just walk up to a guard and declare it? If this is really about him trying to straighten out some unseemly behavior on the part of the school's 'scenario staff,' and *not* just some grandstand attempt at making himself look tougher than he's already proven himself to not be, then wouldn't it be simpler, more direct, and *far* more productive to just call *Student Situation* on them? He'd sure as hell get all the attention he ever wanted, and then some. Right? But…

"I am a superior-grade officer in the United States Air Force, goddammit! And you will *not* turn that hose on *me*, or anyone else in…!"

"*You are a prisoner of war!,*" the megaphone squawks right back, "*and an enemy of the people of this nation! And we are done talking! Hose Team, extinguish that fire!*"

Even from the far side of the circle, I can see the hose plump and stiffen as the valve is cracked, ramming water toward its nozzle. And I can see the 'nozzle man' bracing himself for the thrust.

The major clearly cannot believe this complete disregard for his rank and station. "*Son of a bitch! Are you people deaf?!! I said…!*"

Water, a solid shaft of it, explodes from the hose head like a cannon shot, bowling over the two guys in front (although not the major, of course), and sending up a deflected fan of spray into the convergence of spotlights.

It looks like fireworks bursting beyond a line of silhouetted spectators.

A roar of indignation from the major is instantly smothered by the shrieks of the women and the wailing of the men in closest proximity to the splash zone. But the human sea parts in a mad scramble, giving the stream a clear shot at our bonfire. And it slams into it like a bowling ball plowing through a flaming set of ten pins. It does as much damage from the *impact* as it does from the extinguishing qualities of the water, blowing the base out from beneath the pile at the same time that it douses the flames and rakes the back of my legs with liquid buckshot. Steam boils out of the tumbling conflagration and swallows me whole. *Wow!*

I can hear Rocky laughing like the asylum's poster child off in the mists to my right. But I've got to admit, this was worth hanging around for.

As quickly as the bedlam began though, it abruptly ends. Garbled shouts and commands from the far side of our late great fire seem to suck the noise right out of the air. The shocked screaming just stops, as does the thunder of the high-pressure hose, leaving behind only the hiss and crackle of the drowned bonfire, and a burble of stunned laughter percolating through the fog from both sides. I hear the word, "*Damn!*"—pronounced, "*DAY-yomm!*" in this case—whispered and muttered and spat all around me.

The searchlight beams split apart, sweeping over the disintegrating throng, as the bullhorn bleats again in *faux*-Serbian.

"*Now, disperse this crowd immediately, or we will turn the hose on you again! Disperse and return to your houses! All of you! All work details are canceled, as is all above-ground movement! By order of the Commandant, this camp is now in lockdown and restricted to quarters!*

"*Disperse immediately, and return to your quarters...!*"

The message goes on, repeating itself and keeping up a constant background din of cranked-up badgering, more for atmosphere and ambience than anything else, I suspect. After all, we're all in the same place here, all caught up in the same little drama at the same time. So I'm pretty sure that everyone got the message the first time they screamed it at us. But the circle of guards charges into the group anyway, shoving people into motion, and herding them away from the smoldering ruin of the fire.

In the distance, with a single spotlight tracking them the whole way, I can see the major, in the middle of a fast-marching scrum of guards, being hustled off toward the doublewide's gate. They've got him gripped under the armpits and hoisted half off his feet by the fistful of his jacket collar that one of them is clutching. My guess is that he's finally going to get to see the damned commandant.

I hope he can still remember what it was that was so important for them to talk about, because not only is he about to spend some quality time in a Torture Position or two, I'm sure, but the rest of us—after acting under his 'orders' to strike—are now being marched back to our frozen underground hovels to contemplate our own misdeeds. And there are many among us quivering in their wet uniforms.

I apparently caught a few stray splatters myself. My field jacket is freckled with water spots, and I'm using my sleeve to mop off the moisture from the side of my neck and ear. And that small amount of 'collateral damage' is chilling me out pretty quickly. I can't imagine how cold those guys must be that are completely drenched.

But in the meantime, we are *hours* past the time when this should have ended. And now it's looking like we've got several *more* hours to go to pay for our sins. Hell, for all I know, we might just be spending the whole friggin' night out here again.

Jesus! There's not even any furniture in our 'house!' What are we supposed to sleep on?

Images of me curled up on the cold dirt floor, at the foot of that dead stove, go shuddering through my mind like ice chips down my collar.

I've tried this sort of thing before, you know—on overnight 'field deployments,' and so-called 'hasty bivouacs'—and I know just how it'll go. I won't be able to sleep a wink. And every second that I lie there will shrug past in miserable slow motion. I'll check my watch a hundred times an hour, and swear that it must have stopped... only tonight, I don't even *have* a watch.

Goddammit!

From out of the colorless shadows, the 'door'—the *mouth*—of our 'house' yawns open at my feet, like the gawping underbite of a huge ugly grouper sucking in food. And at the 'coaxing' of the guards, I follow my roomies down into the frigid darkness again.

Son of a bitch! I'm supposed to be home right now!

2
SALVATION

IT FEELS LIKE ABOUT forty-five minutes have passed. Maybe even an hour. But who knows. Still no watch.

For all I can tell, it could very well have been only ten minutes. And I've spent that time, much like everyone else, just pacing and circling and breathing steam trails into the lonely wedge of light spearing down through the door hole.

The two PJs, always thinking and working together, had managed to smuggle in a few shards of the busted-up pallet wood to stoke the 'fire,' such as it was. But even the last of the brightest embers, throbbing in the belly of the stove when we'd first arrived here, had died by the time we got back. And needless to say, nobody thought to smuggle any *matches*. So the 'house' has stayed frosty and dark.

Now, shouted voices cut through the snow-deadened silence outside, and we all begin to migrate toward the door. *What now?*

The first words of conjecture have barely been exchanged between us, when a shadow leaps into the shaft of light. A loud body bustles down the top couple of steps, and barks at us—again in pathetic cartoon-Russian—to get out of the house *now!*

"Form up at the flagpole! Let's go! *Now*, animals!"

We follow his retreating shadow up and out into the falling snow.

All around the yard, prisoners are streaming from their holes like gophers flushed from their warrens by a flood. Two channels of human traffic fill the aisles between the stone hummocks of our 'houses,' coerced and bullied toward the open ground at the front of the camp by the guards. We pass the doghouse, and I eye it longingly, dreaming of how warm I and a couple of other prisoners—preferably female, of course—could make it right now. Then we're at the base of the flagpole.

Our captor's half-assed flag—with its lone red star in the middle of a field of black, part of a matching set with their letterhead and evil 'Dark Side' berets—flutters high in the bubble of light fed by the perimeter floodlights. Almost *out* of the light, actually, as if scraping the apex of a thoroughly stirred-up snow globe. So tall, it's basically *overshot* the nexus of all those criss-crossing beams.

We're herded into a square formation in front of an impromptu 'stage,' of sorts. It looks like a basic flatbed trailer that was wheeled in by hand while we were huddled in our little frozen quarry holes. We turn our backs to the flagpole, and face the stage. They call us to attention, and we stand there, rigid, frigid, and shivering in the ice-flecked breeze. A line of camp officials strolls up onto the platform while we wait, then pivots to face us. I recognize 'Capt. Lickspittle' near the center. And there's old 'Maj. Meatneck,' my *first* interrogator. I resist the urge to wave.

Oh great. They brought the 'first shift' back in.
Must be a long night ahead of us.

* * *

A VERY SENIOR GENTLEMAN, with a silver crew cut capped by his ebony beret, and hard lines carved into his face, steps forward to the front of the stage, and passes a disgusted eye over the lot of us. I've never seen this guy before, but I'm guessing that he's the much ballyhooed Camp Commandant about whom I've *heard*—and *for* whom I've *paid*—so much. And he sure is taking his sweet old time getting this little ceremony underway.

Come on, dammit! It's friggin' cold out here!

"To this day," he suddenly (and *finally*) shouts in a husky baritone, and with an accent authentic enough to suggest that he might just be a real Soviet citizen-soldier, "it amazes me that anyone would actually *seek* to live in America! In a so-called '*democratic*' society in general! And worse, in a *capitalistic smelter* like the United States! Amazing! Truly astonishing!"

'Capitalistic smelter?' Seriously? Are those the kinds of phrases they're *teaching Russian kids in their English classes nowadays? Not just the usual mangled paraphrases for things like "My pen is red," or "Which way is the nearest toilet?" Really?*

"Even moreso that they might take some perverse *pleasure* in doing so! But most astonishing—and *disgusting*—of all, is that they would actually *take up arms* for that 'democracy!' And even worse yet, against *my homeland!*"

He sighs, and shakes his head with great (though amateurish) drama. "The corruption must run so deep."

Oh great. It's time for another "Yay Communism! Boo Capitalism!" speech, apparently.

They dragged us out of our iceboxes, and into the blizzard for this?

We apparently weren't cold or miserable enough for them yet. Now we've got to stand out here, in the falling snow, and at *attention*, no less, to listen to this same canned lecture all over again? The same one 'Colonel Jakinov' already laid on me during my sixth interrogation? The 'no-brainer' one that I got through just by feigning delirium? *What the hell?* Plus some of us are still soaking wet!

Hey, if I've heard this one before, can I go home?

But this guy actually sounds like he means it! He seems legitimately puzzled by our allegiance.

"To serve a nation founded on pure greed and selfishness, to go to *war* on its behalf, and against the people of the only true system of equality on the planet! The only place where every man, woman, and child shares equally in the riches of the community as a whole! Not just the wealthy elite, or the privileged few, but *everyone!*"

Oh, gawd! If I run straight at that guard over there, I wonder if I can impale myself on his bayonet before anyone can stop me.

But the Commandant continues on, oblivious to our misery, unaware of the snowfall that's steadily thickening between us, and eerily passionate about his message.

Communism works, he says. That's why it's spreading across the globe in mighty strides. Democracy, on the other hand, is doomed to fail. That's why it clings to life in but a handful of besieged pockets around the world. The illusion of a government '*of* the people, *by* the people, and *for* the people' is just that... *an illusion*. No man, in a position of such power as our 'duly elected' president would ever care a lick about the opinions, needs, or desires of the masses below him. But all he'd need to do to maintain his place at the pinnacle—particularly over a society so rotten with the emptiness and lies of a Hollywood-based morality—is *act* like he's one of them. The cameras and the editors and the directors would take care of the rest.

But Communism... *whoa...!*

The chill has reached my core. I'm starting to shiver, *hard*. I can't imagine how cold the *really* drenched people must be. But I am a believer now... a believer that this is never going to end.

The shoulders of the people in front of me are dusted with snow, with more drifting down through the lights as I watch. Pennants of backlit steam skirl away from the dozens of noses and mouths arrayed before me, making the stiffly braced ranks of prisoners look like a field of rockets boiling liquid oxygen into the cold night air before a mass launch.

I didn't notice it before now, but beyond the blathering commandant, I can see that they've gotten our bonfire going again. *I wonder why.* Maybe once this 'enlightening' harangue is done, they'll allow us to take some of that burning wood with us back to our house stoves.

"Imagine doctors," the Commandant continues, "practicing medicine *not* for the sole purpose of becoming independently wealthy, but for the good of their communities! Businessmen creating companies and goods *not* for the tax breaks, but to fulfill the needs of their friends and neighbors! This is what communism offers to those who truly embrace it... citizenry of the purest motivation!"

This is the purest load of corn-studded diarrhea I've ever heard in my entire life, actually. But I'll give you my spleen if you'll just shut up and let me stand next to that fire for two minutes.

Silence suddenly drops over our little parade ground, as Herr Commandant pauses to look us all over again. The snow continues unabated. The light wind sniffles around us, stirring tiny ice flecks into flight like sparks, looking for open seams and wet skin. But his lone shouting voice is gone... for the moment.

Then, "You have much to think about, and plenty of time in which to do it! Take that time to look at yourselves, and consider how better to spend your lives!" Then he wheels to his right, and strides off the stage.

That's it? That's what they made me come back out in the snow for?

Lickspittle steps forward as the commandant passes, and throws his own weasely little voice into the wind.

"Sergeant! Return the prisoners to their houses!"

Shit! That is *it! They're sending us back to our ice caves now! I can't believe this!*

Off to my left, another muddled pseudo-Slavic voice barks, "Prisoners in the yard! About... *face!*"

Damn!

Toe to heel, fifty-or-so rumpled figures pirouette to face the rear, and wobble to a stop. Even at attention now, we look cowed and defeated.

But no follow-up command is issued. No "*Dismissed!*" No "*Fall out!*," or "*Forward march!*" Not even a "*Get the hell out of here!*" Just silence.

Eyes start to dart around. Mine included. *Are we dismissed, or not?*

Then somebody gasps. And I hear someone else's awed whisper.

"*Son of a bitch.*"

* * *

IN FRONT OF ME, a couple of heads tilt back. Then several more. Then a wave of lifting chins rolls back toward me, until my own gaze is pulled upward, just to see what everyone else is looking at.

And suddenly, *there it is!*

My breath hitches in my chest, and my shocked little lurch makes me backstep to catch myself.

At the top of the flagpole, the enemy's black flag, with its single red star, is gone. In its place, lolling in the anorexic breeze, is our very own *Stars and Stripes. Old Glory.*

Somewhere during the commandant's torturously long-winded speech, they managed to lower the one and raise the other, right behind our backs, without us knowing.

And now... *there it is.*

I don't think I've ever seen anything so beautiful in all my life. *Ever.*

A clear, unflavored, all-American voice abruptly shouts, "*Group! Atten... HUT!*" (that means '*Attention*')

I don't know whether it's the voice of a brazen student-prisoner, or one of our instructor-guards at last relieved of his stupid 'Russian' accent, but the response is a thunderclap of martial ardor. Boot heels whack together as one. Spines stiffen, shoulders are thrown *back*, chests are thrown *out*.

"*Present... HAWMS!*" (that means, '*present arms*,' or '*salute now*')

And as a single multi-armed organism, half-a-hundred electrified salutes are launched in perfect synchronization. The air *swishes* with the passage of fifty twanging arms. And time stops. I swear it does.

The world goes completely silent. *Soundless*, actually.

For a long lingering moment, even the snow seems to retreat, as if buffeted aside by some force field radiating from those proud colors.

I swear to God, that thing is singing to me! Right now! I can hear it!

And I can *feel* it, tickling at my heart with the fluttering feathers of a bird desperate to escape its cage. A plump bundle of emotion suddenly bloats inside my chest and swells to bursting. The shuddering pressure quickly overwhelms my defenses, and vents out through my tear ducts like the juice of a ruptured orange.

The spill of tears catches me completely by surprise. I didn't see it coming, and I'm helpless to contain it. Truth be told though, right now *that's just fine with me*. For one thing, I'm not the only one. The perfect silence is slowly giving way to all the hiccups, gulps, and sniffles of a bunch of weepy and exhausted brothers-in-arms, and no one is exempt. And for another, *it just feels so good to let it go*.

There is a tangible current of something—call it pride, comfort, familiarity, 'love,' maybe just *home*—streaming from that flag and coursing through me right now in a ghostly torrent, and I just want to scream for the sheer joy of it.

This is much more than mere relief over the damned POW scenario finally coming to an end. This is something entirely different, something much bigger, something... I don't know... something *soaring*. I mean, it really feels like I'm being lifted off my feet by something huge and light and airy inflating inside my chest. It's not just that I can't *help* crying... it's that I *want* to cry!

I want to bawl!

I hold my ramrod salute without a twitch though, just like everyone else, for what feels like an eternity. A proud, grateful, *thankful* eternity.

That magnificent standard up there is waving down to me, so much more than just a whistle blowing at quitting time, more than just permission to release our long-held breaths. It is *salvation incarnate!* And not just from this tiresome scenario either. That is the salvation of *humankind* up there! I can see that now. I might have intellectually acknowledged the existence of some vague, undefined, 'higher meaning' to it before—all the while wincing at the melodrama of such a smarmy statement—but now it's living and breathing right there before me, as true as life itself and as obvious as a newborn child that was only a hope a moment before.

I've just spent the last fifteen minutes listening to an all too plausible argument on behalf of communism—*communism, people!*—well practiced and refined with repetition. And based on *nothing.* All the grand concepts and noble wishing of a 'well-intentioned' dream (if I'm giving its creators the benefit of the doubt), one that was starting to sound so good, so hopeful, and so believable in that moment of weariness, hopelessness, and confusion. But it was all just so much shit! All such a labor of strained logic, selective reasoning, and broad sweeping gray strokes, just to make it marginally palatable to the desperate ear. Especially against this siren Truth now, waving so confidently from the top of its pole.

You're home again, it's saying. *At last. Be at peace.*

And I am.

Until a lone voice shatters the silence.

"*Ordah! HAHMS!*" (which means '*order arms,*' or '*stop saluting now*')

This time the response is less enthusiastic, a lot of people clearly not yet ready to relinquish their salutes. But once the entire class is back at attention, still and quiet save for the scattered sounds of sniffing and throat clearing, that same voice calls out, "*Group! About... HACE!*" ('*about face*')

As a far more cohesive unit now, we pivot back around to face the stage again.

*　　*　　*

THE CADRE IS STILL there, still at attention themselves. And the 'commandant' is back among them. But their black berets are gone, replaced by regular old standard-issue green fatigue caps. And oddly enough, it doesn't look right... as if now they're faking being *Americans.*

A strange 'reverent' moment passes then, with both sides at attention, facing each other, immobile and waiting for something... until the so-called 'commandant' nods.

Off to the side, the voice again barks, "*Group! Parade... HEST!*"

All hands snap together behind their backs, and every left foot steps aside to assume a broader stance. After another pause for 'dramatic effect,' I'm guessing, the 'commandant' finally speaks.

"At ease! At ease!" And our postures relax.

"Gentlemen! And ladies! As I'm sure you've already deduced on your own, this concludes the POW portion of this Survival School class!"

There is a tentative 'rustle' in the formation, as if a 'spontaneous cheer' is *about* to erupt. But it dies quickly, stillborn. Everyone here is *done*, and just wants to go home. Ebullience is not really an option anymore.

"You'll receive a *formal* debrief and an evaluation tomorrow morning, as part of the graduation ceremony! But we felt it important to give you this *in*formal one right now, right here, while this experience is still fresh and real in your minds!"

Oo, damn. How 'bout we do this aboard one of those heated buses we know you've got idling back there in the woods? 'Cause it ain't gettin' no warmer out here, ya' know.

"We kept you out here, three-and-a-half hours past the normal completion time, not because you did anything 'wrong,' *per se*, but because you weren't doing anything *at all!*"

What?! You're blaming the extra time we've all had to spend out here on US?!

"Your primary objective out here in this camp was to *resist!* To impress upon your enemies that yours was a will that could not be broken!"—*No, it wasn't!*—"But with the exception of this last little rebellion around the bonfire, you did basically nothing!"

What do you mean, 'nothing'? I went into that doghouse—twice!—for something, buddy!

"We gave you all kinds of opportunities to show some kind of initiative, some effort towards resistance! We created visual blind-spots for you by clumping the guards, and leaving some areas unmonitored! We sometimes had them walk among you *alone!* And in some cases, even *unarmed!*"

Well, what the hell were we supposed to do with that? Beat them up? Hold a couple of them hostage until the camp leadership bowed to our demands? And what would those demands have been anyway? Come on!

"We even sent some of you *outside the wire!* Guarded by your own fellow prisoners! We even gave some of you *weapons!* And still, *nothing!*"

What's that supposed to mean? We weren't allowed *to escape! Remember? Just five people on the 'Escape Committee,' that's all! Your rules, not ours! Now I'm getting confused.*

We endured all this extra grief because we followed the rules? You can't say we didn't do anything. We resisted when the opportunities presented themselves. We adapted (for the most part) to the conditions granted to us. And perhaps most importantly, we *avoided torture!* The *real* 'prime directive,' I thought. We gave them nothing, divulged no information (presumably). Nobody 'cracked' (except maybe the major, with his little doghouse surrender, and his fixation on avenging the women). But still, aside from that generally uncooperative stance, what we mostly did was *not incite them to the next more brutal (and thereby more 'convincing') level of coercion.*

In other words, we gave them just what we were *supposed* to give them... *nothing!* Not even a reason to treat us worse.

I guess I can see how that would piss them off a little, actually. The instructor cadre, that is. I imagine they probably wanted to see some more flagrant reactions, like the latest 'Major Chickenshit Show'—people driven to self-destructive behavior—just so that they (the instructors) could get to play a more 'malevolent' (*i.e.; more "fun"*) role themselves.

Still we can't be the first ones who ever bored them to death. They had to have seen this before. *So why are we still standing out here in the darkness and the snow and the cold?*

Well, suddenly, *we're not.*

"That's it!," he says rather abruptly, shrugging, and looking up into the snow as if he's only just now realized what all that funny white stuff is that's been sheeting down between us. A half-assed smile crinkles the deep creases of his face as he adds, "Congratulations. Now go get some sleep."

He turns, and begins a tired and very unmilitary trudge off through the deepening snow.

Again, the instant he passes Lickspittle, the runt jumps like a startled chihuahua, and yaps at the rest of us, "*Group! Atten... SHUN!*"

The response is unhurried, laced with relieved sighs, and muted by the snow pack... sufficient, though, for the moment.

Then, "Dismissed...!"

"The main road is right around that corner there, and the buses are waiting there for you! They'll drop you off at the chow hall, which has agreed to stay open for the next half hour, just for you! So if you want to eat, don't waste time by going to your barracks first!"

It never crossed my mind.

We're already streaming past him, most of us breaking into a snow-stumbled trot as the crowd disperses.

Free! I'm free at last!

* * *

I WAS ONLY A prisoner of war for what? Twenty-eight hours or so?

Gawd. I try to imagine living like that for *years*, with no end in sight, certain that no one knows where you are, and that there's no way they could rescue you even if they did... and my mind just laughs at the attempt.

Compared to reality, this experience was *nothing*.

Still, I did it. I pulled it off. I got through another grueling ordeal in the endless upward struggle of this career choice.

I graduated... again. I *survived*... again. And the progression continues.

I just don't know *why* anymore.

For all the pride and satisfaction I can take from this little tribulation, I've never wanted to bail out of this mess more than I do right now.

I mean it. *This is it!* I can't keep hating every moment I'm in, and dreading every one yet to come like this. Without an overarching incentive that's more powerful than all the *dis*incentives, *what's the point?* In any other venue in life, this kind of persistent, unmotivated, and misdirected self-abuse would just be called *stupid*. So what's the difference *here?*

I'm just not interested enough in it—at least not anymore—and the fact is I've *never* taken it seriously enough to justify the effort and sacrifice. It's my own fault, I know, my own weakness of character, but that doesn't change the imperativeness of my backing out of this even one iota.

This whole experience has been enlightening, educational, even *thrilling*, and all that. But I think I've gotten the gist of it by now, and the attendant miseries are just not worth continuing.

Not for *me*, anyway. Not anymore.

So... *(*whew!*)*... I guess that settles that then, doesn't it.

The American flag snaps and pops overhead, as I clomp past its pole. And I look up at it through the swarming snow as I pass.

Yep.

Free at last.

BOOK TWO

EPILOGUE

1

MUSTERING THE WILL... OR NOT

February, 1978
Back with the McChord Combat Control Team
McChord AFB, Tacoma, Washington

I SCRIBBLE MY INITIALS in each of the five check-boxes that Sergeant Mabry indicated, and hand my training records back to him. That makes a total of *eight* items that I've now got checked off...

... eight out of something like seventy-five or eighty. *Dammit.*

(**sigh**)

They say it takes about a year to finish everything listed in your training records. That's the norm, anyway. Combat Control has just got *so* many areas of 'expertise' at which one must exhibit some proficiency, with specializations in all manner of weapons, explosives, communications gear, and of course, parachutes... with aptitudes that need to be refined in all sorts of skill sets, from the martial arts to rappelling, calculating and laying out drop zones, landing zones, and extraction zones, to marksmanship, and of course, air traffic control. All this plus a host of mandatory (and *minimum*) schools, unit-specific training, and broader-perspective exercises. All must be attended, completed, and polished to a high gloss, then tested, graded, and ultimately *signed off* by the team's own evaluators...

which, at McChord, means Sgt. Cole Mabry alone. This is how the year is spent between graduation from Combat Control School and the final anointing of one's Phase III status, the brevetting of that all-important Combat Control *flash* on your beret... the "*First In, Last Out*" signet that lets everyone know *you've made it.*

Phase III, and meant to be, U.S. Air Force CCT.

So yes, my twelve months of team training (also known as '*practice, practice, practice*'), along with minor and major exercises in locations all over the fifty states and even around the world, plus, of course, *schools, schools, and more schools*, began immediately upon my completion of CCS, just before Christmas of last year. And now, two of those twelve months later, I'm just now signing off the fourth through eighth items on my checklist.

And that's just sad.

Just ten more months and seventy-something more items to go!

(**sigh**)

Granted, two of those eight items were for finishing *Basic Survival School* and *POW School* (which even the training records list separately, despite both of them sharing the same two-week time frame), and those together ate up half a month of that year all by themselves. One of the other checked items was just for completing the first block of my CDC course (*Oo, what an over-achiever am I!*). So, in all fairness to myself, I need to allow for the fact that some of these items are time consuming and *can't* be checked off quickly. But still...

The five items I just signed off today were the only ones that showed any 'proof of competence' so far. My *first* ones, actually. A bunch of us newbies spent half a day at a Fort Lewis firing range last week—not even a full business week after surviving Survival School—and between the minimal marksmanship requirements, and the breakdown and reassembly of the weapons themselves (which I just barely got through without humiliating myself... such is my memory), we were, as a group, assessed as 'proficient' at those skills, and so today got to check off those items in our training records.

Yay! We're really cookin' now!

Similarly, after what had felt like nothing more than a simple, casual, off-handed conversation about the weather one day, I found out that I had apparently exhibited a sufficient grasp of the basic weather concepts and criteria—at least as they pertain to our profession—that Cole was impressed enough to affix his own initials to *that* checklist item as well. And I hadn't even known I was being evaluated on that.

But lordy, there's just so much more that I either haven't retained since CCS (like the formulas for wind adjustments, drop zone alignments, and worse, demolition calculations), or stuff that I *never* understood well enough or adapted to in the first place (like *jiu jitsu*, running without cramping, or flying without throwing up), that I just can't imagine how I'm ever going to pass all those evaluations.

Tents *still* don't pitch right for me. Fires don't light, knots don't hold, and sweaty inner layers still freeze on my skin in cold weather, whenever my body comes to rest and stops generating heat. So I'm not feeling any more proficient or comfortable with this stuff than I did a month or two ago.

But, most telling of all, especially after the bludgeoning of CCS, then the torments of the one or two deployments I've had with the Team since then, not to mention the sheer exhaustion and demoralization of Survival School and POW School... I just don't want anything to do with this shit anymore.

It's that simple.

I no longer *care* if I *ever* exhibit the requisite expertise that this training regimen seeks. Because, even if I *am* able to pass every challenge they throw in my path, I'm just not interested in doing anything *with* those skills again! Period. Not anymore. I've done my time, done my dabbling, and satisfied my initial curiosity. So, what else is there to do—that I have an *interest* in doing—anywhere along the remainder of this path?

I don't ever want to be cold again. I don't ever want to be airsick again. I'm dead tired of being exhausted (so to speak), of constantly having to push myself *to* and then *beyond* my max, and I hate being filthy! And as great as all these guys are, what I really want more than anything else is to be back among 'my own kind' again. Nerds, social maladroits... dreamers, writers, *musicians!* Not always having to keep up with professional superheroes in camouflage. It may 'elevate' me as a person, but killing myself to do it is not a worthy trade.

At least not anymore.

The new guy across the hall from me, Leo Roth, has been a great breath of fresh air for me in that regard. Somehow he is freakishly able to be both a stud muffin, uber-trooper, sky warrior by day (*and* night), *and* an astonishingly gifted guitar-playing pencil artist the rest of the time. And that's given us a common ground that I've found nowhere else in this career field. But as helpful and refreshing (and lifesaving) as that is, it's still not enough.

Not by a long shot.

And limping out of POW School barely two weeks ago, well… that didn't help at all. In fact, it pretty well clinched it.

Bottom line then, I just want out. I know I've said this before, even made some half-hearted attempts at following through with that thought, but this time I mean it. I just can't take any more of this.

And compounding that frustration is the fact that I can't ever seem to muster the resolve or find the right moment to actually *say* that to anybody… anybody who'll actually listen, understand, *and* be able to do anything about it anyway.

So what's it going to take to push *that* snowball into downhill motion?

Well, here now is Sgt. Mabry, looking a little sour about my sluggish progress through my training items, but still trying gamely to present the appearance of 'approval,' and maybe even a little encouragement for what little I *have* accomplished.

Gawd, this is so uncomfortable… as always.

* * *

COLE SLIPS MY FOLDER back into its alphabetic slot among all the other training records in the drawer, then spins on his heel, headed for the railing at the edge of this second-story deck.

"Come with me," he says.

Together we trot downstairs, from the cubicle farm atop Cpt. Forth's office down to the hangar floor beside it, then back to the storage cage behind our two parachute packing tables. There, he points to a rumpled pile of parachutes set aside from the more orderly stockpile that lines the back wall.

"See those five chutes over there? Help me get those out to the truck, so we can run 'em over to the riggers at Fort Lewis and swap 'em out."

"Roger that," I reply, and plunge into the task.

The first two chutes I pull out I pass on to Sgt. Mabry. They both seem so sloppily packed, I have to wonder *who packed them?* The third one, which I hang on to, is also very loosely assembled, but comes with a 'torn' shoulder harness strap that looks like someone took a set of pruning shears to it, very nearly severing it altogether. *What the...?*

"Guy named DelVecchio got it caught on something on a C-130's doorframe, as he was going out the door," says Sgt. Mabry, having apparently read my mind. "Smacked him face-first against the outside of the plane and everything. It was actually pretty damned funny. Stopped the rest of the stick from jumping until they could get him free."

Yeh, that sounds *really funny... not.*

"How did he get himself...?"

"Free? Oh, he just kept pushin' and yankin' and twistin' until whatever it was snagged on broke off, or let go, or whatever. And as you can see right there, it held together just enough to finish the jump. But just barely. Couldn't use the chute again, obviously."

Oh, well... Heaven forefend. Hate to waste a good parachute and all.

"Holy shit," I mutter, as I examine the rent strap closer.

"Of course, by the time he tore himself loose, we were like three miles past the DZ, and he had to land in the trees. Took us a while to link up with him again. But it all worked out."

He hoists the two chutes up over one shoulder, then adds, "That was *long* before your time, though. Just never got around to returning it to the riggers. So... grab the rest of those, and let's get going."

Then he turns around, and marches out of the cage. Done talkin' now.

I snap out of my little reverie—imagining what it must have been like for DelVecchio being plastered face-first against the outside of the aircraft by the slipstream *and* the snag in his shoulder strap, wondering what part of the nightmare was going to kill him first—and I slip my other arm through both of the remaining chutes' harnesses. With all three aboard, I lurch my way out through the cage's gate, and stagger after Sgt. Mabry.

Outside, I find him pitching his two chutes onto the bed of the six-pack. Then he walks around to the driver's door without offering a hand to assist me. I act unfazed, but truth be told, *it kinda' pisses me off.* I mean, I know he holds the air traffic control side of the team in some generalized disdain (as opposed to the far nobler and harder working members of his own radio maintenance side), and me, in particular, even more so.

But come on, guy! Show a little subtlety!

I fling my three chutes, one at a time, up onto the bed, and slam the tailgate closed. The engine fires up as I'm circling around to the passenger door, but I dawdle a bit while I wrestle my beret out of my thigh pocket, and torque it squarely onto my head... just to return the favor.

Then I hop up into the cab, and close the door.

* * *

THE DRIVE THROUGH THE BASE is slow and silent. Cole has his elbow resting on the sill of his open window, despite the nip in the air. And he's staring out the windshield as if in a trance.

I know there's more he wants to say. I've *always* felt that Cole looked like he was swallowing words that were ganging up in his throat, like a talented understudy for an appallingly godawful lead actor. But his stoic and laconic nature was content to just leave his opinions trapped there, rotting in his mouth instead.

Well, I suppose it's just as well, since I'm not sure I *want* him to vent everything that's bothering him right now. Especially about *me*.

I don't know—I've *never* known, specifically—what it is that annoys him so much about me, but I've always sensed it, right from the very first second that we met, when he, Monty, and Manny were walking *out* of our hangar just as Skeeter was walking me *in*. Unlike the other two, who'd shaken my hand and given me a thorough update on Skeeter's general uselessness and homosexual proclivities, Cole had stood back in silence, with the rigging tables between us, and merely nodded when he was introduced.

Maybe he just didn't like that I'd arrived unannounced, unexpected, and probably unneeded. Or maybe I just looked to him like I *didn't belong*. Like I'd *never* 'belong.' Too clean-cut, or fresh-faced, or too obviously unscarred, unhardened. Just generally un*suited*. I don't know. But I've always suspected that he might have even had a hand in getting me shipped off to Combat Control School so prematurely, just so that my unready ass could be washed out by the school's high attrition rate, rather than by *him*. Certainly no *proof* of that, mind you, not even any *evidence*. Just an *impression* derived from all the stars that seemed to align so well to that end.

But then I had to go and *graduate* from the damned school, *and* came back wearing the very beret for which he'd never believed me worthy.

And I guarantee *that* did nothing to improve his attitude toward me.

That is, if *any* of this wild supposition holds any water whatsoever.

The thing about it is that I can almost *kinda' sorta'* relate to his scorn for me. He's more of an old-school purist than most of the younger, more 'modern' "action figures" on the team. He's someone who *believes* in THE MISSION, as well as the storied legacies of the teams, and lives by the importance of *both*. And as such, I think he appreciates—even *'embraces'*—only those who truly 'get all that.'

I have a feeling then, that he could *sense*, right from the get-go, that I was *not* one of those… that I was nothing but a dabbler, a wide-eyed looky-loo who just wanted to *play* at the game for a while, and then move on.

Which is, of course, just *exactly* what I am… or *was*, anyway.

These days, I don't even have *that* much curiosity left in me.

It's kind of embarrassing when I stop to think about it, actually… that I could be so conspicuously shallow, so inappropriately (and *insufficiently*) motivated, and worst of all, so *transparent* about it! It makes me worry how many *others* might have seen through me by now, and how many of *them* might actually resent my presence here for those very reasons. I mean, by now it's pretty obvious that I'm *not* right for this job, and that I'm not molding or hardening in the ways I need to in order to fit in with this crew.

So what are they going to do with me? What *can* they do?

And for that matter, what am I going to do with *them*?

The fact is, I *am* here for all the wrong reasons. This job *is* too important, and critical, and dangerous to be treated as nothing more than an exciting little dalliance. And even from *my* point of view, it's way too difficult—*and* critical, *and* dangerous—to be dabbled in 'just for fun.' Too much of it *isn't* fun… and *shouldn't be*. And too many people have to rely on me, and my skills, *and my* motivation just to *stay alive!*

So what the hell am I doing here?

It really is time to go. And when I actually look at it, I do know it, too.

Commit to it then! Speak the damned words you know must be spoken!

I glance over at Cole's stony face, thinking, *You know, if one of us wasn't so implacable and phlegmatic, and the other one wasn't such a goddamned chickenshit, we could probably talk about this, right here and now, and discover that we're both of like minds on this issue! We might actually be able to work together to end this charade!*

But… *nope*. He's going to keep right on swallowing his frustrations, and I'm going to keep on waffling and vacillating and procrastinating until we reach some kind of 'critical mass' some day, and we explode all over each other. And if it ever comes to *that*, no matter how valid my points or perspectives may be, *he's* gonna' win it. And I'm gonna' lose.

Tell him!, my mind screams at my mouth. *Tell him NOW!*

This really is the perfect moment! We're in a *truck*, with no one else around, and no reasons to restrain ourselves, *and* with all the time we need to hash things out. Plus, Sgt. Mabry is probably the *perfect* 'figure of higher authority' with whom to broach this subject. He's one of the senior NCOs on the Team (so he's got the clout), yet he's not in my immediate chain of command (the head of the Radio Maintenance side of the shop, versus *my* position at the end of the Air Traffic Control food chain), so he's not really in a position to inflict anything 'punitive' in the event that he *really* doesn't approve. But he *will* have influence when the matter is discussed at higher levels. He already doesn't like me (so I don't need to worry about his opinion of me taking a nosedive), and he might even find some relief from his annoyances with me if he finds out that I'm willing to leave of my own accord. Hell, he might even *respect* such a gesture.

So TELL HIM! Do us all a favor, and tell him! NOW!

* * *

STILL THE TRUCK ROLLS ON, powerful and rumbling on the outside, silent and stupidly impotent on the inside. It rolls all the way through the base like a camouflaged hearse, past the church and the BX and the Commissary, to the crossroad along its southern fenceline. Then it turns right, cruising past the library and the golf course until it reaches the western gate, where it passes from McChord AFB directly into neighboring Fort Lewis. From there, it prowls westerly past rows of old 'houses' that have been commandeered into offices and peripheral workshops. Until at last, barely ten minutes after leaving The Section, the truck wheels into the moat of parking spaces that surrounds a small, seedy, and depressingly beige 'warehouse,' and shuts down.

Wow! We managed to make it the whole way over here without saying a single friggin' word to each other. Impressive.

We both roll out of our respective doors, and tromp around to the rear of the truck. Sgt. Mabry yanks the tailgate down, and before he's even freed his fingers from the handle, I've vaulted up onto it and walked to the front of the bed where the parachutes are heaped. One at a time then, I toss them aft, allowing them to slide onto the lowered tailgate, where Sgt. Mabry grabs them and sets them on the ground. By the time I get back there myself though, he's already snatched up the same two loosely packed chutes again, and is headed for the building's side door. I drop down without saying a word, slam the tailgate shut, and gather up the remaining chutes. Then I march over to where he's holding the door open for me.

Inside, it's a warren of tired old wooden cubby holes, with the requisite allocation of stock military photos and unread bulletin boards littering the walls. The floors feel spongy underfoot, the hallways are narrow, and everything smells damp and musty.

Just how I imagine every Army building to be.

Cole stops outside an odd interior-corner room, with glass walls that converge at one corner like an oversized movie theater ticket office. I see no one inside, but Cole's obviously been here before, so I trust that this is where we should be. He props his two parachutes against the wall beside its door, and signals me to do the same with mine. Then, in a hushed voice, he tells me that it's probably going to be a few minutes while he makes arrangements, so I might want to go check out the rigging room around the corner while I wait.

And that's exactly what I do.

* * *

THE RIGGING ROOM, unlike the rest of this cluttered and neglected old building, is actually fairly impressive in its dimensions and frenetic activity. It's large(ish)—or at least *long*(ish)—with a broad open bay capable of housing up to eight of the thirty-foot rigging tables, seven of which are in use when I walk in and take up a position against the back wall to watch.

The first things it conjures up though, are memories of *my* having to do this stuff at CCS. And bear in mind, I never got any good at it. I never had *time* to get any good at it. None of us did. We just did our best to memorize the three single-spaced pages of instructions, step by step and line by line, then tried desperately to put those words into action… in less than an hour and ten minutes… just to get past the parachute-packing phase of the course. We fumbled, we backtracked, we corrected, we analyzed our own errors, and attempted to not repeat them. We put *miles* on those floors, marching up and down the lengths of those tables, sorting suspension lines, pleating canopy 'silk' (actually, it's some form of 'rip-stop nylon'), stitching bundles of cord through switchbacks of rubber bands, squashing the springy drogue chutes flat, and tying things together with shoestring.

But only enough to pass.

We—or at least *I*—never got any *good* at it.

These guys, on the other hand, look like human *looms*. Muscle memory refined by so many thousands of hours of repetition. Their arms move so fast, their choreography is so finely honed, that even knowing *what* they're doing, I can't actually *see* them doing it! Things just fly and *swish* around, as if they're twirling paired jump ropes in impossibly complex and overlapping routines. It's amazing… to *watch*, not to *emulate*.

Over the course of the fifteen, maybe twenty minutes that I spend standing there, I watch something like a dozen parachutes being packed, all the way from disheveled heaps to tightly packed rigs. Fully inspected, documented, and prepped for dispersal. It's impressive, even *inspiring*, but *depressing*, all at the same time… depressing, because it's something at which *I'm* going to have to prove myself capable… *again*. And I just don't think I'll ever get it down to the point of being safe and proficient at it.

We just don't pack our own chutes enough for it to become muscle memory, or even anything close to 'second nature.' It isn't 'intuitive' enough for me to be able to 'figure it out,' should I ever forget *how*, and it relies on the very 'rote memorization' that my brain has never mastered. Yet it's (obviously) too important to do poorly.

Sure, I could *practice, practice, practice* over the days leading up to my evaluation, and, much like at Little Rock, that would probably be sufficient to get it checked off in my records. My only real objective during this year-long quest for qualification(s). But I wouldn't retain it… which is the *ultimate* objective in this career field. As soon as I fell back into the Team's regular daily regimen (which has never seen a parachute packed in our shop *even once* in the four-and-a-half months that I've been a member), that data and those skills would simply evaporate again.

And I can see that happening with *all* of these extremely perishable skills. Whether it's remembering the formulae for computing the amount and placement of explosives to cut a *bridge piling* versus a *telephone pole*, or for calculating the wind drift *at altitude* before an air drop... whether it's remembering all the steps and pieces and components in the *dis*assembly, cleaning, and *re*assembly of all the different weapons in our arsenal, or, as displayed right here in this room, all the parts, steps, and moves involved in packing a damned parachute, I am just never going to be able to retain all that. And, as I see now more clearly than ever, I really don't even *want* to.

It has to be either 'logical' or 'intuitive', or it has to be done or used often enough to be hammered into my brain through osmosis. And this kind of stuff is *none* of those things.

So, again, once more re-emphasized *here*, in practice as well as in concept, it's time for me to get out of this business. I'm not right for *it*, and *it's* not right for *me*. And everybody, including me now, knows it.

I sigh, and exit stage-left, and go looking for Sgt. Mabry.

* * *

SO, WITH SIX NEW PARACHUTES riding in the bed of the truck now, freshly, professionally, and *rapidly* packed by the maestros at the Army's rigging shop, Cole and I drive back through the connecting gate into Air Force territory, droning down the road... in absolute silence. Again.

By now, everything in me is *screaming* at the Little Dude working the levers in my head to *Tell Sgt. Mabry! NOW! Now is PERFECT! You know he wants to hear it as badly as you want to say it! So just fucking SAY IT!*

I glance over at the carved granite lines of Sgt. Cole Mabry's face. I take in the leathery 'working man' contours, the sun-seared and dusky color of his skin, and his wind-narrowed eyes. I see in his focused expression the look of a mission-oriented man, a dedicated 'lifer' in *whatever* he takes up as either a pastime or a career. And I see the comfortable and confident gaze of a man for whom there are few mysteries left in this world, who understands what he sees, and has faith in what he does not. For better or worse.

And I realize that I have absolutely *nothing* in common with him. We don't even speak the same language, even when we're saying the exact same thing. Neither of us could explain my unsuitability to the other in words that the 'other' would comprehend, even though both certainly recognize '*it*,' and both find '*it*' an awkward fit among the well-drilled ranks of the McChord Combat Control Team. And so '*it*' continues to go unsaid.

So how *do* I say it? What words do I choose? And what unfortunate turn of phrase might actually make things worse? Maybe come back to haunt me in the future, in some unforeseen way? And perhaps more important still, *what do I have to do to quit over-thinking this shit?*

WHO CARES?! Shut your mental pie-hole, and just start talking! 'Starting words' will lead to 'following words,' which will lead to 'explanatory words,' 'corrective words,' and maybe even 'helpful words!*' The entire conversation doesn't need to be scripted in advance! Just say the obvious! Resign yourself to the inevitable! Commit! Move! Speak! ACT, goddammit!*

The hangar row rolls up alongside us, and Sgt. Mabry turns the truck onto the dirt access road.

NOW! NOW! NOW! Don't wait for a 'better time!' There isn't going to be one! SPEAK! NOOWWWWW!

I look at him again as he brakes the truck to a stop, throws it into Park, and wrenches the key *off* and out. For one fleeting instant, he glances over at me—with a look that says he's wondering if I just shit on my end of the bench—then he's out the door, and striding back to the end of the vehicle.

I don't know if my mouth was actually hanging open *as if to speak* when he looked at me, but it's closed now. And the moment withers and dies.

Again.
(*sigh*)
Maybe tomorrow.
Yeh. Tomorrow, for sure.

Turn the page for an excerpt from
The Pretender, the third and final installment in
Steve Stipp's *In Wolf's Clothing* trilogy.

Coming soon from Next Century...

1
A GRAND ADVENTURE

March, 1978
On the road, somewhere on the Oregon side of the Columbia River Gorge
Enroute to Robins AFB, Warner-Robins, Georgia

* * *

TWILIGHT ON THE COLUMBIA River Gorge.
Gorgeous! (*Get it? As in 'Columbia River Gorge'-ous?*)
Not to mention exciting! And thrilling! Inspirational! Hopeful! Joyful!
And don't forget *satisfying*. And gratifying.
And of course, *fun!*
Damn. I haven't felt this good in, well... too damned long.
Of course, that's not *all* due to just the pink and purple smudges of post-sunset colors that are scuffing the clifftops, igniting the mountains, and sparkling on the water right now. Not all of it, anyway. *Most* of my bubbling elation, in fact, is due to the circumstances that *brought* me and my perky little Datsun B-210 down here to this ridge-running stretch of interstate in the first place, rolling eastbound along the border between Washington state and Oregon.
Because I'm driving *away from Combat Control!* At least for a while.
Hoo-HOO!
And I didn't even have to quit to do it (although I was sure as hell *ready* to give it all up)!

They *sent* me! On a one-man mission, no less! To friggin' *Georgia!* And for at least *four months!* From out of the blue, they just handed me a *third of a year* to spend *not* getting the shit beaten out of me, *not* endangering my life at every turn, and *not* questioning my own sanity!

Can you believe it?! And just in the nick of time, too.

Not only that—*not only THAT!*—but they're sending me there to work in a regular *air traffic control tower! To get my legal air traffic control certification! Can you believe THAT?!!*

Nobody else on the team has gotten to do that. *I'm the first!*

I think I may cry.

Cruising east, away from the Pacific coast, with the last molten dollop of the sun melting at my back, and every star in the universe arched high over my windshield like a standing ovation, it's about all I can do just to keep from bouncing up and down in my seat, giggling and shouting "*Yippee!!*" like a five-year-old on Christmas morning.

In fact, why am I *not* doing that?

It's a reprieve, a reward, and a roadtrip *all in one! A grand adventure!*

For once, all my epic vacillating and indecision finally paid off.

For every day that I awoke, committed to walking into Captain Forth's office and ending this charade with a single sentence, but then held my tongue or deflected my march at the last second because of some tantalizing new distraction or revivifying activity, or just some fleeting moment of pride or pleasure (but usually just because it was too daunting)—*whatever*—now I'm glad that I procrastinated. I'm finally getting my break... a chance to step back, out of the frantic dog race, long enough and far enough to calmly reassess my situation and my decisions, past, present, and future.

My long-awaited 'emotionally neutral interlude.'

Plus I get to drive my new used car clear across the country to boot! And then play with airplanes once I get there! What's not to like?

* * *

I LEFT STRAIGHT FROM WORK this afternoon. My car had sat out in the drizzle and the muddy parking lot all day long, packed to the rafters with just about all my worldly possessions, along with a full tank of gas. But that was just fine with me. The thought of it sitting out there, *waiting for me*, was a pretty profound distraction throughout the day, but who would notice? It's not like my heart's exactly been into my work for quite a while now, anyway.

I guess I could've waited until tomorrow morning to head out, but... *why?* I've been ready to go for a solid week now—ever since they first offered it to me—and it wasn't like I was going to get any more sleep by spending tonight in my barracks room. I've just been too wired and *ready to get going*, and as soon as possible! Besides, I think a big part of me wanted to *make sure* that I could bail out of work and get straight onto the road before someone announced that it was all just a big joke.

Just kidding, Steve! You didn't really think that, with all the air traffic controllers in this unit that need to get their ratings, we'd send YOU to do it first, did you?

And truth be told, I kinda' wondered about that myself.

* * *

I MEAN, I WAS JUST sitting there at that desk, not quite three weeks after getting back from Survival School—rooting muzzily through my CDCs, while my mind wandered and stewed over the fact that I *still* hadn't managed to muster the resolve to tell these people *"I quit!"*—when Skeeter and the LT 'moseyed' into the office area, 'deeply embroiled' in a conversation that, in retrospect, seemed a little too loud. Maybe even a tad 'staged.'

"Well, we gotta' send *some*body," Lt. Kostas had sighed, as he pulled a roster from the wad of papers in Skeeter's hands.

"Yeh, but *who?*," Skeeter responded. "Who?"

Their meandering, by then, had them drifting right past the front of my desk.

"Who's gonna' wanna' be gone for *four months?* And to fuckin' *Georgia*, of all places."

My ears had perked right up... just like they were supposed to, I now suspect. *Did you say Georgia? The one right next to Florida? And for four months? Hmmm.*

"Well, Mutt *can't* go," the LT continued. "Not out of state, anyway. Greg's getting married in May, and Spew? Jesus, I can't send him *anywhere* to represent this team."

Their backs were to me, but I could still hear them clearly.

As was intended, of course.

Skeeter stopped, and tapped the sheet of paper. "What about Rocky?"

I had to act quickly.

"You guys looking for a volunteer for something?," I asked.

They both twisted to look back at me (failing miserably at looking 'perturbed' by my intrusion into their little confab)—the LT even appeared to 'ponder' a wild and crazy new idea that had just 'popped into his head' at that moment—then they looked back at each other, hiked their eyebrows up, pantomimed a 'spontaneous' nod or two, then spun to face me again.

"Would you be *interested* in a little TDY (*'Temporary Duty'*)?," asked Lt. Kostas. "Go get your full tower certification, and all that shit?"

"Absolutely, sir!"

Finally, something I could get genuinely enthusiastic about!

"It'd be clear the hell down at Robins Air Force Base," Skeeter interjected. "Just south of Macon. That's a long way away from here."

Damned straight, it is!, my mind shouted.

"No problem," said my mouth, while my face tried to look more 'dutiful' than desperate.

They looked back at each other, mulling over this new prospect as if the thought had never crossed their minds before. Then Skeeter shrugged.

"It would solve a lot of problems, LT. That way, whenever the *McChord* tower slot finally opens up, we could give that one to Mutt first."

Lt. Kostas nodded again—studiously, 'significantly'—then wheeled back to stand in front of my desk. "Alright then. Can you be ready to go in a week, Airman Stipp?"

"I can be ready to go *tonight*, if you need, sir."

He chuckled. "I'll take that as a 'yes,' then." He held out a hand, and Skeeter dropped another sheet of paper into it. "These are the orders requiring us to fill that slot. Fill out your personal information in the top section, and get it back to Sergeant Murton here ASAP. He should have your orders cut by…"

"Thursday."

"… Thursday. And you can catch a hop out over the weekend. Okay?"

"Yessir," I answered, "But, uhhh…"

"Yes?"

"Any possibility I could just *drive* down there in my own car, sir?"

"Sure, I suppose. If you really wanna'. *I* wouldn't, but all power to ya' if *you* want to."

"Thank-you, sir."
"Have a good trip."
"*Oo-rah.*"

* * *

IT TOOK ME UNTIL this morning, as I was tidying up a few last loose ends around The Shop, before I realized that it had all been a set-up. After years—probably *decades*—of CCT air traffic controllers never even bothering to get their legal tower certifications, some higher authority had apparently decided that it was about time to put their foot down, and *insist* that their controllers meet the minimum regulatory standards of controllers everywhere.

Or at least here at McChord.

I have no idea how pervasive the problem might have been Air Force-wide. For all I know, every *other* CC Team around the world has had their controllers up to snuff. But the McChord team sure as hell hadn't been keeping up. Case in point: the infamous 'Mutt Siegel Show' that I witnessed up at Yakima last year.

Lordy, I still can't believe he got away with that lunacy, especially if it happened on a regular basis, as discussions on the subject implied.

So the mandate apparently came down from on high: *"Make bonafide your air traffic controllers, lest they kill someone who deserveth it not."* And the teams—or at least the McChord Team—suddenly found themselves under the gun to get their controllers rated *somewhere*.

And when you've got the choice of sending an 'Old Head' (worldly in the ways and duties of CCT, but rusty as *hell* with the nuances of regular old ATC), or sending an as yet untested rookie (who not only has as yet to become a fully viable 'asset' to the Team, but is still a recent enough graduate from ATC School that the material won't seem so foreign to him), who would *you* send first?

That's right. You'd ship off the rookie.

And with a half dozen rookies to choose from, who would be *your* first choice?

That's right... the rookiest rookie in the herd... the one least adapted to the life of a Combat Controller, the one whose presence would be missed the least... the one most likely to remember *some* of the teachings of ATC

School, the one most current on contemporary ATC standards... the one who stood the best chance of actually *getting* fully certified in the minimal four-month time constraints, and thereby make the Team look good.

That's right: you'd ship off *moi*.

Thank God, *moi!*

* * *

NIGHT HAS FULLY FALLEN by the time I see a sign for "**Walla Walla, Washington.**"

I bust out laughing... *again*.

www.ingramcontent.com/pod-product-compliance
Lightning Source LLC
Chambersburg PA
CBHW052005070526
44584CB00016B/1622